Machine Learning
with Python
for Everyone

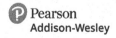

Machine Learning with Python for Everyone

Mark E. Fenner

✦✦Addison-Wesley

Boston • Columbus • New York • San Francisco • Amsterdam • Cape Town
Dubai • London • Madrid • Milan • Munich • Paris • Montreal • Toronto • Delhi • Mexico City
São Paulo • Sydney • Hong Kong • Seoul • Singapore • Taipei • Tokyo

For information about buying this title in bulk quantities, or for special sales opportunities (which may include electronic versions; custom cover designs; and content particular to your business, training goals, marketing focus, or branding interests), please contact our corporate sales department at corpsales@pearsoned.com or (800) 382-3419.

For government sales inquiries, please contact governmentsales@pearsoned.com.

For questions about sales outside the U.S., please contact intlcs@pearson.com.

Visit us on the Web: informit.com/aw

Library of Congress Control Number: 2019938761

Copyright © 2020 Pearson Education, Inc.

Cover image: cono0430/Shutterstock

Pages 58, 87: Screenshot of seaborn © 2012–2018 Michael Waskom.
Pages 167, 177, 192, 201, 278, 284, 479, 493: Screenshot of seaborn heatmap © 2012–2018 Michael Waskom.
Pages 178, 185, 196, 197, 327, 328: Screenshot of seaborn swarmplot © 2012–2018 Michael Waskom.
Page 222: Screenshot of seaborn stripplot © 2012–2018 Michael Waskom.
Pages 351, 354: Screenshot of seaborn implot © 2012–2018 Michael Waskom.
Pages 352, 353, 355: Screenshot of seaborn distplot © 2012–2018 Michael Waskom.
Pages 460, 461: Screenshot of Manifold © 2007–2018, scikit-learn developers.
Page 480: Screenshot of cluster © 2007–2018, scikit-learn developers.
Pages 483, 484, 485: Image of accordion, Vereshchagin Dmitry/Shutterstock.
Page 485: Image of fighter jet, 3dgenerator/123RF.
Page 525: Screenshot of seaborn jointplot © 2012–2018 Michael Waskom.

ISBN-13: 978-0-13-484562-3
ISBN-10: 0-13-484562-5

11 2023

To my son, Ethan—
with the eternal hope of a better tomorrow

Contents

5.5   (Re)Sampling: Making More from Less   128

    5.5.1   Cross-Validation   128

    5.5.2   Stratification   132

    5.5.3   Repeated Train-Test Splits   133

    5.5.4   A Better Way and Shuffling   137

    5.5.5   Leave-One-Out
             Cross-Validation   140

5.6   Break-It-Down: Deconstructing Error into Bias
       and Variance   142

    5.6.1   Variance of the Data   143

    5.6.2   Variance of the Model   144

    5.6.3   Bias of the Model   144

    5.6.4   All Together Now   145

    5.6.5   Examples of Bias-Variance
             Tradeoffs   145

5.7   Graphical Evaluation and Comparison   149

    5.7.1   Learning Curves: How Much Data
             Do We Need?   150

    5.7.2   Complexity Curves   152

5.8   Comparing Learners with
       Cross-Validation   154

5.9   EOC   155

    5.9.1   Summary   155

    5.9.2   Notes   155

    5.9.3   Exercises   157

6 Evaluating Classifiers   159

6.1   Baseline Classifiers   159

6.2   Beyond Accuracy: Metrics
       for Classification   161

    6.2.1   Eliminating Confusion from the
             Confusion Matrix   163

    6.2.2   Ways of Being Wrong   164

    6.2.3   Metrics from the Confusion
             Matrix   165

    6.2.4   Coding the Confusion Matrix   166

    6.2.5   Dealing with Multiple Classes:
             Multiclass Averaging   168

Foreword

Whether it is called statistics, data science, machine learning, or artificial intelligence, learning patterns from data is transforming the world. Nearly every industry imaginable has been touched (or soon will be) by machine learning. The combined progress of both hardware and software improvements are driving rapid advancements in the field, though it is upon software that most people focus their attention.

While many languages are used for machine learning, including R, C/C++, Fortran, and Go, Python has proven remarkably popular. This is in large part thanks to scikit-learn, which makes it easy to not only train a host of different models but to also engineer features, evaluate the model quality, and score new data. The scikit-learn project has quickly become one of Python's most important and powerful software libraries.

While advanced mathematical concepts underpin machine learning, it is entirely possible to train complex models without a thorough background in calculus and matrix algebra. For many people, getting into machine learning through programming, rather than math, is a more attainable goal. That is precisely the goal of this book: to use Python as a hook into machine learning and then add in some math as needed. Following in the footsteps of *R for Everyone* and *Pandas for Everyone*, *Machine Learning with Python for Everyone* strives to be open and accessible to anyone looking to learn about this exciting area of math and computation.

Mark Fenner has spent years practicing the communication of science and machine learning concepts to people of varying backgrounds, honing his ability to break down complex ideas into simple components. That experience results in a form of storytelling that explains concepts while minimizing jargon and providing concrete examples. The book is easy to read, with many code samples so the reader can follow along on their computer.

With more people than ever eager to understand and implement machine learning, it is essential to have practical resources to guide them, both quickly and thoughtfully. Mark fills that need with this insightful and engaging text. *Machine Learning with Python for Everyone* lives up to its name, allowing people with all manner of previous training to quickly improve their machine learning knowledge and skills, greatly increasing access to this important field.

Jared Lander,
Series Editor

Preface

In 1983, the movie *WarGames* came out. I was a preteen and I was absolutely engrossed: by the possibility of a nuclear apocalypse, by the almost magical way the lead character interacted with computer systems, but mostly by the potential of machines that could *learn*. I spent years studying the strategic nuclear arsenals of the East and the West—fortunately with a naivete of a tweener—but it was almost ten years before I took my first serious steps in computer programming. Teaching a computer to do a set process was amazing. Learning the intricacies of complex systems and bending them around my curiosity was a great experience. Still, I had a large step forward to take. A few short years later, I worked with my first program that was explicitly designed to *learn*. I was blown away and I knew I found my intellectual home. I want to share the world of *computer programs that learn* with you.

Audience

Who do I think *you* are? I've written *Machine Learning with Python for Everyone* for the absolute beginner to machine learning. Even more so, you may well have very little college-level mathematics in your toolbox *and I'm not going to try to change that*. While many machine learning books are very heavy on mathematical concepts and equations, I've done my best to *minimize* the amount of mathematical luggage you'll have to carry. I do expect, given the book's title, that you'll have some basic proficiency in Python. If you can *read* Python, you'll be able to get a lot more out of our discussions. While many books on machine learning rely on mathematics, I'm relying on stories, pictures, and Python code to communicate with you. There *will* be the occasional equation. Largely, these can be skipped if you are so inclined. But, if I've done my job well, I'll have given you enough context around the equation to maybe—just *maybe*—understand what it is trying to say.

Why might you have this book in your hand? The least common denominator is that all of my readers want to *learn* about machine learning. Now, you might be coming from very different backgrounds: a student in an introductory computing class focused on machine learning, a mid-career business analyst who all of sudden has been thrust beyond the limits of spreadsheet analysis, a tech hobbyist looking to expand her interests, or a scientist needing to analyze data in a new way. Machine learning is permeating society. Depending on your background, *Machine Learning with Python for Everyone* has different things to offer you. Even a mathematically sophisticated reader who is looking to do a break-in to machine learning using Python can get a lot out of this book.

So, my goal is to take someone with an interest or need to do some machine learning and teach them the *process* and the most important *concepts* of machine learning in a concrete way using the Python scikit-learn library and some of its friends. You'll come away with overall patterns, strategies, pitfalls, and gotchas that will be applicable in every learning system you ever study, build, or use.

Approach

Many books that try to explain mathematical topics, such as machine learning, do so by presenting equations as if they tell a story to the uninitiated. I think that leaves many of us—even those of us who like mathematics!—stuck. Personally, I build a far better mental picture of the process of machine learning by combining visual and verbal descriptions with *running code*. I'm a computer scientist at heart and by training. I love building things. Building things is how I know that I've reached a level where I *really* understand them. You might be familiar with the phrase, "If you really want to know something, teach it to someone." Well, there's a follow-on. "If you really want to know something, teach a computer to do it!" That's my take on how I'm going to teach you machine learning. With minimal mathematics, I want to give you the concepts behind the most important and frequently used machine learning tools and techniques. Then, I want you to immediately see how to make a computer do it. One note: we won't be programming these methods from scratch. We'll be standing on the shoulders of giants and using some very powerful, time-saving, prebuilt software libraries (more on that shortly).

We won't be covering all of these libraries in great detail—there is simply too much material to do that. Instead, we are going to be practical. We are going to use the best tool for the job. I'll explain enough to orient you in the concept we're using—and then we'll get to using it. For our mathematically inclined colleagues, I'll give pointers to more in-depth references they can pursue. I'll save most of this for end-of-the-chapter notes so the rest of us can skip it easily.

If you are flipping through this introduction, deciding if you want to invest time in this book, I want to give you some insight into things that are out-of-scope for us. We aren't going to dive into mathematical proofs or rely on mathematics to explain things. There are many books out there that follow that path and I'll give pointers to my favorites at the ends of the chapters. Likewise, I'm going to assume that you are fluent in basic- to intermediate-level Python programming. However, for more advanced Python topics—and things that show up from third-party packages like NumPy or Pandas—I'll explain enough of what's going on so that you can understand each technique and its context.

Overview

In **Part I**, we establish a foundation. I'll give you some verbal and conceptual introductions to machine learning in Chapter 1. In Chapter 2 we introduce and take a slightly different approach to some mathematical and computational topics that show up repeatedly in machine learning. Chapters 3 and 4 walk you through your first steps in building, training, and evaluating learning systems that classify examples (classifiers) and quantify examples (regressors).

Part II shifts our focus to the most important aspect of applied machine learning systems: evaluating the success of our system in a realistic way. Chapter 5 talks about general evaluation techniques that will apply to all of our learning systems. Chapters 6 and 7 take those general techniques and add evaluation capabilities for classifiers and regressors.

Part III broadens our toolbox of learning techniques and fills out the components of a practical learning system. Chapters 8 and 9 give us additional classification and regression techniques. Chapter 10 describes *feature engineering*: how we smooth the edges of rough data into forms that we can use for learning. Chapter 11 shows how to chain multiple steps together as a single learner and how to tune a learner's inner workings for better performance.

Part IV takes us beyond the basics and discusses more recent techniques that are driving machine learning forward. We look at learners that are made up of multiple little learners in Chapter 12. Chapter 13 discusses learning techniques that incorporate automated feature engineering. Chapter 14 is a wonderful capstone because it takes the techniques we describe throughout the book and applies them to two particularly interesting types of data: images and text. Chapter 15 both reviews many of the techniques we discuss and shows how they relate to more advanced learning architectures—neural networks and graphical models.

Our main focus is on the techniques of machine learning. We will investigate a number of learning algorithms and other processing methods along the way. However, completeness is not our goal. We'll discuss the most common techniques and only glance briefly at the two large subareas of machine learning: graphical models and neural, or deep, networks. However, we will see how the techniques we focus on relate to these more advanced methods.

Another topic we won't cover is implementing specific learning algorithms. We'll build on top of the algorithms that are already available in scikit-learn and friends; we'll create larger solutions using them as components. Still, someone has to implement the gears and cogs inside the black-box we funnel data into. If you are really interested in implementation aspects, you are in good company: I love them! Have all your friends buy a copy of this book, so I can argue I need to write a follow-up that dives into these lower-level details.

Acknowledgments

I must take a few moments to thank several people that have contributed greatly to this book. My editor at Pearson, Debra Williams Cauley, has been instrumental in every phase of this book's development. From our initial meetings, to her probing for a topic that might meet both our needs, to gently shepherding me through many (many!) early drafts, to constantly giving me just enough of a push to keep going, and finally climbing the steepest parts of the mountain at its peak . . . through all of these phases, Debra has shown the highest degrees of professionalism. I can only respond with a heartfelt *thank you*.

My wife, Dr. Barbara Fenner, also deserves more praise and thanks than I can give her in this short space. In addition to the burdens that any partner of an author must bear, she *also* served as my primary draft reader *and* our intrepid illustrator. She did the hard work of drafting all of the non-computer-generated diagrams in this book. While this is not our first joint academic project, it has been turned into the longest. Her patience is, by all appearances, never ending. Barbara, *I thank you!*

My primary technical reader was Marilyn Roth. Marilyn was unfailingly positive towards even my most egregious errors. *Machine Learning with Python for Everyone* is immeasurably better for her input. *Thank you.*

I would also like to thank several members of Pearson's editorial staff: Alina Kirsanova and Dmitry Kirsanov, Julie Nahil, and many other behind-the-scenes folks that I didn't have the pleasure of meeting. This book would not exist without you and your hardworking professionalism. *Thank you.*

Publisher's Note

The text contains unavoidable references to color in figures. To assist readers of the print edition, color PDFs of figures are available for download at http://informit.com/title /9780134845623.

For formatting purposes, decimal values in many tables have been manually rounded to two place values. In several instances, Python code and comments have been slightly modified—all such modifications should result in valid programs.

Online resources for this book are available at https://github.com/mfenner1.

Register your copy of *Machine Learning with Python for Everyone* on the InformIT site for convenient access to updates and/or corrections as they become available. To start the registration process, go to informit.com/register and log in or create an account. Enter the product ISBN (9780134845623) and click Submit. Look on the Registered Products tab for an Access Bonus Content link next to this product, and follow that link to access any available bonus materials. If you would like to be notified of exclusive offers on new editions and updates, please check the box to receive email from us.

About the Author

Mark Fenner, PhD, has been teaching computing and mathematics to adult audiences—from first-year college students to grizzled veterans of industry—since 1999. In that time, he has also done research in machine learning, bioinformatics, and computer security. His projects have addressed design, implementation, and performance of machine learning and numerical algorithms; security analysis of software repositories; learning systems for user anomaly detection; probabilistic modeling of protein function; and analysis and visualization of ecological and microscopy data. He has a deep love of computing and mathematics, history, and adventure sports. When he is not actively engaged in writing, teaching, or coding, he can be found launching himself, with abandon, through the woods on his mountain bike or sipping a post-ride beer at a swimming hole. Mark holds a *nidan* rank in judo and is a certified Wilderness First Responder. He and his wife are graduates of Allegheny College and the University of Pittsburgh. Mark holds a PhD in computer science. He lives in northeastern Pennsylvania with his family and works through his company, Fenner Training and Consulting, LLC.

Part I

First Steps

1

Let's Discuss Learning

1.1 Welcome

From time to time, people trot out a tired claim that computers can "only do what they are told to do." The claim is taken to mean that computers can only do what their programmers know how to do *and* can explain to the computer. This claim is *false*. Computers can perform tasks that their programmers cannot explain to them. Computers can solve tasks that their programmers do not understand. We will break down this paradox with an example of a computer program that *learns*.

I'll start by discussing one of the oldest—if not the oldest known—examples of a programmed machine-learning system. I've turned this into a story, but it is rooted in historical facts. Arthur Samuel was working for IBM in the 1950s and he had an interesting problem. He had to test the big computing machines that were coming off the assembly line to make sure transistors didn't blow up when you turned a machine on and ran a program—people don't like smoke in their workplace. Now, Samuel quickly got bored with running simple toy programs and, like many computing enthusiasts, he turned his attention towards *games*. He built a computer program that let him play checkers against himself. That was fun for a while: he tested IBM's computers by playing checkers. But, as is often the case, he got bored playing two-person games solo. His mind began to consider the possibility of getting a good game of checkers against a *computer opponent*. Problem was, he wasn't good enough at checkers to explain good checkers strategies to a computer!

Samuel came up with the idea of having the computer *learn* how to play checkers. He set up scenarios where the computer could make moves and evaluate the costs and benefits of those moves. At first, the computer was bad, very bad. But eventually, the program started making progress. It was slow going. Suddenly, Samuel had a great two-for-one idea: he decided to let one computer play another and take himself out of the loop. Because the computers could make moves much faster than Samuel could enter his moves—let alone think about them—the result was many more cycles of "make a move and evaluate the outcome" per minute and hour and day.

Here is the amazing part. It didn't take very long for the computer opponent to be able to consistently beat Samuel. *The computer became a better checkers player than its programmer!* How on earth could this happen, if "computers can only do what they are told to do"? The answer to this riddle comes when we analyze *what the computer was told to do*. What Samuel told the computer to do was not the *play-checkers* task; it was the *learn-to-play-checkers* task. Yes, we just went all *meta* on you. *Meta* is what happens when you take a picture of someone taking a picture (of someone else). Meta is what happens when a sentence refers to itself; the next sentence is an example. *This sentence has five words.* When we access the meta level, we step outside the box we were playing in and we get an entirely new perspective on the world. *Learning to play checkers*—a task that develops skill at another task—is a meta task. It lets us move beyond a limiting interpretation of the statement, *computers can only do what they are told*. Computers do what they are told, but they can be told to *develop a capability*. Computers can be told to learn.

1.2   Scope, Terminology, Prediction, and Data

There are many kinds of computational learning systems out there. The academic field that studies these systems is called *machine learning*. Our journey will focus on the current *wunderkind* of learning systems that has risen to great prominence: *learning from examples*. Even more specifically, we will mostly be concerned with *supervised learning from examples*. What is that? Here's an example. I start by giving you several photos of two animals you've never seen before—with apologies to Dr. Seuss, they might be a Lorax or a Who—and then I tell you which animal is in which photo. If I give you a new, unseen photo you might be able to tell me the type of animal in it. Congratulations, *you're doing great!* You just performed supervised learning from examples. When a computer is coaxed to learn from examples, the examples are presented a certain way. Each example is measured on a common group of attributes and we record the values for each attribute on each example. Huh?

Imagine—or glance at Figure 1.1—a cartoon character running around with a basket of different measuring sticks which, when held up to an object, return some characteristic of that object, such as *this vehicle has four wheels, this person has brown hair, the temperature of that tea is 180° F*, and so on *ad nauseam* (that's an archaic way of saying *until you're sick of my examples*).

Figure 1.1   Humans have an insatiable desire to measure all sorts of things.

1.2.1 Features

Let's get a bit more concrete. For example—a meta-example, if you will—a dataset focused on human medical records might record several relevant values for each patient, such as height, weight, sex, age, smoking history, systolic and diastolic (that's the high and low numbers) blood pressures, and resting heart rate. The different people represented in the dataset are our examples. The biometric and demographic characteristics are our attributes.

We can capture this data very conveniently as in Table 1.1.

Table 1.1   A simple biomedical data table. Each row is an example. Each column contains values for a given attribute. Together, each attribute-value pair is a feature of an example.

patient id	height	weight	sex	age	smoker	hr	sys bp	dia bp
007	5'2"	120	M	11	no	75	120	80
2139	5'4"	140	F	41	no	65	115	75
1111	5'11"	185	M	41	no	52	125	75

Notice that each example—each row—is measured on the same attributes shown in the header row. The values of each attribute run down the respective columns.

We call the rows of the table the *examples* of the dataset and we refer to the columns as the *features*. Features are the measurements or values of our attributes. Often, people use "features" and "attributes" as synonyms describing the same thing; what they are referring to are the column of values. Still, some people like to distinguish among three concepts: *what-is-measured*, *what-the-value-is*, and *what-the-measured-value-is*. For those strict folks, the first is an attribute, the second is a value, and the last is a feature—an attribute and a value paired together. Again, we'll mostly follow the typical conversational usage and call the columns *features*. If we are specifically talking about *what-is-measured*, we'll stick with the term *attribute*. You will inevitably see both, used both ways, when you read about machine learning.

Let's take a moment and look at the types of values our attributes—what is measured—can take. One type of value distinguishes between different groups of people. We might see such groups in a census or an epidemiological medical study—for example, sex {*male, female*} or a broad record of ethnic-cultural-genetic heritage {*African, Asian, European, Native American, Polynesian*}. Attributes like these are called discrete, symbolic, categorical, or nominal attributes, but we are *not* going to stress about those names. If you struggled with those in a social science class, you are free to give a hearty huzzah.

Here are two important, or at least practical, points about categorical data. One point is that these values are discrete. They take a small, limited number of possibilities that typically represent one of several options. You're right that small and several are relative terms—just go with it. The second point is that the information in those attributes can be recorded in two distinct ways:

- As a single feature that takes one value for each option, *or*
- As several features, one per option, where one, and only one, of those features is marked as *yes* or *true* and the remainder are marked as *no* or *false*.

Here's an example. Consider

Name	Sex
Mark	Male
Barb	Female
Ethan	Male

versus:

Name	Sex is Female	Sex is Male
Mark	No	Yes
Barb	Yes	No
Ethan	No	Yes

If we had a column for community type in a census, the values might be Urban, Rural, and Suburban with three possible values. If we had the expanded, multicolumn form, it would take up three columns. Generally, we aren't motivated or worried about table size here. What matters is that some learning methods are, shall we say, particular in preferring one form or the other. There are other details to point out, but we'll save them for later.

Some feature values can be recorded and operated on as numbers. We may lump them together under the term *numerical* features. In other contexts, they are known as *continuous* or, depending on other details, *interval* or *ratio* values. Values for attributes like height and weight are typically recorded as decimal numbers. Values for attributes like age and blood pressure are often recorded as whole numbers. Values like counts—say, how many wheels are on a vehicle—are strictly whole numbers. Conveniently, we can perform arithmetic $(+, -, \times, /)$ on these. While we *can* record categorical data as numbers, we can't necessarily perform *meaningful* numerical calculations directly on those values. If two states—say, Pennsylvania and Vermont—are coded as 2 and 14, it probably makes no sense to perform arithmetic on those values. There is an exception: if, by design, those values *mean* something beyond a unique identifier, we might be able to do some or all of the maths. For extra credit, you can find some meaning in the state values I used where mathematics would make sense.

1.2.2 Target Values and Predictions

Let's shift our focus back to the list of biomedical attributes we gathered. As a reminder, the column headings were height, weight, sex, age, smoker, heart rate, systolic blood pressure, and diastolic blood pressure. These attributes might be useful data for a health care provider trying to assess the likelihood of a patient developing cardiovascular heart. To do so, we would need another piece of information: did these folks develop heart disease?

If we have that information, we can add it to the list of attributes. We could capture and record the idea of "developing heart disease" in several different ways. Did the patient:

- Develop any heart disease within ten years: yes/no
- Develop X-level severity heart disease within ten years: None or Grade I, II, III
- Show some level of a specific indicator for heart disease within ten years: percent of coronary artery blockage

We could tinker with these questions based on resources at our disposal, medically relevant knowledge, and the medical or scientific puzzles we want to solve. Time is a precious resource; we might not have ten years to wait for an outcome. There might be medical knowledge about what percent of blockage is a critical amount. We could modify the time horizon or come up with different attributes to record.

In any case, we can pick a concrete, measurable target and ask, "Can we find a predictive relationship between the attributes we have *today* and the outcome that we will see *at some future time*?" We are literally trying to predict the future—maybe ten years from now—from things we know today. We call the concrete outcome our *target feature* or simply our *target*. If our target is a category like {*sick, healthy*} or {*None, I, II, III*}, we call the process of learning the relationship *classification*. Here, we are using the term *classification* in the sense of finding the different classes, or categories, of a possible outcome. If the target is a smooth sweeping of numerical values, like the usual decimal numbers from elementary school {27.2, 42.0, 3.14159, −117.6}, we call the process *regression*. If you want to know why, go and google *Galton regression* for the history lesson.

We now have some handy terminology in our toolbox: most importantly *features*, both either *categorical* or *numerical*, and a *target*. If we want to emphasize the features being used to predict the future unknown outcome, we may call them *input features* or *predictive features*. There are a few issues I've swept under the carpet. In particular, we'll address some alternative terminology at the end of the chapter.

1.3 Putting the Machine in Machine Learning

I want you to create a mental image of a factory machine. If you need help, glance at Figure 1.2. On the left-hand side, there is a conveyor belt that feeds inputs into the machine. On the right-hand side, the machine spits out outputs which are words or numbers. The words might be *cat* or *dog*. The numbers might be {0, 1} or {−2.1, 3.7}. The machine itself is a big hulking box of metal. We can't really see what happens on the inside. But we can see a control panel on the side of the machine, with an operator's seat in front of it. The control panel has some knobs we can set to numerical values and some switches we can flip on and off. By adjusting the knobs and switches, we can make different products appear on the right-hand side of the machine, depending on what came in the left-hand side. Lastly, there is a small side tray beside the operator's chair. The tray can be used to feed additional information, that is not easily captured by knobs and switches, into the machine. Two quick notes for the skeptical reader: our knobs *can* get us

Figure 1.2 Descriptions go in. Categories or other values come out. We can adjust the machine to improve the relationship between the inputs and outputs.

arbitrarily small and large values ($-\infty$ to ∞, if you insist) and we don't *strictly* need on/off switches, since knobs set to precisely 0 or 1 could serve a similar purpose.

Moving forward, this factory image is a great entry point to understand how *learning algorithms* figure out relationships between features and a target. We can sit down as the machine operator and press a magic—probably green—*go* button. Materials roll in the machine from the left and *something* pops out on the right. Our curiosity gets the best of us and we twiddle the dials and flip the switches. Then, *different* things pop out the right-hand side. We turn up KnobOne and the machine pays more attention to the sounds that the input object makes. We turn down KnobTwo and the machine pays less attention to the number of limbs on the input object. If we have a goal—if there is some *known* product we'd like to see the machine produce—hopefully our knob twiddling gets us closer to it.

Learning algorithms are formal rules for how we manipulate our controls. After seeing examples where the target is known, learning algorithms take a given big-black-box and use a well-defined method to set the dials and switches to *good* values. While *good* can be quite a debatable quality in an ethics class, here we have a gold standard: our known target values. If they don't match, we have a problem. The algorithm adjusts the control panel settings so our *predicted outs* match the *known outs*. Our name for the machine is a *learning model* or just a *model*.

An example goes into the machine and, based on the settings of the knobs and switches, a class or a numerical value pops out. Do you want a different output value from the same input ingredients? Turn the knobs to different settings or flip a switch. One machine has a *fixed* set of knobs and switches. The knobs can be turned, but we can't add new knobs. If we add a knob, we have a *different machine*. Amazingly, the differences between knob-based learning methods boil down to answering three questions:

1. What knobs and switches are there: what is on the control panel?
2. How do the knobs and switches interact with an input example: what are the inner workings of the machine?

3. How do we set the knobs from some *known* data: how do we align the inputs with the outputs we want to see?

Many learning models that we will discuss can be described as machines with knobs and switches—with no need for the additional side input tray. Other methods require the side tray. We'll hold off discussing that more thoroughly, but if your curiosity is getting the best of you, flip to the discussion of *nearest neighbors* in Section 3.5.

Each learning method—which we imagine as a black-box factory machine and a way to set knobs on that machine—is really an *implementation* of an *algorithm*. For our purposes, an algorithm is a finite, well-defined sequence of steps to solve a task. An implementation of an algorithm is the specification of those steps in a particular programming language. The algorithm is the abstract idea; the implementation is the concrete existence of that idea—at least, as concrete as a computer program can be! In reality, algorithms *can* also be implemented in hardware—just like our factory machines; it's far easier for us to work with software.

1.4 Examples of Learning Systems

Under the umbrella of supervised learning from examples, there is a major distinction between two things: predicting values and predicting categories. Are we trying (1) to relate the inputs to one of a few possible categories indicated by discrete symbols, or (2) to relate the inputs to a more-or-less continuous range of numerical values? In short, is the target categorical or numerical? As I mentioned, predicting a category is called *classification*. Predicting a numerical value is called *regression*. Let's explore examples of each.

1.4.1 Predicting Categories: Examples of Classifiers

Classifiers are models that take input examples and produce an output that is one of a small number of possible groups or classes:

1. **Image Classification.** From an input image, output the animal (e.g., cat, dog, zebra) that is in the image, or none if there is no animal present. Image analysis of this sort is at the intersection of machine learning and computer vision. Here, our inputs will be a large collection of image files. They might be in different formats (png, jpeg, etc.). There may be substantial differences between the images: (1) they might be at different scales, (2) the animals may be centered or cut-off on the edges of the frame, and (3) the animals might be blocked by other things (e.g., a tree). These all represent challenges for a learning system—and for learning researchers! But, there are some nice aspects to image recognition. Our concept of *cat* and what images constitute a cat is fairly fixed. Yes, there could be blurred boundaries with animated cats—Hobbes, Garfield, Heathcliff, I'm looking at you—but short of evolutionary time scales, cat is a pretty static concept. We don't have a moving target: the *relationship* between the images and our concept of *cat* is fixed over time.

2. **Stock Action.** From a stock's price history, company fundamental data, and other relevant financial and market data, output whether we should buy or sell a stock. This problem adds some challenges. Financial records might only be available in text form. We might be interested in relevant news stories but we have to somehow figure out what's relevant—either by hand or (perhaps!) using another learning system. Once we've figured out the relevant text, we have to interpret it. These steps are where learning systems interact with the field of natural language processing (NLP). Continuing on with our larger task, we have a time series of data—repeated measurements over time. Our challenges are piling up. In financial markets, we probably have a moving target! What worked yesterday to pick a winning stock is almost certainly not going to work tomorrow in the exact same way. We may need some sort of method or technique that accounts for a changing relationship between the inputs and the output. Or, we may simply hope for the best and use a technique that assumes we don't have a moving target. Disclaimer: I am not a financial advisor nor am I offering investment advice.

3. **Medical Diagnosis.** From a patient's medical record, output whether they are sick or healthy. Here we have an even more complicated task. We might be dealing with a combination of text and images: medical records, notes, and medical imaging. Depending on context that may or may not be captured in the records—for example, traveling to tropical areas opens up the possibility of catching certain nasty diseases—different signs and symptoms may lead to very different diagnoses. Likewise, for all our vast knowledge of medicine, we are only beginning to understand some areas. It would be great for our system to read and study, like a doctor and researcher, the latest and greatest techniques for diagnosing patients. Learning to *learn-to-learn* is a meta-task in the extreme.

These are big-picture examples of classification systems. As of 2019, learning systems exist that handle many aspects of these tasks. We will even dive into basic image and language classifiers in Chapter 14. While each of these examples has its own domain-specific difficulties, they share a common task in building a model that separates the target categories in a useful and accurate way.

1.4.2 Predicting Values: Examples of Regressors

Numerical values surround us in modern life. Physical measurements (temperature, distance, mass), monetary values, percents, and scores are measured, recorded, and processed endlessly. Each can easily become a target feature that answers a question of interest:

1. **Student Success.** We could attempt to predict student scores on exams. Such a system might allow us to focus tutoring efforts on struggling students *before* an exam. We could include features like homework completion rates, class attendance, a measure of daily engagement or participation, and grades in previous courses. We could even include opened-ended written assessments and recommendations from prior instructors. As with many regression problems, we could reasonably convert

this regression problem to a classification problem by predicting a pass/fail or a letter grade instead of a raw numerical score.

2. **Stock Pricing.** Similar to the buy/sell stock classifier, we could attempt to predict the future price—dollar value—of a stock. This variation seems like a more difficult task. Instead of being satisfied with a broad estimate of *up* or *down*, we want to predict that the price will be $20.73 in two weeks. Regardless of difficulty, the inputs could be essentially the same: various bits of daily trading information and as much fundamental information—think quarterly reports to shareholders—as we'd like to incorporate.

3. **Web Browsing Behavior.** From an online user's browsing and purchasing history, predict (in percentage terms) how likely the user is to click on an advertising link or to purchase an item from an online store. While the input features of browsing and purchasing history are *not* numerical, our target—a percentage value—is. So, we have a regression problem. As in the image classification task, we have many small pieces of information that each contribute to the overall result. The pieces need context—how they relate to each other—to really become valuable.

1.5 Evaluating Learning Systems

Learning systems are rarely perfect. So, one of our key criteria is measuring how well they do. How *correct* are the predictions? Since nothing comes for free, we also care about the *cost* of making the predictions. What *computational resources* did we invest to get those predictions? We'll look at evaluating both of these aspects of learning system performance.

1.5.1 Correctness

Our key criteria for evaluating learning systems is that they give us correct predictive answers. If we didn't particularly care about correct answers, we could simply flip a coin, spin a roulette wheel, or use a random-number generator on a computer to get our output predictions. We want our learning system—that we are investing time and effort in building and running—to do better than random guessing. So, (1) we need to quantify how well the learner is doing and (2) we want to compare that level of success—or sadly, failure—with other systems. Comparing with other systems can even include comparisons with random guessers. There's a good reason to make that comparison: if we can't beat a random guesser, we need to go back to the drawing board—or maybe take a long vacation.

Assessing correctness is a surprisingly subtle topic which we will discuss in great detail throughout this book. But, for now, let's look at two classic examples of the difficulty of assessing correctness. In medicine, many diseases are—fortunately!—pretty rare. So, a doctor could get a large percentage of correct diagnoses by simply looking at every person in the street and saying, "that person doesn't have the rare disease." This scenario illustrates at least four issues that must be considered in assessing a potential diagnosis:

1. How common is an illness: what's the base rate of sickness?
2. What is the cost of *missing* a diagnosis: what if a patient isn't treated and gets gravely ill?
3. What is the cost of *making* a diagnosis? Further testing might be invasive and costly; worrying a patient needlessly could be very bad for a patient with high levels of anxiety.
4. Doctors typically diagnose patients that come into the office because they are symptomatic. That's a pretty significant difference from a random person in the street.

A second example comes from the American legal system, where there is a presumption of innocence and a relatively high bar for determining guilt. Sometimes this criteria is paraphrased as, "It is better for 99 criminals to go free than for 1 honest citizen to go to jail." As in medicine, we have the issue of rareness. Crime and criminals are relatively rare and getting rarer. We also have different costs associated with failures. We value clearing an honest citizen more than catching every criminal—at least that's how it works in the idealized world of a high-school civics class. Both these domains, legal and medical, deal with unbalanced target classes: disease and guilt are not 50–50 balanced outcomes. We'll talk about evaluating with unbalanced targets in Section 6.2.

One last issue in assessing correctness: two wrongs don't necessarily make a right. If we are predicting rainfall and, in one case, we underpredict by 2 inches while in another case we overpredict by 2 inches, these don't always cancel out. We cannot say, "On average, we were perfect!" Well, in fact, that's *strictly* true and it might be *good enough* in some instances. Usually, however, we do care, and very deeply in other cases, that we were wrong in both predictions. If we were trying to determine the amount of additional water to give some plants, we might end up giving plants a double dose of water that causes them to drown. Brown Thumbs—myself included—might like using that excuse in the next Great Garden Fiasco.

1.5.2 Resource Consumption

In our modern age of disposable everything, it is tempting to apply a consumer-driven strategy to our learning systems: if we hit a barrier, just buy our way through it. Data storage is extremely cheap. Access to phenomenally powerful hardware, such as a computing cluster driven by graphics processors, is just an email or an online purchase away. This strategy begs a question: shouldn't we just throw more hardware at problems that hit resource limits?

The answer *might* be yes—but let's, at least, use quantitative data to make that decision. At each level of increased complexity of a computational system, we pay for the privilege of using that more complex system. We need more software support. We need more specialized human capital. We need more complicated off-the-shelf libraries. We lose the ability to rapidly prototype ideas. For each of these costs, we need to justify the expense. Further, for many systems, there are small portions of code that are a performance bottleneck. It is often possible to maintain the simplicity of the overall system and only have a small kernel that draws on more sophisticated machinery to go *fast*.

With all that said, there are two primary resources that we will measure: time and memory. How long does a computation take? What is the maximum memory it needs? It is often the case that these can be traded off one for the other. For example, I can precompute the answers to common questions and, *presto*, I have very quick answers available. This, however, comes at the cost of writing down those answers and storing them somewhere. I've reduced the time needed for a computation but I've increased my storage requirements.

If you've ever used a lookup table—maybe to convert lengths from imperial to metric—you've made use of this tradeoff. You *could* pull out a calculator, plug values into a formula, and get an answer for *any* specific input. Alternatively, you can just flip through a couple pages of tables and find a precomputed answer up to some number of digits. Now, since the formula method here is quite fast to begin with, we actually end up losing out by using a big table. If the formula were more complicated and expensive to compute, the table could be a big time saver.

A physical-world equivalent of precomputation is when chefs and mixologists premake important components of larger recipes. Then, when they need lime juice, instead of having to locate limes, clean them, and juice them, they simply pull a lime juice cube out of the freezer or pour some lime juice out of a jar. They've traded time at the beginning and some storage space in the refrigerator for faster access to lime juice to make your killer mojito or guacamole.

Likewise, a common computation technique called compression trades off time for space. I can spend some time finding a smaller, compact representation of *Moby Dick*—including the dratted chapter on cetology (the study of whales)—and store the compressed text instead of the raw text of the tome. Now, my hard drive or my bookshelf is less burdened by storage demands. Then, when I get a craving to read about 19th-century whaling adventures, I can do so. But first, I have to pay a computation cost in time because I have to decompress the book. Again, there is a tradeoff between computational time and storage space.

Different learning systems make different tradeoffs between what they *remember* about the data and *how long* they spend processing the data. From one perspective, learning algorithms compress data in a way that is suitable for predicting new examples. Imagine that we are able to take a large data table and reduce it to a few knobs on a machine: as long as we have a copy of that machine around, we only need a few pieces of information to recreate the table.

1.6 A Process for Building Learning Systems

Even in this brief introduction to learning systems, you've probably noticed that there are many, many options that describe a learning system.

- There are different domains where we might apply learning, such as business, medicine, and science.

- There are different tasks within a domain, such as animal image recognition, medical diagnosis, web browsing behavior, and stock market prediction.
- There are different types of data.
- There are different models relating features to a target.

We haven't yet explicitly discussed the different types of models we'll use, but we will in the coming chapters. Rest assured, there are many options.

Can we capture any generalities about building learning systems? Yes. Let's take two different perspectives. First, we'll talk at a high level where we are more concerned with the world around the learning system and less concerned with the learning system itself. Second, we'll dive into some details at a lower level: imagine that we've abstracted away all the complexity of the world around us and are just trying to make a learning system go. More than that, we're trying to find a solid relationship between the features and the target. Here, we've reduced a very open-ended problem to a defined and constrained learning task.

Here are the high-level steps:

1. Develop an understanding of our task (task understanding).
2. Collect and understand our data (data collection).
3. Prepare the data for modeling (data preparation).
4. Build models of relationships in the data (modeling).
5. Evaluate and compare one or more models (evaluation).
6. Transition the model into a deployable system (deployment).

These steps are shown in Figure 1.3. I'll insert a few common caveats here. First, we normally have to iterate, or repeat, these steps. Second, some steps may feed back to prior steps. As with most real-world processes, progress isn't always a straight line forward. These steps are taken from the CRISP-DM flow chart that organizes the high-level steps of building a learning system. I've renamed the first step from *business understanding* to *task understanding* because not all learning problems arise in the business world.

Within the high-level modeling step—that's step 4 above—there are a number of important choices for a supervised learning system:

1. What part of the data is our target and what are the features?
2. What sort of machine, or learning model, do we want to use to relate our input features to our target feature?
3. Do the data and machine have any negative interactions? If so, do we need to do additional data preparation as part of our model building?
4. How do we set the knobs on the machine? What is our algorithm?

While these breakdowns can help us organize our thoughts and discussions about learning systems, they are not the final story. Let's inform the emperor and empress that they are missing their clothes. Abstract models or flow-chart diagrams can never capture the messy reality of the real world. In the real world, folks building learning systems are often called in (1) after there is already a pile of data gathered and (2) after some primary-stake holders—ahem, bosses—have already decided what they want done. From our humble perspective—and from what I want you to get out of this book—that's just

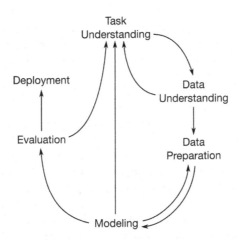

Figure 1.3   A high-level view of machine learning.

fine. We're not going to dive into the details of collecting data, experimental design, and determining good business, engineering, or scientific relationships to capture. We're just going to say, "Go!" We will move from that pile of data to usable examples, applying different learning systems, evaluating the results, and comparing alternatives.

1.7 Assumptions and Reality of Learning

Machine learning is not magic. I can see the look of shock on your faces. But seriously, learning cannot go beyond some fundamental limits. What are those limits? Two of them are directly related to the data we have available. If we are trying to predict heart disease, having information about preferred hair styles and sock colors is—likely—*not* going to help us build a useful model. If we have *no* useful features, we'll only pick up on illusory patterns—random noise—in the data. Even with useful features, in the face of many irrelevant features, learning methods may bog down and stop finding useful relationships. Thus, we have a fundamental limit: we need features that are relevant to the task at hand.

The second data limit relates to quantity. An entire subject called *computational learning theory* is devoted to the details of telling us how many examples we need to learn relationships under certain mathematically idealized conditions. From a practical standpoint, however, the short answer is *more*. We want *more* data. This rule-of-thumb is often summarized as *data is greater than (more important than) algorithms*: data > algorithms. There's truth there, but as is often the case, the details matter. If our data is excessively noisy— whether due to errors or randomness—it might not actually be useful. Bumping up to a stronger learning machine—sort of like bumping up a weight class in wrestling or getting a larger stone bowl for the kitchen—*might* get us better results. Yet, you can be bigger and not *necessarily* better: you might not be a more winning wrestler or make a better guacamole just because you are stronger or have better tools.

Speaking of errors in measurements, not every value we have in a data table is going to be 100% accurate. Our measuring rulers might be off by a bit; our ruler-readers might be rounding off their measurements in different ways. Worse yet, we might ask questions in surveys and receive *lies* in response—the horror! Such is reality. Even when we measure with great attention to detail, there can be differences when we repeat the process. Mistakes and uncertainty happen. The good news is that learning systems *can* tolerate these foibles. The bad news is that with enough *noise* it can be impossible to pick out intelligible patterns.

Another issue is that, in general, we don't know *every* relevant piece of information. Our outcomes may not be known with *complete* accuracy. Taken together, these give us unaccounted-for differences when we try to relate inputs to outputs. Even if we have *every* relevant piece of information measured with *perfect* accuracy, some processes in the world are *fundamentally* random—quarks, I'm looking at you. If the random-walk stock market folks are right, the pricing of stocks is random in a very deep sense. In more macro-scale phenomena, the randomness may be less fundamental but it still exists. If we are missing a critical measurement, it may appear as if the relationship in our data is random. This loss of perspective is like trying to live in a three-dimensional world while only seeing two-dimensional shadows. There are many 3D objects that can give the *same* 2D shadow when illuminated from various angles; a can, a ball, and a coffee cup are all circles from the bird's eye view (Figure 1.4). In the same way, missing measurements can obscure the real, detectable nature of a relationship.

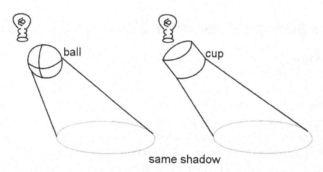

same shadow

Figure 1.4   Perspective can shape our view of reality.

Now for two last technical caveats that we'll hold throughout this book. One is that the relationship between the features and the target is not, itself, a moving target. For example, over time the factors that go into a successful business have presumably changed. In industrial businesses, you need access to raw materials, so being in the right place and the right time is a massive competitive advantage. In knowledge-driven enterprises, the ability to attract high-quality employees from a relatively small pool of talent is a strong competitive advantage. Higher-end students of the mathematical arts call relationships that don't change over time *stationary learning tasks*. Over time, or at least over different examples in our dataset, the underlying relationship is assumed to—we act as if it does—remain the same.

The second caveat is that we don't necessarily assume that nature operates the same way as our machine. All we care about is matching the inputs and the outputs. A more scientific model may seek to *explain* the relationship between inputs and outputs with a mathematical formula that represents *physical laws* of the universe. We aren't going down that rabbit hole. We are content to capture a surface view—a black box or gift-wrapped present—of the relationship. We have our cake, but we can't eat it too.

1.8 End-of-Chapter Material

1.8.1 The Road Ahead

There isn't much to summarize in an introductory chapter. Instead, I'll talk a bit about what we're going through in the four parts of this book.

Part I will introduce you to several types of learning machines and the basics of evaluating and comparing them. We'll also take a brief look at some mathematical topics and concepts that you need to be familiar with to deal with our material. Hopefully, the math is presented in a way that doesn't leave you running for the exits. As you will see, I use a different approach and I hope it will work for you.

Part II dives into detail about evaluating learning systems. My belief is that the biggest risk in developing learning systems is lying to ourselves about how well we are doing. Incidentally, the second biggest risk is blindly using a system without respect for the evolving and complex systems that surround it. Specifically, components in a complex socio-technical system are not swappable like parts in a car. We also need to tread very carefully with the assumption that the future is like the past. As for the first issue, after I get you up and running with some practical examples, we'll take on the issue of evaluation immediately. As to the second issue—good luck with that! In all seriousness, it is beyond the scope of this book and it requires great experience and wisdom to deal with data that acts differently in different scenarios.

Part III fleshes out a few more learning methods and then shifts focus towards manipulating the data so we can use our various learning methods more effectively. We then turn our focus towards fine-tuning methods by manipulating their internal machinery—diving into their inner workings.

Part IV attacks some issues of increasing complexity: dealing with inadequate vocabulary in our data, using images or text instead of a nice table of examples and features, and making learners that are themselves composed of multiple sublearners. We finish by highlighting some connections between different learning systems and with some seemingly far more complicated methods.

1.8.2 Notes

If you want to know more about Arthur Samuel, this brief bio will get you started: http://history.computer.org/pioneers/samuel.html.

The idea of the *meta* level and self-reference is fundamental to higher computer science, mathematics, and philosophy. For a brilliant and broad-reaching look at *meta*, check out

Godel, Escher, Bach: An Eternal Golden Braid by Hofstadter. It is long, but intellectually rewarding.

There are many alternative terms for what we call features and target: inputs/outputs, independent/dependent variables, predictors/outcome, etc.

PA and VT were the 2nd and 14th states to join the United States.

What makes the word *cat* mean the object ★CAT★ and how is this related to the attributes that we take to define a cat: meowing, sleeping in sunbeams, etc.? To dive into this topic, take a look at Wittgenstein (https://plato.stanford.edu/entries/wittgenstein), particularly on language and meaning.

The examples I discussed introduce some of the *really hard* aspects of learning systems. In many cases, this book is about the *easy* stuff (running algorithms) plus some *medium*-difficulty components (feature engineering). The real world introduces complexities that are *hard*.

Outside of supervised learning from examples, there are several other types of learning. *Clustering* is not supervised learning although it does use examples. We will touch on it in later chapters. Clustering looks for patterns in data without specifying a special target feature. There are other, wilder varieties of learning systems; analytic learning and inductive logic programming, case-based reasoning, and reinforcement learning are some major players. See Tom Mitchell's excellent book titled *Machine Learning*. Incidentally, Mitchell has an excellent breakdown of the steps involved in constructing a learning system (the modeling step of the CRISP-DM process).

Speaking of CRISP-DM, Foster Provost and Tom Fawcett have a great book *Data Science for Business Understanding* that dives into machine learning and its role in organizations. Although their approach is focused on the business world, anyone who has to make use of a machine-learning system that is part of a larger system or organization—that's most of them, folks—can learn many valuable lessons from their book. They also have a great approach to tackling technical material. I highly recommend it.

There are many issues that make real-world data hard to process. Missing values is one of these issues. For example, data may be missing randomly, or it may be missing in concert with other values, or it may be missing because our data isn't really a good sample of all the data we might consider. Each of these may require different steps to try to fill in the missing values.

Folks that have background in the social sciences might be wondering why I didn't adopt the classical distinctions of nominal, ordinal, interval, and ratio data. The answer is twofold. First, that breakdown of types misses some important distinctions; search the web for "level of measurement" to get you started. Second, our use of modeling techniques will convert categories, whether ordered or not, to numerical values and then do their thing. Those types aren't treated in a fundamentally different way. However, there are statistical techniques, such as *ordinal regression*, that can account for ordering of categories.

2

Some Technical Background

2.1 About Our Setup

We're about to get down—funk style—with some coding. The chapters in this book started life as Jupyter notebooks. If you're unfamiliar with Jupyter notebooks, they are a very cool environment for working with Python code, text, and graphics in one browser tab. Many Python-related blogs are built with Jupyter notebooks. At the beginning of each chapter, I'll execute some lines of code to set up the coding environment.

The content of `mlwpy.py` is shown in Appendix A. While `from module import *` is generally not recommended, in this case I'm using it specifically to get all of the definitions in `mlwpy.py` included in our notebook environment without taking up forty lines of code. Since scikit-learn is *highly modularized*—which results in many, many `import` lines—the `import *` is a nice way around a long setup block in every chapter. `%matplotlib inline` tells the notebook system to display the graphics made by Python inline with the text.

In [1]:

```
from mlwpy import *
%matplotlib inline
```

2.2 The Need for Mathematical Language

It is very difficult to talk about machine learning (ML) without discussing *some* mathematics. Many ML textbooks take that to an extreme: they are *math* textbooks that happen to discuss machine learning. I'm going to flip that script on its head. I want you to *understand* the math we use and to have some intuition from daily life about what the math-symbol-speak means when you see it. I'm going to minimize the amount of math that I throw around. I also want us—that's you and me together on this wonderful ride—to see the math as code before, or very shortly after, seeing it as mathematical symbols.

Maybe, just maybe, after doing all that you *might* decide you want to dig into the mathematics more deeply. Great! There are endless options to do so. But that's not our game. We care more about the ideas of machine learning than using high-end math to express them. Thankfully, we only need a few ideas from the mathematical world:

- Simplifying equations (algebra),
- A few concepts related to randomness and chance (probability),
- Graphing data on a grid (geometry), and
- A compact notation to express some arithmetic (symbols).

Throughout our discussion, we'll use some algebra to write down ideas precisely and without unnecessary verbalisms. The ideas of probability underlie many machine learning methods. Sometimes this is *very* direct, as in Naive Bayes (NB); sometimes it is less direct, as in Support Vector Machines (SVMs) and Decision Trees (DTs). Some methods rely very directly on a geometric description of data: SVMs and DTs shine here. Other methods, such as NB, require a bit of squinting to see how they can be viewed through a geometric lens. Our bits of notation are pretty low-key, but they amount to a specialized vocabulary that allows us to pack ideas into boxes that, in turn, fit into larger packages. If this sounds to you like refactoring a computer program from a single monolithic script into modular functions, give yourself a prize. That's *exactly* what is happening.

Make no mistake: a deep dive into the arcane mysteries of machine learning requires more, and deeper, mathematics than we will discuss. However, the ideas we *will* discuss are the first steps and the conceptual foundation of a more complicated presentation. Before taking those first steps, let's introduce the major Python packages we'll use to make these abstract mathematical ideas concrete.

2.3   Our Software for Tackling Machine Learning

The one tool I expect you to have in your toolbox is a basic understanding of good, old-fashioned procedural programming in Python. I'll do my best to discuss any topics that are more intermediate or advanced. We'll be using a few modules from the Python standard library that you may not have seen: `itertools`, `collections`, and `functools`.

We'll also be making use of several members of the Python number-crunching and data science stack: `numpy`, `pandas`, `matplotlib`, and `seaborn`. I won't have time to teach you all the details about these tools. However, we won't be using their more complicated features, so nothing should be too mind-blowing. We'll also briefly touch on one or two other packages, but they are relatively minor players.

Of course, much of the reason to use the number-crunching tools is because they form the foundation of, or work well with, scikit-learn. `sklearn` is a great environment for playing with the ideas of machine learning. It implements many different learning algorithms and evaluation strategies and gives you a uniform interface to run them. Win, win, and win. If you've never had the struggle—pleasure?—of integrating several different command-line learning programs . . . you didn't miss anything. Enjoy your world, it's a better place. A side note: scikit-learn is the project's name; `sklearn` is the name of the Python package. People use them interchangeably in conversation. I usually write `sklearn` because it is shorter.

2.4 Probability

Most of us are practically exposed to probability in our youth: rolling dice, flipping coins, and playing cards all give concrete examples of *random events*. When I roll a standard six-sided die—you role-playing gamers know about all the *other*-sided dice that are out there—there are six different outcomes that can happen. Each of those *events* has an equal chance of occurring. We say that the probability of each event is $\frac{1}{6}$. Mathematically, if I—a Roman numeral one, not me, myself, and I—is the case where we roll a one, we'll write that as $P(I) = \frac{1}{6}$. We read this as "the probability of rolling a one is one-sixth."

We can roll dice in Python in a few different ways. Using NumPy, we can generate evenly weighted random events with `np.random.randint`. `randint` is designed to mimic Python's indexing semantics, which means that we *include* the starting point and we *exclude* the ending point. The practical upshot is that if we want values from 1 to 6, we need to start at 1 and end at 7: the 7 will not be included. If you are more mathematically inclined, you can remember this as a half-open interval.

In [2]:

```
np.random.randint(1, 7)
```

Out[2]:

```
4
```

If we want to convince ourselves that the numbers are really being generated with equal likelihoods (as with a perfect, fair die), we can draw a chart of the frequency of the outcomes of many rolls. We'll do that in three steps. We'll roll a die, either a few times or many times:

In [3]:

```
few_rolls  = np.random.randint(1, 7, size=10)
many_rolls = np.random.randint(1, 7, size=1000)
```

We'll count up how many times each event occurred with `np.histogram`. Note that `np.histogram` is designed around plotting buckets of continuous values. Since we want to capture discrete values, we have to create a bucket that surrounds our values of interest. We capture the ones, *I*, by making a bucket between 0.5 and 1.5.

In [4]:

```
few_counts  = np.histogram(few_rolls,  bins=np.arange(.5, 7.5))[0]
many_counts = np.histogram(many_rolls, bins=np.arange(.5, 7.5))[0]

fig, (ax1, ax2) = plt.subplots(1, 2, figsize=(8, 3))
ax1.bar(np.arange(1, 7), few_counts)
ax2.bar(np.arange(1, 7), many_counts);
```

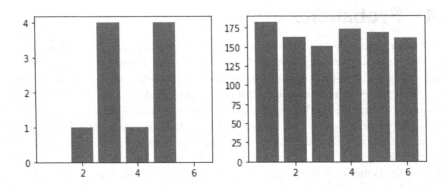

There's an important lesson here. When dealing with random events and overall behavior, a small sample can be misleading. We may need to crank up the number of examples—rolls, in this case—to get a better picture of the underlying behavior. You might ask why I didn't use `matplotlib`'s built-in `hist` function to make the graphs in one step. `hist` works well enough for larger datasets that take a wider range of values but, unfortunately, it ends up obfuscating the simple case of a few discrete values. Try it out for yourself.

2.4.1 Primitive Events

Before experimenting, we assumed that the probability of rolling a one is one out of six. That number comes from $\frac{\text{\#ways this event can occur}}{\text{\#of different events}}$. We can test our understanding of that ratio by asking, "What is the probability of rolling an odd number?" Well, using Roman numerals to indicate the outcomes of a roll, the odd numbers in our space of events are *I*, *III*, *V*. There are three of these and there are six total primitive events. So, we have $P(\text{odd}) = \frac{3}{6} = \frac{1}{2}$. Fortunately, that gels with our intuition.

We can approach this calculation a different way: an odd can occur in three ways and those three ways don't overlap. So, we can add up the individual event probabilities: $P(\text{odd}) = P(I) + P(III) + P(V) = \frac{1}{6} + \frac{1}{6} + \frac{1}{6} = \frac{3}{6} = \frac{1}{2}$. We can get probabilities of *compound events* by *either* counting primitive events *or* adding up the probabilities of primitive events. It's the same thing done in two different ways.

This basic scenario gives us an *in* to talk about a number of important aspects of probability:

- The sum of the probabilities of all possible primitive events in a universe is 1. $P(I) + P(II) + P(III) + P(IV) + P(V) + P(VI) = 1$.
- The probability of an event *not* occurring is 1 minus the probability of it occurring. $P(\text{even}) = 1 - P(\text{not even}) = 1 - P(\text{odd})$. When discussing probabilities, we often write "not" as ¬, as in $P(\neg\text{even})$. So, $P(\neg\text{even}) = 1 - P(\text{even})$.
- There are nonprimitive events. Such a compound event is a combination of primitive events. The event we called *odd* joined together three primitive events.

- A roll will be even or odd, but not both, and all rolls are either even or odd. These two compound events cover all the possible primitive events without any overlap. So, $P(\text{even}) + P(\text{odd}) = 1$.

Compound events are also recursive. We can create a compound event from other compound events. Suppose I ask, "What is the probability of getting an odd or a value greater than 3 or *both*?" That group of events, taken together, is a larger group of primitive events. If I attack this by counting those primitive events, I see that the odds are odd = $\{I, III, V\}$ and the big values are big = $\{IV, V, VI\}$. Putting them together, I get $\{I, III, IV, V, VI\}$ or $\frac{5}{6}$. The probability of this compound event is a bit different from the probability of *odds* being $\frac{1}{2}$ and the probability of *greater-than-3* being $\frac{1}{2}$. I can't just add those probabilities. Why not? Because I'd get a sum of one—meaning we covered everything—but that only demonstrates the error. The *reason* is that the two compound events overlap: they share primitive events. Rolling a five, V, occurs in both subgroups. Since they overlap, we can't just add the two together. We have to add up everything in both groups individually and then remove one of whatever was double- counted. The double-counted events were in both groups—they were odd *and* big. In this case, there is just one double-counted event, V. So, removing them looks like $P(\text{odd}) + P(\text{big})$ $- P(\text{odd and big})$. That's $\frac{1}{2} + \frac{1}{2} - \frac{1}{6} = \frac{5}{6}$.

2.4.2 Independence

If we roll two dice, a few interesting things happen. The two dice don't communicate or act on one another in any way. Rolling a I on one die does not make it more or less likely to roll any value on the other die. This concept is called independence: the two events—rolls of the individual dice—are independent of each other.

For example, consider a different set of outcomes where each event is the *sum* of the rolls of two dice. Our sums are going to be values between 2 (we roll two Is) and 12 (we roll two VIs). What is the probability of getting a sum of 2? We can go back to the counting method: there are 36 total possibilities (6 for each die, times 2) and the only way we can roll a total of 2 is by rolling two Is which can *only* happen one way. So, $P(2) = \frac{1}{36}$. We can also reach that conclusion—because the dice don't communicate or influence each other—by rolling I on die 1 and I on die 2, giving $P(I_1)P(I_2) = \frac{1}{6} \cdot \frac{1}{6} = \frac{1}{36}$. If events are independent, we can multiply their probabilities to get the joint probability of both occurring. *Also*, if we multiply the probabilities and we get the same probability as the overall resulting probability we calculated by counting, we *know* the events must be independent. Independent probabilities work both ways: they are an *if-and-only-if*.

We can combine the ideas of (1) summing the probabilities of different events and (2) the independence of events, to calculate the probability of getting a total of three $P(3)$. Using the event counting method, we figure that this event can happen in two different ways: we roll (I, II) or we roll (II, I) giving $2/36 = 1/18$. Using probability calculations, we can write:

$$P(3) = P((I, II)) + P((II, I))$$
$$= P(I)P(II) + P(II)P(I)$$
$$= \frac{1}{6} \cdot \frac{1}{6} + \frac{1}{6} \cdot \frac{1}{6} = \frac{2}{36} = \frac{1}{18}$$

Phew, that was a lot of work to verify the answer. Often, we can make use of shortcuts to reduce the number of calculations we have to perform. Sometimes these shortcuts are from knowledge of the problem and sometimes they are clever applications of the rules of probability we've seen so far. If we see multiplication, we can mentally think about the two-dice scenario. If we have a scenario like the dice, we can multiply.

2.4.3 Conditional Probability

Let's create one more scenario. In classic probability-story fashion, we will talk about two *urns*. Why urns? I guess that, before we had buckets, people had urns. So, if you don't like urns, you can think about buckets. I digress.

The first urn U_I has three red balls and one blue ball in it. The second urn U_{II} has two red balls and two blue balls. We flip a coin and then we pull a ball out of an urn. If the coin comes up heads, we pick from U_I; otherwise, we pick from U_{II}. We end up at U_I half the time and then we pick a red ball $\frac{3}{4}$ of those times. We end up at U_{II} the other half of the time and we pick a red ball $\frac{2}{4}$ of those times. This scenario is like wandering down a path with a few intersections. As we walk along, we are presented with a different set of options at the next crossroads.

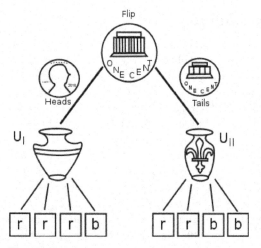

Figure 2.1   A two-step game from coins to urns.

If we sketch out the paths, it looks like Figure 2.1. If we count up the possibilities, we will see that under the whole game, we have five red outcomes and three blue outcomes. $P(\text{red}) = \frac{5}{8}$. Simple, right? Not so fast, speedy! This counting argument *only* works when we have equally likely choices at each step. Imagine we have a very wacky coin that causes me to end up at Urn *I* 999 out of 1000 times: then our chances of picking a red ball would end up quite close to the chance of just picking a red ball from Urn *I*. It would be similar to *almost* ignoring the existence of Urn *II*. We should account for this difference and, at the same time, make use of updated information that might come along the way.

If we play a partial game and we know that we're at Urn I—for example, after we've flipped a head in the first step—our odds of picking a red ball are different. Namely, the probability of picking a red ball—*given* that we are picking from Urn I—is $\frac{3}{4}$. In mathematics, we write this as $P(\text{red} \mid U_I) = \frac{3}{4}$. The vertical bar, $|$, is read as "given". Conditioning—a commonly verbed noun in machine learning and statistics—constrains us to a subset of the primitive events that could possibly occur. In this case, we condition on the occurrence of a head on our coin flip.

How often do we end up picking a red ball from Urn I? Well, to do that we have to (1) get to Urn I by flipping a head, and then (2) pick a red ball. Since the coin doesn't affect the events in Urn I—it picked Urn I, not the balls *within* Urn I—the two are independent and we can multiply them to find the joint probability of the two events occurring. So, $P(\text{red and } U_I) = P(\text{red} \mid U_I)P(U_I) = \frac{1}{2} \cdot \frac{3}{4} = \frac{3}{8}$. The order here may seem a bit weird. I've written it with the later event—the event that depends on U_I—first and the event that kicks things off, U_I, second. This order is what you'll usually see in written mathematics. Why? Largely because it places the $\mid U_I$ next to the $P(U_I)$. You can think about it as reading from the bottom of the diagram back towards the top.

Since there are two nonoverlapping ways to pick a red ball (either from Urn I or from Urn II), we can *add* up the different possibilities. Just as we did for Urn I, for Urn II we have $P(\text{red and } U_{II}) = P(\text{red} \mid U_{II})P(U_{II}) = \frac{1}{2} \cdot \frac{2}{4} = \frac{2}{8}$. Adding up the alternative ways of getting red balls, either out of Urn I or out of Urn II, gives us: $P(\text{red}) = P(\text{red} \mid U_I)P(U_I) + P(\text{red} \mid U_{II})P(U_{II}) = \frac{3}{8} + \frac{2}{8} = \frac{5}{8}$. *Mon dieu!* At least we got the same answer as we got by the *simple* counting method. But now, you know what that important vertical bar, $P(\mid)$, means.

2.4.4 Distributions

There are many different ways of assigning probabilities to events. Some of them are based on direct, real-world experiences like dice and cards. Others are based on hypothetical scenarios. We call the mapping between events and probabilities a *probability distribution*. If you give me an event, then I can look it up in the probability distribution and tell you the probability that it occurred. Based on the rules of probability we just discussed, we can also calculate the probabilities of more complicated events. When a group of events shares a common probability value—like the different faces on a fair die—we call it a *uniform distribution*. Like Storm Troopers in uniform, they all look the same.

There is one other, very common distribution that we'll talk about. It's so fundamental that there are multiple ways to approach it. We're going to go back to coin flipping. If I flip a coin many, many times and count the number of heads, here's what happens as we increase the number of flips:

```
In [5]:
import scipy.stats as ss


b = ss.distributions.binom
for flips in [5, 10, 20, 40, 80]:
```

```
# binomial with .5 is result of many coin flips
success = np.arange(flips)
our_distribution = b.pmf(success, flips, .5)
plt.hist(success, flips, weights=our_distribution)
plt.xlim(0, 55);
```

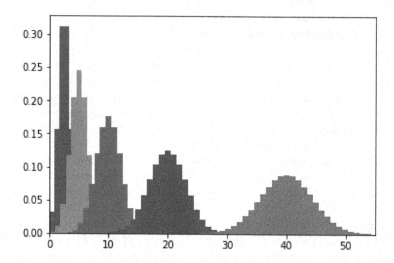

If I ignore that the whole numbers are *counts* and replace the graph with a smoother curve that takes values everywhere, instead of the stair steps that climb or descend at whole numbers, I get something like this:

In [6]:

```
b = ss.distributions.binom
n = ss.distributions.norm

for flips in [5, 10, 20, 40, 80]:
    # binomial coin flips
    success = np.arange(flips)
    our_distribution = b.pmf(success, flips, .5)
    plt.hist(success, flips, weights=our_distribution)

    # normal approximation to that binomial
    # we have to set the mean and standard deviation
    mu      = flips * .5,
    std_dev = np.sqrt(flips * .5 * (1-.5))

    # we have to set up both the x and y points for the normal
```

```
# we get the ys from the distribution (a function)
# we have to feed it xs, we set those up here
norm_x = np.linspace(mu-3*std_dev, mu+3*std_dev, 100)
norm_y = n.pdf(norm_x, mu, std_dev)
plt.plot(norm_x, norm_y, 'k');

plt.xlim(0, 55);
```

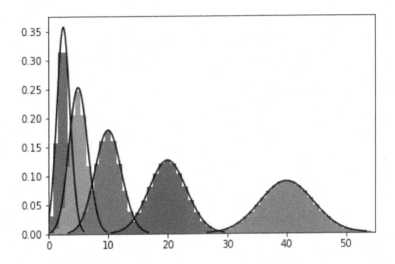

You can think about increasing the number of coin flips as increasing the accuracy of a measurement—we get more decimals of accuracy. We see the difference between 4 and 5 out of 10 and then the difference between 16, 17, 18, 19, and 20 out of 40. Instead of a big step, it becomes a smaller, more gradual step. The step-like sequences become progressively better approximated by the smooth curves. Often, these smooth curves are called *bell-shaped curves*—and, to keep the statisticians happy, yes, there are other bell-shaped curves out there. The specific bell-shaped curve that we are stepping towards is called the *normal distribution*.

The *normal distribution* has three important characteristics:

1. Its midpoint has the most likely value—the hump in the middle.
2. It is symmetric—can be mirrored—about its midpoint.
3. As we get further from the midpoint, the values fall off more and more quickly.

There are a variety of ways to make these characteristics mathematically precise. It turns out that with suitable mathese and small-print details, those characteristics also lead to the normal distribution—the smooth curve we were working towards! My mathematical colleagues may cringe, but the primary feature we need from the normal distribution is its shape.

2.5 Linear Combinations, Weighted Sums, and Dot Products

When mathematical folks talk about a linear combination, they are using a technical term for what we do when we check out from the grocery store. If your grocery store bill looks like:

Product	Quantity	Cost Per
Wine	2	12.50
Orange	12	.50
Muffin	3	1.75

you can figure out the total cost with some arithmetic:

In [7]:
```
(2 * 12.50) + (12 * .5) + (3 * 1.75)
```

Out[7]:
```
36.25
```

We might think of this as a *weighted sum*. A *sum* by itself is simply adding things up. The total number of items we bought is:

In [8]:
```
2 + 12 + 3
```

Out[8]:
```
17
```

However, when we buy things, we pay for each item based on its cost. To get a total cost, we have to add up a sequence of costs times quantities. I can phrase that in a slightly different way: we have to weight the quantities of different items by their respective prices. For example, each orange costs $0.50 and our total cost for oranges is $6. Why? Besides the invisible hand of economics, the grocery store does not want us to pay the same amount of money for the bottle of wine as we do for an orange! In fact, we don't want that either: $10 oranges aren't really a thing, are they? Here's a concrete example:

In [9]:
```
# pure python, old-school
quantity = [2, 12, 3]
costs    = [12.5, .5, 1.75]
partial_cost = []
for q,c in zip(quantity, costs):
```

```
    partial_cost.append(q*c)
sum(partial_cost)
```

Out[9]:

36.25

In [10]:

```
# pure python, for the new-school, cool kids
quantity = [2, 12, 3]
costs    = [12.5, .5, 1.75]
sum(q*c for q,c in zip(quantity,costs))
```

Out[10]:

36.25

Let's return to computing the total cost. If I line up the quantities and costs in NumPy arrays, I can run the same calculation. I can also get the benefits of data that is more organized under the hood, concise code that is easily extendible for more quantities and costs, and better small- and large-scale performance. *Whoa!* Let's do it.

In [11]:

```
quantity = np.array([2, 12, 3])
costs    = np.array([12.5, .5, 1.75])
np.sum(quantity * costs) # element-wise multiplication
```

Out[11]:

36.25

This calculation can also be performed by NumPy with `np.dot`. `dot` multiplies the elements pairwise, selecting the pairs in lockstep down the two arrays, and then adds them up:

In [12]:

```
print(quantity.dot(costs),      # dot-product way 1
      np.dot(quantity, costs),  # dot-product way 2
      quantity @ costs,         # dot-product way 3
                                # (new addition to the family!)

      sep='\n')
```

36.25
36.25
36.25

If you were ever exposed to dot products and got completely lost when your teacher started discussing geometry and cosines and vector lengths, I'm so, so sorry! Your teacher wasn't wrong, but the idea is no more complicated than checking out of the grocery store. There are two things that make the linear combination (expressed in a dot product): (1) we multiply the values pairwise, and (2) we add up all those subresults. These correspond to (1) a single multiplication to create subtotals for each line on a receipt and (2) adding those subtotals together to get your final bill.

You'll also see the dot product written mathematically (using q for `quantity` and c for `cost`) as $\sum_i q_i c_i$. If you haven't seen this notation before, here's a breakdown:

1. The $\sum$, a capital Greek *sigma*, means add up,
2. The $q_i c_i$ means multiply two things, and
3. The i ties the pieces together in lockstep like a sequence index.

More briefly, it says, "add up *all* of the element-wise multiplied q and c." Even more briefly, we might call this the *sum product* of the quantities and costs. At our level, we can use sum product as a synonym for dot product.

So, combining NumPy on the left-hand side and mathematics on the right-hand side, we have:

$$\texttt{np.dot(quantity,cost)} = \sum_i q_i c_i$$

Sometimes, that will be written as briefly as qc. If I want to emphasize the dot product, or remind you of it, I'll use a bullet (•) as its symbol: $q \bullet c$. If you are uncertain about the element-wise or lockstep part, you can use Python's `zip` function to help you out. It is designed precisely to march, in lockstep, through multiple sequences.

In [13]:

```
for q_i, c_i in zip(quantity, costs):
    print("{:2d} {:5.2f} --> {:5.2f}".format(q_i, c_i, q_i * c_i))

print("Total:",
      sum(q*c for q,c in zip(quantity,costs))) # cool-kid method
```

```
 2 12.50 --> 25.00
12  0.50 -->  6.00
 3  1.75 -->  5.25
Total: 36.25
```

Remember, we normally let NumPy—via `np.dot`—do that work for us!

2.5.1 Weighted Average

You might be familiar with a simple average—and now you're wondering, "What is a weighted average?" To help you out, the simple average—also called the mean—is an equally weighted average computed from a set of values. For example, if I have three values $(10, 20, 30)$, I divide up my weights equally among the three values and, *presto*, I get thirds: $\frac{1}{3}10 + \frac{1}{3}20 + \frac{1}{3}30$. You might be looking at me with a distinct side eye, but if I rearrange that as $\frac{10+20+30}{3}$ you might be happier. I simply do `sum(values)/3`: add them all up and divide by the number of values. Look what happens, however, if I go back to the more expanded method:

In [14]:

```
values  = np.array([10.0, 20.0, 30.0])
weights = np.full_like(values, 1/3) # repeated (1/3)

print("weights:", weights)
print("via mean:", np.mean(values))
print("via weights and dot:", np.dot(weights, values))
```

```
weights: [0.3333 0.3333 0.3333]
via mean: 20.0
via weights and dot: 20.0
```

We can write the mean as a weighted sum—a sum product between values and weights. If we start playing around with the weights, we end up with the concept of *weighted averages*. With weighted averages, instead of using equal portions, we break the portions up any way we choose. In some scenarios, we insist that the portions add up to one. Let's say we weighted our three values by $\frac{1}{2}, \frac{1}{4}, \frac{1}{4}$. Why might we do this? These weights could express the idea that the first option is *valued twice as much* as the other two and that the other two are valued equally. It might also mean that the first one is *twice as likely* in a random scenario. These two interpretations are close to what we would get if we applied those weights to underlying costs or quantities. You can view them as two sides of the same double-sided coin.

In [15]:

```
values  = np.array([10,  20,  30])
weights = np.array([.5,  .25,  .25])

np.dot(weights, values)
```

Out[15]:

17.5

One special weighted average occurs when the values are the different outcomes of a random scenario and the weights represent the probabilities of those outcomes. In this case, the weighted average is called the *expected value* of that set of outcomes. Here's a simple game. Suppose I roll a standard six-sided die and I get $1.00 if the die turns out odd and I lose $.50 if the die comes up even. Let's compute a dot product between the payoffs and the probabilities of each payoff. My expected outcome is to make:

In [16]:

```
                              # odd, even
payoffs = np.array([1.0, -.5])
probs   = np.array([ .5,    .5])
np.dot(payoffs, probs)
```

Out[16]:

0.25

Mathematically, we write the expected value of the game as $E(\text{game}) = \sum_i p_i v_i$ with p being the probabilities of the events and v being the values or payoffs of those events. Now, in any *single* run of that game, I'll *either* make \$1.00 or lose \$.50. But, if I were to play the game, say 100 times, I'd expect to come out ahead by about \$25.00 — the expected gain per game times the number of games. In reality, this outcome is a *random* event. Sometimes, I'll do better. Sometimes, I'll do worse. But \$25.00 is my best guess before heading into a game with 100 tosses. With many, many tosses, we're *highly likely* to get *very close* to that expected value.

Here's a simulation of 10000 rounds of the game. You can compare the outcome with `np.dot(payoffs, probs) * 10000`.

In [17]:

```
def is_even(n):
    # if remainder 0, value is even
    return n % 2 == 0

winnings = 0.0
for toss_ct in range(10000):
    die_toss = np.random.randint(1, 7)
    winnings += 1.0 if is_even(die_toss) else -0.5
print(winnings)
```

2542.0

2.5.2 Sums of Squares

One other, very special, sum-of-products is when both the *quantity* and the *value* are *two copies of the same thing*. For example, $5 \cdot 5 + (-3) \cdot (-3) + 2 \cdot 2 + 1 \cdot 1 = 5^2 + 3^2 + 2^2 + 1^2 = 25 + 9 + 4 + 1 = 39$. This is called a *sum of squares* since each element, multiplied by itself, gives the square of the original value. Here is how we can do that in code:

In [18]:

```
values = np.array([5, -3, 2, 1])
squares = values * values # element-wise multiplication
print(squares,
      np.sum(squares),    # sum of squares.  ha!
      np.dot(values, values), sep="\n")
```

```
[25  9  4  1]
39
39
```

If I wrote this mathematically, it would look like: $\mathtt{dot(values, values)} = \sum_i v_i v_i = \sum_i v_i^2$.

2.5.3 Sum of Squared Errors

There is another very common summation pattern, the sum of squared errors, that fits in here nicely. In this case of mathematical terminology, the red herring is both *red* and a *herring*. If I have a known value `actual` and I have your guess as to its value `predicted`, I can compute your error with `error = predicted - actual`.

Now, that error is going to be positive or negative based on whether you over- or underestimated the actual value. There are a few mathematical tricks we can pull to make the errors positive. They are useful because when we measure errors, we don't want two wrongs—overestimating by 5 and underestimating by 5—to cancel out and make a right! The trick we will use here is to square the error: an error of $5 \rightarrow 25$ and an error of $-5 \rightarrow 25$. If you ask about your total squared error after you've guessed 5 and -5, it will be $25 + 25 = 50$.

In [19]:

```
errors = np.array([5, -5, 3.2, -1.1])
display(pd.DataFrame({'errors':errors,
                      'squared':errors*errors}))
```

	errors	squared
0	5.0000	25.0000
1	-5.0000	25.0000
2	3.2000	10.2400
3	-1.1000	1.2100

So, a squared error is calculated by $error^2 = (predicted - actual)^2$. And we can add these up with $\sum_i (predicted_i - actual_i)^2 = \sum_i error_i^2$. This sum reads left to right as, "the sum of (open paren) errors which are squared (close paren)." It can be said more succinctly: the sum of squared errors. That looks a lot like the `dot` we used above:

```
In [20]:
np.dot(errors, errors)
```

```
Out[20]:
61.45
```

Weighted averages and sums of squared errors are probably the most common summation forms in machine learning. By knowing these two forms, you are now prepared to understand what's going on mathematically in many different learning scenarios. In fact, much of the notation that obfuscates machine learning from beginners—while that same notation *facilitates* communication amongst experts!—is really just compressing these summation ideas into fewer and fewer symbols. You now know how to pull those ideas apart.

You might have a small spidey sense tingling at the back of your head. It might be because of something like this: $c^2 = a^2 + b^2$. I can rename or rearrange those symbols and get $\text{distance}^2 = \text{len}_1^2 + \text{len}_2^2$ or $\text{distance} = \sqrt{\text{run}^2 + \text{rise}^2} = \sqrt{\sum_i x_i^2}$. Yes, our old friends—or nemeses, if you prefer—Euclid and Pythagoras can be wrapped up as a sum of squares. Usually, the a and b are distances, and we can compute distances by subtracting two values—just like we do when we compare our actual and predicted values. Hold on to your seats. An error is just a length—a distance—between an actual and a predicted value!

2.6 A Geometric View: Points in Space

We went from checking out at the grocery store to discussing sums of squared errors. That's quite a trip. I want to start from another simple daily scenario to discuss some basic geometry. I promise you that this will be the least geometry-class-like discussion of geometry you have ever seen.

2.6.1 Lines

Let's talk about the cost of going to a concert. I hope that's suitably nonacademic. To start with, if you drive a car to the concert, you have to park it. For up to 10 (good) friends going to the show, they can all fit in a minivan—packed in like a clown car, if need be. The group is going to pay one flat fee for parking. That's good, because the cost of parking is usually pretty high: we'll say $40. Let's put that into code and pictures:

```
In [21]:
people = np.arange(1, 11)
total_cost = np.ones_like(people) * 40.0

ax = plt.gca()

ax.plot(people, total_cost)
```

```
ax.set_xlabel("# People")
ax.set_ylabel("Cost\n(Parking Only)");
```

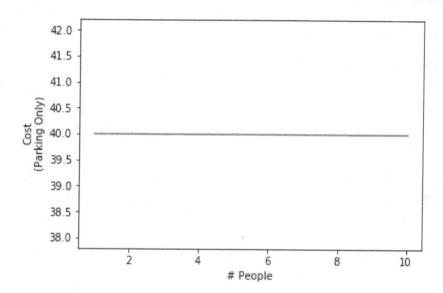

In a math class, we would write this as total_cost = 40.0. That is, regardless of the number of people—moving back and forth along the x-axis at the bottom—we pay the same amount. When mathematicians start getting abstract, they reduce the expression to simply $y = 40$. They will talk about this as being "of the form" $y = c$. That is, the height or the y-value is equal to *some constant*. In this case, it's the value 40 everywhere. Now, it doesn't do us much good to park at the show and not buy tickets—although there is something to be said for tailgating. So, what happens if we have to pay $80 per ticket?

In [22]:

```
people = np.arange(1, 11)
total_cost = 80.0 * people + 40.0
```

Graphing this is a bit more complicated, so let's make a table of the values first:

In [23]:

```
# .T (transpose) to save vertical space in printout
display(pd.DataFrame({'total_cost':total_cost.astype(np.int)},
                     index=people).T)
```

	1	2	3	4	5	6	7	8	9	10
total_cost	120	200	280	360	440	520	600	680	760	840

And we can plot that, point-by-point:

```
In [24]:
ax = plt.gca()
ax.plot(people, total_cost, 'bo')
ax.set_ylabel("Total Cost")
ax.set_xlabel("People");
```

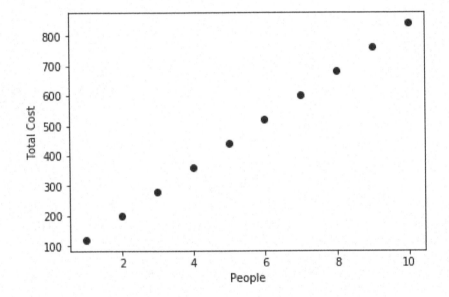

So, if we were to write this in a math class, it would look like:

$$\text{total\_cost} = \text{ticket\_cost} \times \text{people} + \text{parking\_cost}$$

Let's compare these two forms—a constant and a line—and the various ways they might be written in Table 2.1.

Table 2.1   Examples of constants and lines at different levels of language.

Name	Example	Concrete	Abstract	Mathese
Constant	total = parking	total = $40	$y = 40$	$y = c$
Line	total = ticket × person + parking	total = 80 × person + 40	$y = 80x + 40$	$y = mx + b$

I want to show off one more plot that emphasizes the two defining components of the lines: m and b. The m value—which was the $80 ticket price above—tells how much more we pay for each person we add to our trip. In math-speak, it is the *rise*, or increase in y for a single-unit increase in x. A unit increase means that the number of people on the x-axis goes from x to $x + 1$. Here, I'll control m and b and graph it.

```
In [25]:
```

```
# paint by number
# create 100 x values from -3 to 3
xs = np.linspace(-3, 3, 100)

# slope (m) and intercept (b)
m, b = 1.5, -3

ax = plt.gca()

ys = m*xs + b
ax.plot(xs, ys)

ax.set_ylim(-4, 4)
high_school_style(ax) # helper from mlwpy.py

ax.plot(0, -3,'ro') # y-intercept
ax.plot(2,  0,'ro') # two steps right gives three steps up

# y = mx + b with m=0 gives y = b
ys = 0*xs + b
ax.plot(xs, ys, 'y');
```

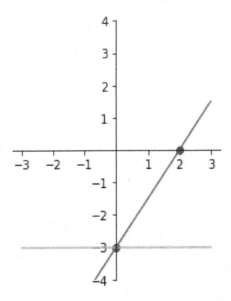

Since our slope is 1.5, taking two steps to the *right* results in us gaining three steps *up*. Also, if we have a *line* and we set the slope of the line m to 0, all of a sudden we are back to a constant. Constants are a specific, restricted type of *horizontal* line. Our yellow line which passes through $y = -3$ is one.

We can combine our ideas about `np.dot` with our ideas about lines and write some slightly different code to draw this graph. Instead of using the pair (m, b), we can write an array of values $w = (w_1, w_0)$. One trick here: I put the w_0 second, to line up with the b. Usually, that's how it is written in mathese: the w_0 is the constant.

With the ws, we can use `np.dot` *if* we augment our `xs` with an extra column of ones. I'll write that augmented version of `xs` as `xs_p1` which you can read as "exs plus a column of ones." The column of ones serves the role of the 1 in $y = mx + b$. Wait, you don't see a 1 there? Let me rewrite it: $y = mx + b = mx + b \cdot 1$. See how I rewrote $b \rightarrow b \cdot 1$? That's the same thing we need to do to make `np.dot` happy. `dot` wants to multiply *something* times w_1 and *something* times w_0. We make sure that whatever gets multiplied by w_0 is a 1.

I call this process of tacking on a column of ones the *plus-one trick* or *+1 trick* and I'll have more to say about it shortly. Here's what the plus-one trick does to our raw data:

In [26]:

```
# np.c_[] lets us create an array column-by-column
xs    = np.linspace(-3, 3, 100)
xs_p1 = np.c_[xs, np.ones_like(xs)]

# view the first few rows
display(pd.DataFrame(xs_p1).head())
```

	0	1
0	-3.0000	1.0000
1	-2.9394	1.0000
2	-2.8788	1.0000
3	-2.8182	1.0000
4	-2.7576	1.0000

Now, we can combine our data and our weights very concisely:

In [27]:

```
w  = np.array([1.5, -3])
ys = np.dot(xs_p1, w)

ax = plt.gca()
ax.plot(xs, ys)

# styling
ax.set_ylim(-4, 4)
high_school_style(ax)
```

```
ax.plot(0, -3,'ro')  # y-intercept
ax.plot(2,  0,'ro'); # two steps to the right should be three whole steps up
```

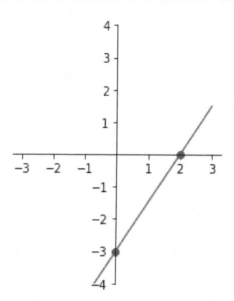

Here are the two forms we used in the code: `ys = m*xs + b` and
`ys = np.dot(xs_p1, w)`. Mathematically, these look like $y = mx + b$ and $y = wx^+$. Here,
I'm using x^+ as an abbreviation for the x that has ones tacked on to it. The two forms
defining `ys` mean the same thing. They just have some differences when we implement
them. The first form has each of the components standing on its own. The second form
requires x^+ to be augmented with a 1 and allows us to conveniently use the dot product.

2.6.2 Beyond Lines

We can extend the idea of lines in at least two ways. We can progress to wiggly curves and
polynomials—equations like $f(x) = x^3 + x^2 + x + 1$. Here, we have a *more complex*
computation on *one input value* x. Or, we can go down the road to multiple dimensions:
planes, hyperplanes, and beyond! For example, in $f(x, y, z) = x + y + z$ we have *multiple
input values* that we combine together. Since we will be *very* interested in multivariate
data—that's multiple inputs—I'm going to jump right into that.

Let's revisit the rock concert scenario. What happens if we have more than one kind of
item we want to purchase? For example, you might be surprised to learn that people
like to consume beverages at concerts. Often, they like to consume what my mother
affectionately refers to as "root beer." So, what if we have a cost for parking, a cost for the
tickets, and a cost for each root beer our group orders. To account for this, we need a new
formula. With `rb` standing for root beer, we have:

$$\text{total\_cost} = \text{ticket\_cost} \times \text{number\_people} + \text{rb\_cost} \times \text{number\_rbs} + \text{parking\_cost}$$

If we plug in some known values for parking cost, cost per ticket, and cost per root beer, then we have something more concrete:

$$total\_cost = 80 \times number\_people + 10 \times number\_rbs + 40$$

With one item, we have a simple two-dimensional plot of a line where one axis direction comes from the input "how many people" and the other comes from the output "total cost". With two items, we now have two *how many's* but still only one `total_cost`, for a total of three dimensions. Fortunately, we can still draw that somewhat reasonably. First, we create some data:

In [28]:

```
number_people = np.arange(1, 11) # 1-10 people
number_rbs    = np.arange(0, 20) # 0-19 rootbeers

# numpy tool to get cross-product of values (each against each)
# in two paired arrays.  try it out: np.meshgrid([0, 1], [10, 20])
# "perfect" for functions of multiple variables
number_people, number_rbs = np.meshgrid(number_people, number_rbs)

total_cost = 80 * number_people + 10 * number_rbs + 40
```

We can look at that data from a few different angles—literally. Below, we show the same graph from five different viewpoints. Notice that they are all flat surfaces, but the apparent tilt or slope of the surface looks different from different perspectives. The flat surface is called a plane.

In [29]:

```
# import needed for 'projection':'3d'
from mpl_toolkits.mplot3d import Axes3D
fig,axes = plt.subplots(2, 3,
                        subplot_kw={'projection':'3d'},
                        figsize=(9, 6))

angles = [0, 45, 90, 135, 180]
for ax,angle in zip(axes.flat, angles):
    ax.plot_surface(number_people, number_rbs, total_cost)
    ax.set_xlabel("People")
    ax.set_ylabel("RootBeers")
    ax.set_zlabel("TotalCost")
    ax.azim = angle

# we don't use the last axis
```

```
axes.flat[-1].axis('off')
fig.tight_layout()
```

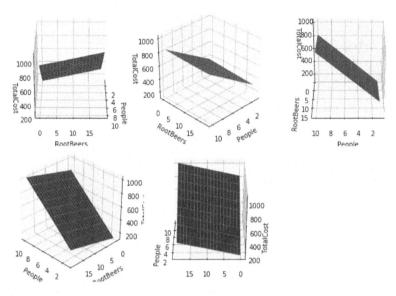

It is pretty straightforward, in code and in mathematics, to move beyond three dimensions. However, if we try to plot it out, it gets very messy. Fortunately, we can use a good old-fashioned tool—that's a GOFT to those in the know—and make a table of the outcomes. Here's an example that also includes some food for our concert goers. We'll chow on some hotdogs at $5 per hotdog:

$$\text{total\_cost} = 80 \times \text{number\_people} + 10 \times \text{number\_rbs} + 5 \times \text{number\_hotdogs} + 40$$

We'll use a few simple values for the counts of things in our concert-going system:

```
In [30]:
```

```
number_people  = np.array([2, 3])
number_rbs     = np.array([0, 1, 2])
number_hotdogs = np.array([2, 4])

costs = np.array([80, 10, 5])

columns = ["People", "RootBeer", "HotDogs", "TotalCost"]
```

I pull off combining several numpy arrays in all possible combinations, similar to what itertools's combinations function does, with a helper np_cartesian_product. It involves a bit of black magic, so I've hidden it in mlwpy.py. Feel free to investigate, if you dare.

```
In [31]:
```

```
counts = np_cartesian_product(number_people,
                              number_rbs,
                              number_hotdogs)

totals = (costs[0] * counts[:, 0] +
          costs[1] * counts[:, 1] +
          costs[2] * counts[:, 2] + 40)

display(pd.DataFrame(np.c_[counts, totals],
                     columns=columns).head(8))
```

	People	RootBeer	HotDogs	TotalCost
0	2	0	2	210
1	2	0	4	220
2	3	0	2	290
3	3	0	4	300
4	2	1	2	220
5	2	1	4	230
6	3	1	2	300
7	3	1	4	310

The assignment to `totals`—on lines 6–8 in the previous cell—is pretty ugly. Can we improve it? Think! Think! There must be a better way! What is going on there? We are adding several things up. And the things we are adding come from being multiplied together element-wise. Can it be? Is it a dot product? Yes, it is.

```
In [32]:
```

```
costs = np.array([80, 10, 5])
counts = np_cartesian_product(number_people,
                              number_rbs,
                              number_hotdogs)

totals = np.dot(counts, costs) + 40
display(pd.DataFrame(np.column_stack([counts, totals]),
                     columns=columns).head(8))
```

	People	RootBeer	HotDogs	TotalCost
0	2	0	2	210
1	2	0	4	220
2	3	0	2	290
3	3	0	4	300
4	2	1	2	220
5	2	1	4	230
6	3	1	2	300
7	3	1	4	310

Using the dot product gets us two wins: (1) the line of code that assigns to `total` is drastically improved and (2) we can more or less arbitrarily extend our costs and counts *without modifying our calculating code at all.* You might notice that I tacked the $+40$ on there by hand. That's because I didn't want to go back to the $+1$ trick—but I could have.

Incidentally, here's what would have happened in a math class. As we saw with the code-line compression from repeated additions to `dot`, details often get abstracted away or moved behind the scenes when we break out advanced notation. Here's a detailed breakdown of what happened. First, we abstract by removing detailed variable names and then replacing our known values by generic identifiers:

$$y = 80x_3 + 10x_2 + 5x_1 + 40$$
$$y = w_3x_3 + w_2x_2 + w_1x_1 + w_0 \cdot 1$$

We take this one step further in code by replacing the wx sums with a dot product:

$$y = w_{[3,2,1]} \bullet x + w_0 \cdot 1$$

The weird $[3, 2, 1]$ subscript on the w indicates that we aren't using *all* of the weights. Namely, we are *not using* the w_0 in the left-hand term. w_0 is in the right-hand term multiplying 1. It is only being used once. The final *coup de grâce* is to perform the $+1$ trick:

$$y = wx^+$$

To summarize, instead of $y = w_3x_3 + w_2x_2 + w_1x_1 + w_0$, we can write $y = wx^+$.

2.7 Notation and the Plus-One Trick

Now that you know what the plus-one trick is, I want to show a few different ways that we can talk about a table of data. That data might be made of values, such as our expense sheet for the trip to the ball park. We can take the table and draw some brackets around it:

$$D = \begin{pmatrix} x_2 & x_1 & y \\ 3 & 10 & 3 \\ 2 & 11 & 5 \\ 4 & 12 & 10 \end{pmatrix}$$

We can also refer to the parts of it: $D = (\boldsymbol{x}, y)$. Here, $\boldsymbol{x}$ means *all of the input features* and y means the *output target feature*. We can emphasize the columns:

$$D = (\boldsymbol{x}, y) = (x_f, ..., x_1, y)$$

f is the number of features. We're counting backwards to synchronize our weights with the discussion in the prior section. In turn, the weights were backwards so we could count down to the constant term at w_0. It is quite a tangled web.

We can also emphasize the rows:

$$D = \begin{bmatrix} e_1 \\ e_2 \\ \cdots \\ e_n \end{bmatrix}$$

Think of e_i as one example. n is the number of examples.

Also, for mathematical convenience—really—we will often use the augmented versions, the plus-one trick, of D and x:

$$D^+ = (x^+, y) = \begin{pmatrix} x_2 & x_1 & x_0 & y \\ 3 & 10 & 1 & 3 \\ 2 & 11 & 1 & 5 \\ 4 & 12 & 1 & 10 \end{pmatrix}$$

Let's break that down:

$$x = \begin{pmatrix} x_2 & x_1 \\ 3 & 10 \\ 2 & 11 \\ 4 & 12 \end{pmatrix}$$

If we want to use that with a 2D formula, we end up writing: $y = w_2 x_2 + w_1 x_1 + w_0$. And we can compress that as: $y = w_{[2,1]} \bullet x + w_0$. Again, the $w_{[2,1]}$ is hinting that we aren't using w_0 in the $\bullet$. Still, there is a certain ugliness about the w_0 tacked on at the end. We can compress even further if we use an augmented version of x:

$$x^+ = \begin{pmatrix} x_2 & x_1 & x_0 \\ 3 & 10 & 1 \\ 2 & 11 & 1 \\ 4 & 12 & 1 \end{pmatrix}$$

Now, our 2D formula looks like $y = w_2x_2 + w_1x_1 + w_0x_0$. Note the additional x_0. That fits nicely into $y = w \bullet x^+$, where w is (w_2, w_1, w_0). The augmented version of w now includes w_0, which was previously a weight without a home. When I want to remind you that we are dealing with x^+ or D^+, I'll say *we are using the +1 trick*. We'll connect this mathematical notation to our Python variables in Section 3.3.

2.8 Getting Groovy, Breaking the Straight-Jacket, and Nonlinearity

So, we just took an unsuspecting line and extended it past its comfort zone—maybe past yours as well. We did it in one very specific way: *we added new variables*. These new variables represented new graphical dimensions. We moved from talking about lines to talking about planes and their higher-dimensional cousins.

There is another way in which we can extend the idea of a line. Instead of adding new information—more variables or features—we can add complexity to the information we already have. Imagine moving from $y = 3$ to $y = 2x + 3$ to $y = x^2 + 2x + 3$. In each case, we've added a term to the equation. As we add terms there, we go from a flat line to a sloped line to a parabola. I'll show these off graphically in a second. The key point is: we still only have *one* input variable. We're simply using that single input in different ways.

Mathematicians talk about these extensions as adding *higher-order* or *higher-power terms* of the original variable to the equation. As we extend our powers, we get all sorts of fancy names for the functions: constant, linear, quadratic, cubic, quartic, quintic, etc. Usually, we can just call them n-th degree polynomials, where n is the highest non-zero power in the expression. A 2nd degree polynomial—for example, $y = x^2 + x + 1$—is also called a quadratic polynomial. These give us single-bend curves called parabolas.

`np.poly1d` gives us an easy helper to define polynomials by specifying the leading coefficients on each term in the polynomial. For example, we specify $2x^2 + 3x + 4$ by passing in a list of [2, 3, 4]. We'll use some random coefficients to get some interesting curves.

In [33]:

```
fig, axes = plt.subplots(2, 2)
fig.tight_layout()

titles = ["$y=c_0$",
          "$y=c_1x+c_0$",
          "$y=c_2x^2+c_1x+c_0$",
          "$y=c_3x^3+c_2x^2+c_1x+c_0$"]

xs = np.linspace(-10, 10, 100)
for power, (ax, title) in enumerate(zip(axes.flat, titles), 1):
    coeffs = np.random.uniform(-5, 5, power)
```

```
poly = np.poly1d(coeffs)
ax.plot(xs, poly(xs))
ax.set_title(title)
```

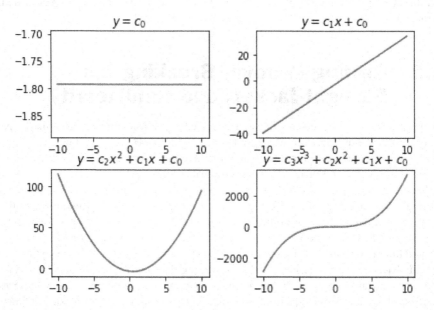

Massaging the general forms of these equations towards our earlier linear equation $y_1 = c_1x + c_0$ gets us to things like $y_2 = c_2x^2 + c_1x + c_0$. One quick note: $x = x^1$ and $1 = x^0$. While I can insert suitable mathese here, trust me that there are very good reasons to define $0^0 = 1$. Taken together, we have

$$y_2 = c_2x^2 + c_1x^1 + c_0x^0 = \sum_{i=0}^{2} c_ix^i$$

You know what I'm about to say. Go ahead, play along and say it with me. You can do it. It's a dot product! We can turn that equation into code by breaking up the x_i and the coefficients c_i and then combining them with a `np.dot`.

In [34]:

```
plt.Figure((2, 1.5))

xs = np.linspace(-10, 10, 101)
coeffs = np.array([2, 3, 4])
ys = np.dot(coeffs, [xs**2, xs**1, xs**0])

# nice parabola via a dot product
plt.plot(xs, ys);
```

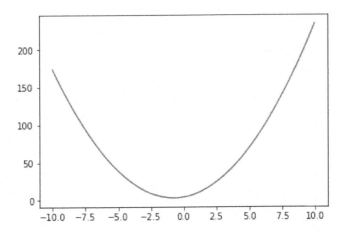

2.9 NumPy versus "All the Maths"

Since the dot product is *so fundamental* to machine learning and since NumPy's `np.dot` has to deal with the practical side of Pythonic computation—as opposed to the pure, Platonic, mathematical world of ideals—I want to spend a few minutes exploring `np.dot` and help you understand how it works in some common cases. More importantly, there is one common form that we'd *like* to use but can't without some minor adjustments. I want you to know why. Here goes.

We talked about the fact that `np.dot` multiples things element-wise and then adds them up. Here's just about the most basic example with a 1D array:

In [35]:

```
oned_vec = np.arange(5)
print(oned_vec, "-->", oned_vec * oned_vec)
print("self dot:", np.dot(oned_vec, oned_vec))
```

```
[0 1 2 3 4] --> [ 0  1  4  9 16]
self dot: 30
```

The result is the sum of squares of that array. Here's a simple example using a row and a column:

In [36]:

```
row_vec = np.arange(5).reshape(1, 5)
col_vec = np.arange(0, 50, 10).reshape(5, 1)
```

Notice that `row_vec` is shaped like a single example and `col_vec` is shaped like a single feature.

```
In [37]:
print("row vec:", row_vec,
      "col_vec:", col_vec,
      "dot:", np.dot(row_vec, col_vec), sep='\n')
```

```
row vec:
[[0 1 2 3 4]]
col_vec:
[[ 0]
 [10]
 [20]
 [30]
 [40]]
dot:
[[300]]
```

So, far, we're mostly good. But what happens if we swap the order? You might expect to get the same answer: after all, in basic arithmetic $3 \times 5 = 5 \times 3$. Let's check it out:

```
In [38]:
out = np.dot(col_vec, row_vec)
print(out)
```

```
[[  0   0   0   0   0]
 [  0  10  20  30  40]
 [  0  20  40  60  80]
 [  0  30  60  90 120]
 [  0  40  80 120 160]]
```

Cue Dorothy: "Toto, I've a feeling we're not in Kansas anymore." What happened here? We'll focus on one output element—the 20 in the second-from-the-top row—to get a handle on the craziness we unleashed. Where does it comes from? Well, we never really defined how the output is produced—except to say that it does a sum product on two 1D arrays. Let's remedy that.

Pick an element in the output, `out[1, 2]`. That's row 1 and column 2, if we start our counting from zero. `out[1, 2]` has the value 20. Where does this 20 come from? It comes from taking a dot product on row 1 of col_vec with column 2 of `row_vec`. That's actually *the definition* of what `np.dot` does. The source values are `col_vec[1,:]` which is [10] and `row_vec[:, 2]` which is [2]. Putting those together gives $10 \times 2 \to 20$ with no additional summing needed because we only have one value in each. You can go through a similar process for the other entries.

Mathematically, this is written as $\text{out}_{ij} = \text{dot}(\text{left}_{i.}, \text{right}_{.j})$ where dot is our friendly sum product over 1D things. So, the output row i comes from the left input's row i and the output's column j comes from the right input column j. Taking from each row and each column gives a 5×5 result.

If we apply the same logic to the to the row-column case, we see

```
In [39]:

out = np.dot(row_vec, col_vec)
out
```

```
Out[39]:

array([[300]])
```

The result is 1×1, so out[0, 0] comes from row 0 of row_vec and column 0 of col_vec. Which is exactly the sum product over [0, 1, 2, 3, 4] and [0, 10, 20, 30, 40], which gives us 0*0 + 1*10 + 2*20 + 3*30 + 4*40. Great.

2.9.1 Back to 1D versus 2D

However, when we use a mix of 1D and 2D inputs, things are more confusing because the input arrays are not taken at face value. There are two important consequences for us: (1) the order matters in multiplying a 1D and a 2D array and (2) we have to investigate the rules np.dot follows for handling the 1D array.

```
In [40]:

col_vec = np.arange(0, 50, 10).reshape(5, 1)
row_vec = np.arange(0, 5).reshape(1, 5)

oned_vec = np.arange(5)

np.dot(oned_vec, col_vec)
```

```
Out[40]:

array([300])
```

If we trade the order, Python blows up on us:

```
In [41]:

try:
    np.dot(col_vec, oned_vec) # *boom*
except ValueError as e:
    print("I went boom:", e)
```

```
I went boom: shapes (5,1) and (5,) not aligned: 1 (dim 1) != 5 (dim 0)
```

So, np.dot(oned_vec, col_vec) works and np.dot(col_vec, oned_vec) fails. What's going on? If we look at the shapes of the guilty parties, we can get a sense of where things break down.

```
In [42]:

print(oned_vec.shape,
      col_vec.shape, sep="\n")
```

```
(5,)
(5, 1)
```

You might consider the following exercise: create a 1D `numpy` array and look at its shape using `.shape`. Transpose it with `.T`. Look at the resulting shape. Take a minute to ponder the mysteries of the NumPy universe. Now repeat with a 2D array. These might not be entirely what you were expecting.

`np.dot` is particular about how these shapes align. Let's look at the row cases:

```
In [43]:

print(np.dot(row_vec, oned_vec))
try: print(np.dot(oned_vec, row_vec))
except: print("boom")
```

```
[30]
boom
```

Here is a summary of what we found:

form	left-input	right-input	success?
np.dot(oned_vec, col_vec)	(5,)	(5, 1)	works
np.dot(col_vec, oned_vec)	(5, 1)	(5,)	fails
np.dot(row_vec, oned_vec)	(1, 5)	(5,)	works
np.dot(oned_vec, row_vec)	(5,)	(1, 5)	fails

For the working cases, we can see what happens if we force-reshape the 1D array:

```
In [44]:

print(np.allclose(np.dot(oned_vec.reshape(1, 5), col_vec),
                  np.dot(oned_vec,                col_vec)),
      np.allclose(np.dot(row_vec, oned_vec.reshape(5, 1)),
                  np.dot(row_vec, oned_vec)))
```

```
True True
```

Effectively, for the cases that work, the 1D array is bumped up to $(1, 5)$ if it is on the left and to $(5, 1)$ if it is on the right. Basically, the 1D receives a placeholder dimension on the side it shows up in the `np.dot`. Note that this bumping is *not* using NumPy's full, generic broadcasting mechanism between the two inputs; it is more of a special case.

Broadcasting two arrays against each other in NumPy will result *in the same shape* whether you are broadcasting **a** against **b** or **b** against **a**. Even so, you can *mimic* `np.dot(col_vec, row_vec)` with broadcasting and multiplication. If you do that, you get the "big array" result: it's called an *outer product*.

With all of that said, why do we care? Here's why:

In [45]:

```
D = np.array([[1, 3],
              [2, 5],
              [2, 7],
              [3, 2]])
weights = np.array([1.5, 2.5])
```

This works:

In [46]:

```
np.dot(D,w)
```

Out[46]:

```
array([ -7.5, -12. , -18. ,  -1.5])
```

This fails:

In [47]:

```
try:
    np.dot(w,D)
except ValueError:
    print("BOOM. :sadface:")
```

```
BOOM. :sadface:
```

And sometimes, we just want the code to look like our math:

$$y = wD$$

What do we do if we don't like the interface we are given? If we are willing to (1) maintain, (2) support, (3) document, and (4) test an alternative, then we can make an interface that we prefer. Usually people only think about the implementation step. That's a costly mistake.

Here is a version of **dot** that plays nicely with a 1D input as the first argument that is shaped like a column:

```
In [48]:

def rdot(arr,brr):
    'reversed-argument version of np.dot'
    return np.dot(brr,arr)
rdot(w, D)
```

```
Out[48]:

array([ -7.5, -12. , -18. ,  -1.5])
```

You might complain that we are going through contortions to make the code look like the math. That's fair. Even in math textbooks, people will do all sorts of weird gymnastics to make this work: *w* might be transposed. In NumPy, this is fine, if it is 2D. Unfortunately, if it is only a 1D NumPy array, transposing does *nothing*. Try it yourself! Another gymnastics routine math folks will perform is to transpose the data—that is, they make each feature a row. Yes, really. I'm sorry to be the one to tell you about that. We'll just use `rdot`—short for "reversed arguments to `np.dot`"—when we want our code to match the math.

Dot products are ubiquitous in the mathematics of learning systems. Since we are focused on investigating learning systems through Python programs, it is *really important* that we (1) understand what is going on with `np.dot` and (2) have a convenient and consistent form for using it. We'll see `rdot` in our material on linear and logistic regression. It will also play a role in several other techniques. Finally, it is fundamental in showing the similarities of a wide variety of learning algorithms.

2.10   Floating-Point Issues

Prepare yourself to be grumpy.

```
In [49]:

1.1 + 2.2 == 3.3
```

```
Out[49]:

False
```

I can hear you now. You want your money back—for this book, for your Python program, for *everything*. It's all been a lie. Drama aside, what is happening here? The issue is floating-point numbers and our expectations. In the Python code above, all of the values are `floats`:

```
In [50]:

type(1.1), type(2.2), type(1.1+2.2), type(3.3)
```

```
Out[50]:
```

```
(float, float, float, float)
```

float is short for *floating-point number*, and floats are how decimal values are usually represented on a computer. When we use floats in our programs, we are often thinking about two different types of numbers: (1) simple decimal values like 2.5 and (2) complicated *real* numbers like π which go on forever, even though we may get away with approximations like 3.14. Both of these have complications when we go from *our* thoughts about these numbers to the *computer's* number-crunching machinery.

Here are a few facts:

1. Computer memory is finite. We can't physically store an infinite number of digits for any numerical value.
2. Some numbers that interest us have an infinite number of decimal places ($\frac{1}{9}$ and π, I'm looking at you).
3. Computers store all of their information in bits—that's base-2 numbers, or *binary*.
4. There are *different* infinite-digit numbers when we write them in decimal versus binary.

Because of points one and two, we have to *approximate* the values we store. We can get *close*, but we can never be *exact*. Because of points three and four, when we convert from a seemingly innocent decimal number like 3.3 to binary, it may become much more complicated—it might have repeating digits, like $\frac{1}{9}$ does in a decimal representation. Putting these pieces together means that *we can't rely on exact comparisons for floating-point values*.

So, what can we do? We can ask if values are *close enough*:

```
In [51]:
```

```
np.allclose(1.1 + 2.2, 3.3)
```

```
Out[51]:
```

```
True
```

Here, numpy is checking if the numbers are the same for many, many decimal places—out to the point where the difference is insignificant. If we care, we can define our own tolerance for what is and isn't significant.

2.11 EOC

2.11.1 Summary

We covered a lot of ideas in this chapter and laid the groundwork to talk about learning in an intelligent way. In many cases, we won't be diving into mathematical details of learning algorithms. However, when we talk about them, we will often appeal to probability, geometry, and dot products in our descriptions. Hopefully, you now have better intuitions about what these terms and symbols mean—particularly if no one has taken the time to explain them to you in a concrete fashion before.

2.11.2 Notes

While we took an intuitive approach to describing distributions, they have concrete mathematical forms which can be extended to multiple dimensions. The discrete uniform distribution looks like:

$$f(x) = \frac{1}{k}$$

Here, k is the number of possible events—six for a typical die or two for a coin flip. The equation for the normal distribution is

$$f(x) = \frac{1}{v_m \text{spread}} e^{-\frac{1}{2}\left(\frac{x - \text{center}}{\text{spread}}\right)^2}$$

The e, combined with a negative power, is responsible for the fast dropoff away from the center. v_m, a *magic value*, is really just there to make sure that all the possibilities sum up to one like all good distributions: it is $v_m = \sqrt{2\pi}$ but I won't quiz you on that. The *center* and *spread* are normally called the *mean* and *standard deviation* and written with μ and σ which are the lowercase Greek *mu* and *sigma*. The normal distribution shows up *everywhere* in statistics: in error functions, in binomial approximations (which we used to generate our normal shapes), and in central limit theorems.

Python uses 0-based indexing while mathematicians often use 1-based indexing. That's because mathematicians are generally *counting* things and computer scientists have historically cared about offsets: from the start, how many steps do I need to move forward to get to the item I need? If I'm at the start of a list or an array, I have to take zero steps to get the first item: I'm already there. A very famous computer scientist, Edsger Dijkstra, wrote an article called "Why numbering should start at zero." Check it out if you are interested and want to win on a computer-science trivia night.

In my mathematical notation, I'm following classic Python's lead and letting both ( ) and [] represent ordered things. { } is used for unordered groups of things—imagine putting things in a large duffel bag and then pulling them back out. The duffel bag doesn't remember the order things were put in it. In a relatively recent change, Python dictionaries in Python 3.7 now have some ordering guarantees to them. So, strictly speaking—after upgrading to the latest Python—I'm using the curly braces in the mathematical **set** sense.

The phrase "there must be a better way!"—particularly in the Python community—deserves a hat tip to Raymond Hettinger, a core Python developer. His Python talks are legendary: find them on YouTube and you'll learn something new about Python.

Predicting Categories: Getting Started with Classification

In [1]:

```
# setup
from mlwpy import *
%matplotlib inline
```

3.1 Classification Tasks

Now that we've laid a bit of groundwork, let's turn our attention to the main attraction: building and evaluating learning systems. We'll start with classification and we need some data to play with. If that weren't enough, we need to establish some evaluation criteria for success. All of these are just ahead.

Let me squeeze in a few quick notes on terminology. If there are only two target classes for output, we can call a learning task *binary classification*. You can think about {*Yes, No*}, {*Red, Black*}, or {*True, False*} targets. Very often, binary problems are described mathematically using $\{-1, +1\}$ or $\{0, 1\}$. Computer scientists love to encode {*False, True*} into the numbers $\{0, 1\}$ as the output values. In reality, $\{-1, +1\}$ or $\{0, 1\}$ are both used for mathematical convenience, and it won't make much of a difference to us. (The two encodings often cause head-scratching if you lose focus reading two different mathematical presentations. You might see one in a blog post and the other in an article and you can't reconcile them. I'll be sure to point out any differences in *this* book.) With more than two target classes, we have a *multiclass* problem.

Some classifiers try to make a decision about the output in a direct fashion. The direct approach gives us great flexibility in the relationships we find, but that very flexibility means that we aren't tied down to assumptions that might lead us to better decisions. These assumptions are similar to limiting the suspects in a crime to people that were near where the crime occurred. Sure, we could start with no assumptions at all and equally consider suspects from London, Tokyo, and New York for a crime that occurred in

Nashville. But, adding an assumption that the suspect is in Tennessee should lead to a better pool of suspects.

Other classifiers break the decision into a two-step process: (1) build a model of how likely the outcomes are and (2) pick the most likely outcome. Sometimes we prefer the second approach because we care about the grades of the prediction. For example, we might want to know how likely it is that someone is sick. That is, we want to know that there is a 90% chance someone is sick, versus a more generic estimate "yes, we think they are sick." That becomes important when the real-world cost of our predictions is high. When cost matters, we can combine the probabilities of events with the costs of those events and come up with a decision model to choose a real-world action that balances these, possibly competing, demands. We will consider one example of each type of classifier: Nearest Neighbors goes directly to an output class, while Naive Bayes makes an intermediate stop at an estimated probability.

3.2   A Simple Classification Dataset

The *iris* dataset is included with `sklearn` and it has a long, rich history in machine learning and statistics. It is sometimes called Fisher's Iris Dataset because Sir Ronald Fisher, a mid-20th-century statistician, used it as the sample data in one of the first academic papers that dealt with what we now call classification. Curiously, Edgar Anderson was responsible for gathering the data, but his name is not as frequently associated with the data. Bummer. History aside, what is the *iris* data? Each row describes one iris—that's a flower, by the way—in terms of the length and width of that flower's sepals and petals (Figure 3.1). Those are the big flowery parts and little flowery parts, if you want to be highly technical. So, we have four total measurements per iris. Each of the measurements is a length of one aspect of that iris. The final column, our classification target, is the particular species—one of three—of that iris: *setosa*, *versicolor*, or *virginica*.

We'll load the *iris* data, take a quick tabular look at a few rows, and look at some graphs of the data.

In [2]:

```
iris = datasets.load_iris()

iris_df = pd.DataFrame(iris.data,
                       columns=iris.feature_names)
iris_df['target'] = iris.target
display(pd.concat([iris_df.head(3),
                   iris_df.tail(3)]))
```

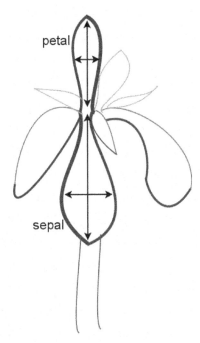

Figure 3.1   An iris and its parts.

	sepal length (cm)	sepal width (cm)	petal length (cm)	petal width (cm)	target
0	5.1000	3.5000	1.4000	0.2000	0
1	4.9000	3.0000	1.4000	0.2000	0
2	4.7000	3.2000	1.3000	0.2000	0
147	6.5000	3.0000	5.2000	2.0000	2
148	6.2000	3.4000	5.4000	2.3000	2
149	5.9000	3.0000	5.1000	1.8000	2

In [3]:

```
sns.pairplot(iris_df, hue='target', size=1.5);
```

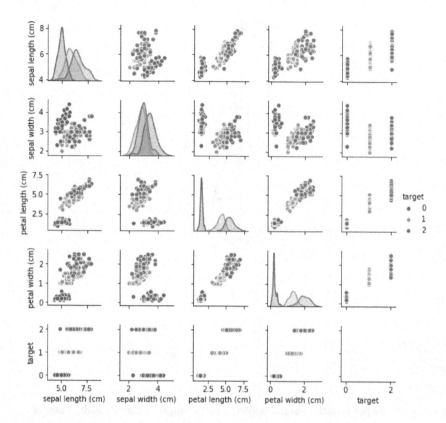

`sns.pairplot` gives us a nice panel of graphics. Along the diagonal from the top-left to bottom-right corner, we see histograms of the frequency of the different types of iris differentiated by color. The off-diagonal entries—everything *not* on that diagonal—are scatter plots of pairs of features. You'll notice that these pairs occur twice—once above and once below the diagonal—but that each plot for a pair is flipped axis-wise on the other side of the diagonal. For example, near the bottom-right corner, we see *petal width* against *target* and then we see *target* against *petal width* (across the diagonal). When we flip the axes, we change up-down orientation to left-right orientation.

In several of the plots, the blue group (target 0) seems to stand apart from the other two groups. Which species is this?

In [4]:

```
print('targets: {}'.format(iris.target_names),
      iris.target_names[0], sep="\n")
```

```
targets: ['setosa' 'versicolor' 'virginica']
setosa
```

So, looks like *setosa* is easy to separate or partition off from the others. The *vs, versicolor* and *virginica*, are more intertwined.

3.3 Training and Testing: Don't Teach to the Test

Let's briefly turn our attention to how we are going to use our data. Imagine you are taking a class (Figure 3.2). Let's go wild and pretend you are studying machine learning. Besides wanting a good grade, when you take a class to learn a subject, you want to be able to use that subject in the real world. Our grade is a surrogate measure for how well we will do in the real world. Yes, I can see your grumpy faces: grades can be very bad estimates of how well we do in the real world. Well, we're in luck! We get to try to make *good* grades that really tell us how well we will do when we get out there to face reality (and, perhaps, our student loans).

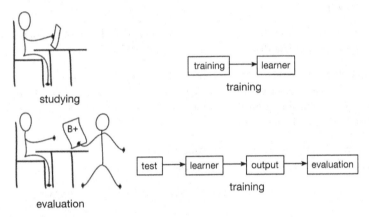

Figure 3.2   School work: training, testing, and evaluating.

So, back to our classroom setting. A common way of evaluating students is to teach them some material and then test them on it. You might be familiar with the phrase "teaching to the test." It is usually regarded as a bad thing. Why? Because, if we teach to the test, the students will do better on the test than on other, new problems they have never seen before. They know the specific answers for the test problems, but they've missed out on the *general* knowledge and techniques they need to answer *novel* problems. Again, remember our goal. We want to do well in the real-world use of our subject. In a machine learning scenario, we want to do well on *unseen* examples. Our performance on unseen examples is called *generalization*. If we test ourselves on data we have already seen, we will have an overinflated estimate of our abilities on novel data.

Teachers prefer to assess students on novel problems. Why? Teachers care about how the students will do on new, never-before-seen problems. If they practice on a specific problem and figure out what's right or wrong about their answer to it, we want that new nugget of knowledge to be something general that they can apply to other problems. If we want to estimate how well the student will do on novel problems, we have to evaluate them on novel problems. Are you starting to feel bad about studying old exams yet?

I don't want to get into too many details of too many tasks here. Still, there is one complication I feel compelled to introduce. Many presentations of learning start off using a teach-to-the-test evaluation scheme called *in-sample evaluation* or *training error*. These have their uses. However, not teaching to the test is such an important concept in learning systems that *I refuse to start you off on the wrong foot!* We just can't take an easy way out. We are going to put on our big girl and big boy pants and do this like adults with a real, *out-of-sample* or *test error* evaluation. We can use these as an estimate for our ability to generalize to unseen, future examples.

Fortunately, `sklearn` gives us some support here. We're going to use a tool from `sklearn` to avoid teaching to the test. The `train_test_split` function segments our dataset that lives in the Python variable `iris`. Remember, that dataset has two components already: the *features* and the *target*. Our new segmentation is going to split it into two buckets of examples:

1. A portion of the data that we will use to study and build up our understanding and
2. A portion of the data that we will use to test ourselves.

We will only study—that is, learn from—the *training* data. To keep ourselves honest, we will only evaluate ourselves on the *testing* data. We promise not to peek at the testing data. We started by breaking our dataset into two parts: features and target. Now, we're breaking each of those into two pieces:

1. Features → training features and testing features
2. Targets → training targets and testing targets

We'll get into more details about `train_test_split` later. Here's what a basic call looks like:

In [5]:

```
# simple train-test split
(iris_train_ftrs, iris_test_ftrs,
 iris_train_tgt,  iris_test_tgt) = skms.train_test_split(iris.data,
                                                         iris.target,
                                                         test_size=.25)
print("Train features shape:", iris_train_ftrs.shape)
print("Test features shape:",  iris_test_ftrs.shape)
```

```
Train features shape: (112, 4)
Test features shape: (38, 4)
```

So, our training data has 112 examples described by four features. Our testing data has 38 examples described by the same four attributes.

If you're confused about the two splits, check out Figure 3.3. Imagine we have a box drawn around a table of our total data. We identify a special column and put that special column on the right-hand side. We draw a vertical line that separates that rightmost column from the rest of the data. That vertical line is the split between our predictive

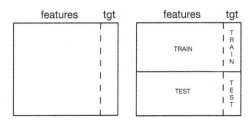

Figure 3.3   Training and testing with features and a target in a table.

features and the target feature. Now, somewhere on the box we draw a horizontal line—maybe three quarters of the way towards the bottom.

The area above the horizontal line represents the part of the data that we use for training. The area below the line is—you got it!—the testing data. And the vertical line? That single, special column is our target feature. In some learning scenarios, there might be multiple target features, but those situations don't fundamentally alter our discussion. Often, we need relatively more data to learn from and we are content with evaluating ourselves on somewhat less data, so the training part might be greater than 50 percent of the data and testing less than 50 percent. Typically, we sort data into training and testing *randomly*: imagine shuffling the examples like a deck of cards and taking the top part for training and the bottom part for testing.

Table 3.1 lists the pieces and how they relate to the *iris* dataset. Notice that I've used both some English phrases and some abbreviations for the different parts. I'll do my best to be consistent with this terminology. You'll find some differences, as you go from book A to blog B and from article C to talk D, in the use of these terms. That isn't the end of the world and there are usually close similarities. Do take a moment, however, to orient yourself when you start following a new discussion of machine learning.

Table 3.1   Relationship between Python variables and *iris* data components.

iris Python variable	Symbol	Phrase
iris	D_{all}	(total) dataset
iris.data	D_{ftrs}	train and test features
iris.target	D_{tgt}	train and test targets
iris_train_ftrs	D_{train}	training features
iris_test_ftrs	D_{test}	testing features
iris_train_tgt	$D_{train_{tgt}}$	training target
iris_test_tgt	$D_{test_{tgt}}$	testing target

One slight hiccup in the table is that `iris.data` refers to all of the input *features*. But this is the terminology that scikit-learn chose. Unfortunately, the Python variable name `data` is sort of like the mathematical x: they are both generic identifiers. `data`, as a name, can refer to just about any body of information. So, while scikit-learn is using a specific sense of the word *data* in `iris.data`, I'm going to use a more specific indicator, D_{ftrs}, for the *features* of the whole dataset.

3.4 Evaluation: Grading the Exam

We've talked a bit about how we want to design our evaluation: we don't teach to the test. So, we train on one set of questions and then evaluate on a new set of questions. How are we going to compute a grade or a score from the exam? For now—and we'll dive into this later—we are simply going to ask, "Is the answer correct?" If the answer is *true* and we predicted *true*, then we get a point! If the answer is *false* and we predicted *true*, we don't get a point. Cue :sadface:. Every correct answer will count as one point. Every missed answer will count as zero points. Every question will count equally for one or zero points. In the end, we want to know the percent we got correct, so we add up the points and divide by the number of questions. This type of evaluation is called *accuracy*, its formula being $\frac{\#correct\ answers}{\#questions}$. It is very much like scoring a multiple-choice exam.

So, let's write a snippet of code that captures this idea. We'll have a very short exam with four true-false questions. We'll imagine a student who finds themselves in a bind and, in a last act of desperation, answers every question with **True**. Here's the scenario:

In [6]:

```
answer_key       = np.array([True, True, False, True])
student_answers = np.array([True, True, True, True]) # desperate student!
```

We can calculate the accuracy by hand in three steps:

1. Mark each answer right or wrong.
2. Add up the correct answers.
3. Calculate the percent.

In [7]:

```
correct = answer_key == student_answers
num_correct = correct.sum() # True == 1, add them up
print("manual accuracy:", num_correct / len(answer_key))
```

manual accuracy: 0.75

Behind the scenes, sklearn's **metrics.accuracy_score** is doing an equivalent calculation:

In [8]:

```
print("sklearn accuracy:",
      metrics.accuracy_score(answer_key,
                             student_answers))
```

sklearn accuracy: 0.75

So far, we've introduced two key components in our evaluation. First, we identified which material we study from and which material we test from. Second, we decided on a method to score the exam. We are now ready to introduce our first learning method, train it, test it, and evaluate it.

3.5 Simple Classifier #1: Nearest Neighbors, Long Distance Relationships, and Assumptions

One of the simpler ideas for making predictions from a labeled dataset is:

1. Find a way to describe the similarity of two different examples.
2. When you need to make a prediction on a new, unknown example, simply take the value from the most similar known example.

This process is the nearest-neighbors algorithm in a nutshell. I have three friends *Mark, Barb, Ethan* for whom I know their favorite snacks. A new friend, Andy, is most like Mark. Mark's favorite snack is Cheetos. I predict that Andy's favorite snack is the same as Mark's: Cheetos.

There are many ways we can modify this basic template. We may consider more than *just* the single most similar example:

1. Describe similarity between pairs of examples.
2. Pick several of the most-similar examples.
3. Combine those picks to get a single answer.

3.5.1 Defining Similarity

We have complete control over what *similar* means. We could define it by calculating a *distance* between pairs of examples: `similarity = distance(example_one, example_two)`. Then, our idea of similarity becomes encoded in the way we calculate the distance. Similar things are close—a small distance apart. Dissimilar things are far away—a large distance apart.

Let's look at three ways of calculating the similarity of a pair of examples. The first, *Euclidean* distance, harkens back to high-school geometry or trig. We treat the two examples as points in space. Together, the two points define a line. We let that line be the hypotenuse of a right triangle and, armed with the Pythagorean theorem, use the other two sides of the triangle to calculate a distance (Figure 3.4). You might recall that $c^2 = a^2 + b^2$ or $c = \sqrt{a^2 + b^2}$. Or, you might just recall it as painful. Don't worry, we don't have to *do* the calculation. `scikit-learn` can be told, "Do that *thing* for me." By now, you might be concerned that my next example can only get *worse*. Well, frankly, it could. The *Minkowski* distance would lead us down a path to Einstein and his theory of relativity . . . but we're going to avoid that black (rabbit) hole.

Instead, another option for calculating similarity makes sense when we have examples that consist of simple *Yes, No* or *True, False* features. With Boolean data, I can compare two examples very nicely by counting up the number of features that are *different*. This simple idea is clever enough that it has a name: the *Hamming* distance. You might recognize this as a close cousin—maybe even a sibling or evil twin—of accuracy. Accuracy is the percent *correct*—the percent of answers the *same* as the target—which is $\frac{correct}{total}$. Hamming distance is the number of *differences*. The practical implication is that when two sets of answers agree

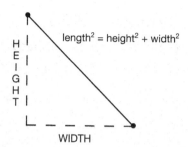

length² = height² + width²

Figure 3.4   Distances from components.

completely, we want the accuracy to be high: 100%. When two sets of features are identical, we want the similarity distance between them to be low: 0.

You might have noticed that these notions of similarity have names—Euclid(-ean), Minkowski, Hamming Distance—that all fit the template of *FamousMathDude Distance*. Aside from the math dude part, the reason they share the term *distance* is because they obey the mathematical rules for what constitutes a distance. They are also called *metrics* by the mathematical wizards-that-be—as in *distance metric* or, informally, a distance measure. These mathematical terms will sometimes slip through in conversation and documentation. `sklearn`'s list of possible distance calculators is in the documentation for `neighbors.DistanceMetric`: there are about twenty metrics defined there.

3.5.2 The k in k-NN

Choices certainly make our lives complicated. After going to the trouble of choosing how to measure our local neighborhood, we have to decide how to combine the different opinions in the neighborhood. We can think about that as determining who gets to vote and how we will combine those votes.

Instead of considering only *the* nearest neighbor, we might consider some small number of nearby neighbors. Conceptually, expanding our neighborhood gives us more perspectives. From a technical viewpoint, an expanded neighborhood protects us from noise in the data (we'll come back to this in far more detail later). Common numbers of neighbors are 1, 3, 10, or 20. Incidentally, a common name for this technique, and the abbreviation we'll use in this book, is *k-NN* for "k-Nearest Neighbors". If we're talking about k-NN for classification and need to clarify that, I'll tack a C on there: *k-NN-C*.

3.5.3 Answer Combination

We have one last loose end to tie down. We must decide how we combine the known values (votes) from the close, or similar, neighbors. If we have an animal classification problem, four of our nearest neighbors might vote for *cat*, *cat*, *dog*, and *zebra*. How do we respond for our test example? It seems like taking the most frequent response, *cat*, would be a decent method.

In a very cool twist, we can use the exact same neighbor-based technique in *regression* problems where we try to predict a numerical value. The only thing we have to change is how we combine our neighbors' targets. If three of our nearest neighbors gave us numerical values of 3.1, 2.2, and 7.1, how do we combine them? We could use any statistic we wanted, but the mean (average) and the median (middle) are two common and useful choices. We'll come back to k-NN for regression in the next chapter.

3.5.4 *k*-NN, Parameters, and Nonparametric Methods

Since k-NN is the first model we're discussing, it is a bit difficult to compare it to other methods. We'll save some of those comparisons for later. There's one major difference we can dive into *right now*. I hope that grabbed your attention.

Recall the analogy of a learning model as a machine with knobs and levers on the side. Unlike many other models, k-NN outputs—the predictions—can't be computed from an input example and the values of a small, fixed set of adjustable knobs. We need *all* of the training data to figure out our output value. Really? Imagine that we throw out just one of our training examples. That example might be *the* nearest neighbor of a new test example. Surely, missing that training example will affect our output. There are other machine learning methods that have a similar requirement. Still others need some, but not *all*, of the training data when it comes to test time.

Now, you might argue that for a fixed amount of training data there could be a fixed number of knobs: say, 100 examples and 1 knob per example, giving 100 knobs. Fair enough. But then I add one example—and, poof, you now need 101 knobs, and that's a *different* machine. In this sense, the number of knobs on the k-NN machine depends on the number of examples in the training data. There is a better way to describe this dependency. Our factory machine had a side tray where we could feed additional information. We can treat the training data as this additional information. Whatever we choose, if we need either (1) a growing number of knobs or (2) the side-input tray, we say the type of machine is *nonparametric*. k-NN is a nonparametric learning method.

Nonparametric learning methods can have parameters. (Thank you for nothing, formal definitions.) What's going on here? When we call a method *nonparametric*, it means that with this method, the relationship between features and targets cannot be captured solely using a *fixed* number of parameters. For statisticians, this concept is related to the idea of parametric versus nonparametric statistics: nonparametric statistics assume less about a basket of data. However, recall that we are *not* making any assumptions about the way our black-box factory machine relates to reality. Parametric models (1) make an assumption about the form of the model and then (2) pick a specific model by setting the parameters. This corresponds to the two questions: what knobs are on the machine, and what values are they set to? We don't make assumptions like that with k-NN. However, k-NN *does* make and rely on assumptions. The most important assumption is that our similarity calculation is related to the *actual* example similarity that we want to capture.

3.5.5 Building a *k*-NN Classification Model

k-NN is our first example of a *model*. Remember, a supervised model is anything that captures the relationship between our features and our target. We need to discuss a few concepts that swirl around the idea of a model, so let's provide a bit of context first. Let's write down a small process we want to walk through:

1. We want to use 3-NN—three nearest neighbors—as our model.
2. We want that model to capture the relationship between the iris training features and the iris training target.
3. We want to use that model to *predict*—on previously unseen test examples—the iris target species.
4. Finally, we want to evaluate the quality of those predictions, using accuracy, by comparing predictions against reality. We didn't peek at these known answers, but we can use them as an answer key for the test.

There's a diagram of the flow of information in Figure 3.5.

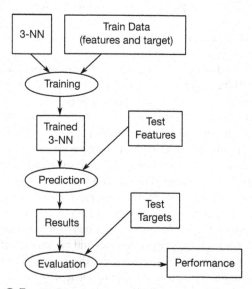

Figure 3.5   Workflow of training, testing, and evaluation for 3-NN.

As an aside on `sklearn`'s terminology, in their documentation an *estimator* is *fit* on some data and then used to *predict* on some data. If we have a training and testing split, we *fit* the *estimator* on *training data* and then use the *fit-estimator* to *predict* on the *test data*. So, let's

1. Create a 3-NN model,
2. Fit that model on the training data,
3. Use that model to predict on the test data, and
4. Evaluate those predictions using accuracy.

In [9]:

```
# default n_neighbors = 5
knn    = neighbors.KNeighborsClassifier(n_neighbors=3)
fit    = knn.fit(iris_train_ftrs, iris_train_tgt)
preds = fit.predict(iris_test_ftrs)

# evaluate our predictions against the held-back testing targets
print("3NN accuracy:",
      metrics.accuracy_score(iris_test_tgt, preds))
```

3NN accuracy: 1.0

Wow, 100%. We're doing great! This machine learning stuff seems pretty easy—except when it isn't. We'll come back to that shortly. We can abstract away the details of k-NN classification and write a simplified workflow template for building and assessing models in sklearn:

1. Build the model,
2. Fit the model using the training data,
3. Predict using the fit model on the testing data, and
4. Evaluate the quality of the predictions.

We can connect this workflow back to our conception of a model as a machine. The equivalent steps are:

1. Construct the machine, including its knobs,
2. Adjust the knobs and feed the side-inputs appropriately to capture the training data,
3. Run new examples through the machine to see what the outputs are, and
4. Evaluate the quality of the outputs.

Here's one last, quick note. The 3 in our 3-nearest-neighbors is not something that we adjust by training. It is part of the *internal* machinery of our learning machine. There is no knob on our machine for turning the 3 to a 5. If we want a 5-NN machine, we have to build a completely different machine. The 3 is not something that is adjusted by the k-NN training process. The 3 is a *hyperparameter*. *Hyperparameters* are not trained or manipulated by the learning method they help define. An equivalent scenario is agreeing to the rules of a game and then playing the game under that *fixed* set of rules. Unless we're playing Calvinball or acting like Neo in *The Matrix*—where the flux of the rules is the point—the rules are static for the duration of the game. You can think of hyperparameters as being predetermined and fixed in place before we get a chance to do anything with them while learning. Adjusting them involves conceptually, and literally, working outside the learning box or the factory machine. We'll discuss this topic more in Chapter 11.

3.6   Simple Classifier #2: Naive Bayes, Probability, and Broken Promises

Another basic classification technique that draws directly on probability for its inspiration and operation is the Naive Bayes classifier. To give you insight into the underlying probability ideas, let me start by describing a scenario.

There's a casino that has two tables where you can sit down and play games of chance. At either table, you can play a dice game and a card game. One table is fair and the other table is rigged. Don't fall over in surprise, but we'll call these *Fair* and *Rigged*. If you sit at *Rigged*, the dice you roll have been tweaked and will only come up with six pips—the dots on the dice—one time in ten. The rest of the values are spread equally likely among 1, 2, 3, 4, and 5 pips. If you play cards, the scenario is even worse: the deck at the rigged table has no face cards—kings, queens, or jacks—in it. I've sketched this out in Figure 3.6. For those who want to nitpick, you can't tell these modifications have been made because the dice are visibly identical, the card deck is in an opaque card holder, and you make no physical contact with either the dice or the deck.

No K, Q, J
Bad Dice

Regular Deck
Fair Dice

Figure 3.6   Fair and rigged tables at a casino.

Suppose I tell you—truthfully!—that you are sitting at *Rigged*. Then, when you play cards for a while and never see a face card, you aren't surprised. You also won't expect to see sixes on the die very often. Still, if you *know* you are at *Rigged*, neither of the outcomes of the dice or card events is going to *add* anything to your knowledge about the other. We *know* we are at *Rigged*, so *inferring* that we are *Rigged* doesn't add a new fact to our knowledge—although in the real world, confirmation of facts is nice.

Without knowing what table we are at, when we start seeing outcomes we receive information that indicates which table we are at. That can be turned into concrete predictions about the dice and cards. If we *know* which table we're at, that process is short-circuited and we can go directly to predictions about the dice and cards. The information about the table cuts off any gains from seeing a die or card outcome. The story is similar at *Fair*. If I tell you that you just sat down at the fair table, you would expect all the dice rolls to happen with the same probability and the face cards to come up every so often.

Now, imagine you are blindfolded and led to a table. You only know that there are two tables and you know what is happening at both—you know *Rigged* and *Fair* exist.

However, you don't know whether you are at *Rigged* or *Fair*. You sit down and the blindfold is removed. If you are dealt a face card, you immediately know you are at the *Fair* table. When we knew the table we were sitting at, knowing something about the dice didn't tell us anything additional about the cards or vice versa. Now that we don't know the table, we might get some information about the dice from the cards. If we see a face card, which doesn't exist at *Rigged*, we know we *aren't* at *Rigged*. We *must* be at *Fair*. (That's double negative logic put to good use.) As a result, we know that sixes are going to show up regularly.

Our key takeaway is that *there is no communication or causation between the dice and the cards at one of the tables*. Once we sit at *Rigged*, picking a card doesn't adjust the dice odds. The way mathematicians describe this is by saying the cards and the dice are *conditionally independent given the table*.

That scenario lets us discuss the main ideas of Naive Bayes (NB). The key component of NB is that it treats the features as if they are conditionally independent of each other given the class, just like the dice and cards at one of the tables. Knowing the table solidifies our ideas about what dice and cards we'll see. Likewise, knowing a class sets our ideas about what feature values we expect to see.

Since independence of probabilities plays out mathematically as multiplication, we get a very simple description of probabilities in a NB model. The likelihood of features for a given class can be calculated from the training data. From the training data, we store the probabilities of seeing particular features within each target class. For testing, we look up probabilities of feature values associated with a potential target class and multiply them together along with the overall class probability. We do that for each possible class. Then, we choose the class with the highest overall probability.

I constructed the casino scenario to explain what is happening with NB. However, when we use NB as our classification technique, *we assume that the conditional independence between features holds, and then we run calculations on the data*. We could be wrong. The assumptions might be broken! For example, we might not know that every time we roll a specific value on the dice, the dealers—who are *very* good card sharks—are manipulating the deck we draw from. If that were the case, there *would* be a connection between the deck and dice; our assumption that there is no connection would be *wrong*. To quote a famous statistician, George Box, "All models are wrong but some are useful." Indeed.

Naive Bayes can be *very* useful. It turns out to be unreasonably useful in text classification. This is almost mind-blowing. It seems obvious that the words in a sentence depend on each other and on their order. We don't pick words at random; we intentionally put the right words together, in the right order, to communicate specific ideas. How can a method which *ignores* the relationship between words—which are the basis of our features in text classification—be so useful? The reasoning behind NB's success is two-fold. First, Naive Bayes is a relatively *simple* learning method that is hard to distract with irrelevant details. Second, since it is particularly simple, it benefits from having *lots* of data fed into it. I'm being slightly vague here, but you'll need to jump ahead to the discussion of *overfitting* (Section 5.3) to get more out of me.

Let's build, fit, and evaluate a simple NB model.

```
In [10]:
nb    = naive_bayes.GaussianNB()
fit   = nb.fit(iris_train_ftrs, iris_train_tgt)
preds = fit.predict(iris_test_ftrs)

print("NB accuracy:",
      metrics.accuracy_score(iris_test_tgt, preds))
```

```
NB accuracy: 1.0
```

Again, we are perfect. Don't be misled, though. Our success says more about the ease of the dataset than our skills at machine learning.

3.7   Simplistic Evaluation of Classifiers

We have everything lined up for the fireworks! We have data, we have methods, and we have an evaluation scheme. As the Italians say, *"Andiamo!"* Let's go!

3.7.1   Learning Performance

Shortly, we'll see a simple Python program to compare our two learners: *k*-NN and NB. Instead of using the names imported by our setup statement `from mlwpy import *` at the start of the chapter, it has its `imports` written out. This code is what you would write in a stand-alone script or in a notebook that *doesn't* import our convenience setup. You'll notice that we rewrote the `train_test_split` call and we also made the test set size significantly bigger. Why? Training on less data makes it a harder problem. You'll also notice that I sent an extra argument to `train_test_split: random_state=42` hacks the randomness of the train-test split and gives us a repeatable result. Without it, every run of the cell would result in different evaluations. Normally we want that, but here I want to be able to talk about the results *knowing* what they are.

```
In [11]:
# stand-alone code
from sklearn import (datasets, metrics,
                     model_selection as skms,
                     naive_bayes, neighbors)

# we set random_state so the results are reproducible
# otherwise, we get different training and testing sets
# more details in Chapter 5
iris = datasets.load_iris()
```

```
(iris_train_ftrs, iris_test_ftrs,
 iris_train_tgt, iris_test_tgt) = skms.train_test_split(iris.data,
                                                        iris.target,
                                                        test_size=.90,
                                                        random_state=42)

models = {'kNN': neighbors.KNeighborsClassifier(n_neighbors=3),
          'NB' : naive_bayes.GaussianNB()}

for name, model in models.items():
    fit = model.fit(iris_train_ftrs, iris_train_tgt)
    predictions = fit.predict(iris_test_ftrs)

    score = metrics.accuracy_score(iris_test_tgt, predictions)
    print("{:>3s}: {:0.2f}".format(name,score))
```

```
kNN: 0.96
 NB: 0.81
```

With a test set size of 90% of the data, k-NN does fairly well and NB does a bit *meh* on this train-test split. If you rerun this code many times without `random_state` set and you use a more moderate amount of testing data, we get upwards of 97+% accuracy on both methods for many repeated runs. So, from a learning performance perspective, *iris* is a fairly easy problem. It is reasonably easy to distinguish the different types of flowers, based on the measurements we have, using very simple classifiers.

3.7.2 Resource Utilization in Classification

Everything we do on a computer comes with a cost in terms of processing time and memory. Often, computer scientists will talk about memory as storage space or, simply, space. Thus, we talk about the *time and space* usage of a program or an algorithm. It may seem a bit old-fashioned to worry about resource usage on a computer; today's computer are orders of magnitude faster and larger in processing and storage capabilities than their ancestors of even a few years ago—let alone the behemoth machines of the 1960s and 1970s. So why are we going down a potentially diverting rabbit hole? There are two major reasons: extrapolation and the limits of theoretical analysis.

3.7.2.1 Extrapolation

Today, much of data science and machine learning is driven by *big data*. The very nature of big data is that it pushes the limits of our computational resources. Big data is a relative term: what's big for you might not be too big for someone with the skills and budget to compute on a large cluster of machines with GPUs (graphics processing units). One possible breaking point after which I *don't* have *small* data is when the problem is so large that I can't solve it on my laptop in a "reasonable" amount of time.

If I'm doing my prototyping and development on my laptop—so I can sip a mojito under a palm tree in the Caribbean while I'm working—how can I know what sort of resources I will need when I scale up to the full-sized problem? Well, I can take measurements of smaller problems of increasing sizes and make some educated guesses about what will happen with the full dataset. To do that, I need to quantify what's happening with the smaller data in time and space. In fairness, it is only an estimate, and adding computational horsepower doesn't always get a one-to-one payback. Doubling my available memory won't always double the size of the dataset I can process.

3.7.2.2   Limits of Theory

Some of you might be aware of a subfield of computer science called *algorithm analysis* whose job is to develop equations that relate the time and memory use of a computing task to the size of that task's input. For example, we might say that the new learning method *Foo* will take $2n + 27$ steps on n input examples. (That's a drastic simplification: we almost certainly care about how many features there are in these examples.)

So, if there is a theoretical way to know the resources needed by an algorithm, why do we care about measuring them? I'm glad you asked. Algorithm analysis typically abstracts away certain mathematical details, like constant factors and terms, that can be practically relevant to real-world run times. Algorithm analysis also (1) makes certain strong or mathematically convenient assumptions, particularly regarding the average case analysis, (2) can ignore implementation details like system architecture, and (3) often uses algorithmic idealizations, devoid of real-world practicalities and necessities, to reach its conclusions.

In short, the only way to *know* how a real-world computational system is going to consume resources, short of some specialized cases that don't apply here, is to run it and measure it. Now, it is just as possible to screw this up: you could run and measure under idealized or nonrealistic conditions. We don't want to throw out algorithmic analysis altogether. My critiques are *not* failures of algorithm analysis; it's simply open-eyed understanding its limits. Algorithm analysis will always tell us some fundamental truths about how different algorithms compare and how they behave on bigger-and-bigger inputs.

I'd like to show off a few methods of comparing the resource utilization of our two classifiers. A few caveats: quantifying program behavior can be very difficult. Everything occurring on your system can potentially have a significant impact on your learning system's resource utilization. Every difference in your input can affect your system's behavior: more examples, more features, different types of features (numerical versus symbolic), and different hyperparameters can all make the same learning algorithm behave differently and consume different resources.

3.7.2.3   Units of Measure

We need to make one small digression. We're going to be measuring the resources used by computer programs. Time is measured in seconds, and space is measured in bytes. One byte is eight bits: it can hold the answers to eight yes/no questions. Eight bits can distinguish between 256 different values—so far, so good. However, we'll be dealing with values that are significantly larger or smaller than our normal experience. I want you to be able to connect with these values.

We need to deal with SI prefixes. SI is short for the International Standard of scientific abbreviations—but, coming from a Romance language, the adjective is *after* the noun, so the IS is swapped. The prefixes that are important for us are in Table 3.2. Remember that the exponent is the x in 10^x; it's also the number of "padded zeros" on the right. That is, *kilo* means $10^3 = 1000$ and 1000 has three zeros on the right. The examples are distances that would be reasonable to measure, using that prefix, applied to meters.

Table 3.2 SI prefixes and length scale examples.

Prefix	Verbal	Exponent	Example Distance
T	tera	12	orbit of Neptune around the Sun
G	giga	9	orbit of the Moon around the Earth
M	mega	6	diameter of the Moon
K	kilo	3	a nice walk
		0	1 meter $\sim$ 1 step
m	milli	−3	mosquito
μ	micro	−6	bacteria
n	nano	−9	DNA

There is another complicating factor. Computers typically work with base-2 amounts of storage, not base-10. So, instead of 10^x we deal with 2^x. Strictly speaking—and scientists are nothing if not strict—we need to account for this difference. For memory, we have some additional prefixes (Table 3.3) that you'll see in use soon.

Table 3.3 SI base-two prefixes and memory scale examples.

Prefix	Verbal Prefix	Number of Bytes	Example
KiB	kibi	2^{10}	a list of about 1000 numbers
MiB	mebi	2^{20}	a short song as an MP3
GiB	gibi	2^{30}	a feature-length movie
TiB	tebi	2^{40}	a family archive of photos and movies

So, 2 MiB is *two mebi-bytes* equal to 2^{20} bytes. You'll notice that the base-2 prefixes are also pronounced differently. Ugh. You might wonder why these step up by 10s, not by 3s as in the base-10 values. Since $2^{10} = 1024 \sim 1000 = 10^3$, multiplying by ten 2s is fairly close to multiplying by three 10s. Unfortunately, these binary prefixes, defined by large standards bodies, haven't necessarily trickled down to daily conversational use. The good news is that within one measuring system, you'll probably only see MiB or MB, not both. When you see MiB, just know that it isn't quite MB.

3.7.2.4 Time

In a Jupyter notebook, we have some nice tools to measure execution times. These are great for measuring the time use of small snippets of code. If we have two different ways of coding a solution to a problem and want to compare their speed, or just want to measure how long a snippet of code takes, we can use Python's `timeit` module. The Jupyter cell magic `%timeit` gives us a convenient interface to time a line of code:

In [12]:

```
%timeit -r1 datasets.load_iris()
```

```
1000 loops, best of 1: 1.4 ms per loop
```

The `-r1` tells `timeit` to measure the timing of the snippet once. If we give a higher `r`, for repeats, the code will be run multiple times and we will get statistics. Recent versions of Jupyter default to calculating the mean and standard deviation of the results. Fortunately, for a single result we just get that single value. If you are concerned about the `1000 loops`, check out my note on it at the end of the chapter.

`%%timeit`—the two-percents make it a *cell magic*—applies the same strategy to the entire block of code in a cell:

In [13]:

```
%%timeit -r1 -n1
(iris_train_ftrs, iris_test_ftrs,
 iris_train_tgt,  iris_test_tgt) = skms.train_test_split(iris.data,
                                                         iris.target,
                                                         test_size=.25)
```

```
1 loop, best of 1: 638 µs per loop
```

And now let's point our chronometer (`timeit`) at our learning workflow:

In [14]:

```
%%timeit -r1

nb    = naive_bayes.GaussianNB()
fit   = nb.fit(iris_train_ftrs, iris_train_tgt)
preds = fit.predict(iris_test_ftrs)

metrics.accuracy_score(iris_test_tgt, preds)
```

```
1000 loops, best of 1: 1.07 ms per loop
```

In [15]:

```
%%timeit -r1

knn   = neighbors.KNeighborsClassifier(n_neighbors=3)
fit   = knn.fit(iris_train_ftrs, iris_train_tgt)
preds = fit.predict(iris_test_ftrs)

metrics.accuracy_score(iris_test_tgt, preds)
```

```
1000 loops, best of 1: 1.3 ms per loop
```

If we just want to time one line in a cell—for example, we only want to see how long it takes to fit the models—we can use a single-percent version, called a *line magic*, of `timeit`:

In [16]:

```
# fitting
nb = naive_bayes.GaussianNB()
%timeit -r1 fit   = nb.fit(iris_train_ftrs, iris_train_tgt)

knn = neighbors.KNeighborsClassifier(n_neighbors=3)
%timeit -r1 fit = knn.fit(iris_train_ftrs, iris_train_tgt)
```

```
1000 loops, best of 1: 708 µs per loop
1000 loops, best of 1: 425 µs per loop
```

In [17]:

```
# predicting
nb   = naive_bayes.GaussianNB()
fit  = nb.fit(iris_train_ftrs, iris_train_tgt)
%timeit -r1 preds = fit.predict(iris_test_ftrs)

knn   = neighbors.KNeighborsClassifier(n_neighbors=3)
fit   = knn.fit(iris_train_ftrs, iris_train_tgt)
%timeit -r1 preds = fit.predict(iris_test_ftrs)
```

```
1000 loops, best of 1: 244 µs per loop
1000 loops, best of 1: 644 µs per loop
```

There seems to be a bit of a tradeoff. *k*-NN is faster to fit, but is slower to predict. Conversely, NB takes a bit of time to fit, but is faster predicting. If you're wondering why I didn't reuse the `knn` and `nb` from the prior cell, it's because when you `%timeit`, variable assignment are trapped inside the `timeit` magic and don't leak back out to our main code. For example, trying to use `preds` as "normal" code in the prior cell will results in a `NameError`.

3.7.2.5   Memory

We can also do a very similar sequence of steps for quick-and-dirty measurements of memory use. However, two issues raise their ugly heads: (1) our tool isn't built into Jupyter, so we need to install it and (2) there are technical details—err, opportunities?—that we'll get to in a moment. As far as installation goes, install the `memory_profiler` module with `pip` or `conda` at your terminal command line:

```
pip install memory_profiler
conda install memory_profiler
```

Then, in your notebook you will be able to use `%load_ext`. This is Jupyter's command to load a Jupyter extension module—sort of like Python's `import`. For `memory_profiler`, we use it like this:

```
%load_ext memory_profiler
```

Here it goes:

In [18]:

```
%load_ext memory_profiler
```

Use it is just like `%%timeit`. Here's the cell magic version for Naive Bayes:

In [19]:

```
%%memit
nb    = naive_bayes.GaussianNB()
fit   = nb.fit(iris_train_ftrs, iris_train_tgt)
preds = fit.predict(iris_test_ftrs)
```

```
peak memory: 144.79 MiB, increment: 0.05 MiB
```

And for Nearest Neighbors:

In [20]:

```
%%memit
knn   = neighbors.KNeighborsClassifier(n_neighbors=3)
fit   = knn.fit(iris_train_ftrs, iris_train_tgt)
preds = fit.predict(iris_test_ftrs)
```

```
peak memory: 144.79 MiB, increment: 0.00 MiB
```

3.7.2.6   Complicating Factors

You may never have considered what happens with memory on your computer. In the late 2010s, you might have 4 or 8GB of system memory, RAM, on your laptop. I have 32GB on my workhorse powerstation—or workstation powerhorse, if you prefer. Regardless, that system memory is shared by each and every running program on your computer. It is the job of the operating system—Windows, OSX, Linux are common culprits—to manage that memory and respond to applications' requests to use it. The OS has to be a bit of a playground supervisor to enforce sharing between the different programs.

Our small Python programs, too, are playing on that playground. We have to share with others. As we request resources like memory—or time on the playground swing—the OS will respond and give us a block of memory to use. We might actually get *more* memory than we request (more on that in a second). Likewise, when we are done with a block of memory—and being the polite playground children that we are—we will return it to the playground monitor. In both our request for memory and our return of the memory, the process incurs management overhead. Two ways that OSes simplify the process and reduce the overhead are (1) by granting memory in blocks that might be more than we need and (2) by possibly letting us keep using memory, after we've said we're done with it, until someone else *actively* needs it. The net result of this is that determining the actual amount of memory that we are using—versus the amount the operating system has walled off for us—can be very tricky. Measuring additional requests within a running program is even more difficult.

Another issue further complicates matters. Python is a memory-managed language: it has its own memory management facilities on top of the OS. If you were to rerun the above cells in a Jupyter notebook, you might see a memory increment of 0.00 MiB and wonder what circuits just got fried. In that case, the old memory we used was released by us—and the operating system never shuffled it off to someone else. So, when we needed more memory, we were able to reuse the old memory and didn't need any new memory from the OS. It is almost as if the memory was released and reclaimed by us so quickly that it was never actually gone! Now, whether or not we see an increment is also dependent on (1) what the notebook cell is doing, (2) what other memory our program has claimed and is using, (3) every other program that is running on the computer, and (4) the exact details of the operating system's memory manager. To learn more, check out a course or textbook on operating systems.

3.7.3 Stand-Alone Resource Evaluation

To minimize these concerns and to reduce confounding variables, it is extremely useful to write small, stand-alone programs when testing memory use. We can make the script general enough to be useful for stand-alone timing, as well.

In [21]:

```
!cat scripts/knn_memtest.py
```

```
import memory_profiler, sys
from mlwpy import *


@memory_profiler.profile(precision=4)
```

```
def knn_memtest(train, train_tgt, test):
    knn   = neighbors.KNeighborsClassifier(n_neighbors=3)
    fit   = knn.fit(train, train_tgt)
    preds = fit.predict(test)

if __name__ == "__main__":
    iris = datasets.load_iris()
    tts = skms.train_test_split(iris.data,
                                iris.target,
                                test_size=.25)
    (iris_train_ftrs, iris_test_ftrs,
     iris_train_tgt,  iris_test_tgt) = tts
    tup = (iris_train_ftrs, iris_train_tgt, iris_test_ftrs)
    knn_memtest(*tup)
```

There are a few ways to use `memory_profiler`. We've seen the line and cell magics in the previous section. In `knn_memtest.py`, we use the `@memory_profiler.profile` *decorator*. That extra line of Python tells the memory profiler to track the memory usage of `knn_memtest` on a line-by-line basis. When we run the script, we see memory-related output for each line of `knn_memtest`:

In [22]:

```
!python scripts/knn_memtest.py
```

```
Filename: scripts/knn_memtest.py
# output modified for formatting purposes

Line #    Mem usage    Increment    Line Contents
================================================
     4 120.5430 MiB 120.5430 MiB    @memory_profiler.profile(precision=4)
     5                              def knn_memtest(train, train_tgt, test):
     6 120.5430 MiB   0.0000 MiB        knn   = neighbors.
                                            KNeighborsClassifier(n_neighbors=3)
     7 120.7188 MiB   0.1758 MiB        fit   = knn.fit(train, train_tgt)
     8 120.8125 MiB   0.0938 MiB        preds = fit.predict(test)
```

Here's another stand-alone script to measure the memory usage of Naive Bayes:

In [23]:

```
import functools as ft
import memory_profiler
from mlwpy import *

def nb_go(train_ftrs, test_ftrs, train_tgt):
    nb    = naive_bayes.GaussianNB()
```

```
    fit   = nb.fit(train_ftrs, train_tgt)
    preds = fit.predict(test_ftrs)

def split_data(dataset):
    split = skms.train_test_split(dataset.data,
                                  dataset.target,
                                  test_size=.25)
    return split[:-1] # don't need test tgt

def msr_mem(go, args):
    base = memory_profiler.memory_usage()[0]
    mu = memory_profiler.memory_usage((go, args),
                                      max_usage=True)[0]
    print("{:<3}: ~{:.4f} MiB".format(go.__name__, mu-base))

if __name__ == "__main__":
    msr = msr_mem
    go = nb_go

    sd = split_data(datasets.load_iris())
    msr(go, sd)
```

```
nb_go: ~0.0078 MiB
```

nb_go has the *model-fit-predict* pattern we saw above. split_data just wraps
train_test_split in a convenient way to use with nb_go. The new piece is setting up the
timing wrapper in msr_mem. Essentially, we ask what memory is used now, run nb_go, and
then see the maximum memory used along the way. Then, we take that max, subtract
what we were using before, max-baseline, and that's the peak memory used by nb_go.
nb_go gets passed in to msr_mem as go and then finds its way to memory_usage.

We can write a similar msr_time driver to evaluate time, and we can write a similar
knn_go to kick off a *k*-NN classifier for measuring time and memory. Here are all four
pieces in a single script:

In [24]:

```
!cat scripts/perf_01.py
```

```
import timeit, sys
import functools as ft
import memory_profiler
from mlwpy import *


def knn_go(train_ftrs, test_ftrs, train_tgt):
    knn   = neighbors.KNeighborsClassifier(n_neighbors=3)
    fit   = knn.fit(train_ftrs, train_tgt)
```

```
    preds = fit.predict(test_ftrs)

def nb_go(train_ftrs, test_ftrs, train_tgt):
    nb    = naive_bayes.GaussianNB()
    fit   = nb.fit(train_ftrs, train_tgt)
    preds = fit.predict(test_ftrs)

def split_data(dataset):
    split = skms.train_test_split(dataset.data,
                                  dataset.target,
                                  test_size=.25)
    return split[:-1] # don't need test tgt

def msr_time(go, args):
    call = ft.partial(go, *args)
    tu = min(timeit.Timer(call).repeat(repeat=3, number=100))
    print("{:<6}: ~{:.4f} sec".format(go.__name__, tu))

def msr_mem(go, args):
    base = memory_profiler.memory_usage()[0]
    mu = memory_profiler.memory_usage((go, args),
                                      max_usage=True)[0]
    print("{:<3}: ~{:.4f} MiB".format(go.__name__, mu-base))

if __name__ == "__main__":
    which_msr = sys.argv[1]
    which_go  = sys.argv[2]

    msr = {'time': msr_time, 'mem':msr_mem}[which_msr]
    go = {'nb' : nb_go, 'knn': knn_go}[which_go]

    sd = split_data(datasets.load_iris())
    msr(go, sd)
```

With all this excitement, let's see where we end up using Naive Bayes:

In [25]:

```
!python scripts/perf_01.py mem nb
!python scripts/perf_01.py time nb
```

```
nb_go: ~0.1445 MiB
nb_go : ~0.1004 sec
```

And with *k*-NN:

```
In [26]:

!python scripts/perf_01.py mem knn
!python scripts/perf_01.py time knn


knn_go: ~0.3906 MiB
knn_go: ~0.1035 sec
```

In summary, our learning and resource performance metrics look like this (the numbers may vary a bit):

Method	Accuracy	~Time(s)	~Memory (MiB)
k-NN	0.96	0.10	.40
NB	0.80	0.10	.14

Don't read too much into the accuracy scores! I'll tell you why in a minute.

3.8 EOC

3.8.1 Sophomore Warning: Limitations and Open Issues

There are several caveats to what we've done in this chapter:

- We compared these learners on a single dataset.
- We used a very simple dataset.
- We did *no* preprocessing on the dataset.
- We used a single train-test split.
- We used accuracy to evaluate the performance.
- We didn't try different numbers of neighbors.
- We only compared two simple models.

Each one of these caveats is great! It means we have more to talk about in the forthcoming chapters. In fact, discussing *why* these are concerns and figuring out *how* to address them is the point of this book. Some of these issues have no fixed answer. For example, no one learner is best on *all* datasets. So, to find a good learner *for a particular problem*, we often try several different learners and pick the one that does the best *on that particular problem*. If that sounds like teaching-to-the-test, you're right! We have to be very careful in how we select the model we use from many potential models. Some of these issues, like our use of accuracy, will spawn a long discussion of how we quantify and visualize the performance of classifiers.

3.8.2 Summary

Wrapping up our discussion, we've seen several things in this chapter:

1. *iris*, a simple real-world dataset
2. Nearest-neighbors and Naive Bayes classifiers
3. The concept of training and testing data
4. Measuring learning performance with accuracy
5. Measuring time and space usage within a Jupyter notebook and via stand-alone scripts

3.8.3 Notes

If you happen to be a botanist or are otherwise curious, you can read Anderson's original paper on irises: www.jstor.org/stable/2394164. The version of the *iris* data with `sklearn` comes from the UCI Data repository: https://archive.ics.uci.edu/ml/datasets/iris.

The Minkowski distance isn't really as scary as it seems. There's another distance called the Manhattan distance. It is the distance it would take to walk as directly as possible from one point to the other, if we were on a fixed grid of streets like in Manhattan. It simply adds up the absolute values of the feature differences without squares or square roots. All Minkowski does is extend the formulas so we can pick Manhattan, Euclidean, or other distances by varying a value p. The weirdness comes in when we make p very, very big: $p \to \infty$. Of course, that has its own name: the Chebyshev distance.

If you've seen theoretical resource analysis of algorithms before, you might remember the terms *complexity analysis* or *Big-O* notation. The Big-O analysis simplifies statements on the upper bounds of resource use, as input size grows, with mathematical statements like $\mathcal{O}(n^2)$—hence the name Big-O.

I briefly mentioned graphics processing units (GPUs). When you look at the mathematics of computer graphics, like the visuals in modern video games, it is all about describing points in space. And when we play with data, we often talk about examples as points in space. The "natural" mathematical language to describe this is *matrix algebra*. GPUs are designed to perform matrix algebra at warp speed. So, it turns out that machine learning algorithms can be run very, very efficiently on GPUs. Modern projects like Theano, TensorFlow, and Keras are designed to take advantage of GPUs for learning tasks, often using a type of learning model called a *neural network*. We'll briefly introduce these in Chapter 15.

In this chapter, we used Naive Bayes on discrete data. Therefore, learning involved making a table of how often values occurred for the different target classes. When we have continuous numerical values, the game is a bit different. In that case, learning means figuring out the center and spread of a distribution of values. Often, we assume that a *normal* distribution works well with the data; the process is then called *Gaussian Naive Bayes*—Gaussian and normal are essentially synonyms. Note that we are making an *assumption*—it might work well but we might also be *wrong*. We'll talk more about GNB in Section 8.5.

In any chapter that discusses performance, I would be remiss if I didn't tell you that "premature optimization is the root of all evil . . . in programming." This quote is from an essay form of Donald Knuth's 1974 Turing Award—the Nobel Prize of Computer Science—acceptance speech. Knuth is, needless to say, a giant in the discipline. There are two points that underlie his quote. Point one: in a computer system, the majority of the execution time is usually tied up in a small part of the code. This observation is a form of the Pareto principle or the 80–20 rule. Point two: optimizing code is hard, error-prone, and makes the code more difficult to understand, maintain, and adapt. Putting these two points together tells us that we can waste an awful lot of programmer time optimizing code that isn't contributing to the overall performance of our system. So, what's the better way? (1) Write a good, solid, *working* system and then measure its performance. (2) Find the bottlenecks—the slow and/or calculation-intensive portions of the program. (3) Optimize those bottlenecks. We only do the work that we *know* needs to be done and has a chance at meeting our goals. We also do as little of this intense work as possible. One note: *inner loops*—the innermost nestings of repetition—are often the most fruitful targets for optimization because they are, by definition, code that is repeated the most times.

Recent versions of Jupyter now report a mean and standard deviation for `%timeit` results. However, the Python core developers and documenters prefer a different strategy for analyzing `timeit` results: they prefer either (1) taking the minimum of several repeated runs to give an idea of best-case performance, which will be more consistent for comparison sake, or (2) looking at all of the results as a whole, without summary. I think that (2) is *always* a good idea in data analysis. The mean and standard deviation are not *robust*; they respond poorly to outliers. Also, while the mean and standard deviation completely characterize normally distributed data, other distributions will be characterized in very different ways; see Chebyshev's inequality for details. I would be far happier if Jupyter reported medians and inter-quartile ranges (those are the 50th percentile and the 75th–25th percentiles). These are robust to outliers and are not based on distributional assumptions about the data.

What was up with the `1000 loops` in the `timeit` results? Essentially, we are stacking multiple runs of the same, potentially short-lived, task one after the other so we get a longer-running pseudo-task. This longer-running task plays more nicely with the level of detail that the timing functions of the operating system support. Imagine measuring a 100-yard dash using a sundial. It's going to be very hard because there's a mismatch between the time scales. As we repeat the task multiple times—our poor sprinters might get worn out but, fortunately, Python keeps chugging along—we may get more meaningful measurements. Without specifying a `number`, `timeit` will attempt to find a good number for you. In turn, this may take a while because it will try increasing values for `number`. There's also a `repeat` value you can use with `timeit`; `repeat` is an *outer loop* around the whole process. That's what we discussed computing statistics on in the prior paragraph.

3.8.4 Exercises

You might be interested in trying some classification problems on your own. You can follow the model of the sample code in this chapter with some other classification datasets from `sklearn`: `datasets.load_wine` and `datasets.load_breast_cancer` will get you started. You can also download numerous datasets from online resources like:

- The UCI Machine Learning Repository,
  https://archive.ics.uci.edu/ml/datasets.html
- Kaggle, www.kaggle.com/datasets

Predicting Numerical Values: Getting Started with Regression

In [1]:

```
# setup
from mlwpy import *
%matplotlib inline
```

4.1 A Simple Regression Dataset

Regression is the process of predicting a finely graded numerical value from inputs. To illustrate, we need a simple dataset that has numerical results. `sklearn` comes with the *diabetes* dataset that will serve us nicely. The dataset consists of several biometric and demographic measurements. The version included with `sklearn` has been modified from raw numerical features by subtracting the mean and dividing by the standard deviation of each column. That process is called *standardizing* or *z-scoring* the features. We'll return to the standard deviation later; briefly, it is a measure of how spread out a set of values are.

The net result of standardizing the columns is that each column has a mean of 0 and a standard deviation of 1. We standardize, or otherwise rescale, the data so that differences in feature ranges—heights within 50–100 inches or incomes from \$20,000 to \$200,000— don't incur undo weight penalties or benefits just from their scale. We'll discuss standardization and scaling more in Section 10.3. The categorical values in *diabetes* were recorded numerically as $\{0, 1\}$ and then standardized. I mention it to explain why there are *negative* ages (the mean age is zero after standardizing) and why the sexes are coded, or recorded, as $\{0.0507, -0.0446\}$ instead of $\{M, F\}$.

In [2]:

```
diabetes = datasets.load_diabetes()

tts = skms.train_test_split(diabetes.data,
                            diabetes.target,
                            test_size=.25)

(diabetes_train_ftrs, diabetes_test_ftrs,
 diabetes_train_tgt,  diabetes_test_tgt) = tts
```

We can dress the dataset up with a `DataFrame` and look at the first few rows:

In [3]:

```
diabetes_df = pd.DataFrame(diabetes.data,
                           columns=diabetes.feature_names)
diabetes_df['target'] = diabetes.target
diabetes_df.head()
```

Out[3]:

	age	sex	bmi	bp	s1	s2	s3	s4	s5	s6	target
0	0.04	0.05	0.06	0.02	-0.04	-0.03	-0.04	0.00	0.02	-0.02	151.00
1	0.00	-0.04	-0.05	-0.03	-0.01	-0.02	0.07	-0.04	-0.07	-0.10	75.00
2	0.09	0.05	0.04	-0.01	-0.05	-0.03	-0.03	0.00	0.00	-0.03	141.00
3	-0.09	-0.04	-0.01	-0.04	0.01	0.02	-0.04	0.03	0.02	-0.01	206.00
4	0.01	-0.04	-0.04	0.02	0.00	0.02	0.01	0.00	-0.03	-0.05	135.00

Aside from the odd values for seemingly categorical measures like age and sex, two of the other columns are quickly explainable; the rest are more specialized and somewhat underspecified:

- *bmi* is the *body mass index*, computed from height and weight, which is an approximation of body-fat percentage,
- *bp* is the *blood pressure*,
- *s1–s6* are six *blood serum measurements*, and
- *target* is a numerical score measuring the progression of a patient's illness.

As we did with the *iris* data, we can investigate the bivariate relationships with Seaborn's `pairplot`. We'll keep just a subset of the measurements for this graphic. The resulting mini-plots are still fairly small, but we can still glance through them and look for overall patterns. We can always redo the `pairplot` with all the features if we want to zoom out for a more global view.

In [4]:

```
sns.pairplot(diabetes_df[['age', 'sex', 'bmi', 'bp', 's1']],
             size=1.5, hue='sex', plot_kws={'alpha':.2});
```

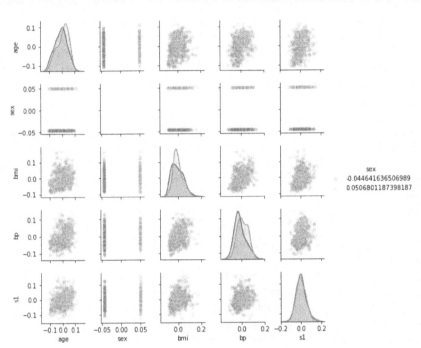

4.2 Nearest-Neighbors Regression and Summary Statistics

We discussed nearest-neighbor classification in the previous chapter and we came up with the following sequence of steps:

1. Describe similarity between pairs of examples.
2. Pick several of the most-similar examples.
3. Combine the picked examples into a single answer.

As we shift our focus from predicting a class or category to predicting a numerical value, steps 1 and 2 can stay the same. Everything that we said about them still applies. However, when we get to step 3, we have to make adjustments. Instead of simply voting for candidate answers, we now need to take into account the quantities represented by the outputs. To do this, we need to combine the numerical values into a single, representative answer. Fortunately, there are several handy techniques for calculating a single summary value from a set of values. Values computed from a set of data are called *statistics*. If we are trying to represent—to summarize, if you will—the overall dataset with one of these, we call it a *summary statistic*. Let's turn our attention to two of these: the median and the mean.

4.2.1 Measures of Center: Median and Mean

You may be familiar with the average, also called the arithmetic mean. But I'm going start with a—seemingly!—less math-heavy alternative: the median. The median of a group of numbers is the *middle* number when that group is written in order. For example, if I have three numbers, listed in order as $[1, 8, 10]$, then 8 is the middle value: there is one number above it and one below. Within a group of numbers, the median has the same count of values below it and above it. To put it another way, if all the numbers have equal weight, regardless of their numerical value, then a scale placed at the median would be balanced (Figure 4.1). Regardless of the biggest value on the right—be it 15 or 40—the median stays the same.

You might be wondering what to do when we have an *even* number of values, say $[1, 2, 3, 4]$. The usual way to construct the median is to take the middle *two* values—the 2 and 3—and take their average, which gives us 2.5. Note that there are still the same number of values, two, above and below this median.

Using the median as a summary statistic has one wonderful property. If I fiddle with the values of the numbers at the start or end of the sorted data, the median stays the same. For example, if my data recorder is fuzzy towards the tails—i.e., values far from the median—and instead of $[1, 8, 10]$, I record $[2, 8, 11]$, my median is the same! This resilience in the face of differing measured values is called *robustness*. The median is a *robust* measure of center.

Now, there are scenarios where we care about the actual numbers, not just their in-order positions. The other familiar way of estimating the center is the *mean*. Whereas the median balances the *count* of values to the left and right, the mean balances the total distances to the left and right. So, the mean is the value for which `sum(distance(s,mean) for s in smaller)` is equal to `sum(distance(b,mean) for b in bigger)`. The only value that meets this constraint is `mean=sum(d)/len(d)` or, as the mathematicians say, mean $= \bar{x} = \frac{\sum_i x_i}{n}$. Referring back to Figure 4.1, if we trade the 15 for a 40, we get a different balance point: the mean has increased because the sum of the values has increased.

The benefit of the mean is that it accounts for the specific numeric values of the numbers: the value 3 is five units below the mean of 8. Compare to the median which

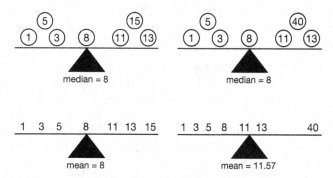

Figure 4.1 Comparing mean and median with balances.

abstracts distance away in favor of ordering: the value 3 is less than the median 8. The problem with the mean is that if we get an outlier—a rare event near the tails of our data—it can badly skew our computation precisely because the specific value matters.

As an example, here's what happens if we shift one value by "a lot" and recompute the mean and median:

In [5]:

```
values = np.array([1, 3, 5, 8, 11, 13, 15])
print("no outlier")
print(np.mean(values),
      np.median(values))

values_with_outlier = np.array([1, 3, 5, 8, 11, 13, 40])
print("with outlier")
print("%5.2f" % np.mean(values_with_outlier),
      np.median(values_with_outlier))
```

```
no outlier
8.0 8.0
with outlier
11.57 8.0
```

Beyond the mean and median, there are many possible ways to combine the nearest-neighbor answers into an answer for a test example. One combiner that builds on the idea of the mean is a *weighted* mean which we discussed in Section 2.5.1. In the nearest-neighbor context, we have a perfect candidate to serve as the weighting factor: the distance from our new example to the neighbor. So, instead of neighbors contributing just their values $[4.0, 6.0, 8.0]$, we can also incorporate the distance from each neighbor to our example. Let's say those distances are $[2.0, 4.0, 4.0]$, i.e. the second and third training examples are twice as far from our test example as the first one. A simple way to incorporate the distance is to compute a *weighted average* using

In [6]:

```
distances = np.array([2.0, 4.0, 4.0])
closeness = 1.0 / distances              # element-by-element division
weights = closeness / np.sum(closeness)  # normalize sum to one
weights
```

Out[6]:

```
array([0.4, 0.2, 0.2])
```

Or, in mathese:

$$\frac{\frac{1}{distances}}{\sum \left(\frac{1}{distances} \right)}$$

as the weights. We use $\frac{1}{\text{distances}}$ since if you are *closer*, we want a *higher* weight; if you are *further*, but still a nearest neighbor, we want a *lower* weight. We put the entire sum into the numerator to normalize the values so they sum to one. Compare the mean with the weighted mean for these values:

In [7]:

```
values = np.array([4, 6, 8])

mean = np.mean(values)
wgt_mean = np.dot(values, weights)

print("Mean:", mean)
print("Weighted Mean:", wgt_mean)
```

```
Mean: 6.0
Weighted Mean: 6.4
```

Graphically—see Figure 4.2—our balance diagram now looks a bit different. The examples that are downweighted (contribute less than their fair share) move closer to the pivot because they have less mechanical leverage. Overweighted examples move away from the pivot and gain more influence.

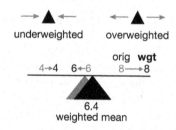

Figure 4.2   The effects of weighting on a mean.

4.2.2   Building a *k*-NN Regression Model

Now that we have some mental concepts to back up our understanding of *k*-NN regression, we can return to our basic `sklearn` workflow: build, fit, predict, evaluate.

In [8]:

```
knn   = neighbors.KNeighborsRegressor(n_neighbors=3)
fit   = knn.fit(diabetes_train_ftrs, diabetes_train_tgt)
preds = fit.predict(diabetes_test_ftrs)

# evaluate our predictions against the held-back testing targets
metrics.mean_squared_error(diabetes_test_tgt, preds)
```

Out[8]:

3471.41941941942

If you flip back to the previous chapter and our k-NN classifier, you'll notice only two differences.

1. We built a different model: this time we used `KNeighborsRegressor` instead of `KNeighborsClassifier`.
2. We used a different evaluation metric: this time we used `mean_squared_error` instead of `accuracy_score`.

Both of these reflect the difference in the targets we are trying to predict—numerical values, not Boolean categories. I haven't explained `mean_squared_error` (MSE) yet; it's because it is deeply tied to our next learning method, linear regression, and once we understand linear regression, we'll basically understand MSE for free. So, just press pause on evaluating regressors with MSE for a few minutes. Still, if you need *something* to make you feel comfortable, take a quick look at Section 4.5.1.

To put the numerical value for MSE into context, let's look at two things. First, the MSE is approximately 3500. Let's take its square root—since we're adding up squares, we need to scale back to nonsquares:

In [9]:
```
np.sqrt(3500)
```

Out[9]:

59.16079783099616

Now, let's look at the range of values that the target can take:

In [10]:
```
diabetes_df['target'].max() - diabetes_df['target'].min()
```

Out[10]:

321.0

So, the target values span about 300 units and our predictions are off—in some average sense—by 60 units. That's around 20%. Whether or not that is "good enough" depends on many other factors which we'll see in Chapter 7.

4.3 Linear Regression and Errors

We're going to dive into linear regression (LR)—which is just a fancy name for drawing a straight line through a set of data points. I'm really sorry to bring up LR, particularly if you are one of those folks out there who had a bad experience studying LR previously. LR has a long history throughout math and science. You may have been exposed to it before. You may have seen LR in an algebra or statistics class. Here's a very different presentation.

4.3.1 No Flat Earth: Why We Need Slope

Do you like to draw? (If not, please just play along.) Take a pen and draw a bunch of dots on a piece of paper. Now, draw a single straight line through the dots. You might have encountered a problem already. If there were more than two dots, there are many, many different lines you could potentially draw. The idea of *drawing a line through the dots* gets a general idea across, but it doesn't give us a reproducible way of specifying or completing the task.

One way of picking a specific line through the dots is to say we want a *best* line—problem solved. We're done. Let's go for five o'clock happy hour. Oh, wait, I have to define what *best* means. Rats! Alright, let's try this. I want the line that stays closest to the dots based on the *vertical* distance from the dots to the line. Now we're getting somewhere. We have something we can calculate to compare different alternatives.

Which line is best under that criteria? Let me start by simplifying a little bit. Imagine we can only draw lines that are parallel to the bottom of the piece of paper. You can think about moving the line like raising or lowering an Olympic high-jump bar: it stays parallel to the ground. If I start sliding the line up and down, I'm going to start far away from all the points, move close to some points, slide onwards to a great, just-right middle ground, move close to other points, and finally end up far away from everything. Yes, the idea of a happy medium—too hot, too cold, and just right—applies here. We'll see this example in code and graphics in just a moment. At the risk of becoming too abstract too quickly, we are limited to drawing lines like $y = c$. In English, that means the height of our bar is always equal to some constant, fixed value.

Let's draw a few of these high-jump bars and see what happens.

In [11]:

```
def axis_helper(ax, lims):
    'clean up axes'
    ax.set_xlim(lims); ax.set_xticks([])
    ax.set_ylim(lims); ax.set_yticks([])
    ax.set_aspect('equal')
```

We're going to use some trivial data to show what's happening.

In [12]:

```
# our data is very simple:  two (x, y) points
D = np.array([[3, 5],
              [4, 2]])

# we'll take x as our "input" and y as our "output"
x, y = D[:, 0], D[:, 1]
```

Now, let's graph what happens as we move a horizontal line up through different possible values. We'll call these values our *predicted* values. You can imagine each raised bar as being a possible set of predictions for our example data points. Along the way, we'll also keep track of what our error values are. The errors are the differences between the horizontal line and the data points. We'll also calculate a few values from the errors: the sum of errors, the *sum of squares* of the errors (abbreviated SSE), and the *square root of the sum of squared errors*. You might want to look at the output first, before trying to understand the code.

In [13]:

```
horizontal_lines = np.array([1, 2, 3, 3.5, 4, 5])

results = []
fig, axes = plt.subplots(1, 6, figsize=(10, 5))
for h_line, ax in zip(horizontal_lines, axes.flat):
    # styling
    axis_helper(ax, (0, 6))
    ax.set_title(str(h_line))

    # plot the data
    ax.plot(x, y, 'ro')

    # plot the prediction line
    ax.axhline(h_line, color='y') # ax coords; defaults to 100%

    # plot the errors
    # the horizontal line *is* our prediction; renaming for clarity
    predictions = h_line
    ax.vlines(x, predictions, y)

    # calculate the error amounts and their sum of squares
    errors = y - predictions
    sse = np.dot(errors, errors)

    # put together some results in a tuple
    results.append((predictions,
                    errors, errors.sum(),
                    sse, np.sqrt(sse)))
```

We start very far away from one point and not too far from another. As we slide the bar up, we hit a nice middle ground between the points. Yet we keep sliding the bar; we end up on the top point, fairly far away from the bottom point. Perhaps the ideal tradeoff is somewhere in the middle. Let's look at some numbers.

In [14]:

```
col_labels = "Prediction", "Errors", "Sum", "SSE", "Distance"
display(pd.DataFrame.from_records(results,
                          columns=col_labels,
                          index="Prediction"))
```

Prediction	Errors	Sum	SSE	Distance
1.0000	[4.0, 1.0]	5.0000	17.0000	4.1231
2.0000	[3.0, 0.0]	3.0000	9.0000	3.0000
3.0000	[2.0, -1.0]	1.0000	5.0000	2.2361
3.5000	[1.5, -1.5]	0.0000	4.5000	2.1213
4.0000	[1.0, -2.0]	-1.0000	5.0000	2.2361
5.0000	[0.0, -3.0]	-3.0000	9.0000	3.0000

Our table includes the raw errors that can be positive or negative—we might over- or underestimate. The sums of those raw errors don't do a great job evaluating the lines. Errors in the opposite directions, such as $[2, -1]$, give us a total of 1. In terms of our overall prediction ability, we don't want these errors to cancel out. One of the best ways to address that is to use a *total distance*, just like we used distances in the nearest-neighbors method above. That means we want something like $\sqrt{(\text{prediction} - \text{actual})^2}$. The SSE column is the *sum of squared errors* which gets us most of the way towards calculating distances. All that's left is to take a square root. The line that is best, under the rules so far, is the horizontal line at the mean of the points based on their vertical component: $\frac{5+2}{2} = 3.5$. The mean is the best answer here for the same reason it is the pivot on the balance beams we showed earlier: it perfectly balances off the errors on either side.

4.3.2 Tilting the Field

What happens if we keep the restriction of drawing straight lines but remove the restriction of making them horizontal? My apologies for stating the possibly obvious, but now we can draw lines that aren't flat. We can draw lines that are pointed up or down, as needed. So, if the cluster of dots that you drew had an overall growth or descent, like a plane taking off or landing, a sloped line can do better than a flat, horizontal runway. The form of these sloped lines is a classic equation from algebra: $y = mx + b$. We get to adjust m and b so that when we know a point's left-rightedness—the x value—we can get as close as possible on its up-downness y.

How do we define close? The same way we did above—with distance. Here, however, we have a more interesting line with a slope. What does the distance from a point to our line look like? It's just `distance(prediction, y) = distance(m*x + b,y)`. And what's our total distance? Just add those up for all of our data: `sum(distance(mx + b, y)` `for x, y in D)`. In mathese, that looks like

$$\sum_{x,y \in D} \left((mx + b) - y\right)^2$$

I promise code and graphics are on the way! A side note: it's possible that for a set of dots, the best line *is* flat. That would mean we want an answer that is a simple, horizontal line—just what we discussed in the previous section. When that happens, we just set m to zero and head on our merry way. Nothing to see here, folks. Move along.

Now, let's repeat the horizontal experiment with a few, select tilted lines. To break things up a bit, I've factored out the code that draws the graphs and calculates the table entries into a function called `process`. I'll admit `process` is a *horrible* name for a function. It's up there with *stuff* and *things*. Here, though, consider it the processing we do with our small dataset and a simple line.

In [15]:

```python
def process(D, model, ax):
    # make some useful abbreviations/names
    # y is our "actual"
    x, y = D[:, 0], D[:, 1]
    m, b = model

    # styling
    axis_helper(ax, (0, 8))

    # plot the data
    ax.plot(x, y, 'ro')

    # plot the prediction line
    helper_xs = np.array([0, 8])
    helper_line = m * helper_xs + b
    ax.plot(helper_xs, helper_line, color='y')

    # plot the errors
    predictions = m * x + b
    ax.vlines(x, predictions, y)

    # calculate error amounts
    errors = y - predictions

    # tuple up the results
```

```
    sse = np.dot(errors, errors)
    return (errors, errors.sum(), sse, np.sqrt(sse))
```

Now we'll make use of **process** with several different prediction lines:

In [16]:

```
# our data is very simple:  two (x, y) points
D = np.array([[3, 5],
              [4, 2]])


#                   m    b  --> predictions = mx + b
lines_mb = np.array([[ 1,  0],
                     [ 1,  1],
                     [ 1,  2],
                     [-1,  8],
                     [-3, 14]])

col_labels = ("Raw Errors", "Sum", "SSE", "TotDist")
results = []

# note: plotting occurs in process()
fig, axes = plt.subplots(1, 5, figsize=(12, 6))
records = [process(D, mod, ax) for mod,ax in zip(lines_mb, axes.flat)]
df = pd.DataFrame.from_records(records, columns=col_labels)
display(df)
```

	Raw Errors	Sum	SSE	TotDist
0	[2, -2]	0	8	2.8284
1	[1, -3]	-2	10	3.1623
2	[0, -4]	-4	16	4.0000
3	[0, -2]	-2	4	2.0000
4	[0, 0]	0	0	0.0000

So, we have a progression in calculating our measure of success:

- `predicted = m*x + b`
- `error = (m*x + b) - actual = predicted - actual`
- `SSE = sum(errors**2) = sum(((m*x+b) - actual)**2 for x,actual in data)`
- `total_distance = sqrt(SSE)`

The last line precisely intersects with both data points. Its predictions are 100% correct; the vertical distances are zero.

4.3.3 Performing Linear Regression

So far, we've only considered what happens with a single predictive feature x. What happens when we add more features—more columns and dimensions—into our model? Instead of a single slope m, we now have to deal with a slope for each of our features. We have some contribution to the outcome from each of the input features. Just as we learned how our output changes with one feature, we now have to account for different relative contributions from different features.

Since we have to track many different slopes—one for each feature—we're going to shift away from using m and use the term *weights* to describe the contribution of each feature. Now, we can create a linear combination—as we did in Section 2.5—of the weights and the features to get the prediction for an example. The punchline is that our prediction is `rdot(weights_wo, features) + wgt_b` if `weights_wo` is *without* the b part included. If we use the plus-one trick, it is `rdot(weights, features_p1)` where `weights` includes a b (as `weights[0]`) and `features_p1` includes a column of ones. Our error still looks like `distance(prediction, actual)` with `prediction=rdot(weights, features_p1)`. The mathese form of a prediction (with a prominent dot product) looks like:

$$y_{\text{pred}} = \sum_{\text{ftrs}} w_f x_f = w \bullet x$$

```
In [17]:

lr    = linear_model.LinearRegression()
fit   = lr.fit(diabetes_train_ftrs, diabetes_train_tgt)
preds = fit.predict(diabetes_test_ftrs)

# evaluate our predictions against the unseen testing targets
metrics.mean_squared_error(diabetes_test_tgt, preds)
```

```
Out[17]:

2848.2953079329427
```

We'll come back to `mean_squared_error` in just a minute, but you are already equipped to understand it. It is the average distance of the errors in our prediction.

4.4   Optimization: Picking the Best Answer

Picking the best line means picking the best values for m and b or for the *weights*. In turn, that means setting factory knobs to their best values. How can we choose these *bests* in a well-defined way?

Here are four strategies we can adopt:

1. Random guess: Try lots of possibilities at random, take the best one.
2. Random step: Try one line—pick an m and a b—at random, make several random adjustments, pick the adjustment that helps the most. Repeat.
3. Smart step: Try one line at random, see how it does, adjust it in some smart way. Repeat.
4. Calculated shortcut: Use fancy mathematics to prove that if Fact A, Fact B, and Fact C are all true, then the One Line To Rule Them All must be the best. Plug in some numbers and use The One Line To Rule Them All.

Let's run through these using a really, really simple constant-only model. Why a constant, you might ask. Two reasons. First, it is a simple horizontal line. After we calculate its value, it is the same everywhere. Second, it is a simple baseline for comparison. If we do well with a simple constant predictor, we can just call it a day and go home. On the other hand, if a more complicated model does as well as a simple constant, we might question the value of the more complicated model. As Yoda might say, "A simple model, never underestimate."

4.4.1   Random Guess

Let's make some simple data to predict.

In [18]:

```
tgt = np.array([3, 5, 8, 10, 12, 15])
```

Let's turn Method 1—random guessing—into some code.

In [19]:

```
# random guesses with some constraints
num_guesses = 10
results = []

for g in range(num_guesses):
    guess = np.random.uniform(low=tgt.min(), high=tgt.max())
    total_dist = np.sum((tgt - guess)**2)
    results.append((total_dist, guess))
best_guess = sorted(results)[0][1]
best_guess
```

```
Out[19]:
```

```
8.228074784134693
```

Don't read too much into this specific answer. Just keep in mind that, since we have a simple value to estimate, we only need to take a few shots to get a good answer.

4.4.2 Random Step

Method 2 starts with a single random guess, but then takes a random step up or down. If that step is an improvement, we keep it. Otherwise, we go back to where we were.

```
In [20]:
```

```python
# use a random choice to take a hypothetical
# step up or down:  follow it, if it is an improvement
num_steps = 100
step_size = .05

best_guess = np.random.uniform(low=tgt.min(), high=tgt.max())
best_dist  = np.sum((tgt - best_guess)**2)

for s in range(num_steps):
    new_guess = best_guess + (np.random.choice([+1, -1]) * step_size)
    new_dist = np.sum((tgt - new_guess)**2)
    if new_dist < best_dist:
        best_guess, best_dist = new_guess, new_dist
print(best_guess)
```

```
8.836959712695537
```

We start with a single guess and then try to improve it by random stepping. If we take enough steps and those steps are individually small enough, we should be able to find our way to a solid answer.

4.4.3 Smart Step

Imagine walking, blindfolded, through a rock-strewn field or a child's room. You might take tentative, test steps as you try to move around. After a step, you use your foot to probe the area around you for a clear spot. When you find a clear spot, you take that step.

```
In [21]:
```

```python
# hypothetically take both steps (up and down)
# choose the better of the two
# if it is an improvement, follow that step
```

```
num_steps = 1000
step_size = .02

best_guess = np.random.uniform(low=tgt.min(), high=tgt.max())
best_dist  = np.sum((tgt - best_guess)**2)
print("start:", best_guess)
for s in range(num_steps):
    # np.newaxis is needed to align the minus
    guesses = best_guess + (np.array([-1, 1]) * step_size)
    dists   = np.sum((tgt[:,np.newaxis] - guesses)**2, axis=0)

    better_idx = np.argmin(dists)

    if dists[better_idx] > best_dist:
        break

    best_guess = guesses[better_idx]
    best_dist  = dists[better_idx]
print("  end:", best_guess)
```

```
start: 9.575662598977047
  end: 8.835662598977063
```

Now, unless we get stuck in a bad spot, we should have a better shot at success than random stepping: at any given point we check out the legal alternatives and take the best of them. By effectively cutting out the random steps that don't help, we should make progress towards a good answer.

4.4.4 Calculated Shortcuts

If you go to a statistics textbook, you'll discover that for our SSE evaluation criteria, there is a *formula* for the answer. To get the smallest sum of squared errors, what we need is precisely the *mean*. When we said earlier that the mean balanced the distances to the values, we were merely saying the same thing in a different way. So, we don't actually have to search to find our best value. The fancy footwork is in the mathematics that demonstrates that the mean is the right answer to this question.

In [22]:

```
print("mean:", np.mean(tgt))
```

```
mean: 8.833333333333334
```

4.4.5 Application to Linear Regression

We can apply these same ideas to fitting a sloped line, or finding many weights (one per feature), to our data points. The model becomes a bit more complicated—we have to twiddle more values, either simultaneously or in sequence. Still, it turns out that an equivalent to our Method 4, *Calculated Shortcut*, is the standard, classical way to find the best line. When we fit a line, the process is called *least-squares fitting* and it is solved by the *normal equations*—you don't have to remember that—instead of just the *mean*. Our Method 3, *Smart Step*, using some mathematics to limit the direction of our steps, is common when dealing with very big data where we can't run all the calculations needed for the standard method. That method is called *gradient descent*. Gradient descent (GD) uses some smart calculations—instead of probing steps—to determine directions of improvement.

The other two methods are not generally used to find a best line for linear regression. However, with some additional details, Method 2, *Random Step*, is close to the techniques of *genetic algorithms*. What about Method 1, *Random Guessing*? Well, it isn't very useful by itself. But the idea of random starting points *is* useful when combined with other methods. This discussion is just a quick introduction to these ideas. We'll mention them throughout the book and play with them in Chapter 15.

4.5 Simple Evaluation and Comparison of Regressors

Earlier, I promised we'd come back to the idea of mean squared error (MSE). Now that we've discussed sum of squared errors and total distances from a regression line, we can tie these ideas together nicely.

4.5.1 Root Mean Squared Error

How can we quantify the performance of regression predictions? We're going to use some mathematics that are almost identical to our criteria for finding good lines. Basically, we'll take the average of the squared errors. Remember, we can't just add up the errors themselves because then a +3 and a −3 would cancel each other out and we'd consider those predictions perfect when we're really off by a total of 6. Squaring and adding those two values gives us a total error of 18. Averaging gives us a mean squared error of 9. We'll take one other step and take the *square root* of this value to get us back to the same scale as the errors themselves. This gives us the *root mean squared error*, often abbreviated *RMSE*. Notice that in this example, our RMSE is 3: precisely the amount of the error(s) in our individual predictions.

That reminds me of an old joke for which I can't find specific attribution:

> Two statisticians are out hunting when one of them sees a duck. The first takes aim and shoots, but the bullet goes sailing past six inches too high. The second statistician also takes aim and shoots, but this time the bullet goes sailing past six inches too low. The two statisticians then give one another high fives and exclaim, "Got him!"

Groan all you want, but that is the fundamental tradeoff we make when we deal with averages. Please note, no ducks were harmed in the making of this book.

4.5.2 Learning Performance

With data, methods, and an evaluation metric in hand, we can do a small comparison between *k*-NN-R and LR.

In [23]:

```
# stand-alone code
from sklearn import (datasets, neighbors,
                     model_selection as skms,
                     linear_model, metrics)

diabetes = datasets.load_diabetes()
tts =  skms.train_test_split(diabetes.data,
                             diabetes.target,
                             test_size=.25)
(diabetes_train, diabetes_test,
 diabetes_train_tgt, diabetes_test_tgt) = tts

models = {'kNN': neighbors.KNeighborsRegressor(n_neighbors=3),
          'linreg' : linear_model.LinearRegression()}

for name, model in models.items():
    fit   = model.fit(diabetes_train, diabetes_train_tgt)
    preds = fit.predict(diabetes_test)

    score = np.sqrt(metrics.mean_squared_error(diabetes_test_tgt, preds))
    print("{:>6s} : {:0.2f}".format(name,score))
```

```
   kNN : 54.85
linreg : 46.95
```

4.5.3 Resource Utilization in Regression

Following Section 3.7.3, I wrote some stand-alone test scripts to get an insight into the resource utilization of these regression methods. If you compare the code here with the earlier code, you'll find only two differences: (1) different learning methods and (2) a different learning performance metric. Here is that script adapted for *k*-NN-R and LR:

```
In [24]:

!cat scripts/perf_02.py


import timeit, sys
import functools as ft
import memory_profiler
from mlwpy import *

def knn_go(train_ftrs, test_ftrs, train_tgt):
    knn = neighbors.KNeighborsRegressor(n_neighbors=3)
    fit   = knn.fit(train_ftrs, train_tgt)
    preds = fit.predict(test_ftrs)

def lr_go(train_ftrs, test_ftrs, train_tgt):
    linreg = linear_model.LinearRegression()
    fit   = linreg.fit(train_ftrs, train_tgt)
    preds = fit.predict(test_ftrs)

def split_data(dataset):
    split = skms.train_test_split(dataset.data,
                                  dataset.target,
                                  test_size=.25)
    return split[:-1] # don't need test tgt

def msr_time(go, args):
    call = ft.partial(go, *args)
    tu = min(timeit.Timer(call).repeat(repeat=3, number=100))
    print("{:<6}: ~{:.4f} sec".format(go.__name__, tu))

def msr_mem(go, args):
    base = memory_profiler.memory_usage()[0]
    mu = memory_profiler.memory_usage((go, args),
                                      max_usage=True)[0]
    print("{:<3}: ~{:.4f} MiB".format(go.__name__, mu-base))

if __name__ == "__main__":
    which_msr = sys.argv[1]
    which_go = sys.argv[2]

    msr = {'time': msr_time, 'mem':msr_mem}[which_msr]
    go = {'lr' : lr_go, 'knn': knn_go}[which_go]

    sd = split_data(datasets.load_iris())
    msr(go, sd)
```

When we execute it, we see

```
In [25]:
```

```
!python scripts/perf_02.py mem lr
!python scripts/perf_02.py time lr
```

```
lr_go: ~1.5586 MiB
lr_go : ~0.0546 sec
```

```
In [26]:
```

```
!python scripts/perf_02.py mem knn
!python scripts/perf_02.py time knn
```

```
knn_go: ~0.3242 MiB
knn_go: ~0.0824 sec
```

Here's a brief table of our results that might vary a bit over different runs:

Method	RMSE	Time (s)	Memory (MiB)
k-NN-R	55	0.08	0.32
LR	45	0.05	1.55

It may be surprising that linear regression takes up so much memory, especially considering that *k*-NN-R requires keeping all the data around. This surprise highlights an issue with the way we are measuring memory: (1) we are measuring the *entire* fit-and-predict process as one unified task and (2) we are measuring the *peak* usage of that unified task. Even if linear regression has one brief moment of high usage, that's what we are going to see. Under the hood, this form of linear regression—which optimizes by Method 4, *Calculated Shortcut*—isn't super clever about how it does its calculations. There's a critical part of its operation—solving those normal equations I mentioned above—that is very memory hungry.

4.6 EOC

4.6.1 Limitations and Open Issues

There are several caveats to what we've done in this chapter—and many of them are the same as the previous chapter:

- We compared these learners on a single dataset.
- We used a very simple dataset.
- We did *no* preprocessing on the dataset.
- We used a single train-test split.

- We used accuracy to evaluate the performance.
- We didn't try different numbers of neighbors.
- We only compared two simple models.

Additionally, linear regression is quite sensitive to using standardized data. While *diabetes* came to us prestandardized, we need to keep in mind that *we* might be responsible for that step in other learning problems. Another issue is that we can often benefit from restricting the weights—the $\{m, b\}$ or w—that a linear regression model can use. We'll talk about why that is the case and how we can do it with `sklearn` in Section 9.1.

4.6.2 Summary

Wrapping up our discussion, we've seen several things in this chapter:

1. *diabetes*: a simple real-world dataset
2. Linear regression and an adaptation of nearest-neighbors for regression
3. Different measures of center—the mean and median
4. Measuring learning performance with root mean squared error (RMSE)

4.6.3 Notes

The *diabetes* data is from a paper by several prominent statisticians which you can read here: http://statweb.stanford.edu/~tibs/ftp/lars.pdf.

4.6.4 Exercises

You might be interested in trying some classification problems on your own. You can follow the model of the sample code in this chapter with another regression dataset from `sklearn`: `datasets.load_boston` will get you started!

Part II

Evaluation

5

Evaluating and Comparing Learners

In [1]:

```
# setup
from mlwpy import *
diabetes = datasets.load_diabetes()
%matplotlib inline
```

5.1 Evaluation and Why Less Is More

Lao Tzu: Those that know others are wise. Those that know themselves are Enlightened.

The biggest risk in developing a learning system is *overestimating how well it will do when we use it*. I touched on this risk in our first look at classification. Those of us that have studied for a test and *thought* we had a good mastery of the material, and then *bombed* the test, will be intimately familiar with this risk. It is very, very easy to (1) think we know a lot and will do well on an exam and (2) not do very well on the exam. On a test, we may discover we need details when we only remember a general idea. I know it happened in mid-nineteenth century, but was it 1861 or 1862!? Even worse, we might focus on some material at the expense of other material: we might miss studying some information entirely. Well, *nuts*: we needed to know her name but not his birth year.

In learning systems, we have two similar issues. When you study for the test, you are *limited* in what you can remember. Simply put, your brain gets full. You don't have the *capacity* to learn each and every detail. One way around this is to remember the big picture instead of many small details. It is a great strategy—until you need one of those details! Another pain many of us have experienced is that when you're studying for a test, your friend, spouse, child, *anyone* hollers at you, "I need your attention now!" Or it might be a new video game that comes out: "Oh look, a shiny bauble!" Put simply, you get *distracted by noise*. No one is judging, we're all human here.

These two pitfalls—limited capacity and distraction by noise—are shared by computer learning systems. Now, typically, a learning system won't be distracted by the latest YouTube sensation or Facebook meme. In the learning world, we call these sources of error by different names. For the impatient, they are *bias* for the capacity of what we can squeeze into our head and *variance* for how distracted we get by noise. For now, squirrel away that bit of intuition and don't get distracted by noise.

Returning to the issue of overconfidence, what can we do to protect ourselves from . . . ourselves? Our most fundamental defense is *not teaching to the test*. We introduced this idea in our first look at classification (Section 3.3). To avoid teaching to the test, we use a very practical three-step recipe:

- Step one: split our data into separate training and testing datasets.
- Step two: *learn* on the training data.
- Step three: *evaluate* on the testing data.

Not using *all* the data to *learn* may seem counterintuitive. Some folks—certainly none of *my* readers—could argue, "Wouldn't building a model on more data lead to better results?" Our humble skeptic has a good point. Using more data *should* lead to better estimates by our learner. The learner should have better parameters—better knob settings on our factory machine. However, there's a really big consequence of using *all* of the data for learning. *How would we know that a more-data model is better than a less-data model?* We have to *evaluate* both models somehow. If we teach to the test by learning and evaluating on *all* of the data, we are likely to overestimate our ability once we take our system into the big, scary, complex real world. The scenario is similar to studying a specific test from last year's class—wow, multiple choice, easy!—and then being tested on this year's exam which is *all essays*. Is there a doctor in the house? A student just passed out.

In this chapter, we will dive into general evaluation techniques that apply to both regression and classification. Some of these techniques will help us avoid teaching to the test. Others will give us ways of comparing and contrasting learners in very broad terms.

5.2 Terminology for Learning Phases

We need to spend a few minutes introducing some vocabulary. We need to distinguish between a few different phases in the machine learning process. We've hit on *training* and *testing* earlier. I want to introduce another phase called *validation*. Due to some historical twists and turns, I need to lay out clearly what I mean by these three terms—training, validation, and testing. Folks in different disciplines can use these terms with slight variations in meaning which can trip the unwary student. I want you to have a clear walking path.

5.2.1 Back to the Machines

I want you to return to the mental image of our factory learning machine from Section 1.3. The machine is a big black box of knobs, inputs, and outputs. I introduced that machine to give you a concrete image of what learning algorithms are doing and how we have control over them. We can continue the story. While the machine itself seems to be *part* of a factory, in reality, we are a business-to-business (that's B2B to you early 2000s business students) provider. Other companies want to make use of our machine. However, they want a completely hands-off solution. We'll build the machine, set all the knobs as in Figure 5.1, and send the machine to the customer. They won't do anything other than feed it inputs and see what pops out the other side. This delivery model means that when we hand off the machine to our customer, it needs to be fully tuned and ready to rock-and-roll. Our challenge is to ensure the machine can perform adequately after the hand-off.

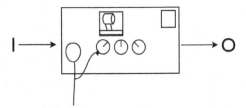

Figure 5.1   Learning algorithms literally dial-in—or optimize—a relationship between input and output.

In our prior discussion of the machine, we talked about relating inputs to outputs by setting the knobs and switches on the side of the machine. We established that relationship because we had some *known* outputs that we were expecting. Now, we want to avoid teaching to the test when we set the dials on our machine. We want the machine to do well for us, but more importantly, we want it to do well for our customer. Our strategy is to hold out some of the input-output pairs and save them for later. We will *not* use the saved data to set the knobs. We will use the saved data, *after* learning, to evaluate how well the knobs are set. Great! Now we're completely set and have a good process for making machines for our customers.

You know what's coming. Wait for it. Here it comes. Houston, we have a problem. There are many different types of machines that relate inputs to outputs. We've already seen two classifiers and two regressors. Our customers might have some preconceived ideas about what sort of machine they want because they heard that Fancy Silicon Valley Technologies, Inc. was using one type of machine. FSVT, Inc. might leave it entirely up to us to pick the machine. Sometimes we—or our corporate overlords—will choose between different machines based on characteristics of the inputs and outputs. Sometimes we'll choose based on resource use. Once we select a broad class of machines (for example, we decide we need a widget maker), there may be several physical machines we can pick (for example, the Widget Works 5000 or the WidgyWidgets Deluxe Model W would both work nicely). Often, we will pick the machine we use based on its learning performance (Figure 5.2).

Let me step out of the metaphor for a moment. A concrete example of a factory machine is a *k*-Nearest Neighbors (*k*-NN) classifier. For *k*-NN, different values of *k* are entirely different physical machines. *k* is *not* a knob we adjust on the machine. *k* is *internal*

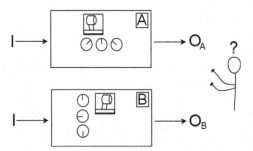

Figure 5.2　If we can build and optimize different machines, we select one of them for the customer.

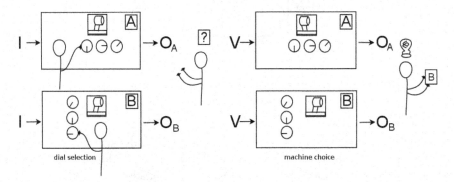

Figure 5.3　Optimization (dial-setting) and selection (machine choice) as steps to create a great machine for our customer.

to the machine. No matter what inputs and outputs we see, we can't adjust k directly on one machine (see Section 11.1 for details). It's like looking at the transmission of a car and wanting a different gearing. That modification is at a level beyond the skillsets of most of us. But all is not lost! We can't modify our car's transmission, but we *can* buy a different car. We are free to have *two different machines*, say 3-NN and 10-NN. We can go further. The machines could also be completely different. We could get two sedans and one minivan. With learning models, they don't all have to be k-NN variants. We could get a 3-NN, a 10-NN, and a Naive Bayes. To pick among them, we run our input-output pairs through the models to train them. Then, we evaluate how they perform on the held-out data to get a better—less trained on the test—idea of how our machines will perform for the customer (Figure 5.3).

Hurray! We're done. High-fives all around, it's time for coffee, tea, soda, or beer (depending on your age and doctor's advice).

Not so fast. We still have a problem. Just as we can teach to the test in setting the knobs on the machines, we can also teach to the test in terms of *picking a machine*. Imagine that we use our held-out data as the basis for picking the best machine. For k-NN that means picking the best k. We could potentially try all the values of k up to the size of our dataset. Assuming 50 examples, that's all values of k from 1 to 50. Suppose we find that 27 is the best. That's great, except we've been looking at the same held-out data every time we try a different k. We no longer have an *unseen* test to give us a fair evaluation of the machine we're going to hand off to our customer. We used up our hold-out test set and fine-tuned our performance towards it. What's the answer now?

The answer to teaching-to-the-test with knobs—tuning a given machine—was to have a separate set of held-out data that isn't used to set the knobs. Since that worked pretty well there, let's just do that again. We'll have *two* sets of held-out data to deal with two separate steps. One set will be used to *pick the machine*. The second set will be used to *evaluate how well the machine will work for the customer* in a fair manner, without peeking at the test. Remember, we also have the non-held-out data that is used to tune the machine.

5.2.2 More Technically Speaking . . .

Let's recap. We now have three distinct sets of data. We can break the discussion of our needs into three distinct phases. We'll work from the outside to the inside—that is, from our final goal towards fitting the basic models.

1. We need to provide a single, well-tuned machine to our customer. We want to have a final, no-peeking evaluation of how that machine will do for our customer.
2. After applying some thought to the problem, we select a few candidate machines. With those candidate machines, we want to evaluate and compare them without peeking at the data we will use for our final evaluation.
3. For each of the candidate machines, we need to set the knobs to their best possible settings. We want to do that without peeking at either of the datasets used for the other phases. Once we select one machine, we are back to the basic learning step: we need to set its knobs.

5.2.2.1 Learning Phases and Training Sets

Each of these three phases has a component of evaluation in it. In turn, each different evaluation makes use of a specific set of data containing different known input-output pairs. Let's give the phases and the datasets some useful names. Remember, the term *model* stands for our metaphorical factory machine. The phases are

1. *Assessment*: final, last-chance estimate of how the machine will do when operating in the wild
2. *Selection*: evaluating and comparing different machines which may represent the same broad type of machine (different k in k-NN) or completely different machines (k-NN and Naive Bayes)
3. *Training*: setting knobs to their optimal values and providing auxiliary side-tray information

The datasets used for these phases are:

1. Hold-out test set
2. Validation test set
3. Training set

We can relate these phases and datasets to the factory machine scenario. This time, I'll work from the inside out.

1. The training set is used to adjust the knobs on the factory machine.
2. The validation test set is used to get a non-taught-to-the-test evaluation of that finely optimized machine and help us pick between different optimized machines.
3. The hold-out test set is used to make sure that *the entire process of building one or more factory machines, optimizing them, evaluating them, and picking among them* is evaluated fairly.

The last of these is a *big* responsibility: there are many ways to peek and be misled by distractions. If we train and validation-test over and over, we are building up a strong idea of what works and doesn't work in the validation test set. It may be indirect, but we are effectively *peeking* at the validation test set. The hold-out test set—data we have never used before in any training or validation-testing for this problem—is necessary to protect us from this *indirect peeking* and to give us a fair evaluation of how our final system will do with novel data.

5.2.2.2 Terms for Test Sets

If you check out a number of books on machine learning, you'll find the term *validation set* used, fairly consistently, for *Selection*. However, when you *talk* to practitioners, folks will verbally use the phrase *test set* for both datasets used for *Selection* and for *Assessment*. To sweep this issue under the carpet, if I'm talking about evaluation and it is either (1) clear from context or (2) doesn't particularly matter, I'll use the generic phrase *testing* for the data used in either *Assessment* or *Selection*. The most likely time that will happen is when we aren't doing *Selection* of models—we are simply using a basic train-test split, training a model and then performing a held-out evaluation, *Assessment*, on it.

If the terms *do* matter, as when we're talking about both phases together, I'll be a bit more precise and use more specific terms. If we need to distinguish these datasets, I'll use the terms *hold-out test set* (HOT) and *validation set* (ValS). Since *Assessment* is a one-and-done process—often at the end of all our hard work applying what we know about machine learning—we'll be talking about the HOT relatively infrequently. That is not to say that the HOT is unimportant—quite the contrary. Once we use it, we can never use it as a HOT again. We've peeked. Strictly speaking, we've contaminated both ourselves and our learning system. We can delete a learning system and start from scratch, but it is very difficult to erase our own memories. If we do this repeatedly, we'd be right back into teaching to the test. The only solution for breaking the lockbox of the HOT is to gather new data. On the other hand, we are not obligated to use all of the HOT at once. We can use half of it, find we don't like the results and go back to square one. When we develop a new system that we need to evaluate before deployment, we still have the other half the HOT for *Assessment*.

5.2.2.3 A Note on Dataset Sizes

A distinctly practical matter is figuring out how big each of these sets should be. It is a difficult question to answer. If we have *lots* of data, then all three sets can be very large and there's no issue. If we have very little data, we have to be concerned with (1) using enough data in training to build a good model and (2) leaving enough data for the testing phases. To quote one of the highest-quality books in the field of machine and statistical learning, *Elements of Statistical Learning*, "It is difficult to give a general rule on how to choose the number of observations in each of the three parts." Fortunately, Hastie and friends immediately take pity on us poor practitioners and give a generic recommendation of 50%–25%–25% for training, validation testing, and held-out testing. That's about as good of a baseline split as we can get. With cross-validation, we could possibly consider a 75–25 split with 75% being thrown into the basket for cross-validation—which will be repeatedly split into training and validation-testing sets—and 25% saved away in a lockbox for final assessment. More on that shortly.

If we go back to the 50–25–25 split, let's drill into that 50%. We'll soon see evaluation tools called *learning curves*. These give us an indication of what happens to our validation-testing performance as we train on more and more examples. Often, at some high enough number of training examples, we will see a plateau in the performance. If that plateau happens within the 50% split size, things are looking pretty good for us. However, imagine a scenario where we need 90% of our available data to get a decent performance. Then, our 50–25–25 split is *simply not going to give a sufficiently good classifier* because we need more training data. We need a learner that is more efficient in its use of data.

5.2.2.4 Parameters and Hyperparameters

Now is the perfect time—I might be exaggerating—to deal with two other terms: parameters and hyperparameters. The knobs on a factory machine represent model parameters set by a learning method during the training phase. Choosing between different machines (3-NN or 10-NN) in the same overall class of machine (*k*-NN) is selecting a hyperparameter. Selecting hyperparameters, like selecting models, is done in the selection phase. Keep this distinction clear: *parameters* are set as *part of the learning method* in the training phase while *hyperparameters* are beyond the control of the learning method.

For a given run of a learning method, the available parameters (knobs) and the way they are used (internals of the factory machine) are fixed. We can only adjust the values those parameters take. Conceptually, this limitation can be a bit hard to describe. If the phases described above are talked about from outer to inner—in analogy with outer and inner loops in a computer program—the order is *Assessment, Selection, Training*. Then, adjusting hyperparameters means stepping out one level from adjusting the parameters—stepping out from Training to Selection. We are thinking outside the box, if you will. At the same time—from a different perspective—we are *diving into* the inner workings of the machine like a mechanic. As is the case with rebuilding car engines, the training phase just doesn't go there.

With that perfect moment passed, we're going to minimize the discussion of hyperparameters for several chapters. If you want to know more about hyperparameters *right now*, go to Section 11.1. Table 5.1 summarizes the pieces we've discussed.

Table 5.1   Phases and datasets for learning.

Phase	Name	Dataset Used	Machine	Purpose
inner	training	training set	set knobs	optimize parameters
middle	selection	validation test set	choose machines	select model, hyperparameters
outer	assessment	hold-out test set	evaluate performance	assess future performance

For the middle phase, selection, let me emphasize just how easily we can mislead ourselves. We've only considered two kinds of classifiers so far: NB and *k*-NN. While *k* could grow arbitrarily big, we commonly limit it to relatively small values below 20 or so. So, maybe we are considering 21 total possible models (20 *k*-NN variants and 1 Naive Bayes model). Still, there are *many* other methods. In this book, we'll discuss about a half dozen. Several of these have almost *infinite* tunability. Instead of choosing between a *k* of 3, 10, or 20, some models have a *C* with any value from zero to infinity. Over many models and many tuning options, it is conceivable that we might hit the jackpot and find one combination that is *perfect* for our inner and middle phases. However, we've been indirectly peeking—homing in on the target by systematic guessing. Hopefully, it is now clear why the outer phase, assessment, is necessary to prevent ourselves from teaching to the test.

5.3   Major Tom, There's Something Wrong: Overfitting and Underfitting

Now that we've laid out some terminology for the learning phases—training, selection, and assessment—I want to dive into things that can go wrong with learning. Let's turn back to the exam scenario. *Mea culpa.* Suppose we take an exam and we don't do as well as we'd like. It would be nice if we could attribute our failure to something more specific than "bad, don't do that again." Two distinct failures are (1) not bringing enough raw horsepower—capacity—to the exam and (2) focusing too much on irrelevant details. To align this story with our earlier discussion, number two is really just a case of being distracted by noise—but it makes us feel better about ourselves than binging on Netflix. These two sources of error have technical names: *underfitting* and *overfitting*. To investigate them, we're going to cook up a simple practice dataset.

5.3.1 Synthetic Data and Linear Regression

Often, I prefer to use real-world datasets—even if they are small—for examples. But in this case, we're going to use a bit of synthetic, genetically modified data. Creating synthetic data is a good tool to have in your toolbox. When we develop a learning system, we might need some data that we completely control. Creating our own data allows us to control the *true* underlying relationship between the inputs and the outputs and to manipulate how noise affects that relationship. We can specify both the type and amount of noise.

Here, we'll make a trivial dataset with one feature and a target, and make a train-test split on it. Our noise is chosen uniformly (you might want to revisit our discussion of distributions in Section 2.4.4) from values between -2 and 2.

In [2]:

```
N = 20
ftr = np.linspace(-10, 10, num=N)            # ftr values
tgt = 2*ftr**2 - 3 + np.random.uniform(-2, 2, N) # tgt = func(ftr)

(train_ftr, test_ftr,
 train_tgt, test_tgt) = skms.train_test_split(ftr, tgt, test_size=N//2)

display(pd.DataFrame({"ftr":train_ftr,
                      "tgt":train_tgt}).T)
```

	0	1	2	3	4	5	6	7	8	9
ftr	-1.58	-6.84	-3.68	1.58	-7.90	3.68	7.89	4.74	5.79	-0.53
tgt	2.39	91.02	22.38	3.87	122.58	23.00	121.75	40.60	62.77	-1.61

Now we can take a look at that data visually. We have our known data points—the training set—in blue dots. The red pluses show the input feature values for the test set. We need to figure out how high up we should take each of those values.

In [3]:

```
plt.plot(train_ftr, train_tgt, 'bo')
plt.plot(test_ftr, np.zeros_like(test_ftr), 'r+');
```

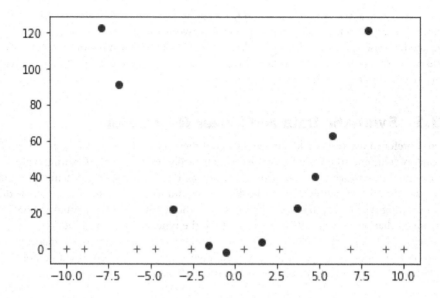

The numbers are a fairly straightforward example of a regression task. We have a numerical target value that we want to predict from an input. Now, we only have a few regression tools in our toolbox at this point. So, let's pull out linear regression (LR) and see what happens:

```
In [4]:
```

```
# note: sklearn *really* wants 2D inputs (a table)
# so we use rehape here.
sk_model = linear_model.LinearRegression()
sk_model.fit(train_ftr.reshape(-1, 1), train_tgt)
sk_preds = sk_model.predict(test_ftr.reshape(-1, 1))
sk_preds[:3]
```

```
Out[4]:
```

```
array([53.218 , 41.4552, 56.8374])
```

We're not evaluating these predictions in any way. But at least—like our training targets—they are positive values.

5.3.2 Manually Manipulating Model Complexity

Up until now, we've relied entirely on `sklearn` to do all the heavy lifting for us. Basically, `sklearn`'s methods have been responsible for setting the knob values on all the machines we've been using for our demonstrations. But there are *many* other packages for finding those ideal knob values. Some of those packages are specifically geared towards machine learning. Others are geared towards specialized areas of mathematics and engineering.

One of those alternatives is the `polyfit` routine in NumPy. It takes input and output values, our features and a target, and a *degree of polynomial* to align with the data. It figures out the right knob values—actually, the coefficients of polynomials we discussed in Section 2.8—and then `np.poly1d` turns those coefficients into a function that can take inputs and produce outputs. Let's explore how it works:

In [5]:

```
# fit-predict-evaluate a 1D polynomial (a line)
model_one = np.poly1d(np.polyfit(train_ftr, train_tgt, 1))
preds_one = model_one(test_ftr)
print(preds_one[:3])
```

```
[53.218  41.4552 56.8374]
```

Interesting. The first three predictions are the same as our LR model. Are all of the predictions from these inputs the same? Yes. Let's demonstrate that and calculate the RMSE of the model:

In [6]:

```
# the predictions come back the same
print("all close?", np.allclose(sk_preds, preds_one))

# and we can still use sklearn to evaluate it
mse = metrics.mean_squared_error
print("RMSE:", np.sqrt(mse(test_tgt, preds_one)))
```

```
all close? True
RMSE: 86.69151817350722
```

Great. So, two take-home messages here. Message one: we can use alternative systems, not just `sklearn`, to learn models. We can even use those alternative systems *with* `sklearn` to do the evaluation. Message two: `np.polyfit`, as its name implies, can easily be manipulated to produce any degree of polynomial we are interested in. We have just fit a relatively simple line, but we can move beyond that to more complicated patterns. Let's explore that now.

One way to manipulate the complexity of linear regression is to ask, "What happens if we break out of our straight jacket and allow bends?" We can start answering that by looking at what happens when we add a single bend. For the non-mathphobic, a curve with one bend in it—called a parabola—is described by a degree-two polynomial. Instead of fitting a straight line to the points and picking the line with the lowest squared error, we're going to hold up parabolas—curves with a single bend—to the training data and find the one that fits best. The mathematics are surprisingly, or at least comfortingly, similar. As a result, our code only requires a minor tweak.

In [7]:

```
# fit-predict-evaluate a 2D polynomial (a parabola)
model_two = np.poly1d(np.polyfit(train_ftr, train_tgt, 2))
preds_two = model_two(test_ftr)
print("RMSE:", np.sqrt(mse(test_tgt, preds_two)))
```

RMSE: 1.2765992188881117

Hey, our test error improved quite a bit. Remember, error is like heat going out of your windows in the winter: we want very little of it! If one bend helped so well, maybe we just need a little more wiggle in our lives? Let's allow up to eight bends. If one was good, eight must be great! We can get eight bends from a degree-9 polynomial. You will really impress your dinner party guests if you tell them that a degree-9 polynomial is sometimes referred to as a *nonic*. Here's our degree-9 model's MSE:

In [8]:

```
model_three = np.poly1d(np.polyfit(train_ftr, train_tgt, 9))
preds_three = model_three(test_ftr)
print("RMSE:", np.sqrt(mse(test_tgt, preds_three)))
```

RMSE: 317.3634424235501

The error is significantly higher—worse—than we saw with the parabola. That might be unexpected. Let's investigate.

5.3.3 Goldilocks: Visualizing Overfitting, Underfitting, and "Just Right"

That didn't exactly go as planned. We didn't just get worse. We got utterly, terribly, horribly worse. What went wrong? We can break down what happened in the training and testing data visually:

In [9]:

```
fig, axes = plt.subplots(1, 2, figsize=(6, 3), sharey=True)

labels = ['line', 'parabola', 'nonic']
models = [model_one, model_two, model_three]
train = (train_ftr, train_tgt)
test  = (test_ftr, test_tgt)

for ax, (ftr, tgt) in zip(axes, [train, test]):
    ax.plot(ftr, tgt, 'k+')
```

```
for m, lbl in zip(models, labels):
    ftr = sorted(ftr)
    ax.plot(ftr, m(ftr), '-', label=lbl)

axes[1].set_ylim(-20, 200)
axes[0].set_title("Train")
axes[1].set_title("Test");
axes[0].legend(loc='upper center');
```

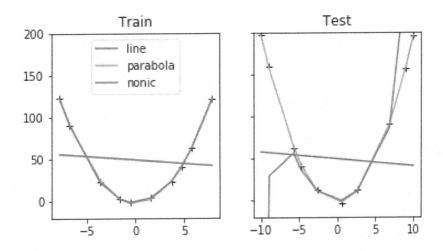

model_one, the straight line, has great difficulty because our real model follows a curved trajectory. model_two eats that up: it follows the curve just about perfectly. model_three *seems* to do wonderfully when we train. It basically overlaps with both model_two and the real outputs. However, it has problems when we go to testing. It starts exploding out of control near ftr=-7. For ease of comparison, we can rerun the models and gather up the results in one table. Since it is easy to add another midway model, I'll also throw in a degree-6 model.

In [10]:

```
results = []
for complexity in [1, 2, 6, 9]:
    model = np.poly1d(np.polyfit(train_ftr, train_tgt, complexity))
    train_error = np.sqrt(mse(train_tgt, model(train_ftr)))
    test_error = np.sqrt(mse(test_tgt, model(test_ftr)))
    results.append((complexity, train_error, test_error))
```

```
columns = ["Complexity", "Train Error", "Test Error"]
results_df = pd.DataFrame.from_records(results,
                                       columns=columns,
                                       index="Complexity")

results_df
```

Out[10]:

Complexity	Train Error	Test Error
1	45.4951	86.6915
2	1.0828	1.2766
6	0.2819	6.1417
9	0.0000	317.3634

Let's review what happened with each of the three models with complexity 1, 2, and 9.

- Model one (Complexity 1—a straight line). Model one was *completely* outclassed. It brought a tricycle to a Formula One race. It was doomed from the beginning. The model doesn't have enough raw horsepower, or capacity, to capture the complexity of a target. It is too biased towards flatness. The model is *underfitting*.
- Model three (Complexity 9—a wiggly 9-degree polynomial). Model three certainly had enough horsepower. We see that it does very well on the training data. In fact, it gets to the point where it is *perfect* on the training data. But it completely falls apart when it comes to testing. Why? Because it memorized the *noise*—the randomness in the data. It varies too much with the data. We call this *overfitting*.
- Model two (Complexity 2—a parabola). Here we have the Goldilocks solution: it's not too hot, it's not too cold, it's just right. We have enough horsepower, but not so much that we can't control it. We do well enough on the training data and we see that we are at the lowest *testing* error. If we had set up a full validation step to select between the three machines with different complexity, we would be quite happy with model two. Model two doesn't *exactly* capture the training patterns because the training patterns include *noise*.

Let's graph out the results on the train and test sets:

In [11]:

```
results_df.plot();
```

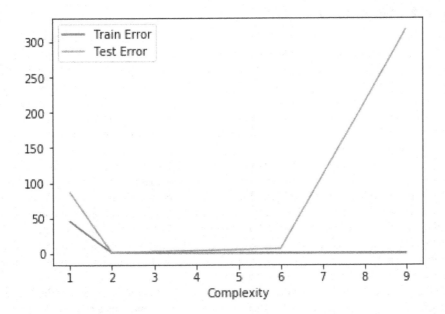

The key take-away from the graph is that as we ratchet up the complexity of our model, we get to a point where we can make the training error very, very small—perhaps even zero. It is a Pyrrhic victory. Where it really counts—on the test set—we get worse. Then, we get terrible. We get to give up and go home bad. To highlight the important pieces of that graph, a version with helpful labels is shown in Figure 5.4.

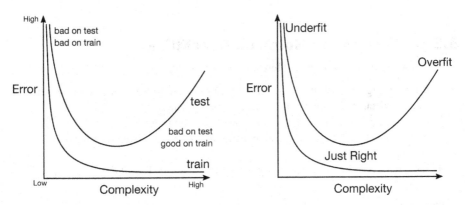

Figure 5.4 As complexity increases, we generally move from underfitting to just right to overfitting.

5.3.4   Simplicity

Let's spend one more minute talking about complexity and its good friend, simplicity. We just saw a concrete example of added complexity making our performance worse. That's because the added complexity wasn't used for the right reasons. It was spent following the noise instead of the true pattern. We don't really get to choose how complexity is used by our learners. They *have* a complexity—which can be used for good or bad. So, if we had several learners that all performed the same but had differing complexities, the potential abuse of power—by which I mean complexity—might lead us to prefer the simplest of these equal-performing models.

The underlying idea—simplicity is an important rule-of-thumb—is known throughout science and philosophy as Occam's razor (Ockham's razor for you historians) from a quote by William of Ockham, "Entities are not to be multiplied without necessity." (That's translated from Latin.) For us, the message is that we don't want more complexity in our model unless there is a reason. Put concretely, we don't want a higher-degree polynomial unless it pays us back in lower *test* error. Paraphrasing a much longer actual quote from Einstein, "Make things as simple as possible, but no simpler." (Hey, if I'm going to name-drop, I'm not going to stop at a philosopher who lived around 1300!)

Here's a thought that might keep you awake tonight. There is a learning method, which we will discuss later in Section 12.4, that can continue improving its test set performance even after it has *apparently* mastered the training set. Students of machine learning say it has driven the training error to zero but it is still improving. What's a real-life equivalent? You might imagine smoothing out your own rough edges in a public performance. Even after you've completed rehearsing a scene or preparing a dish well enough for friends and family, there is more you can do before you are ready for the public. Before your opening night on stage, you want to be *on point* for the harshest critic. Amazingly, there's a learning system that can transition from a friends-and-family rehearsal to a Broadway show.

5.3.5   Take-Home Notes on Overfitting

This section has a lot to consider. Here are the key points:

- Underfitting: A very simple model may not be able to learn the pattern in the training data. It also does poorly on the testing data.
- Overfitting: A very complex model may learn the training data perfectly. However, it does poorly on the testing data because it also learned irrelevant relationships in the training data.
- Just-right: A medium-complexity model performs well on the training and testing data.

We need the right tradeoff between simplicity and complexity to find a just-right model.

5.4 From Errors to Costs

In our discussion of overfitting and underfitting, we compared model complexity and error rates. We saw that as we vary the complexity of a class of models—the degree of our polynomials—we have different training and test performance. These two aspects, error and complexity, are intimately tied together. As we wander deeper into the zoo of learning methods, we'll see that some methods can explicitly trade off training error for complexity. In terms of our factory machine, we can consider *both* our success in copying the input-output relationship *and* the values we set on the knobs. Separating out these two aspects of "model goodness" lets us speak pretty generally about both regression and classification problems. When we progress a bit more, we'll also be able to *describe* many different algorithms in terms of a just a few choices. How a method treats errors and complexity are two of those choices.

5.4.1 Loss

So, what is our breakdown? First, we'll construct a *loss function* that quantifies what happens when our model is wrong on a single example. We'll use that to build a *training loss* function that measures how well our model does on the entire training set. More technical write-ups call this the *empirical loss*. Empirical simply means "by observation" or "as seen," so it's a loss based on the data we've seen. The training loss is the sum of the losses on each example. We can write that in code as:

In [12]:

```
def training_loss(loss, model, training_data):
    ' total training_loss on train_data with model under loss'
    return sum(loss(model.predict(x.reshape(1, -1)), y)
                           for x, y in training_data)
def squared_error(prediction, actual):
    ' squared error on a single example '
    return (prediction - actual)**2

# could be used like:
# my_training_loss = training_loss(squared_error, model, training_data)
```

A generic mathematical way to write this is:

$$\text{TrainingLoss}_{\text{Loss}}(m, D_{\text{train}}) = \sum_{x,y \in D_{\text{train}}} \text{Loss}(m(x), y)$$

and for the specific case of squared-error (SE) on 3-NN, where 3-NN(x) represents the prediction of 3-NN on an example x:

$$\text{TrainingLoss}_{\text{SE}}(\text{3-NN}, D_{\text{train}}) = \sum_{x,y \in D_{\text{train}}} \text{SE}(\text{3-NN}(x), y) = \sum_{x,y \in D_{\text{train}}} (\text{3-NN}(x) - y)^2$$

We can put that to use with:

In [13]:

```
knn = neighbors.KNeighborsRegressor(n_neighbors=3)
fit = knn.fit(diabetes.data, diabetes.target)

training_data = zip(diabetes.data, diabetes.target)

my_training_loss = training_loss(squared_error,
                                 knn,
                                 training_data)
print(my_training_loss)
```

[863792.3333]

If we use `sklearn`'s `mean_squared_error` and multiply it by the number of training examples—to undo the `mean` part—we get the same answer.

In [14]:

```
mse = metrics.mean_squared_error(diabetes.target,
                                 knn.predict(diabetes.data))
print(mse*len(diabetes.data))
```

863792.3333333333

The somewhat scary equation for TraingingLoss is a fundamental principle that underlies the evaluation calculations we use. We will also add on to that equation, literally, to deal with the problem of determining a good model complexity.

5.4.2   Cost

As we saw with overfitting, if we make our model more and more complex, we can capture *any* pattern—even pattern that is really noise. So, we need something that works against complexity and rewards simplicity. We do that by adding a value to the training loss to create a total notion of *cost*. Conceptually, cost = loss + complexity, but we have to fill in some details. The term we add to deal with complexity has several technical names: regularization, smoothing, penalization, or shrinkage. We'll just call it *complexity*. In short, the total cost we pay to use a model on some data depends on (1) how well it does and (2) how complicated it is. You can think of the complexity part as a baseline investment. If we have a very high initial investment, we better not have many errors. Conversely, if we have a low initial investment, we might have some room to allow for error. All of this is because we want good performance on unseen data. The term for performance on novel, unseen data is *generalization*.

One last comment. We don't have to have a fixed idea of how to trade off error and complexity. We can leave it as an open question and it will become part of the way our machine is built. In technical terms, it's just another hyperparameter. To use a traditional naming scheme—and to help break mathphobias—I'm going to use a lower-case Greek letter, λ, pronounced "lamb-da" as in "it's a lamb, duh." Lambda represents that tradeoff. While it can be unnatural to phrase some learners strictly in terms of loss and complexity, it is very broadly possible. We'll discuss that idea more in Chapter 15. We can choose a good value of λ by performing several rounds of validation testing and taking the λ that leads to the lowest cost.

In [15]:

```
def complexity(model):
    return model.complexity

def cost(model, training_data, loss, _lambda):
    return training_loss(m,D) + _lambda * complexity(m)
```

Mathematically, that looks like

$$\text{Cost}(m, D_{\text{train}}, \text{Loss}, \lambda) = \text{TrainingLoss}_{\text{Loss}}(m, D_{\text{train}}) + \lambda \text{Complexity}(m)$$

That is, our cost goes up (1) if we make more mistakes and (2) if we invest resources in more expensive, but also more flexible, models. If we take $\lambda = 2$, one unit of complexity is comparable to two units of loss. If we take $\lambda = .5$, two units of complexity are comparable to one unit of loss. Shifting λ adjusts how much we care about errors and complexity.

5.4.3 Score

You will also see the term *score* or *scoring function*. Scoring functions—at least in `sklearn`'s lexicon—are a variation on quantifying loss where bigger values are better. For our purpose, we can consider losses and scores to be inverses: as one goes up, the other goes down. So, we generally want a *high score* or a *low loss*. It simply depends on which sort of measurement we are using; they are two different ways of saying the same thing. Another set of opposites is that we will want to *minimize* a loss or loss function but we will *maximize* a score or scoring function. To summarize:

- Score: higher is better, try to maximize.
- Loss, error, and cost: lower is better, try to minimize.

Once again, if we have two models, we can compare their costs. If we have many different models, we can use some combination of brute force, blind or clever search, and mathematical trickery to pick the lowest-cost models among those—we discussed these alternatives in Section 4.4. Of course, we might be wrong. There might be models we didn't consider that have even lower cost. Our cost might not be the ideal way of evaluating the models' performance in the real world. Our complexity measure, or our tradeoff for complexity, might be too high or too low. All of these factors are working behind the scenes when we haltingly say, "We picked the *best* model and hyperparameters." Well, we did, at least up to the guesses, assumptions, and constraints we used.

We'll discuss the practical side of picking good, or at least better, model hyperparameters in Section 11.2. As we will see, modern machine learning software such as `sklearn` makes it *very easy* to try many models and combinations of hyperparameters.

5.5 (Re)Sampling: Making More from Less

If we content ourselves with a single train-test split, that single step provides and determines both the data we can train from and our testing environment. It is a simple method, for sure. However, we might get (un)lucky and get a very *good* train-test split. Imagine we get very *hard* training data and very *easy* testing data. Boom—all of a sudden, we are *overestimating* how well we will do in the big, bad real world. If overconfidence is our real concern, we'd actually like a worst-case scenario: easy training and hard testing that would lead us to underestimate the real-world performance. Enough with single-evaluation scenarios, however. Is there a way we could do better? If we ask people to estimate the number of beans in a jar, they will individually be wrong. But if we get many, many estimates, we can get a better overall answer. Hurray for the wisdom of crowds. So, how do we generate multiple estimates for evaluation? We need multiple datasets. But we only have one dataset available. How can we turn one dataset into many?

5.5.1 Cross-Validation

The machine learning community's basic answer to generating multiple datasets is called *cross-validation*. Cross-validation is like a card game where we deal out all the cards to three players, play a round of the game, and then shift our cards to the player on the right—and repeat that process until we've played the game with each of the three different sets of cards. To figure out our overall score, we take the individual scores from each different hand we played with and combine them, often with an average.

Let's go directly to an example. Cross-validation takes a number of *folds* which is like the number of players we had above. With three players, or three folds, we get three different attempts to play the game. For 3-fold cross-validation, we'll take an entire set of labeled data and shake it up. We'll let the data fall randomly—as evenly as possible—into the three buckets in Figure 5.5 labeled with Roman numerals: B_I, B_{II}, and B_{III}.

Now, we perform the following steps shown in Figure 5.6:

1. Take bucket B_I and put it to the side. Put B_{II} and B_{III} together and use them as our training set. Train a model—we'll call it *ModelOne*—from that combined training set. Now, evaluate *ModelOne* on bucket B_I and record the performance as *EvalOne*.

2. Take B_{II} and put it to the side. Put buckets B_I and B_{III} together and use them as our training set. Train *ModelTwo* from that combined training set. Now, evaluate *ModelTwo* on bucket B_{II} and record the performance as *EvalTwo*.

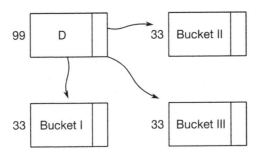

Figure 5.5 Our setup for cross-validation splits the data into approximately equal buckets.

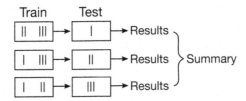

Figure 5.6 We use each cross-validation bucket, in turn, as our test data. We train on the remainder.

3. Take bucket B_{III} and put it to the side. Put B_I and B_{II} together as our training set. Train *ModelThree* from that combined training set. Now, evaluate *ModelThree* on B_{III} and record the performance as *EvalThree*.

Now, we've recorded three performance values. We can do several things with the values, including graphing them and summarizing them statistically. Graphing them can help us understand how variable our performance is with respect to different training and testing datasets. It tells us something about how our model, our training sets, and our testing sets interact. If we see a very wide spread in our performance measures, we would be justified in being skeptical of any single performance score for our system. On the other hand, if the scores are all similar, we have some certainty that, regardless of the specific train-test split, our system's performance will be similar. One caveat: our random sampling is done without replacement and the train-test splits are all dependent on each other. This breaks some of the usual assumptions we make in statistics land. If you are concerned about it, you might want to see Section 5.5.3.

What we've described is 3-fold cross-validation. The general name for CV techniques is k-fold cross-validation—I'll usually abbreviate it as k-fold CV or just k-CV. The amount of cross-validation we do depends on a few factors including the amount of data we have. 3-, 5-, and 10-fold CV are commonly used and recommended. But we're getting ahead of ourselves. Here's a simple example of *5*-fold CV with `sklearn`:

```
In [16]:
# data, model, fit & cv-score
model = neighbors.KNeighborsRegressor(10)
skms.cross_val_score(model,
                     diabetes.data,
                     diabetes.target,
                     cv=5,
                     scoring='neg_mean_squared_error')
# notes:
# defaults for cross_val_score are
# cv=3 fold, no shuffle, stratified if classifier
# model.score by default (regressors: r2, classifiers: accuracy)
```

```
Out[16]:
array([-3206.7542, -3426.4313, -3587.9422, -3039.4944, -3282.6016])
```

The default value for the cv argument to **cross_val_score** is None. To understand what that means, we have to look into the documentation for **cross_val_score**. Here is the relevant part, cleaned up and simplified a bit:

cv: int or None or others. Determines the cross-validation splitting strategy. Possible inputs for cv are:

- None, to use the default 3-fold cross validation,
- Integer, to specify the number of folds in a **(Stratified)KFold**,
- Others.

For integer/None inputs, if the estimator is a classifier and y is either binary or multiclass, **StratifiedKFold** is used. In all other cases, **KFold** is used.

We haven't discussed stratification yet—we'll get to it after the next commercial break—but there are two take-home lessons: (1) by default we're doing 3-fold CV and (2) for classification problems, **sklearn** uses stratification.

So, what's up with the **scoring='neg_mean_squared_error'** argument? You might recall mean squared error (MSE) being a thing. You are in the right ballpark. However, we have to reconcile "error up, bad" with "score up, good." To do that, **sklearn** negates the MSE to go from an error measure to a score. The scores are all *negative*, but a bigger score is better. Think of it as losing less money: instead of being down $100, you are only down $7.50.

One last bit on regression and scoring: the default scoring for regressors is r2 (R^2 for the math folks). It is well known in statistics under the name *coefficient of determination*. We'll discuss it in Section 7.2.3 but for now, let me simply say that *it is very, very easy to misuse and abuse* R^2. You may be carrying R^2 baggage with you—please leave it at the door. This is not your classic R^2.

We haven't talked about what value of k to use. The dirtiest secret of k-CV is that we need to balance three things. The first issue: how long does it take to train and test our

n Buckets

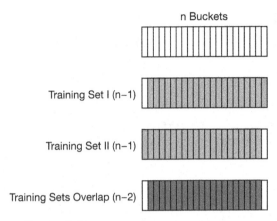

Figure 5.7   Overlap in n-fold cross-validation.

models? A bigger k means more buckets which in turn means more training and testing phases. There are some *incremental/decremental* learning methods that can be implemented to minimize the amount of work necessary to train and test different models. Unfortunately, most common models are *not* implemented or interfaced with cross-validation routines in a way that allows this efficiency. To make matters even more interesting, training on smaller datasets is *faster* than training on larger datasets. So, we are comparing many small trainings (and large testings) with fewer larger trainings (and smaller testings). The run times will depend on the specific learning methods you use.

The second issue to balance is that the value of k slides up and down between two extremes. The smallest useful value is $k = 2$, which makes two buckets of data and two estimates of our test error. The largest value k can take is the number of data points we have, $k = n$. This results in each example being in its own bucket and n total models and estimates. In addition, when we have two buckets, we never train on the same data. With three buckets, we have some overlap—half the training set used to create the model tested on B_I is in common with the training sets used to create the model tested on B_{II}. Specifically, the common elements are those in B_{III}. With n buckets, between any two of our models, they are trained on the *same* $n - 2$ examples (see Figure 5.7). To get to the full n examples, there's one more example for training that is different in the two CV folds and another example that is reserved for testing.

The net effect is that the data in the training folds for $k = 2$ is *very different* and the data in the training folds for $k = n$ is *almost the same*. This means the estimates we get out of $k = 2$ will be quite different—if there is a difference to be found. The estimates out of $k = n$ will be very similar, because they are doing *almost* the same thing!

The third issue is that small values of k—relatively few folds—will result in training set sizes ranging from 50% ($k = 2$) to 90% ($k = 10$) of the data. Whether this is acceptable— whether learning on that much data will be sufficient—depends on the problem at hand. We can evaluate that graphically using learning curves, as in Section 5.7.1. If the learning curve flattens out at the percent of data we are trying to learn from—if that much data is enough to get us to a sufficient performance threshold—we are probably OK using the related number of folds.

5.5.2 Stratification

Let's turn to a quick example of cross-validation in a classification context. Here, we tell `cross_val_score` to use 5-fold CV.

In [17]:

```
iris = datasets.load_iris()
model = neighbors.KNeighborsClassifier(10)
skms.cross_val_score(model, iris.data, iris.target, cv=5)
```

Out[17]:

```
array([0.9667, 1.    , 1.    , 0.9333, 1.    ])
```

As mentioned above, the cross-validation was done in a *stratified* manner because it is the default for classifiers in `sklearn`. What does that mean? Basically, stratification means that when we make our training-testing splits for cross-validation, we want to respect the proportions of the targets that are present in our data. Huh? Let's do an example. Here's a tiny dataset targeting cats and dogs that we'll take two-fold training samples from:

In [18]:

```
# not stratified
pet = np.array(['cat', 'dog', 'cat',
                'dog', 'dog', 'dog'])
list_folds = list(skms.KFold(2).split(pet))
training_idxs = np.array(list_folds)[:, 0, :]

print(pet[training_idxs])
```

```
[['dog' 'dog' 'dog']
 ['cat' 'dog' 'cat']]
```

Out cat-loving readers will notice that there were no cats in the first fold. That's not great. If that were our target, we would have no examples to learn about cats. Simply put, that can't be good. Stratified sampling enforces fair play among the cats and dogs:

In [19]:

```
# stratified
# note: typically this is behind the scenes
# making StratifiedKFold produce readable output
# requires some trickery. feel free to ignore.
pet = np.array(['cat', 'dog', 'cat', 'dog', 'dog', 'dog'])
```

```
idxs = np.array(list(skms.StratifiedKFold(2)
                         .split(np.ones_like(pet), pet)))
training_idxs = idxs[:, 0, :]
print(pet[training_idxs])
```

```
[['cat' 'dog' 'dog']
 ['cat' 'dog' 'dog']]
```

Now, both folds have a balanced number of cats and dogs, equal to their proportion in the overall dataset. Stratification ensures that we have the same (or nearly the same, once we round off uneven splits) *percent* of dogs and cats in each of our training sets as we do in our entire, available population. Without stratification, we could end up having too few (or even none) of a target class—in our nonstratified example, the first training set had no cats. We don't expect that training data to lead to a good model.

Stratification is particularly useful when (1) we have limited data overall or (2) we have classes that are poorly represented in our dataset. Poor representation might be due to rareness—if we're talking about an uncommon disease or winning lottery tickets—or it might be due to our data collection processes. Having a limited total amount of data makes *everything* rare, in a sense. We will discuss more issues around rare classes in Section 6.2.

How does the default stratification apply to the *iris* dataset in Chapter 3? It means that when we perform the cross-validation splits, we can be sure that each of the training sets has a balanced representation from each of the three possible target flowers. What if we don't want stratification? It's slightly more tricky, but we can do it:

In [20]:

```
# running nonstratified CV
iris = datasets.load_iris()
model = neighbors.KNeighborsClassifier(10)
non_strat_kf = skms.KFold(5)
skms.cross_val_score(model,
                     iris.data,
                     iris.target,
                     cv=non_strat_kf)
```

Out[20]:

```
array([1.    , 1.    , 0.8667, 0.9667, 0.7667])
```

We can make an educated guess that the last fold probably had a bad distribution of flowers. We probably didn't see enough of one of the species to learn patterns to identify it.

5.5.3 Repeated Train-Test Splits

Here's another example of the train-test split with an added twist. (That's a train-test twist, if you're keeping track.) Our twist is that we are going to do some repeated coin flipping to generate several train-test splits. Why do we want to *repeat* the fundamental train-test split step? Any time we rely on randomness, we are subject to variation: several different train-test splits might give different results. Some of those might turn out wonderfully and some may turn out horribly. In some scenarios, like playing the lottery, the *vast majority* of outcomes are very similar—you don't win money. In others, we don't know ahead of time what the outcomes are. Fortunately, we have an extremely useful tool at our disposal that we can pull out when confronted with unknown randomness. Do the random thing many times and see what happens. Stand back, we're about to try science!

In the case of train-test splits, we generally don't know ahead of time how well we expect to perform. Maybe the problem is really easy and almost all of the train-test splits will give a good learner that performs well on the test set. Or maybe it is a very hard problem and we happen to select an easy subset of training data—we do great in training, but perform horribly in testing. We can investigate the variation due to the train-test split by making many train-test splits and looking at different results. We do that by randomly resplitting several times and evaluating the outcomes. We can even compute statistics—the mean, median, or variance—of the results if we really want to get technical. However, I am always a fan of *looking at the data* before we get into *summarizing the data* with statistics.

The multiple values—one per train-test split—get us a distribution of the results and how often they occur. Just like drawing a graph of the heights of students in a classroom gets us a distribution of those heights, repeated train-test splits get us a distribution of our evaluation measure—whether it is accuracy, root-mean-squared-error, or something else. The distribution is *not* over *every* possible source of variation. It is simply taking into account one difference due to randomness: how we picked the training and testing data. We can see how *variable* our result is *due to* the randomness of making a train-test split. Without further ado, let's look at some results.

In [21]:

```
# as a reminder, these are some of the imports
# that are hidden behind: from mlwpy import *
# from sklearn import (datasets, neighbors,
#                      model_selection as skms,
#                      linear_model, metrics)
# see Appendix A for details

linreg   = linear_model.LinearRegression()
diabetes = datasets.load_diabetes()

scores = []
for r in range(10):
    tts = skms.train_test_split(diabetes.data,
                                diabetes.target,
                                test_size=.25)
```

```
      (diabetes_train_ftrs, diabetes_test_ftrs,
       diabetes_train_tgt,  diabetes_test_tgt) = tts

      fit   = linreg.fit(diabetes_train_ftrs, diabetes_train_tgt)
      preds = fit.predict(diabetes_test_ftrs)

      score = metrics.mean_squared_error(diabetes_test_tgt, preds)
      scores.append(score)

scores = pd.Series(np.sqrt(sorted(scores)))
df = pd.DataFrame({'RMSE':scores})
df.index.name = 'Repeat'
display(df.T)
```

Repeat	0	1	2	3	4	5	6	7	8	9
RMSE	49.00	50.19	51.97	52.07	53.20	55.70	56.25	57.49	58.64	58.69

You can certainly take *looking at the data* to an extreme. A raw list is only useful for
relatively few values—people don't scale well to reading too many numbers. Let's make
a plot. `swarmplot`, from the Seaborn library, is very useful here. It makes a single value
plot—also called a stripplot—and stacks repeated values horizontally so you get a feel for
where there are clumps of values.

```
In [22]:
ax = plt.figure(figsize=(4, 3)).gca()
sns.swarmplot(y='RMSE', data=df, ax=ax)
ax.set_xlabel('Over Repeated\nTrain-Test Splits');
```

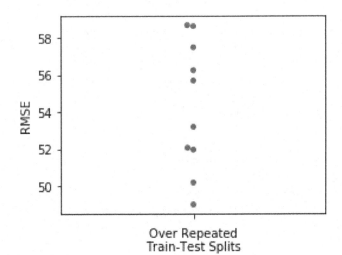

In [23]:

```
display(df.describe().T)
```

	count	mean	std	min	25%	50%	75%	max
RMSE	10.000	54.322	3.506	49.003	51.998	54.451	57.182	58.694

When evaluating plots like this, always orient yourself to the scale of the data. At first, we might think that this data is pretty spread out, but upon further review, we see that it is clustered in the mid-to-upper 50s. Whether that is "a lot" depends on size of the RMSE values—the mean is near 55, so we are in the ballpark of $\pm 10\%$. That's large enough to warrant our attention.

As a quick Python lesson, here's a way we can rewrite the score-computing code above with a list comprehension instead of a loop. The basic strategy is to (1) take the contents of the loop and turn it into a function and (2) use that function repeatedly in a list comprehension. This rewrite gets us a bit of performance gain—but I'm not doing it for the resource optimization. The biggest win is that we've given a *name* to our process of making a train-test split, fitting, predicting, and evaluating. As in the book of Genesis, naming is one of the most powerful things we can do in a computer program. Defining a function also gives us a single entity that we can test for resource use and *reuse* in other code.

In [24]:

```
def tts_fit_score(model, data, msr, test_size=.25):
    ' apply a train-test split to fit model on data and eval with MSR '
    tts = skms.train_test_split(data.data,
                                data.target,
                                test_size=test_size)

    (train_ftrs, test_ftrs, train_tgt,  test_tgt) = tts

    fit   = linreg.fit(train_ftrs, train_tgt)
    preds = fit.predict(test_ftrs)

    score = msr(test_tgt, preds)
    return score

linreg   = linear_model.LinearRegression()
diabetes = datasets.load_diabetes()
scores = [tts_fit_score(linreg, diabetes,
                        metrics.mean_squared_error) for i in range(10)]
print(np.mean(scores))
```

3052.540273057884

I'll leave you with one final comment on repeated train-test splits and cross-validation. With *k*-CV, we will get one, and only one, prediction for each and every example. Each example is in precisely one test bucket. The predictions for the *whole* dataset will be aggregated from the *k* models that are developed on different sets of data. With repeated train-test splits, we may completely ignore training or predicting on some examples and make repeated predictions on other examples as we see in Figure 5.8. In repeated train-test splits, it is all subject to the randomness of our selection process.

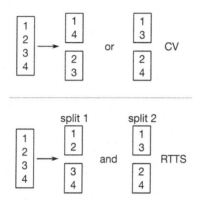

Figure 5.8   RTTS may have duplication between repeats.

5.5.4 A Better Way and Shuffling

Managing the repeated looping to make multiple train-test splits was a bit annoying. It was not heart- or back-breaking, but there are many places we could make a mistake. It would be nice if someone wrapped the process up in a single stand-alone function. Fortunately, `sklearn` has done that. If we pass in a `ShuffleSplit` data-splitter to the cv argument of `cross_val_score`, we get precisely the algorithm we hand-coded above.

In [25]:

```
linreg   = linear_model.LinearRegression()
diabetes = datasets.load_diabetes()

# nondefault cv= argument
ss = skms.ShuffleSplit(test_size=.25) # default, 10 splits
scores = skms.cross_val_score(linreg,
                              diabetes.data, diabetes.target,
                              cv=ss,
                              scoring='neg_mean_squared_error')

scores = pd.Series(np.sqrt(-scores))
df = pd.DataFrame({'RMSE':scores})
df.index.name = 'Repeat'
```

```
display(df.describe().T)

ax = sns.swarmplot(y='RMSE', data=df)
ax.set_xlabel('Over Repeated\nTrain-Test Splits');
```

	count	mean	std	min	25%	50%	75%	max
RMSE	10.000	55.439	3.587	50.190	52.966	55.397	58.391	60.543

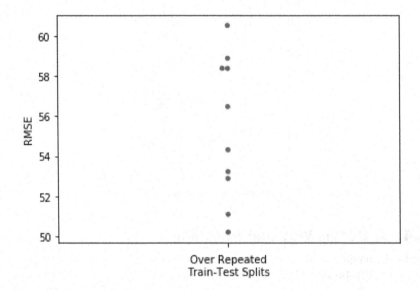

The slight differences with our manual version are due to randomly selecting the train-test splits.

Now, I want to talk about another way that randomness affects us as intrepid students of machine learning. It's the kind of randomness that the computer uses when we ask it to do random things. Here's what's going on behind the scenes with ShuffleSplit. Don't worry, I'll explain random_state in just a second.

In [26]:

```
ss = skms.ShuffleSplit(test_size=.25, random_state=42)

train, test = 0, 1
next(ss.split(diabetes.data))[train][:10]
```

Out[26]:

```
array([ 16, 408, 432, 316,   3,  18, 355,  60, 398, 124])
```

By the way, I use `next` because `ShuffleSplit` relies on a Python generator to produce one split after another. Saying `next` provides me with the next data split. After fetching the next data split, I pick out the training data `[train]` and then the first ten examples `[:10]`.

Good enough. Let's try again.

In [27]:

```
ss = skms.ShuffleSplit(test_size=.25, random_state=42)
next(ss.split(diabetes.data))[train][:10]
```

Out[27]:

```
array([ 16, 408, 432, 316,   3,  18, 355,  60, 398, 124])
```

That can't be good. Someone call—someone! We need help. The results are the same. Wasn't this supposed to be random? The answer is yes . . . and no. Randomness on a computer is often pseudo-random. It's a long list of numbers that, when put together, are random enough to fake their randomness. We start at some point in that list and start taking values. To an outside observer, they seem pretty random. But if you know the mechanism, you could actually know what values are coming ahead of time. Thus, (1) the values we generate will *look* mostly random, but (2) the process used to generate them is actually deterministic. This determinism has a nice side effect that we can take advantage of. If we specify a starting point for the sequence of pseudo-random numbers, we can get a reproducible list of the not-so-random values. When we use `random_state`, we are setting a starting point for `ShuffleSplit` to use when it asks for randomness. We'll end up getting the same outputs. Repeatable train-test splitting is very useful for creating reproducible test cases, sharing examples with students, and eliminating some degrees of freedom when chasing down bugs.

While we're at it, here's another place where a similar issue comes up. Let's do two separate runs of `KFolding`.

In [28]:

```
train, test = 0, 1
kf = skms.KFold(5)
next(kf.split(diabetes.data))[train][:10]
```

Out[28]:

```
array([89, 90, 91, 92, 93, 94, 95, 96, 97, 98])
```

In [29]:

```
kf = skms.KFold(5)
next(kf.split(diabetes.data))[train][:10]
```

Out[29]:

```
array([89, 90, 91, 92, 93, 94, 95, 96, 97, 98])
```

The lack of randomness, in places we *want* randomness, is starting to get a little old. The issue here is the default parameters to `KFold`:

```
skms.KFold(n_splits=3, shuffle=False, random_state=None)
```

`shuffle=False`, the default, means that we *don't* shake up the examples before distributing them to different folds. If we *want* them shaken up, we need to say so. To keep the examples a bit more readable, we'll switch back to the simple `pet` targets.

In [30]:

```
pet = np.array(['cat', 'dog', 'cat',
                'dog', 'dog', 'dog'])

kf = skms.KFold(3, shuffle=True)

train, test = 0, 1
split_1_group_1 = next(kf.split(pet))[train]
split_2_group_1 = next(kf.split(pet))[train]

print(split_1_group_1,
      split_2_group_1)
```

```
[0 1 4 5] [0 1 3 5]
```

If we set a `random_state`, it's shared by the splitters:

In [31]:

```
kf = skms.KFold(3, shuffle=True, random_state=42)

split_1_group_1 = next(kf.split(pet))[train]
split_2_group_1 = next(kf.split(pet))[train]
print(split_1_group_1,
      split_2_group_1)
```

```
[2 3 4 5] [2 3 4 5]
```

5.5.5 Leave-One-Out Cross-Validation

I mentioned above that we could take an extreme approach to cross-validation and use as many cross-validation buckets as we have examples. So, with 20 examples, we could potentially make 20 train-test splits, do 20 training fits, do 20 testing rounds, and get 20 resulting evaluations. This version of CV is called *leave-one-out cross-validation* (LOOCV) and it is interesting because *all* of the models we generate are going to have *almost all* of their training data in common. With 20 examples, 90% of the data is shared between any two training runs. You might refer back to Figure 5.7 to see it visually.

```
In [32]:
linreg   = linear_model.LinearRegression()
diabetes = datasets.load_diabetes()

loo = skms.LeaveOneOut()
scores = skms.cross_val_score(linreg,
                             diabetes.data, diabetes.target,
                             cv=loo,
                             scoring='neg_mean_squared_error')

scores = pd.Series(np.sqrt(-scores))
df = pd.DataFrame({'RMSE':scores})
df.index.name = 'Repeat'

display(df.describe().T)

ax = sns.swarmplot(y='RMSE', data=df)
ax.set_xlabel('Over LOO\nTrain-Test Splits');
```

	count	mean	std	min	25%	50%	75%	max
RMSE	442.000	44.356	32.197	0.208	18.482	39.547	63.973	158.236

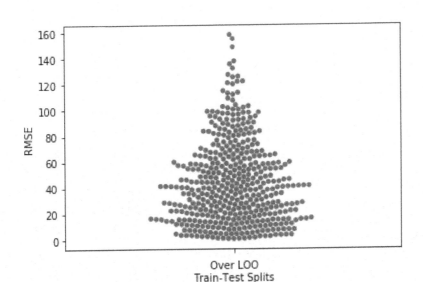

Curiously, there are three noticeable points with a high RMSE and there are about twenty points that form a distinct peak above the main body of the errors (RMSE > 100). That means there are about twenty points that are resistant to prediction with the model we are building using almost all of the data. It would be worthwhile to investigate any common factors in those difficult examples.

LOOCV is a deterministic evaluation method. There's no randomness in the selection because everything is used in the same way every time we run LOOCV. This determinism can be useful for comparing and testing correctness of learning algorithms. However, it can be expensive to run LOOCV because we need to train the model once for each left-out example. Some models have mathematical tricks that can used to drastically reduce the overhead of retraining. On the evaluation side, the net effect of incorporating lots of training data—all but one example—in every CV partition is that LOOCV gives a relatively unbiased estimate of the real error rate. Because the single-example predictions are so closely related—most of the training data is shared and piped into the same learning algorithm—the estimates of our performance error on *new* examples can vary widely. Overall, a general recommendation is to prefer 5- or 10-fold CV to LOOCV.

5.6 Break-It-Down: Deconstructing Error into Bias and Variance

Let's imagine that we are at a race track and we start taking some basic measurements. We see cars zooming around the track and we measure where the cars are at and how fast they are going. Let's say we record two lap times for a total distance $d = 2$. We'll also record an average speed s. If I have a table of these values and I don't remember any high-school physics, I can start trying to relate the different columns together. For example, from the two times and the total time I might come up with the fact that $t_1 + t_2 = t_{total}$. Again, imagine we *forgot* everything we learned in high-school physics or maybe even fourth-grade math.

Driver	t_1	t_2	t_{total}	s	d
Mario	35	75	110	.018	2
Luigi	20	40	60	.033	2
Yoshi	40	50	90	.022	2

Let's consider some variations in trying to relate the columns. First, are the measurements *perfect* or are there errors in how we recorded them? Second, what relationships—what mathematical operations—am I allowed to use to relate the columns? To keep things under control, we'll limit ourselves to two simple operations, addition and multiplication, and see what happens with them. Lastly, we'll consider relationships between different sets of columns as inputs and outputs.

In Table 5.2, I've laid out the different possibilities and some assessments of how perfectly they can describe the data and what goes wrong.

Table 5.2 Sources of errors in learning.

Inputs	Output	Measurement errors	True Relationship	Try to Relate With	Perfect?	Why?
t_1, t_2	t_{total}	no	add	add	yes	
t_1, t_2	t_{total}	yes	add	add	no	measurement errors
t_{total}, s	d	no	multiply	add	no	can't get right form

Two of these three cases are subpar. The two cases where we end up with "Perfect? No!" are equivalent to two sources of error that we must address when we develop learning systems. A third source of error is the interaction between the training data and the learner. We saw hints of this interaction when we saw the different results from training on different training sets. Together, these three examples of error give us a great foundation to break down the ways we can make mistakes in predictions. Measurement errors—the second line in Table 5.2—reduce our ability to relate values clearly, but those errors may be difficult to control. They may not even be our fault if someone else did the measuring; we're doing the modeling. But the third line, where we have a mismatch between *reality* and our chosen *model*, is a problem of our own making.

5.6.1 Variance of the Data

When we make a mistake—when we have an incorrect class or a MSE greater than zero—there can be a few different causes. One of these causes—the actual randomness in the relationship between the input features and the output target—we have no real control over. For example, not every college graduate that majored in economics and has five years of professional work experience earns the same amount of money. There is a wide range of possibilities for their income. If we include more information, such as selectiveness of their undergrad school, we may be able to narrow down that range. However, randomness will still remain. Similarly, depending on our timing devices and user error at the race track, we may record the times more or less precisely (repeatably).

Having a range of outputs is a fundamental difference between the mathematical functions you saw in high school and random processes. Instead of one input having one-and-only-one output, a single input can have a range—that's a distribution—of outputs. We've wrapped back around to rolling a die or flipping a coin: dealing with randomness. The degree to which our data is affected by randomness—either in measurement or in real-world differences—is called the *variance of the data*.

5.6.2   Variance of the Model

There are some sources of error we *can* control in a learning system, but there may be limits on our control. When we pick a single model—say, linear regression—and go through a training step, we set the values of the parameters of that model. We are setting the values on the knobs of our factory machine. If we choose our training and testing datasets at random, which we should, we lose some control over the outcome. The parameters of our model—the values of our knobs—are subject to the coin-flipping choice of training data. If we flip the coins again, we get different training data. With different training data we get a different trained model. The way models vary due to the random selection of the data we train on is called the *variance of the model*.

A trained model will give us different answers when we use it on test cases and in the wild. Here's a concrete example. If we have one very bad data point, with 1-Nearest Neighbors, most of our training and testing examples will be unaffected by it. However, for anyone that *is* the nearest neighbor of the bad example, things will go wrong. Conversely, if we used a large number of neighbors, the effect of that example would be diluted out among many other training examples. We've ended up with a tradeoff: being able to account for tricky examples also leaves us exposed to following bad examples. Our racetrack example did *not* include an example of variance due to the model training.

5.6.3   Bias of the Model

Our last source of error is where we have the most control. When I choose between two models, one may have a fundamentally better resonance with the relationship between the inputs and outputs. We've already seen one example of poor resonance in Section 5.3.2: a line has great difficulty following the path of a parabola.

Let's tie this idea to our current discussion. We'll start by eliminating noise—the inherent randomness—we discussed a few paragraphs back. We eliminate it by considering only a best-guess output for any given input. So, while an input example made from level of education, degree program, and years post-graduation {*college, economics,* 5} *actually* has a range of possible income predictions, we'll take one best value to represent the possible outputs. Now, we ask, "How well can model one line up with that single value?" and "How well can model two line up with that single value?" Then, we expand that process to *all* of our inputs—{*secondary, vocational,* 10}, {*grad, psychology,* 8}—and ask how well do the models match the single best guesses for every possible input.

Don't worry, we'll make these ideas more concrete in a moment.

We say that a model that cannot match the *actual* relationship between the inputs and outputs—after we ignore the inherent noisiness in the data—has higher *bias*. A highly biased model has difficulty capturing complicated patterns. A model with low bias can follow more complicated patterns. In the racetrack example, when we wanted to relate speed and time to come up with a distance, we couldn't do it with *addition* because the true relationship between them is *multiplication*.

5.6.4 All Together Now

These three components give us a fundamental breakdown of the sources of errors in our predictions. The three components are (1) the inherent variability in our data, (2) the variability in creating our predicting model from training data, and (3) the bias of our model. The relationship between these and our overall error is called the *bias-variance decomposition*, written mathematically as

$$\text{Error} = \text{Bias}_{\text{Learner}} + \text{Variance}_{\text{Learner(Training)}} + \text{Variance}_{\text{Data}}$$

I'm sweeping many details of this equation under the carpet. But take heart! Even graduate-level, mathematically inclined textbooks sweep details of this particular equation under the carpet. Of course, they call it "removing unnecessary details," but we won't hold it against them. I'll just say that we're in good company. Before we look at some examples, let's reiterate one more time. The errors in our predictions are due to randomness in the data, variability in building our model from training data, and the difference between what relationships our model can express and the actual, *true* relationship.

5.6.5 Examples of Bias-Variance Tradeoffs

Let's examine a few concrete examples of the bias-variance tradeoff by looking at how it applies to *k*-Nearest Neighbors, Linear Regression, and Naive Bayes.

5.6.5.1 Bias-Variance for *k*-NN

Let's think about what happens with *k*-NN as we vary the number of neighbors. Start by going to extremes. The fewest number of neighbors we could use is one. This amounts to saying, "If I'm a new example, then find who is most like me and label me with their target." 1-NN, as a strategy, has the potential to have a very jagged or wiggly border. Every training example gets to have its own say without consulting anyone else! From the opposite perspective, once we find the closest example, we ignore what everyone else says. If there were ten training examples, once we find our closest neighbor, nothing about the other nine matters.

Now, let's go to the opposite extreme. Let's say we have ten examples and we do 10-NN. Our strategy becomes "I'm a new example. Find my ten closest neighbors and average their target. That's my predicted target." Well, with just ten total examples, every new example we come across is going to have exactly those ten nearest neighbors. So, regardless of the example, we are averaging *everyone's* target value. This is equivalent to saying, "Make my predicted target the overall training mean." Our predictions here have no border: they are all exactly the same. We predict the same value regardless of the input predictor values. The only more biased prediction would be predicting some constant—say, 42—that isn't computed from the data at all.

Figure 5.9 summarizes the bias-variance tradeoff for *k*-NN. Increasing the number of neighbors increases our bias and decreases our variance. Decreasing the number of neighbors increases our variance and decreases our bias.

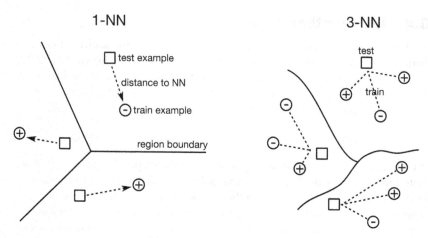

Figure 5.9   Bias in k-NN.

5.6.5.2 Bias-Variance for Linear Regression

What is the comparable analysis for linear regression? There are two different ways to think about it and I want to simplify both of them for now. Let's modify a plain-vanilla linear regression in two ways:

- Restricting the features that are included
- *Adding* new pseudo-features that have a simple relationship to the original features

We'll start with two possible linear regression models. *ConstantLinear* is just predicting a flat horizontal line or surface. The second model, *PlainLinear*, is our standard line or plane-like model that can incline and tilt. In terms of the weights we discussed in Section 4.3.2, the first model sets all weights except w_0 to zero and gives the same output value regardless of input. It says, "I'm afraid of change, don't confuse me with data." The second model says, "It's a party, invite everyone!" You can imagine a middle ground between these two extremes: pick and choose who to invite to the party. That is, set *some* of the weights to zero. So, we have four variations on the linear regression model:

- Constant linear: include no features, $w_i = 0$ for all $i \neq 0$.
- Few: include a few features, most $w_i = 0$.
- Many: include many features, a few $w_i = 0$.
- Plain linear: include all features, no $w_i = 0$.

These give us a similar spectrum of complexities for our linear regression model as we saw with k-NN. As we include fewer features by setting more weights to zero, we lose our ability to distinguish between differences represented in the lost features. Put another way, our world gets *flatter* with respect to the missing dimensions. Think about taking a soda can and flattening it like a pancake. Any of the *height* information about the can has been completely lost. Even irregularities in the can—like that little lip that collects spilled out soda—are gone. Shining a light on objects (as in Figure 5.10) gives us an analogy for how differences are hidden when we lose information.

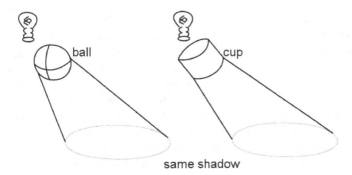

Figure 5.10   Losing features (dimensions) restricts our view of the world
and increases our bias.

Knocking out some of the features completely, by setting w_i's to zero, is quite extreme. We'll see a more gradual process of making the weights smaller, but not necessarily zero, in Section 9.1.

Now let's turn to *extending* the features we include. As we saw earlier in this chapter, by adding more *polynomial* terms—x^2, x^3, and friends—we can accommodate more bends or wiggles in our data (Figure 5.11). We can use those bends to capture examples that appear to be oddities. As we also saw, that means we can be fooled by noise.

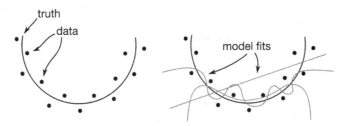

Figure 5.11   Adding complex terms lets our model wiggle more, but that
variance might follow noise.

In linear regression, adding features—like polynomial terms—decreases bias but increases variance. Conversely, forcing the weights of features to zero increases bias and decreases variances.

5.6.5.3 Relating k-NN and Linear Regression

There is a nice connection between the different linear regression models and the k-NN spectrum. The constant linear model—the simplest and most biased model—predicts a single value everywhere: *the mean*. Similarly, a k-NN system that has k equal to the number of examples in the training dataset takes into account all of the data and summarizes it. That summary can be *the mean*. The most biased linear regression and nearest-neighbors models *both predict the mean*.

On the other end of the spectrum—the end with less bias—we get complexity in two very different ways. *PlainLinear* includes information from all the features, but trades off feature values, based on parameter weights, to get to a "central" predicted value. *1-NN* includes information from all the *features* in the distance calculation, but then it only considers the closest *example* to get the prediction value.

It is amazingly interesting—at least to me—that consulting *more examples* in nearest neighbors leads to *more bias*, yet consulting *more features* in linear regression leads to *less bias*. An explanation is that in nearest neighbors, the only thing we do when we consult someone else is average away the differences between examples—we are smoothing out the rough edges. So, it has as much to do with our method of combining information as it does with the fact that we are consulting more examples.

5.6.5.4 Bias-Variance for Naive Bayes

There's an elephant in the room. We've discussed each of the methods we introduced in Part I, except Naive Bayes (NB). So, what about the bias-variance of NB? Describing the tradeoffs with NB is a little different because Naive Bayes is more like a single point on a spectrum of assumptions. The spectrum that NB lives on has *the number of conditional independence assumptions* on its x axis for complexity. Naive Bayes makes almost as many of these as possible: everything is conditionally independent given the class (Figure 5.12).

If class is independent of all the features—the ultimate independence assumption—the best we can do is guess based on the distribution of the class. For a continuous target, it implies that we guess the mean. We are back to a mean-only model for our least complex, most biased, most-assumptions model within a class of models. That's pretty convenient. Other, more complicated models that try to add complexity to NB could make fewer and fewer independence assumptions. These would come with more and more complicated claims about dependency. Eventually, we get the most complicated type of dependency: the dreaded *full joint distribution*. Among other problems, if we want to adequately capture the distinctions in a fully dependent joint distribution, we need an amount of data that is exponential in the number of features of the data. For each additional feature we need something like—I'm taking liberties with the values—another factor-of-10 examples. If we need 100 examples for two features, we would need 1000 for three features. Yikes. Suffice it to say, that is not good for us.

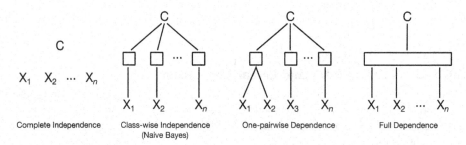

Complete Independence   Class-wise Independence   One-pairwise Dependence   Full Dependence
(Naive Bayes)

Figure 5.12   Naive Bayes is one bias-variance point on a spectrum of possibilities.

5.6.5.5 Summary Table

It might be surprising that three learning methods, each motivated by different priorities and conceptualizations of the data, all have a common starting point: in a simple enough scenario, they predict the *mean*. Nearest neighbors with every example? It predicts a mean, if that's our summary calculation. Linear regression with only w_0? Yup, that w_0 ends up being the mean! A simpler form of Naive Bayes—Even Naiver Bayes?—is exactly the mean (or the most frequent value for a classification problem) of the output target. Each method extends that in different ways, however. Table 5.3 shows how the models have different tradeoffs in terms of bias-variance and under- and overfitting.

Table 5.3 Tradeoffs between bias and variance.

Scenario	Example	Good	Bad	Risk
high bias & low variance	more neighbors	resists noise	misses pattern	underfit
	low-degree polynomial	forced to generalize		
	smaller or zero linear regression coefficients			
	more independence assumptions			
low bias & high variance	fewer neighbors	follows complex patterns	follows noise	overfit
	high-degree polynomial		memorizes training data	
	bigger linear regression coefficients			
	fewer independence assumptions			

5.7 Graphical Evaluation and Comparison

Our discussion has turned a bit towards the theoretical. You can probably tell because we haven't seen any code for a while. I want to remedy that by going immediately to evaluating performance *visually*. In additional to being fun, evaluating learners visually answers important questions in ways that can be hard to boil down to a single number. Remember, single numbers—mean, median, I'm looking at *you*—can be highly misleading.

5.7.1   Learning Curves: How Much Data Do We Need?

One of the simplest questions we can ask about a learning system is how its learning performance increases as we give it more training examples. If the learner *never* gets good performance, even when we give it a lot of data, we might be barking up the wrong proverbial tree. We could also see that when we use more, or all, of our training data, we continue improving our performance. That might give us confidence to spend some real-world effort to obtain more data to train our model. Here's some code to get us started. `sklearn` provides `learning_curve` to do the calculations we need.

In [33]:

```
iris = datasets.load_iris()

# 10 data set sizes:  10% - 100%
# (that much data is piped to a 5-fold CV)
train_sizes = np.linspace(.1, 1.0, 10)
nn = neighbors.KNeighborsClassifier()

(train_N,
 train_scores,
 test_scores) = skms.learning_curve(nn, iris.data, iris.target,
                                    cv=5, train_sizes=train_sizes)

# collapse across the 5 CV scores; one result for each data set size
df = pd.DataFrame(test_scores, index=(train_sizes*100).astype(np.int))
df['Mean 5-CV'] = df.mean(axis='columns')
df.index.name = "% Data Used"

display(df)
```

% Data Used	0	1	2	3	4	Mean 5-CV
10	0.3333	0.3333	0.3333	0.3333	0.3333	0.3333
20	0.3333	0.3333	0.3333	0.3333	0.3333	0.3333
30	0.3333	0.3333	0.3333	0.3333	0.3333	0.3333
40	0.6667	0.6667	0.6667	0.6667	0.6667	0.6667
50	0.6667	0.6667	0.6667	0.6667	0.6667	0.6667
60	0.6667	0.6667	0.6667	0.6667	0.6667	0.6667
70	0.9000	0.8000	0.8333	0.8667	0.8000	0.8400
80	0.9667	0.9333	0.9000	0.9000	0.9667	0.9333
90	0.9667	1.0000	0.9000	0.9667	1.0000	0.9667
100	0.9667	1.0000	0.9333	0.9667	1.0000	0.9733

`learning_curve` returns arrays with two dimensions: the number of training sizes by the number of cv-folds. I'll call these `(percents, folds)`. In the code above, the values are `(10, 5)`. Unfortunately, turning those values—from the table immediately above—into graphs can be a bit of a headache.

Fortunately, Seaborn has—or had, it's being deprecated—a helper we can use. We're going to send the results to `tsplot`. `tsplot` creates multiple overlaid graphs, one for each condition, and it gives us a center and a range based on the repeated measurements we have. Remember how our college grads might have a range of possible incomes? It's the same idea here. `tsplot` is geared towards plotting time series. It expects data with three components: times, conditions, and repeats. In turn, these three components become the x axis, the grouper (one line), and the repeats (the width around the line). The grouping serves to keep certain data points together; since we're drawing multiple plots on one figure, we need to know which data belongs together in *one* shade. The repeats are the multiple assessments of the same scenario subject to some random variation. Do it again and you get a slightly different result. `tsplot` expects these components in the following order: `(repeats, times, conds)`.

If we take the results of `learning_curve` and stack `train_scores` and `test_scores` on the outermost dimension, we end up with data that is structured like `(train/test condition, percents, folds)`. We just need those dimensions turned inside out since `(folds, percents, conditions)` lines up with `tsplot`'s `(repeats, times, conditions)`. The way we do this is with `np.transpose`.

In [34]:

```
# tsplot expects array data to have these dimensions:
# (repeats, times, conditions)
# for us, those translate to:
# (CV scores, percents, train/test)
joined = np.array([train_scores, test_scores]).transpose()

ax = sns.tsplot(joined,
                time=train_sizes,
                condition=['Train', 'Test'],
                interpolate=False)

ax.set_title("Learning Curve for 5-NN Classifier")
ax.set_xlabel("Number of Samples used for Training")
ax.set_ylabel("Accuracy");
```

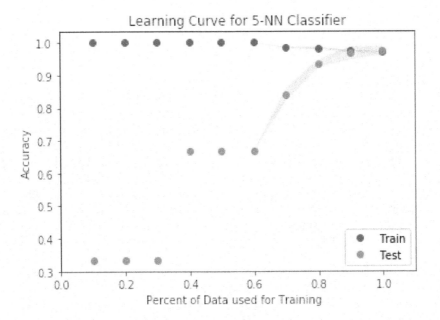

We see some distinct steps in the testing error. Using up to about 30% of the data for training gives very poor test performance—just above 30% accuracy. Bumping the training data to 40–50% ups our test performance to 70%, a big step in the right direction. As we move from 70% to 100% of the data used for training, the test performance starts to flatten out near a respectable percent in the high 90s. What about the training side? Why does it decrease? With few enough examples, there is apparently a simple enough pattern that our 5-NN can capture all of the training data—until we get to about 60%. After that, we start losing a bit of ground on the training performance. But remember—what we really care about is the test performance.

One other takeaway: we can convert this percent into a minimum number of examples we think we need for adequate training. For example, we needed almost 100% *of the joined training folds* to get reasonable 5-CV testing results. That translates into needing 80% of the full dataset for training. If this was inadequate, we could consider fewer CV splits which would up the amount of training data.

5.7.2 Complexity Curves

Earlier, when we discussed under- and overfitting, we drew a graph that showed what happened to our training and testing performance as we varied the complexity of our model. Graphing that was buried deep inside some nested loops and drawing functions. We can appropriate `tsplot`, as we did for sample curves, to make the process fit in five logical lines of code. Since we're not playing code-golf—not trying to minimize the number of lines of code to win a prize—I won't literally write it in five lines.

```
In [35]:
num_neigh = [1, 3, 5, 10, 15, 20]
KNC = neighbors.KNeighborsClassifier
tt = skms.validation_curve(KNC(),
                           iris.data, iris.target,
                           param_name='n_neighbors',
                           param_range=num_neigh,
                           cv=5)

# stack and transpose trick (as above)
ax = sns.tsplot(np.array(tt).transpose(),
                time=num_neigh,
                condition=['Train', 'Test'],
                interpolate=False)

ax.set_title('5-fold CV Performance for k-NN')
ax.set_xlabel("\n".join(['k for k-NN',
                         'lower k, more complex',
                         'higher k, less complex']))
ax.set_ylim(.9, 1.01)
ax.set_ylabel('Accuracy');
```

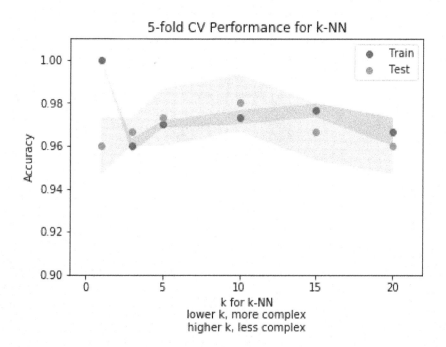

Now, I'll leave you with a small puzzle to think about. Why does 1-NN get 100% training accuracy? Is that a good thing? When *might* it be a good thing? What does it mean that we seem to have the best validation test performance in the middle of the curve, near 10-NN?

I'm about to give you the answers. Look away if you want to think about them for yourself. With 1-NN, the training points are classified exactly as their own target value: they are exactly their own nearest neighbor. It's potentially overfitting in the extreme. Now, if there is little or no noise, it might be OK. 10-NN might be a good value for our final system to deliver to our customer—it seems to make a good tradeoff between underfitting (bias) and overfitting (variance). We should assess it on a hold-out test set.

5.8 Comparing Learners with Cross-Validation

One of the benefits of CV is that we can see the variability with respect to training on different training sets. We can only do that if we keep each evaluation as a stand-alone value because we need to compare individual values against each other. That is, we need to keep each fold separated and graphically distinct. We can do that with a simple plot.

In [36]:

```
classifiers = {'gnb' : naive_bayes.GaussianNB(),
               '5-NN' : neighbors.KNeighborsClassifier(n_neighbors=5)}

iris = datasets.load_iris()

fig, ax = plt.subplots(figsize=(6, 4))
for name, model in classifiers.items():
    cv_scores = skms.cross_val_score(model,
                                     iris.data, iris.target,
                                     cv=10,
                                     scoring='accuracy',
                                     n_jobs=-1) # use all cores
    my_lbl = "{} {:.3f}".format(name, cv_scores.mean())
    ax.plot(cv_scores, '-o', label=my_lbl) # marker=next(markers)
ax.set_ylim(0.0, 1.1)
ax.set_xlabel('Fold')
ax.set_ylabel('Accuracy')
ax.legend(ncol=2);
```

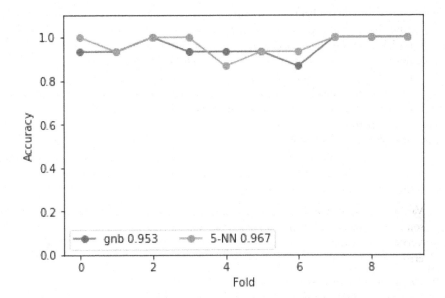

We see that we have a lot of similar outcomes. 5-NN appears to win on three folds, while GNB wins on one. The others are visual ties. We would be unable to do this sort of "who won" comparison on stripplots or from calculated means. The stripplot loses the connection to the fold and the mean compresses all the comparative information in the individual folds.

5.9 EOC

5.9.1 Summary

We have become more sophisticated in the machinery we use to compare different learners: instead of single train-test splits, we make multiple splits. That's good. We also dove into one of the fundamental theoretical issues in learning: the bias-variance tradeoff. Lastly, we've looked at two graphical methods learning curves, complexity curves, and comparing learners across several folds of cross-validation. However, we're still using only a small toolbox of methods and we're not really selecting hyperparameters for those methods in a structured way. More to come!

5.9.2 Notes

External Issues in Evaluation   When we build a bridge, we want to make certain that it is safe. We want to ensure that it can handle the weight and wind—hi Tacoma Narrows!—that it will experience. Yet, before we even start construction, someone needs to ask, "Should we build a bridge?" Are there other, better alternatives? Could we build a road around a bay? Could we build a tunnel under a channel? Could we make do with daily ferries? Would it be better to *do nothing now* and wait until technology advances or, perhaps, more users are in need of the crossing? Each of these options may be different when measured in different ways: construction cost, durability, maintenance cost, maximum weight per vehicle, maximum throughput of vehicles, total expected lifespan, expansion cost, and travel time for the end users. There are many, many ways of comparing alternatives.

In engineering terms, these two types of assessment have specific names. When we ask "Assuming we need to build a bridge, is the bridge safe?" we are talking about *verifying* that the bridge is safe. When we ask "Should we build a bridge or a road or a tunnel?", we are *validating* which solution we should use.

- Validation: are we building the right thing to solve a problem? Should we build something else, or solve the problem a different way?
- Verification: is the thing we built doing its job the right way? Does it have a low error, or make few mistakes, or not fall apart?

In this chapter, we discussed the issue of verification as it is called by engineers. Assuming that we want a learning system, how can we assess its capabilities? I hope that I've reminded you to think outside the box (that you're building): maybe you would be better off seeking an alternative solution. I have one confusing footnote to add. These terms—verification and validation—come out of a specific engineering context. But within the machine learning and related communities, some of the techniques by which we *verify* our systems have names that include *validation*. For example, the machine learning evaluation technique known as *cross-validation* is, in the engineering terms we just introduced, *verifying* the operation of the system. All I can do is say, "I'm sorry."

General Notes   What we've referred to as training is also, under the hood, solving some sort of *optimization problem*. Setting the dials on our machines is really about finding some suitable *best* values for the dials under some constraints.

There's an interaction between the representational power of our learning systems—our bias and variance—and the raw data we have available. For example, two points define a line. If I only have two data points, I can't really justify anything more wiggly than a straight line. But, there are—literally!—an infinite number of ways I could generate two data points. Almost all of those are not a simple straight line.

Another interesting aspect of nearest neighbor bias is considering what happens to 1-NN when there are very many features. You may have heard that in space, no one can hear you scream. When we have many features—as the cool kids say, "When we are in high-dimensional space"—that is true. In high-dimensional space, everyone is very far from everyone else, so no one is close enough to hear you. This phenomenon is one aspect of the *Curse of Dimensionality*. In a learning sense, this means that no one is close enough to really know what value you should take. Our predictions don't have enough subtlety to them: we are too biased.

There are many different ways to resample data for evaluation purposes. We discussed cross-validation and repeated train-test splitting (RTTS). RTTS is also called *Monte Carlo cross-validation*. When you see Monte Carlo (a famous gambling town) in a learning or statistical phrase, feel free to substitute the phrase "repeated random rolls." Here, Monte Carlo refers to the repeated randomness of selecting train-test splits—as opposed to the one-and-done randomness of standard cross-validation. Each of the resampling evaluators is making an estimate of a target quantity. Mind-blowingly enough, this means they themselves have a *bias* and a *variance*. On dear, we've slipped into the meta world again! If you'd like to learn more, you can start with this mathematically dense paper by Kohavi, "A study of cross-validation and bootstrap for accuracy estimation and model selection."

There are other, related resampling methods called the *jackknife* and the *bootstrap*. The jackknife is very similar to leave-one-out style evaluation. We'll discuss bootstrapping in a slightly different context—essentially using repeated sampling *with replacement* to build models—in Section 12.3.1. When we want to account for hyperparameters, we need another level of cross-validation: *nested cross-validation*. We'll discuss it in Section 11.3.

The quote from *Elements of Statistical Learning* (ESL) is from the first edition, page 196. Likewise, if you'd like to see the details that were swept under the carpet in the bias-variance equation, ESL has those details starting on that same page. Funny, that. Be warned, it is not easy reading. A nice answer on *CrossValidated*—an online statistics and machine learning community—has some useful discussion also: https://stats.stackexchange.com/a/164391/1704.

If you're wondering why I took the time to hack through using `tsplot`, you can check out the `sklearn` docs example for making a learning curve: http://scikit-learn.org/stable /auto_examples/model_selection/plot_learning_curve.html. Drawing the graph by hand just didn't interest me for some reason.

5.9.3 Exercises

We've introduced a number of evaluation techniques. We never compared them directly to each other. Can you directly compare leave-one-out with two-, three-, five-, and ten-fold cross-validation on a learning problem? Do you see any patterns as the number of folds increases?

A quick example of the variance in model estimates is the difference in training (calculating) a mean and a median from a random sample of a larger dataset. Make a small dataset with 20 random values in it. Randomly select 10 of those values and compute the mean and median of the 10 values. Repeat randomly selecting 10 values five times and compute the mean and median. How different are the 5 means? How different are the 5 medians? How do those values compare to the mean and median of the original 20 values?

Evaluating Classifiers

```
In [1]:
# setup
from mlwpy import *
%matplotlib inline

iris = datasets.load_iris()

tts = skms.train_test_split(iris.data, iris.target,
                            test_size=.33, random_state=21)

(iris_train_ftrs, iris_test_ftrs,
 iris_train_tgt,  iris_test_tgt) = tts
```

In the previous chapter, we discussed evaluation issues that pertain to both classifiers and regressors. Now, I'm going to turn our attention to evaluation techniques that are appropriate for classifiers. We'll start by examining baseline models as a standard of comparison. We will then progress to different metrics that help identify different types of mistakes that classifiers make. We'll also look at some graphical methods for evaluating and comparing classifiers. Last, we'll apply these evaluations on a new dataset.

6.1 Baseline Classifiers

I've emphasized—and the entire previous chapter reinforces—the notion that we must not lie to ourselves when we evaluate our learning systems. We discussed fair evaluation of single models and comparing two or more alternative models. These steps are great. Unfortunately, they miss an important point—it's an easy one to miss.

Once we've invested time in making a fancy—new and improved, folks!—learning system, we are going to feel some obligation to *use* it. That obligation may be to our boss, or our investors who paid for it, or to ourselves for the time and creativity we invested in it. However, rolling a learner into production use presumes that the shiny, new, improved system is needed. It might not be. Sometimes, simple old-fashioned technology is more effective, and more cost-effective, than a fancy new product.

How do we know whether we need a campfire or an industrial stovetop? We figure that out by comparing against the simplest ideas we can come up with: *baseline methods*. `sklearn` calls these *dummy methods*.

We can imagine four levels of learning systems:

1. Baseline methods—prediction based on simple statistics or random guesses,
2. Simple off-the-shelf learning methods—predictors that are generally less resource-intensive,
3. Complex off-the-shelf learning methods—predictors that are generally more resource-intensive, and
4. Customized, boutique learning methods.

Most of the methods in this book fall into the second category. They are simple, off-the-shelf systems. We'll glance at more complex systems in Chapter 15. If you need boutique solutions, you should hire someone who has taken a deeper dive into the world of machine learning and statistics—like your humble author. The most basic, baseline systems help us decide if we need a complicated system and if that system is better than something primitive. If our fancy systems are no better than the baseline, we may need to revisit some of our fundamental assumptions. We may need to gather more data or change how we are representing our data. We'll talk about adjusting our representation in Chapters 10 and 13.

In `sklearn`, there are four baseline classification methods. We'll actually show code for five, but two are duplicates. Each of the methods makes a prediction when given a test example. Two baseline methods are random; they flip coins to make a prediction for the example. Two methods return a constant value; they always predict the same thing. The random methods are (1) `uniform`: choose evenly among the target classes based on the *number* of classes and (2) `stratified`: choose evenly among the target classes based on *frequency* of those classes. The two constant methods are (1) `constant` (surprise?): return one target class that we've picked out and (2) `most_frequent`: return the single most likely class. `most_frequent` is also available under the name `prior`.

The two random methods will behave differently when a dataset has rare occurrences, like a rare disease. Then, with two classes—plentiful healthy people and rare sick people—the `uniform` method picks evenly, 50%–50%, between sick and healthy. It ends up picking way more sick people than there are in reality. For the `stratified` method, we pick in a manner similar to stratified sampling. It picks healthy or sick as the target based on the percents of healthy and sick people in the data. If there are 5% of sick people, it would pick sick around 5% of the time and healthy 95% of the time.

Here's a simple use of a `most_frequent` baseline method:

In [2]:

```
# normal usage: build-fit-predict-evaluate
baseline = dummy.DummyClassifier(strategy="most_frequent")
baseline.fit(iris_train_ftrs, iris_train_tgt)
base_preds = baseline.predict(iris_test_ftrs)
```

```
base_acc = metrics.accuracy_score(base_preds, iris_test_tgt)
print(base_acc)
```

```
0.3
```

Let's compare the performance of these simple baseline strategies against each other:

```
In [3]:
```

```
strategies = ['constant', 'uniform', 'stratified',
              'prior', 'most_frequent']

# set up args to create different DummyClassifier strategies
baseline_args = [{'strategy':s} for s in strategies]
baseline_args[0]['constant'] = 0 # class 0 is setosa

accuracies = []
for bla in baseline_args:
    baseline = dummy.DummyClassifier(**bla)
    baseline.fit(iris_train_ftrs, iris_train_tgt)
    base_preds = baseline.predict(iris_test_ftrs)
    accuracies.append(metrics.accuracy_score(base_preds, iris_test_tgt))

display(pd.DataFrame({'accuracy':accuracies}, index=strategies))
```

	accuracy
constant	0.3600
uniform	0.3800
stratified	0.3400
prior	0.3000
most_frequent	0.3000

`uniform` and `stratified` will return different results when rerun multiple times on a fixed train-test split because they are *randomized* methods. The other strategies will always return the same values for a fixed train-test split.

6.2 Beyond Accuracy: Metrics for Classification

We've discussed a grand total of two metrics so far: accuracy for classification and root-mean-squared-error (RMSE) for regression. `sklearn` has a plethora of alternatives:

In [4]:

```
# helpful stdlib tool for cleaning up printouts
import textwrap
print(textwrap.fill(str(sorted(metrics.SCORERS.keys())),
                    width=70))
```

```
['accuracy', 'adjusted_mutual_info_score', 'adjusted_rand_score',
'average_precision', 'balanced_accuracy', 'brier_score_loss',
'completeness_score', 'explained_variance', 'f1', 'f1_macro',
'f1_micro', 'f1_samples', 'f1_weighted', 'fowlkes_mallows_score',
'homogeneity_score', 'mutual_info_score', 'neg_log_loss',
'neg_mean_absolute_error', 'neg_mean_squared_error',
'neg_mean_squared_log_error', 'neg_median_absolute_error',
'normalized_mutual_info_score', 'precision', 'precision_macro',
'precision_micro', 'precision_samples', 'precision_weighted', 'r2',
'recall', 'recall_macro', 'recall_micro', 'recall_samples',
'recall_weighted', 'roc_auc', 'v_measure_score']
```

Not all of these are designed for classifiers and we're not going to discuss all of them. But, to a slightly different question, how can we identify the scorer used for a particular classifier—say, *k*-NN? It's not too difficult, although the answer *is* a bit verbose. You can see the whole output with `help(knn.score)`, but I'll trim it down to the good bits:

In [5]:

```
knn = neighbors.KNeighborsClassifier()

# help(knn.score) # verbose, but complete

print(knn.score.__doc__.splitlines()[0])
print('\n---and---\n')
print("\n".join(knn.score.__doc__.splitlines()[-6:]))
```

```
Returns the mean accuracy on the given test data and labels.

---and---

        Returns
        -------
        score : float
            Mean accuracy of self.predict(X) wrt. y.
```

The punch line is that the default evaluation for *k*-NN is mean accuracy. Accuracy has some fundamental limits and we are going to move into discussing `precision`, `recall`, `roc_auc`, and `f1` from the extensive list of metrics we just saw. Why discuss these metrics and what's wrong with accuracy? Is it not accurate? I'm glad you asked. Let's get right to answering your questions.

Here's a quick example of the issue with accuracy. Remember, accuracy is basically a count of how often we are right. Let's imagine a dataset where we have 100 patients and a rare disease. We're happy the disease is rare, because it is very deadly. In our dataset, we have 98 healthy people and 2 sick people. Let's take a simple baseline strategy and predict *everyone is healthy*. Our accuracy is 98%. That's really good, right? Well, not really. In fact, on the people that we need to identify—so they can get proper medical care—we find exactly zero of them. That's a very real problem. If we had a more complex learning system that failed in the same way, we'd be very unhappy with its performance.

6.2.1 Eliminating Confusion from the Confusion Matrix

When we have a dataset and we make a classifier that predicts a target from features, we have our prediction and reality. As any of you with young children know, beliefs and reality don't always line up. Children—and adults too, let's be honest—love to interpret things around them in a self-serving way. The current metric we have for assessing how well our guess or prediction matches with reality is *accuracy*: where are they the same? If I were predicting the outcome of a hockey game and I said "My team will win" and they lost, then we have an error—no accuracy points for me.

We can break down our errors in two ways. Here's an example. I see a pot on the stove and it has metal handles. If it's hot and I grab it, I'm going to get a nasty surprise. That's a painful mistake. But, if the pot is cold and I leave it there—and don't clean it like my significant other asked me—I'm going to get in trouble. Another mistake. "But sweetie, I thought it was hot" is going to sound a lot like an excuse. These two types of errors show up in many different guises: guessing that it's hot when it is cold and guessing that it's cold when it is hot. Both mistakes can get us in trouble.

When we talk about abstract problems in learning, hot and cold become *positive* and *negative* outcomes. These terms aren't necessarily *moral* judgments. Often, what we call positive is either (1) the more risky, (2) the less likely, or (3) the more interesting outcome. For an example in medicine, when a test comes back positive, it means that something interesting is happening. That could be a good or bad outcome. The ambiguity is the source of many medical jokes. "Oh no, the test is negative. I'm going to an early grave." *Cue Mark fainting.* "No Mark, we wanted the test to be negative, you don't have the disease!" *Phew.*

Let's turn back to the example of the hot and cold pot. We get to pick which outcome we consider positive. While I don't want to get in trouble with my significant other, I'm *more* concerned about burning my hands. So, I'm going to say that the hot pot is positive. Just like in the medical case, I don't want a test indicating a bad medical condition.

6.2.2 Ways of Being Wrong

So, here are the ways I can be right and wrong:

	I think: **pot is hot**	*I think*: **pot is cold**
pot *is* hot	I thought hot it is hot I'm right	I thought cold it isn't cold I'm wrong
pot *is* cold	I thought hot it isn't hot I'm wrong	I thought cold it is cold I'm right

Now, we're going to replace those *pot-specific* terms with some general terms. We're going to replace right/wrong with True/False. *True* means you did good, you got it right, you matched the *real* state of the world. False means :sadface:, you made a mistake. We're also going to introduce the terms *Positive* and *Negative*. Remember, we said that hot pot—the pot being hot—was our *Positive*. So, we are going to say that *my positive claim*, "I thought hot," is going to be filled with the word "Positive". Here goes:

	I think: **pot is hot (Positive)**	*I think*: **pot is cold (Negative)**
pot *is* hot	True (predicted) Positive	False (predicted) Negative
pot *is* cold	False (predicted) Positive	True (predicted) Negative

To pick this apart: the top left corner, *True Positive*, means that (1) I was correct (*True*) when (2) I claimed the pot was hot (*Positive*). Likewise, *True Negative* means that I was correct—the *True* part—when I claimed the pot was cold—the *Negative* part. In the top right corner, *False Negative* means I was wrong (*False*) when I claimed the pot was cold (*Negative*).

Now, let's remove all of our training wheels and create a general table, called a *confusion matrix*, that will fit any binary classification problem:

	Predicted Positive (PredP)	**Predicted Negative (PredN)**
Real Positive (RealP)	True Positive (TP)	False Negative (FN)
Real Negative (RealN)	False Positive (FP)	True Negative (TN)

Comparing with the previous table, T, F, P, N stand for *True*, *False*, *Positive*, and *Negative*. There are a few mathematical relationships here. The state of the real world is captured in the rows. For example, when the real world is *Positive*, we are dealing with cases in the top row. In real-world terms, we have: $RealP = TP + FN$ and $RealN = FP + TN$. The columns represent the breakdown with respect to our predictions. For example, the first column captures how we do when we predict a positive example. In terms of our predictions, we have: $PredP = TP + FP$ and $PredN = FN + TN$.

6.2.3 Metrics from the Confusion Matrix

We can ask and answer questions from the confusion matrix. For example, if we are doctors, we care how well we're able to find people who are, in reality, sick. Since we defined sick as our positive case, these are people in the first row. We are asking how well do we do on RealP: how many, within the actual real-world sick people, do we correctly detect: $\frac{TP}{TP+FN} = \frac{TP}{RealP}$. The term for this is *sensitivity*. You can think of it as "how well dialed-in is this test to finding sick folks"— where the emphasis is on the sick people. It is also called *recall* by folks coming from the information retrieval community.

Different communities came up with this idea independently, so they gave it different names. As a way to think about recall, consider getting hits from a web search. Of the really valuable or interesting hits, RealP, how many did we find, or recall, correctly? Again, for sensitivity and recall we care about correctness in the real-world positive, or interesting, cases. Sensitivity has one other common synonym: the *true positive rate* (TPR). Don't scramble for your pencils to write that down, I'll give you a table of terms in a minute. The TPR is the true positive rate with respect to *reality*.

There's a complement to caring about the sick or interesting cases we got right: the sick folks we got *wrong*. This error is called a *false negative*. With our abbreviations, the sick people we got wrong is $\frac{FN}{TP+FN}$. We can add up the sick people we got right and the sick people we got wrong to get *all* of the sick people total. Mathematically, that looks like $\frac{TP}{TP+FN} + \frac{FN}{TP+FN} = \frac{TP+FN}{TP+FN} = 1 = 100\%$. These equations say that I can break up all 100% of the sick people into (1) sick people that I think are sick and (2) sick people that I think are healthy.

We can also ask, "How well do we do on healthy people?" Our focus is now on the second row, RealN. If we are doctors, we want to know what the value of our test is when people are healthy. While the risk is different, there is still risk in misdiagnosing healthy people. We—playing doctors, for a second—don't want to be telling people they are sick when they are healthy. Not only do we give them a scare and a worry, we might end up treating them with surgery or drugs they don't need! This mistake is a case of a *false positive* (FP). We can evaluate it by looking at how correct we are on healthy people: $\frac{TN}{FP+TN} = \frac{TN}{RealN}$. The diagnostic term for this is the *specificity* of the test: does the test only raise a flag in the specific cases we want it to. Specificity is also known as the *true negative rate* (TNR). Indeed, it's the true negative rate with respect to reality.

One last combination of confusion matrix cells takes the *prediction* as the primary part and reality as the secondary part. I think of it as answering "What is the value of our test when it comes back *positive*?" or, more briefly, "What's the value of a hit?" Well, hits are the PredP. Inside PredP, we'll count the number correct: TP. We then have $\frac{TP}{PredP} = \frac{TP}{TP+FP}$, which is called *precision*. Try saying, "How precise are our positive predictions?" ten times quickly.

Figure 6.1 shows the confusion matrix along with our metrics for assessing it.

One last comment on the confusion matrix. When reading about it, you may notice that some authors swap the axes: they'll put reality on the columns and the predictions in the rows. Then, TP and TN will be the same boxes, but FP and FN will be flipped. The unsuspecting reader may end up very, very perplexed. Consider yourself warned when you read other discussions of the confusion matrix.

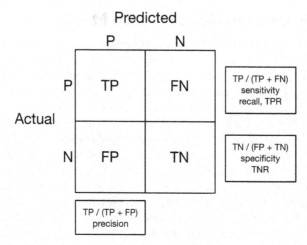

Figure 6.1   The confusion matrix of correct and incorrect predictions.

6.2.4   Coding the Confusion Matrix

Let's see how these evaluations work in `sklearn`. We'll return to our trusty *iris* dataset and do a simple train-test split to remove some complication. As an alternative, you could wrap these calculations up in a cross-validation to get estimates that are less dependent on the specific train-test split. We'll see that shortly.

If you haven't seen method chaining formatted like I'm doing in lines 1–3 below, it may look a bit jarring at first. However, it is my preferred method for long, chained method calls. Using it requires that we add parentheses around the whole expression to make Python happy with the internal line breaks. When I write chained method calls like this, I prefer to indent to the method access dots `.`, because it allows me to visually connect method 1 to method 2 and so on. Below, we can quickly read that we move from `neighbors` to `KNeighborsClassifiers` to `fit` to `predict`. We *could* rewrite this with several temporary variable assignments and achieve the same result. However, method chaining without unnecessary variables is becoming a common style of coding in the Python community. Stylistic comments aside, here goes:

```
In [6]:

tgt_preds = (neighbors.KNeighborsClassifier()
                      .fit(iris_train_ftrs, iris_train_tgt)
                      .predict(iris_test_ftrs))

print("accuracy:", metrics.accuracy_score(iris_test_tgt,
                                           tgt_preds))

cm = metrics.confusion_matrix(iris_test_tgt,
                              tgt_preds)
print("confusion matrix:", cm, sep="\n")
```

```
accuracy: 0.94
confusion matrix:
[[18  0  0]
 [ 0 16  1]
 [ 0  2 13]]
```

Yes, the confusion matrix is really a table. Let's make it a *pretty* table:

In [7]:

```
fig, ax = plt.subplots(1, 1, figsize=(4, 4))
cm = metrics.confusion_matrix(iris_test_tgt, tgt_preds)
ax = sns.heatmap(cm, annot=True, square=True,
                 xticklabels=iris.target_names,
                 yticklabels=iris.target_names)
ax.set_xlabel('Predicted')
ax.set_ylabel('Actual');
```

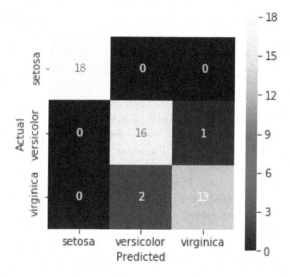

Now we can literally see what's going on. In some respects *setosa* is easy. We get it 100% right. We have some mixed signals on *versicolor* and *virginica*, but we don't do too badly there either. Also, the errors with *versicolor* and *virginica* are confined to misclassifying between those two classes. We don't get any cross-classification back into *setosa*. We can think about *setosa* as being a clean category of its own. The two *v* species have some overlap that is harder to sort out.

6.2.5 Dealing with Multiple Classes: Multiclass Averaging

With all that prettiness, you might be forgiven if you forgot about precision and recall. But if you do remember about them, you might have gone all wide-eyed by now. *We don't have two classes.* This means our dichotomous, two-tone formulas break down, fall flat on their face, and leave us with a problem. How do we *compress* the rich information in a many-values confusion matrix into simpler values?

We made three mistakes in our classification. We predicted one *versicolor* as *virginica* and we predicted two *virginica* as *versicolor*. Let's think in terms of *value of a prediction* for a moment. In our two-class metrics, it was the job of precision to draw out information from the positive prediction column. When we predict *versicolor*, we are correct 16 times and wrong 2. If we consider *versicolor* on one side and everyone else on the other side, we can calculate something very much like precision. This gives us $\frac{16}{18} \approx .89$ for a one-versus-rest—me-against-the-world—precision for *versicolor*. Likewise, we get $\frac{13}{14} \approx .93$ for our one-versus-rest precision for *virginica*.

Those breakdowns don't seem *too* bad, but how do we combine them into a *single* value? We've talked about a few options for summarizing data; let's go with the *mean*. Since we're perfect when we predict *setosa*, that contributes 1.0. So, the mean of $\{\frac{16}{18}, \frac{13}{14}, 1\}$ is about .9392. This method of summarizing the predictions is called `macro` by `sklearn`. We can calculate the *macro precision* by computing a value for each column and then dividing by the number of columns. To compute the value for one column, we take the diagonal entry in the column—where we are correct—and divide by the sum of all values in the column.

In [8]:

```
macro_prec = metrics.precision_score(iris_test_tgt,
                                     tgt_preds,
                                     average='macro')
print("macro:", macro_prec)


cm = metrics.confusion_matrix(iris_test_tgt, tgt_preds)
n_labels = len(iris.target_names)
print("should equal 'macro avg':",
      # correct            column            # columns
      (np.diag(cm) / cm.sum(axis=0)).sum() / n_labels)
```

```
macro: 0.9391534391534391
should equal 'macro avg': 0.9391534391534391
```

Since that method is called the `macro` average, you're probably chomping at the bit to find out about the `micro` average. I actually find the name `micro` a bit counterintuitive. Even the `sklearn` docs say that `micro` "calculates metrics globally"! That doesn't sound *micro* to me. Regardless, the `micro` is a broader look at the results. `micro` takes all the *correct* predictions and divides by *all* the predictions we made. These come from (1) the sum of the values on the diagonal of the confusion matrix and (2) the sum of all values in the confusion matrix:

In [9]:

```
print("micro:", metrics.precision_score(iris_test_tgt,
                                         tgt_preds,
                                         average='micro'))

cm = metrics.confusion_matrix(iris_test_tgt, tgt_preds)
print("should equal avg='micro':",
      # TP.sum()          / (TP&FP).sum() -->
      # all correct       / all preds
      np.diag(cm).sum() / cm.sum())
```

```
micro: 0.94
should equal avg='micro': 0.94
```

`classification_report` wraps several of these pieces together. It computes the one-versus-all statistics and then computes a *weighted* average of the values—like `macro` except with different weights. The weights come from the *support*. In learning context, the support of a classification rule—*if x is a cat and x is striped and x is big, then x is a tiger*—is the count of the examples where that rule applies. So, if 45 out of 100 examples meet the constraints on the left-hand side of the *if*, then the support is 45. In `classification_report`, it is the "support in reality" of our examples. So, it's equivalent to the total counts in each *row* of the confusion matrix.

In [10]:

```
print(metrics.classification_report(iris_test_tgt,
                                    tgt_preds))
# average is a weighted macro average (see text)

# verify sums-across-rows
cm = metrics.confusion_matrix(iris_test_tgt, tgt_preds)
print("row counts equal support:", cm.sum(axis=1))
```

	precision	recall	f1-score	support
0	1.00	1.00	1.00	18
1	0.89	0.94	0.91	17
2	0.93	0.87	0.90	15
micro avg	0.94	0.94	0.94	50
macro avg	0.94	0.94	0.94	50
weighted avg	0.94	0.94	0.94	50

```
row counts equal support: [18 17 15]
```

We see and confirm several of the values that we calculated by hand.

6.2.6 F_1

I didn't discuss the `f1-score` column of the classification report. F_1 computes a different kind of average from the confusion matrix entries. By average, I mean a measure of center. You know about *the* mean (arithmetic average or arithmetic mean) and median (the middle-most of sorted values). There are other types of averages out there. The ancient Greeks actually cared about three averages or means: the arithmetic mean, the geometric mean, and the harmonic mean. If you google these, you'll find geometric diagrams with circles and triangles. That is singularly unhelpful for understanding these from our point of view. In part, the difficulty is because the Greeks had yet to connect geometry and algebra. That connection was left for Descartes to discover (or create, depending on your view of mathematical progress) centuries later.

A more helpful view for us is that the special means—the geometric mean and the harmonic mean—are just wrappers around a converted arithmetic mean. In the case of the geometric mean, it is computed by taking the arithmetic mean of the logarithms of the values and then exponentiating the value. Now you know why it has a special name—that's a mouthful. Since we're concerned with the harmonic mean here, the equivalent computation is (1) take the arithmetic mean of the reciprocals and then (2) take the reciprocal of that. The harmonic mean is very useful when we need to summarize rates like speed or compare different fractions.

F_1 is a harmonic mean with a slight tweak. It has a constant in front—but don't let that fool you. We're just doing a harmonic mean. It plays out as

$$F_1 = 2 \times \frac{1}{\frac{1}{\text{precision}} + \frac{1}{\text{recall}}}$$

If we apply some algebra by taking common denominators and doing an invert-and-multiply, we get the usual textbook formula for F_1:

$$F_1 = 2\frac{\text{precision} \times \text{recall}}{\text{precision} + \text{recall}}$$

The formula represents an *equal* tradeoff between precision and recall. In English, that means we want to be equally right in the value of our predictions and with respect to the real world. We can make other tradeoffs: see the End-of-Chapter Notes on F_β.

6.3   ROC Curves

We haven't talked about it explicitly, but our classification methods can do more than just slap a label on an example. They can give a probability to each prediction—or some score for how certain they are that a cat is, really, a cat. Imagine that after training, a classifier comes up with scores for ten individuals who might have the disease. These scores are .05, .15, ..., .95. Based on training, it is determined that .7 is the best break point between folks that have the disease (higher scores) and folks that are healthy (lower scores). This is illustrated in Figure 6.2.

Figure 6.2 A medium-high threshold produces a low number of claimed hits (diseases).

What happens if I move my bar to the left (Figure 6.3)? Am I claiming more people are sick or healthy?

thresh

0.05 0.15 0.25 0.35 0.45 | 0.55 0.65 0.75 0.85 0.95

0.5

5
scores
below

5
scores
above

Figure 6.3 A lower threshold—an easier bar to clear—leads to more claimed hits (diseases).

Moving the bar left—lowering the numerical break point—increases the number of hits (sick claims) I'm making. As of right now, we haven't said anything about whether these people are *really* sick or healthy. Let's augment that scenario by adding some truth. The entries in the table are the scores of individuals from our classifier.

	PredP	**PredN**
RealP	.05 .15 .25	.55 .65
RealN	.35 .45	.75 .85 .95

Take a moment to think back to the confusion matrix. Imagine that we can move the bar between predicted positives PredP and predicted negatives PredN to the left or right. I'll call that bar the PredictionBar. The PredictionBar separates PredP from PredN: PredP are to the left and PredN are to the right. If we move the PredictionBar far enough to the right, we can push examples that fell on the right of the bar to the left of the bar. The flow of examples changes predicted negatives to predicted positives. If we slam the PredictionBar all the way to the right, we are saying that we predict everything as a PredP. As a side effect, there would be no PredN. This is great! We have absolutely no false negatives.

Here's a reminder of the confusion matrix entries:

	PredP	**PredN**
RealP	TP	FN
RealN	FP	TN

Hopefully, some of you are raising an eyebrow. You might recall the old adages, "There's no such thing as a free lunch," or "You get what you pay for," or "You don't get something for nothing." In fact, if you raised an eyebrow, you were wise to be skeptical. Take a closer look at the bottom row of the confusion matrix. The row has the examples which are real negatives. By moving the prediction bar all the way to the right, we've emptied out the true negative bucket by pushing all of its contents to the false positive bucket. Every real negative is now a false positive! By predicting everything PredP, we do great on real positives and horrible on real negatives.

You can imagine a corresponding scenario by moving the PredictionBar all the way to the left. Now, there are no PredP. Everything is a predicted negative. For the top row—real positives—it is a disaster! At least things are looking better in the bottom row: all of those real negatives are correctly predicted negative—they are true negatives. You might be wondering: what is an equivalent setup with a *horizontal* bar between real positives and real negatives? It's sort of a trick question—there isn't one. For the sorts of data we are discussing, a particular example can't go from being real positive to real negative. Real cats can't become real dogs. Our predictions can change; reality can't. So, it doesn't make sense to talk about moving that line.

You may be sensing a pattern by now. In learning systems, there are often tradeoffs that must be made. Here, the tradeoff is between how many false positives we will tolerate versus how many false negatives we will tolerate. We can control this tradeoff by moving our prediction bar, by setting a threshold. We can be hyper-risk-averse and label everyone sick so we don't miss catching a sick person. Or, we can be penny-pinchers and label everyone healthy, so we don't have to treat anyone. Either way, there are two questions:

1. How do we evaluate and select our threshold? How do we pick a specific tradeoffs between false positives and false negatives?
2. How do we compare two different classification systems, both of which have a whole range of possible tradeoffs?

Fortunately, there is a nice graphical tool that lets us answer these questions: the *ROC curve*. The *ROC curve*—or, with its very, very long-winded name, the *Receiver Operating Characteristic curve*—has a long history in classification. It was originally used to quantify radar tracking of bombers headed towards England during World War II. This task was, perhaps, slightly more important than our classification of irises. Regardless, they needed to determine whether a blip on the radar screen was a real threat (a bomber) or not (a ghosted echo of a plane or a bird): to tell true positives from false positives.

ROC curves are normally drawn in terms of *sensitivity* (also called *true positive rate*, TPR). $1 - specificity$ is called the *false positive rate* (FPR). Remember, these both measure performance *with respect to the breakdown in the real world*. That is, they care how we do based on what is out there in reality. We want to have a *high* TPR: 1.0 is perfect. We want a *low* FPR: 0.0 is great. We've already seen that we can game the system and guarantee a high TPR by making the prediction bar so low that we say *everyone* is positive. But what does that do to our FPR? Exactly! It sends it up to one: fail. The opposite case—cheating towards saying no one is sick—gets us a great FPR of zero. There are no false claims of sickness, but our TPR is no good. It's also zero, while we wanted that value to be near 1.0.

6.3.1 Patterns in the ROC

In Figure 6.4 we have an abstract diagram of an ROC curve. The bottom-left corner of the graph represents a FPR of zero and a TPR of zero. The top-right corner represents TPR and FPR both equal to one. Neither of these cases are ideal. The top-left corner represents an FPR of 0 and a TPR of 1—perfection. In `sklearn`, a low threshold means moving the PredictionBar all the way to the right of the confusion matrix: we make everything positive. This occurs in the top-right corner of the ROC graph. A high threshold means we make many things negative—our PredictionBar is slammed all the way left in the confusion matrix. It's hard to get over a high bar to be a positive. This is what happens in the bottom-left corner of the ROC graph. We have no false positives because we have no positives at all! As the threshold decreases, it gets easier to say something is positive. We move across the graph from bottom-left to top-right.

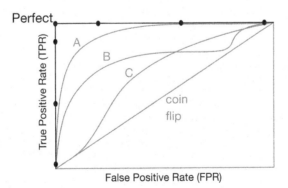

Figure 6.4   An abstract look at an ROC curve.

Four things stand out in the ROC graph.

1. The $y = x$ line from the bottom-left corner to the top-right corner represents coin flipping: randomly guessing the target class. Any decent classifier should do better than this. Better means pushing towards the top-left of the diagram.

2. A perfect classifier lines up with the left side and the top of the box.

3. Classifier A does *strictly* better than B and C. A is more to the top-left than B and C, everywhere.

4. B and C flip-flop. At the higher thresholds B is better; at lower thresholds C is better.

The second point (about a perfect classifier) is a bit confusing. As we move the threshold, don't some predictions go from *right* to *wrong*? Ever? Well, in fact, remember that a threshold of zero is nice because everything is positive. Of the real positives, we get all of them correct even though we get all the real negatives wrong. A threshold of one has some benefit because everything is predicted negative. Of the real negatives, we get them all, even though we get all the real positives wrong. Those errors are due to the extreme thresholds—not our classifier. Any classifier would suffer under the thumb of these authoritarian thresholds. They are just "fixed points" on *every* ROC graph.

Let's walk across the ROC curve for our *perfect* classifier. If our threshold is at one, even if we give something a correct score, it is going to get thrown in as negative, regardless of the score. We are stuck at the bottom-left corner of the ROC curve. If we slide our threshold down a bit, some examples can become positives. However, since we're perfect, none of them are *false* positives. Our TPR is going to creep up, while our FPR stays 0: we are climbing the left side of the ROC box. Eventually, we'll be at the ideal threshold that balances our FPR of zero and achieves a TPR of 1. This balance point is the *correct* threshold for our perfect classifier. If we move beyond this threshold, again, the threshold itself becomes the problem (it's you, not me!). Now, the TPR will stay constant at 1, but the FPR will increase—we're moving along the top of the ROC box now—because our threshold is forcing us to claim more things as positive regardless of their reality.

6.3.2 Binary ROC

OK, with conceptual discussion out of the way, how do we make ROC work? There's a nice single call, `metrics.roc_curve`, to do the heavy lifting after we do a couple of setup steps. But we need to do a couple of setup steps. First, we're going to convert the iris problem into a *binary* classification task to simplify the interpretation of the results. We'll do that by converting the target class from the standard three-species problem to a binary yes/no question. The three species question asks, "Is it *virginica*, *setosa*, or *versicolor*?" The answer is one of the three species. The binary question asks, "Is it *versicolor*?" The answer is yes or no.

Second, we need to invoke the classification scoring mechanism of our classifier so we can tell who is on which side of our prediction bar. Instead of outputting a class like *versicolor*, we need to know some score or probability, such as a .7 likelihood of *versicolor*. We do that by using `predict_proba` instead of our typical `predict`. `predict_proba` comes back with probabilities for *False* and *True* in two columns. We need the probability from the *True* column.

In [11]:

```
# warning: this is 1 "one" not 1 "ell"
is_versicolor = iris.target == 1

tts_1c = skms.train_test_split(iris.data, is_versicolor,
                               test_size=.33, random_state = 21)
(iris_1c_train_ftrs, iris_1c_test_ftrs,
(iris_1c_train_ftrs, iris_1c_test_ftrs,
 iris_1c_train_tgt,  iris_1c_test_tgt) = tts_1c

# build, fit, predict (probability scores) for NB model
gnb = naive_bayes.GaussianNB()
prob_true = (gnb.fit(iris_1c_train_ftrs, iris_1c_train_tgt)
                .predict_proba(iris_1c_test_ftrs)[:, 1]) # [:, 1]=="True"
```

With the setup done, we can do the calculations for the ROC curve and display it. Don't get distracted by the auc. We'll come back to that in a minute.

In [12]:

```
fpr, tpr, thresh = metrics.roc_curve(iris_1c_test_tgt,
                                     prob_true)
auc = metrics.auc(fpr, tpr)
print("FPR : {}".format(fpr),
      "TPR : {}".format(tpr), sep='\n')

# create the main graph
fig, ax = plt.subplots(figsize=(8, 4))
ax.plot(fpr, tpr, 'o--')
ax.set_title("1-Class Iris ROC Curve\nAUC:{:.3f}".format(auc))
ax.set_xlabel("FPR")
ax.set_ylabel("TPR");

# do a bit of work to label some points with their
# respective thresholds
investigate = np.array([1, 3, 5])
for idx in investigate:
    th, f, t = thresh[idx], fpr[idx], tpr[idx]
    ax.annotate('thresh = {:.3f}'.format(th),
                xy=(f+.01, t-.01), xytext=(f+.1, t),
                arrowprops = {'arrowstyle':'->'})
```

```
FPR : [0.    0.     0.     0.0606 0.0606 0.1212 0.1212 0.1818 1.     ]
TPR : [0.    0.0588 0.8824 0.8824 0.9412 0.9412 1.     1.     1.     ]
```

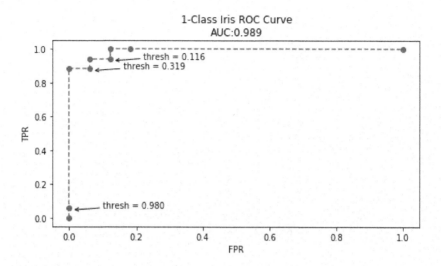

Notice that most of the FPR values are between 0.0 and 0.2, while the TPR values quickly jump into the range of 0.9 to 1.0. Let's dive into the calculation of those values. Remember, each point represents a different confusion matrix based on its own unique threshold. Here are the confusion matrices for the second, fourth, and sixth thresholds which are also labeled in the prior graph. Thanks to zero-based indexing, these occur at indices 1, 3, and 5 which I assigned to the variable investigate in the previous cell. We could have picked any of the eight thresholds that sklearn found. Verbally, we can call these a high, middle, and low bar for being sick—or, in this case, for our positive class of *is_versicolor* (predicted true).

Bar	Medical Claim	Prediction
Low	Easy to call sick	Easy to predict True
Mid		
High	Hard to call sick	Hard to predict False

Let's look at these values.

In [13]:

```
title_fmt = "Threshold {}\n~{:5.3f}\nTPR : {:.3f}\nFPR : {:.3f}"

pn = ['Positive', 'Negative']
add_args = {'xticklabels': pn,
            'yticklabels': pn,
            'square':True}

fig, axes = plt.subplots(1, 3, sharey = True, figsize=(12, 4))
for ax, thresh_idx in zip(axes.flat, investigate):
```

```
preds_at_th = prob_true < thresh[thresh_idx]
cm = metrics.confusion_matrix(1-iris_1c_test_tgt, preds_at_th)
sns.heatmap(cm, annot=True, cbar=False, ax=ax,
            **add_args)


ax.set_xlabel('Predicted')
ax.set_title(title_fmt.format(thresh_idx,
                              thresh[thresh_idx],
                              tpr[thresh_idx],
                              fpr[thresh_idx]))

axes[0].set_ylabel('Actual');
# note: e.g. for threshold 3
# FPR = 1-spec = 1 - 31/(31+2) = 1 - 31/33 = 0.0606...
```

Getting these values lined up takes a bit of trickery. When `prob_true` is below threshold, we are predicting a *not-versicolor*. So, we have to negate our target class using `1-iris_1c_test_tgt` to get the proper alignment. We also hand-label the axes so we don't have `0` as the positive class. It simply looks too weird for me. Notice that as we lower our threshold—move PredictionBar to the right—there is a flow of predictions from the right of the confusion matrix to the left. We predict more things as positive as we lower the threshold. You can think of examples as spilling over the prediction bar. That happens in the order given to the examples by the `probas`.

6.3.3 AUC: Area-Under-the-(ROC)-Curve

Once again, I've left a stone unturned. You'll notice that we calculated `metrics.auc` and printed out its values in the graph titles above. What am I hiding now? We humans have an insatiable appetite to simplify—that is partially why means and measures of center are so (ab)used. Here, we want to simplify by asking, "How can we summarize an ROC curve as a single value?" We answer by calculating the *area under the curve* (AUC) that we've just drawn.

Recall that the perfect ROC curve is mostly just a point in the top-left. If we include the extreme thresholds, we also get the bottom-left and top-right points. These points trace the left and upper perimeter of the box. The area under the lines connecting these points is 1.0—because they surround a square with side lengths equal to 1. As we cover less of the whole TPR/FPR square, our area decreases. We can think of the uncovered parts of the square as defects. If our classifier gets as bad as random coin flipping, the line from bottom-left to top-right will cover half of the square. So, our reasonable range of values for AUC goes from 0.5 to 1.0. I said reasonable because we *could* see a classifier that is reliably worse than coin flipping. Think about what a constant prediction of a low-occurrence target class—always predicting sick in the case of a rare disease—would do.

The AUC is an *overall* measure of classifier performance at a series of thresholds. It summarizes a lot of information and subtlety into one number. As such, it should be approached with caution. We saw in the abstract ROC diagram that the behavior and rank order of classifiers may change at different thresholds. The scenario is like a race between two runners: the lead can go back and forth. Hare is fast out of the gate but tires. Slow-and-steady Tortoise comes along, passes Hare, and wins the race. On the other hand, the benefit of single-value summaries is that we can very easily compute other statistics on them and summarize them graphically. For example, here are several cross-validated AUCs displayed simultaneously on a strip plot.

In [14]:

```
fig,ax = plt.subplots(1, 1, figsize=(3, 3))
model = neighbors.KNeighborsClassifier(3)
cv_auc = skms.cross_val_score(model, iris.data, iris.target==1,
                              scoring='roc_auc', cv=10)
ax = sns.swarmplot(cv_auc, orient='v')
ax.set_title('10-Fold AUCs');
```

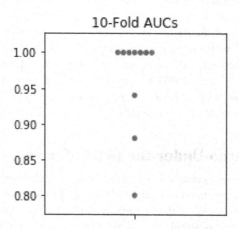

Many of the folds have perfect results.

6.3.4 Multiclass Learners, One-versus-Rest, and ROC

`metrics.roc_curve` is ill-equipped to deal with multiclass problems: it yells at us if we try. We can work around it by recoding our tri-class problem into a series of me-versus-the-world or one-versus-rest (OvR) alternatives. OvR means we want to compare each of the following binary problems: 0 versus $[1, 2]$, 1 versus $[0, 2]$, and 2 versus $[0, 1]$. Verbally, it is one target class versus all of the others. It is similar to what we did above in Section 6.3.2 by pitting *versicolor* against all other species: 1 versus $[0, 2]$. The difference here is that we'll do it for all three possibilities. Our basic tool to encode these comparisons into our data is `label_binarize`. Let's look at examples 0, 50, and 100 from the original multiclass data.

In [15]:

```
checkout = [0, 50, 100]
print("Original Encoding")
print(iris.target[checkout])
```

```
Original Encoding
[0 1 2]
```

So, examples 0, 50, and 100 correspond to classes 0, 1, and 2. When we binarize, the classes become:

In [16]:

```
print("'Multi-label' Encoding")
print(skpre.label_binarize(iris.target, [0, 1, 2])[checkout])
```

```
'Multi-label' Encoding
[[1 0 0]
 [0 1 0]
 [0 0 1]]
```

You can interpret the new encoding as columns of Boolean flags—yes/no or true/false—for "Is it class x?" The first column answers, "Is it class 0?" For the first row (example 0), the answers are yes, no, and no. It is a really complicated way to break down the statement "I am class 0" into three questions. "Am I class 0?" *Yes.* "Am I class 1?" *No.* "Am I class 2?" *No.* Now, we add a layer of complexity to our classifier. Instead of a *single* classifier, we are going to make one classifier for each target class—that is, one for each of the three new target columns. These become (1) a classifier for class 0 versus rest, (2) a classifier for class 1 versus rest, and (3) a classifier for class 2 versus rest. Then, we can look at the individual performance of those three classifiers.

```
In [17]:

iris_multi_tgt = skpre.label_binarize(iris.target, [0, 1, 2])

# im --> "iris multi"

(im_train_ftrs, im_test_ftrs,
 im_train_tgt,  im_test_tgt) = skms.train_test_split(iris.data,
                                                     iris_multi_tgt,
                                                     test_size=.33,
                                                     random_state=21)

# knn wrapped up in one-versus-rest (3 classifiers)
knn        = neighbors.KNeighborsClassifier(n_neighbors=5)
ovr_knn    = skmulti.OneVsRestClassifier(knn)
pred_probs = (ovr_knn.fit(im_train_ftrs, im_train_tgt)
                     .predict_proba(im_test_ftrs))

# make ROC plots
lbl_fmt = "Class {} vs Rest (AUC = {:.2f})"
fig,ax = plt.subplots(figsize=(8, 4))
for cls in [0, 1, 2]:
    fpr, tpr, _ = metrics.roc_curve(im_test_tgt[:,cls],
                                    pred_probs[:,cls])
    label = lbl_fmt.format(cls, metrics.auc(fpr,tpr))
    ax.plot(fpr, tpr, 'o--', label=label)
ax.legend()
ax.set_xlabel("FPR")
ax.set_ylabel("TPR");
```

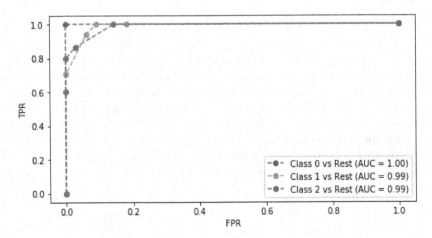

All three of these classifiers are pretty respectable: they have few defects compared to a perfect classifier that follows the graph borders. We saw earlier that *Class 0* (*setosa*) was fairly easy to separate, so we aren't too surprised at it doing well here. Each of the other classifiers get very good TPR rates at pretty minimal FPR rates (below .18 or so). Incidentally, this analysis is the exact strategy we can use to pick a threshold. We can identify an acceptable TPR and then choose the threshold that gets us the best FPR for that TPR. We can also work the other way around if we care more about FPR than TPR. For example, we may only want to identify people that are suitably likely to be sick to prevent unnecessary, invasive, and costly medical procedures.

6.4 Another Take on Multiclass: One-versus-One

There's another approach to dealing with the sometimes negative interaction between multiclass problems and learning systems. In one-versus-rest, we chunk off apples against all other fruit in one grand binary problem. For apples, we create *one* one-versus-rest classifier.

An alternative is to chuck off apple-versus-banana, apple-versus-orange, apple-versus-pineapple, and so forth. Instead of one grand Boolean comparison for apples, we make $n - 1$ of them where n is the number of classes we have. We call this alternative *one-versus-one*. How do we wrap those one-versus-one winners into a grand winner for making a single prediction? A simple answer is to take the sums of the individual wins as we would in a round-robin competition. sklearn does some normalization on this, so it is a little hard to see—but the punch line is that the class with the biggest number of wins is the class we predict.

The one-versus-one wrapper gives us *classification scores* for each individual class. These values are *not* probabilities. We can take the index of the maximum classification score to find the single best-predicted class.

In [18]:

```
knn         = neighbors.KNeighborsClassifier(n_neighbors=5)
ovo_knn     = skmulti.OneVsOneClassifier(knn)
pred_scores = (ovo_knn.fit(iris_train_ftrs, iris_train_tgt)
                      .decision_function(iris_test_ftrs))
df = pd.DataFrame(pred_scores)
df['class'] = df.values.argmax(axis=1)
display(df.head())
```

	0	1	2	class
0	-0.5000	2.2500	1.2500	1
1	2.0000	1.0000	0.0000	0
2	2.0000	1.0000	0.0000	0
3	2.0000	1.0000	0.0000	0
4	-0.5000	2.2500	1.2500	1

To see how the predictions line up with the votes, we can put the *actual* classes beside the one-versus-one classification scores:

In [19]:

```
# note: ugly to make column headers
mi = pd.MultiIndex([['Class Indicator', 'Vote'], [0, 1, 2]],
                [[0]*3+[1]*3,list(range(3)) * 2])
df = pd.DataFrame(np.c_[im_test_tgt, pred_scores],
              columns=mi)
display(df.head())
```

	Class Indicator			**Vote**		
	0	1	2	0	1	2
0	0.0000	1.0000	0.0000	-0.5000	2.2500	1.2500
1	1.0000	0.0000	0.0000	2.0000	1.0000	0.0000
2	1.0000	0.0000	0.0000	2.0000	1.0000	0.0000
3	1.0000	0.0000	0.0000	2.0000	1.0000	0.0000
4	0.0000	1.0000	0.0000	-0.5000	2.2500	1.2500

You might be wondering why there were three classifiers for both one-versus-rest and one-versus-one. If we have n classes, for one-versus-rest we will have n classifiers—one for each class against everyone else; that's why there are 3 there. For one-versus-one, we have a classifier for each pair of classes. The formula for the number of pairs of n things is $\frac{n(n-1)}{2}$. For three classes, this is $\frac{3 \times 2}{2} = 3$. You can think of the formula this way: pick a person (n), pick all their possible dance partners ($n - 1$, no dancing with yourself), and then remove duplicates (divide by two) because Chris dancing with Sam is the same as Sam with Chris.

6.4.1   Multiclass AUC Part Two: The Quest for a Single Value

We can make use of the one-versus-one idea in a slightly different way. Instead of different *classifiers* competing in one-versus-one, *Karate Kid* style tournament, we'll have a *single classifier* apply itself to the whole dataset. Then, we'll pick out pairs of targets and see how the single classifier *does on each possible pairing*. So, we compute a series of mini-confusion matrices for pairs of classes with a class i serving as *Positive* and another class j serving as *Negative*. Then, we can calculate an AUC from that. We'll do that both ways—each of the pair serving as positive and negative—and take the average of all of those AUCs. Basically, AUC is used to quantify the chances of a true cat being less likely to be called a dog than a random dog. Full details of the logic behind this technique—I'll call it the Hand and Till M—are available in a reference at the end of the chapter.

The code itself is a bit tricky, but here's some pseudocode to give you an overall idea of what is happening:

1. Train a model.
2. Get classification scores for each example.
3. Create a blank table for each pairing of classes.
4. For each pair of classes c_1 and c_2:
    (1) Find AUC of c_1 against c_2.
    (2) Find AUC of c_2 against c_1.
    (3) Entry for c_1, c_2 is the average of these AUCs.
5. Overall value is the average of the entries in the table.

The trickiest bit of code is selecting out just those examples where the two classes of interest interact. For one iteration of the control loop, we need to generate an ROC curve for those two classes. So, we need the examples where either of them occurs. We track these down by doing a `label_binarize` to get indicator values, 1s and 0s, and then we pull out the particular columns we need from there.

In [20]:

```
def hand_and_till_M_statistic(test_tgt, test_probs, weighted=False):
    def auc_helper(truth, probs):
        fpr, tpr, _ = metrics.roc_curve(truth, probs)
        return metrics.auc(fpr, tpr)

    classes   = np.unique(test_tgt)
    n_classes = len(classes)

    indicator = skpre.label_binarize(test_tgt, classes)
    avg_auc_sum = 0.0

    # comparing class i and class j
    for ij in it.combinations(classes, 2):
        # use use sum to act like a logical OR
        ij_indicator = indicator[:,ij].sum(axis=1,
                                           dtype=np.bool)

        # slightly ugly, can't broadcast these as indexes
        # use .ix_ to save the day
```

```
    ij_probs    = test_probs[np.ix_(ij_indicator, ij)]
    ij_test_tgt = test_tgt[ij_indicator]

    i,j = ij
    auc_ij = auc_helper(ij_test_tgt==i, ij_probs[:, 0])
    auc_ji = auc_helper(ij_test_tgt==j, ij_probs[:, 1])

    # compared to Hand and Till reference
    # no / 2 ... factor is out since it will cancel
    avg_auc_ij = (auc_ij + auc_ji)

    if weighted:
        avg_auc_ij *= ij_indicator.sum() / len(test_tgt)
    avg_auc_sum += avg_auc_ij

# compared to Hand and Till reference
# no * 2 ... factored out above and they cancel
M = avg_auc_sum / (n_classes * (n_classes-1))
return M
```

To *use* the Hand and Till method we've defined, we need to pull out the
scoring/ordering/probaing trick. We send the *actual* targets and our scoring of the classes
into `hand_and_till_M_statistic` and we get back a value.

In [21]:

```
knn = neighbors.KNeighborsClassifier()
knn.fit(iris_train_ftrs, iris_train_tgt)
test_probs = knn.predict_proba(iris_test_ftrs)
hand_and_till_M_statistic(iris_test_tgt, test_probs)
```

Out[21]:

```
0.9915032679738562
```

There's a great benefit to writing `hand_and_till_M_statistic` the way we did. We can
use a helper routine from `sklearn` to turn our Hand and Till code into a *scoring function*
that plays nicely with `sklearn` cross-validation routines. Then, doing things like a 10-fold
CV with our new evaluation metric is just a stroll in the park:

In [22]:

```
fig,ax = plt.subplots(1, 1, figsize=(3, 3))
htm_scorer = metrics.make_scorer(hand_and_till_M_statistic,
                                 needs_proba=True)
cv_auc = skms.cross_val_score(model,
                              iris.data, iris.target,
                              scoring=htm_scorer, cv=10)
```

```
sns.swarmplot(cv_auc, orient='v')
ax.set_title('10-Fold H&T Ms');
```

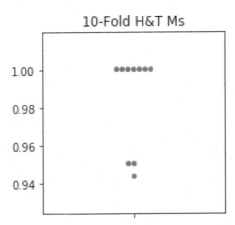

We'll also use `make_scorer` when we want to pass a `scoring` argument that isn't using `sklearn`'s predefined default values. We'll see examples of that shortly.

Since Hand and Till M method uses one, and only one, classifier for evaluation, we have a direct connection between the performance of the classifier and the classifier itself. When we use a one-versus-rest wrapper around a classifier, we lose the direct connection; instead we see how classifiers *like* the one we are interested in behave in a similar scenarios on a shared dataset. In short, the M method here has a stronger relationship to a multiclass prediction use case. On the other hand, some learning methods cannot be used directly on multiclass problems. These methods *need* one-versus-rest or one-versus-one classifiers to do multiclass prediction. In that case, the one-versus setups give us finer details of the pairwise performance of the classifier.

6.5   Precision-Recall Curves

Just as we can look at the tradeoffs between sensitivity and specificity with ROC curves, we can evaluate the tradeoffs between precision and recall. Remember from Section 6.2.3 that precision is the value of a positive prediction and recall is how effective we are on examples that are positive in reality. You can chant the following phrases: "precision positive prediction" and "recall positive reality."

6.5.1   A Note on Precision-Recall Tradeoff

There is a *very* important difference between the sensitivity-specificity curve and the precision–recall curve. With sensitivity-specificity, the two values represent portions of the row totals. The tradeoff is between performance on real-world positives and negatives. With precision-recall, we are dealing a *column* piece *and* a *row* piece out of the confusion matrix. So, they can vary more independently of each other. More importantly, an increasing precision does not imply an increasing recall. Note, sensitivity and $1 -$ specificity are traded off: as we draw our ROC curve from the bottom left, we can move up or to the right. We never move down or left. A precision-recall curve can regress: it might take a step down instead of up.

Here's a concrete example. From this initial state with a precision of $5/10$ and a recall of $5/10$:

	PredP	PredN
RealP	5	5
RealN	5	5

consider what happens when we raise the threshold for calling an example a positive. Suppose that two from each of the predicted positive examples—two of the actually positive and two of the predicted positive, actually negative—move to predicted negative:

	PredP	PredN
RealP	3	7
RealN	3	7

Our precision is now $3/6 = .5$—the same—but our recall has gone to $3/10$ which is less than $.5$. It got *worse*.

For comparison, here we raise the threshold so that only one case moves from TP to FN.

	PredP	PredN
RealP	4	6
RealN	5	5

Our precision becomes $4/9$, which is about $.44$. The recall is $4/10 = .4$. So, both are less than the original example.

Probably the easiest way to visualize this behavior is by thinking what happens when you move the prediction bar. Very importantly, moving the prediction bar *does not affect the state of reality at all*. No examples move up or down between rows. However, moving the prediction bar may—by definition!—move the predictions: things may move between columns.

6.5.2 Constructing a Precision-Recall Curve

Those details aside, the technique for calculating and displaying a PR curve (PRC) is very similar to the ROC curve. One substantial difference is that both precision and recall should be high—near 1.0. So, a point at the top right of the PRC is perfect for us. Visually, if one classifier is better than another, it will be pushed more towards the top-right corner.

```
In [23]:

fig,ax = plt.subplots(figsize=(6, 3))
for cls in [0, 1, 2]:
    prc = metrics.precision_recall_curve
    precision, recall, _ = prc(im_test_tgt[:,cls],
                               pred_probs[:,cls])
    prc_auc = metrics.auc(recall, precision)
    label = "Class {} vs Rest (AUC) = {:.2f})".format(cls, prc_auc)
    ax.plot(recall, precision, 'o--', label=label)
ax.legend()
ax.set_xlabel('Recall')
ax.set_ylabel('Precision');
```

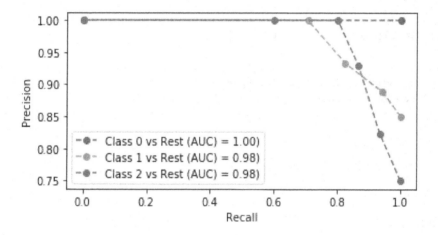

The PRC for class 0, *setosa*, versus the rest is perfect.

6.6 Cumulative Response and Lift Curves

So far, we've examined performance metrics in a fairly isolated setting. What happens when the real world encroaches on our ivory tower? One of the biggest real-world factors is *limited resources*, particularly of the noncomputational variety. When we deploy a system into the real world, we often can't do *everything* the system might recommend to us. For example, if we decide to treat all folks predicted to be sick with a probability greater than 20%, we might overwhelm certain health care facilities. There might be too many patients to treat or too many opportunities to pursue. How can we choose? Cumulative response and lift curves give us a nice visual way to make these decisions. I'm going to hold off on verbally describing these because words don't do them justice. The code that we'll see in a second is a far more precise, compact definition.

The code to make these graphs is surprisingly short. We basically compute our classification scores and order our predictions by those scores. That is, we want the most likely cat to be the first thing we call a cat. We'll discuss that more in a moment. To make this work, we (1) find our preferred order of the test examples, starting from the one with the highest `proba` and moving down the line, then (2) use that order to rank our known, real outcomes, and (3) keep a running total of how well we are doing with respect to those real values. We are comparing a running total of our predictions, ordered by score, against the real world. We graph our running percent of success against the total amount of data we used up to that point. One other trick is that we treat the known targets as zero-one values and add them up. That gets us a running *count* as we incorporate more and more examples. We convert the count to a percent by dividing by the final, total sum. Voilà, we have a running percent. Here goes:

In [24]:

```
# negate b/c we want big values first
myorder = np.argsort(-prob_true)

# cumulative sum then to percent (last value is total)
realpct_myorder = iris_1c_test_tgt[myorder].cumsum()
realpct_myorder = realpct_myorder / realpct_myorder[-1]

# convert counts of data into percents
N = iris_1c_test_tgt.size
xs = np.linspace(1/N, 1, N)

print(myorder[:3])
```

```
[ 0 28 43]
```

This says that the first three examples I would pick to classify as hits are 0, 28, and 43.

In [25]:

```
fig, (ax1, ax2) = plt.subplots(1, 2, figsize=(8, 4))
fig.tight_layout()

# cumulative response
ax1.plot(xs, realpct_myorder, 'r.')
ax1.plot(xs, xs, 'b-')
ax1.axes.set_aspect('equal')

ax1.set_title("Cumulative Response")
ax1.set_ylabel("Percent of Actual Hits")
ax1.set_xlabel("Percent Of Population\n" +
               "Starting with Highest Predicted Hits")
```

```
# lift
# replace divide by zero with 1.0
ax2.plot(xs, realpct_myorder / np.where(xs > 0, xs, 1))


ax2.set_title("Lift Versus Random")
ax2.set_ylabel("X-Fold Improvement") # not cross-fold!
ax2.set_xlabel("Percent Of Population\n" +
               "Starting with Highest Predicted Hits")
ax2.yaxis.tick_right()
ax2.yaxis.set_label_position('right');
```

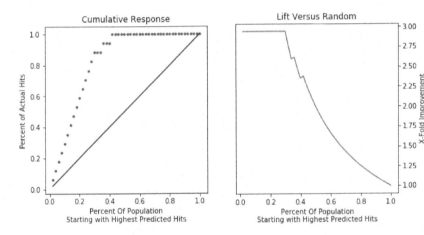

First, let's discuss the Cumulative Response curve. The y-axis is effectively our true positive rate: how well we are doing with respect to reality. The x-axis is a bit more complicated to read. At a given point on the x-axis, we are targeting the "predicted best" x% of the population and asking how well we did. For example, we can see that when we are allowed to use the first 40% of the population (our top 40% predictions), we get 100% of the hits. That can represent a tremendous real-world savings.

Imagine that we are running a fundraising campaign and sending letters to potential donors. Some recipients will read our letter and throw it in the trash. Others will read our letter and respond with a sizable and appreciated check or PayPal donation. If our mailing had a predictive model as good as our model here, we could save quite a bit on postage stamps. Instead of spending $10,000.00 on postage for everyone, we could spend $4,000.00 and target just that predicted-best 40%. If the model is really that good, we'd still hit *all* of our target donors who would contribute.

The Lift Versus Random curve—sometimes called a lift curve or a gain curve—simply divides the performance of our smart classifier against the performance of a baseline random classifier. You can think of it as taking a vertical slice up and down from the Cumulative Response graph, grabbing the red-dot value, and dividing it by the blue-line value. It is reassuring to see that when we start out, we are doing far better than random. As we bring in more of the population—we commit to spending more on postage—it gets harder to win by much over random. After we've targeted all of the actual hits, we can only lose ground. In reality, we should probably stop sending out more requests.

6.7 More Sophisticated Evaluation of Classifiers: Take Two

We've come a long way now. Let's apply what we've learned by taking the binary *iris* problem and seeing how our current basket of classifiers performs on it with our more sophisticated evaluation techniques. Then, we'll turn to a different dataset.

6.7.1 Binary

In [26]:

```
classifiers = {'base'  : baseline,
               'gnb'   : naive_bayes.GaussianNB(),
               '3-NN'  : neighbors.KNeighborsClassifier(n_neighbors=10),
               '10-NN' : neighbors.KNeighborsClassifier(n_neighbors=3)}
```

In [27]:

```
# define the one_class iris problem so we don't have random ==1 around
iris_onec_ftrs = iris.data
iris_onec_tgt  = iris.target==1
```

In [28]:

```
msrs = ['accuracy', 'average_precision', 'roc_auc']

fig, axes = plt.subplots(len(msrs), 1, figsize=(6, 2*len(msrs)))
fig.tight_layout()

for mod_name, model in classifiers.items():
    # abbreviate
    cvs = skms.cross_val_score
    cv_results = {msr:cvs(model, iris_onec_ftrs, iris_onec_tgt,
                          scoring=msr, cv=10) for msr in msrs}

    for ax, msr in zip(axes, msrs):
        msr_results = cv_results[msr]
        my_lbl = "{:12s} {:.3f} {:.2f}".format(mod_name,
                                               msr_results.mean(),
                                               msr_results.std())
```

```
ax.plot(msr_results, 'o--', label=my_lbl)
ax.set_title(msr)
ax.legend(loc='lower center', ncol=2)
```

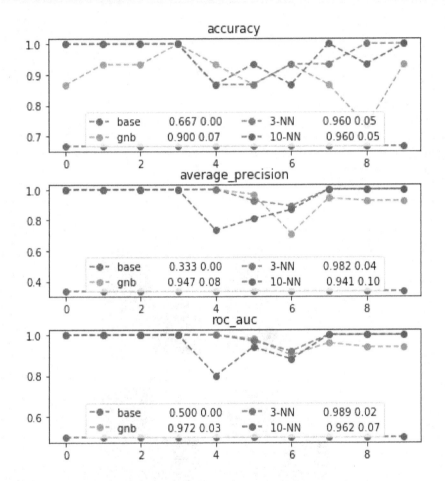

Here, we've jumped right to summaries. It's heartening that our coin-flipping baseline method gets 50% on the AUC measure. Not much else is super interesting here, but we do see that there's one CV-fold where Naive Bayes does really poorly.

To see more details on where the precision comes from or what the ROC curves look like, we need to peel back a few layers.

In [29]:

```
fig, axes = plt.subplots(2, 2, figsize=(4, 4), sharex=True, sharey=True)
fig.tight_layout()
```

```
for ax, (mod_name, model) in zip(axes.flat, classifiers.items()):
    preds = skms.cross_val_predict(model,
                                   iris_onec_ftrs, iris_onec_tgt,
                                   cv=10)

    cm = metrics.confusion_matrix(iris.target==1, preds)
    sns.heatmap(cm, annot=True, ax=ax,
                cbar=False, square=True, fmt="d")

    ax.set_title(mod_name)

axes[1, 0].set_xlabel('Predicted')
axes[1, 1].set_xlabel('Predicted')
axes[0, 0].set_ylabel('Actual')
axes[1, 0].set_ylabel('Actual');
```

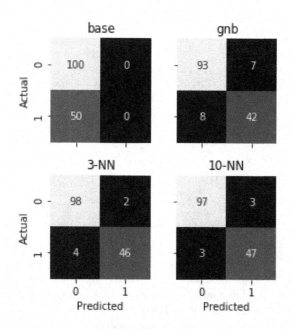

To dive into the ROC curves, we can make use of an argument to `cross_val_predict` that lets us extract the classification scores directly from the aggregate cross-validation classifiers. We do that with `method='predict_proba'` below. Instead of returning a single class, we get back the class scores.

In [30]:

```
fig, ax = plt.subplots(1, 1, figsize=(6, 4))

cv_prob_true = {}
for mod_name, model in classifiers.items():
    cv_probs = skms.cross_val_predict(model,
                                      iris_onec_ftrs, iris_onec_tgt,
                                      cv=10, method='predict_proba')
    cv_prob_true[mod_name] = cv_probs[:, 1]

    fpr, tpr, thresh = metrics.roc_curve(iris_onec_tgt,
                                         cv_prob_true[mod_name])

    auc = metrics.auc(fpr, tpr)
    ax.plot(fpr, tpr, 'o--', label="{}:{}".format(mod_name, auc))

ax.set_title('ROC Curves')
ax.legend();
```

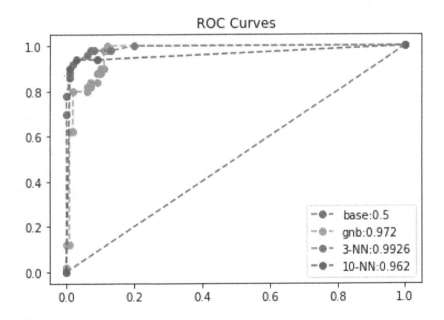

Based on the ROC graph, we are probably most interested in our 3-NN model right now because of its slightly better AUC. We'll make use of the cv_prob_trues from last example to create our lift curve:

In [31]:

```
fig, (ax1,ax2) = plt.subplots(1, 2, figsize=(10, 5))

N = len(iris_onec_tgt)
xs = np.linspace(1/N, 1, N)

ax1.plot(xs, xs, 'b-')

for mod_name in classifiers:
    # negate so big values come first
    myorder = np.argsort(-cv_prob_true[mod_name])

    # cumulative sum then to percent (last value is total)
    realpct_myorder = iris_onec_tgt[myorder].cumsum()
    realpct_myorder = realpct_myorder / realpct_myorder[-1]

    ax1.plot(xs, realpct_myorder, '.', label=mod_name)

    ax2.plot(xs,
             realpct_myorder / np.where(xs > 0, xs, 1),
             label=mod_name)
ax1.legend()
ax2.legend()

ax1.set_title("Cumulative Response")
ax2.set_title("Lift versus Random");
```

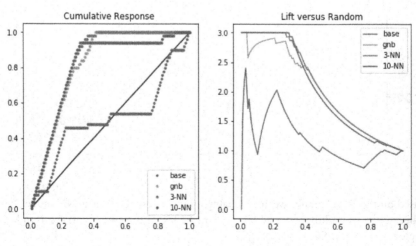

Here, we see gains similar to what we saw in the earlier lift chart. After targeting about 40% of the population, we can probably stop trying to find more *veritosa*. We have some different leaders at different times: GNB falls off and then surpasses 10-NN. GNB and 3-NN both peak out when targeting 40% of the population. 10-NN seems to hit a lull and doesn't hit 100% success (y-axis) success until a near-100% targeting rate on the x axis.

6.7.2 A Novel Multiclass Problem

Let's turn our attention to a new problem and, while we're at it, deal with—instead of ignoring—the issues with multiclass problems. Our dataset was gathered by Cortez and Silva (see the End-of-Chapter Notes for the full reference) and I downloaded it from the UCI data repository here: https://archive.ics.uci.edu/ml/datasets/student+performance.

The data measures the student achievement in two secondary education subjects: math and language. The two subjects are described in different CSV files; we are only going to look at the math data. The data attributes include student grades, demographic, social, and school-related features collected by using school reports and questionnaires. For our example here, I preprocessed the data to (1) remove non-numerical features and (2) produce a discrete target class for classification. The code to reproduce my preprocessing is shown at the end of the chapter.

In [32]:

```
student_df = pd.read_csv('data/portugese_student_numeric_discrete.csv')
student_df['grade'] = pd.Categorical(student_df['grade'],
                                categories=['low', 'mid', 'high'],
                                ordered=True)
```

In [33]:

```
student_ftrs = student_df[student_df.columns[:-1]]
student_tgt  = student_df['grade'].cat.codes
```

We'll start things off gently with a simple 3-NN classifier evaluated with accuracy. We've discussed its limitations—but it is still a simple method and metric to get us started. If the target classes aren't too unbalanced, we might be OK with accuracy.

In [34]:

```python
fig,ax = plt.subplots(1, 1, figsize=(3, 3))
model = neighbors.KNeighborsClassifier(3)
cv_auc = skms.cross_val_score(model,
                              student_ftrs, student_tgt,
                              scoring='accuracy', cv=10)
ax = sns.swarmplot(cv_auc, orient='v')
ax.set_title('10-Fold Accuracy');
```

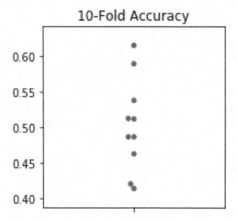

Now, if we want to move on to precision, we have to go beyond the simple `scoring="average_precision"` argument to `cross_val_score` interface that `sklearn` provides. That average is really an average for a *binary* classification problem. If we have multiple target classes, we need to specify *how* we want to average the results. We discussed *macro* and *micro* strategies earlier in the chapter. We'll use `macro` here and pass it as an argument to a `make_scorer` call.

In [35]:

```python
model = neighbors.KNeighborsClassifier(3)
my_scorer = metrics.make_scorer(metrics.precision_score,
                                average='macro')
cv_auc = skms.cross_val_score(model,
                              student_ftrs, student_tgt,
                              scoring=my_scorer, cv=10)
fig,ax = plt.subplots(1, 1, figsize=(3, 3))
sns.swarmplot(cv_auc, orient='v')
ax.set_title('10-Fold Macro Precision');
```

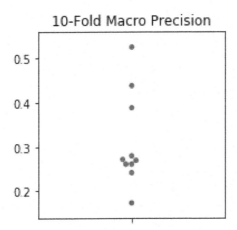

Following a very similar strategy, we can use our Hand and Till *M* evaluator.

In [36]:

```
htm_scorer = metrics.make_scorer(hand_and_till_M_statistic,
                                 needs_proba=True)
cv_auc = skms.cross_val_score(model,
                              student_ftrs, student_tgt,
                              scoring=htm_scorer, cv=10)

fig,ax = plt.subplots(1, 1, figsize=(3, 3))
sns.swarmplot(cv_auc, orient='v')
ax.set_title('10-Fold H&T Ms');
```

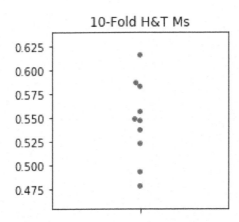

Now, we can compare a few different classifiers with a few different metrics.

In [37]:

```
classifiers = {'base'  : dummy.DummyClassifier(strategy="most_frequent"),
               'gnb'   : naive_bayes.GaussianNB(),
               '3-NN'  : neighbors.KNeighborsClassifier(n_neighbors=10),
               '10-NN' : neighbors.KNeighborsClassifier(n_neighbors=3)}
```

In [38]:

```
macro_precision = metrics.make_scorer(metrics.precision_score,
                                      average='macro')
macro_recall    = metrics.make_scorer(metrics.recall_score,
                                      average='macro')
htm_scorer = metrics.make_scorer(hand_and_till_M_statistic,
                                 needs_proba=True)

msrs = ['accuracy', macro_precision,
        macro_recall, htm_scorer]

fig, axes = plt.subplots(len(msrs), 1, figsize=(6, 2*len(msrs)))
fig.tight_layout()

for mod_name, model in classifiers.items():
    # abbreviate
    cvs = skms.cross_val_score
    cv_results = {msr:cvs(model, student_ftrs, student_tgt,
                          scoring=msr, cv=10) for msr in msrs}

    for ax, msr in zip(axes, msrs):
        msr_results = cv_results[msr]
        my_lbl = "{:12s} {:.3f} {:.2f}".format(mod_name,
                                               msr_results.mean(),
                                               msr_results.std())
        ax.plot(msr_results, 'o--')
        ax.set_title(msr)
        # uncomment to see summary stats (clutters plots)
        #ax.legend(loc='lower center')
```

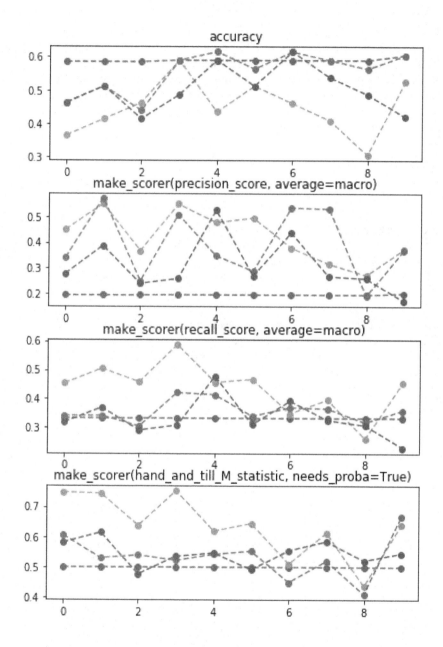

It appears we made a pretty hard problem for ourselves. Accuracy, precision, and recall all seem to be pretty downright awful. That cautions us in our interpretation of the Hand and Till *M* values. A few folds of GNB have some values that aren't awful, but half of the fold values for GNB end up near 0.6. Remember the preprocessing we did? By throwing out features and discretizing, we've turned this into a very hard problem.

We know things aren't good, but there is a glimmer of hope—maybe we do well on some classes, but just poorly overall?

In [39]:

```
fig, axes = plt.subplots(2, 2, figsize=(5, 5), sharex=True, sharey=True)
fig.tight_layout()

for ax, (mod_name, model) in zip(axes.flat,
                                 classifiers.items()):
    preds = skms.cross_val_predict(model,
                                   student_ftrs, student_tgt,
                                   cv=10)

    cm = metrics.confusion_matrix(student_tgt, preds)
    sns.heatmap(cm, annot=True, ax=ax,
                cbar=False, square=True, fmt="d",
                xticklabels=['low', 'med', 'high'],
                yticklabels=['low', 'med', 'high'])

    ax.set_title(mod_name)
axes[1, 0].set_xlabel('Predicted')
axes[1, 1].set_xlabel('Predicted')
axes[0, 0].set_ylabel('Actual')
axes[1, 0].set_ylabel('Actual');
```

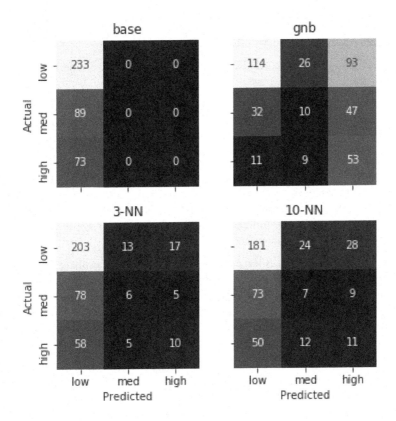

Not so much. A large part of our problem is that we're simply predicting the low class (even with our nonbaseline methods) an awful lot of the time. We need more information to tease apart the distinguishing characteristics of the target classes.

6.8 EOC

6.8.1 Summary

We've added *many* techniques to our quiver of classification evaluation tools. We can now account for unbalanced numbers of target classes, assess our learners with respect to reality and predictions (separately and jointly), and we can dive into specific class-by-class failures. We can also determine the overall benefit that a classification system gets us over guessing a random target.

6.8.2 Notes

If you need an academic reference on ROC curves, check out:

- Fawcett, Tom (2004). "ROC Graphs: Notes and Practical Considerations for Researchers." *Pattern Recognition Letters* 27 (8): 882–891.

AUC has some direct relationships to well-known statistical measures. In particular, the *Gini index*—which measures the difference of two ranges of outcomes—and AUC are related by Gini $+ 1 = 2 \times$ AUC. The Mann-Whitney U statistic is related to AUC as $\frac{U}{n_1 n_2} =$ AUC where n_i is the number of elements in class i. If you aren't a stats guru, don't worry about these.

We discussed F_1 and said it was an evenly balanced way to combine precision and recall. There are a range of alternatives called F_β that can weight precision more or less depending on whether you care more about performance with respect to reality or more about the performance of a prediction.

Here are two crazy facts. (1) A learning method called *boosting* can take any learner that is minutely better than coin flipping and make it arbitrarily good—if we have enough good data. (2) If a learner for a Boolean problem is reliably bad—reliably worse than coin flipping—we can make it reliably good by flipping its predictions. Putting these together, we can take any consistent *initial* learning system and make it as good as we want. In reality, there are mathematical caveats here—but the existence of this possibility is pretty mind-blowing. We'll discuss some practical uses of boosting in Section 12.4.

Some classifier methods don't play well with multiple target classes. These *require* that we do one-versus-one or one-versus-rest to wrap up their predictions to work in multiclass scenarios. Support vector classifiers are an important example which we will discuss in Section 8.3.

The Hand and Till M is defined in:

- Hand, David J. and Till, Robert J. (2001). "A Simple Generalisation of the Area Under the ROC Curve for Multiple Class Classification Problems." *Machine Learning* 45 (2): 171–186.

Although, as is often the case when you want to use a research method, I had to dig into an implementation of it to resolve a few ambiguities. It seems likely that the same technique could be used with precision-recall curves. If you happen to be looking for a master's thesis, fame, or just glory and honor, run it past your advisor or manager.

We saw that accuracy was the default metric for k-NN. In fact, accuracy is the default metric for all `sklearn` classifiers. As is often the case, there's an asterisk here: *if* the classifier inherits from the `ClassifierMixin` class, *then* they use mean accuracy. If not, they could use something else. `ClassifierMixin` is an internal `sklearn` class that defines the basic, shared functionality of `sklearn`'s classifiers. *Inheriting*—a concept from object-oriented programming (OOP)—shares that behavior with other classes. The `sklearn` documentation doesn't have a literal table of classifiers and scorers.

The school data we used came from:

- Cortez, P. and Silva, A. "Using Data Mining to Predict Secondary School Student Performance." In: A. Brito and J. Teixeira (eds), *Proceedings of 5th FUture BUsiness TEChnology Conference (FUBUTEC 2008)*, pp. 5-12, Porto, Portugal, April, 2008, EUROSIS.

Here's the code to download and preprocess it into the form used in this chapter:

In [40]:

```
student_url = ('https://archive.ics.uci.edu/' +
               'ml/machine-learning-databases/00320/student.zip')
def grab_student_numeric_discrete():
    # download zip file and unzip
    # unzipping unknown files can be a security hazard
    import urllib.request, zipfile
    urllib.request.urlretrieve(student_url,
                               'port_student.zip')
    zipfile.ZipFile('port_student.zip').extract('student-mat.csv')

    # preprocessing
    df = pd.read_csv('student-mat.csv', sep=';')

    # g1 & g2 are highly correlated with g3;
    # dropping them makes the problem significantly harder
    # we also remove all non-numeric columns
    # and discretize the final grade by 0-50-75-100 percentile
    # which were determined by hand
    df = df.drop(columns=['G1', 'G2']).select_dtypes(include=['number'])
    df['grade'] = pd.cut(df['G3'], [0, 11, 14, 20],
                         labels=['low', 'mid', 'high'],
                         include_lowest=True)
    df.drop(columns=['G3'], inplace=True)

    # save as
    df.to_csv('portugese_student_numeric_discrete.csv', index=False)
```

6.8.3 Exercises

Try applying our classification evaluation techniques against the wine or breast cancer datasets which you can pull in with `datasets.load_wine` and `datasets.load_breast_cancer`.

Evaluating Regressors

```
In [1]:

# Setup
from mlwpy import *
%matplotlib inline

diabetes = datasets.load_diabetes()

tts = skms.train_test_split(diabetes.data,
                            diabetes.target,
                            test_size=.25,
                            random_state=42)

(diabetes_train_ftrs, diabetes_test_ftrs,
 diabetes_train_tgt,  diabetes_test_tgt) = tts
```

We've discussed evaluation of learning systems and evaluation techniques specific to classifiers. Now, it is time to turn our focus to evaluating regressors. There are fewer ad-hoc techniques in evaluating regressors than in classifiers. For example, we don't have confusion matrices and ROC curves, but we'll see an interesting alternative in residual plots. Since we have some extra mental and physical space, we'll spend a bit of our time in this chapter on some auxiliary evaluation topics: we'll create our own `sklearn`-pluggable evaluation metric and take a first look at processing pipelines. Pipelines are used when learning systems require multiple steps. We'll use a pipeline to *standardize* some data before we attempt to learn from it.

7.1 Baseline Regressors

As with classifiers, regressors need simple baseline strategies to compete against. We've already been exposed to predicting the *middle* value, for various definitions of middle. In `sklearn`'s bag of tricks, we can easily create baseline models that predict the mean and the median. These are fixed values for a given training dataset; once we train on the dataset, we get a single value which serves as our prediction for all examples. We can also pick arbitrary constants out of a hat. We might have background or domain knowledge that gives us a reason to think some value—a minimum, maximum, or maybe 0.0—is a reasonable baseline. For example, if a rare disease causes fever and most people are healthy, a temperature near 98.6 degrees Fahrenheit could be a good baseline temperature prediction.

A last option, `quantile`, generalizes the idea of the `median`. When math folks say generalize, they mean that a specific thing can be phrased within a more general template. In Section 4.2.1, we saw that the median is the sorted data's middle value. It had an interesting property: half the values are less than it and half the values are greater than it. In more general terms, the median is one specific percentile—it is called the 50th percentile. We can take the idea of a median from a halfway point to an arbitrary midway point. For example, the 75th percentile has 75% of the data less than it and 25% of the data greater.

Using the `quantile` strategy, we can pick an arbitrary percent as our break point. Why's it called `quantile` and not `percentile`? It's because `quantile` refers to *any* set of evenly spaced break points from 0 to 100. For example, quartiles—phonetically similar to quarters—are the values 25%, 50%, 75%, and 100%. Percentiles are *specifically* the 100 values from 1% to 100%. Quantiles can be more finely grained than single-percent steps—for example, the 1000 values 0.1%, 0.2%, . . . , 1.0%, . . . , 99.8%, 99.9%, 100.0%.

In [2]:

```
baseline = dummy.DummyRegressor(strategy='median')
```

In [3]:

```
strategies = ['constant', 'quantile', 'mean', 'median', ]
baseline_args = [{"strategy":s} for s in strategies]

# additional args for constant and quantile
baseline_args[0]['constant'] = 50.0
baseline_args[1]['quantile'] =  0.75

# similar to ch 5, but using a list comprehension
# process a single argument package (a dict)
def do_one(**args):
    baseline = dummy.DummyRegressor(**args)
    baseline.fit(diabetes_train_ftrs, diabetes_train_tgt)
    base_preds = baseline.predict(diabetes_test_ftrs)
    return metrics.mean_squared_error(base_preds, diabetes_test_tgt)

# gather all results via a list comprehension
mses = [do_one(**bla) for bla in baseline_args]

display(pd.DataFrame({'mse':mses}, index=strategies))
```

	mse
constant	14,657.6847
quantile	10,216.3874
mean	5,607.1979
median	5,542.2252

7.2 Additional Measures for Regression

So far, we've used *mean squared error* as our measure of success—or perhaps more accurately, a measure of failure—in regression problems. We also modified MSE to the *root mean squared error* (RMSE) because the scale of MSE is a bit off compared to our predictions. MSE is on the same scale as the squares of the errors; RMSE moves us back to the scale of the errors. We've done this conversion in an ad-hoc manner by applying square roots here and there. However, RMSE is quite commonly used. So, instead of hand-spinning it—manually writing code—all the time, let's integrate RMSE more deeply into our `sklearn`-fu.

7.2.1 Creating Our Own Evaluation Metric

Generally, `sklearn` wants to work with scores, where bigger is better. So we'll develop our new regression evaluation metric in three steps. We'll define an error measure, use the error to define a score, and use the score to create a scorer. Once we've defined the scorer function, we can simply pass the scorer with a `scoring` parameter to `cross_val_score`. Remember: (1) for *errors* and *loss functions*, lower values are better and (2) for *scores*, higher values are better. So, we need some sort of inverse relationship between our error measure and our score. One of the easiest ways to do that is to negate the error. There is a mental price to be paid. For RMSE, all our scores based on it will be negative, and being *better* means being closer to zero while still negative. That can make you turn your head sideways, the first time you think about it. Just remember, it's like losing *less* money than you would have otherwise. If we must lose some money, our ideal is to lose zero.

Let's move on to implementation details. The error and scoring functions have to receive three arguments: a fit model, predictors, and a target. Yes, the names below are a bit odd; `sklearn` has a naming convention that "smaller is better" ends with `_error` or `_loss` and "bigger is better" ends with `_score`. The `*_scorer` form is responsible for applying a model on features to make predictions and compare them with the actual known values. It quantifies the success using an error or score function. It is not necessary to define all three of these pieces. We could pick and choose which RMS components we implement. However, writing code for all three demonstrates how they are related.

In [4]:

```python
def rms_error(actual, predicted):
    ' root-mean-squared-error function '
    # lesser values are better (a < b means a is better)
    mse = metrics.mean_squared_error(actual, predicted)
    return np.sqrt(mse)

def neg_rmse_score(actual, predicted):
    ' rmse based score function '
    # greater values are better  (a < b means b better)
    return -rms_error(actual, predicted)

def neg_rmse_scorer(mod, ftrs, tgt_actual):
    ' rmse scorer suitable for scoring arg '
    tgt_pred = mod.predict(ftrs)
    return neg_rmse_score(tgt_actual, tgt_pred)

knn = neighbors.KNeighborsRegressor(n_neighbors=3)
skms.cross_val_score(knn,
                     diabetes.data, diabetes.target,
                     cv=skms.KFold(5, shuffle=True),
                     scoring=neg_rmse_scorer)
```

Out[4]:

```
array([-58.0034, -64.9886, -63.1431, -61.8124, -57.6243])
```

Our `hand_and_till_M_statistic` from Section 6.4.1 acted like a score and we turned it into a scorer with `make_scorer`. Here, we've laid out all the `sklearn` subcomponents for RMSE: an error measure, a score, and a scorer. `make_scorer` can be told to treat larger values as the *better* result with the `greater_is_better` argument.

7.2.2 Other Built-in Regression Metrics

We saw the laundry list of metrics in the last chapter. As a reminder, they were available through `metrics.SCORERS.keys()`. We can check out the default metric for linear regression by looking at `help(lr.score)`.

In [5]:

```
lr = linear_model.LinearRegression()

# help(lr.score) # for full output
print(lr.score.__doc__.splitlines()[0])
```

```
Returns the coefficient of determination R^2 of the prediction.
```

The default metric for linear regression is R^2. In fact, R^2 is the default metric for all regressors. We'll have more to say about R^2 in a few minutes. The other major built-in performance evaluation metrics for regressors are mean absolute error, mean squared error (which we've been using), and median absolute error.

We can compare mean absolute error (MAE) and mean squared error (MSE) from a practical standpoint. We'll ignore the M (mean) part for the moment, since in both cases it simply means—ha!—dividing by the number of examples. MAE penalizes large and small differences from *actual* by the same amount as the size of the error. Being off by 10 gets you a penalty of 10. However, MSE penalizes bigger errors more: being off by 10 gets a penalty of 100. Going from an error of 2 to 4 in MAE goes from a penalty of 2 to a penalty of 4; in MSE, we go from a penalty of 4 to penalty of 16. The net effect is that larger errors become *really large* penalties. One last take: if two predictions are off by 5—their errors are 5 each—the contributions to MAE are $5 + 5 = 10$. With MSE, the contributions from two errors of 5 are $5^2 + 5^2 = 25 + 25 = 50$. With MAE, we could have 10 data points off by 5 (since $5 * 10 = 50$), two points off by 25 each, or one point off by 50. For MSE, we could only have one point off by about 7 since $7^2 = 49$. Even worse, for MSE a single data point with an error of 50 will cost us $50^2 = 2500$ *squared error points*. I think we're broke.

Median absolute error enters in a slightly different way. Recall our discussion of mean and median with balances in Section 4.2.1. The reason to use median is to protect us from single large errors overwhelming other well-behaved errors. If we're OK with a few real whammies of wrongness—as long as the rest of the predictions are on track—MAE may be a good fit.

7.2.3 R^2

R^2 is an inherently statistical concept. It comes with a large amount of statistical baggage—but this is not a book on statistics per se. R^2 is also conceptually tied to linear regression—and this is not a book on linear regression per se. While these topics are certainly within the scope of a book on machine learning, I want to stay focused on the big-picture issues and not get held up on mathematical details—especially when there are books, classes, departments, and disciplines that deal with it. So, I'm only going to offer a few words on R^2. Why even bother? Because R^2 is the default regression metric in `sklearn`.

What is R^2? I'll define it in the manner that `sklearn` computes it. To get to that, let me first draw out two quantities. Note, this is not the exact phrasing you'll see in a statistics textbook, but I'm going to describe R^2 in terms of two models. Model 1 is *our model of interest*. From it, we can calculate how well we do with our model using the *sum of squared errors* which we saw back in Section 2.5.3.

$$\text{SSE}_{\text{ours}} = \sum_i \text{our\_errors}_i^2 = \sum_i (\text{our\_preds}_i - \text{actual}_i)^2$$

Our second model is a simple baseline model that always predicts the *mean* of the target. The sum of squared errors for the mean model is:

$$\text{SSE}_{\text{mean}} = \sum_i \text{mean\_errors}_i^2 = \sum_i (\text{mean\_preds}_i - \text{actual}_i)^2 = \sum_i (\text{mean} - \text{actual}_i)^2$$

Sorry to drop all of those Σ's on you. Here's the code view:

In [6]:

```
our_preds  = np.array([1, 2, 3])
mean_preds = np.array([2, 2, 2])
actual     = np.array([2, 3, 4])


sse_ours = np.sum(( our_preds - actual)**2)
sse_mean = np.sum((mean_preds - actual)**2)
```

With these two components, we can compute R^2 just like `sklearn` describes in its documentation. Strictly speaking, we're doing here something slightly different which we'll get to in just a moment.

In [7]:

```
r_2 = 1 - (sse_ours / sse_mean)
print("manual r2:{:5.2f}".format(r_2))
```

manual r2: 0.40

The formula referenced by the `sklearn` docs is:

$$R^2 = 1 - \frac{\text{SSE}_{\text{ours}}}{\text{SSE}_{\text{mean}}}$$

What is the second term there? $\frac{\text{SSE}_{\text{ours}}}{\text{SSE}_{\text{mean}}}$ is the ratio between how well we do versus how well a simple model does, when both models are measured in terms of sum of squared errors. In fact, the specific baseline model is the `dummy.DummyRegressor(strategy='mean')` that we saw at the start of the chapter. For example, if the errors of our fancy predictor were 2500 and the errors of simply predicting the mean were 10000, the ratio between the two would be $\frac{1}{4}$ and we would have $R^2 = 1 - \frac{1}{4} = \frac{3}{4} = 0.75$. We are *normalizing*, or rescaling, our model's performance to a model that always predicts the mean target value. Fair enough. But, what is *one minus* that ratio?

7.2.3.1 An Interpretation of R^2 for the Machine Learning World

In the linear regression case, that second term $\frac{\text{SSE}_{\text{ours}}}{\text{SSE}_{\text{mean}}}$ will be between zero and one. At the high end, if the linear regression uses only a constant term, it will be identical to the mean and the value will be 1. At the low end, if the linear regression makes no errors on the data, it will be zero. A linear regression model, when fit to the training data and evaluated on the training data, can't do worse than the mean model.

However, that limitation is *not necessarily* the case for us because we are *not necessarily* using a linear model. The easiest way to see this is to realize that our "fancy" model could be *worse* than the mean. While it is hard to imagine failing that badly on the training data, it starts to seem plausible on *test* data. If we have a worse-than-mean model and we use sklearn's formula for R^2, all of a sudden we have a *negative* value. For a value labeled R^2, this is really confusing. Squared numbers are usually positive, right?

So, we had a formula of $1-$ *something* and it looked like we could read it as "100% minus something"—which would give us the leftovers. We can't do that because our *something* might be positive *or* negative and we don't know what to call a value above a *true* maximum of 100% that accounts for all possibilities.

Given what we're left with, how can we think about sklearn's R^2 in a reasonable way? The ratio between the SSEs gives us a normalized performance versus a standard, baseline model. Under the hood, the SSE is really the same as our mean squared error but without the mean. Interestingly, we can put to work some of the algebra you never thought you'd need. If we divide both SSEs in the ratio by n, we get

$$R^2 = 1 - \frac{\frac{\text{SSE}_{\text{ours}}}{n}}{\frac{\text{SSE}_{\text{mean}}}{n}} = 1 - \frac{\text{MSE}_{\text{ours}}}{\text{MSE}_{\text{mean}}}$$

We see that we've really been working with ratios of MSEs in disguise. Let's get rid of the $1-$ to ease our interpretation of the right-hand side:

$$R^2 = 1 - \frac{\text{SSE}_{\text{ours}}}{\text{SSE}_{\text{mean}}} = 1 - \frac{\text{MSE}_{\text{ours}}}{\text{MSE}_{\text{mean}}}$$

$$1 - R^2 = \frac{\text{SSE}_{\text{ours}}}{\text{SSE}_{\text{mean}}} = \frac{\text{MSE}_{\text{ours}}}{\text{MSE}_{\text{mean}}}$$

The upshot is that we can view $1 - R^2$ (for arbitrary machine learning models) as a MSE that is normalized by the MSE we get from a simple, baseline model that predicts the mean. If we have two models of interest and if we compare (divide) the $1 - R^2$ of our model 1 and the $1 - R^2$ of our model 2, we get:

$$\frac{1 - R^2_{\text{M1}}}{1 - R^2_{\text{M2}}} = \frac{\frac{\text{MSE}_{\text{M1}}}{\text{MSE}_{\text{mean}}}}{\frac{\text{MSE}_{\text{M2}}}{\text{MSE}_{\text{mean}}}} = \frac{\text{MSE}_{\text{M1}}}{\text{MSE}_{\text{M2}}}$$

which is just the ratios of MSEs—or SSEs—between the two models.

7.2.3.2 A Cold Dose of Reality: sklearn's R^2

Let's compute a few simple R^2 values manually and with sklearn. We compute r2_score from actuals and test set predictions from a simple predict-the-mean model:

In [8]:

```
baseline = dummy.DummyRegressor(strategy='mean')

baseline.fit(diabetes_train_ftrs, diabetes_train_tgt)
base_preds = baseline.predict(diabetes_test_ftrs)

# r2 is not symmetric because true values have priority
# and are used to compute target mean
base_r2_sklearn = metrics.r2_score(diabetes_test_tgt, base_preds)
print(base_r2_sklearn)
```

-0.014016723490579253

Now, let's look at those values with some manual computations:

In [9]:

```
# sklearn-train-mean to predict test tgts
base_errors    = base_preds - diabetes_test_tgt
sse_base_preds = np.dot(base_errors, base_errors)

# train-mean to predict test targets
train_mean_errors = np.mean(diabetes_train_tgt) - diabetes_test_tgt
sse_mean_train    = np.dot(train_mean_errors, train_mean_errors)

# test-mean to predict test targets (Danger Will Robinson!)
test_mean_errors = np.mean(diabetes_test_tgt) - diabetes_test_tgt
sse_mean_test    = np.dot(test_mean_errors, test_mean_errors)

print("sklearn train-mean model SSE(on test):", sse_base_preds)
print(" manual train-mean model SSE(on test):", sse_mean_train)
print(" manual test-mean  model SSE(on test):", sse_mean_test)
```

```
sklearn train-mean model SSE(on test): 622398.9703179051
 manual train-mean model SSE(on test): 622398.9703179051
 manual test-mean  model SSE(on test): 613795.5675675676
```

Why on Earth did I do the third alternative? I calculated the mean of the *test* set and looked at my error against the test targets. Not surprisingly, since we are teaching to the test, we do a bit better than the other cases. Let's see what happens if we use those taught-to-the-test values as our baseline for computing r2:

In [10]:

```
1 - (sse_base_preds / sse_mean_test)
```

Out[10]:

-0.014016723490578809

Shazam. Did you miss it? I'll do it one more time.

In [11]:

```
print(base_r2_sklearn)
print(1 - (sse_base_preds / sse_mean_test))
```

-0.014016723490579253
-0.014016723490578809

sklearn's R^2 is specifically calculating its base model—the mean model—from the true values we are testing against. We are not comparing the performance of my_model.fit(train) and mean_model.fit(train). With sklearn's R^2, we are comparing my_model.fit(train) with mean_model.fit(test) and evaluating them against test. Since that's counterintuitive, let's draw it out the long way:

In [12]:

```
#
# WARNING!  Don't try this at home, boys and girls!
# We are fitting on the *test* set... to mimic the behavior
# of sklearn R^2.
#
testbase = dummy.DummyRegressor(strategy='mean')
testbase.fit(diabetes_test_ftrs, diabetes_test_tgt)
testbase_preds = testbase.predict(diabetes_test_ftrs)
testbase_mse = metrics.mean_squared_error(testbase_preds,
                                          diabetes_test_tgt)

models = [neighbors.KNeighborsRegressor(n_neighbors=3),
          linear_model.LinearRegression()]
results = co.defaultdict(dict)
for m in models:
    preds = (m.fit(diabetes_train_ftrs, diabetes_train_tgt)
              .predict(diabetes_test_ftrs))

    mse = metrics.mean_squared_error(preds, diabetes_test_tgt)
    r2  = metrics.r2_score(diabetes_test_tgt, preds)
    results[get_model_name(m)]['R^2'] = r2
    results[get_model_name(m)]['MSE'] = mse

print(testbase_mse)
```

```
df = pd.DataFrame(results).T
df['Norm_MSE'] = df['MSE'] / testbase_mse
df['1-R^2'] = 1-df['R^2']
display(df)
```

5529.689797906013

	MSE	R^2	Norm_MSE	1-R^2
KNeighborsRegressor	3,471.4194	0.3722	0.6278	0.6278
LinearRegression	2,848.2953	0.4849	0.5151	0.5151

So, $1 - R^2$ computed by `sklearn` is equivalent to the MSE of our model normalized by the *fit-to-the-test-sample* mean model. If we *knew* the mean of our test targets, the value tells us how well we would do in comparison to predicting that known mean.

7.2.3.3   Recommendations on R^2

With all that said, I'm going to recommend against using R^2 unless you are an advanced user and you believe you know what you are doing. Here are my reasons:

1. R^2 has a lot of scientific and statistical baggage. When you say R^2, people may think you mean more than the calculations given here. If you google R^2 by its statistical name, the *coefficient of determination*, you will find thousands of statements that don't apply to our discussion here. Any statements that include "percent" or "linear" or "explained" should be viewed with *extreme* skepticism when applied to `sklearn`'s R^2. Some of the statements are true, under certain circumstances. But not always.
2. There are a number of formulas for R^2 — `sklearn` uses one of them. The multiple formulas for R^2 are equivalent when using a linear model with an intercept, but there are other scenarios where they are *not* equivalent. This Babel of formulas drives the confusion with the previous point. We have a calculation for R^2 that, under *certain circumstances*, means things beyond what we use it for with `sklearn`. We don't care about those additional things right now.
3. R^2 has a simple relationship to a very weird thing: a *normalized MSE computed on a test-sample-trained mean model*. We can avoid the baggage by going straight to the alternative.

Instead of R^2, we will simply use MSE or RMSE. If we *really* want to normalize these scores, we can compare our regression model with a training-set-trained mean model.

7.3   Residual Plots

We took a deep dive into some mathematical weeds. Let's step back and look at some graphical techniques for evaluating regressors. We're going to develop a regression analog of confusion matrices.

7.3.1 Error Plots

To get started, let's graph an actual, true target value against a predicted value. The graphical distance between the two represents our error. So, if a particular example was *really* 27.5 and we *predicted* 31.5, we'd need to plot the point $(x = 27.5, y = 31.5)$ on axes labeled (Reality, Predicted). One quick note: *perfect* predictions would be points along the line $y = x$ because for each output, we'd be predicting exactly that value. Since we're usually not perfect, we can calculate the error between what we predicted and the actual value. Often, we throw out the signs of our errors by squaring or taking absolute value. Here, we'll keep the directions of our errors for now. If we predict too high, the error will be positive; if we predict too low, the error will be negative. Our second graph will simply swap the predicted-actual axes so our point above will become $(x = 31.5, y = 27.5)$: (Predicted, Reality). It may all sound too easy—stay tuned.

In [13]:

```python
ape_df = pd.DataFrame({'predicted' : [4, 2, 9],
                       'actual'    : [3, 5, 7]})

ape_df['error'] = ape_df['predicted'] - ape_df['actual']

ape_df.index.name = 'example'
display(ape_df)
```

	predicted	actual	error
example			
0	4	3	1
1	2	5	-3
2	9	7	2

In [14]:

```python
def regression_errors(figsize, predicted, actual, errors='all'):
    ''' figsize -> subplots;
        predicted/actual data -> columns in a DataFrame
        errors -> "all" or sequence of indices '''
    fig, axes = plt.subplots(1, 2, figsize=figsize,
                             sharex=True, sharey=True)
    df = pd.DataFrame({'actual':actual,
                       'predicted':predicted})

    for ax, (x,y) in zip(axes, it.permutations(['actual',
                                                'predicted'])):
        # plot the data as '.'; perfect as y=x line
        ax.plot(df[x], df[y], '.', label='data')
```

```
    ax.plot(df['actual'], df['actual'], '-',
            label='perfection')
    ax.legend()

    ax.set_xlabel('{} Value'.format(x.capitalize()))
    ax.set_ylabel('{} Value'.format(y.capitalize()))
    ax.set_aspect('equal')

axes[1].yaxis.tick_right()
axes[1].yaxis.set_label_position("right")

# show connecting bars from data to perfect
# for all or only those specified?
if errors == 'all':
    errors = range(len(df))
if errors:
    acts  = df.actual.iloc[errors]
    preds = df.predicted.iloc[errors]
    axes[0].vlines(acts, preds, acts, 'r')
    axes[1].hlines(acts, preds, acts, 'r')

regression_errors((6, 3), ape_df.predicted, ape_df.actual)
```

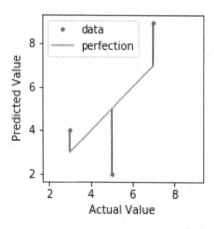 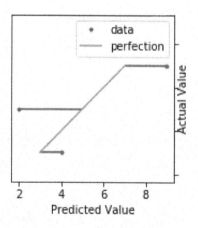

In both cases, the orange line ($y = x$ which in this case is `predicted = actual`) is conceptually an omniscient model where the predicted value is the true actual value. The error on that line is zero. On the left graph, the difference between prediction and reality is vertical. On the right graph, the difference between prediction and reality is horizontal. Flipping the axes results in flipping the datapoints over the line $y = x$. By the wonderful virtue of reuse, we can apply that to our diabetes dataset.

In [15]:

```
lr   = linear_model.LinearRegression()
preds = (lr.fit(diabetes_train_ftrs, diabetes_train_tgt)
            .predict(diabetes_test_ftrs))

regression_errors((8, 4), preds, diabetes_test_tgt, errors=[-20])
```

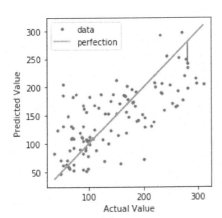 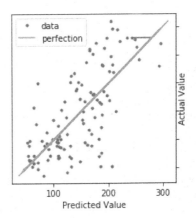

The difference between these graphs is that the left-hand graph is an answer to the question "Compared to reality (*Actual Value*), how did we do?" The right-hand graph is an answer to "For a given prediction (*Predicted Value*), how do we do?" This difference is similar to that between sensitivity (and specificity) being calculated with respect to the *reality of sick*, while precision is calculated with respect to a *prediction of sick*. As an example, when the actual value ranges from 200 to 250, we seem to consistently predict low. When the predicted value is near 200, we have real values ranging from 50 to 300.

7.3.2 Residual Plots

Now, we are ready to introduce *residual plots*. Unfortunately, we're about to run smack into a wall of terminological problems. We talked about the *error* of our predictions: error = predicted − actual. But for *residual plots*, we need the mirror image of these: residuals = actual − predicted. Let's make this concrete:

In [16]:

```
ape_df = pd.DataFrame({'predicted' : [4, 2, 9],
                       'actual'    : [3, 5, 7]})

ape_df['error'] = ape_df['predicted'] - ape_df['actual']
ape_df['resid'] = ape_df['actual'] - ape_df['predicted']
```

```
ape_df.index.name = 'example'
display(ape_df)
```

	predicted	actual	error	resid
example				
0	4	3	1	-1
1	2	5	-3	3
2	9	7	2	-2

When talking about *errors*, we can interpret the value as how much we over- or undershot by. An error of 2 means our prediction was over by 2. We can think about it as *what happened*. With residuals, we are thinking about what adjustment we need to do to *fix up* our prediction. A residual of -2 means that we need to subtract 2 to get to the right answer.

Residual plots are made by graphing the predicted value against the residual for that prediction. So, we need a slight variation of the right graph above (predicted versus actual) but written in terms of *residuals*, not *errors*. We're going to take the residual values—the signed distance from predicted back to actual—and graph them against their predicted value.

For example, we predict 31.5 for an example that is actually 27.5. The residual is -4.0. So, we'll have a point at $(x = \text{predicted} = 31.5, y = \text{residual} = -4.0)$. Incidentally, these can be thought of as *what's left over after we make a prediction*. What's left over is sometimes called a *residue*—think the green slime in *Ghostbusters*.

Alright, two graphs are coming your way: (1) actual against predicted and (2) predicted against residual.

In [17]:

```
def regression_residuals(ax, predicted, actual,
                         show_errors=None, right=False):
    ''' figsize -> subplots;
        predicted/actual data -> columns of a DataFrame
        errors -> "all" or sequence of indices '''
    df = pd.DataFrame({'actual':actual,
                       'predicted':predicted})
    df['error'] = df.actual - df.predicted
    ax.plot(df.predicted, df.error, '.')
    ax.plot(df.predicted, np.zeros_like(predicted), '-')

    if right:
        ax.yaxis.tick_right()
        ax.yaxis.set_label_position("right")
```

```
    ax.set_xlabel('Predicted Value')
    ax.set_ylabel('Residual')

    if show_errors == 'all':
        show_errors = range(len(df))
    if show_errors:
        preds = df.predicted.iloc[show_errors]
        errors = df.error.iloc[show_errors]
        ax.vlines(preds, 0, errors, 'r')

fig, (ax1, ax2) = plt.subplots(1, 2, figsize=(8, 4))

ax1.plot(ape_df.predicted, ape_df.actual, 'r.', # pred vs actual
         [0, 10], [0, 10], 'b-')                 # perfect line
ax1.set_xlabel('Predicted')
ax1.set_ylabel('Actual')
regression_residuals(ax2, ape_df.predicted, ape_df.actual,
                     'all', right=True)
```

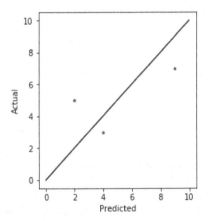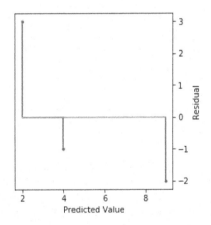

Now, we can compare two different learners based on their residual plots. I'm going to shift to using a proper train-test split, so these residuals are called *predictive residuals*. In a traditional stats class, the plain vanilla residuals are computed from the training set (sometimes called *in sample*). That's not our normal method for evaluation: we prefer to evaluate against a test set.

```
In [18]:

lr  = linear_model.LinearRegression()
knn = neighbors.KNeighborsRegressor()

models = [lr, knn]

fig, axes = plt.subplots(1, 2, figsize=(10, 5),
                         sharex=True, sharey=True)
fig.tight_layout()

for model, ax, on_right in zip(models, axes, [False, True]):
    preds = (model.fit(diabetes_train_ftrs, diabetes_train_tgt)
                  .predict(diabetes_test_ftrs))

    regression_residuals(ax, preds, diabetes_test_tgt, [-20], on_right)

axes[0].set_title('Linear Regression Residuals')
axes[1].set_title('k-NN-Regressor Residuals');
```

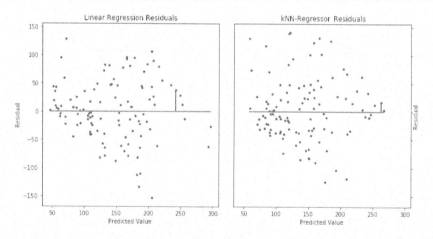

A few comments are in order. Since the two models predict different values for our point of interest, it shows up at different spots on the horizontal x axis. With the linear regression model, the value is predicted a hint under 250. With the k-NN-R model, the value is predicted to be a bit above 250. In both cases, it is underpredicted (remember, residuals tell us how to fix up the prediction: we need to add a bit to these predictions). The actual value is:

```
In [19]:

print(diabetes_test_tgt[-20])
```

```
280.0
```

If either of our models predicted 280, the residual would be zero.

In a classical stats class, when you look at residual plots, you are trying to diagnose if the assumptions of linear regression are violated. Since we're using linear regression as a black box prediction method, we're less concerned about meeting assumptions. However, we can be very concerned about trends among the residuals with respect to the predicted values. Potential trends are exactly what these graphs give us a chance to evaluate. At the very low end of the predicted values for the linear regression model, we have pretty consistent negative error (positive residual). That means when we predict a small value, we are probably undershooting. We also see undershooting in the predicted values around 200 to 250. For k-NN-R, we see a wider spread among the negative errors while the positive errors are a bit more clumped around the zero error line. We'll discuss some methods of improving model predictions by diagnosing their residuals in Chapter 10.

7.4 A First Look at Standardization

I'd like to analyze a different regression dataset. To do that, I need to introduce the concept of normalization. Broadly, normalization is the process of taking different measurements and putting them on a directly comparable footing. Often, this involves two steps: (1) adjusting the center of the data and (2) adjusting the scale of the data. Here's a quick warning that you may be getting used to: some people use normalization in this general sense, while others use this term in a more specific sense—and still others even do both.

I'm going to hold off on a more general discussion of normalization and standardization until Section 10.3. You'll need to wait a bit—or flip ahead—if you want a more thorough discussion. For now, two things are important. First, some learning methods *require* normalization before we can reasonably press "Go!" Second, we're going to use one common form of normalization called *standardization*. When we *standardize* our data, we do two things: (1) we *center* the data around zero and (2) we scale the data so it has a standard deviation of 1. Those two steps happen by (1) subtracting the mean and then (2) dividing by the standard deviation. Standard deviation is a close friend of variance from Section 5.6.1: we get standard deviation by taking the square root of variance. Before we get into the calculations, I want to show you what this looks like graphically.

```
In [20]:
# 1D standardization
# place evenly spaced values in a dataframe
xs = np.linspace(-5, 10, 20)
df = pd.DataFrame(xs, columns=['x'])

# center ( - mean) and scale (/ std)
df['std-ized'] = (df.x - df.x.mean()) / df.x.std()

# show original and new data; compute statistics
fig, ax = plt.subplots(1, 1, figsize=(3, 3))
```

```
sns.stripplot(data=df)
display(df.describe().loc[['mean', 'std']])
```

	x	std-ized
mean	2.5000	0.0000
std	4.6706	1.0000

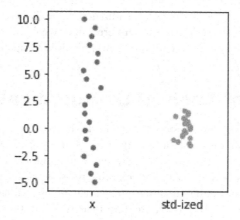

That's all well and good, but things get far more interesting in two dimensions:

In [21]:

```
# 2 1D standardizations
xs = np.linspace(-5, 10, 20)
ys = 3*xs + 2 + np.random.uniform(20, 40, 20)

df = pd.DataFrame({'x':xs, 'y':ys})
df_std_ized = (df - df.mean()) / df.std()

display(df_std_ized.describe().loc[['mean', 'std']])
```

	x	y
mean	0.0000	-0.0000
std	1.0000	1.0000

We can look at the original data and the standardized data on two different scales: the natural scale that `matplotlib` wants to use for the data and a simple, fixed, zoomed-out scale:

```
In [22]:

fig, ax = plt.subplots(2, 2, figsize=(5, 5))

ax[0,0].plot(df.x, df.y, '.')
ax[0,1].plot(df_std_ized.x, df_std_ized.y, '.')
ax[0,0].set_ylabel('"Natural" Scale')

ax[1,0].plot(df.x, df.y, '.')
ax[1,1].plot(df_std_ized.x, df_std_ized.y, '.')

ax[1,0].axis([-10, 50, -10, 50])
ax[1,1].axis([-10, 50, -10, 50])

ax[1,0].set_ylabel('Fixed/Shared Scale')
ax[1,0].set_xlabel('Original Data')
ax[1,1].set_xlabel('Standardized Data');
```

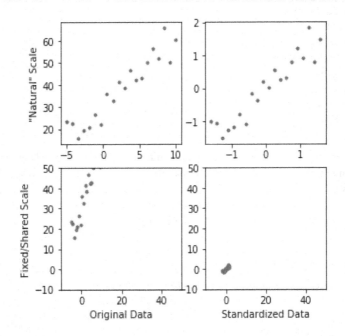

From our grid-o-graphs, we can see a few things. After standardizing, the shape of the data stays the same. You can see this clearly in the top row—where the data are on different scales and in different locations. In the top row, we let `matplotlib` use different scales to emphasize that the *shape* of the data is the same. In the bottom row, we use a fixed common scale to emphasize that the *location* and the *spread* of the data are different. Standardizing shifts the data to be centered at zero and scales the data so that the resulting values have a standard deviation and variance of 1.0.

We can perform standardization in `sklearn` using a special "learner" named
`StandardScaler`. Learning has a special meaning in this case: the learner figures out the
mean and standard deviation from the training data and applies these values to transform
the training or test data. The name for these critters in `sklearn` is a *Transformer*. `fit`
works the same way as it does for the learners we've seen so far. However, instead of
`predict`, we use `transform`.

In [23]:

```
train_xs, test_xs = skms.train_test_split(xs.reshape(-1, 1), test_size=.5)

scaler = skpre.StandardScaler()
scaler.fit(train_xs).transform(test_xs)
```

Out[23]:

```
array([[ 0.5726],
       [ 0.9197],
       [ 1.9608],
       [ 0.7462],
       [ 1.7873],
       [-0.295 ],
       [ 1.6138],
       [ 1.4403],
       [-0.1215],
       [ 1.0932]])
```

Now, managing the train-test splitting *and* multiple steps of fitting *and then* multiple
steps of predicting by hand would be quite painful. Extending that to cross-validation
would be an exercise in frustration. Fortunately, `sklearn` has support for building a
sequence of training and testing steps. These sequences are called *pipelines*. Here's how we
can standardize and then fit a model using a pipeline:

In [24]:

```
(train_xs, test_xs,
 train_ys, test_ys)= skms.train_test_split(xs.reshape(-1, 1),
                                            ys.reshape(-1, 1),
                                            test_size=.5)

scaler = skpre.StandardScaler()
lr     = linear_model.LinearRegression()

std_lr_pipe  = pipeline.make_pipeline(scaler, lr)

std_lr_pipe.fit(train_xs, train_ys).predict(test_xs)
```

```
Out[24]:

array([[17.0989],
       [29.4954],
       [41.8919],
       [36.9333],
       [61.7263],
       [24.5368],
       [31.9747],
       [49.3298],
       [51.8091],
       [59.247 ]])
```

The pipeline itself acts just like any other learner we've seen: it has `fit` and `predict` methods. We can use a pipeline as a plug-in substitute for any other learning method. The consistent interface for learners is probably the single biggest win of `sklearn`. We use the *same interface* whether the learners are stand-alone components or built up from primitive components. This consistency is the reason we should all buy the `sklearn` developers celebratory rounds at conferences.

A detail on pipelines: even though the `StandardScaler` uses `transform` when it is applied stand-alone, the overall pipeline uses `predict` to apply the transformation. That is, calling `my_pipe.predict()` will do the transformations necessary to get to the final predict step.

Finally, I'll leave you with one last warning. You may have noticed that we are learning the parameters we use to standardize (our training mean and standard deviation). We do that from the *training* set. Just like we don't want to peek with a full-blown learner, we don't want to peek with our preprocessing. There may be some wiggle room around what *exactly* constitutes peeking. Still, for safety's sake, I encourage you *never* to peek—in any way, shape, or form—unless there is (1) a formal proof that peeking won't bias or invalidate your results and (2) you understand the limits of the formal proof and when it may *not* apply—so that, again, you're back in a scenario where you shouldn't peek. Be cool, be safe, don't peek.

7.5 Evaluating Regressors in a More Sophisticated Way: Take Two

We're going to turn back to the Portuguese student data for our larger example. We have the same data we used in Chapter 6, except we've kept the target feature as a numerical value. So, we have just the numerical features from the original dataset and the `G3` column as our target.

In [25]:

```
student_df = pd.read_csv('data/portugese_student_numeric.csv')
display(student_df[['absences']].describe().T)
```

	count	mean	std	min	25%	50%	75%	max
absences	395.00	5.71	8.00	0.00	0.00	4.00	8.00	75.00

In [26]:

```
student_ftrs = student_df[student_df.columns[:-1]]
student_tgt  = student_df['G3']
```

7.5.1   Cross-Validated Results on Multiple Metrics

The following code uses `skms.cross_validate` to score over multiple metrics. This is a very nice convenience function: it allows us to evaluate multiple metrics with one call. It also does some work to capture the amount of time spent to fit and predict with the given model. We're going to ignore those other pieces and simply make use of the multiple metric evaluations that it returns. Like `skms.cross_val_score`, it requires `scorers` passed into the `scoring` argument.

In [27]:

```
scaler = skpre.StandardScaler()

lr      = linear_model.LinearRegression()
knn_3   = neighbors.KNeighborsRegressor(n_neighbors=3)
knn_10  = neighbors.KNeighborsRegressor(n_neighbors=10)

std_lr_pipe     = pipeline.make_pipeline(scaler, lr)
std_knn3_pipe   = pipeline.make_pipeline(scaler, knn_3)
std_knn10_pipe  = pipeline.make_pipeline(scaler, knn_10)

# mean with/without Standardization should give same results
regressors = {'baseline'  : dummy.DummyRegressor(strategy='mean'),
              'std_knn3'   : std_knn3_pipe,
              'std_knn10'  : std_knn10_pipe,
              'std_lr'     : std_lr_pipe}

msrs = {'MAE' : metrics.make_scorer(metrics.mean_absolute_error),
        'RMSE' : metrics.make_scorer(rms_error)}

fig, axes = plt.subplots(2, 1, figsize=(6, 4))
fig.tight_layout()
```

```
for mod_name, model in regressors.items():
    cv_results = skms.cross_validate(model,
                                     student_ftrs, student_tgt,
                                     scoring = msrs, cv=10)

    for ax, msr in zip(axes, msrs):
        msr_results = cv_results["test_" + msr]

        my_lbl = "{:12s} {:.3f} {:.2f}".format(mod_name,
                                               msr_results.mean(),
                                               msr_results.std())
        ax.plot(msr_results, 'o--', label=my_lbl)
        ax.set_title(msr)
        # ax.legend() # uncomment for summary stats
```

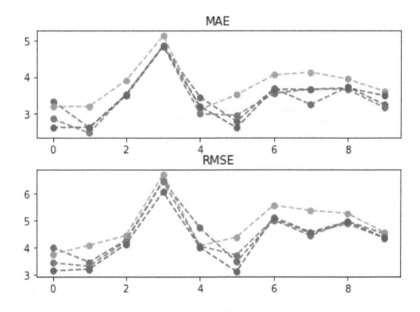

A few things stand out here. 3-NN is not serving us very well in this problem: the baseline method generally has less error than 3-NN. For several folds, 10-NN and LR perform very similarly and their overall performance is mostly on par with one another and slightly better than baseline.

We can tease out some of the close values—and get a more direct comparison with the baseline regressor—by looking at the ratio of the MSEs: $\frac{\sqrt{MSE_{me}}}{\sqrt{MSE_{baseline}}}$.

In [28]:

```
fig,ax = plt.subplots(1, 1, figsize=(6, 3))
baseline_results = skms.cross_val_score(regressors['baseline'],
                            student_ftrs, student_tgt,
                            scoring = msrs['RMSE'], cv=10)

for mod_name, model in regressors.items():
    if mod_name.startswith("std_"):
        cv_results = skms.cross_val_score(model,
                                student_ftrs, student_tgt,
                                scoring = msrs['RMSE'], cv=10)

        my_lbl = "{:12s} {:.3f} {:.2f}".format(mod_name,
                                    cv_results.mean(),
                                    cv_results.std())

        ax.plot(cv_results / baseline_results, 'o--', label=my_lbl)
ax.set_title("RMSE(model) / RMSE(baseline)\n$<1$ is better than baseline")
ax.legend();
```

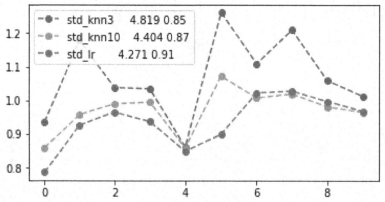

Here, it is quite clear that 3-NN is generating substantially more error than baseline (its ratios are bigger than 1) and it is worse than the other two regressors. We also see that LR seems to be a bit of a winner on more folds, although 10-NN does eek out a few victories in folds 6–9.

Although it is easily abused (as we discussed in Section 7.2.3), let's see the default R^2 scoring for this problem:

```
In [29]:

fig, ax = plt.subplots(1, 1, figsize=(6, 3))
for mod_name, model in regressors.items():
    cv_results = skms.cross_val_score(model,
                                      student_ftrs, student_tgt,
                                      cv=10)
    my_lbl = "{:12s} {:.3f} {:.2f}".format(mod_name,
                                           cv_results.mean(),
                                           cv_results.std())

    ax.plot(cv_results, 'o--', label=my_lbl)
ax.set_title("$R^2$");
# ax.legend(); # uncomment for summary stats
```

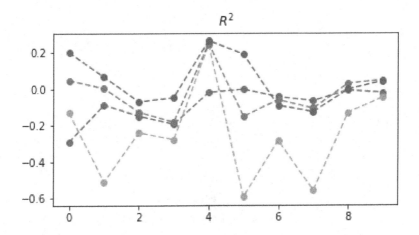

There are two interesting patterns here. The first is that our linear regression seems to be consistently better than k-NN-R. Secondly, the pattern between our two metrics appears pretty consistent. Certainly the *order* of the winners on each fold—remember that R^2 approaching 1 is a better value—seems to be the same. Given the relationships between R^2 and MSE we saw above, we probably aren't too surprised by that.

Second, if you've been paying close attention, you might wonder why the baseline model—which was a mean predictor model—doesn't have an R^2 of zero. By the way, you get a gold star for noticing. Can you figure out why? As we discussed, there's going to be different values for the means of training and testing sets. Since we're doing train-test splitting wrapped up in cross-validation, our training and testing means are going to be a bit off from each other, but not too much. You'll notice that most of the R^2 values for the mean model are in the vicinity of zero. That's the price we pay for randomness and using R^2.

7.5.2 Summarizing Cross-Validated Results

Another approach to cross-validated predictions is to view the entire cross-validation process as a single learner. If you dig through your notes, you might find that when we do cross-validation, each example is in *one and only one* testing scenario. As a result, we can simply gather up all the predictions—made by a basket of learners training on different partitions of the data—and compare them with our known targets. Applying an evaluation metric to these predictions and targets gives us a net result of a *single* value for each model and metric. We access these predictions with `cross_val_predict`.

In [30]:

```
msrs = {'MAD'  : metrics.mean_absolute_error,
        'RMSE' : rms_error} # not scorer, no model

results = {}
for mod_name, model in regressors.items():
    cv_preds = skms.cross_val_predict(model,
                                      student_ftrs, student_tgt,
                                      cv=10)
    for ax, msr in zip(axes, msrs):
        msr_results = msrs[msr](student_tgt, cv_preds)
        results.setdefault(msr, []).append(msr_results)
df = pd.DataFrame(results, index=regressors.keys())
df
```

Out[30]:

	MAD	RMSE
baseline	3.4470	4.6116
std_knn3	3.7797	4.8915
std_knn10	3.3666	4.4873
std_lr	3.3883	4.3653

7.5.3 Residuals

Since we did some basic residual plots earlier, let's make this interesting by (1) looking at the residuals of our baseline model and (2) using the standardized, preprocessed data.

In [31]:

```
fig, axes = plt.subplots(1, 4, figsize=(10, 5),
                         sharex=True, sharey=True)
fig.tight_layout()
```

```
for model_name, ax in zip(regressors, axes):
    model = regressors[model_name]
    preds = skms.cross_val_predict(model,
                                   student_ftrs, student_tgt,
                                   cv=10)

    regression_residuals(ax, preds, student_tgt)
    ax.set_title(model_name + " residuals")
pd.DataFrame(student_tgt).describe().T
```

Out[31]:

	count	mean	std	min	25%	50%	75%	max
G3	395.00	10.42	4.58	0.00	8.00	11.00	14.00	20.00

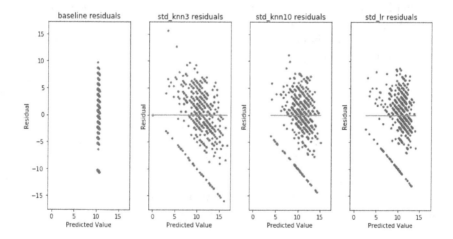

A few interesting points:

- Even though we are using the mean model as our baseline model, we have multiple means—there's one for each training-split. But take heart, our predicted values only have a slight variation for the mean-only model(s).
- The residuals for our standardize-then-fit models have some striking patterns.
  1. They all show banding. The banding is due to the integer values of the target: there are target values of 17 and 18, but not 17.5. So, we have distinct gaps.
  2. The overall patterns seem quite similar for each of the nonbaseline models.
  3. There's a whole band of "error outliers" where all of the residuals are negative and keep decreasing with the amount of the prediction. Negative residuals are positive errors. They indicate we are overpredicting. On the right, we predict 15 and we're over by about 15, as the actual is near zero. On the left, we predict near 5 and we're over by about 5; the actual is, again, near zero. So, the

reason we see that band is that it shows us our *maximum* error (minimum residual) at each possible predicted value. If we predict x and the actual value is zero, our error is x (residual of $-x$).

7.6 EOC

7.6.1 Summary

We've added a few tools to our toolkit for assessing regression methods: (1) baseline regression models, (2) residual plots, and (3) some appropriate metrics. We've also explained some of the difficulties in using these metrics. We took a first look at pipelines and standardization, which we'll come back to in more detail later.

7.6.2 Notes

In the residual plots, you might have noticed that the (actual, predicted) points are equidistant from the $y = x$ line in *both* the horizontal and vertical directions. That regularity, *if unexpected*, might indicate that something is wrong. However, it turns out that we *should* expect that regularity.

Any triangle made up of one 90-degree angle and two 45-degree angles is going to have its short sides (those are the bases, not the hypotenuse) of the same length. (Ah, what a stroll down the memory line to high school geometry.) Conceptually, this means that the distance (1) *from actual to predicted* is the same as the distance (2) *from predicted to actual*. That's not surprising. The distance from Pittsburgh to Philadelphia is the same as the distance from Philadelphia to Pittsburgh. Nothing to see here, carry on.

When we see troublesome patterns in a residual plot, we might ask, "What do we do to fix it?" Here are some recommendations that come out of the statistical world (see, for example, Chapter 3 of *Applied Linear Statistical Models* by Kutner and friends)—with the caveat that these recommendations are generally made with respect to linear regression and are merely starting points. Your mileage might vary.

- If the spread of the residuals is pretty even, transform the inputs (not the outputs).
- If the spread of the residuals is increasing (they look like a funnel), taking the logarithm of the output can force it back to an even spread.
- If there is a clear functional relationship in the residuals (for example, if we try to model a true x^2 with a linear regression, our residuals would look like $x^2 - (mx + b)$, which in turn looks like a parabola), then transforming the inputs may help.

We'll talk about performing these tasks in Chapter 10.

Statisticians—there they go again—like to work with something called *Studentized* residuals. Studentization *depends* on using a linear regression (LR) model. Since we don't necessarily have a LR model, we can use *semi-Studentized* residuals simply by dividing our errors—the residuals—by the root-mean-squared error $\frac{\text{errors}}{\text{RMSE}}$. Basically, we are normalizing their size to the average-ish error size.

If you insist on a statistical approach to comparing algorithms—that's t-tests, comparing means, and so forth—you may want to check out:

- Dietterich, Thomas G. (1998). "Approximate Statistical Tests for Comparing Supervised Classification Learning Algorithms." *Neural Computation* 10 (7): 1895–1923.

We'll make use of another idea from that paper—5 × 2 cross-validation—in Section 11.3.

In a 2010 article "What You Can and Can't Properly Do with Regression," Richard Berk describes three levels of application of linear regression.

- The first is as a purely descriptive model. This is how we are generally using models throughout this book. We say, "We are going to get the best description of the relationship between the predictors and the target using a linear model." We don't make any assumptions about how the data came to be, nor do we have a preconceived idea of the relationship. We just hold up a ruler and see how well it measures what we are seeing.
- Level two is statistical inference: computing confidence intervals and constructing formal tests of statistical hypotheses. To access level two, our data must be a suitable random sampling of a larger population.
- Level three involves making claims about *causality*: the predictors *cause* the target. A follow-on is that *if we manipulate the predictor values, we can tell you what the change in the target will be*. This is a very strong statement of belief and *we are not going there*. If we could intervene in our variables and generate test cases to see the outcomes (also known as performing experiments), we could potentially rule out things like confounding factors and illusory correlations.

More Comments on R^2   Strictly speaking, R^2 is `sklearn`'s default metric for classes that inherit from `sklearn`'s parent regression class `RegressorMixin`. Discussing inheritance is beyond the scope of this book; the quick summary is that we can place common behavior in a *parent* class and access that behavior without reimplementing it in a *child* class. The idea is similar to how genetic traits are inherited from parent to child.

If you want to dive into some of the limitations of R^2, start here:

- Kvalseth, Tarald O. (1985). "Cautionary Note about R2." *The American Statistician* 39 (4): 279–285.
- Anscombe, F. J. (1973). "Graphs in Statistical Analysis." *American Statistician* 27 (1): 17–21.

Yes, they are both statistical journals. No, I'm not sorry. The first is primarily about calculations surrounding R^2 and the second is about interpreting its value. Above, I limited my critiques of R^2 to its use in predictive evaluation of learning systems. But in the larger statistical context, (1) even in cases where it is completely appropriate to use R^2, people often have strong misconceptions about its interpretation and (2) it is often applied inappropriately. Basically, lots of people are running around with scissors, just waiting to trip and hurt themselves. If you'd like to fortify yourself against some of the most common misuses, check out Chapter 2 of *Advanced Data Analysis* by Shalizi.

R^2, as it is used by many scientists, means *much more* than the specific calculation I've presented here. To many folks in the wide academic world, R^2 is inherently tied to *our model* being a *linear* model—that is, a linear regression. There are often additional assumptions placed on top of that. Thus, you will commonly hear phrases like "R^2 is the percentage of variance explained by a *linear* relationship between the predictors and the target." That statement is true, *if you are using a linear model as your prediction model*. We are interested in models that go beyond a typical linear regression.

Fetching the Student Data   Here is the code to download and preprocess the data we used in the final example.

In [32]:

```
student_url = ('https://archive.ics.uci.edu/' +
               'ml/machine-learning-databases/00320/student.zip')
def grab_student_numeric():
    # download zip file and unzip
    # unzipping unknown files can be a security hazard
    import urllib.request, zipfile
    urllib.request.urlretrieve(student_url,
                               'port_student.zip')
    zipfile.ZipFile('port_student.zip').extract('student-mat.csv')

    # preprocessing
    df = pd.read_csv('student-mat.csv', sep=';')

    # g1 & g2 are highly correlated with g3;
    # dropping them makes the problem significantly harder
    # we also remove all non-numeric columns
    df = df.drop(columns=['G1', 'G2']).select_dtypes(include=['number'])

    # save as
    df.to_csv('portugese_student_numeric.csv', index=False)

# grab_student_numeric()
```

7.6.3 Exercises

Try applying our regression evaluation techniques against the boston dataset that you can pull in with `datasets.load_boston`.

Here's a more thought-provoking question: what relationship between true and predicted values would give a *linear* residual plot as the result?

Part III

More Methods and Fundamentals

More Classification Methods

```
In [1]:

# setup
from mlwpy import *
%matplotlib inline

iris = datasets.load_iris()

# standard iris dataset
tts = skms.train_test_split(iris.data, iris.target,
                            test_size=.33, random_state=21)
(iris_train_ftrs, iris_test_ftrs,
 iris_train_tgt,  iris_test_tgt) = tts

# one-class variation
useclass = 1
tts_1c = skms.train_test_split(iris.data, iris.target==useclass,
                               test_size=.33, random_state = 21)
(iris_1c_train_ftrs, iris_1c_test_ftrs,
 iris_1c_train_tgt,  iris_1c_test_tgt) = tts_1c
```

8.1 Revisiting Classification

So far, we've discussed two classifiers: Naive Bayes (NB) and k-Nearest Neighbors (k-NN). I want to add to our classification toolkit—but first, I want to revisit what is happening when we classify data. In some ways, classification is *easy*. What? If it is so easy, why on Earth are there hundreds of books and thousands of research articles written on it? Why am I writing about it now? OK, you raise some fair points. Let me be a bit more specific about what I mean by *easy*. If I asked my son Ethan—currently a 12-year-old—to *draw* some circles, lines, or boxes that separated some Xs and Os in diagram, he could do it as in Figure 8.1. If a 12-year-old can do it, it must be easy. Q.E.D.—*quod erat demonstrandum—thus it has been shown* that classification is easy. Or, perhaps not. What details am I glossing over?

There are a number of pieces that we need to specify in the separating process. We can talk about them as instructions to Ethan:

1. What rules do I give Ethan when he starts drawing? Can he use straight lines? Can he use more than one line? Do they have to be parallel to the edges of the paper? Can he use curves? If so, how curvy can they be? Can he pick up his pencil or must he make one, and only one, continuous boundary before he stops?

2. When I say, "Good job, Ethan!" what do I mean by *good job*? How do I evaluate the separation that he's made? If *X*s and *O*s show up in the same region—apparently a flaw in his drawing—is that fundamentally because of the rules I gave Ethan, or because of the nature of the *X*s and *O*s, or both?

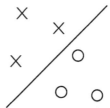

Figure 8.1   Separating shapes in space.

Classification methods differ in two fundamental ways: (1) they have different constraints on how to draw their boundaries and (2) they have different ways to evaluate those boundaries. These differences are side effects of the underlying mathematics of the methods. In reality, a mathematical alchemist, creating a new method, makes some *assumptions* or constraints about what is happening with the data and how we will separate it. Then, she works through some more or less complicated mathematics. Eventually, out pops some equation that defines a separating boundary. In turn, the boundary lets us classify an example as *X* or *O*. Since the nice connection between algebra and geometry lets us turn equations and examples into geometric, drawable objects, we can skip right to discussing these methods in terms of geometric pictures. There *are* some wonderful mathematical ways to talk about the relationships among these methods. As I've said, I want to avoid relying on those mathematics in describing the methods to you—but if you are interested, I'll give you a taste of it in Chapter 15.

Once we've drawn our *good* boundaries—you could think of them as fences separating sheep from unruly cows—we can ask simple questions to figure out the class of a new example: "Are we inside or outside the fenced area?" or "Which side of a very long fence are we on?" These questions can be simple, mathematical comparisons between a value computed from an example and a constant:

1. Which side of a fence are we on? Is some value greater than 0?
2. Which of the two possibilities is the answer? Is some value 0 or 1? Is some value −1 or 1?
3. Is one event the more likely of two? Is some value greater than $\frac{1}{2}$?
4. Am I the most likely of several alternatives? Is some value the greatest in a set of values?

The first two questions are very similar. Often, the choice has to do with simplifying the underlying mathematics that we are setting aside for now. The third is a bit more general—not only can we say *which* outcome we prefer, but we can say *by how much* we prefer it. If we don't have strict probabilities (instead we have generic scores), we might have a different threshold than one-half. The fourth comes into play when we select between more than two classes. These questions are in their simplest forms. Sometimes we do a bit of additional processing before asking them.

In this chapter, we will look at four different methods for classification: decision trees, support vector classifiers, logistic regression, and discriminant analysis. In that order, these methods introduce increasing numbers of assumptions. As we saw with Naive Bayes, the assumptions don't *prevent* us from applying a method: we are free to use *any* method with *any* data. Often, we won't know what assumptions are met before we apply the method. The better the alignment between the assumptions of a method and the patterns in the data, the better we expect a method to perform. Since we don't know, we may try multiple methods, cross-validate, and use the method with the best cross-validated results as our final tool.

8.2 Decision Trees

Did you know that retired spies like to play tennis? I didn't know that either. But they do. As much as they might like to keep their personal security—PerSec, to those in the know—under tight control, they still prefer to play outdoors and outdoor sports are subject to weather. Since old spies can be hard to find, information about when a former spy will be playing a few sets is quite valuable to both friends and foes. Suppose a ball-fetcher—we'll call her Belle—at a tennis club were to overhear a spy talking about an old war story. She decides to be sleuthy herself and to *predict* when the spy will show up to play tennis. Belle starts recording whether the spy played tennis on a given day and the weather. From the weather, we predict tennis play. This classification example, without the James Bond backstory, is due to Ross Quinlan. He developed one of the two main branches of decision tree learning systems.

Our intrepid spy recorded values for *Cloudy*, *Precip(itation)*, *Windy*, *Temp(erature)*, and *Play(edTennis)*. Here is some of the data that Belle recorded:

Cloudy	Precip	Windy	Temp	Play
Yes	Yes	Yes	45	No
Yes	No	No	75	Yes
No	No	No	30	No
No	No	Yes	85	Yes
No	No	No	85	No
No	No	No	65	Yes

After recording the data for a while, Belle noticed that the most important single predictor of whether James Bond—I mean Jeffrey Billings—was playing tennis was whether it was sunny out (*Cloudy* = *No*); everything else seemed to matter less. Then there were other similar patterns that emerged after breaking the data up into sunny and non-sunny days. Belle recorded sequences of questions that led to whether James . . . err, Jeffrey . . . was playing tennis. The result looked like Figure 8.2.

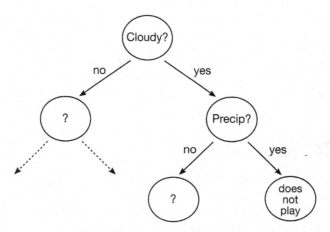

Figure 8.2   A simple decision tree.

What do we make of this diagram? For starters, it is called a *decision tree* (DT). Yes, it is upside down: it grows from the top down. I do apologize—academics are nothing if not counterintuitive. But just think of the hanging planter at grandma and grandpa's house with the plant growing downwards over the sides. I guess Decision Shrubs didn't catch on as a name.

The single question at the top, *Cloudy?*, is called the *root* of the tree. The scattered nodes at the bottom are called the *leaves*. At each leaf, we have some—possibly mixed—set of outcomes. Imagine that Belle recorded 30 cases of playing, and 5 cases of not playing, when the recorded data indicated sunny, the temperature between 60 and 75, no rain, and no wind. I'm told that those conditions are nearly ideal for playing tennis. On the flip side, weather of *Cloudy*, *Temp* < 60, *Precip*, *Windy* had 0 cases of playing and 20 cases of not playing. Some might call those the worst conditions where you *could* play tennis, but you would never *want* to. When it's even colder or more windy, the club shuts down the courts and everyone goes to the tiki lounge.

If you look at most of the leaves in the tree, the outcomes are mixed: there are examples of playing and not playing. We can get conflicting results for several reasons:

- The actual decision to play tennis has some inherent randomness. Even on two days that are in all observable ways the same, the decision might be left to chance.
- There may be observable features that we *could* measure but we didn't. For example, if we had a history of how many days of tennis were played in the last week, we might see that above some threshold our spy gets tired and prefers to rest. Or, on days with a doctor's appointment, tennis just doesn't happen.
- There could be errors in our measurements. Belle may have made mistakes in recording the weather. Mistakes could have a relatively large effect if bad handwriting translated a cloudy day to a sunny day. Mistakes could also be relatively minor if a temperature of 67 degrees was recorded as 66.

Here's one other interesting phenomenon that occurs in several different learning methods, but it shows up very prominently with decision trees. Imagine we had a column that identified the day Belle recorded the weather. It has a sequence of increasing values: $1, 2, 3, 4, \ldots, 100$. We *could* use this identifier to *perfectly* learn the training data. Simply make splits in the tree that lead to leaf nodes for every uniquely numbered day. Now, we have a lookup table encoded in a tree (see Figure 8.3). Day 17, *Didn't Play*. Done.

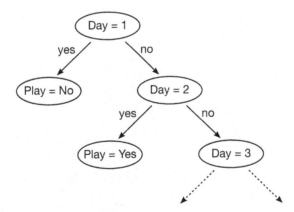

Figure 8.3   A decision tree that has memorized a table.

Think for a moment about how well this generalizes to future days. Unique identifiers are just that: *unique*. They don't tell us anything about the nature of a *different* example. Would a unique identifying column be of any help when we need to predict a *new* day identified with the value 101? Always be careful with labels—which don't represent measurements—in your data. If you could swap the values in a column with your favorite list of unique names—Fido, Lassie, etc.—and not add or lose any information, you should consider excluding the column from your training data.

Incidentally, the *reason* trees are particularly vulnerable to unique identifiers is that they have very high capacity and very low bias. The consequence is that they are *prone to overfitting*. We reduce this tendency primarily by limiting the *depth* to which a tree can grow.

8.2.1 Tree-Building Algorithms

Tree-building methods result in a model that can be thought of as a *patchwork of constant predictors*. The differences among decision tree (DT) methods revolve around (1) how they break down the entire space of the data into smaller and smaller regions and (2) when they stop the breakdown. Here's how a decision tree classifier (DTC) breaks down the *iris* data when it only considers the first two features (*sepal length* and *sepal width*):

In [2]:

```
tree_classifiers = {'DTC' : tree.DecisionTreeClassifier(max_depth=3)}

fig, ax = plt.subplots(1,1,figsize=(4,3))
for name, mod in tree_classifiers.items():
    # plot_boundary only uses specified columns
    # [0,1] [sepal len/width] to predict and graph
    plot_boundary(ax, iris.data, iris.target, mod, [0,1])
    ax.set_title(name)
plt.tight_layout()
```

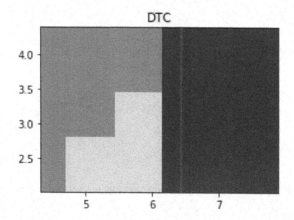

The red region (on the right) is *setosa*. The blue (top left) and gray (lower center) are the two *v* classes. Note that the boundaries are all made with lines that are parallel to the *x* or *y* axes. Also, I'm sneaking in a `max_depth=3` argument to the DT constructor. We'll go into more detail on that shortly. For now, `max_depth` is simply the maximum number of questions I can ask of any example before I classify it. You might remember playing a game called Twenty Questions. That's a bit like a `max_depth=20` constraint.

Breaking up the whole space creates a *partition*. We predict the class of an example based on the color of the region the example falls into. Mathematically, we can write

$$\text{target} = \sum_{R \in P} c_R I(\text{example} \in R)$$

That equation is a bit of symbol-soup. I would apologize for showing it, but I want to take a few sentences to convince you that it is a very odd-looking dot product. Here goes. Let's start by defining the letters. R is a region of our graph; P is the group of *all* of the regions. Summing over all of the $R \in P$ means that we add up some values over the whole graph. c_R is the predicted class for the region R: for example, one of the types of irises. I is an *indicator function* which gives us a value of one if an example is in R and zero otherwise. Taken together, c_R and $I(\text{example} \in R)$ give us c_R when an example is in R and give us zero everywhere else. Together, these pieces look like $\sum c_R I$ which is exactly a pretty convoluted dot product.

Trees create blocky—think Legos or Tetris—regions of colored space from our features. The partition—the shapes of the regions—is pretty constrained from one point of view. It is made of overlaid rectangles where only the topmost rectangle counts. Overlaying cards as in Figure 8.4 gives us boundaries like those in Figure 8.5. You can imagine neatly spreading out a few decks of cards on a rectangular table. The cards are of different sizes and they must be horizontally and vertically aligned with the sides of

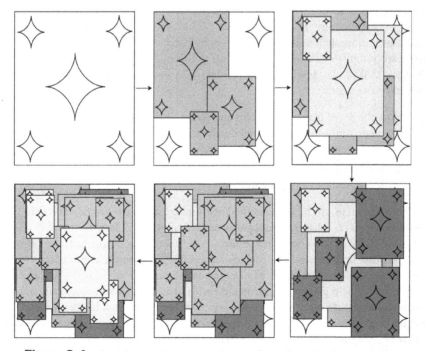

Figure 8.4   Decision tree boundaries form regions of overlapping rectangles.

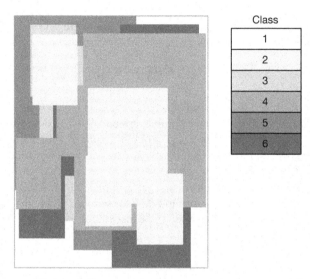

Class
1
2
3
4
5
6

Figure 8.5   End result of overlapping rectangles.

the table. The cards can overlap. When cards of the same suit (clubs, hearts, diamonds, spades) are touching one another, they form a larger region for that suit. To create those regions from points in space, we create simple yes/no answers by thresholding. For example, we test a feature *Temp* against a value 55. Choosing the values to split on is the trickiest aspect of implementing decision trees by hand.

There are a number of major tree-building algorithms. ID3, C4.5, and C5.0 were made by Quinlan. CART was developed independently. In general, the tree-building algorithms use the following steps:

1. Evalute the set of features and splits and pick a "best" feature-and-split.
2. Add a node to the tree that represents the feature-split.
3. For each descendant, work with the matching data and either:

    (1) If the targets are similar enough, return a predicted target.
    (2) If not, return to step 1 and repeat.

Each of these steps can be implemented and limited in different ways. The DT algorithms control (1) what splits and partitions are allowed, (2) how feature-splits are evaluated, (3) what makes targets in a group similar enough to form a leaf, and (4) other limits. The other limits commonly include an absolute limit on the depth of the tree and the minimum number of examples at a leaf to make a prediction, regardless of similarity. These constraints help prevent overfitting. As with identifying labels, if we can continually break down the feature space until we have single examples in each bucket, we'll get perfect training accuracy—but we'll lose generalization. Unconstrained trees have very little bias, but they do suffer from high variance. We'll see examples of this shortly.

8.2.2 Let's Go: Decision Tree Time

We can take a quick look at how trees do on the basic *iris* dataset.

In [3]:

```
dtc = tree.DecisionTreeClassifier()
skms.cross_val_score(dtc,
                     iris.data, iris.target,
                     cv=3, scoring='accuracy') # sorry
```

Out[3]:

```
array([0.9804, 0.9216, 0.9792])
```

Overall, they do quite well.

If we have a fit tree, we can view it graphically using one of two different methods. The first needs an additional Python library, `pydotplus`, which you may not have installed on your computer. The second requires an additional command-line program, `dot`, which you may have to install. `dot` is a program for drawing diagrams specified by text files, sort of like using HTML to specify how something looks on screen. These outputs have a *Gini* value listed—I'll discuss that very briefly at the end of Chapter 13. For now, just think of it as measuring how *pure* the class split is at that point. If there is only one class represented, the *Gini* value is 0.0.

We'll use the simplified single-class iris problem here: it only results in a single split, even if we allow the tree the freedom to grow more deeply.

In [4]:

```
iris_1c_tree = (tree.DecisionTreeClassifier()
                    .fit(iris_1c_train_ftrs, iris_1c_train_tgt))
```

In [5]:

```
# using an additional library:
# conda install pydotplus
# pip install pydotplus
import pydotplus
dot_data = tree.export_graphviz(iris_1c_tree, out_file=None)
graph = pydotplus.graph_from_dot_data(dot_data)
graph.write_png("outputs/iris_1c.png")
Image("outputs/iris_1c.png", width=75, height=75)
```

Out[5]:

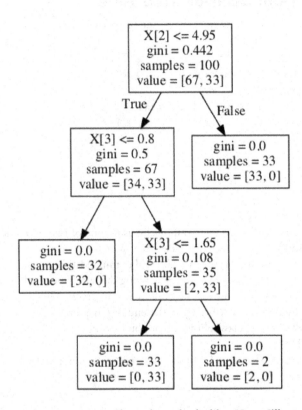

We can also see what a more complicated tree looks like. Here, I'll use the other tree drawing method. We'll specify additional arguments to `export_graphviz` so we can make the output a bit more presentable.

In [6]:

```
iris_tree = (tree.DecisionTreeClassifier()
                   .fit(iris_train_ftrs, iris_train_tgt))
```

In [7]:

```
# no added library to produce .dot file
with open("outputs/iris.dot", 'w') as f:
    dot_data = tree.export_graphviz(iris_tree, out_file=f,
                             feature_names=iris.feature_names,
                             class_names=iris.target_names,
                             filled=True, rounded=True)
```

```
# the following '!' lines are "shell" commands
# uses the 'dot' program to convert dot -> png
!dot -Tpng outputs/iris.dot -o outputs/iris.png
!rm outputs/iris.dot

Image("outputs/iris.png", width=140, height=140)
```

Out[7]:

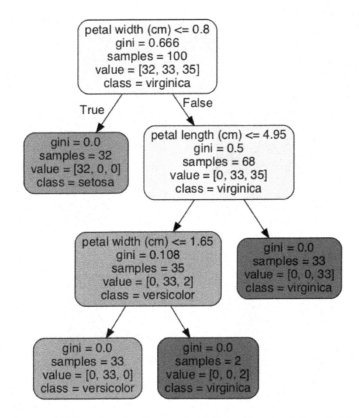

We can also get a feeling for what happens with increasing depth in a decision tree. Let's take a look at the default tree from `DecisionTreeClassifier` and trees limited to depths 1, 2, and 3. Remember, even at a `max_depth=2`, we'll have three splits: one split for the root node and one split at each of the two children. We expect to see these three splits as three cuts across our feature space. The default setting, `max_depth=None`, implies not constraining the depth at all, as if `max_depth` = ∞ (the sideways 8 means *infinity*).

In [8]:

```
fig, axes = plt.subplots(2,2,figsize=(4,4))

depths = [1, 2, 3, None]
for depth, ax in zip(depths, axes.flat):
    dtc_model = tree.DecisionTreeClassifier(max_depth=depth)
    # plot_boundary only uses specified columns [0,1]
    # so we are only predicting with sepal length and width
    plot_boundary(ax, iris.data, iris.target, dtc_model, [0,1])
    ax.set_title("DTC (max_depth={})".format(dtc_model.max_depth))

plt.tight_layout()
```

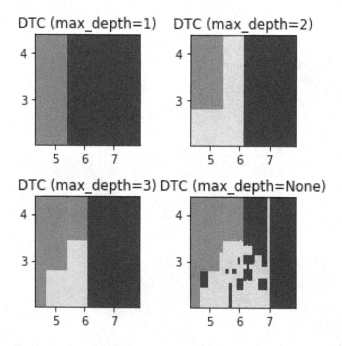

As a sanity check for our intuition about how the tree maps to separation in space, you can look at the top-right figure. Red is on the right, blue is in the top-left, and gray is the remainder. It has the three boundary lines—cuts or divisions—we expect: one between gray and red, one horizontally between gray and blue, and one vertically between gray and blue. The two gray-blue edges come from two different splits. Also, look at how many mini-regions there are in the bottom-right, max_depth=None, figure. Test yourself: as the max depth increases, are we moving towards overfitting or underfitting?

8.2.3 Bias and Variance in Decision Trees

If we start with a wide open, no-depth-limit tree, we'll have a model that is very flexible and can capture *any* finite pattern that doesn't have coin-flipping randomness built into it. While that might seem ideal, you've learned enough to know that there is a tradeoff. If we use unconstrained trees, we will likely overfit, and when we try to generalize, we'll have poor test performance. If you need a reminder about that tradeoff, see Section 5.6. So, how can we *bias* our trees or place limits on them to prevent overfitting? We can take several steps.

1. We can limit the depth of the trees. We allow fewer questions before categorizing.
2. We can require more examples at leaves. This constraint forces us to group together examples that might be different. Since we aren't allowed to separate them them, it effectively smoothes out some of our boundaries.
3. We can limit the number of features we consider when we ask questions of the examples. This constraint has the added benefit of speeding up our learning process.

8.3 Support Vector Classifiers

In a few minutes, we'll see a great oddity of logistic regression classifiers: the underlying mathematics fail with perfectly separable data. If drawing a line between the Xs and Os on paper is as simple as possible, the mathematics simply fall apart. It's a case of being in a desert and drowning in fresh water. Let's take a closer look at the perfectly separable case. What would *you* do with all the data points falling neatly on either side of a set of tracks? Here are three possible lines:

In [9]:

```
fig, ax = plt.subplots(1,1,figsize=(4,3))

# fancy way to get cross product of points
left  = np.mgrid[1:4.0, 1:10].reshape(2, -1).T
right = np.mgrid[6:9.0, 1:10].reshape(2, -1).T

# data points
ax.scatter(left[:,0] , left[:,1] , c='b', marker='x')
ax.scatter(right[:,0], right[:,1], c='r', marker='o')

# separating lines
ax.plot([3.5, 5.5], [1,9], 'y', label='A')
ax.plot([4.5, 4.5], [1,9], 'k', label='B')
ax.plot([3.5, 5.5], [9,1], 'g', label='C')
ax.legend(loc='lower center');
```

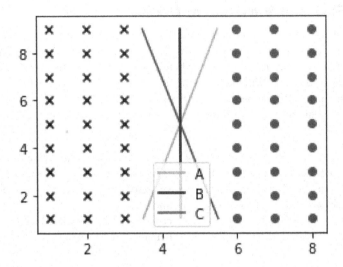

We can create an infinite number of lines by gradually sweeping from the green line (pointing up-left) to the yellow line (pointing up-right). All of these lines will give us perfect results and score perfectly on various (training) evaluation metrics. We could also gradually sweep the center black line left and right a bit, while keeping it vertical: so many lines, so little time. Perhaps there is another standard—beyond simple correctness—we can use to compare the separating lines.

What line has a strong case for being *the best around*? Cue the soundtrack from *The Karate Kid*. I'm a big fan of the black line, *B*. Why? It does the best job of staying far away from the data. In some ways it is the most cautious line: it is always splitting the difference between the Xs and Os. You can think of the empty middle space between the classes as a no-man's land or, perhaps, a river between two countries. The empty space has a fancy name in the machine learning community. It is the *margin* between the two countries— err, classes. The *B* line has a special name: it is the *maximum margin separator* between the classes because it keeps both classes as far from itself as possible.

Here's a related point. If I change the problem slightly by keeping only those points on the borders of the two class clusters, I get something like

```
In [10]:
```

```
fig, ax = plt.subplots(1,1,figsize=(4,3))

# fancy way to get cross-product of points
left  = np.mgrid[1:4:2, 1:10].reshape(2, -1).T
right = np.mgrid[6:9:2, 1:10].reshape(2, -1).T
```

```
ax.scatter(left[:,0] , left[:,1] , c='b', marker='x')
ax.scatter([2,2], [1,9], c='b', marker='x')
ax.scatter(right[:,0], right[:,1], c='r', marker='o')
ax.scatter([7,7], [1,9], c='r', marker='o')
ax.set_xlim(0,9);
```

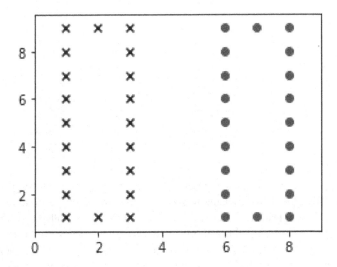

From a certain perspective, we haven't lost anything. We still have the outline—often called a hull, in analogy with the hull of a ship—of our classes intact. We can continue reducing the data we need to form that max-margin separating line. Really, we don't need the *entire* border of both classes. Only the boundary points facing the opposing class really matter. So, I can drop the non-facing points, as well. We are left with two opposing lines of contestants facing off before a game.

In [11]:

```
fig, ax = plt.subplots(1,1,figsize=(4,3))

left  = np.mgrid[3:4, 1:10].reshape(2, -1).T
right = np.mgrid[6:7, 1:10].reshape(2, -1).T

ax.scatter(left[:,0] , left[:,1] , c='b', marker='x')
ax.scatter(right[:,0], right[:,1], c='r', marker='o')
ax.set_xlim(0,9);
```

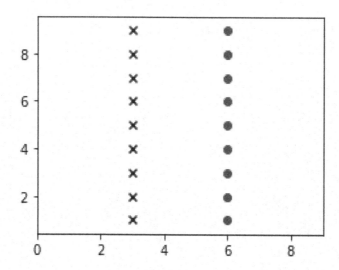

We've worked our way down to a potentially much smaller set of data points. In essence, we can throw out a lot of our data and just focus on the points that matter. The points that matter are called the *support vectors*. It would be great if they were called *supporting examples*, but alas, no one asked me. We'll talk more about examples as vectors in Section 13.3.

We are ready to talk about Support Vector Classifiers (SVCs). The heart of a SVC is to (1) find the *support vectors*—the border points—and then (2) do the mathematics necessary to figure out the *maximum margin separator* between those points. SVCs try to balance off two competing concerns: getting the biggest margin between the example classes and minimizing the number of training errors. Our examples above had no *hard* training examples—everything fell on its own side of the tracks. But we'll dive into more difficult cases in a few minutes.

Two additional notes. First, we want a big margin because—under certain assumptions—it leads to good generalization and good test set error. Second, there are really two things that drive the need for more support vectors: additional complexity in the boundary between the classes and examples that don't play nicely with the proposed boundaries.

Our discussion, so far, is a nice conceptual introduction to SVCs and their elder siblings, Support Vector Machines (SVMs). We'll talk about SVMs more in Section 13.2.4. While we've stayed out of the realm of the usual math-heavy presentation of SVCs, they do have some very nice mathematical and practical properties:

1. They are sparse: they focus on the hard training examples near the margin. They can adapt by storing more examples if necessary. Contrast this with *k*-NN which *always* needs to store *all* of the training examples to make predictions.
2. The form of the SVC classification boundary is simple: it's a line. The boundary can be made more complicated in a convenient way that we'll discuss when we talk about SVMs.

3. SVCs generalize well to novel test data because they try to leave as much cushioning between classes as possible—that's the maximum-margin principle coming to the rescue.

4. The underlying optimization problem—finding the best line—leads to *the* best line given our constraints. We don't get a suboptimal line.

8.3.1 Performing SVC

There are a few practical details that go along with using SVC:

- SVCs aren't naturally suited to multiclass classification. They are typically wrapped up in either one-versus-one (OvO) or one-versus-rest (OvR) systems. We talked about these differences in Sections 6.3.4 and 6.4. Note, *you* don't have to add this capability to SVMs. It is done behind the scenes for you. As of `scikit-learn` version `0.19`, these methods are all standardized on using OvR. Prior to that, there was a mix of OvO and OvR.

- There are four ways (actually more) that we can get a SVC in `sklearn`: (1) using `LinearSVC`, (2) using `SVC` with a *linear kernel*, (3) using `SVC` with a *polynomial kernel* of degree 1 (a line in disguise), and (4) using a `NuSVC` with a linear kernel. These four methods don't necessarily lead to the *exact* same results due to mathematical, implementation, and default-argument differences. Reconciling the differences is painful; I have some notes about it at the end of the chapter. Also, we haven't discussed kernels yet and we'll hold off on discussion them until Section 13.2.4. For now, consider them a coding detail—although they are far more than that.

8.3.1.1 Just the Facts: Running SVCs

Here, I'll focus on just two of these SVC options: `SVC` and `NuSVC`. I'll get into the `nu` parameter in just a moment, but I selected its value of `.9` to get a result close to that of the `SVC`.

In [12]:

```
sv_classifiers = {"SVC(Linear)"   : svm.SVC(kernel='linear'),
                  "NuSVC(Linear)" : svm.NuSVC(kernel='linear', nu=.9)}
```

In [13]:

```
fig, axes = plt.subplots(1,2,figsize=(6,3))
for (name, mod), ax in zip(sv_classifiers.items(), axes.flat):
    plot_boundary(ax, iris.data, iris.target, mod, [0,1])
    ax.set_title(name)
plt.tight_layout()
```

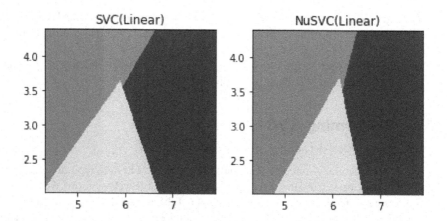

To a quick glance, SVC and NuSVC are pretty similar, but the precise angles of the region boundaries are not identical.

8.3.1.2   Parameters for SVCs

SVC relies on one primary parameter, C, to control its bias-variance tradeoff. C can be difficult to interpret directly. NuSVC solves the same task as SVC, but it relies on different mathematics. We bother with it because the primary parameter for NuSVC, ν — pronounced like *new* and written in English as *nu*—has a simple meaning: *at least ν%* of the data will be kept as a support vector. It also has a consequence on errors, but errors of a special type: *margin errors*. Margin errors are points that are (1) either on the wrong side of the separator (a classification error) or (2) on the correct side of the separator (correctly classified) *but* within the margin. So, the other effect of ν is that we tolerate *at most ν%* margin errors in our training data. Under certain circumstances, margin errors increase to ν and support vectors decrease to ν. Values of ν are in the range $[0, 1]$ which we interpret as a percent from 0% to 100%. While harder to interpret, SVC has better runtime characteristics than NuSVC.

The parameters for SVCs have a bit of occultness to them: they are hidden secrets known only to the alchemists. In truth, you have to dive deeply into some heavy mathematics to see what they mean. Still, we can explore their effects on some small examples. (I said small, not easy.) Let's look at how varying C and ν affects the boundary between classes.

In [14]:

```
def do_linear_svc_separators(svc_maker, pname, params, ax):
    'create svc(params) and draw seperation boundary'
    xys = (np.linspace(2,8,100),
           np.linspace(2,8,100))

    for p in params:
```

```
        kwargs = {pname:p, 'kernel':'linear'}
        svc = svc_maker(**kwargs).fit(ftrs, tgt)
        # plot_separator is in mlwpy.py
        plot_separator(svc, *xys,
                       '{}={:g}'.format(pname, p), ax=ax)
```

In [15]:

```
ftrs = np.array([[3,3],
                 [3,6],
                 [7,3],
                 [7,6],
                 [6,3]])
tgt  = np.array([0,0,1,1,0])
colors = np.array(['r', 'b'])


Cs = [.1, 1.0, 10]
nus = [.3, .4, .5]


fig, axes = plt.subplots(1,3,figsize=(12,4),
                         sharex=True, sharey=True)
for ax in axes:
    ax.scatter(ftrs[:,0], ftrs[:,1], c=colors[tgt])
ax.set_xlim(2,8); ax.set_ylim(2,7)


do_linear_svc_separators(svm.SVC,    "C",  Cs, axes[1])
do_linear_svc_separators(svm.NuSVC, "nu", nus, axes[2])


axes[0].set_title("No Boundary")
axes[1].set_title("C Boundaries")
axes[2].set_title(r"$\nu$ Boundaries");


# the two right most points are blue
# the remaining three points are red
```

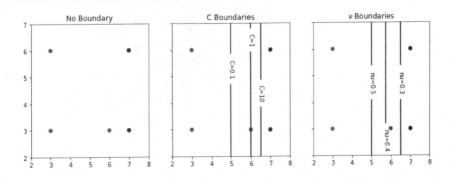

There are two take-home messages here:

1. A bigger ν and a smaller C have approximately the same effect. The *scales* of ν and C are quite different, however. We're using orders of magnitude in C and we're using linear, one-tenth, steps in ν.
2. Bigger ν and smaller C can get us a SVC that to some extent *ignores* misclassification.

8.3.2 Bias and Variance in SVCs

One last set of comments is appropriate here. Let's look at how our parameters—ν in NuSVC and C in SVC—relate to bias and variance. We'll start by creating some data:

In [16]:

```
ftrs, tgt = datasets.make_blobs(centers=2,
                                n_features=3,
                                n_samples=200,
                                center_box = [-2.0, 2.0],
                                random_state=1099)

# note: using three features, but graphing only two dimensions
fig, ax = plt.subplots(1,1,figsize=(4,3))
ax.scatter(ftrs[:, 0], ftrs[:, 1],
           marker='o', c=tgt, s=25, edgecolor='k')
ax.axis('off');

# generally the yellow class is on top
# and the purple class is on bottom
```

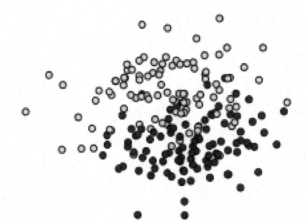

Now, we'll look at the effect of ν:

In [17]:

```
nus = np.linspace(0.05, 1.0, 10)
tt = skms.validation_curve(svm.NuSVC(kernel='linear'),
                           ftrs, tgt,
                           param_name='nu',
                           param_range=nus,
                           cv=5)

fig,ax = plt.subplots(1,1,figsize=(4,3))
ax = sns.tsplot(np.array(tt).transpose(),
                time=nus,
                condition=['Train', 'Test'],
                interpolate=False)

ax.set_title('5-fold CV Performance for NuSVC')
ax.set_xlabel("\n".join([r'$\nu$ for $\nu$-SVC']))
ax.set_ylim(.3, 1.01)
ax.legend(loc='lower center');
```

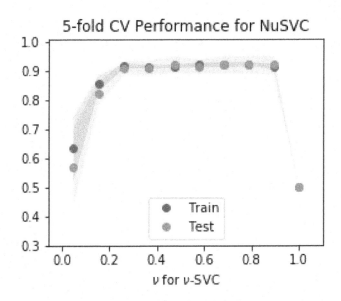

Here we see that a very large ν is basically awful for training and testing. We can't capture enough of the pattern to do anything—we are too biased. On the other end, decreasing ν lets us capture *some* pattern—but when we go to test, we simply don't do very well. We aren't generalizing because we have overfit the training data. Broadly speaking, a small ν is equivalent to a large C, although the scales differ.

In [18]:

```
cs = [0.0001, 0.001, 0.01, .1, 1.0, 10, 100, 1000]
tt = skms.validation_curve(svm.SVC(kernel='linear'),
                           ftrs, tgt,
                           param_name='C',
                           param_range=cs,
                           cv=5)

fig,ax = plt.subplots(1,1,figsize=(4,3))
ax = sns.tsplot(np.array(tt).transpose(),
                time=cs,
                condition=['Train', 'Test'],
                interpolate=False)

ax.set_title('5-fold CV Performance for SVC')
ax.set_xlabel("\n".join([r'C for SVC']))
ax.set_ylim(.8, 1.01)
ax.set_xlim(.00001, 10001)
ax.set_xscale('log')
```

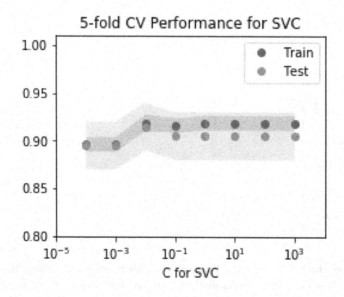

On the left, at small C values, both our training and testing performance is relatively poor. On the right, at large C, our training performance is better than our test. Putting these together, high values of C lead to overfitting and low values of C lead to underfitting. While C is harder to interpret than ν, it trades off between the complexity of our model and the errors we make. A bigger C means that we care more about errors compared to complexity. With a really big C, even the smallest errors matter a lot. So, we build a model with a lot of complexity to cover those errors. We'll make our view of this tradeoff more concrete in Chapter 15.

8.4 Logistic Regression

To start with, let's just point out the elephant in the room. Logistic regression is a linear classification technique. It gets worse. Logistic regression is both a regression technique and a classification technique. I can hear some of my colleagues now, "But Mark, it's a classification technique!" In mathematics, something called a *red herring* might not be red and it might not even be a fish! That aside, logistic regression is a *classification* method that uses *regression* as an internal component. Logistic regression works in two stages: (1) it computes something closely related to the probabilities of being in each target class and (2) it labels an example with the highest-probability class. Step one is a regression from the predictors to the not-quite-probabilities. Taking a threshold against the not-quite-probabilities—or taking a maximum among several values—gives us a class.

We have to dive into a bit of street math to explain what is happening. Once we do, you'll see a very tight relationship between linear regression and logistic regression. The key concept we need to bridge the two is something called the *log-odds*. Now, we're not talking about betting on the outcomes at the lumberjack games—but our story *will* begin with a bet. The log-odds are the not-quite-probabilities I mentioned in the previous paragraph.

8.4.1 Betting Odds

My friends that like to bet—on basement poker, at the casino, or on the ponies at the racetrack—are *very* familiar with thinking in terms of odds. I . . . am not. So, let's spend a couple of minutes talking about probabilities and odds. Here's a very simple example of the relationship between probabilities and odds. Imagine our probability—we'll say *of winning*—is 10%. That means if we play a game ten times, we expect to win once. We can break that down another way: of ten total attempts we expect one win and nine losses. If we create the ratio of those two numbers, we get $\frac{1}{9} \approx .1111$. These are the *odds* of winning. We'll also write those odds as $1 : 9$. Be very careful: even though this is the *odds* and we calculate it from a *ratio*, this value *is not* the *odds-ratio*—that is a *different* concept.

Back to odds: how can we interpret them? Why do my betting friends like to think in terms of odds? To answer that, let's ask another question. For a given set of odds, what is a *fair bet* for those odds? Specifically, if the odds of winning are .1111, what amount of money do the participants need to wager so that, in the long run, the game is fair. To keep this from getting too abstract, let's design a game that matches the 10% probability—or $\frac{1}{9}$ odds—of winning.

We'll start by taking nine spades and one heart from a deck of cards. I'll sit down with my friend, Andy. We'll shuffle the cards and then my friend deals me one card. If it is the heart, I win! If not, Andy wins. This setup gives us a game with a 10% probability, or 1 : 9 odds, of *MarkWins*—go, me! How much money should Andy and I be willing to risk on this simple game if we want to have a fair outcome? In the long run, what is the break-even point where we both expect to win the same amount of money? Note that we talk about playing the game many times to reduce the effect of chance variability. If we only play one round, only one person will win that round—probably Andy! If we play 100 times, we expect to see something closer to a 90–10 split for Andy winning. There is no guarantee, though.

To figure out the break-even point, let's start with some concrete numbers. Here's an example where we both wager $10.

$$\text{MarkWinnings} = (.1 \times +10) + (.9 \times -10) = 1 - 9 = -8$$
$$\text{AndyWinnings} = (.9 \times +10) + (.1 \times -10) = 9 - 1 = 8$$

To compute the winnings, we took the two possible outcomes—a win and a loss—and combined (1) the two probabilities of those outcomes and (2) the two monetary results of those outcomes together with a—tada!—dot product. Writing that out mathematically gives us $\sum_{\text{outcome}} p_{\text{outcome}} v_{\text{outcome}}$, where p and v are the probabilities and the dollar-values for each outcome. This particular dot product is called the *expected value* of winnings when someone plays the game.

Notice that since no money disappears, we have a true *zero-sum game* and our total winnings must balance out to zero. So, if we both risk an equal amount of money—$10 for each of us—I, Mark, am really going to be in the hole. Let's sanity-check that result—do the numbers make sense? Remember, my odds of winning were only 1:9. Sadly, I don't have a very good chance of winning. To balance things out, I should stake *less money* than Andy because I have lower odds of winning. What is the break-even point for a bet? We could perform some algebra to calculate the answer, but let's do it experimentally with some code. We'll look at pairs of bets from $1 to $11 in steps of $2 and compute Mark's winnings.

We'll make use of two helper functions:

In [19]:

```
def simple_argmax(arr):
    ' helper to convert np.argmax into something usable '
    return np.array(np.unravel_index(np.argmax(arr),
                                     arr.shape))


def df_names(df, idxs):
    ' helper to convert number of index/column labels '
    r,c = idxs
    return df.index[r], df.columns[c]
```

Then, we'll create a table of the outcomes for several combinations of betting:

```
In [20]:

base_bets = np.arange(1,12,2)
mark_bet, andy_bet = np.meshgrid(base_bets, base_bets)

mark_winnings = .1 * andy_bet + .9 * -mark_bet

df = pd.DataFrame(mark_winnings,
                  index  =base_bets,
                  columns=base_bets)
df.index.name = "Andy Bet"
df.columns.name = "Mark Bet"

print("Best Betting Scenario (for Mark) for These Values:")
print("(Andy, Mark):", df_names(df, simple_argmax(mark_winnings)))

display(df)
```

```
Best Betting Scenario (for Mark) for These Values:
(Andy, Mark): (11, 1)
```

Mark Bet Andy Bet	1	3	5	7	9	11
1	-0.8000	-2.6000	-4.4000	-6.2000	-8.0000	-9.8000
3	-0.6000	-2.4000	-4.2000	-6.0000	-7.8000	-9.6000
5	-0.4000	-2.2000	-4.0000	-5.8000	-7.6000	-9.4000
7	-0.2000	-2.0000	-3.8000	-5.6000	-7.4000	-9.2000
9	0.0000	-1.8000	-3.6000	-5.4000	-7.2000	-9.0000
11	0.2000	-1.6000	-3.4000	-5.2000	-7.0000	-8.8000

That's pretty interesting. Recall from our discussion above: if my overall expected winnings are zero, so are Andy's. The best outcome for me, not surprisingly, is in the lower-left corner of that table. It occurs when I wager $1 and Andy wagers $11. That's my lowest bet and Andy's highest bet. Now, if Andy is willing to play a game where I bet $1 and he bets $99, things are looking very different for me. I win 10% of the time, so I'm looking at $.1 \times \$99 + .9 \times -\$1 = 9$. If we played this game with these bets many times, I'd start coming out ahead. Things are looking up for ol' Marco.

What about the break-even point? That's where the winnings for both of us are the same, $0.00. It's close to the bottom-left corner: I wager $1 and Andy wagers $9. Compare that to my odds of winning: 1 : 9. The break-even point is the bet where the amount of money you stake is equal to your odds of winning. Andy is a 9 : 1 favorite: he bets $9 for every $1 Mark bets. I am a 1 : 9 long-shot. I'll only bet $1 for every $9 that Andy bets.

Here's one last take-home message from betting. If two players had an equal probability of winning, the probabilities would be .5 each. These correspond to an odds of 1 : 1 which we write as odds = 1. These values are the tipping point between winning and losing. Higher values (.75, odds 3 : 1) make one event or winner *more* likely and the other *less* likely.

8.4.2 Probabilities, Odds, and Log-Odds

Hopefully, you now have some understanding of how odds work. Earlier, I mentioned that we care about the *log-odds*. I'll explain why in a minute. Let's start by creating a table of some probability values with their corresponding odds and log-odds. The log-odds are literally just that: the mathematical logarithm applied to the odds values: log(odds).

In [21]:

```
tail_probs = [0.0, .001, .01, .05, .10, .25, 1.0/3.0]

lwr_probs = np.array(tail_probs)
upr_probs = 1-lwr_probs[::-1]
cent_prob = np.array([.5])

probs = np.concatenate([lwr_probs, cent_prob, upr_probs])

# much better than geterr/seterr/seterr
with np.errstate(divide='ignore'):
    odds     = probs / (1-probs)
    log_odds = np.log(odds)

index=["{:4.1f}%".format(p) for p in np.round(probs,3)*100]

polo_dict = co.OrderedDict([("Prob(E)",        probs),
                            ("Odds(E:not E)", odds),
                            ("Log-Odds",        log_odds)])
polo_df = pd.DataFrame(polo_dict, index=index)
polo_df.index.name="Pct(%)"
polo_df
```

Out[21]:

Pct(%)	Prob(E)	Odds(E:not E)	Log-Odds
0.0%	0.0000	0.0000	-inf
0.1%	0.0010	0.0010	-6.9068
1.0%	0.0100	0.0101	-4.5951
5.0%	0.0500	0.0526	-2.9444
10.0%	0.1000	0.1111	-2.1972
25.0%	0.2500	0.3333	-1.0986
33.3%	0.3333	0.5000	-0.6931
50.0%	0.5000	1.0000	0.0000
66.7%	0.6667	2.0000	0.6931
75.0%	0.7500	3.0000	1.0986
90.0%	0.9000	9.0000	2.1972
95.0%	0.9500	19.0000	2.9444
99.0%	0.9900	99.0000	4.5951
99.9%	0.9990	999.0000	6.9068
100.0%	1.0000	inf	inf

If you prefer a graphical view, let's look at the relationship between probabilities and odds (expressed as fractions):

In [22]:

```
def helper(ax,x,y,x_name,y_name):
    ax.plot(x,y, 'r--o')
    ax.set_xlabel(x_name)
    ax.set_ylabel(y_name)

# note, we trim the values above 90% [index -5] b/c
# the scale of the plots gets too compressed
# (huh, log-scale takes care of that! funny .....)
fig, (ax0, ax1) = plt.subplots(1,2, figsize=(9,3))
helper(ax0, probs[:-5], odds[:-5], 'probability', 'odds')
helper(ax1, odds[:-5], probs[:-5], 'odds', 'probability')
```

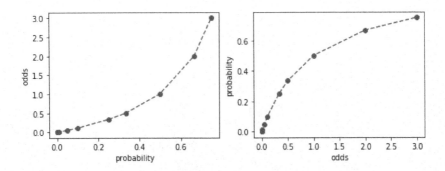

and the relationship between probabilities and log-odds:

In [23]:

```
fig, (ax0, ax1) = plt.subplots(1,2, figsize=(9,3))
helper(ax0, probs, log_odds, 'probability', 'log-odds')
helper(ax1, log_odds, probs, 'log-odds', 'probability')
```

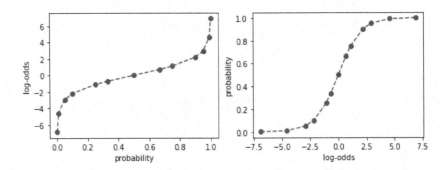

If you look at the first and last rows of the table, you can see the extreme values for each of the probabilities, odds, and log-odds. The min and max probabilities correspond with events that are either impossibilites or guarantees. Of course, we know there are rarely such things. (You can now meditate on the impossibility of impossibilities and then come back to your happy place.)

Here are the ranges of values:

In [24]:

```
pd.DataFrame([polo_df.min(axis=0),
              polo_df.max(axis=0)], index=['min', 'max']).T
```

```
Out[24]:
```

	min	max
Prob(E)	0.0000	1.0000
Odds(E:not E)	0.0000	inf
Log-Odds	-inf	inf

There are a few important points here. The ranges of our values go from $[0, 1]$ to $(0, \infty)$ to $(-\infty, \infty)$ as we move from probabilities to odds to log-odds. Now, I'm ready to drop a bombshell on you. If we predict the log-odds from our input features, logistic regression and linear regression are basically doing the same thing! I do have a weasel word, *basically*, in there because there are a few caveats.

You might recall from Section 4.3.3 our calculation for the predicted linear regression value: `predicted_value=rdot(w, x)`. For logistic regression, the equivalent calculation is `predicted_log_odds = rdot(w, x)`. And now you know why logistic regression has *regression* in its name. The mathese way to write this is $\text{LO} = \sum_{\text{ftrs}} w_f x_f$. Actually, stats folks like to write $\widehat{\text{LO}}$ with a *hat* for *predicted* or *estimated* values. But I'm going to leave that out.

In *linear* regression, we are predicting a target output value that can range anywhere from a large-magnitude negative value ($-1{,}000{,}000$ or less) to a large-magnitude positive value ($+1{,}000{,}000$ or more). Probabilities don't do that—they go from zero to one. Odds don't do that—they go from zero to large, positive values. But log-odds? Yes, they can do that! Log-odds are a version of probabilities that go from very small negative values to very large positive values. Log-odds are just the type of value that linear regression needs for a well-behaved target. We can leverage that for our devious *logistic* regression purposes.

Of course, we aren't usually satisfied by getting the log-odds. For classification problems, we want to predict the outcome class: {cat, dog} or {False, True}. So, we need a little more machinery. Let me write out the longer form of two mathematical abbreviations we are going to use. We're going to simplify things a bit and assume we are dealing with a binary classification problem—there are only two classes, so if something is *not-a-cat* it must be *dog*. We care about (1) the probability that an example belongs to a target class and (2) the log-odds that an example belong to a target class. We can write these as:

- The probability of targethood for an example x: $\text{P}(x \text{ is-a tgt}) = \text{P}_{\text{tgt}}(x)$.
- The log-odds of targethood for an example x: $\text{LO}(x \text{ is-a tgt}) = \text{LO}_{\text{tgt}}(x)$.

Think about each x that follows as *an example*. We can get away with focusing on a single target, since if something is *not* that target, then it must be the other class. We'll drop the tgt subscript and we're left with $\text{P}(x)$ and $\text{LO}(x)$. Based on our discussion of betting and our table of equivalent values, we know that we'll lean towards our chosen target when $\text{P}(x) > .5$ or $\text{LO}(x) > 0$.

We can fill in some math for our `rdot(w,x)` and write out:

$$\sum_{\text{ftrs}} w_f x_f = \text{LO}(x) = \log \frac{\text{P}(x)}{1 - \text{P}(x)} = \text{logit}\left(\text{P}(x)\right)$$

The second equality comes from the definition of the log-odds: it's the log of the odds and the odds are the inner fraction on that right-hand side. The logit is simply a name given to converting probabilities to log-odds. A probability, like $P(x)$, goes in and its log-odds, $LO(x)$, comes out. Since I love arrows, the logit takes $P(x) \rightarrow \log \frac{P(x)}{1-P(x)}$ $= LO(x)$. We actually used code for this above when we created the table of probabilities, odds, and log-odds. I'm sneaky like that. Here's what it looks like as a stand-alone function:

In [25]:

```
def logit(probs):
    odds = probs / (1-probs)
    log_odds = np.log(odds)
    return log_odds
```

We can also solve for $P(x)$ and see what happens. Note that exp and log are opposites of each other: one undoes the other. It's a little clunky to write out exp, the exponential function, like this, but it prevents confusion from too many superscripts.

$$\log \frac{P(x)}{1 - P(x)} = LO(x)$$

$$\frac{P(x)}{1 - P(x)} = \exp\left(LO(x)\right)$$

$$P(x) = \left(1 - P(x)\right) \exp\left(LO(x)\right)$$

$$P(x) = \exp\left(LO(x)\right) - P(x) \exp\left(LO(x)\right)$$

$$P(x) + P(x) \exp\left(LO(x)\right) = \exp\left(LO(x)\right)$$

$$P(x)\left(1 + \exp\left(LO(x)\right)\right) = \exp\left(LO(x)\right)$$

$$P(x) = \frac{\exp(LO(x))}{1 + \exp(LO(x))} = \text{logistic}\left(LO(x)\right) \quad \star$$

The logistic function is a special name for taking $LO(x) \rightarrow \frac{\exp(LO(x))}{1+\exp(LO(x))} = P(x)$. So now we have two functions that work in opposite directions:

- logit($P(x)$) takes us from a probability to the log-odds
- logistic($LO(x)$) takes us from log-odds to a probability

Why do we care? Because we have to make a decision. If the log-odds are greater than 0, $LO(x) > 0$, then the odds favor *tgt*. That means we're in the case when the odds are greater than one and the probability is greater than 50%. If the log-odds are less than 0, $LO(x) < 0$, the odds favor the other of the two targets, *not-tgt* or $\neg tgt$. That means that when $LO(x) = 0$, we are at the boundary between the two. That boundary is precisely

$$\sum_{\text{ftrs}} w_f x_f = LO(x) = 0$$

When that left-hand sum—a dot product—is zero, we are essentially at a loss to pick between *tgt* and $\neg tgt$.

8.4.3 Just Do It: Logistic Regression Edition

sklearn has several methods for performing logistic regression. We call them through LogisticRegression and SGDClassifier. In Section 4.4, we talked about four ways of picking a "preferred" set of parameters. The methods used by sklearn for logistic regression are smart step methods: from a starting point, make some adjustments, and repeat as necessary until the answer is *good enough*. SGD stands for *Stochastic Gradient Descent* and it is one way of performing smart steps. It makes its adjustments by looking at the errors in the current guess and using those to lower the error of the next guess. We tell SGDClassifier to use a *log-loss* model of the errors which gives us logistic-regression-like behavior. Other losses lead to other classification methods which we'll see in Chapter 15. SGDClassifier can handle very large problems, but it takes multiple iterations to do so and, because of its internal use of randomness, every run may result in a different answer. With enough data and small enough error tolerance, SGDClassifier should reach, or converge to, similar answers on different runs.

The other logistic regression method we'll use is LogisticRegression with method='saga'. I'll save futher discussion of saga for the end notes—but briefly, saga allows us to use a full multiclass model instead of wrapping a binary classification with a one-versus-rest.

In [26]:
```
# Both options come with "regularization" turned ON
# we'll ignore that for now, but see Chapter 9 for more details
LogReg = linear_model.LogisticRegression
SGD    = linear_model.SGDClassifier
logreg_classifiers = {'LogReg(saga)': LogReg(solver='saga',
                                             multi_class='multinomial',
                                             max_iter=1000),
                      'LogReg(SGD)' :  SGD(loss='log', max_iter=1000)}

fig, axes = plt.subplots(1,2,figsize=(12,4))
axes = axes.flat
for (name, mod), ax in zip(logreg_classifiers.items(), axes):
    plot_boundary(ax, iris.data, iris.target, mod, [0,1])
    ax.set_title(name)
plt.tight_layout()
```

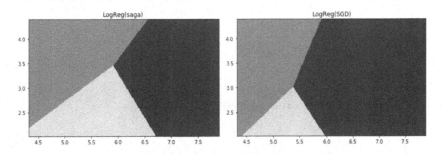

8.4.4   A Logistic Regression: A Space Oddity

Here's an oddity of logistic regression: if all the data falls nicely into two clusters, then there is an infinite number of lines we can draw between the clusters. Logistic regression doesn't have a built-in answer to picking one of these infinite alternatives. Trying to solve a perfectly separable classification problem with logistic regression may lead to problematic answers. Fortunately, (1) those problems are more serious for statisticians than they are for us using logistic regression as a black-box prediction method and (2) for practical purposes in interesting problems, we will never have perfectly separable data. Still, here's an example of the issue.

In [27]:

```
fig, ax = plt.subplots(1,1,figsize=(4,1))

x = np.array([1,2,5,10]).reshape(-1, 1)
y = ['red', 'blue', 'red', 'blue']
ax.scatter(x,np.zeros_like(x), c=y);
```

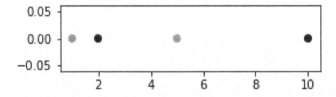

This is a typical scenario: the two classes are intertwined. We'll use a non-`sklearn` method to perform logistic regression. This method is a bit old-school, but it will expose our issue clearly.

In [28]:

```
import statsmodels.formula.api as sm

x = np.c_[x, np.ones_like(x)] # +1 trick
tgt = (np.array(y) == 'red')

# sm.Logit is statsmodels name for logistic regression
(sm.Logit(tgt, x, method='newton')
  .fit()
  .predict(x)) # training predictions
```

```
Optimization terminated successfully.
         Current function value: 0.595215
         Iterations 5
```

```
Out[28]:

array([0.7183, 0.6583, 0.4537, 0.1697])
```

Everything seems pretty well behaved, so far. Now, look what happens with a seemingly minor change to the data.

```
In [29]:

fig, ax = plt.subplots(1,1,figsize=(4,1))

x = np.array([1,4,6,10]).reshape(-1, 1)
y = ['red', 'red', 'blue', 'blue']
ax.scatter(x, np.zeros_like(x), c=y);
```

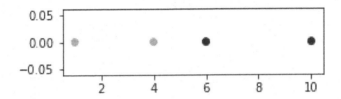

```
In [30]:

x = np.c_[x, np.ones_like(x)] # +1 trick
tgt = (np.array(y) == 'red')
try:
    sm.Logit(tgt, x, method='newton').fit().predict(x) # in-sample predictions
except Exception as e:
    print(e)
```

```
Perfect separation detected, results not available
```

Surprisingly, `Logit` refuses to solve the problem for us. It warns us that there was perfect separation between the classes and there are no results to use. It seems like drawing the perfect line would be easy. It isn't. The problem is that there is an infinite number of lines that we could draw and our old-school logistic regression doesn't have a built-in way to pick between them. In turn, some methods don't do well with that uncertainty and can give very bad answers. Hence, `Logit` stops with a *fail*.

8.5 Discriminant Analysis

There is a group of classifiers, coming from the field of statistics, that we will broadly call *discriminant analysis* (DA) methods. Here, discriminant is used in the sense of "Gloria has a very discriminating palate": she can tell subtle differences in flavors. We are hoping to find subtle differences that will allow us to classify things.

DA methods are very interesting for at least three reasons:

1. They have a wonderfully clear mathematical connection with Naive Bayes on continuous features (Gaussian Naive Bayes, GNB).
2. Like GNB, discriminant analysis methods model the features and the target *together*.
3. DA methods arise from particularly simple — or perhaps mathematically convenient — assumptions about the data. The different DA methods make slightly different assumptions.

Without going into great mathematical detail, we will discuss four different DA methods. I won't introduce them by name, yet. Each of these methods works by making *assumptions* about the *true* nature of the data. *Those assumptions could be wrong!* Every method we use makes assumptions of one kind or another. However, DA methods make a specific set of stronger and stronger assumptions about the relationships between the features and their relationship to the target. We'll talk about these as a group of friends. Suppose there are three friends: Feature One, Feature Two, and Class. They don't always talk to each other as much as they'd like to, so they don't know as much about each other as they'd like. Here are the sorts of assumptions these methods make:

1. Features One and Two talk to each other. They care what Class has to say.
2. Features One and Two talk to each other. They don't care what Class has to say.
3. Feature One doesn't talk to Feature Two *directly*. Anything Feature One knows comes from talking to Class. That knowledge, in turn, *might* give some information — gossip — about Feature Two.
4. We can combine 2 and 3: Feature One doesn't talk directly to Feature Two *nor* does it care what Class has to say.

In fact, these assumptions aren't just about the communication between Feature One and Feature Two. They are about the communication between *all pairs* of features: $\{\text{Ftr}_i, \text{Ftr}_j\}$.

These assumptions lead to different models. Make no mistake: we can *assume* any of these scenarios and build a model of our data that relies on its assumptions. It might work out; it might not. We might have perfect knowledge that leads us to choose one of these sets of assumptions correctly. If so, we'd expect it to work better than the others. Short of omniscience, we can try each set of assumptions. Practically, that means we fit several different DA models, cross-validate, and see which performs the best. Then we assess on a hold-out set to make sure we haven't misled ourselves.

8.5.1   Covariance

To understand the differences between the DA methods, you need to know about *covariance*. Covariance describes one way in which the features are related — or not — to each other. For example, if we are looking at physiological data on medical patients, our models might make good use of the fact that height and weight have a strong relationship. The covariance encodes the different ways features may metaphorically communicate with each other.

A quick point: in this section and this chapter, we are talking about the use of covariance as an internal widget of a learning machine. Different constraints on covariance lead to different learning machines. On the other hand, you might be familiar with the difficulties some models have when features are *too* closely related. We are not addressing those issues here; we'll talk about it when we discuss feature selection in Section 13.1.

We'll start our discussion by talking about *variance*. If you remember our discussions in Chapter 2, you'll recall that the variance is the *sum of squared errors* of a model that predicts the mean value. You might even be able to come up with an equation for that. Before you scramble for pencil and paper, for a feature X that formula looks like:

$$\text{Var}(X) = \frac{1}{n} \sum_{x \in X} (x - \bar{X})^2$$

Remember that $\bar{X} = \frac{1}{n} \sum x$ is the mean of the set of data X. This formula is what I will call the *common* formula for variance. (Footnote: I'm ignoring the difference between variance of a random variable, variance of a population, and variance of a finite sample. If you are uneasy, take a deep breath and check out the End-of-Chapter Notes.) You might recognize a dot product in the formula for variance: `var_X = dot(x-mean_X, x-mean_X) / n`. If we write the variance out as code for the sum of squared errors from the mean, it might be even more familiar.

```
In [31]:
X = np.array([1,3,5,10,20])
n = len(X)

mean_X = sum(X) / n
errors = X - mean_X
var_X = np.dot(errors, errors) / n

fmt = "long way: {}\nbuilt in: {}\n   close: {}"
print(fmt.format(var_X,
                 np.var(X),
                 np.allclose(var_X, np.var(X)))) # phew
```

```
long way: 46.16
built in: 46.16
   close: True
```

8.5.1.1 The Classic Approach

Now, if we have two variables, we don't get quite the same easy verbal phrasing of comparing with a mean model. Still, if I said that we take *two* models that predict the means for the two variables and *multiply* them together, you might come up with something like:

$$\text{Cov}(X, Y) = \frac{1}{n} \sum_{\substack{x \in X \\ y \in Y}} (x - \bar{X})(y - \bar{Y})$$

I apologize for using X and Y as two potential features. I'd use subscripts, but they are easily lost in the shuffle. I'm only going to do that in this section. In code, that turns into:

In [32]:

```
X = np.array([1,3,5,10,20])
Y = np.array([2,4,1,-2,12])

mean_X = sum(X) / n
mean_Y = sum(Y) / n

errors_X = X - mean_X
errors_Y = Y - mean_Y

cov_XY = np.dot(errors_X, errors_Y) / n
print("long way: {:5.2f}".format(cov_XY))
print("built in:", np.cov(X,Y,bias=True)[0,1])
# note:
# np.cov(X,Y,bias=True) gives [Cov(X,X), Cov(X,Y)
#                              Cov(Y,X), Cov(Y,Y)]
```

```
long way: 21.28
built in: 21.28
```

Now, what happens if we ask about the covariance of a feature with itself? That means we can set $Y = X$, filling in X for Y, and we get:

$$\text{Cov}(X, X) = \frac{1}{n} \sum_{x \in X} (x - \bar{X})(x - \bar{X}) = \frac{1}{n} \sum_{x \in X} (x - \bar{X})^2 = \text{Var}(X)$$

That's all well and good, but we've gotten pretty far off the track of giving you some *intuition* about what happens here. Since the variance is a sum of squares, we know it is a sum of positive values because squaring individual positive or negative numbers always results in positives. Adding many positive numbers also gives us a positive number. So, the variance is always positive (strictly speaking, it can also be zero). The covariance is a bit different. The individual terms in the covariance sum will be positive if *both* x and y are greater than their means *or* if *both* x and y are less than their means (Figure 8.6). If they are on different sides of their means (say, $x > \bar{X}$ and $y < \bar{Y}$), the sign of *that term* will be negative. Overall, we could have a bunch of negative terms or a bunch of positive terms or a mix of the two. The overall covariance could be positive or negative, close to zero or far away.

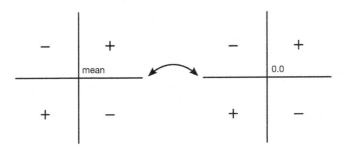

Figure 8.6   The quadrants around the mean are the like quadrants around (0, 0).

8.5.1.2   An Alternative Approach

What I've said so far isn't too different than what you'd see in a statistics textbook. That's not bad, but I love alternative approaches. There is a different, but equivalent, formula for the covariance. The alternative form can give us some insight into what the covariance represents. Basically, we'll take all the unique pairs of X values, compute the difference between them, and square them. Then, we'll add those values up. For the variance, that process looks like

In [33]:

```
var_x = 0
n = len(X)
for i in range(n):
    for j in range(i, n): # rest of Xs
        var_x += (X[i] - X[j])**2
print("Var(X):", var_x / n**2)
```

Var(X): 46.16

The value we calculated is the same as the one we got earlier. That's great. But you might notice some ugliness in the Python code: we used indexing to access the X[i] values. We didn't use direct iteration over X. We'll fix that in a minute.

Here's the equivalent snippet for covariance. We'll take X and Y values for each pair of features and do a similar computation. We take the differences and multiply them; then we add up all of those terms.

In [34]:

```
cov_xy = 0
for i in range(len(X)):
    for j in range(i, len(X)): # rest of Xs, Ys
        cov_xy += (X[i] - X[j])*(Y[i]-Y[j])
print("Cov(X,Y):", cov_xy / n**2)
```

Cov(X,Y): 21.28

Again, we get the same answer—although the Python code is still hideously relying on range and [i] indexing. Give me one more second on that.

Let's look at the *formulas* for these alternate forms of the covariance. They assume we keep our X and Y values in order and use subscripts to access them—just like we did with the code above. This subscripting is very common in mathematics as well as in languages like C and Fortran. It is less common in well-written Python.

$$\text{Var}(X) = \frac{1}{n^2} \sum_i \sum_{j>i} (x_i - x_j)^2$$

$$\text{Cov}(X,Y) = \frac{1}{n^2} \sum_i \sum_{j>i} (x_i - x_j)(y_i - y_j)$$

$$= \frac{1}{2n^2} \sum_{i,j} (x_i - x_j)(y_i - y_j) \quad \star$$

I wrote the Python code to most directly replicate these equations. If you look at the subscripts, you notice that they are trying to avoid each other. The purpose of $j > i$ is to say, "I want *different* pairs of xs and ys." I don't want to double-count things. When we take that out (in the last ⋆ed equation), we *do* double-count in the sum so we have to *divide by two* to get back to the correct answer. The benefit of that last form is that we can simply add up over *all* the pairs of xs and then fix up the result. There is a cost, though: we are adding in things we will just discard momentarily. Don't worry, we'll fix that too.

For the last equation, the Python code is much cleaner:

In [35]:

```
cov_XY = 0.0
xy_pairs = it.product(zip(X,Y), repeat=2)
for (x_i, y_i), (x_j, y_j) in xy_pairs:
    cov_XY += (x_i - x_j) * (y_i - y_j)
print("Cov(X,Y):", cov_XY / (2 * n**2))
```

Cov(X,Y): 21.28

We can do even better. it.product takes the complete element-by-element pairing of all the zip(X,Y) pairs. (Yes, that's pairs of pairs.) it.combinations can ensure we use one, and only one, copy of each pair against another. Doing this saves us $\frac{1}{2}$ of the repetitions through our loop. Win! So here, we don't have to divide by two.

In [36]:

```
cov_XX = 0.0
for x_i, x_j in it.combinations(X, 2):
    cov_XX += (x_i - x_j)**2
print("Cov(X,X) == Var(X):", cov_XX / (n**2))
```

Cov(X,X) == Var(X): 46.16

```
In [37]:

cov_XY = 0.0
for (x_i, y_i), (x_j,y_j) in it.combinations(zip(X,Y), 2):
    cov_XY += (x_i - x_j) * (y_i - y_j)
print("Cov(X,Y):", cov_XY / (n**2))
```

```
Cov(X,Y): 21.28
```

Back to the last equation: $\frac{1}{2n^2} \sum_{i,j}(x_i - x_j)(y_i - y_j)$. Using this form, we get a very nice way to interpret covariance. Can you think of a simple calculation that takes xs and ys, subtracts them, and multiplies them? I'll grab a sip of water while you think about it. Here's a hint: subtracting values can often be interpreted as a *distance*: from mile marker 5 to mile marker 10 is $10 - 5 = 5$ miles.

OK, time's up. Let me rewrite the equation by ignoring the leading fraction for a moment: $\text{Cov}(X, Y) = c_{\text{magic}} \sum_{ij}(x_i - x_j)(y_i - y_j)$. If you've been following along, once again, we have an ever-present dot product. It has a very nice interpretation. If I have a rectangle defined by two points, $\{x_i, y_i\}$ and $\{x_j, y_j\}$, I can get length $= x_i - x_j$ and height $= y_i - y_j$. From these, I can get the area $=$ length $\times$ height $= (x_i - x_j)(y_i - y_j)$. So, if we ignore c_{magic}, the covariance is simply a *sum of areas of rectangles* or a *sum product of distances*. That's not so bad, is it? The covariance is very closely related to the sum of areas created by looking at each pair of points as corners of a rectangle.

We saw c_{magic} earlier, so we can deal with the last pain point. Let's rip the bandage off quickly: c_{magic} is $\frac{1}{2n^2}$. If there were n terms being added up and we had $\frac{1}{n}$, we'd be happy talking about the *average* area. In fact, that's what we have here. The squared value, $\frac{1}{n^2}$, comes from the double summation. Looping i from 1 to n and j from 1 to n means we have n^2 total pieces. Averaging means we need to divide by n^2. The $\frac{1}{2}$ comes from not wanting to double-count rectangles.

If we include $c_{\text{magic}} = \frac{1}{2n^2}$, the covariance is simply the average area of the rectangles defined by all pairs of points. The area is *signed*, it has a $+$ or a $-$, depending on whether the line connecting the points is pointed up or down as it moves left-to-right—the same pattern we saw in Figure 8.6. If the idea of a *signed area*—an area with a sign attached to it—is making you scratch your head, you're in good company. We'll dive into this more with examples and graphics in the following section.

8.5.1.3 Visualizing Covariance

Let's visualize what is going on with these rectangle areas and covariances. If we can think of covariance as areas of rectangles, let's *draw* these rectangles. We'll use a simple example with three data points and two features. We'll draw the diagonal of each of the three rectangles and we'll color in the total contributions at each region of the grid. Red indicates a positive overall covariance; blue indicates a negative covariance. Darker colors indicate more covariance in either the positive or negative direction: lighter colors, leading to white, indicate a lack of covariance. Our technique to get the coloring right is to (1) build a NumPy `array` with the proper values and (2) use matplotlib's `matshow`, matrix show, to display that matrix.

We have a few helpers for "drawing" the rectangles. I use scare-quotes because we are *really* filling in values in an array. Later, we'll use that array for the actual drawing.

In [38]:

```
# color coding
# -inf -> 0; 0 -> .5; inf -> 1
# slowly at the tails; quickly in the middle (near 0)
def sigmoid(x):
    return np.exp(-np.logaddexp(0, -x))


# to get the colors we need, we have to build a raw array
# with the correct values; we are really "drawing"
# inside a numpy array, not on the screen
def draw_rectangle(arr, pt1, pt2):
    (x1,y1),(x2,y2) = pt1,pt2
    delta_x, delta_y = x2-x1, y2-y1
    r,c = min(y1,y2), min(x1,x2)   # x,y -> r,c
    # assign +/- 1 to each block in the rectangle.
    # total summation value equals area of rectangle (signed for up/down)
    arr[r:r+abs(delta_y),
        c:c+abs(delta_x)] += np.sign(delta_x * delta_y)
```

Now, we'll create our three data points and "draw"—fill in the array—the three rectangles that the points define:

In [39]:

```
# our data points:
pts = [(1,1), (3,6), (6,3)]
pt_array = np.array(pts, dtype=np.float64)


# the array we are "drawing" on:
draw_arr = np.zeros((10,10))
ct = len(pts)
c_magic = 1 / ct**2 # without double counting


# we use the clever don't-double-count method
for pt1, pt2 in it.combinations(pts, 2):
    draw_rectangle(draw_arr, pt1, pt2)
draw_arr *= c_magic
```

In [40]:

```
# display the array we drew
from matplotlib import cm
fig, ax = plt.subplots(1,1,figsize=(4,3))
```

```
ax.matshow(sigmoid(draw_arr), origin='lower', cmap=cm.bwr, vmin=0, vmax=1)
fig.tight_layout()

# show a diagonal across each rectangles
# the array elements are centered in each grid square
ax.plot([ .5, 2.5],[ .5, 5.5], 'r')  # from 1,1 to 3,6
ax.plot([ .5, 5.5],[ .5, 2.5], 'r')  # from 1,1 to 6,3
ax.plot([2.5, 5.5],[5.5, 2.5], 'b'); # from 3,6 to 6,3
```

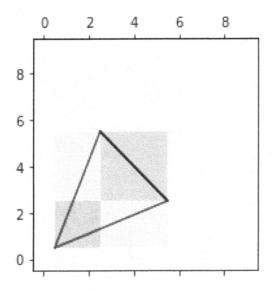

That graphic represents three datapoints defined by two features each.

```
In [41]:

np_cov = np.cov(pt_array[:,0], pt_array[:,1], bias=True)[0,1]
print("Cov(x,y) -    from numpy: {:4.2f}".format(np_cov))

# show the covariance, as calculated from our drawing
print("Cov(x,y) - our long way: {:4.2f}".format(draw_arr.sum()))
```

```
Cov(x,y) -    from numpy: 1.22
Cov(x,y) - our long way: 1.22
```

In the diagram, red indicates a *positive* relationship between two data points: as x goes up, y goes up. Note that if I flip the points and draw the line backwards, this is the same as saying as x goes down, y goes down. In either case, the *sign* of the terms is the same. Reds contribute to a positive covariance. On the other hand, blues indicate an opposing relationship between x and y: x up, y down or x down, y up. Finally, the intensity of the color indicates the strength of the positive or negative relationship for the two points that define that rectangle. The total covariance for the pair of points is divided equally among the squares of the rectangle. To get the final color, we add up all the contributions we've gotten along the way. Dark red is a big positive contribution, light blue is a small negative contribution, and pure white is a zero contribution. Finally, we divide by the number of points squared.

Here's what the raw numbers look like. The value in a grid square is precisely what controls the color in that grid square.

In [42]:

```
plt.figure(figsize=(4.5,4.5))
hm = sns.heatmap(draw_arr, center=0,
                 square=True, annot=True,
                 cmap='bwr', fmt=".1f")
hm.invert_yaxis()
hm.tick_params(bottom=False, left=False)
```

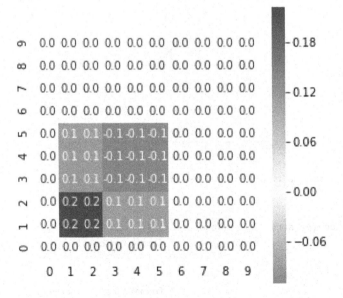

Our discussion has been limited to the covariance between two features: X and Y. In our datasets, we might have many features—$X, Y, Z, \ldots$—so we can have covariances between all pairs of features: $\mathrm{Cov}(X, Y)$, $\mathrm{Cov}(X, Z)$, $\mathrm{Cov}(Y, Z)$, and so on. Here's an important point: the covariance formula for two features we used above relied on calculations between pairs of data points $\{(x_1, y_1), (x_2, y_2)\}$ for those two features. When we talk about *all* the covariances, we are talking about the relationships between all pairs of features and we need to record them in a table of some sort. That table is called a *covariance matrix*. Don't be scared. It is simply a table listing the covariances—the average sums of rectangle areas—between different pairs of variables. The covariance between X and Y is the same as the covariance between Y and X, so the table is going to have repeated entries.

Here's an example that has relatively little *structure* in the data. What do I mean by structure? When we look at the covariance matrix, there aren't too many patterns in it. But there is one. I'll let you find it.

In [43]:

```
data = pd.DataFrame({'X':[ 1, 3, 6],
                     'Y':[ 1, 6, 3],
                     'Z':[10, 5, 1]})
data.index.name = 'examples'

# it's not critical to these examples, but Pandas' cov is
# "unbiased" and we've been working with "biased" covariance
# see EOC notes for details
display(data)
print("Covariance:")
display(data.cov())
```

examples	X	Y	Z
0	1	1	10
1	3	6	5
2	6	3	1

Covariance:

	X	Y	Z
X	6.3333	1.8333	-11.1667
Y	1.8333	6.3333	-5.1667
Z	-11.1667	-5.1667	20.3333

I'll talk about the values in that matrix with respect to the main diagonal—the 6.3, 6.3, and 20.3 values. (Yes, there are two diagonals. The "main" diagonal we care about is the one running from top-left to bottom-right.)

You may have noticed two things. First, the elements are mirrored across the main diagonal. For example, the top-right and bottom-left values are the *same* (−11.1667). That is not a coincidence; *all* covariance matrices are *symmetric* because, as I pointed out above, $\mathrm{Cov}(X, Y) = \mathrm{Cov}(Y, X)$ for all pairs of features. Second, you may have picked up on the fact that both X and Y have the *same* variance. It shows up here as $\mathrm{Cov}(X, X)$ and $\mathrm{Cov}(Y, Y)$.

Now, imagine that our different features are not directionally related to each other. There's no set pattern: as one goes up, the other can either go up *or* down. We might be trying to relate three measurements that we really don't expect to be related at all: height, SAT scores, and love of abstract art. We get something like this:

In [44]:

```
data = pd.DataFrame({'x':[ 3, 6, 3, 4],
                     'y':[ 9, 6, 3, 0],
                     'z':[ 1, 4, 7, 0]})
data.index.name = 'examples'
display(data)
print("Covariance:")
display(data.cov()) # biased covariance, see EOC
```

	x	y	z
examples			
0	3	9	1
1	6	6	4
2	3	3	7
3	4	0	0

Covariance:

	x	y	z
x	2.0000	0.0000	0.0000
y	0.0000	15.0000	0.0000
z	0.0000	0.0000	10.0000

The data numbers don't *look* so special, but that's a weird covariance matrix. What's going on here? Let's plot the data values:

In [45]:

```
fig, ax = plt.subplots(1,1,figsize=(4,3))
data.plot(ax=ax)
ax.vlines([0,1,2,3], 0, 10, colors=".5")

ax.legend(loc='lower center', ncol=3)

plt.box(False)
ax.set_xticks([0,1,2,3])
ax.set_ylabel("values");
```

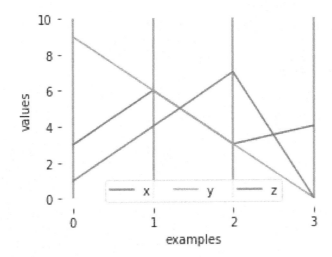

We see that we never get a *consistent* pattern. It is not as simple as "if X goes up, Y goes up." We also don't see any consistency between X and Z or Y and Z—there's no simple pattern of "you go up, I go down." There's always some segment where it goes the other way. For example, blue and green go up together in segment one, but work against each other in segments two and three. I constructed the data so that not only are the covariances low, they cancel out more or less exactly: all of the off-diagonal covariances in the matrix are zero. The only non-zero entries are on the *diagonal* of the table. We call this a *diagonal covariance matrix*. X, Y, and Z all have their *own* variance, but they have no pairwise covariance. If their own variances were zero, that would mean that the *sum of rectangle sizes* was zero. That only happens if all the values are the same. For example, with $x_1 = x_2 = x_3 = 42.314$, the not-quite-a-rectangle we construct from these xs would be a single point with no length or width.

All of this discussion has been about one covariance matrix. In a few minutes, we'll take about how that matrix influences our DA methods. But we can't always rely on one matrix to carry all of the information we need. If we have multiple classes, you can imagine two scenarios: one where there is a single covariance matrix that is the same for every class—that is, one covariance is enough to describe everything. The second case is where we need a different covariance matrix for each class. We'll ignore middle grounds and either have one matrix overall or have one for each class.

Let's summarize what we've learned about the covariance. In one interpretation, the covariance simply averages the sizes of pairwise rectangles constructed from two features. Bigger rectangles mean bigger values. If the rectangle is built by moving up-and-right, its value is positive. If a pair of features moves essentially independently of each other—any coordinated increase is always offset by a corresponding decrease—their covariance is zero.

8.5.2 The Methods

Now, we are equipped to talk about the differences between the four variations of discriminant analysis (DA): QDA, LDA, GNB, and DLDA. Q stands for quadratic, L stands for linear, DL stands for diagonal linear, and GNB is our old friend Gaussian Naive Bayes . . . that's Naive Bayes on smoothly valued features. These techniques make different *assumptions* about the covariances—the average rectangle sizes we dove into above.

1. QDA *assumes* that the covariances between different features are *unconstrained*. There can be class-wise differences between the covariance matrices.
2. LDA adds a constraint. It says that the covariances between features are all *the same* regardless of the *target classes*. To put it another way, LDA assumes that regardless of target class, the same covariance matrix does a good job describing the data. The entries in that single matrix are unconstrained.
3. GNB *assumes* something slightly different: it says that the covariances between *distinct* features—for example, Feature One and Feature Two—are all zero. The covariance matrices have entries on their main diagonal and zeros *everywhere else*. As a technical note, GNB really assumes that pairs of features are independent within that class—which implies, or leads to, a Feature One versus Feature Two covariance of zero. There may be different matrices for each different target class.
4. DLDA combines LDA and GNB: the covariances are *assumed* to be the same for each class—there's only one covariance matrix—*and* $\text{Cov}(X, Y)$ is zero between pairs of nonidentical features ($X \neq Y$).

I really emphasized the role of the assumptions in this process. Hopefully, it is clear: it is an assumption of the method, *not necessarily* the state of the world that produced the data. Do you have that all straight? No? That's OK. Here's a faster run through of the assumptions:

1. QDA: possibly different covariance matrices per class,
2. LDA: same covariance matrix for all classes,
3. GNB: different diagonal covariance matrices per class, and
4. DLDA: same diagonal covariance matrix for all classes.

Let's make the idea of *classwise covariance matrices* and *different covariance matrices per class* concrete. Suppose I have a simple table of data with measurements on cats and dogs. The target class is whether we have a cat or dog. The features are length and weight. You can probably come up with two different ways to calculate the *variance* of the weights: either calculate the variance over *all* of the pets at once or calculate the variance over the cats and dogs *separately* so we keep track of two values. Calculating over *all* is similar to what we do with covariance in LDA and DLDA. Calculating separately per cats and dogs is what we do with covariance QDA and GNB. That is, in LDA and DLDA we would calculate the covariance of length and weight over cats and dogs *together*; in QDA and GNB, we would calculate the covariances *separately* for each pet type.

Here's a summary Table 8.1, with some mathese for those that are so inclined.

Table 8.1 Summary of discriminant analysis methods and assumptions. Σ is a covariance matrix (CM). Σ_c is a covariance matrix for a class c.

Abbreviation	Name	Assumptions	Description
QDA	Quadratic Discriminant Analysis	any Σ_c	per class, arbitrary CM
LDA	Linear Discriminant Analysis	$\Sigma_c = \Sigma$	shared, arbitrary CM
GNB	Gaussian Naive Bayes	$\Sigma_c = \text{diag}_c$	per class, diagonal CM
DLDA	Diagonal LDA	$\Sigma_c = \text{diag}$	shared, diagonal CM

8.5.3 Performing DA

So, let's look at the operation of the DA methods. We'll do a simple train-test split and look at the confusion matrices from each of the four methods.

```
In [46]:

qda  = discriminant_analysis.QuadraticDiscriminantAnalysis()
lda  = discriminant_analysis.LinearDiscriminantAnalysis()
nb   = naive_bayes.GaussianNB()
dlda = DLDA() # from mlwpy.py

da_methods = [qda, lda, nb, dlda]
names = ["QDA", "LDA", "NB", "DLDA"]

fig, axes = plt.subplots(2,2, figsize=(4.5, 4.5),
                         sharex=True, sharey = True)
for ax, model, name in zip(axes.flat, da_methods, names):
    preds = (model.fit(iris_train_ftrs, iris_train_tgt)
                  .predict(iris_test_ftrs))
    cm = metrics.confusion_matrix(iris_test_tgt, preds)
    sns.heatmap(cm, annot=True, cbar=False, ax=ax)
    ax.set_title(name)

axes[0,0].set_ylabel('Actual')
axes[1,0].set_xlabel('Predicted');
```

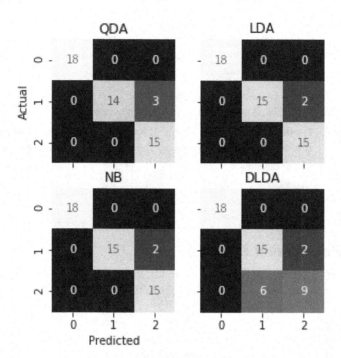

We should be wary of reading too much into the differences here because they are not substantial. However, there seems to be something to LDA as a sweet spot of the assumptions—based on Occam's razor, we make the *fewest* assumptions that get the job done. There's a bit of variation in the results when you rerun with multiple train-test splits, so I would never recommend hard-selling the success of LDA here. However, in a larger problem, it would be worthwhile to explore it in more detail. Let's look at the borders these methods create.

In [47]:

```
fig, axes = plt.subplots(2,2,figsize=(4.5, 4.5))
axes = axes.flat

for model, ax, name in zip(da_methods, axes, names):
    # plot boundary only uses the specified (two) dimensions to predict
    plot_boundary(ax, iris.data, iris.target, model, [0,1])
    ax.set_title(name)
plt.tight_layout()
```

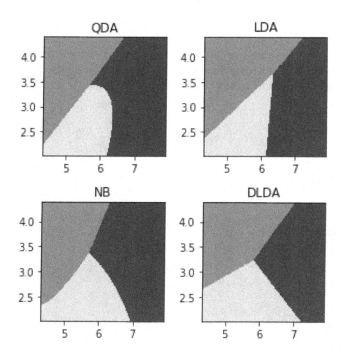

Both QDA and GNB have nonlinear boundaries—they curve a bit. LDA and DLDA both have linear borders between the classes.

8.6 Assumptions, Biases, and Classifiers

Before we get to our grand-finale comparison of classifiers, I want to pull together some thoughts on the differences between the classification methods we've seen so far.

One issue we haven't discussed yet is that of *linearity*. That's a technical term, but you can probably see its root: *line*. That means that in two dimensions, such as on a usual *xy*-graph, we can draw a line and break the plane of that graph into two halves: above/below or perhaps left/right of the line. The idea also applies in higher dimensions. We can split a 3D space with a 2D thing: a plane. We can repeat that same process in higher and higher dimensions—even when we can't really draw or conceive of these things with our intuition. The line, the plane, and their higher-dimension cousins are all *linear forms* in a specific mathematical sense. They are simple, straight ahead, without wiggles.

What if we *need* wiggles? Perhaps we know we need a model with a curve, a parabola, or a circle? These forms take us to the realm of *nonlinear* techniques. We've actually seen a few nonlinear techniques, I just haven't made a big deal about them. Nearest neighbors and decision trees can both capture relationships that are more wiggly than linear forms allow. Many, even most, other techniques can be extended naturally to deal with nonlinear data: linear regression, logistic regression, and SVCs. You are well justified if you want to run and hide when mathematicians say *naturally*. In this case, *naturally* means that we replace the notion of similarity rooted in the covariance matrix with another called a *kernel*. We'll discuss kernels in detail in Section 13.2.

We moved from a very unbiased classifier—decision trees—through a variety of classifiers that make primarily linear borders (although GNB and QDA allow curved boundaries). Here's how DTs and SVCs treat a simple example (is $y > x$):

In [48]:

```
ftrs = np.mgrid[1:10, 1:10].T.reshape(-1,2)
tgt  = ftrs[:,0] > ftrs[:,1]


fig, axes = plt.subplots(1,3,figsize=(9,3))
axes = axes.flat


svc = svm.SVC(kernel='linear')
dt_shallow = tree.DecisionTreeClassifier(max_depth=3)
dt_deep    = tree.DecisionTreeClassifier()
models = [svc, dt_shallow, dt_deep]

for model, ax in zip(models, axes):
    # plot boundary only uses the specified (two) dimensions to predict
    plot_boundary(ax, ftrs, tgt, model, [0,1])
    ax.set_title(get_model_name(model))
plt.tight_layout()
```

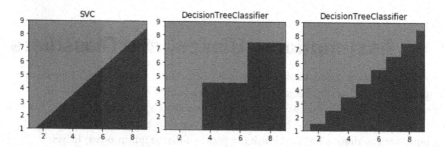

The first decision tree is hampered by the fact that we only allowed it to make a few splits in the middle pane. As we let it ask more and more questions—`max_depth` gets larger—it staircases its way to heaven. If we had sufficient data, that would look more and more like a straight line with the step heights getting really, really tiny.

Unlike logistic regression and the various discriminant analysis methods, SVCs don't have any underlying notion of probability built into them. This does not make SVCs any better or any worse than DAs: it makes them *different*. If some data happens to fall nicely into the feature-wise independence assumption—that's the diagonal covariance matrix—of GNB, then yes, GNB is going to be a win. Unfortunately, we almost never *know* ahead of time what assumptions will hold. Instead, what we do is apply a modeling method, like GNB, that comes with some assumptions; the better the assumptions line up with reality, the better the method will do on that problem. But there are just as many problems out there where those assumptions are not met. If the assumptions are met, we'd prefer GNB and we'd probably see it perform better classification. If those assumptions are not met, we can fall back to SVC. From a certain perspective, SVCs make the fewest assumptions of these three models (the DA methods, logistic regression, and SVCs), so they are the most flexible. However, that means that the other methods may do better when the assumptions *are* met.

As we move from SVCs to logistic regression to DA, we move from (1) minimal assumptions about the data to (2) a primitive data model that relates features and targets to (3) varying degrees of assumptions about how the features are distributed, their relationships to the target, and the base rates of the targets. Logistic regression attempts to capture the relationship between the inputs and the output. In particular, it captures the probability of the output given what we know about the inputs. However, it ignores any self-contained information from the target class. For example, it would ignore knowledge from the data that a particular disease is very, very rare. In contrast, the discriminant analysis methods model both a relationship between inputs and outputs *and* the base probabilities of the outputs. In particular, they capture the probability of the inputs given what we know about an output *and* (2) stand-alone information about the output. Weird, right? I'm intentionally being a bit vague about these relationships, but you can check the notes at the end of the chapter for some hints about what's happening.

8.7 Comparison of Classifiers: Take Three

With significant new tools in our classification toolbox, let's attack a problem that's a bit more difficult than the irises.

8.7.1 Digits

Here we're going to make use of the *digits* dataset that ships with `sklearn`.

In [49]:

```
digits = datasets.load_digits()
```

The data represents simple images of handwritten digits. For example, the first digit is

In [50]:

```
print("Shape:", digits.images[0].shape)
plt.figure(figsize=(3,3))
plt.imshow(digits.images[0], cmap='gray');
```

Shape: (8, 8)

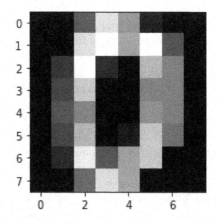

and it has a target value of

```
In [51]:
```

```
digits.target[0]
```

```
Out[51]:
```

```
0
```

The dataset comes in two forms. One (`digits.images`) is appropriate for display purposes; I used it just above. The other (`digits.data`) is appropriate for use in learning. That form is a flattened row of the information in the square 64×64 images.

Now we can construct our learning problem.

```
In [52]:
```

```
classifier_parade = \
    {'LogReg(1)' : linear_model.LogisticRegression(max_iter=1000),
     'LogReg(2)' : linear_model.SGDClassifier(loss='log',
                                              max_iter=1000),

     'QDA' : discriminant_analysis.QuadraticDiscriminantAnalysis(),
     'LDA' : discriminant_analysis.LinearDiscriminantAnalysis(),
     'GNB' : naive_bayes.GaussianNB(),

     'SVC(1)' : svm.SVC(kernel="linear"),
     'SVC(2)' : svm.LinearSVC(),

     'DTC' : tree.DecisionTreeClassifier(),
     '5NN-C' : neighbors.KNeighborsClassifier(),
     '10NN-C' : neighbors.KNeighborsClassifier(n_neighbors=10)}
```

```
baseline = dummy.DummyClassifier(strategy="uniform")

base_score = skms.cross_val_score(baseline,
                                  digits.data, digits.target==1,
                                  cv=10,
                                  scoring='average_precision',
                                  n_jobs=-1)
```

We evaluate our solutions with cross-validation on the *digits* dataset.

In [53]:

```
fig, ax = plt.subplots(figsize=(6,4))
ax.plot(base_score, label='base')
for name, model in classifier_parade.items():
    cv_scores = skms.cross_val_score(model,
                                     digits.data, digits.target,
                                     cv=10,
                                     scoring='f1_macro',
                                     n_jobs=-1) # all CPUs
    my_lbl = "{} {:.3f}".format(name, cv_scores.mean())
    ax.plot(cv_scores, label=my_lbl, marker=next(markers))
ax.set_ylim(0.0, 1.1)
ax.set_xlabel('Fold')
ax.set_ylabel('Accuracy')
ax.legend(loc='lower center', ncol=2);
```

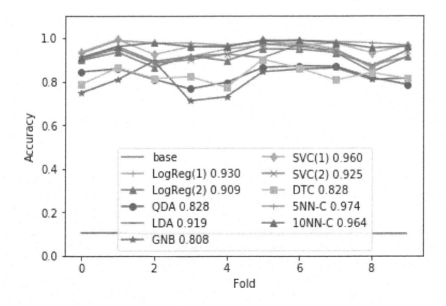

Frankly, there is really too much going on here to easily summarize. Still, there are some overall trends. You can see that a classical method, Logistic Regression, is competing nicely with a very modern method, SVCs. And our drop-dead simple Nearest Neighbors methods are doing even better. It would be great practice to dive into comparing different classifiers on different metrics for this problem. You might also be interested in comparing the resource utilization of the different methods on *digits*.

8.8 EOC

8.8.1 Summary

We've now added a variety of methods to our classification toolbox. Decision trees are highly flexible models that find common regions of space. Logistic regression and discriminant analysis variations use different probabilistic models of the data to assign likelihoods to classes. Support Vector Classifiers look directly for a linear separation between classes. Along with Naive Bayes and nearest neighbors, we have eight different types of classifiers we can use.

How do we pick? Sometimes outside concerns drive our choice. Decision trees are generally readable by humans. Logistic regression models can be interpreted as the change in log-odds based on variable values. SVCs? SVCs don't really *do* interpretation in the same way. We can *use* them, but they have a lot going on inside their black box. Now, even if we *know* that we need to use a DT for understanding, we might still fit other models to see how the DT performance stacks up to the other cool kids.

8.8.2 Notes

The idea that there is *No One Method to Rule Them All* (and in the darkness, bind them) is called the *No Free Lunch Theorem*. I'd prefer the *No One Ring Theorem*, but alas, they didn't ask Tolkien or me.

Decision Trees   While we've talked about decision trees leading to a *class*, we can also ask them about the *probability distribution* at the leaves. Then, if we wanted, we could flip coins to get a distribution similar to what we saw at each leaf. We don't have to make a concrete decision if we don't want to.

To answer the mid-tree quiz: "As the max depth increases, are we moving towards overfitting or underfitting?" The answer is *overfitting*.

There are several characteristics of trees that are *not* fundamental to DTs—they just happen to be the way things are. We could, for instance, allow decisions to be made on functions of the features. Among other things, this would allow non-parallel or non-perpendicular value splits. Instead of splitting on $x > 5$, we could split on $2x + 3 > 5$: we now have an off-axis comparison. We could also allow comparisons like *is color in {red, blue, green}? (no).* We *can* capture that sort of relationship with a sequence of binary questions: *is red? (no), is green? (no), is blue? (no).* But that comes at the cost of subdividing regions that might be light on data to begin with. There is a tradeoff between expressiveness and verbosity that different authors have disagreed on. I'll take a pragmatic approach: if you think you need a fancy technique, try it—and then cross-validate.

If you happen to be a more advanced reader making your way through this book, you might be interested in a recent (2015) paper: *Efficient non-greedy optimization of decision trees* by Norouzi and friends. The methods of tree-building I've described in this chapter are *greedy*: they take individual steps that seem to be the best. But, of course, without an overall map, individual steps can lead you astray. That paper describes a non-greedy way to build trees.

SVCs   We'll talk much more about some of the coolest aspects of SVMs in Chapter 13. Quickly, we move from a SVC to a SVM by introducing a *kernel*. To tide you over, I'll mention that `sklearn` has an interface to `liblinear` which is a very powerful program for computing SVCs (linear SVMs) as well as logistic regression models. At a minimum, to run it as a standard SVC, comparable to what we used above, you'll make a call like: `svm.LinearSVC(loss='hinge')`. The `LinearSVC` has some nice benefits when working with large datasets (greater than about 10,000 examples).

`SVC` and `NuSVC` use another program, `libsvm`, under the hood. `libsvm` is about as close to a *de facto* standard implementation of SVCs and SVMs as we have in the machine learning community. When talking about `NuSVC`, people often make the mistake of talking about ν in terms of *training errors*. ν is related to *margin errors*. ν *is not* directly related to training errors. If you want to see for yourself, read pages 1225–1226 of *New Support Vector Algorithms* by Scholkpf.

Trying to get `LinearSVC` and `SVC` and `NuSVC` to produce the same boundaries is quite difficult. `libsvm` and `liblinear` do slightly different things from a mathematical and computational perspective. At a minimum, `LinearSVC` includes the +1 trick column when it performs *regularization*. Furthermore, `LinearSVC` and `SVC` place their own defaults on top of the underlying defaults. If you want a comparison, be prepared to do some digging. These might get you started:

- https://stackoverflow.com/a/23507404/221602
- https://stackoverflow.com/q/33843981/221602
- https://stackoverflow.com/q/35076586/221602

Logistic Regression   Mathematical clarity can sometimes be quite opaque. For example, the following equation $\frac{1}{1+e^{-x}} = \frac{e^x}{1+e^x}$ leads to two quite different-looking ways of writing out a logistic function. And that, in turn, can lead to different ways of expressing logistic regression. Good luck.

The assumptions of logistic regression are strongly related to the assumptions of linear regression with the exception that the linear relationship is between the log-odds of the target classes and the input features. Otherwise, we still need the errors to be well behaved and we need to avoid redundancy in the features. See Chapter 10 for details.

We haven't really addressed *how* logistic regression works. We've explained log-odds and built a linear-regression-like model from it, but what makes it go? A classic way to find the answer—the best coefficients—is called *iteratively reweighted least squares* (IRLS). Basically, it follows the same method as classic linear regression, but it has to repeat that process multiple times. This process ends up being equivalent to a *Newton's Method*: if I'm up a hill, aim towards a place where I cross the x axis by pointing downhill and taking a step towards it based on the steepness of the slope. Newton's Method is called a second-order method because we need to find an extreme point in a function—where it's at a peak or a valley—and to do *that* we need to find the slope that will get us to that point. So, we sort of need the slope of a slope—hence "second order" or "second derivative" if you are familiar. The other major class of methods, called *Gradient Descent*, basically says: aim yourself downhill and take a small step that way.

The `statsmodels` method we used above uses the good old IRLS technique. We can perform logistic regression in several ways in `sklearn`. `liblinear` uses a very fancy version of Newton's Method called Trust Region Newton's Method. That's the default call to `LogisticRegression`. `SGDClassifier` uses a fast version of Gradient Descent that doesn't process *all* of the data at each step downhill. The `saga` argument to `LogisticRegression` uses a—surprise!—SAGA method that performs like SGD but also remembers some history of prior steps. Gradient Descent uses all the data at each step, while Stochastic Gradient Descent uses some or only one example at each step and SAGA remembers some history of steps while using only some data at each new step.

More disturbingly, you may have noticed that we didn't discuss the role of bias and variance with logistic regression. We will revisit this in Chapter 15.

Discriminant Analysis Methods

At the risk of offending my statistician friends, I dreadfully glossed over some details about variance. In reality, what we've discussed is either the population variance or the biased sample variance. There are a few different ways of dealing with the biasedness; the most common is to divide by $n - 1$ instead of n.

I have to credit a member of StackOverflow, *whuber*, for a comment and graphic which brought a graphical method of exploring covariance to my attention. You can see it here: https://stats.stackexchange.com/a/18200/1704. Tracking down some of those ideas led me to an article by Hayes from 2011 titled "A Geometrical Interpretation of an Alternative Formula for the Sample Covariance."

There are many ways to relate different methods to one another. For example, a technique called *Nearest Shrunken Centroids* (NSC) is related to DLDA: if you center and standardize your data and then perform NSC, you should get results that are equivalent to a form of regularized (smoothed) DLDA. See *Elements of Statistical Learning* by Hastie and friends, second edition, page 651. As always, there may be mathematical and implementation differences that prevent you from achieving complete equivalence. As a note, `sklearn`'s current (as of May 2019) implementation of `NearestCentroids` doesn't fully account for distance metrics and won't quite solve this for us.

If you are familiar with Naive Bayes and are wondering why it is called a linear method, the reason is that for *discrete*—technically, *multinomial*—Naive Bayes, the boundaries created *are* linear. However, for *continuous*—technically, Gaussian—Naive Bayes, as we have seen in this chapter, the boundaries are not linear.

8.8.3 Exercises

Here are some questions to keep you up at night:

1. Under what scenarios would an identifying variable, such as a unique number for each day, be *useful* for learning a target value? How could we apply it when we need to predict truly never-seen data—beyond even a hold-out test set?
2. Play around with SVM boundaries and example points. Make a few positive and negative examples—you can color them red and blue if you like. Make some patterns with the examples. Now, graph and look at the resulting linear boundaries that get created when you train an SVM. How do the boundaries change as you go from well-separated classes to having outliers across the obvious separation?
3. Compare the runtimes of of `NuSVC` and `SVC` under different learning scenarios and parameters.
4. Compare the DA methods with 20 repeated train-test splits. Use the same TTSs for each method. Count up the winners. Try with a different dataset.
5. You now have a bigger toolbox. Try to find better predictive models of the student data from the end of Chapter 6.
6. Our examples of bias and variance with SVCs were a bit weak. If you want to see very clear examples of bias-variance—overfitting and underfitting—redo those examples with a *Gaussian kernel*. Don't know what that is? Stay tuned or turn to Chapter 13.

More Regression Methods

```
In [1]:

#setup
from mlwpy import *
%matplotlib inline

diabetes = datasets.load_diabetes()

d_tts = skms.train_test_split(diabetes.data,
                              diabetes.target,
                              test_size=.25,
                              random_state=42)

(diabetes_train_ftrs, diabetes_test_ftrs,
 diabetes_train_tgt,  diabetes_test_tgt) = d_tts
```

We are going to dive into a few additional techniques for regression. All of these are variations on techniques we've seen before. Two are direct variations on linear regression, one splices a support vector classifier with linear regression to create a Support Vector Regressor, and one uses decision trees for regression instead of classification. As such, much of what we'll talk about will be somewhat familiar. We'll also discuss how to build a learner of our own that plugs directly into sklearn's usage patterns. Onward!

9.1 Linear Regression in the Penalty Box: Regularization

As we briefly discussed in Section 5.4, we can conceptually define the goodness of a model as a cost that has two parts: (1) what we lose, or spend, when we make a mistake and (2) what we invest, or spend, into the complexity of our model. The math is pretty easy here: $cost = loss(errors) + complexity$. Keeping mistakes low keeps us accurate. If we keep the complexity low, we also keep the model simple. In turn, we also improve our ability to generalize. Overfitting has a high complexity and low training loss. Underfitting has low complexity and high training loss. At our sweet spot, we use just the right amount of complexity to get a low loss on training *and* testing.

Controlling the complexity term—keeping the complexity low and the model simple—is called *regularization*. When we discussed overfitting, we talked about some wiggly graphs being *too* wiggly: they overfit and follow noise instead of pattern. If we reduce some of the wiggliness, we do a better job of following the signal—the interesting pattern—and ignoring the noise.

When we say we want to regularize, or *smooth*, our model, we are really putting together a few ideas. Data is noisy: it combines noisy distractions with the real useful signal. Some models are powerful enough to capture both signal *and* noise. We hope that the pattern in the signal is reasonably smooth and regular. If the features of two examples are fairly close to each other, we hope they have similar target values. Excessive jumpiness in the target between two close examples is, *hopefully*, noise. We don't want to capture noise. So, when we see our model function getting too jagged, we want to force it back to something smooth.

So, how can we reduce roughness? Let's restrict ourselves to talking about one type of model: linear regression. I see a raised hand in the back of the classroom. "Yes?" "But Mark, if we are choosing between different straight lines, they *all seem to be equally rough!*" That's a fair point. Let's talk about what it might mean for one line to be simpler than another. You may want to review some of the geometry and algebra of lines from Section 2.6.1. Remember the basic form of a line: $y = mx + b$. Well, if we get rid of mx, we can have something that is even *simpler*, but still a line: $y = b$. A concrete example is $y = 3$. That is, for any value of x we (1) ignore that value of x—it plays no role now— and (2) just take the value on the right-hand side, 3. There are two ways in which $y = b$ is simpler than $y = mx + b$:

- $y = b$ can only be a 100% correct predictor for a single data point, unless the other target values are *cooperative*. If an *adversary* is given control over the target values, they can easily break $y = 3$ by choosing a second point that has any value besides 3, say 42.
- To fully specify a model $y = b$, I need one value: b. To fully specify a model $y = mx + b$, I need two values: m and b.

A quick point: if either (1) we set $m = 0$, getting back to $y = b$, or (2) we set $b = 0$ and we get $y = mx$, we have reduced our capacity to follow true patterns in the data. We've simplified the models we are willing to consider. If $m = 0$, we are *literally* back to the $y = b$ case: we can only capture one adversarial point. If $b = 0$, we are in a slightly different scenario, but again, we can only capture one adversarial point. The difference in the second case is that we have an *implicit* y-intercept—usually specified by an explicit value for b—of zero. Specifically, the line will start at $(0, 0)$ instead of $(0, b)$. In both cases, if we take the zero as a given, we only need to remember one other value. Here's the key idea: setting weights to zero simplifies a linear model by reducing the number of points it can follow *and* reducing the number of weights it has to estimate.

Now, what happens when we have more than one input feature? Our linear regression now looks like $y = w_2 x_2 + w_1 x_1 + w_0$. This equation describes a plane in 3D instead of a line in 2D. One way to reduce the model is to pick some ws—say, w_1 and w_0—and set them to zero. That gives us $y = w_2 x_2$ which effectively says that we don't care about the value of x_1 and we are content with an intercept of zero. Completely blanking out values seems a bit heavy-handed. Are there more gradual alternatives? Yes, I'm glad you asked.

Instead of introducing zeros, we can ask that the *total size* of the weights be relatively small. Of course, this constraint brings up problems—or, perhaps, opportunities. We must define *total size* and *relatively small*. Fortunately, *total* hints that we need to add several things up with sum. Unfortunately, we have to pick what we feed to sum.

We want the sum to represent an amount and we want things far away from zero to be counted equally—just as we have done with errors. We'd like 9 and −9 to be counted equally. We've dealt with this by (1) squaring values or (2) taking absolute values. As it turns out, we can reasonably use either here.

In [2]:
```
weights = np.array([3.5, -2.1, .7])
print(np.sum(np.abs(weights)),
      np.sum(weights**2))
```

6.3 17.15

Now we have to define some criteria for *relatively small*. Let's return to our goal: we want to simplify our model to move from overfitting and towards *just right*. Our just-right values cannot operate on their own, in a vacuum. They must be connected to how well we are fitting the data—we just want to tone down the *over* part of *overfitting*. Let's return to the way we account for the quality of our fit. To investigate, let's create a bit of data where we specifically control the errors in it:

In [3]:
```
x_1 = np.arange(10)
m, b = 3, 2
w = np.array([m,b])

x = np.c_[x_1, np.repeat(1.0, 10)] # the plus-one trick

errors = np.tile(np.array([0.0, 1.0, 1.0, .5, .5]), 2)

print(errors * errors)
print(np.dot(errors, errors))

y_true = rdot(w,x)
y_msr  = y_true + errors

D = (x,y_msr)
```

```
[0.   1.   1.   0.25 0.25 0.   1.   1.   0.25 0.25]
5.0
```

Here's how the truth compares to our noisy data points:

In [4]:

```
fig, ax = plt.subplots(1,1,figsize=(4,3))
ax.plot(x_1, y_true, 'r', label='true')
ax.plot(x_1, y_msr , 'b', label='noisy')
ax.legend();
```

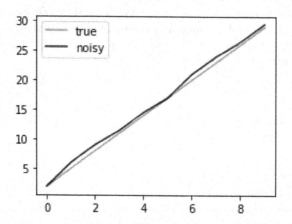

Now, I'm going to take a shortcut. I'm not going to go through the process of fitting and finding good parameters from the data. We're not going to rerun a linear regression to pull out ws (or $\{m, b\}$). But imagine that I did and I got back the perfect parameter values—the ones we used to *create* the data above. Here's what our sum of squared errors would look like:

In [5]:

```
def sq_diff(a,b):
        return (a-b)**2
```

In [6]:

```
predictions = rdot(w,x)
np.sum(sq_diff(predictions, y_msr))
```

Out[6]:

```
5.0
```

As a reminder, that comes from this equation:

$$loss = \sum_{x,y \in D} (wx - y)^2$$

We need to account for our ideas about keeping the weights small. In turn, this constraint is a surrogate for simplifying—regularizing—the model. Let's say that instead of just making *predictions* we'll have a total *cost* associated with our model. Here goes:

In [7]:

```
predictions = rdot(w,x)

loss = np.sum(sq_diff(predictions, y_msr))

complexity_1 = np.sum(np.abs(weights))
complexity_2 = np.sum(weights**2) # == np.dot(weights, weights)

cost_1 = loss + complexity_1
cost_2 = loss + complexity_2

print("Sum(abs) complexity:", cost_1)
print("Sum(sqr) complexity:", cost_2)
```

```
Sum(abs) complexity: 11.3
Sum(sqr) complexity: 22.15
```

Remember, we've pulled two fast ones. First, we didn't actually work from the data *back to* the weights. Instead, we just used the same weights to make the data and to make our not-quite-predictions. Our second fast one is that we used the *same weights* in both cases, so we have the *same losses* contributing to both costs. We can't compare these two: normally, we use one or the other to *compute the cost* which helps us find a good set of weights under one calculation for loss and complexity.

There's one last piece I want to introduce before showing a fundamental relationship of learning. Once we define a cost and say that we want to have a low cost, we are really making another tradeoff. I can lower the cost by making fewer errors—leading to a lower loss—or by having less complexity. Am I willing to do both equally or do I consider one more important? Is halving complexity worth doubling the errors I make? Our *real goal* is trying to make few errors in the future. That happens by making few errors now—on training data—*and* by keeping model complexity down.

To this end, it is valuable to add a way to trade off towards fewer errors or towards lower complexity. We do that like this:

In [8]:

```
predictions = rdot(w,x)
errors = np.sum(sq_diff(predictions, y_msr))
complexity_1 = np.sum(np.abs(weights))

C = .5
```

```
cost = errors + C * complexity_1
cost
```

Out[8]:

8.15

Here, I'm saying that as far as cost is concerned, one point of increase in complexity is only worth $\frac{1}{2}$ of a point increase in loss. That is, losses are twice as costly, or twice as important, as complexity. If we use C to represent that tradeoff, we get the following math-heavy equations:

$$\text{Cost}_1 = \sum_{x,y \in D} (wx - y)^2 + C \sum_j |w_j|$$

$$\text{Cost}_2 = \sum_{x,y \in D} (wx - y)^2 + C \sum_j w_j^2$$

Finding the best line with Cost_1 is called L_1-regularized regression, or the *lasso*. Finding the best line with Cost_2 is called the L_2-regularized regression, or *ridge regression*.

9.1.1 Performing Regularized Regression

Performing regularized linear regression is no more difficult than the good old-fashioned (GOF) linear regression.

The default value for our C, the total weight of the complexity penalty, is `1.0` for both `Lasso` and `Ridge`. In `sklearn`, the C value is set by the parameter `alpha`. So, for $C = 2$, we would call `linear_model.Lasso(alpha=2.0)`. You'll see λ, α, and C in discussions of regularization; they are all serving a similar role, but you do have to pay attention for authors using slight variations in meaning. For our purposes, we can basically consider them all the same.

In [9]:

```
models = [linear_model.Lasso(),          # L1 regularized; C=1.0
          linear_model.Ridge()]          # L2 regularized; C=1.0

for model in models:
    model.fit(diabetes_train_ftrs, diabetes_train_tgt)
    train_preds = model.predict(diabetes_train_ftrs)
    test_preds  = model.predict(diabetes_test_ftrs)
    print(get_model_name(model),
          "\nTrain MSE:",metrics.mean_squared_error(diabetes_train_tgt,
                                                    train_preds),
          "\n Test MSE:", metrics.mean_squared_error(diabetes_test_tgt,
                                                    test_preds))
```

```
Lasso
Train MSE: 3947.899897977698
 Test MSE: 3433.1524588051197
Ridge
Train MSE: 3461.739515097773
 Test MSE: 3105.468750907886
```

Using these is so easy, we might move on without *thinking* about when and why to use them. Since the default of linear regression is to operate *without* regularization, we can easily switch to a regularized version and see if it improves matters. We might try that when we train on some data and see an overfitting failure. Then, we can try different amounts of regularization—different values for C—and see what works best on cross-validated runs. We'll discuss tools to help us pick a C in Section 11.2.

With very noisy data, we might be tempted to make a complex model that is likely to overfit. We have to *tolerate* a fair bit of error in the model to reduce our complexity. That is, we pay less for complexity and pay a bit more for errors. With noiseless data that captures a linear pattern, we have little need for complexity control and we should see good results with GOF linear regression.

9.2 Support Vector Regression

We've introduced the idea of a fundamental tradeoff in learning: our cost comes from both the mistakes and the complexity of our learner. Support Vector Regression (SVR) makes use of this in a same-but-different manner. We regularized GOF linear regression by adding a complexity factor to its loss. We can continue down this path and tweak linear regression even further. We can modify its loss also. Remember: *cost = loss + complexity*. The standard loss in linear regression is the sum of squared errors called the *squared error loss*. As we just saw, that form is also called L_2—in this case, the L_2 loss. So, you might think, "Aha! Let's use L_1, the sum of absolute values." You are close. We're going to use L_1, but we're going to tweak it. Our tweak is to use L_1 and ignore small errors.

9.2.1 Hinge Loss

In our first look at Support Vector Classifiers (SVCs) from Section 8.3, we didn't discuss the underlying magic that lets a SVC do its tricks. It turns out that the magic is very similar for the SVC and SVR: both make use of a slightly different loss than linear regression (either kind). In essence, we want to measure what happens when we are *wrong* and we want to ignore small errors. Putting these two pieces together gives us the idea of the *hinge loss*. For starters, here's what the absolute values of the errors look like:

In [10]:

```
#  here, we don't ignore small errors
error = np.linspace(-4, 4, 100)
```

```
loss = np.abs(error)

fig, ax = plt.subplots(1,1,figsize=(4,3))
ax.plot(error, loss)

ax.set_xlabel('Raw Error')
ax.set_ylabel('Abs Loss');
```

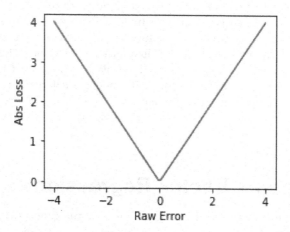

How can we ignore errors up to a certain threshold? For example, let's write code that ignores absolute errors that are less than 1.0:

In [11]:

```
an_error = .75
abs_error = abs(an_error)
if abs_error < 1.0:
    the_loss = 0.0
else:
    the_loss = abs_error
print(the_loss)
```

0.0

Now we are going to get fancy. Pay close attention. We can rewrite that with some clever mathematics. Here's our strategy:

1. Subtract the threshold value from the absolute error.
2. If the result is is bigger than zero, keep it. Otherwise, take zero instead.

```
In [12]:

an_error = 0.75
adj_error = abs(an_error) - 1.0
if adj_error < 0.0:
    the_loss = 0.0
else:
    the_loss = adj_error
print(the_loss)
```

```
0.0
```

Can we summarize that with a single mathematical expression? Look at what happens based on adjusted error. If `adj_error < 0.0`, we get 0. If `adj_error >= 0.0`, we get `adj_error`. Together, those two outcomes are equivalent to taking the bigger value of `adj_error` or 0. We can do that like:

```
In [13]:

error = np.linspace(-4, 4, 100)

# here, we ignore errors up to 1.0 by taking bigger value
loss = np.maximum(np.abs(error) - 1.0,
                  np.zeros_like(error))

fig, ax = plt.subplots(1,1,figsize=(4,3))
ax.plot(error, loss)

ax.set_xlabel("Raw Error")
ax.set_ylabel("Hinge Loss");
```

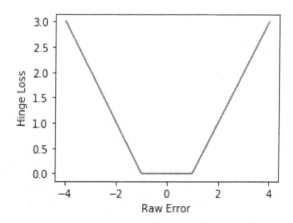

Mathematically, we encode it like this: $loss = \max(|error| - threshold, 0)$. Let's take one more second to deconstruct it. First, we subtract the amount of error we are willing to ignore from the raw error. If it takes us to a negative value, then maxing against zero will throw it out. For example, if we have an absolute error of .5 (from a raw error of .5 *or* −.5) and we subtract 1, we end up with an adjusted error of −1.5. Maxing with 0, we take the 0. We're left with zero—no cost. If you squint your eyes a bit, and turn your head sideways, you might be able to see a pair of doors with hinges at the kinks in the prior graph. That's where the name for the *hinge loss* comes from. When we apply the hinge loss around a known target, we get a band where we don't care about small differences.

In [14]:

```
threshold = 2.5

xs = np.linspace(-5,5,100)
ys_true = 3 * xs + 2

fig, ax = plt.subplots(1,1,figsize=(4,3))
ax.plot(xs, ys_true)
ax.fill_between(xs, ys_true-threshold, ys_true+threshold,
                color=(1.0,0,0,.25))

ax.set_xlabel('Input Feature')
ax.set_ylabel('Output Target');
```

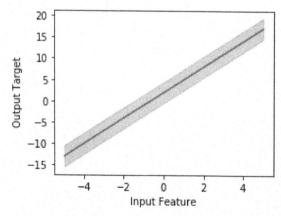

Now, imagine that instead of knowing the relationship (the blue line above), we only have some data that came from noisy measurements around that true line:

In [15]:

```
threshold = 2.5

xs = np.linspace(-5,5,100)
ys = 3 * xs + 2 + np.random.normal(0, 1.5, 100)
```

```
fig, ax = plt.subplots(1,1,figsize=(4,3))
ax.plot(xs, ys, 'o',  color=(0,0,1.0,.5))
ax.fill_between(xs, ys_true - threshold, ys_true + threshold,
                color=(1.0,0,0,.25));
```

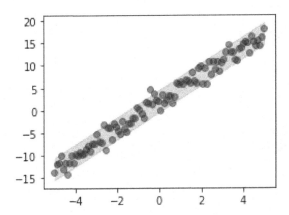

We might consider many potential lines to fit this data. However, the band around the central line captures most of the noise in the data and *throws all of those small errors* out. The coverage of the band is close to perfect—there are only a few points out of 100 that have enough of a mistake to matter. Admittedly, we cheated when we drew this band: we based it on information (the true line) that we normally don't have available. The central line may remind you of the maximum margin separator in SVCs.

9.2.2 From Linear Regression to Regularized Regression to Support Vector Regression

We can develop a progression from GOF linear regression to regularized regression to support vector regression. At each of the steps, we add or tweak some part of the basic recipe. Using the **xs** and **ys** from above, we can define a few terms and see the progression. We'll image that we estimated the w_1 parameter to be 1.3 and we'll take $C = 1.0$. Our band of ignorance—the threshold on the amount of error we tolerate—is $\varepsilon = .25$. That's a baby Greek *epsilon*.

In [16]:

```
# hyperparameters for the scenario
C, epsilon = 1.0, .25


# parameters
weights = np.array([1.3])
```

We can make our `predictions` from that w and look at the three losses—square-error, absolute, and hinge losses. I won't use the absolute loss any further—it's just there for comparison sake.

In [17]:
```
# prediction, error, loss
predictions = rdot(weights, xs.reshape(-1, 1))
errors = ys - predictions

loss_sse   = np.sum(errors ** 2)
loss_sae   = np.sum(np.abs(errors))
loss_hinge = np.sum(np.max(np.abs(errors) - epsilon, 0))
```

We can also compute the two complexity penalties we need for L_1 and L_2 regularization. Note the close similarity to the calculations for the *losses*, except we calculate the complexity from the *weights* instead of the *errors*.

In [18]:
```
# complexity penalty for regularization
complexity_saw = np.sum(np.abs(weights))
complexity_ssw = np.sum(weights**2)
```

Finally, we have our total costs:

In [19]:
```
# cost
cost_gof_regression   = loss_sse   + 0.0
cost_L1pen_regression = loss_sse   + C * complexity_saw
cost_L2pen_regression = loss_sse   + C * complexity_ssw
cost_sv_regression    = loss_hinge + C * complexity_ssw
```

Now, as that code is written, it only calculates a cost for each type of regression for *one* set of weights. We would have to run that code over and over—with different sets of weights—to find a good, better, or best set of weights.

Table 9.1 shows the mathematical forms that are buried in that code. If we let $L_1 = \sum |v_i|$ and $L_2 = \sum v_i^2$ be the sum of absolute values and the sum of squared values, respectively, then we can summarize these in the smaller, more readable form of Table 9.2. Remember, the loss applies to the raw errors. The penalty applies to the parameters or weights.

I want to congratulate. By reading Table 9.2, you can see the fundamental differences between these four regression methods. In reality, we don't *know* the right assumptions to choose between learning methods—for example, the discriminant methods or these varied regression methods—so we don't *know* whether the noise and underlying complexity of data is going to be best suited to one or another of these techniques. But we skirt around this problem by cross-validating to pick a preferred method for a given

Table 9.1 The different mathematical forms for penalized regression and SVR.

Name	Penalty	Math
GOF Linear Regression	None	$\sum_i (y_i - wx_i)^2$
Lasso	L_1	$\sum_i (y_i - wx_i)^2 + C \sum_j w_j$
Ridge	L_2	$\sum_i (y_i - wx_i)^2 + C \sum_j w_j^2$
SVR	L_1	$\sum_i \max(|y_i - wx_i| - \varepsilon, 0) + C \sum_j w_j$

Table 9.2 Common losses and penalties in regression models.

Name	Loss	Penalty
GOF LR	L_2	0
Lasso (L_1-Penalty LR)	L_2	L_1
Ridge (L_2-Penalty LR)	L_2	L_2
SVR	Hinge	L_2

dataset. As a practical matter, the choice between these models may depend on outside constraints. For some statistical goals—like significance testing, which we aren't discussing in this book—we might prefer *not* using SVR. On very complex problems, we probably don't even bother with GOF linear regression—although it might be a good baseline comparison. If we have lots of features, we may choose the lasso—L_1-penalized—to eliminate features entirely. Ridge has a more moderate approach and reduces—but doesn't eliminate—features.

9.2.3 Just Do It—SVR Style

There are two main options for SVR in `sklearn`. We won't dive into the theory, but you can control different aspects with these two different regressors:

- ε-SVR (Greek letter *epsilon*-SVR): you set the error band tolerance. ν is determined implicitly by this choice. This is what you get with the default parameters to `SVR` in `sklearn`.
- ν-SVR (Greek letter *nu*-SVR): you set ν, the proportion of kept support vectors with respect to the total number of examples. ε, the error band tolerance, is determined implicitly by this choice.

```
In [20]:
svrs = [svm.SVR(),    # default epsilon=0.1
        svm.NuSVR()] # default nu=0.5

for model in svrs:
    preds = (model.fit(diabetes_train_ftrs, diabetes_train_tgt)
                  .predict(diabetes_test_ftrs))
    print(metrics.mean_squared_error(diabetes_test_tgt, preds))
```

5516.346206774444
5527.520141195904

9.3 Piecewise Constant Regression

All of the linear regression techniques we've looked at have one common theme: they assume that a suitably small variation of the inputs will lead to a small variation in the output. You can phrase this in several different ways, but they are all related to the concept of *smoothness*. The output never jumps around. In classification, we *expect* the outputs to make leaps: at some critical point we move from predicting *dog* to predicting *cat*. Methods like logistic regression have smooth transitions from one class to the next; decision tree classifiers are distinctly dog-or-cat. In mathese, if we have a numerical output value that is not sufficiently smooth, we say we have a *discontinuous target*.

Let's draw up a concrete example. Suppose there is a hotdog stand that wants to be cash-only but doesn't want to deal with coins. They want to be *literally* paper-cash only. So, when a customer gets a bill of $2.75, they simply round up and charge the customer $3.00. We won't discuss how the customers feel about this. Here's a graph that converts the raw bill to a collected bill:

In [21]:

```
raw_bill = np.linspace(.5, 10.0, 100)
collected = np.round(raw_bill)

fig, ax = plt.subplots(1,1,figsize=(4,3))
ax.plot(raw_bill, collected, '.')
ax.set_xlabel("raw cost")
ax.set_ylabel("bill");
```

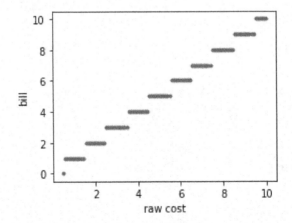

The graph looks a bit like a set of stairs. It simply isn't possible for our smooth regression lines to capture the pattern in this relationship. A single line through this dataset will have problems. We could connect the fronts of the steps, the backs of the steps, the middles of the steps: none of these will be quite right. We could connect the front of the bottom step to the back of the top step. Again, we still can't make it work perfectly. If we use GOF linear regression, we'll capture the middle points fairly well, but the ends of each step will be missed. To put it bluntly, the bias of linear regression puts a fundamental limit on our ability to follow the pattern.

You might be thinking that a decision tree could break down the inputs into little buckets. You'd be completely right—we'll talk about that in the next section. But I'd like to take a middle ground between using linear regression and modifying decision trees to perform regression. We're going to do *piecewise* linear regression in the simplest possible way: with *piecewise constant regression*. For each region of the input features, we're going to predict a simple horizontal line. That means we're predicting a single constant value for that region.

Our raw cost-versus-bill graph was one example where this is an appropriate model. Here's another example that has a less consistent relationship. Instead of constantly working our way up, we move both up and down as x increases. We start by defining some split points. If we wanted four lines, we'd define three split points (remember, when you cut a rope, you go from one piece of rope to two). Imagine we split at a, b, and c. Then, we'll fit four lines on the data: (1) from very small up to a, (2) from a to b, (3) from b to c, and (4) from c onwards to very big. Making that slightly more concrete, imagine `a,b,c=3,8,12`. The result might look like

In [22]:

```
fig, ax = plt.subplots(1,1,figsize=(4,3))
ax.plot([0,3],    [0,0],
        [3,8],    [5,5],
        [8,12],   [2,2],
        [12,15],  [9,9])
ax.set_xticks([3,8,12]);
```

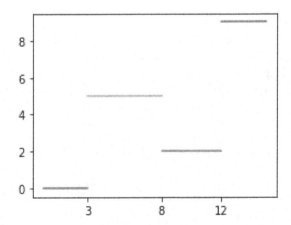

You might be able to make some educated guesses about how the number of splits relates to bias. If there are no splits, we are simply performing linear regression without a slope—predicting a constant value everywhere using the mean. If we go to the other

extreme, we'll have n data points and make $n - 1$ mini–lines. Would that model exhibit good training performance? What about applying it to predict on a test set? This model would be great in training, but it would be very bad in testing: it overfits the data.

In some respects, piecewise constant regression is like k-Nearest Neighbors Regression (k-NN-R). However, k-NN-R considers examples based on relative distance instead of raw numeric value. We claim a new testing example is like training examples 3, 17, or 21 because they are close to the new example, regardless of the raw numeric value. Piecewise constant regression gives examples the same target value based on a preset range of splits: I'm like the examples with values between 5 and 10 because my value is 6, even if I'm closer to an example with value 4.

In data science, we use the phrase *let the data speak for itself*. Here, that idea is front and center: with k-NN-R the data determines the boundary between predictions *and* those boundaries move with the density of the data. Denser regions get more potential boundaries. With piecewise constant regression, our splits are predetermined. There's no wiggle room for areas with high or low densities of data. The net effect is that we may do very well when choosing splits for piecewise regression if we have some strong background information about the data. For example, in the US, tax brackets are set by predetermined break points. If we don't have the right information, our splits may do much worse than k-NN-R.

9.3.1 Implementing a Piecewise Constant Regressor

So far, we've only made use of prebuilt models. In the spirit of full disclosure, I snuck in a custom-made diagonal LDA model at the end of the previous chapter, but we didn't discuss the implementation at all. Since `sklearn` doesn't have a built-in piecewise regression capability, we'll take this as an opportunity to implement a learner of our own. The code to do so is not too bad: it has about 40 lines and it makes use of two main ideas. The first idea is relatively straightforward: to perform each constant regression for the individual pieces, we'll simply reuse `sklearn`'s built-in linear regression on a rewritten form of the data. The second idea is that we need to map from the input feature—we'll limit ourselves to just one for now—to the appropriate section of our rope. This mapping is a bit more tricky, since it has two steps.

Step one involves using `np.searchsorted`. `searchsorted` is itself sort of tricky, but we can summarize what it does by saying that it finds an insertion point for a new element into a sorted sequence of values. In other words, it says where someone should enter a line of people ordered by height to maintain the ordering. We want to be able to translate a feature value of 60 to segment, or rope piece, 3. We need to do this in both the training and testing phases.

Step two is that we convert the rope pieces to true/false indicators. So, instead of *Piece* = 3, we have $Piece_1 = False$, $Piece_2 = False$, $Piece_3 = True$. Then, we learn a regression model from the piece indicators to the output target. When we want to predict a new example, we simply run it through the mapping process to get the right piece indicator and then pipe it to the constant linear regression. The remapping is all wrapped up in the `_recode` member function in the code below.

9.3.2 General Notes on Implementing Models

The `sklearn` docs discuss how to implement custom models. We're going to ignore some of the possible alternatives and lay out a simplified process.

- Since we're implementing a regressor, we'll inherit from `BaseEstimator` and `RegressorMixin`.
- We will *not* do anything with the model arguments in `__init__`.
- We'll define `fit(X,y)` and `predict(X)` methods.
- We can make use of `check_X_y` and `check_array` to verify arguments are valid in the `sklearn` sense.

Two quick comments on the code:

- The following code only works for a single feature. Extending it to multiple features would be a fun project. We'll see some techniques in Chapter 10 that might help.
- If no cut points are specified, we use one cut point for every ten examples and we choose the cut points at evenly spaced percentiles of the data.

  If we have two regions, the one split would be at 50%, the median. With three or four regions, the splits would be at 33–67% or 25–50–75%. Recall that percentiles are where x% of the data is less than that value. For example, if 50% of our data is less than 5'11", than 5'11" is the 50th percentile value. Ironically, a single split at 50% might be particularly bad if the data is concentrated in the middle, as might be the case with heights.

In [23]:

```
from sklearn.base import BaseEstimator, RegressorMixin
from sklearn.utils.validation import (check_X_y,
                                       check_array,
                                       check_is_fitted)


class PiecewiseConstantRegression(BaseEstimator, RegressorMixin):
    def __init__(self, cut_points=None):
        self.cut_points = cut_points

    def fit(self, X, y):
        X, y = check_X_y(X,y)
        assert X.shape[1] == 1 # one variable only

        if self.cut_points is None:
            n = (len(X) // 10) + 1
            qtiles = np.linspace(0.0, 1.0, n+2)[1:-1]
            self.cut_points = np.percentile(X, qtiles, axis=1)
        else:
            # ensure cutpoints in order and in range of X
            assert np.all(self.cut_points[:-1] < self.cut_points[1:])
```

```
              assert (X.min() < self.cut_points[0] and
                      self.cut_points[-1] < X.max())

        recoded_X = self._recode(X)
        # even though the _inner_ model is fit without an intercept,
        # our piecewise model *does* have a constant term (but see notes)
        self.coeffs_ = (linear_model.LinearRegression(fit_intercept=False)
                                    .fit(recoded_X, y).coef_)
    def _recode(self, X):
        cp = self.cut_points
        n_pieces = len(cp) + 1
        recoded_X = np.eye(n_pieces)[np.searchsorted(cp, X.flat)]
        return recoded_X

    def predict(self, X):
        check_is_fitted(self, 'coeffs_')
        X = check_array(X)
        recoded_X = self._recode(X)
        return rdot(self.coeffs_, recoded_X)
```

To test and demonstrate that code, let's generate a simple example dataset we can train on.

In [24]:

```
ftr = np.random.randint(0,10,(100,1)).astype(np.float64)
cp = np.array([3,7])
tgt = np.searchsorted(cp, ftr.flat) + 1

fig, ax = plt.subplots(1,1,figsize=(4,3))
ax.plot(ftr, tgt, '.');
```

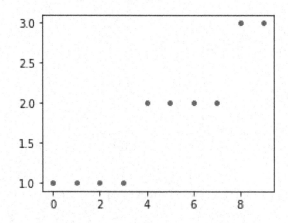

Since we played by the rules and wrote a learner that plugs directly into the `sklearn` usage pattern (that's also called an *API* or application programming interface), our use of the code will be quite familiar.

In [25]:

```
# here, we're giving ourselves all the help we can by using
# the same cut points as our data were generated with
model = PiecewiseConstantRegression(cut_points=np.array([3, 7]))
model.fit(ftr, tgt)
preds = model.predict(ftr)
print("Predictions equal target?", np.allclose(preds, tgt))
```

```
Predictions equal target? True
```

As written, `PiecewiseConstantRegression` is defined by some hyperparameters (the cut points) and some parameters (the constants associated with each piece). The constants are computed when we call `fit`. The overall fit of the model is very, very sensitive to the number and location of the split points. If we are thinking about using piecewise methods, we either (1) hope to have background knowledge about where the jumps are or (2) are willing to spend time trying different hyperparameters and cross-validating the results to get a good end product.

Now, even though I'm taking the easy way out and talking about piecewise constants—the individual lines have a b but no mx—we could extend this to piecewise lines, piecewise parabolas, etc. We could also require that the end points meet. This requirement would get us a degree of continuity, but not necessarily smoothness. Phrased differently, we could connect the piecewise segments but there might still be sharp turns. We could enforce an even higher degree of smoothness where the turns have to be somewhat gentle. Allowing more bends in the piecewise components reduces our bias. Enforcing constraints on the meeting points regularizes—smooths—the model.

9.4 Regression Trees

One of the great aspects of decision trees is their flexibility. Since they are conceptually straightforward—find regions with similar outputs, label everything in that region in some way—they can be easily adapted to other tasks. In case of regression, if we can find regions where a single numerical value is a good representation of the whole region, we're golden. So, at the leaves of tree, instead of saying *cat* or *dog*, we say *27.5*.

9.4.1 Performing Regression with Trees

Moving from piecewise constant regression to decision trees is a straightforward conceptual step. Why? Because you've already done the heavy lifting. Decision trees give us a way to zoom in on regions that are sufficiently similar and, having selected a region, we predict a constant. That zoom-in happens as we segment off regions of space.

Eventually, we get to a small enough region that behaves in a nicely uniform way. Basically, using decision trees for regression gives us an automatic way of picking the number and location of split points. These splits are determined by computing the loss when a split breaks the current set of data at a node into two subsets. The split that leads to the immediate lowest squared error is the chosen breakpoint for that node. Remember that tree building is a greedy process and it is not guaranteed to be a globally best step—but a sequence of greedy steps is often good enough for day-to-day use.

In [26]:

```
dtrees = [tree.DecisionTreeRegressor(max_depth=md) for md in [1, 3, 5, 10]]

for model in dtrees:
    preds = (model.fit(diabetes_train_ftrs, diabetes_train_tgt)
                  .predict(diabetes_test_ftrs))
    mse = metrics.mean_squared_error(diabetes_test_tgt, preds)
    fmt = "{} {:2d} {:4.0f}"
    print(fmt.format(get_model_name(model),
                     model.get_params()['max_depth'],
                     mse))
```

```
DecisionTreeRegressor  1 4341
DecisionTreeRegressor  3 3593
DecisionTreeRegressor  5 4312
DecisionTreeRegressor 10 5190
```

Notice how adding depth helps and then hurts. Let's all say it together: *overfitting*! If we allow too much depth, we split the data into too many parts. If the data is split too finely, we make unneeded distinctions, we overfit, and our test error creeps up.

9.5 Comparison of Regressors: Take Three

We'll return to the student dataset and apply some of our fancier learners to it.

In [27]:

```
student_df = pd.read_csv('data/portugese_student_numeric.csv')
student_ftrs = student_df[student_df.columns[:-1]]
student_tgt  = student_df['G3']
```

```
In [28]:
student_tts = skms.train_test_split(student_ftrs, student_tgt)

(student_train_ftrs, student_test_ftrs,
 student_train_tgt,  student_test_tgt) = student_tts
```

We'll pull in the regression methods we introduced in Chapter 7:

```
In [29]:
old_school = [linear_model.LinearRegression(),
              neighbors.KNeighborsRegressor(n_neighbors=3),
              neighbors.KNeighborsRegressor(n_neighbors=10)]
```

and add some new regressors from this chapter:

```
In [30]:
# L1, L2 penalized (abs, sqr), C=1.0 for both
penalized_lr = [linear_model.Lasso(),
                linear_model.Ridge()]

# defaults are epsilon=.1 and nu=.5, respectively
svrs = [svm.SVR(), svm.NuSVR()]

dtrees = [tree.DecisionTreeRegressor(max_depth=md) for md in [1, 3, 5, 10]]

reg_models = old_school + penalized_lr + svrs + dtrees
```

We'll compare based on root mean squared error (RMSE):

```
In [31]:
def rms_error(actual, predicted):
    ' root-mean-squared-error function '
    # lesser values are better (a<b means a is better)
    mse = metrics.mean_squared_error(actual, predicted)
    return np.sqrt(mse)
rms_scorer = metrics.make_scorer(rms_error)
```

and we'll standardize the data before we apply our models:

```
In [32]:

scaler = skpre.StandardScaler()

scores = {}
for model in reg_models:
    pipe = pipeline.make_pipeline(scaler, model)
    preds = skms.cross_val_predict(pipe,
                                   student_ftrs, student_tgt,
                                   cv=10)
    key = (get_model_name(model) +
           str(model.get_params().get('max_depth', "")) +
           str(model.get_params().get('n_neighbors', "")))
    scores[key] = rms_error(student_tgt, preds)

df = pd.DataFrame.from_dict(scores, orient='index').sort_values(0)
df.columns=['RMSE']
display(df)
```

	RMSE
DecisionTreeRegressor1	4.3192
Ridge	4.3646
LinearRegression	4.3653
NuSVR	4.3896
SVR	4.4062
DecisionTreeRegressor3	4.4298
Lasso	4.4375
KNeighborsRegressor10	4.4873
DecisionTreeRegressor5	4.7410
KNeighborsRegressor3	4.8915
DecisionTreeRegressor10	5.3526

For the top four models, let's see some details about performance on a fold-by-fold basis.

```
In [33]:

better_models = [tree.DecisionTreeRegressor(max_depth=1),
                 linear_model.Ridge(),
                 linear_model.LinearRegression(),
                 svm.NuSVR()]
```

```
fig, ax = plt.subplots(1, 1, figsize=(8,4))
for model in better_models:
    pipe = pipeline.make_pipeline(scaler, model)
    cv_results = skms.cross_val_score(pipe,
                                      student_ftrs, student_tgt,
                                      scoring = rms_scorer,
                                      cv=10)

    my_lbl = "{:s} ({:5.3f}$\pm${:.2f})".format(get_model_name(model),
                                                cv_results.mean(),
                                                cv_results.std())
    ax.plot(cv_results, 'o--', label=my_lbl)
    ax.set_xlabel('CV-Fold #')
    ax.set_ylabel("RMSE")
    ax.legend()
```

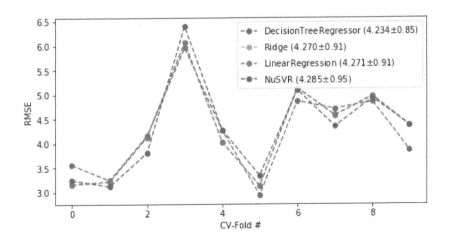

Each of these goes back and forth a bit. They are all very close in learning performance. The range of the means $(4.23, 4.29)$ is not very wide and it's also a bit less than the standard deviation. There's still work that remains to be done. We didn't actually work through different values for regularization. We can do that by hand, in a manner similar to the complexity curves we saw in Section 5.7.2. However, we'll approach that in a much more convenient fashion in Section 11.2.

9.6 EOC

9.6.1 Summary

At this point, we've added a number of distinctly different regressors to our quiver of models. Decision trees are highly flexible; regularized regression and SVR update the linear regression to compete with the cool kids.

9.6.2 Notes

We talked about L_1 and L_2 regularization. There is a method in `sklearn` called `ElasticNet` that allows us to blend the two together.

While we were satisfied with a constant-value prediction for each region at the leaf of a tree, we *could*—standard methods *don't*—make mini-regression lines (or curves) at each of the leaves.

Trees are one example of an *additive model*. Classification trees work by (1) picking a region and (2) assigning a class to examples from that region. If we pick one and only one region for each example, we can write that as a peculiar sum, as we did in Section 8.2.1. For regression, it is a sum over region selection and target value. There are many types of models that fall under the additive model umbrella—such as the piecewise regression line we constructed, a more general version of piecewise regression called *splines*, and more complicated friends. Splines are interesting because advanced variations of splines can move the choice of decision points from a hyperparameter to a parameter: the decision points become part of the best solution instead of an input. Splines also have nice ways of incorporating regularization—there it is generally called *smoothness*.

Speaking of smoothness, continuity, and discontinuity: these topics go very, very deep. I've mostly used smoothness in an everyday sense. However, in math, we can define smoothness in many different ways. As a result, in mathematics, some continuous functions might *not* be smooth. Smoothness can be an *additional* constraint, beyond continuity, to make sure functions are very well behaved.

For more details on implementing your own `sklearn`-compatible learners, see http://scikit-learn.org/stable/developers/contributing.html#rolling-your-own-estimator. Be aware that the class parameters they discuss there are *not* the model parameters we have discussed. Instead, they are the model hyperparameters. Part of the problem is the double meaning of *parameter* in computer science (for information passed into a function) and mathematics (for knobs a machine-model adjusts). For more details, see Section 11.2.1.

After we get through Chapter 10—coming up next, stay tuned—we'll have some additional techniques that would let us do more general piecewise linear regression that works on multiple features.

9.6.3 Exercises

1. Build a good old-fashioned, ridge, and lasso regression on the same dataset. Examine the coefficients. Do you notice any patterns? What if you vary the amount of regularization to the ridge and lasso?

2. Create data that represents a step function: from zero to one, it has value of zero; from one to two, it has a value of one; from two to three, it has the value two, and so on. What line is estimated when you fit a good old-fashioned linear regression to it? Conceptually, what happens if you draw a line through the fronts of the steps? What about the backs? Are any of these lines distinctly better from an error or residual perspective?

3. Here's a conceptual question. If you're making a piecewise linear regression, what would it mean for split points to underfit or overfit the data? How would you assess if either is happening? Follow up: what would a complexity curve for piecewise regression look like? What would it assess?

4. Evaluate the resource usage for the different learners on the student dataset.

5. Compare the performance of our regression methods on some other datasets. You might look at the digits via `datasets.load_digits`.

6. Make a simple, synthetic regression dataset. Examine the effect of different values of ν (nu) when you build a `NuSVR`. Try to make some systematic changes to the regression data. Again, vary ν. Can you spot any patterns? (Warning: patterns that arise in 1, 2, or just a few dimensions—that is, with just a few features—may not hold in higher dimensions.)

7. Conceptual question. What would *piecewise parabolas* look like? What would happen if we require them to connect at the ends of their intervals?

Manual Feature Engineering: Manipulating Data for Fun and Profit

```
In [1]:
# setup
from mlwpy import *
%matplotlib inline

iris = datasets.load_iris()
(iris_train,      iris_test,
 iris_train_tgt, iris_test_tgt) = skms.train_test_split(iris.data,
                                                        iris.target,
                                                        test_size=.25)
# remove units ' (cm)' from names
iris.feature_names = [fn[:-5] for fn in iris.feature_names]

# dataframe for convenience
iris_df = pd.DataFrame(iris.data, columns=iris.feature_names)
iris_df['species'] = iris.target_names[iris.target]
```

10.1 Feature Engineering Terminology and Motivation

We are going to turn our attention away from expanding our catalog of models and instead take a closer look at the data. *Feature engineering* refers to manipulation—addition, deletion, combination, mutation—of the features. Remember that features are attribute-value pairs, so we could add or remove columns from our data table and modify values within columns. Feature engineering can be used in a broad sense and in a narrow sense.

I'm going to use it in a broad, inclusive sense and point out some gotchas along the way. Here are some concrete examples:

- *Scaling* and *normalization* means adjusting the range and center of data to ease learning and improve the interpretation of our results. You might recall that the *diabetes* dataset (Section 4.1) in `sklearn` comes to us pre-*standardized*, which is one form of scaling.
- *Filling missing values*. Real-world datasets can be missing values due to the difficulty of collecting *complete* datasets and because of errors in the data collection process. Missing values can be filled in based on expert knowledge, heuristics, or by some machine learning techniques.
- *Feature selection* means removing features because they are unimportant, redundant, or outright counterproductive to learning. Sometimes we simply have *too many* features and we need fewer. An example of a counterproductive feature is an identification variable which doesn't help in generalization. We saw in Section 8.2 how unique identifiers can lead a decision tree all the way from the root to unique leaves for *every* training example. The problem is that a new unique identifier of a test example *won't be anywhere in the tree*. Fail.
- *Feature coding* involves choosing a set of symbolic values to represent different categories. We discussed this as far back as Chapter 1. The concept of *WithPartner* can be captured with a single column taking values *WithPartner* or *Single*, or it can be captured with two columns *WithPartner* and *Single*, one of which is *True* and the other *False*. Strictly speaking, this is a form of feature construction.
- *Feature construction* creates new feature(s) from one or more other features. For example, from a flower's sepal length and width, we can create the flower's *sepal area*.
- *Feature extraction* means moving from low-level features that are unsuitable for learning—practically speaking, we get poor testing results—to higher-level features which *are* useful for learning. Often feature extraction is valuable when we have specific data formats—like images or text—that have to be converted to a tabular row-column, example-feature format. Feature extraction and feature construction differ in the complexity of transformations they make, but conceptually they are doing the same thing.

10.1.1 Why Engineer Features?

Two drivers of feature engineering are (1) background knowledge from the domain of the task and (2) inspection of the data values. The first case includes a doctor's knowledge of important blood pressure thresholds or an accountant's knowledge of tax bracket levels. Another example is the use of body mass index (BMI) by medical providers and insurance companies. While it has limitations, BMI is quickly calculated from body weight and height and serves as a surrogate for a characteristic that is *very hard* to accurately measure: proportion of lean body mass. Inspecting the values of a feature means looking at a histogram of its distribution. For distribution-based feature engineering, we might see multimodal distributions—histograms with multiple humps—and decide to break the humps into bins.

10.1.2 When Does Engineering Happen?

A major distinction we can make in feature engineering is *when* it occurs. Our primary question here is whether the feature engineering is performed inside the cross-validation loop or not. Feature engineering that is done during the modeling process will typically be done within a cross-validation loop. Cross-validation can protect us from overfitting.

We can also modify the features before we start the modeling process. Often, these modifications are part of exporting data from a storage system like a database. My readers that work with databases will be familiar with an extract-transform-load (ETL) paradigm. Feature engineering can also be part of *data cleaning* as an intermediate step between exporting/importing data and learning. If we manipulate the data before building a model, we need to be very careful that we don't peek at the relationship between the predictive features and the target. We also need to be careful so we don't unintentionally *introduce* a relationship that isn't there in the raw data. There are many, many ways we can slip up and fail.

So, if we *are* going to perform premodeling feature engineering, we should be very careful to squirrel away a hold-out test set *before* we start playing with the data. The test set will allow us to evaluate the results of both our premodeling feature engineering *and* the direct modeling steps. We can use the hold-out test set to protect us from dangerous feature engineering outside of a cross-validation loop. We proceed as usual and see what happens with our training and testing errors. If our training errors are good but we see our testing errors aren't improving—or are even getting *worse*—then we can assume that we are overfitting. In that case, we probably want to move some of our feature engineering into the cross-validation loop to detect the overfitting earlier.

Now, we have two competing concerns. If your feature engineering *needs* to be in the cross-validation loop, the easiest programming hooks mean you'll probably want to perform it with `sklearn`. But if your feature engineering is complicated and not already implemented in `sklearn`, you probably *don't* want to use `sklearn`—you probably want to use `pandas` or other custom Python tools. Now for the real kicker: if you have complicated feature engineering that needs to be in the CV loop, my best wishes are with you. Meeting these two needs at once is difficult. In seriousness, you might want to factor out some of the most complicated portions as preprocessing. Still, you may be able to write helper code that can be placed in the CV loop. In Section 9.3.1, we defined a custom learner. You can also define a custom transformer and we'll see that shortly.

A practical take on the *whens* of feature engineering gives us an overall timeline:

1. Pull the data from external sources, possibly using helper code written in Python and making use of packages for interfacing with other systems like databases.
2. Separate out a hold-out test set. Don't peek at it.
3. Perform any initial data cleaning with the external system and/or pure Python.
4. Place the data in a Pandas `DataFrame` and do any additional premodeling *data wrangling*. Data wrangling is a common term for feature engineering done before the learning steps.
5. Design the learning and within-CV loop feature engineering steps with `sklearn`.
6. Pipe the data from `pandas` to `sklearn` and press *Go*.
7. Evaluate the results.

8. Repeat as necessary.
9. When ready to take over the world or save lives, verify the system on the hold-out test set.
10. Cross fingers and deploy system.

10.1.3   How Does Feature Engineering Occur?

Another breakdown is *how* the feature engineering occurs. Our focus in this chapter is on feature engineering that is explicitly defined and manually applied. An example of an explicitly defined feature engineering task is creating the ratio between heights and weights that creates a BMI value. If we are *literally* responsible for calculating that value and adding a column to our dataset, I call that *manually applied* feature engineering—in this case, manual feature construction. If we set up a pipeline (as in the next chapter) that constructs all possible ratios between pairs of features, I'll call that *automatically applied*.

There are learning methods that incorporate feature engineering as part of their operation. Some of these methods—like Support Vector Machines (Section 13.2.4)—use the reengineered features behind the scenes without our intervention. Others—like principal components analysis (Section 13.3)—require us to make use of their outputs as inputs to another learning step. In both cases, we perform steps similar to the learning algorithms we've seen so for: we fit a model to training data and then we transform the testing data.

10.2   Feature Selection and Data Reduction: Taking out the Trash

One of the most blunt tools we have in feature engineering is removing data. We might remove data because of redundancy, irrelevance, or overload. (A quick side note: I'm discussing this from the perspective of removing *features* from our dataset. We could equally well consider removing *examples*—that is, rows instead of columns—from our dataset.)

There are practical and technical reasons that redundancy is a problem. We will see some technical reasons later in this chapter. From a practical perspective, if two columns represent the same concept—or, worse, the same literal values—we are pushing around and storing more numbers then we need to. The information is available to the learning system in more than one form. Some learning systems can't handle this effectively.

Irrelevant features are even worse. Not only do they take up space, they also lead us down training paths that won't do well when we turn to testing. Imagine several columns of random data. We can probably put enough random columns into our dataset to uniquely identify each example. Then, we can memorize a lookup table from these pseudo-identifiers to correct targets. But then, what do we do with a new example? If we just fill in several random values, the target will be equally random. It won't have any relationship between the useful features—the nonrandom ones—and the target. We discussed this difficulty in the context of decision trees in Section 8.2.

By overload, I mean simply that in a very large dataset—with many, many features—we may have no choice but to reduce the number of features we consider due to processing time and memory constraints. So, if we need to dump some data, how do we do it? There are three major strategies: manual techniques based on our knowledge of the problem and the data, random sampling techniques that use coin flipping to keep or discard data, and model-based techniques that attempt to keep features that interact well with our learning model. Sometimes these methods are combined: we can use random feature selection to build models and then combine the resulting models. We'll discuss that in Chapter 12.

Manual and randomized feature selection is conceptually simple. Drop a column from a table—either based on a principled argument (we know the two columns are measuring the same thing) or based on a randomness. Done. I don't have a *but* here. Selecting or discarding data based on learning models makes up for the simplicity of the other two options. There are forests worth of books and articles written on the topic. We can only scratch the surface. However, here are some examples.

Some feature selection strategies are internal components of learning techniques. For example, decision trees have to pick a feature to split on at each node. One type of decision tree uses a measure called *information gain* to decide on a good feature. We can extend that idea to rank features of a larger dataset. We can also use the results of modeling to evaluate features. For example, we can look at features with low linear regression coefficients and declare that they are relatively unimportant to the overall model. This doesn't necessarily save us work in the first model-building process, but it might save substantial time in future models. We can also build many models and ask what the commonalities among those models are. Features that show up in many models may be more likely to be important to the relationship with the target.

One of our regularized forms of linear regression—L_1-regularized regression or the *lasso*—has a tendency to push the learned coefficients to zero. The result is that models built using the lasso might drop out some features. So, we say that the lasso method is performing feature selection as an implicit part of its operation. We can use the lasso as our final model or we can use it as a feature selection phase before using other models.

10.3 Feature Scaling

We are going to discuss two ways to rescale and recenter features that don't consider any relationships with other features or the target. Rescaling means that we translate the values so that the extremes are different and the intermediate values are moved in some consistent way. Recentering the data means that we translate the values so that the extremes are different and the intermediate values are moved in some consistent way. Often, rescaling will also result in recentered data. The two major ways of rescaling are either by changing on a *fixed* scale or changing the values with respect to some statistic computed from the data. Whoa, did Mark just go off the deep end? It's OK. We'll bring it back in.

Here's an example of fixed rescaling. If you convert between Fahrenheit and Celsius temperatures, you would take $220°$F to $100°$C and $32°$F to $0°$C. Temperatures in the middle—say, $104°$F converting to $40°$C—follow a fixed rule. At least this is a bit more concrete, but what is the fixed value we are using to convert these? Well, that comes from the formula for converting temperatures: $C = \frac{5(F-32)}{9}$. A little algebra turns that into $C = \frac{5}{9}F - 17.7$, which is our friendly old $y = mx + b$ in a different form. If you never noticed, converting values with a linear formula simply stretches and shifts the values; m is responsible for the stretching and b is responsible for the shift.

In [2]:

```
fig, ax = plt.subplots(1,1,figsize=(4,3))
f_temps = np.linspace(0, 212, 100)
c_temps = (5/9) * (f_temps - 32)
plt.plot(f_temps, f_temps, 'r',   # F -> F
         f_temps, c_temps, 'b');  # F -> C
```

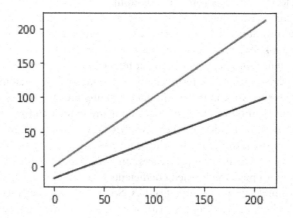

Notice how the upper red line is compressed vertically from 0 to 212 to around -18 to 100 on the lower blue line. The central value also moves from 106 to 59. Outside of unit conversions—Celsius to Fahrenheit or meters to feet—the most common *fixed* scalings are mapping $\{min, max\}$ values to $\{0, 1\}$ or to $\{-1, 1\}$ and spreading the other values out evenly between them.

Standardization, a statistical rescaling, is a bit trickier. Instead of stretching out from the source to the target based on a fixed, prior value (like $\frac{5}{9}$ to convert Fahrenheit to Celsius), it compresses values based on the spread—measured by the variance or standard deviation—of the source values. The difference is probably best explained with a graphic. Here we use sklearn's StandardScaler to do the heavy lifting. fit_transform evaluates the training data *and* modifies it in one go. It is similar to our usual model.fit().predict() except it does not use a separate target in the fit() step. It simply learns—in this case, a mean and a standard deviation—and then applies itself to them. After being fit, it can also transform testing data. I've colored bins of data points so you can see how the points move around due to the transformation.

```
In [3]:
fig, ax = plt.subplots(1,1,figsize=(4,3))
original = np.random.uniform(-5, 5, 100)
scaled = skpre.StandardScaler().fit_transform(original.reshape(-1,1))[:,0]
bins = np.floor(original).astype(np.uint8) + 5

df = pd.DataFrame({'original':original,
                   'scaled':scaled,
                   'hue':bins})
df = pd.melt(df, id_vars='hue', var_name='scale')

sns.swarmplot(x='scale', y='value', hue='hue', data=df).legend_.remove()
```

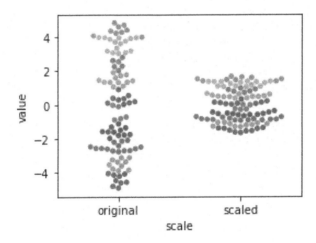

Here, the unit of measurement isn't Fahrenheit or Celsius: it's units of the *standard deviation*. The standard deviation tells us about the spread of our data. The more spread-out our data is, the bigger the standard deviation is. We are *still* on a linear scale after we standardize. That might be surprising. Here's the formula: $\text{scaled} = \frac{\text{orig}-\text{mean}(\text{orig})}{\text{stddev}(\text{orig})}$ $= \frac{1}{\text{stddev}(\text{orig})} \text{orig} - \frac{\text{mean}(\text{orig})}{\text{stddev}(\text{orig})}$. There's a $y = mx + b$ hidden in there. The new center of our data is zero.

In a curious twist of events, standardization doesn't change the overall shape of the data—it may not look the same at first sight, but here's another take. In our example, we had data from a uniform or flat-ish distribution. When we standardize it, it is still uniform. Visually, the shape has relatively flat sides. It just happens to be more compressed. As another example—try it yourself—if the data looks like a two-humped camel and we standardize it, it would *still* have two humps. Basically, we can evenly stretch or squeeze the graph of the data, but we can't distort it more than that.

Let's look into the *how* of scaling. Here are simple examples of `MinMaxScaler` and `StandardScaler`. To follow the example points as they move around, I'm going to color them by their percentile bin. I'm using Pandas `cut` method to do this. I don't want to get hung up on that, but just know that it is similar to the encoding technique we used when we made our piecewise constant regression model in Section 9.3. Here, we make use of Pandas *categorical* capabilities to create a coloring value:

In [4]:

```
iris_df = pd.DataFrame(iris.data, columns=iris.feature_names)

bins = pd.cut(iris_df['sepal width'],
              np.percentile(iris_df['sepal width'],
                            [25, 50, 75, 100])).cat.codes

df = pd.DataFrame({'orig':iris_df['sepal width'],
                   'hue':bins})

scalers = [('std', skpre.StandardScaler()),
           ('01' , skpre.MinMaxScaler()),
           ('-1,1', skpre.MinMaxScaler((-1,1)))]

for name, scaler in scalers:
    # ugly:  [[]] to keep 2D for sklearn
    #        reshape(-1) to go back to 1D for seaborn   :(
    df[name] = scaler.fit_transform(df[['orig']]).reshape(-1)

df = pd.melt(df, id_vars='hue', var_name='scale')
sns.swarmplot(x='scale', y='value', hue='hue', data=df).legend_.remove()
```

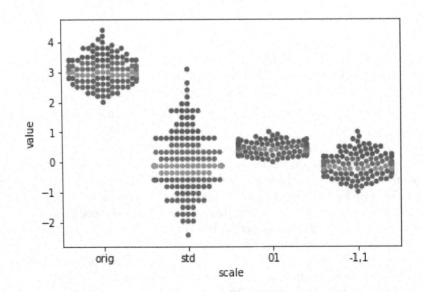

The most common motivation for rescaling is that we don't want arbitrary measurement scales to influence our outcomes. For example, if we measure someone's height in meters, instead of nanometers, the values will be much smaller—one meter is an awful lot of nano-whatevers. But that shouldn't really effect the fundamental information in the measurements. The easiest way to keep things fair between values measured on very different scales is to rescale them to an approximately common scale. Another example occurs when different types of measurements are in the same model. For example, household income is often tens of thousands of dollars—but cars per household is typically measured in single digits. Numerically, these values have very different weight. We offset that by placing them on a common scale. Some of the benefits of rescaling become more prominent when we move beyond predictive modeling and start making statistical or causal claims.

10.4 Discretization

We've already seen discretization—the process of sorting a range of continuous values into some finite, or discrete, buckets of values—when we implemented piecewise constant regression. There, we had to pick an output value—a line segment—based on the input value's bucket. Discretization also shows up as part of decision tree value splits: *height* > 5'7" is either true or false. There are a number of *automated* methods for discretizing data; some of them look at the relationship between a feature's values, the *ideal* split points to break those features at, and the value of those breaks to good classification. It is crucial that these methods be used inside of cross-validation to prevent overfitting on the training data. You can think of sufficiently advanced discretization strategies as micro-learners of their own—imagine if they could discretize right into the correct classification buckets! For now, let's consider some *manual* approaches to discretization with the *iris* data.

In [5]:

```
iris_df = pd.DataFrame(iris.data, columns=iris.feature_names)
iris_df['species'] = iris.target_names[iris.target]
display(iris_df.iloc[[0,50,100]])
```

	sepal length	sepal width	petal length	petal width	species
0	5.1000	3.5000	1.4000	0.2000	setosa
50	7.0000	3.2000	4.7000	1.4000	versicolor
100	6.3000	3.3000	6.0000	2.5000	virginica

If we look at a smoothed plot of the sepal lengths, we see it is a pretty well-behaved bump.

```
In [6]:
```

```
plt.subplots(1,1,figsize=(4,3))
ax = sns.distplot(iris_df['sepal length'], hist=False, rug=True)
ax.set_ylabel("Approximate %");
```

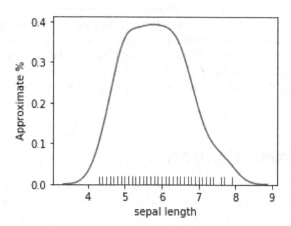

A simple way to discretize is to break the values into *low* and *high* at the mean or median.

```
In [7]:
```

```
# apply binary threshold to numeric with sklearn is tricky
column = iris_df[['sepal length']] # keep 2Dness because sk complains
col_mean = column.mean().values    # and sk fails with Series/DF

both = column.copy()
both['> Mean'] = skpre.binarize(column, col_mean).astype(np.bool)

print('Column Mean:', col_mean)
display(both.iloc[[0,50,100]])
```

Column Mean: [5.8433]

	sepal length	> Mean
0	5.1000	False
50	7.0000	True
100	6.3000	True

We can also do the same discretization using the `pd.cut` function we showed off a minute or two ago.

```
In [8]:

sep_len_series = iris_df['sepal length']
breaks = [sep_len_series.mean(),
          sep_len_series.max()]

# ugly to extract
print(pd.cut(sep_len_series, breaks).cat.codes[[0, 50, 100]])
```

```
0      -1
50      0
100     0
dtype: int8
```

But, frankly, going to raw `np` results in a fairly readable solution that involves minimal behind-the-scenes magic.

```
In [9]:

# an easy button:
np.where(column > column.mean(), True, False)[[0,50,100]]
```

```
Out[9]:

array([[False],
       [ True],
       [ True]])
```

Even though we pushed that computation through, does it make sense to break such well-behaved data right in the middle? Two very similar sepal length values—mean plus a little and mean minus a little—are forced into different buckets. The big hump also means most of the values are in that region around the mean. Do we want them together or split apart? Only our prediction problem can tell us for sure. But, personally, I'd be more comfortable keeping the middle together and partitioning the particularly long and short into their own buckets. So, we'd have short, medium, and long with *most* of the examples falling into the medium bucket.

If we have domain knowledge, we might have other reasons to pick certain split points. For example, an accountant might introduce split points at tax bracket thresholds. Here, there is strong information available and we likely don't need to worry about overfitting. We can always cross-validate and compare. If we have no source of expert information, we might try a range of split point possibilities and cross-validate them to make sure we don't overfit.

Let's get practical for a moment. Which technique should you use? Now, I'm going to get up to my old tricks. The answer is *it depends*. You may not be a NumPy ninja, so the last option may not make sense to you. But if you have more complex numerical data, you might get some other wins by using NumPy. There's a bit more of a tradeoff with the Pandas and `sklearn` options. The Pandas option isn't going to be super convenient to place inside of a cross-validation loop. The `sklearn` method will plug directly into cross-validation using pipelines. However, if you need to do data exploration and processing to come up with the split points, stick with Pandas.

10.5   Categorical Coding

So far, we've been using the *iris* dataset in the exact form it was given to us: we predict the species from numerical measurements of the flowers. But we can rearrange the data and do other learning tasks. For example, imagine we want to predict petal length from the other features, including the species. Now, we take the species as a *known* input feature and the petal length as an *unknown* target. Here's what the data looks like:

In [10]:

```
# close your eyes Francis, this is about to get ugly
# this pandas voodoo is simply to produce a labeled dataframe
# so you can *see* the learning problem I am describing in the text

new_iris_df = pd.DataFrame(iris_df, columns=['petal length',
                                             'petal width',
                                             'species'])

new_iris_df.columns = pd.MultiIndex([['input ftrs', 'target ftr'],
                                     new_iris_df.columns],
                                    [[1, 0, 0], [0,1,2]])

new_iris_df.sort_index(axis='columns', inplace=True)
display(new_iris_df.iloc[[0,50,100]])
```

	input ftrs		target ftr
	petal width	species	petal length
0	0.2000	setosa	1.4000
50	1.4000	versicolor	4.7000
100	2.5000	virginica	6.0000

Species does not have a direct numerical interpretation. There isn't a defined ordering that we can use to say setosa = 1 < versicolor = 2. We *could* use numbers to represent categories—think class 0, class 1, class 2. However, if we pass this column to linear regression, what would it mean for a species coefficient to be multiplied by these different values? We'd be treating the *categories* as numerical values when they are really just class identifiers. We *don't* want a numerical difference of 1 to be interpreted as adding or subtracting anything from a predicted petal length.

Our general technique for encoding discrete data is called *coding categorical variables*. We'll examine it in a broader context in a few minutes. For now, let's start with a useful technique that gives old-school statisticians fits: *one-hot coding*. It translates a single column with multiple values into multiple columns with one, and only one, *on* value. The *on* value for an example is usually a binary 1 (or True) with the other column values being 0 (or False). Here are the iris species in a one-hot encoding:

In [11]:

```
# start with category numbers
print("Numerical categories:",
      iris.target[[0, 50, 100]], sep='\n')

# produces sparse representation
sparse = skpre.OneHotEncoder().fit_transform(iris.target.reshape(-1,1))

# densify it
print("One-hot coding:",
      sparse[[0,50,100]].todense(), sep="\n")
```

```
Numerical categories:
[0 1 2]
One-hot coding:
[[1. 0. 0.]
 [0. 1. 0.]
 [0. 0. 1.]]
```

Several technical points are worth mentioning here. `OneHotEncoder` requires numerical inputs. It isn't happy with strings. It also requires a 2D input—hence the call to `reshape`. Finally, if we go one-hot, there are many, many zeros in the result. Remember, only one value per example is turned on over all the expanded columns. A source column with even just a few legal values leads to *lots* of zeros—all but one of the options *aren't* used for every example. So, `sklearn` is clever and stores the data in a compressed format that deals well with *sparsity*—a technical term for data with lots of zeros. Instead of recording values everywhere, it records just the nonzero entries and assumes everything else is zero.

There are some learning methods that can work efficiently with sparse data; they know that many values are zero and are smart about not doing extra work. If we want to see the data in its usual, complete form, we have to ask to make it dense. You can imagine that when we fill out the sparse form, we have a table that is a bit like Swiss cheese: it has lots of holes in it. We have to fill those holes—values that were assumed to be zero—in with *actual* zeros. Then we have a solid—dense—table with entries everywhere. We do that with the `.todense()` call in the last line.

We can also perform one-hot encoding with `pandas`. One benefit is that we can ask it to give nice labels to the one-hot columns.

In [12]:

```
# can use drop_first to get treatment coding
# can request sparse storage
encoded = pd.get_dummies(iris_df, prefix="is")
encoded.iloc[[0,50,100]]
```

Out[12]:

	sepal length	sepal width	petal length	petal width	is_ setosa	is_ versicolor	is_ virginica
0	5.1000	3.5000	1.4000	0.2000	1	0	0
50	7.0000	3.2000	4.7000	1.4000	0	1	0
100	6.3000	3.3000	6.0000	2.5000	0	0	1

We can merge the one-hot species with the original data for fun and profit. We may want to visualize the relationship between the encoding and the original species values. Here goes:

In [13]:

```
# splicing dataframes together by merging
# recall `iris.target` is in terms of 0, 1, 2, not symbolic (setosa, etc).
encoded_species = pd.get_dummies(iris.target)
encoded_df = pd.merge(iris_df, encoded_species,
                      right_index=True, left_index=True)
encoded_df.iloc[[0,50,100]]
```

Out[13]:

	sepal length	sepal width	petal length	petal width	species	0	1	2
0	5.1000	3.5000	1.4000	0.2000	setosa	1	0	0
50	7.0000	3.2000	4.7000	1.4000	versicolor	0	1	0
100	6.3000	3.3000	6.0000	2.5000	virginica	0	0	1

10.5.1 Another Way to Code and the Curious Case of the Missing Intercept

Here's one other way to achieve the one-hot coding. In the statistical world, the one-hot coding goes by the names of *treatment* or *dummy coding*. There are details I'm going to tap-dance around, but I'll leave a few more notes at the end of the chapter. patsy is a nice system that allows us to specify a number of feature engineering and modeling ideas in a convenient way. Here's a long-hand version we'll use in a minute:

```
In [14]:
import patsy.contrasts as pc

levels = iris.target_names
coding = (pc.Treatment(reference=0)
                .code_with_intercept(list(levels)))
print(coding)
```

```
ContrastMatrix(array([[1., 0., 0.],
                      [0., 1., 0.],
                      [0., 0., 1.]]),
               ['[setosa]', '[versicolor]', '[virginica]'])
```

My reason for bringing *yet another option* up is not to overwhelm you with alternatives. In reality, I want to segue into talking about a few useful feature engineering tasks we can do with patsy and also deepen your understanding of the implications of categorical encodings. Now, I claimed it was a *nice* system for doing things like one-hot encoding. But, for crying out loud, that previous cell is hideous. Let's press the easy button.

```
In [15]:
encoded = patsy.dmatrix('species-1',
                        iris_df,
                        return_type='dataframe')
display(encoded.iloc[[0,50,100]])
```

	species[setosa]	species[versicolor]	species[virginica]
0	1.0000	0.0000	0.0000
50	0.0000	1.0000	0.0000
100	0.0000	0.0000	1.0000

What's happening with that -1 in 'species-1'? Let's see what happens when we leave it out.

```
In [16]:
encoded = patsy.dmatrix('species',
                        iris_df,
                        return_type='dataframe')
display(encoded.iloc[[0,50,100]])
```

	Intercept	species[T.versicolor]	species[T.virginica]
0	1.0000	0.0000	0.0000
50	1.0000	1.0000	0.0000
100	1.0000	0.0000	1.0000

We get *two* of the features coded explicitly *and* we get a column of all ones under the name *Intercept*. By the way, `patsy` is literally performing the +1 trick for us and giving it the name *Intercept*. So, why do we have to do the `-1` to get the simple result? Why does the `dmatrix` for `species` give us a column of ones *and*—seemingly!—ignore one of the species (there's no column for *setosa*)? We'll come back to this in moment.

10.5.1.1 Patsy Models

Let's point a flashlight at what just happened. We were building design matrices—`dmatrix` critters—with two main elements: (1) some specification of a modeling idea and (2) the data we want to run through that model. A design matrix tells us how we get from raw data to the form of the data we want to run through the underlying number-crunching of a modeling process. It's definitely example time.

We might specify that we want to predict petal length from petal width and species—our regression twist on the *iris* data. If our column names had underscores (`petal_length`) instead of spaces (`petal length`), that specification would be written as `'petal_length ~ petal_width + C(species, Treatment)'`. This specification says to run a linear regression with the left-hand side of the tilde `~` as the target and the right-hand side terms as the input features. The `C()` indicates that we want to encode the `species` before running the linear regression. Having spaces in the names complicates matters slightly, but we'll fix that in a moment.

Here's a quick reference of basic things we can do with `patsy` formulas:

- `tgt ~ ftr_1 + ftr_2 + ftr_3`: model `tgt` from the right-hand side features.
- `tgt ~ Q('ftr 1') + Q('ftr 2') + Q('ftr 3')`: Quote funky names.
- `tgt ~ ftr_1 + C(cat_ftr, Some_Coding)`: model `tgt` on `ftr_1` and the Categorically encoded `cat_ftr`.
- `tgt ~ ftr_1 - 1`: model `tgt` on `ftr_1` *without* an intercept. By default, the formulas include an intercept: we have to remove it by hand. We can also remove features from the RHS: `tgt ~ ftr_1 + ftr_2 - ftr_1` is equivalent to `tgt ~ ftr_2`. There are useful cases for feature removal.

Now, I want to investigate what happens with including—or not—certain variable codings. To do so, we need some trivial data we can process in our heads. Here we go:

In [17]:

```
pet_data = pd.DataFrame({'pet' :['cat', 'cat', 'dog'],
                         'cost':[20.0,   25.0,  40.0]})

pet_df = pd.get_dummies(pet_data)
display(pet_df)
```

	cost	pet_cat	pet_dog
0	20.0000	1	0
1	25.0000	1	0
2	40.0000	0	1

In this example, the cat costs are 20 and 25. The single dog example has a cost of 40. Make a quick mental note that the average cat cost is 22.50.

10.5.1.2 Model (Seemingly) without Intercept

We've almost never taken a concrete look at the knob values that are set on our factory machine. Let's do that here. After we `fit`, linear regression will have chosen particular knob values, the ws or m, b. Below, you might notice that I snuck a `fit_intercept=False` into the linear regression constructor. There's a very good reason for it, and I'll get back to it in a few minutes. It is intimately tied to the default `dmatrix` having a column of all ones and *not* coding all three species explicitly. Just keep in mind that we didn't explicitly fit a `b` term (the constant or intercept).

In [18]:

```
def pretty_coeffs(sk_lr_model, ftr_names):
    ' helper to display sklearn results in a nice dataframe '
    lr_coeffs = pd.DataFrame(sk_lr_model.coef_,
                             columns=ftr_names,
                             index=['Coeff'])
    lr_coeffs['intercept'] = sk_lr_model.intercept_
    return lr_coeffs
```

Let's do a bit of data massaging to make our modeling step happy:

In [19]:

```
# massage
sk_tgt  = pet_df['cost'].values.reshape(-1,1)
sk_ftrs = pet_df.drop('cost', axis='columns')

# build model
sk_model = (linear_model.LinearRegression(fit_intercept=False)
                        .fit(sk_ftrs, sk_tgt))
display(pretty_coeffs(sk_model, sk_ftrs.columns))
```

	pet_cat	pet_dog	intercept
Coeff	22.5000	40.0000	0.0000

We didn't fit an intercept—that equivalent to fixing its value at zero. A quick comment on interpreting the `pet` entries. One, and only one, of the two feature values (for *pet_cat* and *pet_dog*) is not zero. Basically, we pick one of those columns and the result chooses our cost. You might also notice that the cat value is the average of the two cat cases; the dog value is the single dog value. For both, we've turned the dummy coding of zeros and ones into a switchable weight—only one of which is turned on—to add to our pet-care cost model.

Back to my main story. Here's another way to generate *the same* model and knob settings.

In [20]:

```
import statsmodels as sm
import statsmodels.formula.api as smf
```

In [21]:

```
# patsy formula that explicitly removes an intercept
formula = 'cost ~ pet - 1'
sm_model = smf.ols(formula, data=pet_data).fit()
display(pd.DataFrame(sm_model.params).T)
```

	pet[cat]	pet[dog]
0	22.5000	40.0000

These two methods work out to the same coefficients—we're pretty happy about that. Let's go back to the question of the missing intercept. I left it out with `fit_intercept=False` in the `sklearn` example. If you start playing around with these `patsy` formulas, you'll find out that it is very difficult to get an explicit three-column dummy coding for the species *and* a column of all ones for the intercept. I'll finally answer:

- Why does coding a categorical variable, by default, appear to leave one variable value out?
- Why does the default formula include an intercept?

10.5.1.3 Model with Definite Intercept

Let's recreate the `sklearn` model, this time *with* an intercept:

In [22]:

```
sk_tgt  = pet_df['cost'].values.reshape(-1,1)
sk_ftrs = pet_df.drop('cost', axis='columns')
sk_model = (linear_model.LinearRegression()  # fit_intercept=True by default!
                       .fit(sk_ftrs, sk_tgt))
display(pretty_coeffs(sk_model, sk_ftrs.columns))
```

	pet_cat	pet_dog	intercept
Coeff	-8.7500	8.7500	31.2500

Now, let's do *the same* model building with `patsy` and `statsmodels`. We have to do some trickery to convince statsmodels to (1) use the fully explicit, one-hot coding for the pets and (2) *also* use a column of all ones. We'll do that by: (1) `pet - 1` to code the pets with both cats and dogs and (2) we'll use an artificial column of **ones** to force an intercept.

```
In [23]:

pet_data_p1 = pet_data.copy()  # don't muck the original data
pet_data_p1['ones'] = 1.0       # manual +1 trick

# remove coding intercept ..... add manual ones == add manual intercept
formula = 'cost ~ (pet - 1) + ones'
sm_model = smf.ols(formula, data=pet_data_p1).fit()
display(pd.DataFrame(sm_model.params).T)
```

	pet[cat]	pet[dog]	ones
0	1.6667	19.1667	20.8333

Something seems to be wrong, Major Tom. The coefficients are different. Let's take a quick look at the predictions from both models:

```
In [24]:

# row-slicing is annoying, but have to get to single-D things
# and .flat gives a warning in the DF constructor
df = pd.DataFrame({'predicted_sk' : sk_model.predict(sk_ftrs)[:,0],
                   'predicted_sm' : sm_model.predict(pet_data_p1),
                   'actual'       : sk_tgt[:,0]})
display(df)
```

	predicted_sk	predicted_sm	actual
0	22.5000	22.5000	20.0000
1	22.5000	22.5000	25.0000
2	40.0000	40.0000	40.0000

Yet the predictions are the same. What on Earth is going on?

10.5.1.4 Solving the Riddle

Let's look under the hood at what happens when we specify a `pet` formula without an intercept. Here's our data including the column of ones:

```
In [25]:

display(pet_data_p1)
```

	pet	cost	ones
0	cat	20.0000	1.0000
1	cat	25.0000	1.0000
2	dog	40.0000	1.0000

The encoding for that data—without an intercept from the categorical coding—gives us

```
In [26]:
print('pet - 1 coding')
print(patsy.dmatrix('pet - 1', data=pet_data_p1))


pet - 1 coding
[[1. 0.]
 [1. 0.]
 [0. 1.]]
```

If we add up across, example-wise, all the coding-created columns, we can verify we only have one "on" value for each example:

```
In [27]:
# what happens when we add up the coding columns
print("column sum:")
full_coding = patsy.dmatrix('pet - 1',
                            data=pet_data_p1,
                            return_type='dataframe')
display(pd.DataFrame(full_coding.sum(axis='columns')))


column sum:
```

	0
0	1.0000
1	1.0000
2	1.0000

If we add up the columns of the fully explicit coding that has columns for both pets, we get a column of all ones. *In addition*, both of our models—the `sklearn` has `fit_intercept=True` by default and our `statsmodels` has the explicit column of ones—*already* have a column of ones in them. So, we have a redundant column of ones buried in our data. This redundancy is *precisely* why there are two different but predictively equivalent answers to the regression models with intercepts. When we remove the intercept but keep the full coding, we *still* have an intercept-like term from the sum of the coding columns.

There are some rules about what constitutes redundancy for a linear model. If a linear combination of some columns is equal to a linear combination of other columns, there is redundancy. Then, we can't accurately get one and only one answer for our linear regression coefficients: there are many—an infinite number of them—equally correct answers. We can add a little bit to one coefficient and subtract a little bit from another and they will balance out. You'll notice that this did not seem to be much of a problem for us in terms of predictions. In the bigger picture, the redundancy issue is called *collinearity* and it is more of a concern when you move above the level of prediction and start entering the realms of statistical and causal reasoning. As I've mentioned, we are sweeping those issues under the carpet in this book. However, those issues are precisely why `statsmodels` makes you go far out of your way to include both full coding and an explicit intercept.

10.6 Relationships and Interactions

Feature construction is very powerful. In fact, it is so powerful, it can actually *replace* the steps we normally perform in model building. Suitably constructed features can mimic the targets we produce when we predict with a model. Here are two examples:

1. In our example of piecewise constant regression, the most difficult step was determining where—in which region or slice—each input value belonged. After we did that, we simply selected the appropriate constant. That's almost like using a Python dictionary with a complicated key. The hard work is generating the key—the lookup is almost trivial. If we preprocess the data into the right bins, our model has almost nothing left to do. We can replace our more complicated model-building process with a somewhat complicated preprocessing step and a trivial model building step.
2. To move from linear regression to polynomial regression—modeling with curvy shapes—we can either spend a lot of effort defining a custom method that fits a polynomial to data *or* we can simply *create* polynomial features and pass them to a standard linear regression fitter.

Many complicated learning methods can be implemented as either (1) a complicated method or (2) feature construction plus a basic method. Often, the later is less labor-intensive. If we separate out the feature engineering, we need to be sure to assess the combined method in the same way we would assess a stand-alone method—usually with cross-validation.

10.6.1 Manual Feature Construction

I've made the claim that feature engineering can be very strong in the sense that it can remove the need to learn. Sufficiently powerful discretization and feature construction methods can *essentially* solve learning problems for us. Let's cut out the handwaving and make that idea more explicit. Here's a classic troublesome learning example. I'm going to create a very simple table of examples for the *xor function*. *xor* is a Boolean function that is true only when one or the other, but not both, of its inputs is true. Here's the data:

```
In [28]:

xor_data = [[0,0,0],
            [0,1,1],
            [1,0,1],
            [1,1,0]]
```

```
xor_df = pd.DataFrame(xor_data,
                      columns=['x1','x2','tgt'])
display(xor_df)
```

	x1	x2	tgt
0	0	0	0
1	0	1	1
2	1	0	1
3	1	1	0

If we try to model *xor* with a simple linear classifier, things don't work out so well. We're getting problems predicting *in-sample* on the training set—we haven't even seen any novel *testing* data yet.

In [29]:

```
model = linear_model.LogisticRegression().fit(xor_df[['x1', 'x2']],
                                              xor_df['tgt'])
model.predict(xor_df[['x1', 'x2']])
```

Out[29]:

```
array([0, 0, 0, 0])
```

How can we be so bad? Well, let's look at a graph of the data values colored by their output.

In [30]:

```
fig, ax = plt.subplots(1,1,figsize=(2,2))
ax.scatter('x1', 'x2', data=xor_df, c='tgt')
ax.set_xlim(-1, 2)
ax.set_ylim(-1, 2);
```

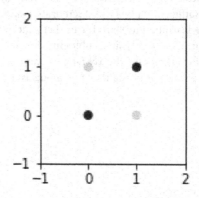

It is fundamentally impossible to use a single line to separate these points and keep them with their like classes only. At a minimum, we need two lines to fence off points on one diagonal from points on the other diagonal. But what if we can create a clever feature?

In [31]:

```
xor_df['new'] = (-1)**xor_df['x1'] * (-1)**xor_df['x2']
xor_df
```

Out[31]:

	x1	x2	tgt	new
0	0	0	0	1
1	0	1	1	-1
2	1	0	1	-1
3	1	1	0	1

Now things are looking pretty nice: even a super simple rule, `xor_df['new'] < 0 == True`, will give us our target. Here's what happens:

In [32]:

```
model = linear_model.LogisticRegression().fit(xor_df[['new']],
                                               xor_df['tgt'])
model.predict(xor_df[['new']])
```

Out[32]:

```
array([0, 1, 1, 0])
```

Sometimes, we need to invent a new vocabulary—constructed columns like `new`—to enable our learning systems to *learn*.

10.6.2 Interactions

One specific type of constructed feature is an *interaction* between existing features. There are two major ways that features interact: (1) by working together like a key in a dictionary that selects a class or target value and (2) by acting together based on their *product* (multiplication) instead of their sum (addition). The second is a really complex way of saying that when we multiply two features together we are considering the way in which they interact. Multiple degrees of interaction can include more and more features.

Here we consider two-way interactions between numerical features—all pairs of numerical features—with `sklearn`:

```
In [33]:
```

```
# parameters:
# degree: degree of terms
# interaction_only: no x**2, only x*y (and x,y)
# include_bias: constant term
quad_inters = skpre.PolynomialFeatures(degree=2,              # degree of terms
                                       interaction_only=True, # no x**2, only x*y
                                       include_bias=False)     # constant term
subset = iris_df.loc[[0, 50, 100], ['sepal length', 'sepal width']]
new_terms = pd.DataFrame(quad_inters.fit_transform(subset),
                         index=[0, 50, 100])
new_terms.set_axis(['sep length', 'sep width', 'sep area'],
                   axis=1, inplace=True)

# note:  creating the interaction *also*
# includes the base terms in the interaction
display(new_terms)
```

	sep length	sep width	sep area
0	5.1000	3.5000	17.8500
50	7.0000	3.2000	22.4000
100	6.3000	3.3000	20.7900

This representation may be good enough, particularly if we want to make these steps part of an `sklearn` pipeline. However, we can get much finer grained control using `patsy`.

10.6.2.1 Interactions via Patsy Formulas

Now we can get a big win from using `patsy` formulas. Patsy lets us specify interactions with either : or *. The difference is that : only includes the interaction—`sepal_width * sepal_length`—between the two, like `interaction_only=True` in `skpre.PolynomialFeatures`.

```
In [34]:
```

```
design_df = patsy.dmatrix("Q('sepal length'):Q('sepal width') - 1",
                          data=iris_df.iloc[[0, 50, 100]],
                          return_type='dataframe')
design_df
```

Out[34]:

	Q('sepal length'):Q('sepal width')
0	17.8500
50	22.4000
100	20.7900

If we use the patsy * to join two features, `ftr_1` * `ftr_2`, we will get three columns: `ftr_1`, `ftr_2`, and the product `ftr_1` x `ftr_2`. Between two categorical features, a patsy * means we take the Cartesian product—all possible combinations of each value. Let's construct a scenario where we might use this.

After we've been talking about sepal length and width for a while, you might start thinking that we could, as an approximation, multiply the two together to get a sepal *area*. Effectively, we are talking about creating a new feature *sepal area = sepal width × sepal length*. We might justify this by appealing to the area of a rectangle or an approximate area of an ellipse when calculated from its major and minor axes. We'd be happy to tie the two primitive concepts of width and length to a more expressive idea. We might be even happier if we talked to a botanist who said that in her expert opinion, yes, the approximation is valid enough *and* the area is more useful in determining the species. This approach is driven by background knowledge—so we probably don't need to go to great lengths to cross-validate it. However, we *would* want a hold-out test set to ensure that we don't mislead ourselves as to the value of areas. Unlike medieval scholastic philosophers who were content to argue and argue without evidence, we insist on demonstrating our claims with data and evaluation.

Let's *also* combine this idea of flower areas with discretization to find the *big* areas. Finally, we'll create combinations of smaller and larger petals and sepals.

In [35]:

```
# create some areas
sepal_area = iris_df['sepal length'] * iris_df['sepal width']
petal_area = iris_df['petal length'] * iris_df['petal width']

# discretize
iris_df['big_sepal'] = sepal_area > sepal_area.median()
iris_df['big_petal'] = petal_area > petal_area.median()
display(iris_df.iloc[[0,50,100]])
```

	sepal length	sepal width	petal length	petal width	species	big_sepal	big_petal
0	5.10	3.50	1.40	0.20	setosa	True	False
50	7.00	3.20	4.70	1.40	versicolor	True	True
100	6.30	3.30	6.00	2.50	virginica	True	True

In [36]:

```
design_df = patsy.dmatrix("big_sepal:big_petal - 1",
                          data=iris_df.iloc[[0, 50, 100]],
                          return_type='dataframe')

# breaking up the long column names
display(design_df.iloc[:, :2])
display(design_df.iloc[:,2: ])
```

	big_sepal[False]:big_petal[False]	big_sepal[True]:big_petal[False]
0	0.0000	1.0000
50	0.0000	0.0000
100	0.0000	0.0000

	big_sepal[False]:big_petal[True]	big_sepal[True]:big_petal[True]
0	0.0000	0.0000
50	0.0000	1.0000
100	0.0000	1.0000

Examples 50 and 100 both have big sepals and petals. Example 0 has a big sepal and a small petal.

When we create an interaction between a categorical and a numerical features, we effectively get one weight for the numerical feature for each of the categories we consider:

In [37]:

```
# we (Q)uote sepal length because it has a space in the name
design_df = patsy.dmatrix("C(species,Treatment):Q('sepal length') - 1",
                          data=iris_df.iloc[[0, 50, 100]],
                          return_type='dataframe')

# breaking up the long column names
display(design_df.iloc[:,[0]])
display(design_df.iloc[:,[1]])
display(design_df.iloc[:,[2]])
```

	C(species, Treatment)[setosa]:Q('sepal length')
0	5.1000
50	0.0000
100	0.0000

C(species, Treatment)[versicolor]:Q('sepal length')	
0	0.0000
50	7.0000
100	0.0000

C(species, Treatment)[virginica]:Q('sepal length')	
0	0.0000
50	0.0000
100	6.3000

If we dive back into the data, we see where those values are coming from—the column value is precisely the selected out value of sepal length when it is in that category. It is an elementwise multiplication of (1) the one-hot encoding of the species *times* (2) the sepal length.

In [38]:

```
print(iris_df.iloc[[0, 50, 100]]['sepal length'])
```

```
0                  5.1000
50                 7.0000
100                6.3000
Name: sepal length, dtype: float64
```

10.6.2.2 From Patsy to sklearn

We can also look at a quick example of connecting `patsy` formulas and `sklearn` models. Essentially, we build a design matrix—that's the mapping between raw features and the data that we use to learn parameters—by hand, apply it by hand, and then run the model.

In [39]:

```
import statsmodels as sm
import statsmodels.formula.api as smf
```

In [40]:

```
# we can build a design matrix and send it to sklearn
design = "C(species,Treatment):petal_area"
design_matrix = patsy.dmatrix(design, data=iris_df)

# intercept is already in design matrix
lr = linear_model.LinearRegression(fit_intercept=False)
```

```
mod = lr.fit(design_matrix, iris_df['sepal width'])
print(mod.coef_)

[ 2.8378  1.402  -0.0034  0.0146]
```

In [41]:

```
# hey, we get the same results!
formula = "Q('sepal width') ~ C(species,Treatment):petal_area"
res1 = smf.ols(formula=formula, data=iris_df).fit()
print(res1.params)
```

```
Intercept                                       2.8378
C(species, Treatment)[setosa]:petal_area        1.4020
C(species, Treatment)[versicolor]:petal_area   -0.0034
C(species, Treatment)[virginica]:petal_area     0.0146
dtype: float64
```

Fortunately, we get the same results—there's some rounding in there—whether we do some manual hacking to feed data to `sklearn` or use a self-contained `statsmodels` approach.

10.6.3 Adding Features with Transformers

If we want tighter integration with `sklearn`, we can define feature transformations using either `FunctionTransformer` for freestanding functions or inherit from `TransformerMixin` for classes. If we don't need to remember or learn anything from a training set to a test set—if the transformation is completely self-contained, like taking the logarithm of the absolute value of the data—then we don't need to add the complexity of a class-based method. We'll start by recreating the initial *area* features in a clean `DataFrame`.

In [42]:

```
iris_df = pd.DataFrame(iris.data, columns=iris.feature_names)
iris_df['species'] = iris.target_names[iris.target]

area_df = pd.DataFrame({"sepal_area" : iris_df['sepal length'] *
                                       iris_df['sepal width'],
                        "petal_area" : iris_df['petal length'] *
                                       iris_df['petal width']})
```

Now, if we simply want comparisons with the median values over the whole dataset—not training and testing differences—we can make a transformer as quickly as:

In [43]:

```
def median_big_small(d):
    return d > np.median(d)

transformer = skpre.FunctionTransformer(median_big_small)
res = transformer.fit_transform(area_df)

print("Large areas as compared to median?")
print(res[[0, 50, 100]])
```

```
Large areas as compared to median?
[[ True False]
 [ True False]
 [ True  True]]
```

If we want to *learn* the medians on the training data and then apply our discretization based on the learned medians to the testing data, we need a little more support. We have to compute the medians on the training data and then apply those medians as a threshold to either the training or testing data.

In [44]:

```
from sklearn.base import TransformerMixin
class Median_Big_Small(TransformerMixin):
    def __init__(self):
        pass
    def fit(self, ftrs, tgt=None):
        self.medians = np.median(ftrs)
        return self
    def transform(self, ftrs, tgt=None):
        return ftrs > self.medians
```

The usage pattern is the same as for a built-in transformer and it is quite similar to a standard learning model. Since we use a `train_test_split`, we get randomly selected examples here.

In [45]:

```
# training-testing split
training, testing = skms.train_test_split(area_df)

# create and run the transformer
transformer = Median_Big_Small()
train_xform = transformer.fit_transform(training)
test_xform  = transformer.transform(testing)

# the dataframes survived!
```

```
print('train:')
display(train_xform[:3])
print('test:')
display(test_xform[ :3])
```

train:

	sepal_area	petal_area
39	True	False
142	True	False
64	True	False

test:

	sepal_area	petal_area
147	True	False
78	True	False
133	True	False

10.7   Target Manipulations

In the context of linear regression models, you may hear the following advice:

- Transforming the input features primarily corrects for nonlinearity in the relationship between the input features and the target.
- Transforming the target value corrects problems with unaccounted-for differences between the input features and the target.

I'll add a few comments. Correcting for nonlinearity means that the *fundamental relationship* between features and target is *not* linear. Linear regression models are looking *specifically* for a best line. Going beyond the constraints of a good line means addressing the *bias* of linear regression.

Problems with unaccounted-for differences are characteristics of the errors between our predictions and reality. These are the residuals of Section 7.3.2. The two patterns we may see are (1) systematic behavior, such as bigger errors with bigger input x values, and (2) being distributed in a *non-normal* way. Non-normality means the errors may be unbalanced above and below the prediction line or the errors don't taper off quickly.

We can go out on a limb and translate these to give general rules of thumb for dealing with modeling problems.

- Manipulating the inputs is primarily about addressing *bias* in our model.
- Manipulating the target is primarily about addressing how noise affects the relationship between inputs and target. This noise occurs in the relationship—it's not variation in our estimation of parameters.

10.7.1 Manipulating the Input Space

Let's make these ideas more concrete by seeing how the first rule—correcting for a nonlinear relationship or, more generally, bias—plays out.

In [46]:

```
x = np.linspace(1,10,50)
n1 = np.random.normal(size=x.shape)

comparison = pd.DataFrame({"x"  : x,
                           "d1" : 2*x+5    + n1,
                           "d2" : 2*x**2+5 + n1})

comparison['x'] = x
melted = pd.melt(comparison, id_vars=['x'])
```

One of the two data columns is not like the other:

In [47]:

```
sns.lmplot(x='x', y='value',
           data=melted, col='variable', ci=None,
           size=3);
```

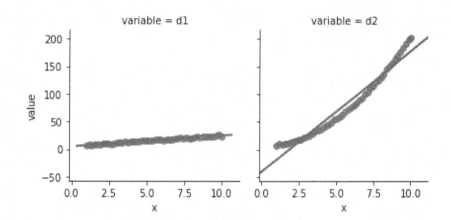

Looking below, the model built to relate d1 and x is well behaved. Its residuals seem somewhat normal-like—although we are only using 50 data points, so we aren't going to see a super smooth normal shape. The residuals from the d2 model simply have no obvious relationship to a normal curve.

In [48]:

```
fig, axes = plt.subplots(1,2,figsize=(8,3))
for ax, variable in zip(axes, ['d1', 'd2']):
    predicted = (smf.ols("{} ~ x".format(variable), data=comparison)
                    .fit()
                    .predict())
    actual = comparison[variable]
    sns.distplot(predicted - actual, norm_hist=True, rug=True, ax=ax)
    ax.set_xlabel(variable)
    ax.set_ylabel('residual')
fig.tight_layout();
```

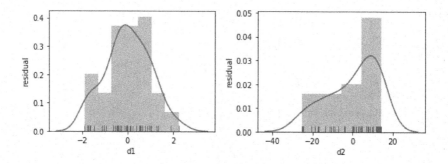

Before we panic, let's see what happens when we try to relate a slighty different version of x, x^2, to d2. We'll look at the residuals, as well.

In [49]:

```
magic = pd.DataFrame({"d2"    : 2*x**2+5+n1,
                      "x_sq" : x**2})
melted = pd.melt(magic, id_vars=['x_sq'])

fig, (ax1, ax2) = plt.subplots(1,2,figsize=(8,3))
sns.regplot(x='x_sq', y='value',
            data=melted, ci=None, ax=ax1)

predicted = (smf.ols("d2 ~ x_sq", data=magic)
                .fit()
                .predict())
actual = comparison['d2']
sns.distplot(predicted - actual, rug=True,
            norm_hist = True, ax=ax2)
```

```
ax2.set_title('histogram')
ax2.set_xlim(-3,3)
ax2.set_ylim(0,.45)
ax2.set_ylabel('residual');
```

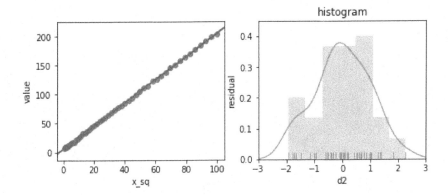

The residuals look great. *Et voilà!* Or, as the British say, "Bob's your uncle." By manipulating the features, we can adjust for unusual—nonlinear—relationships between features and target.

10.7.2 Manipulating the Target

We can do a similar exercise that makes it clear when we should try to manipulate the target. Here, we will inject distinctly different types of noise into our relationship:

In [50]:

```
x = np.linspace(1,10,50)

n1 = np.random.normal(size=x.shape)
n2 = .5*x*np.random.normal(size=x.shape)

comparison = pd.DataFrame({"x"  : x,
                           "d1" : 2*x+5+n1,
                           "d2" : 2*x+5+n2})

comparison['x'] = x
melted = pd.melt(comparison, id_vars=['x'])
```

Again, one of these is not like the other:

In [51]:

```
sns.lmplot(x='x', y='value',
           data=melted, col='variable', ci=None,
           size=3);
```

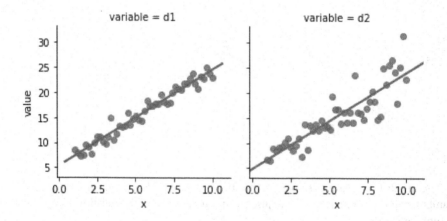

Something seems to be distinctly *off* with the right graph of **d2**. I didn't comment on how we *generated* the data—but let's focus on what we *see*. The errors—the vertical distance from the points to the line—are increasing in magnitude as x increases. Here is a histogram of the residuals for **d1** and **d2**:

In [52]:

```
fig, axes = plt.subplots(1,2,figsize=(8,3))
for ax, variable in zip(axes, ['d1', 'd2']):
    predicted = (smf.ols("{} ~ x".format(variable), data=comparison)
                    .fit()
                    .predict())
    actual = comparison[variable]
    sns.distplot(predicted - actual, norm_hist=True, rug=True, ax=ax)
    ax.set_xlabel(variable)
    ax.set_ylabel('residual')

fig.tight_layout();
```

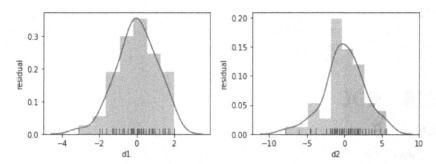

Again, we'll try not to panic. Instead, let's try to perform a bit of magic by taking the logarithm of the target:

In [53]:

```
magic = pd.DataFrame({"log_d2" : np.log(comparison['d2']),
                      "x"      : x})
melted = pd.melt(magic, id_vars=['x'])

fig, (ax1, ax2) = plt.subplots(1,2,figsize=(8,3))
sns.regplot(x='x', y='value', data=melted, ci=None, ax=ax1)

predicted = (smf.ols("log_d2 ~ x", data=magic)
                .fit()
                .predict())
actual = magic['log_d2']
sns.distplot(predicted - actual, rug=True, ax=ax2)

ax2.set_title('histogram')
ax2.set_xlim(-.7, .7)
ax2.set_ylim(0,3)
ax2.set_ylabel('residual');
```

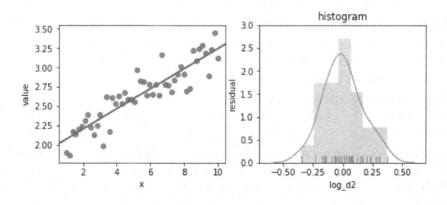

The residuals are pretty well behaved now. These examples are somewhat contrived; you won't *always* see this sort of improvement from simple transformations. But they are easy to try—and you might get *some* improvement from them.

10.8 EOC

10.8.1 Summary

We've added to our toolbox in a very different way. We can now address issues with the *data* itself. These methods are widely useful: regardless of the learning method we apply, these feature engineering steps may be necessary. However, these methods are also limited. They require manual intervention, we need to be careful of overfitting with them, and they only haphazardly account for relationships between targets and features. These methods also need to be supplemented when we start dealing with data that is distinctly nontabular, like images and text.

10.8.2 Notes

`sklearn` has a normalization function whose purpose is to make *rows* sum to one. That's different from what we've been doing: we've been talking about normalization over columns.

We briefly discussed *sparse* data storage. Some learning methods can be written so as to take advantage of sparsity: they'll know that unfilled values are zeros and avoid doing unnecessary mathematics with those entries. I haven't found a convenient list of sparse-aware methods in `sklearn`. You'll have to find the breadcrumbs in the documentation.

We've discussed one-hot—also known as dummy or treatment—coding. There are other methods of encoding categorical variables that avoid the intercept problems. These methods are called *contrast* coding schemes. Instead of relying on one-against-one, they take one value as baseline and compare the others against it. By taking an implicit baseline, they don't have the collinearity problem we discussed above.

A quick search with Google will get you docs for `patsy` and `statsmodels`:

- https://patsy.readthedocs.org/en/latest/quickstart.html
- http://statsmodels.sourceforge.net/devel/example_formulas.html
- http://statsmodels.sourceforge.net

You'll find a lot of information on data transformation—feature engineering—in the statistical literature. It is often restricted to discussing linear regression. Here are a few examples:

- *Data Transformation* from https://onlinecourses.science.psu.edu/stat501/node/318
- Chapter 8 of *Practical Regression and Anova in R* by Faraway
- Section 2.2.4 of *Advanced Data Analysis from an Elementary Point of View* by Shalizi

10.8.3 Exercises

1. What are some of the ways that we might introduce an unintended relationship into our features giving ourselves an undue advantage when we try to predict the target? Put another way, what might we do with our features that represents a grave overfitting that may work in training, but will fail—spectacularly—in practice?

2. What are some examples of knowledge that might lead us to *manually* select features from a dataset? In a large dataset, we might have many different prediction problems from various sets of features to different targets. Depending on target, we might have different constraints imposed by logic, law, science, or other factors. Be creative!

3. Investigate how feature selection based on one method works when used for learning with other methods. Perform feature selection with lasso regression (L_1 regularization), then model with something that isn't based on linear regression, for example k-NN-R or a decision tree regressor.

4. Imagine you have multimodal data—that is, the values of a feature form a two-humped (or more) camel. What happens when you standardize this data? Do it! You can create the two-humped values by merging the results of two different normal distributions (say, one with mean 5 and one with mean 10).

5. We did some pretty basic discretizations with the *iris* data. Can you do better? Here's a hint: try building a decision tree classifier and looking at the split point it uses. Apply some of those by hand and then try a different classifier.

6. Using `mystery_df` (below), graph x against each of the other features. Now, experiment with taking the log (`np.log`) of x, the other variable, or both and then graphing those values. You should be able to visually assess whether a linear regression would do well with these graphs. When would a linear regression be successful?

```
In [54]:
x = np.linspace(1,8,100)
n1 = np.random.normal(size=x.shape)
n2 = x * np.random.normal(size=x.shape)

mystery = {'m1':5 + n1,
           'm2':5 + n2,
           'm3':x + n1,
           'm4':x + n2,
           'm5':np.log2(x) + n1,
           'm6':np.log2(x) + n2,
           'm7':np.exp2(x + n1),
           'm8':np.exp2(x + n2)}

mystery_df = pd.DataFrame(mystery)
mystery_df['x'] = x
```

11

Tuning Hyperparameters and Pipelines

```
In [1]:
# setup
from mlwpy import *
%matplotlib inline

iris     = datasets.load_iris()
diabetes = datasets.load_diabetes()
digits   = datasets.load_digits()
```

We've already introduced models, parameters, and hyperparameters in Section 5.2.2.4. I'm about to bring them up again for two reasons. First, I want you to see a concrete analogy between (1) how we write simple Python functions in different ways by varying their code and arguments and (2) how learning models use parameters and hyperparameters. Second, we'll turn our attention towards choosing good hyperparameters. When we `fit` a model, we are choosing good parameters. We need some sort of well-defined process to choose good hyperparameters. We will press two types of *search*—`GridSearch` and `RandomizedSearch`—into service. Searching is a very general approach to solving or optimizing problems. Often, searching can work in domains that are not mathematically nice. However, the tradeoff—no surprise—is that the answers are not guaranteed to be the absolute best possible answers. Instead, as with heuristics, we hope the answers are *good enough*.

All of this discussion will put us in a great position to look more deeply at constructing *pipelines* of multiple learning components strung end-to-end. Often, the proper use of pipelines requires that we find good hyperparameters for the components of that pipeline. Therefore, diving too deeply into pipelines without also discussing the `Searching` techniques of the `sklearn` API could lead us into bad habits. We can't have that!

11.1 Models, Parameters, Hyperparameters

If you need to refresh yourself on terminology related to models, parameters, and hyperparameters, look back at Section 5.2. I want to expand that discussion with a concrete analogy that builds from very primitive Python functions. Here goes.

One of the difficulties of building machines, including physical computers and software programs, is that there is often more than one way to do it. Here's a simple example:

In [2]:

```
def add_three(x):
    return 3 + x
def add(x, y):
    return x + y


add(10,3) == add_three(10)
```

Out[2]:

True

Whenever a computation relies on a value—3 in this example—we can either (1) hard-code that value, as in `add_three`, or (2) provide that value at runtime by passing an argument, as with the 3 in `add(10,3)`. We can relate this idea to our factory-machine learning models and their knobs. If a knob is on the side of the machine, we can adjust that value when we fit a model. This scenario is like `add(x,y)`: providing the information on the fly. If a value is *inside* the box—it is part of the fixed internal components of the learning machine—then we are in a scenario similar to `add_three(x)`: the 3 is a *fixed in place* part of the code. We can't adjust that component when we fit this particular learning machine.

Here's one other way we can construct the adder-of-three. We can make a function that returns a function. I sincerely hope I didn't just cause you a headache. Our approach will be to pass a value for an *internal* component to our function maker. The function maker will use that internal value when it constructs a shiny new function that we want to use. The scenario is like the process of constructing one of our factory machines. While the machine is being built, we can combine any number of internal cogs and widgets and gizmos. After it is built, it is done, fixed, concrete, solid; we won't be making any more modifications to its internals.

Here's some code:

In [3]:

```
def make_adder(k):
    def add_k(x):
        return x + k
    return add_k
```

```
# a call that creates a function
three_adder = make_adder(3)

# using that created function
three_adder(10) == add_three(10)
```

Out[3]:

True

So, the good news is that *it worked*. The bad news might be that you don't know why. Let's break down what happens in line 7: `three_adder = make_adder(3)`. When we call `make_adder(3)`, we spin up the usual machinery of a function call. The 3 gets associated with the name `k` in `make_adder`. Then, we execute the code in `make_adder`. It does two things: defines the name `add_k`—with function *stuff*—and then returns `add_k`. These two steps are almost like a function that has two lines: `m=10` and then `return 10`. The difference is that we are defining a name `add_k` whose value is a function, not just a simple `int`.

OK, so what does it mean to define `add_k`? It is a function of one argument, `x`. Whatever value is passed into `add_k` will be added to the `k` value that was passed into `make_adder`. But this particular `add_k` *can never add anything else to* `x`. From its perspective, that `k` is a constant value for all time. The only way to get a different `add_k` is to make another call to `make_adder` and create a *different* function.

Let's summarize what we get back from `make_adder`:

- The returned *thing* (strictly, it's a Python object) is a function with one argument.
- When the returned function is called, it (1) computes `k` plus the value it is called with and (2) returns that value.

Let's relate this back to our learning models. When we say `KNeighborsClassifier(3)` we are doing something like `make_adder(3)`. It gives us a concrete object we can `.fit` that has a 3 baked into its recipe. If we want to have 5-NN, we need a new learning machine constructed with a different call: `KNeighborsClassifier(5)`, just like constructing a `five_adder` requires a call to `make_adder(5)`. Now, in the case of `three_adder` and `five_adder` you are probably yelling at me, "Just use `add(x,y)`, dummy!" That's fine, I'm not offended. We can do that. But in the case of k-NN, we can't. The way the algorithm is designed, internally, doesn't allow it.

What is our takeaway message? I drew out the idea of fixed versus parameter-driven behavior to make the following points:

1. After we create a model, we don't modify the internal state of the learning machine. We can modify the values of the knobs and what we feed it with the side input tray (as we saw in Section 1.3).
2. The training step gives us our preferred knob settings and input-tray contents.
3. If we don't like the result of testing after training, we can *also* select an entirely different learning machine with different internals. We can choose machines that are of completely different types. We could switch from k-NN to linear regression. Or, we can stay within the same overall class of learning machines and vary a

hyperparameter: switch from 3-NN to 5-NN. This is the process of *model selection* from Section 5.2.2.1.

11.2 Tuning Hyperparameters

Now let's look at *how* we select good hyperparameters with help from `sklearn`.

11.2.1 A Note on Computer Science and Learning Terminology

In an unfortunate quirk of computer science terminology, when we describe the process of making a function call, the terms *parameters* and *arguments* are often used interchangeably. However, in the strictest sense, they have more specific meanings: arguments are the *actual* values passed into a call while parameters are the *placeholders* that receive values in a function. To clarify these terms, some technical documents use the name *actual* argument/parameter and *formal* argument/parameter. Why do we care? Because when we start talking about tuning hyperparameters, you'll soon hear people talking about *parameter tuning*. Then you'll think I've been lying to you about the difference between the *internal* factory-machine components set by hyperparameter selection and the *external* factory-machine components (knobs) set by parameter optimization.

In this book, I've exclusively used the term *arguments* for the computer-sciency critters. That was specifically to avoid clashing with the machine learning *parameter* and *hyperparameter* terms. I will continue using *parameters* (which are optimized during training) and *hyperparameters* (which are tuned via cross-validation). Be aware that the `sklearn` docs and function-argument names often (1) abbreviate hyperparameter to `param` or (2) use `param` in the computer science sense. In *either case*, in the following code we will be talking about the *actual arguments* to a learning constructor—such as specifying a value for k=3 in a *k*-NN machine. The machine learning speak is that we are setting the *hyperparameter* for *k*-NN to 3.

11.2.2 An Example of Complete Search

To prevent this from getting too abstract, let's look at a concrete example. `KNeighborsClassifier` has a number of arguments it can be called with. Most of these arguments are hyperparameters that control the internal operation of the `KNeighborsClassifier` we create. Here they are:

In [4]:

```
knn = neighbors.KNeighborsClassifier()
print(" ".join(knn.get_params().keys()))
```

```
algorithm leaf_size metric metric_params n_jobs n_neighbors p weights
```

We haven't taken a deep dive into any of these besides n_neighbors. The n_neighbors argument controls the *k* in our *k*-NN learning model. You might remember that a key issue with nearest neighbors is deciding the distance between different examples. These are precisely controlled by some combinations of metric, metric_params, and p. weights determines how the neighbors combine themselves to come up with a final answer.

11.2.2.1 Evaluating a Single Hyperparameter

In Section 5.7.2, we *manually* went through the process of comparing several different values of *k*, n_neighbors. Before we get into more complex examples, let's rework that example with some built-in sklearn support from GridSearch.

In [5]:

```
param_grid = {"n_neighbors" : [1,3,5,10,20]}


knn = neighbors.KNeighborsClassifier()
# warning! this is with accuracy
grid_model = skms.GridSearchCV(knn,
                               return_train_score=True,
                               param_grid = param_grid,
                               cv=10)

grid_model.fit(digits.data, digits.target)
```

Out[5]:

```
GridSearchCV(cv=10, error_score='raise-deprecating',
    estimator=KNeighborsClassifier(algorithm='auto', leaf_size=30,
        metric='minkowski', metric_params=None,
        n_jobs=None, n_neighbors=5, p=2, weights='uniform'),
    fit_params=None, iid='warn', n_jobs=None,
    param_grid={'n_neighbors': [1, 3, 5, 10, 20]},
    pre_dispatch='2*n_jobs', refit=True, return_train_score=True,
    scoring=None, verbose=0)
```

Fortunately, the result of skms.GridSearchCV is *just a model*, so you already know how to make it run: call fit on it. Now, it will take about five times as long as a single *k*-NN run because we are running it for five values of *k*. The result of fit is a pretty enormous Python dictionary. It has entries for each combination of hyperparameters and cross-validation rounds. Fortunately, it can be quickly converted into a DataFrame with pd.DataFrame(grid_model.cv_results_).

```
In [6]:
```

```
# many columns in .cv_results_
# all params are also available in 'params' column as dict
param_cols = ['param_n_neighbors']
score_cols = ['mean_train_score', 'std_train_score',
              'mean_test_score', 'std_test_score']

# look at first five params with head()
df = pd.DataFrame(grid_model.cv_results_).head()

display(df[param_cols + score_cols])
```

	param_n_ neighbors	mean_train_ score	std_train_ score	mean_test_ score	std_test_ score
0	1	1.0000	0.0000	0.9761	0.0180
1	3	0.9933	0.0009	0.9777	0.0161
2	5	0.9907	0.0005	0.9738	0.0167
3	10	0.9861	0.0011	0.9644	0.0208
4	20	0.9806	0.0018	0.9610	0.0233

We can single out some columns of interest and index the `DataFrame` by the parameter we manipulated.

```
In [7]:
```

```
# subselect columns of interest:
# param_* is a bit verbose
grid_df = pd.DataFrame(grid_model.cv_results_,
                       columns=['param_n_neighbors',
                                'mean_train_score',
                                'mean_test_score'])
grid_df.set_index('param_n_neighbors', inplace=True)
display(grid_df)
```

	mean_train_score	mean_test_score
param_n_neighbors		
1	1.0000	0.9761
3	0.9933	0.9777
5	0.9907	0.9738
10	0.9861	0.9644
20	0.9806	0.9610

We can also view it graphically:

In [8]:

```
ax = grid_df.plot.line(marker='.')
ax.set_xticks(grid_df.index);
```

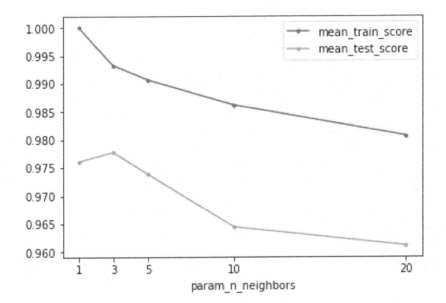

One benefit of this approach—versus what we did manually in Chapter 5—is that we don't have to manage any of the results-gathering by hand. The *major* benefit comes when we start trying to deal with more than one hyperparameter.

11.2.2.2 Evaluating over Multiple Hyperparameters

Even for a simple *k*-NN model, there are quite a few possibilities. If you look at the documentation, you'll see that n_neighbors and p are simply integers. We could try *lots* of different values. Remember, we need to manage training and test sets—an overall cross-validation process—for all of these combinations. Otherwise, we put ourselves at risk to overfit the data with some particular hyperparameters because we never evaluated them on fresh data.

If we were to try that by hand for a model that takes three parameters, it might look like this in quick-and-dirty Pythonic pseudocode:

```
In [9]:

def best_model_hyper_params(make_a_model,
                            some_hyper_params,
                            data):
    results = {}
    for hyper_params in it.combinations(some_hyper_params):
        for train,test in make_cv_split(data):
            model = make_a_model(*hyper_params).fit(train)
            key = tuple(hyper_params)
            if key not in results:
                results[key] = []
            results[key].append(score(test, model.predict(test)))
            # or, rock stars can use this instead of the prior 4 lines:
            # (results.setdefault(tuple(hyper_params), [])
            #         .append(score(test, model.predict(test)))

    best_hp = max(results, key=results.get)
    best_model = make_a_model(*best_hp).fit(data)
    return best_model

def do_it():
    model = pick_a_model # e.g., k-NN

    some_hyper_params = [values_for_hyper_param_1, # e.g., n_neighbors=[]
                         values_for_hyper_param_2,
                         values_for_hyper_param_3]

    best_model_hyper_params(model_type,
                            some_hyper_params,
                            data)
```

Fortunately, evaluating over hyperparameters is a common task in designing and building a learning system. As such, we don't have to code it up ourselves. Let's say we want to try all combinations of these hyperparameters:

Hyperparameter	Values
n_neighbors	$1, ..., 10$
weights	*uniform, distance*
p	$1, 2, 4, 8, 16$

Two notes:

1. *distance* means that my neighbor's contribution is weighted by its distance from *me*. *uniform* means all my neighbors are considered the same with no weighting.

2. `p` is an argument to a *Minkowski distance* constructor. We saw it briefly in the Chapter 2 Notes. Just know that $p = 1$ is a Manhattan distance (L_1-like), $p = 2$ is Euclidean distance (L_2-like), and higher ps approach something called an infinity-norm.

The following code performs the setup to try these possibilities for a k-NN model. It does not get into the actual processing.

In [10]:

```
param_grid = {"n_neighbors" : np.arange(1,11),
              "weights"     : ['uniform', 'distance'],
              "p"           : [1,2,4,8,16]}

knn = neighbors.KNeighborsClassifier()
grid_model = skms.GridSearchCV(knn, param_grid = param_grid, cv=10)
```

This code will take a bit longer than our previous calls to `fit` on a `kNN` with `GridSearch` because we are fitting $10 \times 2 \times 5 \times 10 = 200$ total models (that last 10 is from the multiple fits in the cross-validation step). But the good news is all the dirty work is managed for us.

In [11]:

```
# digits takes ~30 mins on my older laptop
# %timeit -r1 grid_model.fit(digits.data, digits.target)
%timeit -r1 grid_model.fit(iris.data, iris.target)
```

```
1 loop, best of 1: 3.72 s per loop
```

After calling `grid_model.fit`, we have a large basket of results we can investigate. That can be a bit overwhelming to deal with. A little Pandas-fu can get us what we are probably interested in: which models—that is, which sets of hyperparameters—performed the best? This time I'm going to extract the values in a slightly different way:

In [12]:

```
param_df = pd.DataFrame.from_records(grid_model.cv_results_['params'])
param_df['mean_test_score'] = grid_model.cv_results_['mean_test_score']
param_df.sort_values(by=['mean_test_score']).tail()
```

Out[12]:

	n_neighbors	p	weights	mean_test_score
79	8	16	distance	0.9800
78	8	16	uniform	0.9800
77	8	8	distance	0.9800
88	9	16	uniform	0.9800
99	10	16	distance	0.9800

I specifically wanted to look at several of the top results—and not just the single top result—because it is often the case that there are several models with similar performance. That heuristic holds true here—and, when you see this, you'll know not to be too invested in a single "best" classifier. However, there certainly are cases where there is a clear winner.

We can access that best model, its parameters, and its overall score with attributes on the fit `grid_model`. A very important and subtle warning about the result: it is a *new* model that was created using the best hyperparameters and then refit to the entire dataset. Don't believe me? From the `sklearn` docs under the `refit` argument to `GridSearchCV`:

> The refitted estimator is made available at the `best_estimator_` attribute and permits using `predict` directly on this `GridSearchCV` instance.

So, we can take a look at the results of our grid search process:

```
In [13]:
print("Best Estimator:", grid_model.best_estimator_,
      "Best Score:",     grid_model.best_score_,
      "Best Params:",    grid_model.best_params_, sep="\n")


Best Estimator:
KNeighborsClassifier(algorithm='auto', leaf_size=30, metric='minkowski',
                     metric_params=None, n_jobs=None, n_neighbors=8, p=4,
                     weights='uniform')
Best Score:
0.98
Best Params:
{'n_neighbors': 8, 'p': 4, 'weights': 'uniform'}
```

The process (1) uses `GridSearch` to find good hyperparameters and then (2) trains a single model, built with those hyperparameters, on the entire dataset. We can take this model to other, novel data and perform a final hold-out test assessment.

Here's a quick note on the randomization used by `GridSearchCV`. Concerning the use of `shuffle`-ing to `KFold` and friends, the `sklearn` docs emphasize that:

> The `random_state` parameter defaults to `None`, meaning that the shuffling will be different every time `KFold(..., shuffle=True)` is iterated. However, `GridSearchCV` will use the same shuffling for each set of parameters validated by a single call to its `fit` method.

Generally, we want this sameness. We want to compare parameters, not random samples over possible cross-validation data splits.

11.2.3 Using Randomness to Search for a Needle in a Haystack

If we have many hyperparameters, or if the range of possible values for a single hyperparameter is large, we may not be able to exhaustively try all possibilities. Thanks to the beauty of randomization, we can proceed in a different way. We can specify *random combinations* of the hyperparameters—like different dealings from a deck of cards—and ask for a number of these to be tried. There are two ways we can specify these. One is by providing a list of values; these are sampled uniformly, just like rolling a die. The other option is a bit more complicated: we can make use of the random distributions in `scipy.stats`.

Without diving into that too deeply, here are four specific options you can consider:

- For a hyperparameter that you'd prefer to have smaller values, instead of bigger values, you could try `ss.geom`. This function uses a geometric distribution which produces positive values that fall off very quickly. It's based on how long you have to wait, when flipping a coin, to see a head. Not seeing a head for a long time is very unlikely.
- If you have a range of values that you'd like to sample evenly—for example, any value between −1 and 1 should be as likely as any other—use `ss.uniform`.
- If you'd like to try hyperparameter values with a normal distribution, use `ss.normal`.
- For simple integers, use `randint`.

`sklearn` uses `RandomizedSearchCV` to perform the random rolling of hyperparameter values. Internally, it is using the `.rvs(n)` method on the `scipy.stats` distributions. So, if you define something that has a `.rvs(n)` method, you can pass it to `RandomizedSearchCV`. Be warned, I'm not responsible for the outcome.

In [14]:

```
import scipy.stats as ss
knn = neighbors.KNeighborsClassifier()
param_dists = {"n_neighbors" : ss.randint(1,11), # values from [1,10]
               "weights"     : ['uniform', 'distance'],
               "p"           : ss.geom(p=.5)}

mod = skms.RandomizedSearchCV(knn,
                              param_distributions = param_dists,
                              cv=10,
                              n_iter=20) # how many times do we sample?

# fitting 20 models
%timeit -r1 mod.fit(iris.data, iris.target)
print(mod.best_score_)
```

```
1 loop, best of 1: 596 ms per loop
0.98
```

11.3 Down the Recursive Rabbit Hole: Nested Cross-Validation

My most astute readers—you're probably one of them—may be pondering something. If we consider *many* possible sets of hyperparameters, is it possible that we will overfit them? Let me kill the surprise: the quick answer is *yes*. But you say, "What about our hold-out test set?" Indeed, young grasshopper, when we see poor performance on our hold-out test set, we've already *lost the game*. We've peeked into our last-resort data. We need an alternative that will deal with the overfitting in hyperparameter tuning *and* give us insight into the variability and robustness of our estimates. I'll give you two hints about how we'll do it. First, the `*Search` models are *just* models—we can use them just like other simple models. We feed them data, fit them, and can then predict with them. Second, we solved the problem of assessing the variability of performance with respect to the *parameters* with cross-validation. Let's try to combine these ideas: grid search as a model that we assess with cross-validation.

Let's step back a minute to clearly define the problem. As a reminder, here's the setup with respect to *parameters*, *training*, and *validation* before we start considering hyperparameters and `*Search`ing. When we *fit* one of our usual models—3-NN or SVM with $C = 1.0$, for example—on a training set and evaluate it on a validation set, we have variability due to the randomness in selecting the training and validation sets. We might pick particular good-performing or bad-performing pairs. What we really want to know is how we expect to do on one of those selected at random.

This scenario is similar to picking a single student from a class and using her height to represent the whole class. It's not going to work too well. However, taking an *average* of the heights of many students in the class is a far better estimate of the height of a randomly selected student. In our learning case, we take many train-test splits and average their results to get an idea of how our system performs on a randomly selected train-test split. Beyond this, we *also* get a measure of the variability. We might see a tight clustering of performance results; we might see a steep drop-off in learning performance after some clear winners.

11.3.1 Cross-Validation, Redux

Now, we are interested in wrapping that entire method—an entire `GridSearch` process—inside of cross-validation. That seems a bit mind-blowing but Figure 11.1 should help. It shows how things look with our usual, flat CV on a generic model. If we decide we like the CV performance of the model, we can go back and train it on all of the non-hold-out data. That final trained model is what we'd like to use to make new predictions in the future.

There's no difference if we use a primitive model like linear regression (LR) *or* a more complicated model that results from a `GridSearch` as the model we assess with cross-validation. As in Figure 11.2, both simply fill in the *Model* that cross-validation runs on. However, what goes on under the hood is decidedly different.

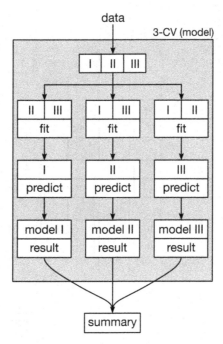

Figure 11.1   Flat cross-validation on a generic model.

The intricate part happens inside of the GridSearch boxes. Inside of one box, there is an entirely self-contained fit process being used by the internal learning models constructed from a single set of hyperparameters. If we call GridSearchCV(LinearRegression), then inside the box we are fitting linear regression parameters. If we call GridSearchCV(3-NN), then inside the box we are building the table of neighbors to use in making predictions. But in either case, the output of GridSearchCV is a model which we can evaluate.

11.3.2   GridSearch as a Model

The usual models that we call fit on are *fully defined* models: we pick the model *and* the hyperparameters to make it *concrete*. So, what the heck happens when we call fit on a GridSearchCV mega-model? When we call fit on a LinearRegression model, we get back a set of values for the inner-parameter weights that are their preferred, optimal values given the training set. When we call GridSearchCV on the n_neighbors of a *k*-NN, we get back a n_neighbors that is the preferred value of that *hyperparameter* given the training data. The two are *doing the same thing* at different levels.

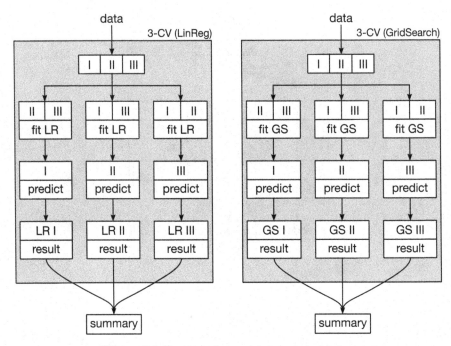

Figure 11.2   Wrapping models in cross-validation.

Figure 11.3 shows a graphical view of a two hyperparameter grid search that highlights the method's output: a fit model and good hyperparameters. It also shows the use of CV as an *internal* component of the grid search. The cross-validation of a single hyperparameter results in an evaluation of that hyperparameter and model combination. In turn, several such evaluations are compared to select a preferred hyperparameter. Finally, the preferred hyperparameter and all of the incoming data are used to train (equivalent to our usual `fit`) a final model. The output is a fit model, just as if we had called `LinearRegression.fit`.

11.3.3 Cross-Validation Nested within Cross-Validation

The `*SearchCV` functions are smart enough to do cross-validation (CV) for all model and hyperparameter combinations they try. This CV is great: it protects us against teaching to the test as we fit the individual model and hyperparameter combinations. However, it is not sufficient to protect us from teaching to the test by `GridSearchCV` *itself*. To do that, we need to place it in its own cross-validation wrapper. The result is a *nested cross-validation*. Figure 11.4 shows the data splitting for a 5-fold outer cross-validation and a 3-fold inner cross-validation.

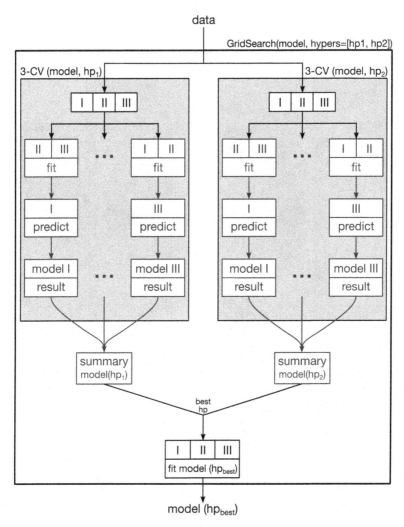

Figure 11.3 GridSearch.

The outer CV is indicated by capital letters. The inner CV splits are indicated by Roman numerals. One sequence of the outer CV works as follows. With the inner CV data (I, II, III) chosen from *part* of the outer CV data (B, C, D, E), we find a good model by CV and then evaluate it on the *remainder* of the outer CV data (A). The good model—with values for its hyperparameters—is a single model, fit to all of (I, II, III), coming from the `grid_model.best_*` friends.

We can implement nested cross-validation without going to extremes. Suppose we perform 3-fold CV within a `GridSearch`—that is, each model and hyperparameter combo is evaluated three times.

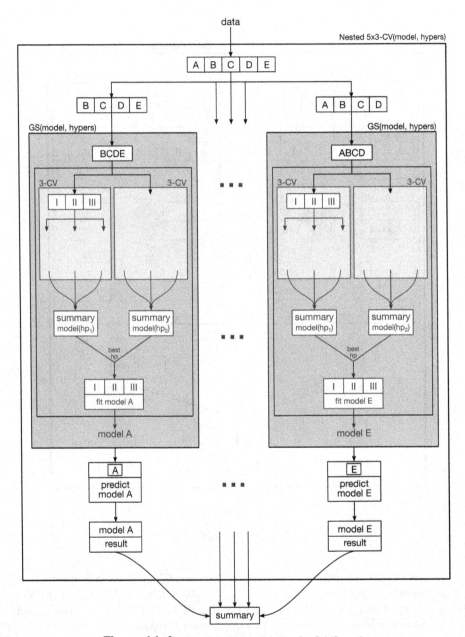

Figure 11.4   Nested cross-validation for GridSearch.

In [15]:

```
param_grid = {"n_neighbors" : np.arange(1,11),
              "weights"     : ['uniform', 'distance'],
              "p"           : [1,2,4,8,16]}

knn = neighbors.KNeighborsClassifier()
grid_knn = skms.GridSearchCV(knn,
                             param_grid = param_grid,
                             cv=3)
```

As happened at the parameter level without cross-validation, now we are unintentionally narrowing in on hyperparameters that work well for this dataset. To undo this peeking, we can wrap the `GridSearchCV(knn)` up in *another* layer of cross-validation with five folds:

In [16]:

```
outer_scores = skms.cross_val_score(grid_knn,
                                    iris.data, iris.target,
                                    cv=5)
print(outer_scores)
```

```
[0.9667 1.     0.9333 0.9667 1.    ]
```

For our example, we've used 5-fold repeats of 3-fold cross-validation for a 5 × 3 nested cross-validation strategy—also called a *double cross* strategy. I chose those numbers for clarity of the examples and diagrams. However, the most common recommendation for nested CV is a 5 × 2 cross-validation scheme, which was popularized by Tom Dietterich. The numbers 5 and 2 are not magical, but Dietterich does provide some practical justification for them. The value 2 is chosen for the inner loop because it makes the training sets disjoint: they don't overlap at all. The value 5 was chosen because Dietterich found that fewer repetitions gave too much variability—differences—in the values, so we need a few more repeats to get a reliable, repeatable estimate. With more than five, there is too much overlap between splits which sacrifices the independence between training sets so the estimates become more and more related to each other. So, five was a happy medium between these two competing criteria.

11.3.4 Comments on Nested CV

To understand what just happened, let me extend the `GridSearch` pseudocode I wrote earlier in Section 11.2.2.2.

In [17]:

```
def nested_cv_pseudo_code(all_data):
    results = []
    for outer_train, test in make_cv_split(all_data):
        for hyper_params in hyper_parameter_possibilities:
            for train, valid in make_cv_split(outer_train):
                inner_score = evaluate(model.fit(train).predict(valid))
            best_mod = xxx # choose model with best inner_score
            preds = best_model.fit(outer_train).predict(test)
            results.append(evaluate(preds))
```

Let me review the process for flat cross-validation. The training phase of learning sets parameters, and we need a train-validation step to assess the performance of those parameters. But, really, we need cross-validation—multiple train-validation splits—to generate a *better* estimate by averaging and to assess the variability of those estimates. We have to extend this idea to our `GridSearch`.

When we use grid search to *select* our preferred values of hyperparameters, we are effectively determining—or, at a different level, *optimizing*—those hyperparameter values. At a minimum, we need the train-validation step of the grid search to assess those outcomes. In reality, however, we want a better estimate of the performance of our overall process. We'd also love to know how certain we are of the results. If we do the process a second time, are we going to get similar results? Similarity can be over several different aspects: (1) are the predictions similar? (2) is the overall performance similar? (3) are the selected hyperparameters similar? (4) do different hyperparameters lead to similar performance results?

In a nested cross-validation, the outer cross-validation tells us *the variability* we can expect when we go through the process of selecting hyperparameters via grid search. It is analogous to a usual cross-validation which tells us how performance varies over different train-test splits when we estimate parameters.

Just as we *do not* use cross-validation to determine the *parameters* of a model—the parameters are set by the training step *within* the CV—we don't use outer cross-validation of the `GridSearch` to pick the best hyperparameters. The best hypers are determined inside of the `GridSearch`. The outer level of CV simply gives us a more realistic estimate of how those inner-level-selected hyperparameters will do when we use them for our final model.

The practical application of nested cross-validation is far easier than trying to conceptualize it. We can use nested CV:

In [18]:

```
param_grid = {"n_neighbors" : np.arange(1,11),
              "weights"     : ['uniform', 'distance'],
              "p"           : [1,2,4,8,16]}

knn = neighbors.KNeighborsClassifier()
```

```
grid_knn = skms.GridSearchCV(knn,
                             param_grid = param_grid,
                             cv=2)

outer_scores = skms.cross_val_score(grid_knn,
                                    iris.data,
                                    iris.target,
                                    cv=5)
# how does this do over all??
print(outer_scores)
```

```
[0.9667 0.9667 0.9333 0.9667 1.    ]
```

These values show us the learning performance we can expect when we randomly segment our data and pass it into the lower-level hyperparameter and parameter computations. Repeating it a few times gives us an idea of the answers we can expect. In turn, that tells us how *variable* the estimate might be. Now, we can actually train our preferred model based on parameters from `GridSearchCV`:

In [19]:

```
grid_knn.fit(iris.data, iris.target)
preferred_params = grid_knn.best_estimator_.get_params()
final_knn = neighbors.KNeighborsClassifier(**preferred_params)
final_knn.fit(iris.data, iris.target)
```

Out[19]:

```
KNeighborsClassifier(algorithm='auto', leaf_size=30, metric='minkowski',
                     metric_params=None, n_jobs=None, n_neighbors=7, p=4,
                     weights='distance')
```

Our estimates of its performance are based on the outer, 5-fold CV we just performed. We can now take `final_knn` and `predict` on novel data, but we should take a moment and point it at a hold-out test set first (see Exercises).

11.4 Pipelines

One of our biggest limitations in feature engineering—our tasks from Chapter 10—is organizing the computations and obeying the rules of not teaching to the test. Fortunately, pipelines allow us to do both. We gave a brief introduction to pipelines in Section 7.4. Here, we will look at a few more details of pipelines and show how they integrate with grid search.

If we return to our factory analogy, we can easily imagine stringing together the outputs of one machine to the inputs of the next. If some of those components are feature-engineering steps (as in Chapter 10), we have a very natural conveyor belt. The conveyor conveniently moves examples from one step to the next.

11.4.1   A Simple Pipeline

In the simplest examples, we can create a pipeline of learning components from multiple models and transformers and then use that pipeline as a model. `make_pipeline` turns this into a one-liner:

In [20]:

```
scaler = skpre.StandardScaler()
logreg = linear_model.LogisticRegression()

pipe = pipeline.make_pipeline(scaler, logreg)
print(skms.cross_val_score(pipe, iris.data, iris.target, cv=10))
```

```
[0.8    0.8667 1.     0.8667 0.9333 0.9333 0.8    0.8667 0.9333 1.    ]
```

If we use the convenient `make_pipeline`, the names for the steps in the pipeline are built from the __class__ attributes of the steps. So, for example:

In [21]:

```
def extract_name(obj):
    return str(logreg.__class__).split('.')[-1][:-2].lower()

print(logreg.__class__)
print(extract_name(logreg))
```

```
<class 'sklearn.linear_model.logistic.LogisticRegression'>
logisticregression
```

The name is translated into lower case and just the alphabetical characters after the last . are kept. The resulting name is the `logisticregression` which we can see here:

In [22]:

```
pipe.named_steps.keys()
```

Out[22]:

```
dict_keys(['standardscaler', 'logisticregression'])
```

If we want to name the steps ourselves, we use the more customizable `Pipeline` constructor:

```
In [23]:

pipe = pipeline.Pipeline(steps=[('scaler', scaler),
                                ('knn', knn)])

cv_scores = skms.cross_val_score(pipe, iris.data, iris.target,
                                 cv=10,
                                 n_jobs=-1) # all CPUs
print(pipe.named_steps.keys())
print(cv_scores)


dict_keys(['scaler', 'knn'])
[1.     0.9333 1.     0.9333 0.9333 1.     0.9333 0.9333 1.     1.    ]
```

A `Pipeline` can be used just as any other `sklearn` model—we can `fit` and `predict` with it, and we can pass it off to `cross_val_score`. This common interface is the number one win of `sklearn`.

11.4.2 A More Complex Pipeline

As we add more steps to a learning task, we get more benefits from using a pipeline. Let's use an example where we have four major processing steps:

1. Standardize the data,
2. Create interaction terms between the features,
3. Discretize these features to big-small, and
4. Apply a learning method to the resulting features.

If we had to manage this all by hand, the result—unless we are rock-star coders—would be a tangled mess of spaghetti code. Let's see how it plays out using pipelines.

Here is the simple big-small discretizer we developed in Section 10.6.3:

```
In [24]:

from sklearn.base import TransformerMixin
class Median_Big_Small(TransformerMixin):
    def __init__(self):
        pass
    def fit(self, ftrs, tgt=None):
        self.medians = np.median(ftrs)
        return self
    def transform(self, ftrs, tgt=None):
        return ftrs > self.medians
```

We can just plug that into our pipeline, along with other prebuilt `sklearn` components:

In [25]:

```
scaler = skpre.StandardScaler()
quad_inters = skpre.PolynomialFeatures(degree=2,
                                       interaction_only=True,
                                       include_bias=False)
median_big_small = Median_Big_Small()
knn = neighbors.KNeighborsClassifier()

pipe = pipeline.Pipeline(steps=[('scaler', scaler),
                                ('inter',  quad_inters),
                                ('mbs',    median_big_small),
                                ('knn',    knn)])

cv_scores = skms.cross_val_score(pipe, iris.data, iris.target, cv=10)

print(cv_scores)
```

```
[0.6    0.7333 0.8667 0.7333 0.8667 0.7333 0.6667 0.6667 0.8    0.8    ]
```

I won't make too many comments about these results but I encourage you to compare these results to some of our simpler learning systems that we applied to the *iris* problem.

11.5   Pipelines and Tuning Together

One of the biggest benefits of using automation—the `*SearchCV` methods—to tune hyperparameters shows up when our learning system is not a single component. With multiple components come multiple sets of hyperparameters that we can tweak. Managing these by hand would be a *real mess*. Fortunately, pipelines play very well with the `*SearchCV` methods since they are *just another (multicomponent) model*.

In the pipeline above, we somewhat arbitrarily decided to use quadratic terms—second-degree polynomials like xy—as inputs to our model. Instead of picking that out of a hat, let's use cross-validation to pick a *good* degree for our polynomials. The major pain point here is that we must preface the parameters we want to set with `pipelinecomponentname__`. That's the name of the component followed by two underscores. Other than that, the steps for grid searching are the same. We create the pipeline:

In [26]:

```
# create pipeline components and pipeline
scaler = skpre.StandardScaler()
poly   = skpre.PolynomialFeatures()
lasso  = linear_model.Lasso(selection='random', tol=.01)
pipe = pipeline.make_pipeline(scaler,
                              poly,
                              lasso)
```

We specify hyperparameter names and values, prefixed with the pipeline step name:

In [27]:

```
# specified hyperparameters to compare
param_grid = {"polynomialfeatures__degree" : np.arange(2,6),
              "lasso__alpha" : np.logspace(1,6,6,base=2)}

from pprint import pprint as pp
pp(param_grid)
```

```
{'lasso__alpha': array([ 2.,   4.,   8.,  16.,  32.,  64.]),
 'polynomialfeatures__degree': array([2, 3, 4, 5])}
```

We can fit the model using our normal `fit` method:

In [28]:

```
# iid to silence warning
mod = skms.GridSearchCV(pipe, param_grid, iid=False, n_jobs=-1)
mod.fit(diabetes.data, diabetes.target);
```

There are results for each step in the pipeline:

In [29]:

```
for name, step in mod.best_estimator_.named_steps.items():
    print("Step:", name)
    print(textwrap.indent(textwrap.fill(str(step), 50), " " * 6))
```

```
Step: standardscaler
      StandardScaler(copy=True, with_mean=True,
      with_std=True)
Step: polynomialfeatures
      PolynomialFeatures(degree=2, include_bias=True,
      interaction_only=False)
```

```
Step: lasso
      Lasso(alpha=4.0, copy_X=True, fit_intercept=True,
      max_iter=1000,   normalize=False, positive=False,
      precompute=False, random_state=None,
      selection='random', tol=0.01, warm_start=False)
```

We are only really interested in the best values for parameters we were considering:

```
In [30]:
```

```
pp(mod.best_params_)
```

```
{'lasso__alpha': 4.0, 'polynomialfeatures__degree': 2}
```

11.6 EOC

11.6.1 Summary

We've now solved two of the remaining issues in building larger learning systems. First, we can build systems with multiple, modular components working together. Second, we can systematically evaluate hyperparameters and select good ones. We can do that evaluation in a non-teaching-to-the-test manner.

11.6.2 Notes

Our function defining a function and setting the value of k is an example of a *closure*. When we fill in k, we close-the-book on defining add_k: add_k is set and ready to go as a well-defined function of one argument x.

The notes on the details of shuffling and how it interacts with GridSearch are from http://scikit-learn.org/stable/modules/cross_validation.html#a-note-on-shuffling.

There are a few nice references on cross-validation that go beyond the usual textbook presentations:

- *Approximate Statistical Tests for Comparing Supervised Classification Learning Algorithms* by Dietterich
- *A Survey of Cross-Validation Procedures for Model Selection* by Arlot and Celisse
- *Cross-Validatory Choice and Assessment of Statistical Predictions* by Stone

One of the most interesting and mind-bending aspects of performance evaluation is that we are *estimating* the performance of a system. Since we are estimating—just like our learning models are estimated by fitting to a training dataset—our estimates are subject to bias and variance. This means that the same concerns that arise in fitting models apply to evaluating performance. That's a bit more *meta* than I want to get in this book—but *On Over-fitting in Model Selection and Subsequent Selection Bias in Performance Evaluation* by Cawley and Talbot tackles this issue head on, if you're intersted.

11.6.3 Exercises

1. Using linear regression, investigate the difference between the best parameters that we see when we build models on CV folds and when we build a model on an entire dataset. You could also try this with as simple a model as calculating the mean of these CV folds and the whole dataset.

2. Pick an example that interests you from Chapters 8 or 9 and redo it with proper hyperparameter estimation. You can do the same with some of the feature engineering techniques form Chapter 10.

3. You can imagine that with 10 folds of data, we could split them as 1×10, 5×2, or 2×5. Perform each of these scenarios and compare the results. Is there any big difference in the resource costs? What about the variability of the metrics that we get as a result? Afterwards, check out *Consequences of Variability in Classifier Performance Estimates* at https://www3.nd.edu/~nchawla/papers/ICDM10.pdf.

4. You may have noticed that I failed to save a hold-out test set in the nested cross-validation examples (Section 11.3). So, we really don't have an independent, final evaluation of the system we developed there. Wrap the entire process we built in Section 11.3 inside of a *simple* train-test split to remedy that.

Part IV

Adding Complexity

12

Combining Learners

```
In [1]:
# setup
from mlwpy import *

digits = datasets.load_digits()
digits_ftrs, digits_tgt = digits.data, digits.target

diabetes = datasets.load_diabetes()
diabetes_ftrs, diabetes_tgt = diabetes.data, diabetes.target

iris = datasets.load_iris()
tts = skms.train_test_split(iris.data, iris.target,
                            test_size=.75, stratify=iris.target)
(iris_train_ftrs, iris_test_ftrs,
 iris_train_tgt,  iris_test_tgt) = tts
```

12.1 Ensembles

Up to this point, we've talked about learning methods as stand-alone, singular entities. For example, when we use linear regression (LR) or a decision tree (DT), that's *the* single and entire model we are using. We might connect it with other preprocessing steps, but the LR or DT is the model. However, there's an interesting variation we can play on this theme. Much like teams draw on different characters of their members to create functional success and choirs draw on different voices to create musical beauty, different learning systems can be combined to improve on their individual components. In the machine learning community, combinations of multiple learners are called *ensembles*.

To draw on our factory analogy, imagine that we are trying to make something like a car. We probably have many factory machines that make the subcomponents of the car: the engine, the body, the wheels, the tires, and the windows. To assemble the car, we send all of these components to a big factory and out pops a working car. The car itself still has all of the stand-alone components, and each component does its own thing—produces power, turns wheels, slows the vehicle—but they all work together to do car things. On the other hand, if we are making mass quantities of an Italian dressing—yes, I prefer homemade too—the components we combine together lose their individual identity. That's one of the wonders of baking, cooking, and mixology—the way the ingredients combine to form new flavors. While the dressing factory might be a bit smaller than the car factory, we could still bring together ingredients that were themselves the output of other machines.

These two scenarios mirror the two main divisions of ensemble methods (Figure 12.1). Some ensemble methods divide work into different components that are responsible for different regions. Taken *together*, the component regions cover *everything*. In other ensemble methods, every component model predicts everywhere—there are no regional divisions—and then those component predictions are combined into a single prediction.

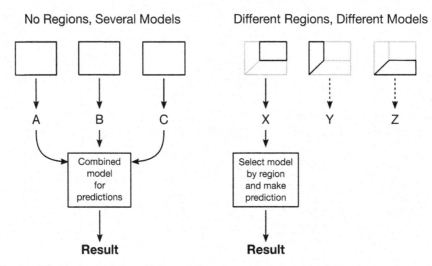

Figure 12.1   On the left, multiple models make predictions everywhere –they are generalists. On the right, different regions are predicted by distinct, specialist models.

Here's another intuitive take on ensembles that emphasizes the way we combine their component learners. At the risk of turning this discussion into a Facebook flamewar, I'll create an analogous scenario with two hypothetical forms of democratic legislature shown in Figure 12.2. In the first form, *SpecialistRepresentation*, every representative is assigned a specialty, such as foreign or domestic issues. When an issue comes up for a vote, reps only vote on their area of specialty. On domestic issues, the foreign specialists will abstain from voting. The hope with this form of government is that reps can become more educated on their particular topic and therefore able to reach better, more informed decisions (don't roll your eyes). On the other side, *GeneralistRepresentation*, every rep votes on everything and we simply take the winning action. Here, the hope is that by averaging many competing and diverse ideas, we end up with some reasonable answer.

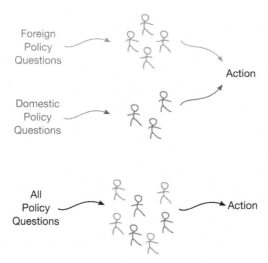

Figure 12.2 Top: representatives only make decisions in their area of expertise. Bottom: every representative makes decisions on every topic – they are all generalists.

Very often, ensembles are constructed from relatively primitive component models. When we start training multiple component models, we have to pay the training cost for each of them. If the component training times are high, our total training time may be very high. On the learning performance side, the result of combining many simple learners gives us a net effect of acting like a more powerful learner. While it might be tempting to use ensembles with more powerful components to create an omnipotent learning algorithm, we won't pursue that path. If you happen to have unlimited computing resources, it might make a fun weekend project. Please be mindful that you don't accidentally turn on Skynet. We rarely need to create custom ensembles; we typically use off-the-shelf ensemble methods. Ensembles underlie several powerful techniques and, if we have multiple learning systems that we need to combine, an ensemble is the perfect way to combine them.

12.2 Voting Ensembles

A conceptually simple way of forming an ensemble is (1) build several different models on the same dataset and then, on a new example, (2) combine the predictions from the different models to get a single final prediction. For regression problems, our combination of predictions can be any of the summary statistics we've seen—for example, the mean or median. When we combined nearest neighbors to make a prediction (Section 3.5), we used these. The analogy with ensembles is that we simply create and train a few models, get a few predictions, and then take the average—whether it's a literal arithmetic mean or some fancier variation. *Presto*, that's our final prediction. For classification, we can take a majority vote, try to get a measure of certainty from the base classifiers and take a weighted vote, or come up with other clever ideas.

```
In [2]:

base_estimators = [linear_model.LogisticRegression(),
                   tree.DecisionTreeClassifier(max_depth=3),
                   naive_bayes.GaussianNB()]
base_estimators = [(get_model_name(m), m) for m in base_estimators]

ensemble_model = ensemble.VotingClassifier(estimators=base_estimators)
skms.cross_val_score(ensemble_model, digits_ftrs, digits_tgt)
```

```
Out[2]:

array([0.8571, 0.8397, 0.8742])
```

Here are two last points. Combining *different* types of models—for example, a linear regression and a decision tree regressor—is called *stacking*. Combining models with different biases can result in a less biased aggregate model.

12.3 Bagging and Random Forests

Let's turn our attention to more complicated ways of combining models. The first is called *random forests* and relies on a technique called *bagging*. The term *bagging* has little to do with physical bags, like a duffel bag or a tote; instead it is a synthetic word, a portmanteau, of the phrase *bootstrap aggregation*. *Aggregation* simply means combining, but we still need to figure out what *bootstrap* means. For that, I'm going to describe how we calculate a simple statistic—the mean—using a *bootstrap* technique.

12.3.1 Bootstrapping

The basic idea of bootstrapping is to find a distribution—a range of possibilities—from a single dataset. Now, if you think about cross-validation, which also takes a single dataset and slices-and-dices it to get multiple results, you aren't far off the mark. They are both instances of *resampling* techniques. I'll have more to say about their relationship in a minute.

Back to bootstrapping. Imagine we have our handy dataset and we want to compute a statistic from it. For convenience, we'll say we want to compute the mean. Of course there is a simple, direct formula for computing the mean: sum the values and divide by the number of values. Mathematically, we write that as $\text{mean}(X) = \frac{\sum x}{n}$. Fair enough. Why bother with any more complexity? Because a single-point estimate—*one* calculated value—of the mean could be misleading. We don't know how variable our estimate of the mean is. In many cases, we want to know how *wrong* we might be. Instead of being satisfied with a single value, we can ask about the *distribution* of the means we could compute from data that is like this dataset. Now, there are some theoretical answers that describe the distribution of the mean—you can find them in any introductory statistics textbook. But, for *other* statistics—up to and including something as fancy as trained classifiers—we don't have nice, pre-canned answers calculated by easy formulas. Bootstrapping provides a direct alternative. To figure out how to compute a bootstrapped value, let's look at some code and some graphics that explain this process.

Sampling with and without Replacement   We need one other idea before we describe the bootstrap process. There are two ways to sample, or select, values from a collection of data. The first is *sampling without replacement*. Imagine we put all of our data in a bag. Suppose we want one sample of five examples from our dataset. We can put our hand in the bag, pull out an example, record it, and *set it to the side*. In this case—*without replacement*—it does *not* go back in the bag. Then we grab a second example from the bag, record it, and put it to the side. Again, it doesn't go back in the bag. We repeat these selections until we've recorded five total examples. It is clear that what we select on the first draw has an effect on what is left for our second, third, and subsequent draws. If an example is out of the bag, it can't be chosen again. Sampling without replacement makes the choices *dependent* on what happened earlier—the examples are not independent of one another. In turn, that affects how statisticians let us talk about the sample.

The other way we can sample from a dataset is by *sampling with replacement*: we pull out an example from the dataset bag, record its value, and *put the example back in the bag*. Then we draw again and repeat until we have the number of samples we want. Sampling with replacement, as in Figure 12.3, gives us an *independent* sequence of examples.

So, how do we use bootstrapping to compute a *bootstrap statistic*? We randomly sample our source dataset, *with replacement*, until we generate a new bootstrap sample with the same number of elements as our original. We compute our statistic of interest on that *bootstrap sample*. We do that several times and then take the mean of those individual bootstrap sample statistics. Figure 12.4 shows the process visually for calculating the bootstrap mean.

Let's illustrate that idea with some code. We'll start with the classic, nonbootstrap formula for the mean.

In [3]:

```
dataset = np.array([1,5,10,10,17,20,35])
def compute_mean(data):
    return np.sum(data) / data.size
compute_mean(dataset)
```

Out[3]:

14.0

Nothing too difficult there. One quick note: we could apply that calculation to the *entire* dataset and get the usual answer to the question, "What is the mean?" We could *also* apply `compute_mean` to other, tweaked forms of that dataset. We'll get different answers to different questions.

Figure 12.3   When we sample with replacement, examples are selected, recorded, and then returned to the cauldron.

Now, let's pivot to the bootstrap technique. We'll define a helper function to take a bootstrap sample—remember, it happens with replacement—and return it.

In [4]:

```
def bootstrap_sample(data):
    N   = len(data)
    idx = np.arange(N)
    bs_idx = np.random.choice(idx, N,
                              replace=True) # default added for clarity
    return data[bs_idx]
```

Now we can see what several rounds of bootstrap sampling and the means for those samples look like:

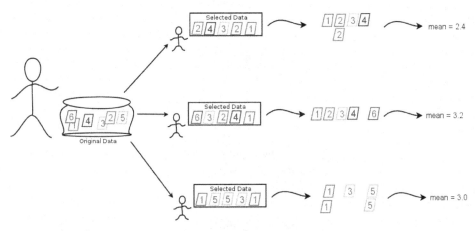

Figure 12.4   We repeatedly calculate the value of the mean on bootstrap samples.
We combine those values by taking *their* mean.

In [5]:

```
bsms = []
for i in range(5):
    bs_sample = bootstrap_sample(dataset)
    bs_mean = compute_mean(bs_sample)
    bsms.append(bs_mean)

    print(bs_sample, "{:5.2f}".format(bs_mean))
```

```
[35 10  1  1 10 10 10] 11.00
[20 35 20 20 20 20 20] 22.14
[17 10 20 10 10  5 17] 12.71
[20  1 10 35  1 17 10] 13.43
[17 10 10 10  1  1 10]  8.43
```

From those bootstrap sample means we can compute a single value—the mean of the
means:

In [6]:

```
print("{:5.2f}".format(sum(bsms) / len(bsms)))
```

```
13.54
```

Here is the bootstrap calculation rolled up into a single function:

In [7]:

```
def compute_bootstrap_statistic(data, num_boots, statistic):
    ' repeatedly calculate statistic on num_boots bootstrap samples'
    # no comments from the peanut gallery
    bs_stats = [statistic(bootstrap_sample(data)) for i in range(num_boots)]
    # return the average of the calculated statistics
    return np.sum(bs_stats) / num_boots

bs_mean = compute_bootstrap_statistic(dataset, 100, compute_mean)
print("{:5.2f}".format(bs_mean))
```

13.86

The really interesting part is that we can compute just about *any* statistic using this same process. We'll follow up on that idea now.

12.3.2 From Bootstrapping to Bagging

When we create a *bagged learner*, we are constructing a much more convoluted statistic: a learner in the form of a trained model. In what sense is a learner a statistic? Broadly, a statistic is any function of a group of data. The mean, median, min, and max are all calculations that we apply to a dataset to get a result. They are all statistics. Creating, fitting, and applying a learner to a new example—while a bit more complicated—is *just* calculating a result from a dataset.

I'll prove it by doing it.

In [8]:

```
def make_knn_statistic(new_example):
    def knn_statistic(dataset):
        ftrs, tgt = dataset[:,:-1], dataset[:,-1]
        knn = neighbors.KNeighborsRegressor(n_neighbors=3).fit(ftrs, tgt)
        return knn.predict(new_example)
    return knn_statistic
```

The one oddity here is that we used a closure—we discussed these in Section 11.1. Here, our statistic is calculated with respect to one specific new example. We need to hold that test example fixed, so we can get down to a single value. Having done that trick, we have a calculation on the dataset—the inner function, knn_statistic—that we can use in the exact same way that we used compute_mean.

In [9]:

```
# have to slightly massage data for this scenario
# we use last example as our fixed test example
diabetes_dataset = np.c_[diabetes_ftrs, diabetes_tgt]
```

```
ks = make_knn_statistic(diabetes_ftrs[-1].reshape(1,-1))
compute_bootstrap_statistic(diabetes_dataset, 100, ks)
```

Out[9]:

74.00666666666667

Just like computing the mean will give us different answers depending on the exact dataset we use, the returned value from `knn_statistic` will depend on the data we pass into it.

We can mimic that process and turn it into our basic algorithm for bagging:

1. Sample the data with replacement.
2. Create a model and train it on that data.
3. Repeat.

To predict, we feed an example into each of the trained models and combine their predictions. The process, using decision trees as the component models, is shown in Figure 12.5.

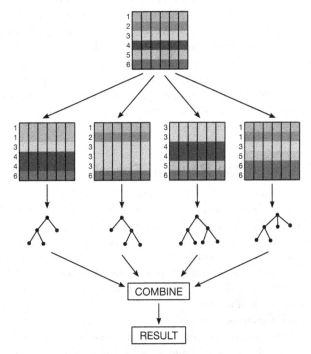

Figure 12.5 As with the bootstrapped mean, we sample the dataset and generate a decision tree from each subdataset. Every tree has a say in the final prediction.

Here's some pseudocode for a classification bagging system:

```
In [10]:

def bagged_learner(dataset, base_model, num_models=10):
    # pseudo-code:  needs tweaks to run
    models = []
    for n in num_models:
        bs_sample = np.random.choice(dataset, N, replace=True)
        models.append(base_model().fit(*bs_sample))
    return models

def bagged_predict_class(models, example):
    # take the most frequent (mode) predicted class as result
    preds = [m.predict(example) for m in models]
    return pd.Series(preds).mode()
```

We can talk about some practical concerns of bagging using the bias-variance terminology we introduced in Section 5.6. (And you thought that was all just theoretical hand-waving!) Our process of combining many predictions is good at balancing out high variance: conceptually, we're OK with *overfitting* in our base model. We'll overfit and then let the averaging—or, here, taking the biggest vote getter with the mode—smooth out the rough edges. Bagging doesn't help with *bias*, but it can help significantly reduce variance. In practice, we want the `base_model` to have a low bias.

Conceptually, since our learners are created from samples that are taken with replacement, the learners are independent of one another. If we really wanted to, we could train each of the different base models on a separate computer and then combine them together at the end. We could use this separation to great effect if we want to use parallel computing to speed up the training process.

12.3.3 Through the Random Forest

Random forests (RFs) are a specific type of a bagged learner built on top of decision trees. RFs use a variation on the decision trees we've seen. Standard decision trees take the best-evaluated feature of *all* the features to create a decision node. In contrast, RFs subselect a random set of features and then take the best of that subset. The goal is to force the trees to be different from each other. You can imagine that even over a random selection of the examples, a single feature might be tightly related to the target. This alpha feature would then be pretty likely to be chosen as the top split point in each tree. Let's knock down the monarch of the hill.

Instead of a single feature being the top decision point in many bootstrapped trees, we'll selectively ignore some features and introduce some randomness to shake things up. The randomness forces different trees to consider a variety of features. The original random forest algorithm relied on the same sort of majority voting that we described for bagging. However, `sklearn`'s version of RFs extracts class probabilities from each tree in the forest and then averages those to get a final answer: the class with the highest average probability is the winner.

If we start with our `bagged_learner` code from above, we still need to modify our tree-creation code—the component-model building step—from Section 8.2. It is a pretty simply modification which I've placed in *italics*:

0. *Randomly select a subset of features* for this tree to consider.
1. Evaluate the selected features and splits and pick the best feature-and-split.
2. Add a node to the tree that represents the feature-split.
3. For each descendant, work with the matching data and either:

    ▪ If the targets are similar enough, return a predicted target.
    ▪ If not, return to step 1 and repeat.

Using that pseudocode as our base estimator, together with the `bagged_learner` code, gets us a quick prototype of a random forest learning system.

Extreme Random Forests and Feature Splits   One other variant—yet another bagged-tree (YABT)—is called an *extreme random forest*. No, this is not the X-Games of decision-tree sports. Here, *extreme* refers to adding yet another degree of randomness to the model creation process. Give a computer scientist an idea—replacing a deterministic method with randomness—and they will apply it everywhere. In extreme random forests, we make the following change to the component-tree building process:

1. Select split points at random and take the best of those.

So, in addition to randomly choosing what features are involved, we also determine what values are important by coin flipping. It's amazing that this technique works—and it can work well indeed. Until now, I have not gone into great detail about the split selection process. I don't really care to, since there are many, many discussions of it around. I particularly like how Foster and Provost approach it in their book that I reference at the end of the chapter.

Let me give you the idea behind making good split points with an example. Suppose we wanted to predict good basketball players from simple biometric data. Unfortunately for folks like myself, height is a really good predictor of basketball success. So, we might start by considering how height is related to a dataset of successful and—like myself—nonsuccessful basketball players. If we order all of the heights, we might find that people from 4'5" to 6'11" have tried to play basketball. If I introduce a split-point at 5'0", I'll probably have lots of unsuccessful players on the less-than side. That's a relatively similar group of people when grouped by basketball success. But, on the greater-than side, I'll probably have a real mix of both classes. We say that we have low *purity* above the split point and high purity below the split point. Likewise, if I set a split point at 6'5", there are probably a lot of successful people on the high side, but the low side is quite mixed. Our goal is to find that *just right* split point on height that gives me as much information about the success measure—for both the taller and shorter folks—as possible. Segmenting off big heights and low heights gets me a lot of information. In the middle, other factors, such as the amount of time playing basketball, matter a lot.

So, extreme random forests don't consider *all possible* split points. They merely choose a random subset of points to consider, evaluate those points, and take the best—of that limited set.

12.4 Boosting

I remember studying for vocabulary and geography tests using *flash cards*. I don't know if the App Generation knows about these things. They were little pieces of paper—two-sided, like most pieces of paper—and on one side you would put a word or a noun or a concept and on the other side you would put a definition or an important characteristic of that thing. For example, one side might be *gatto* and the other side *cat* (for an Italian vocab test), or *Lima* on one side and *capital of Peru* on the other (for a world geography test).

Studying was a simple act of flipping through the flash cards—seeing one side and recalling the other. You could use both sides to go (1) from concept to definition or (2) from definition to concept. Now, typically, I wouldn't keep all the cards in the deck. Some of the definitions and concepts became easy for me and I'd put those cards aside (Figure 12.6) so I could focus on the difficult concepts. Eventually, I whittled the deck down to a fairly small pile—the hard stuff—which I kept studying until the exam.

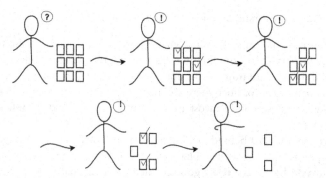

Figure 12.6 When studying with flashcards, we can selectively remove the easy cards and focus our attention on the hard examples. Boosting uses a similar approach.

The process of taking cards out of the deck is a bit like weighting the likelihood of seeing those cards but in an extreme way: it takes the probability down to zero. Now, if I *really* wanted to be thorough, instead of removing the easy cards, I could add duplicates of the hard cards. The effect would be similar: hard cards would be seen more often and easy cards would be seen less. The difference is that the process would be gradual.

We can apply this same idea—focusing on the hard examples—to a learning system. We start by fitting a Simple-McSimple Model to some hard data. Not surprisingly, we get a lot of examples wrong. But surprisingly, we do get a few right. We refocus our efforts on the harder examples and try again. That repeated process of focusing our efforts on harder examples—and considering the easier examples done(-ish)—is the heart of boosting.

12.4.1 Boosting Details

With boosting, we learn a simple model. Then, instead of resampling equally from the base dataset, we focus on the examples that we got wrong and develop another model. We repeat that process until we are satisfied or run out of time. Thus, boosting is a sequential method and the learners developed at later stages depend on what happened at earlier stages. While boosting can be applied to any learning model as the primitive component model, often we use *decision stumps*—decision trees with only one split point. Decision stumps have a depth of one.

We haven't talked about what learning with weighted data means. You can think of it in two different ways. First, if we want to perform weighted training and example A has twice the weight of example B, we'll simply duplicate example A twice in our training set and call it a day. The alternative is to incorporate the weighting in our error or loss measures. We can weight errors by the example weight and get a *weighted error*. Then, we find the best knob settings with respect to the weighted errors, not raw errors.

In a very raw, pseudocode form, these steps look like:

1. Initialize example weights to $\frac{1}{N}$ and m to zero.
2. Repeat until done:
    1. Increment m.
    2. Fit a new classifier (often a stump), C_m, to the weighted data.
    3. Compute weighted error of new classifier.
    4. The classifier weight, wgt_m, is function of weighted errors.
    5. Update example weights based on old example weights, classifier errors, and classifier weights.
3. For new example and m repeats, output a prediction from the majority vote of C weighted by wgt.

We can take some massive liberties (don't try this at home!) and write some Pythonic pseudocode:

```
In [11]:

def my_boosted_classifier(base_classifier, bc_args,
                          examples, targets, M):
    N = len(examples)
    data_weights = np.full(N, 1/N)
    models, model_weights = [], []

    for i in range(M):
        weighted_dataset = reweight((examples,targets),
                                    data_weights)
        this_model = base_classifier(*bc_args).fit(*weighted_dataset)

        errors = this_model.predict(examples) != targets
        weighted_error = np.dot(weights, errors)
```

```
# magic reweighting steps
this_model_wgt = np.log(1-weighted_error)/weighted_error
data_weights  *= np.exp(this_model_wgt * errors)
data_weights  /= data_weights.sum() # normalize to 1.0


models.append(this_model)
model_weights.append(this_model_wgt)

  return ensemble.VotingClassifier(models,
                                   voting='soft',
                                   weights=model_weights)
```

You'll notice a few things here. We picked a value of M out of a hat. Certainly, that gives us a deterministic stopping point: we'll only do M iterations. But we could introduce a bit more flexibility here. For example, `sklearn` stops its discrete AdaBoost—a specific boosting variant, similar to what we used here—when either the accuracy hits 100% or `this_model` starts doing worse than a coin flip. Also, instead of reweighting examples, we could perform weighted bootstrap sampling—it's simply a different way to prioritize some data over another.

Boosting very naturally deals with *bias* in our learning systems. By combining many simple, highly biased learners, boosting reduces the overall bias in the results. Boosting can *also* reduce variance.

In boosting, unlike bagging, we can't build the primitive models in parallel. We need to wait on the results of one pass so we can reweight our data and focus on the hard examples before we start our next pass.

12.4.1.1 Improvements with Boosting Iterations

The two major boosting classifiers in `sklearn` are `GradientBoostingClassifier` and `AdaBoostClassifier`. Each can be told the maximum number of component estimators—our M argument to `my_boosted_classifier`—to use through `n_estimators`. I'll leave details of the boosters to the end notes, but here are a few tidbits. AdaBoost is the classic forebearer of modern boosting algorithms. Gradient Boosting is a new twist that allows us to plug in different loss functions and get different models as a result. For example, if we set `loss="exponential"` with the `GradientBoostingClassifier`, we get a model that is basically AdaBoost. The result gives us code similar to `my_boosted_classifier`.

Since boosting is an iterative process, we can reasonably ask how our model improves over the cycles of reweighting. `sklearn` makes it relatively easy to access that progress through `staged_predict`. `staged_predict` operates like `predict` except it follows the predictions made on examples at each step—or stage—of the learning process. We need to convert those predictions into evaluation metrics if we want to quantify the progress.

In [12]:

```
model = ensemble.AdaBoostClassifier()
stage_preds = (model.fit(iris_train_ftrs, iris_train_tgt)
                    .staged_predict(iris_test_ftrs))
stage_scores = [metrics.accuracy_score(iris_test_tgt,
                                       pred) for pred in stage_preds]
fig, ax = plt.subplots(1,1,figsize=(4,3))
ax.plot(stage_scores)
ax.set_xlabel('# steps')
ax.set_ylabel('accuracy');
```

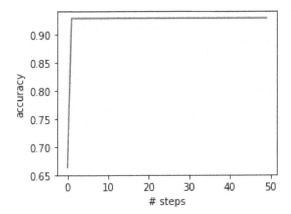

12.5 Comparing the Tree-Ensemble Methods

Let's now compare how these team-based methods work on the *digits* data. We'll start with two simple baselines: a single decision stump (equivalent to a `max_depth=1` tree) and a single `max_depth=3` tree. We'll also build 100 *different* forests with a number of tree stumps going from 1 to 100.

In [13]:

```
def fit_predict_score(model, ds):
    return skms.cross_val_score(model, *ds, cv=10).mean()

stump  = tree.DecisionTreeClassifier(max_depth=1)
dtree  = tree.DecisionTreeClassifier(max_depth=3)
forest = ensemble.RandomForestClassifier(max_features=1, max_depth=1)
```

```
tree_classifiers = {'stump' : stump, 'dtree' : dtree, 'forest': forest}

max_est = 100
data = (digits_ftrs, digits_tgt)
stump_score   = fit_predict_score(stump, data)
tree_score    = fit_predict_score(dtree, data)
forest_scores = [fit_predict_score(forest.set_params(n_estimators=n),
                                   data)
                 for n in range(1,max_est+1)]
```

We can view those results graphically:

In [14]:

```
fig, ax = plt.subplots(figsize=(4,3))

xs = list(range(1,max_est+1))
ax.plot(xs, np.repeat(stump_score, max_est), label='stump')
ax.plot(xs, np.repeat(tree_score, max_est),  label='tree')
ax.plot(xs, forest_scores, label='forest')

ax.set_xlabel('Number of Trees in Forest')
ax.set_ylabel('Accuracy')
ax.legend(loc='lower right');
```

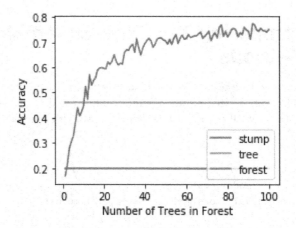

Comparing the forests to the two baselines shows that a single-stump forest acts a lot like—unsurprisingly—a stump. But then, as the number of stumps grows, we quickly outperform even our moderately sized tree.

Now, to see how the boosting methods progress over time *and* to make use of cross-validation—to make sure we're comparing apples to apples—we need to manually manage a bit of the cross-validation process. It's not complicated, but it is slightly ugly. Essentially, we need to generate the fold indices by hand with `StratifiedKFold` (we looked at this in Section 5.5.2) and then *use* those indices to select the proper parts of our dataset. We could simply place this code inline, below, but that really obscures what we're trying to do.

In [15]:

```
def my_manual_cv(dataset, k=10):
    ' manually generate cv-folds from dataset '
    # expect ftrs, tgt tuple
    ds_ftrs, ds_tgt = dataset
    manual_cv = skms.StratifiedKFold(k).split(ds_ftrs,
                                              ds_tgt)
    for (train_idx, test_idx) in manual_cv:
        train_ftrs = ds_ftrs[train_idx]
        test_ftrs  = ds_ftrs[test_idx]
        train_tgt  = ds_tgt[train_idx]
        test_tgt   = ds_tgt[test_idx]

        yield (train_ftrs, test_ftrs,
               train_tgt, test_tgt)
```

For this comparison, we'll use a `deviance` loss for our gradient boosting classifier. The result is that our classifier acts like logistic regression. We tinker with one important parameter to give `AdaBoostClassifier` a legitimate shot at success on the *digits* data. We adjust the `learning_rate` which is an additional factor—literally, a multiplier—on the weights of the estimators. You can think of it as multiplying `this_model_weight` in `my_boosted_classifier`.

In [16]:

```
AdaBC  = ensemble.AdaBoostClassifier
GradBC = ensemble.GradientBoostingClassifier
boosted_classifiers = {'boost(Ada)' : AdaBC(learning_rate=2.0),
                       'boost(Grad)' : GradBC(loss="deviance")}
mean_accs = {}
```

```
for name, model in boosted_classifiers.items():
    model.set_params(n_estimators=max_est)
    accs = []
    for tts in my_manual_cv((digits_ftrs, digits_tgt)):
        train_f, test_f, train_t, test_t = tts
        s_preds = (model.fit(train_f, train_t)
                        .staged_predict(test_f))
        s_scores = [metrics.accuracy_score(test_t, p) for p in s_preds]
        accs.append(s_scores)
    mean_accs[name] = np.array(accs).mean(axis=0)
mean_acc_df = pd.DataFrame.from_dict(mean_accs,orient='columns')
```

Pulling out the individual, stage-wise accuracies is a bit annoying. But the end result is that we can compare the number of models we are combining between the different ensembles.

In [17]:

```
xs = list(range(1,max_est+1))
fig, (ax1, ax2) = plt.subplots(1,2,figsize=(8,3),sharey=True)
ax1.plot(xs, np.repeat(stump_score, max_est), label='stump')
ax1.plot(xs, np.repeat(tree_score, max_est),  label='tree')
ax1.plot(xs, forest_scores, label='forest')
ax1.set_ylabel('Accuracy')
ax1.set_xlabel('Number of Trees in Forest')
ax1.legend()

mean_acc_df.plot(ax=ax2)
ax2.set_ylim(0.0, 1.1)
ax2.set_xlabel('# Iterations')
ax2.legend(ncol=2);
```

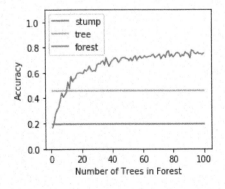
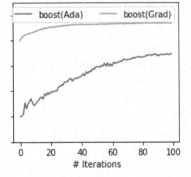

After adding more trees to the forest and letting more iterations pass for AdaBoost, the forest and AdaBoost have broadly similar performance (near 80% accuracy). However, the AdaBoost classifier doesn't seem to perform nearly as well as the GradientBoosting classifier. You can play around with some hyperparameters—`GridSearch` is seeming mighty useful about now—to see if you can improve any or all of these.

12.6 EOC

12.6.1 Summary

The techniques we've explored in this chapter bring us to some of the more powerful models available to the modern machine learning practitioner. They build conceptually and literally on top of the models we've seen throughout our tour of learning methods. Ensembles bring together the best aspects of teamwork to improve learning performance compared to individuals.

12.6.2 Notes

In machine learning, the specialist learning scenario typically has terms like *additive*, *mixture*, or *expert* in the name. The key is that the component models only apply to certain areas of the input. We can extend this to a *fuzzy specialist* scenario where applying to a region need not be a binary yes or no but can be given by a weight. Models can gradually turn on and off in different regions.

Not to get too meta on you, but many simple learners—linear regression and decision trees, I'm looking at you—can be viewed as ensembles of *very simple* learning components combined together. For example, we combine multiple decision stumps to create a standard decision tree. To make a prediction, a decision tree asks questions of its decision stumps and ends up with an answer. Likewise, a linear regression takes the contribution of each feature and then adds up—combines with a dot product, to be specific—those single-feature predictions into a final answer. Now, we don't normally talk about decision trees and linear regression as ensembles. Just keep in mind that there is nothing magical about taking simple answers or predictions and combining them in some interesting and useful ways.

We computed a number of bootstrap estimates of a statistic: first the mean and then classifier predictions. We can use the same technique to compute a bootstrap estimate of variability (variance)—using the usual formula for variance—and we can perform other statistical analyses in a similar manner. These methods are *very* broadly applicable in scenarios that don't lend themselves to simple formulaic calculations. However, they do depend on some relatively weak but extremely technical assumptions—*compact differentiability* is the term to google—to have theoretical support. Often, we charge bravely ahead, even without complete theoretical support.

Boosting   Boosting is really amazing. It can continue to improve its testing performance even after its training performance is perfect. You can think about this as smoothing out unneeded wiggles as it continues iterating. While it is fairly well agreed that bagging reduces variance and boosting reduces bias, it is less well agreed that boosting reduces *variance*. My claim to this end is based on technical report by Breiman, "Bias, Variance, and Arcing Classifiers." Here, *arcing* is a close cousin to boosting. An additional useful point from that report: bagging is most useful for unstable—high-variance— methods like decision trees.

The form of boosting we discussed is called *AdaBoost*—for *adaptive* boosting. The original form of boosting—pre-AdaBoost—was quite theoretical and had issues that rendered it impractical in many scenarios. AdaBoost resolved those issues, and subsequent research connected AdaBoost to fitting models with an *exponential loss*. In turn, substituting other loss functions led to boosting methods appropriate for different kinds of data. In particular, *gradient boosting* lets us swap out a different loss function and get different boosted learners, such as boosted logistic regression. My boosting pseudocode is based on Russell and Norvig's excellent *Artificial Intelligence: A Modern Approach*.

Aside from `sklearn`, there are other boosting implementations out there. `xgboost`—for *extreme gradient boosting*—is the newest kid on the block. It uses a technique—an optimization strategy—that produces better weights as it calculates the weights of the component models. It also uses slightly less tiny component models. Coupling better weighting with more complex component models, `xgboost` has a cult-like following on Kaggle (a social website, with competitions, for machine learning enthusiasts).

We can't always use `xgboost`'s technique but we can use it in common learning scenarios. Here's a super quick code demo:

In [18]:

```
# conda install py-xgboost
import xgboost
# gives us xgboost.XGBRegressor, xgboost.XGBClassifier
# which interface nicely with sklearn
# see docs at
# http://xgboost.readthedocs.io/en/latest/parameter.html
xgbooster = xgboost.XGBClassifier(objective="multi:softmax")
scores = skms.cross_val_score(xgbooster, iris.data, iris.target, cv=10)
print(scores)
```

```
[1.     0.9333 1.     0.9333 0.9333 0.9333 0.9333 0.9333 1.     1.    ]
```

12.6.3 Exercises

1. Ensemble methods are very, very powerful—but they come at a computational cost. Evaluate and compare the resource usage (memory and time) of several different tree-based learners: stumps, decision trees, boosted stumps, and random forests.

2. Create a voting classifier with a few—five—relatively old-school base learners, for example linear regression. You can feed the base learners with datasets produced

by cross-validation, if you're clever. (If not, you can MacGyver something together—but that just means being clever in a different way!) Compare the bias and variance—underfitting and overfitting—of the base method developed on the whole training set and the voting method by assessing them on training and testing sets and overlaying the results. Now, repeat the same process using bagged learners. If you are using something besides decision trees, you might want to look at `sklearn.ensemble.BaggingRegressor`.

3. You can implement a bagged classifier by using some of the code we wrote along with `sklearn`'s `VotingClassifier`. It gives you a choice in how you use the votes: they can be `hard` (everyone gets one vote and majority wins) or `soft` (everyone gives a probability weight to a class and we add those up—the biggest value wins). `sklearn`'s random forest uses the equivalent of `soft`. You can compare that with a `hard` voting mechanism. `soft` is recommended when the probabilities of the base models are *well calibrated*, meaning they reflect the actual probability of the event occurring. We aren't going to get into it, but some models are not well calibrated. They can *classify* well, but they can't give reasonable probabilities. You can think of it as finding a good boundary, but not having insight into what goes on around the boundary. Assessing this would require knowing real-world probabilities and comparing them to the probabilities generated by the model—that's a step beyond simply having target classes.

4. Since we like to use boosting with very simple models, if we turn our attention to linear regression we might think about using simple constant models as our base models. That is just a horizontal line: $y = b$. Compare good old-fashioned linear regression with boosted constant regressions on a regression dataset.

5. What happens if we use deeper trees in ensembles? For example, what happens if you use trees of depth two or three as the base learners in boosting? Do you see any significant improvements or failures?

6. We saw `AdaBoost` lose out to `GradientBoosting`. Use a `GridSearch` to try several different parameter values for each of these ensemble methods and compare the results. In particular, you might try to find a good value for the learning rate.

Models That Engineer Features for Us

In [1]:

```python
# setup
from mlwpy import *
%matplotlib inline

kwargs = {'test_size':.25, 'random_state':42}

iris = datasets.load_iris()
tts = skms.train_test_split(iris.data, iris.target, **kwargs)
(iris_train,      iris_test,
 iris_train_tgt, iris_test_tgt) = tts

wine = datasets.load_wine()
tts = skms.train_test_split(wine.data, wine.target, **kwargs)
(wine_train,      wine_test,
 wine_train_tgt, wine_test_tgt) = tts

diabetes = datasets.load_diabetes()
tts = skms.train_test_split(diabetes.data, diabetes.target, **kwargs)
(diabetes_train_ftrs, diabetes_test_ftrs,
 diabetes_train_tgt,  diabetes_test_tgt) = tts

# these are entire datasets
iris_df = pd.DataFrame(iris.data, columns=iris.feature_names)
wine_df = pd.DataFrame(wine.data, columns=wine.feature_names)
diabetes_df = pd.DataFrame(diabetes.data, columns=diabetes.feature_names)
```

In Chapter 10, we performed feature engineering by hand. For example, we could *manually*—with our own eyes—read through a list of features and say that some more are needed. We could *manually* create a new feature for body mass index (BMI)—from height and weight—by running the necessary calculations. In this chapter, we will talk about *automated ways* of performing feature selection and construction. There are two benefits to automation: (1) we can consider many, many possible combinations of features and operations and (2) we can place these steps within cross-validation loops to prevent overfitting due to feature engineering.

So far in this book, I have preferred to start with some specifics and then talk about things more abstractly. I'm going to flip things around for a few minutes and speak abstractly and then follow up with some intuitive examples. From Chapter 2, you might remember that we can take a geometric view of our data. We act as if each of our examples is a point in some 2D, 3D, or *n*-D space. Things get weird in higher dimensions—but rest assured, theoretical physicists and mathematicians have us covered. If we have a simple scenario of five examples with three features each—five points in 3D space—then there are several ways we might rewrite or reexpress this data:

- We might ask: if I can only keep one of the original dimensions, which one should I keep?
    - We can extend that: if I can keep *n* of the original dimensions, which should I keep?
    - We can reverse it: which dimensions should I get rid of?
- I measured some features in ways which were convenient. Are there *better* ways to express those measurements?
    - Some measurements may overlap in their information: for example, if height and weight are highly correlated, we may not need both.
    - Some measurements may do better when combined: for health purposes, combining height and weight to BMI may be beneficial.
- If I want to reduce the data down to a *best* line, which line should I use?
- If I want to reduce the data down to a *best* plane, which plane should I use (Figure 13.1)?

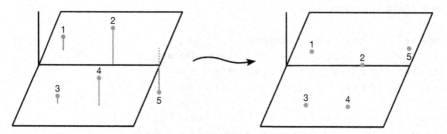

Figure 13.1   Mapping points from 3D to 2D.

We can answer these questions using a variety of techniques. Here's a quick reminder about terminology (which we discussed more thoroughly in Section 10.1). The process of selecting some features to use, and excluding others, is called *feature selection*. The process of reexpressing the given measurements is called *feature construction*. We'll save *feature extraction* for the next chapter. Some learning techniques make use of feature selection and feature construction, *internally*, in their regular operation. We can also perform feature selection and feature construction as stand-alone preprocessing steps.

One major reason to select a subset of features is when we have a *very* large dataset with many measurements that could be used to train several different learning systems. For example, if we had data on housing sales, we might care about predicting values of houses, recommending houses to particular users, and verifying that mortgage lenders are complying with financial and anti-discrimination laws. Some aspects of the dataset might be useful for answering all of these questions; other features might only apply to one or two of those questions. Trimming down the unneeded features can simplify the learning task by removing irrelevant or redundant information.

One concrete example of feature construction is body mass index. It turns out that accurately measuring a person's lean body mass—or, less enthusiastically for some, our nonlean mass—is very difficult. Even in a laboratory setting, taking accurate and repeatable measurements is difficult. On the other hand, there are many well-documented relationships between health concerns and the ratio of lean to nonlean mass. In short, it's very useful for health care providers to have a quick assessment of that ratio.

While it has limitations, BMI is an easy-to-compute result from easy-to-measure values that has a good relationship with health outcomes. It is calculated as $\mathrm{BMI} = \frac{\text{weight}}{\text{height}^2}$ with weight in kilograms and height in meters. Practically speaking, at the doctor's office, you take a quick step on a scale, they put the little stick on your head, and after two quick operations on a calculator, you have a surrogate value for the hard-to-measure concept of lean mass. We can apply similar ideas to bring hard-to-measure or loosely related concepts to the forefront in learning systems.

13.1 Feature Selection

From a high-level viewpoint, there are three ways to pick features:

1. Single-step filtering: evaluate each feature in isolation, then select some and discard the rest.
2. Select-Model-Evaluate-Repeat: select one or more features, build a model, and assess the results. Repeat after adding or removing features. Compared to single-step filtering, this technique lets us account for interactions between features and between features and a model.
3. Embed feature selection within model building: as part of the model building process, we can select or ignore different features.

We'll talk about the first two in more detail in a moment. For the third, feature selection is naturally embedded in several learning techniques. For example:

1. Lasso regression from Section 9.1, and L_1 regularization generally, leads to zeros for regression coefficients which is equivalent to ignoring those features.

2. Decision trees, as commonly implemented, select a single feature at each tree node. Limiting the depth of a tree limits the total number of features that the tree can consider.

13.1.1   Single-Step Filtering with Metric-Based Feature Selection

The simplest method of selecting features is to numerically score the features and then take the top results. We can use a number of statistical or information-based measures to do the scoring. We will look at variance, covariance, and information gain.

13.1.1.1   Variance

The simplest way to choose features to use in a model is to give them scores. We can score features in pure isolation or in relationship to the target. The simplest scoring ignores even the target and simply asks something about a feature in isolation. What characteristics of a feature could be useful for learning but don't draw on the relationship we want to learn? Suppose a feature has the *same* value for every example—an entire column with the value *Red*. That column, literally, has no information to provide. It also happens to have zero variance. Less extremely, the lower variance a feature has, the less likely it is to be useful to distinguish a target value. Low-variance features, as a general rule, are not going to be good for prediction. So, this argument says we can get rid of features with very low variance.

The features from the *wine* dataset have the following variances:

In [2]:

```
print(wine_df.var())
```

```
alcohol                         0.6591
malic_acid                      1.2480
ash                             0.0753
alcalinity_of_ash              11.1527
magnesium                     203.9893
total_phenols                   0.3917
flavanoids                      0.9977
nonflavanoid_phenols            0.0155
proanthocyanins                 0.3276
color_intensity                 5.3744
hue                             0.0522
od280/od315_of_diluted_wines    0.5041
proline                     99,166.7174
dtype: float64
```

You may notice a problem: the scales of the measurements may differ so much that their average squared distance from the mean—that's the variance, by the way—is small compared to the raw measurements on other scales. Here's an example in the *wine* data:

```
In [3]:

print(wine_df['hue'].max() - wine_df['hue'].min())
```

```
1.23
```

The biggest possible difference in `hue` is 1.23; its variance was about 0.05. Meanwhile:

```
In [4]:

print(wine_df['proline'].max() - wine_df['proline'].min())
```

```
1402.0
```

The range of `proline` is just over 1400 and the average squared difference from the average `proline` value is almost 10,000. The two features are simply speaking different languages—or, one is whispering and one is shouting. So, while the argument for selecting based on variance has merits, selecting features in this exact manner is not recommended. Still, we'll march ahead to get a feel for how it works before we add complications.

Here, we'll pick out those features that have a variance greater than one.

```
In [5]:

# variance-selection example without scaling
varsel = ftr_sel.VarianceThreshold(threshold=1.0)
varsel.fit_transform(wine_train)

print("first example")
print(varsel.fit_transform(wine_train)[0],
      wine_train[0, wine_train.var(axis=0) > 1.0], sep='\n')
```

```
first example
[   2.36   18.6   101.      3.24    5.68 1185.   ]
[   2.36   18.6   101.      3.24    5.68 1185.   ]
```

So, running the `VarianceThreshold.fit_transform` is effectively the same as picking the columns with variance greater than one. Good enough. `get_support` gives us a set of Boolean values to select columns.

```
In [6]:

print(varsel.get_support())
```

```
[False  True False  True  True False  True False False  True False False
  True]
```

If we want to know the *names* of the features we kept, we have go back to the dataset's `feature_names`:

```
In [7]:

keepers_idx = varsel.get_support()
keepers = np.array(wine.feature_names)[keepers_idx]
print(keepers)
```

```
['malic_acid' 'alcalinity_of_ash' 'magnesium' 'flavanoids'
 'color_intensity' 'proline']
```

Here's one other conceptual example. Imagine I measured human heights in centimeters versus meters. The differences from the mean, when measured in meters, are going to be relatively small; in centimeters, they are going to be larger. When we *square* those differences—remember, the formula for variance includes an $(x - \bar{x})^2$—they are magnified even more. So, we need the units of the measurements to be comparable. We *don't* want to normalize these measurements by dividing by the standard deviation—if we do that, all the variances will go to 1. Instead, we can rescale them to $[0, 1]$ or $[-1, 1]$.

```
In [8]:

minmax = skpre.MinMaxScaler().fit_transform(wine_train)
print(np.sort(minmax.var(axis=0)))
```

```
[0.0223 0.0264 0.0317 0.0331 0.0361 0.0447 0.0473 0.0492 0.0497 0.0569
 0.058  0.0587 0.071 ]
```

Now, we can assess the variance of those rescaled values. It's not super principled, but we'll apply a threshold of 0.05. Alternatively, you could decide you want to keep some number or percentage of the best features and work backwards from that to an appropriate threshold.

```
In [9]:

# scaled-variance selection example
pipe = pipeline.make_pipeline(skpre.MinMaxScaler(),
                              ftr_sel.VarianceThreshold(threshold=0.05))
pipe.fit_transform(wine_train).shape

# pipe.steps is list of (name, step_object)
keepers_idx = pipe.steps[1][1].get_support()
print(np.array(wine.feature_names)[keepers_idx])
```

```
['nonflavanoid_phenols' 'color_intensity' 'od280/od315_of_diluted_wines'
 'proline']
```

Unfortunately, using variance is troublesome for two reasons. First, we don't have any absolute scale on which to pick a threshold for a good variance. Sure, if the variance is zero, we can probably ditch the feature—but on the other extreme, a feature with unique values for every example is also a problem. In Section 8.2 we saw that we can make a perfect decision tree for training from such a feature, but it has no generalization utility. Second, the value we choose is very much a relative decision based on the features we have in the dataset. If we want to be more objective, we could use a pipeline and grid-search mechanisms to choose a good variance threshold based on the data. Still, if a learning problem has too many features (hundreds or thousands), applying a variance threshold to reduce the features quickly without investing a lot of computational effort may be useful.

13.1.1.2 Correlation

There is a more serious issue with using variance. Considering the variance of an isolated feature *ignores* any information about the target. Ideally, we'd like to incorporate information about how a feature varies together with the target. *Aha!* That sounds a lot like covariance. True, but there are some differences. Covariance has some subtle and weird behavior which makes it slightly difficult to interpret. Covariance becomes easier to understand when we normalize it by the variance of its parts. Essentially, for two features, we ask (1) how the two vary together *compared to*, (2) how the two vary individually. A deep result in mathematics says that the first (varying together) is always less than or equal to the second (varying individually). We can put these ideas together to get the *correlation* between two things—in this case, a feature and a target. Mathematically, $r = \text{cor}(x, y)$ $= \frac{\text{cov}(x,y)}{\sqrt{\text{var}(x)\text{var}(y)}}$. With a feature and a target, we substitute ftr $\to x$ and tgt $\to y$ and get $r = \text{cor}(\text{ftr}, \text{tgt})$.

Correlation has many interpretations; of interest to us here is interpreting it as an answer to: *if we ignore the signs, how close is the covariance to its maximum possible value?* Note that both covariance and correlation can be positive or negative. I'll let one other point slip: when the correlation is 1—and when the covariance is at its maximum—there is a perfect linear relationship between the two inputs. However, while the correlation is all about this linear relationship, the covariance itself cares about more than just linearity. If we rewrite covariance as a multiplication of correlation and covariances—$\text{cov}(x, y)$ $= \text{cor}(x, y)\sqrt{\text{var}(x)\text{var}(y)}$—and squint a bit, we see that (1) spreading out x or y (increasing their variance), (2) increasing the line-likeness (increasing $\text{cor}(x, y)$), and, less obviously, (3) equally distributing a given total variance between x and y will all increase the covariance. While that got a bit abstract, it answers the question of why people often prefer correlation to covariance: correlation is simply about *lines*.

Since correlation can be positive or negative—it's basically whether the line points up or down—comparing raw correlations can cause a slight problem. A line isn't *bad* just because it points down instead of up. We'll adopt one of our classic solutions to plus-minus issues and *square* the correlation value. So, instead of working with r, we'll work with r^2. And now, at long last, we've completed a circle back to topics we first discussed in Section 7.2.3. Our approach earlier was quite different, even though the underlying mathematics of the two are the same. The difference is in the use and interpretation of the results.

One other confusing side note. We are using the correlation as a *univariate feature selection* method because we are picking a single feature with the method. However, the longer name for the correlation value we are computing is the *bivariate correlation between a predictive feature and the target output*. Sorry for the confusion here, but I didn't make up the names. `sklearn` lets us use the correlation between feature and target in a sneaky way: they wrap it up inside of their `f_regression` univariate selection method. I won't go into the mathematical details here (see the End-of-Chapter Notes), but the ordering of features under `f_regression` will be the same if we rank-order the features by their squared correlations.

We'll show that these are equivalent and, while we're at it, we'll also show off computing correlations by hand. First, let's compute the covariances between each feature and the target for the *diabetes* dataset. For this problem, the covariance for one feature will look like $\text{cov}(\text{ftr}, \text{tgt}) = \frac{\text{dot}(\text{ftr}-\text{mean}(\text{ftr}))(\text{tgt}-\text{mean}(\text{tgt}))}{n}$ The code looks pretty similar—we just have to deal with a few `numpy` axis issues.

In [10]:

```
# cov(X,Y) = np.dot(X-E(X), Y-E(Y)) / n
n = len(diabetes_train_ftrs)

# abbreviate names
x = diabetes_train_tgt[np.newaxis,:]
y = diabetes_train_ftrs
cov_via_dot = np.dot(x-x.mean(), y-y.mean()) / n

# compute all covariances, extract the ones between ftr and target
# bias=True to divide by n instead of n-1; np.cov defaults to bias=False
cov_via_np  = np.cov(diabetes_train_ftrs, diabetes_train_tgt,
                     rowvar=False, bias=True)[-1, :-1]
print(np.allclose(cov_via_dot, cov_via_np))
```

True

Now, we can calculate the correlations in two ways: (1) from the covariances we just calculated or (2) from `numpy`'s `np.corrcoef` directly.

In [11]:

```
# np.var default ddof=0 equates to bias=True
# np.corrcoef is a bit of a hot mess to extract values from

# cov()/sqrt(var() var())
cor_via_cov = cov_via_np / np.sqrt(np.var(diabetes_train_tgt) *
                                   np.var(diabetes_train_ftrs, axis=0))
cor_via_np = np.corrcoef(diabetes_train_ftrs, diabetes_train_tgt,
                         rowvar=False)[-1, :-1]
print(np.allclose(cor_via_cov, cor_via_np))
```

True

Lastly, we can confirm that the order of the variables when we calculate the correlations and the order when we use `sklearn`'s `f_regression` is the same.

In [12]:

```
# note: we use the squares of the correlations, r^2
corrs = np.corrcoef(diabetes_train_ftrs,
                    diabetes_train_tgt, rowvar=False)[-1, :-1]
cor_order = np.argsort(corrs**2) # r^2 (!)
cor_names = np.array(diabetes.feature_names)[cor_order[::-1]]

# and sklearn's f_regression calculation
f_scores = ftr_sel.f_regression(diabetes_train_ftrs,
                                diabetes_train_tgt)[0]
freg_order = np.argsort(f_scores)
freg_names = np.array(diabetes.feature_names)[freg_order[::-1]]

# numpy arrays don't like comparing strings
print(tuple(cor_names) == tuple(freg_names))
```

True

If you lost the big picture, here's a recap:

- Variance was OK-ish, but covariance is a big improvement.
- Covariance has some rough edges; correlation r is nice; squared-correlation r^2 is nicer.
- `sklearn`'s `f_regression` orders by r^2 for us.

We can order by r^2 using `f_regression`.

13.1.1.3 Information Measures

Correlation can only directly measure *linear relationships* between its inputs. There are many—even infinitely many—other relationships we might care about. So, there are other useful statistics between columns that we might calculate. A very general way to look at the relationships between features and a target comes from the field of *coding and information theory*. We won't go into details, but let me give you a quick story.

Like many young children, I *loved* flashlights. It didn't take long for me to find out that Morse code allows people to transmit information with blinking flashlights. However, the young me viewed memorizing Morse code as an insurmountable task. Instead, my friends and I made up our own codes for very specific scenarios. For example, when playing capture-the-flag, we wanted to know if it was safe to cross a field. If there were only two answers, *yes* and *no*, then two simple blinking patterns would suffice: one blink for *no* and two blinks for *yes*. Imagine that most of the time the field is safe to cross. Then, most of the time, we'd want to send a *yes* message. But then, we're actually being a bit wasteful by using two blinks for *yes*. If we swap the meaning of our blinks—making it one for *yes* and two for *no*—we'll save some work. In a nutshell, these are the ideas that coding and information theory consider: how do we communicate or transmit information efficiently, considering that some of the messages we want to transmit are more likely than others.

Now, if you didn't nod off, you are probably wondering what this has to do with relating features and targets. Imagine that the feature value is a message that gets sent to the learner (Figure 13.2). The learner needs to decode that message and turn it into a result—our target of interest. Information-theoretic measures take the view of translating a feature to a message which gets decoded and leads to a final target. Then, they quantify how well different features get their message across. One concrete measure from information theory is called *mutual information* and it captures, in a generic sense, how much knowing a value of one outcome tells us about the value of another.

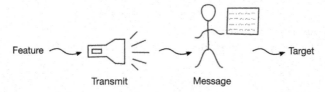

Figure 13.2   Sending messages from features to target via flashlight.

One Useful and One Random Variable   We'll start with a problem that is simple to express but results in a nonlinear classification problem.

```
In [13]:
xs = np.linspace(-10,10,1000).reshape(-1,1)
data = np.c_[xs, np.random.uniform(-10,10,xs.shape)]
tgt = (np.cos(xs) > 0).flatten()
```

Since that is a pretty unintuitive formula, let's look at it graphically:

```
In [14]:
plt.figure(figsize=(4,3))
plt.scatter(data[:,0], tgt);
```

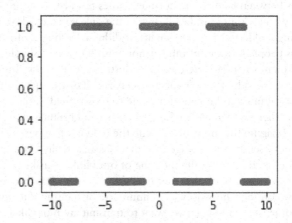

Basically, we have a pattern that turns off and on (0 and 1) at regular intervals. The graph is not that complicated, but it is decidedly nonlinear. In `data`, our first column is evenly spaced values; our second column is random values. We can look at the mutual information for each column against our nonlinear target:

In [15]:

```
mi = ftr_sel.mutual_info_classif(data, tgt,
                                 discrete_features=False)
print(mi)
```

```
[0.6815 0.0029]
```

That's a pretty good sign: we have a small, almost zero, value for the random column and larger value for the informative column. We can use similar measures for regression problems.

In [16]:

```
xs = np.linspace(-10,10,1000).reshape(-1,1)
data = np.c_[xs, np.random.uniform(-10,10,xs.shape)]
tgt = np.cos(xs).flatten()
```

Here's a graph of column one versus our target:

In [17]:

```
plt.figure(figsize=(4,3))
plt.plot(data[:,0], tgt);
```

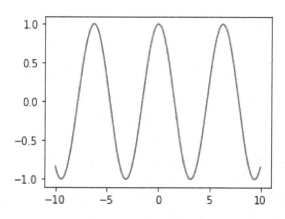

And now we can compare the r^2-like and mutual information techniques:

```
In [18]:
print(ftr_sel.f_regression(data, tgt)[0],
      ftr_sel.mutual_info_regression(data, tgt),
      sep='\n')
```

```
[0. 0.]
[1.9356 0.    ]
```

In this example, both the uninformative, random column and the informative column have a zero *linear* relationship with the target. However, looking at the `mutual_info_regression`, we see a reasonable set of values: the random column gives zero and the informative column gives a positive number.

Two Predictive Variables   Now, what happens when we have more than one informative variable? Here's some data:

```
In [19]:
xs, ys = np.mgrid[-2:2:.2, -2:2:.2]
c_tgt = (ys > xs**2).flatten()

# basically, turn r_tgt off if y<x**2
r_tgt = ((xs**2 + ys**2)*(ys>xs**2))

data = np.c_[xs.flat, ys.flat]

# print out a few examples
print(np.c_[data, c_tgt, r_tgt.flat][[np.arange(0,401,66)]])
```

```
[[[-2.  -2.   0.   0. ]
  [-1.4 -0.8  0.   0. ]
  [-0.8  0.4  0.   0. ]
  [-0.2  1.6  1.   2.6]
  [ 0.6 -1.2  0.   0. ]
  [ 1.2  0.   0.   0. ]
  [ 1.8  1.2  0.   0. ]]]
```

And that leads to two different problems, one classification and one regression.

```
In [20]:
fig,axes = plt.subplots(1,2, figsize=(6,3), sharey=True)
axes[0].scatter(xs, ys, c=np.where(c_tgt, 'r', 'b'), marker='.')
axes[0].set_aspect('equal');

bound_xs = np.linspace(-np.sqrt(2), np.sqrt(2), 100)
bound_ys = bound_xs**2
```

```
axes[0].plot(bound_xs, bound_ys, 'k')
axes[0].set_title('Classification')

axes[1].pcolormesh(xs, ys, r_tgt,cmap='binary')
axes[1].set_aspect('equal')
axes[1].set_title('Regression');
```

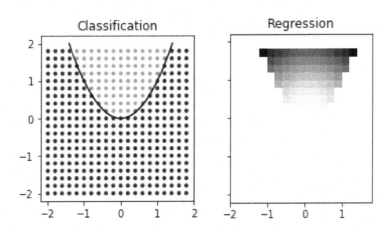

Before we compute any statistics here, let's think about this scenario for a minute. If you tell me the value of y and it is less than zero, I know an awful lot about the result: it's always *blue* (for classification) or *white* (for regression). If y is bigger than zero, we don't get as much of a win, but as y keeps increasing, we get a higher likelihood of *red* (in the left figure) or *black* (in the right figure). For x, a value greater or less than zero doesn't really mean much: things are perfectly balanced about the x-axis.

That said, we can look at the information-based metric for c_tgt which is calculated using mutual_info_classif:

In [21]:
```
print(ftr_sel.mutual_info_classif(data, c_tgt,
                              discrete_features=False, random_state=42))
```

```
[0.0947 0.1976]
```

The relative values for the r_tgt regression problem are broadly similar to those for mutual_info_regression:

In [22]:
```
print(ftr_sel.mutual_info_regression(data, r_tgt.flat,
                              discrete_features=False))
```

```
[0.0512 0.4861]
```

These values line up well with our intuitive discussion.

13.1.1.4   Selecting the Top Features

Practically speaking, when we want to apply a selection metric, we want to rank and then pick features. If we want some fixed number of features, `SelectKBest` lets us do that easily. We can take the top five with the following code:

In [23]:

```
ftrsel = ftr_sel.SelectKBest(ftr_sel.mutual_info_classif, k=5)
ftrsel.fit_transform(wine_train, wine_train_tgt)

# extract names
keepers_idx = ftrsel.get_support()
print(np.array(wine.feature_names)[keepers_idx])
```

```
['flavanoids' 'color_intensity' 'hue' 'od280/od315_of_diluted_wines'
 'proline']
```

That makes it relatively easy to compare two different feature selection methods. We see that most of the top five selected features are the same under `f_classif` and `mutual_info_classif`.

In [24]:

```
ftrsel = ftr_sel.SelectKBest(ftr_sel.f_classif, k=5)
ftrsel.fit_transform(wine_train, wine_train_tgt)

keepers_idx = ftrsel.get_support()
print(np.array(wine.feature_names)[keepers_idx])
```

```
['alcohol' 'flavanoids' 'color_intensity' 'od280/od315_of_diluted_wines'
 'proline']
```

If we'd prefer to grab some percentage of the features, we can use `SelectPercentile`. Combining it with r^2 gives us:

In [25]:

```
ftrsel = ftr_sel.SelectPercentile(ftr_sel.f_regression,
                                  percentile=25)
ftrsel.fit_transform(diabetes_train_ftrs,
                     diabetes_train_tgt)

print(np.array(diabetes.feature_names)[ftrsel.get_support()])
```

```
['bmi' 'bp' 's5']
```

And to use mutual information, we can do this:

```
In [26]:

ftrsel = ftr_sel.SelectPercentile(ftr_sel.mutual_info_regression,
                                  percentile=25)
ftrsel.fit_transform(diabetes_train_ftrs,
                     diabetes_train_tgt)

print(np.array(diabetes.feature_names)[ftrsel.get_support()])
```

```
['bmi' 's4' 's5']
```

Very generally speaking, different feature selection metrics often give similar rankings.

13.1.2 Model-Based Feature Selection

So far, we've been selecting features based either on their stand-alone characteristics (using variance) or on their relationship with the target (using correlation or information). Correlation is nice because it tracks a linear relationship with the target. Information is nicer because it tracks *any*—for some definition of "any"—relationship. Still, in reality, when we select features, we are going to use them *with* a model. It would be nice if the features we used were tailored to that model. Not all models are lines or otherwise linear. The existence of a relationship between a feature and a target does not mean that a particular model can find or make use of it. So, we can naturally ask if there are any feature selection methods that can work *with* models to select features that work well in that model. The answer is yes.

A second issue, up to this point, is that we've only evaluated *single* features, not *sets* of features. Models work with whole sets of features in one go. For example, linear regressions have coefficients on each feature, and decision trees compare values of some features after considering all features. Since models work with multiple features, we can use the performance of models on different baskets of features to assess the value of those features to the models.

Combinatorics—the sheer number of ways of picking a subset of features from a bigger set—is what usually prevents us from testing each and every possible subset of features. There are simply too many subsets to evaluate. There are two major ways of addressing this limitation: randomness and greediness. It sounds like we are taking yet another trip to a casino.

Randomness is fairly straightforward: we take subsets of the features at random and evaluate them. Greediness involves starting from some initial set of features and adding or removing features from that starting point. Here, *greed* refers to the fact that we may take steps that individually look good, but we may end up in a less-than-best final spot. Think of it this way. If you are wandering around a big city without a map, looking for the zoo, you might proceed by walking to a corner and asking, "Which way to the zoo?" You get an answer and follow the directions to a next corner. If people are honest—we can hope—you might end up at the zoo after quite a long walk. Unfortunately, different people might have different ideas about how to take you to the zoo, so you might end up backtracking or going around in circles for a bit. If you had a map, however, you could take yourself there directly via a shortest path. When we have a limited view of the total problem—whether standing on a street corner or only considering *some* features to add or delete—we may not reach an optimal solution.

In practice, greedy feature selection gives us an overall process that looks like this:

1. Select some initial set of features.
2. Build a model with the current features.
3. Evaluate the importance of the features to the model.
4. Keep the best features or drop the worst features from the current set. Systematically or randomly add or remove features, if desired.
5. Repeat from step 2, if desired.

Very often, the starting point is either (1) a single feature, with us working *forward* by adding features, or (2) *all* the features, with us working *backward* by removing features.

13.1.2.1 Good for Model, Good for Prediction

Without the repetition step (step 5), we only have a single model-building step. Many models give their input features an importance score or a coefficient. `SelectFromModel` uses these to rank and select features. For several models, the default is to keep the features with the score above the mean or average.

In [27]:

```
ftrsel = ftr_sel.SelectFromModel(ensemble.RandomForestClassifier(),
                                 threshold='mean') # default
ftrsel.fit_transform(wine_train, wine_train_tgt)
print(np.array(wine.feature_names)[ftrsel.get_support()])
```

```
['alcohol' 'flavanoids' 'color_intensity' 'hue'
 'od280/od315_of_diluted_wines' 'proline']
```

For models with L_1 regularization—that's what we called the *lasso* in Section 9.1—the default threshold is to throw out *small* coefficients.

In [28]:

```
lmlr = linear_model.LogisticRegression
ftrsel = ftr_sel.SelectFromModel(lmlr(penalty='l1'))
    # thesh is "small" coeffs
ftrsel.fit_transform(wine_train, wine_train_tgt)

print(np.array(wine.feature_names)[ftrsel.get_support()])
```

```
['alcohol' 'malic_acid' 'ash' 'alcalinity_of_ash' 'magnesium' 'flavanoids'
 'proanthocyanins' 'color_intensity' 'od280/od315_of_diluted_wines'
 'proline']
```

Note that we don't have any easy way to *order* the selected features unless we go back to the coefficients or importances from the underlying model. `SelectFromModel` gives us a binary—yes or no—look at whether to keep features or not.

13.1.2.2 Let a Model Guide Decision

Going beyond a one-step process, we can let the basket of features grow or shrink based on repeated model-building steps. Here, the repetition of step 5 (from two sections back) *is desired*. Imagine we build a model, evaluate the features, and then drop the worst feature. Now, we repeat the process. Since features can interact with each other, the entire ordering of the features may now be different. We drop the worst feature under the new ordering. We continue on until we've dropped as many features as we want to drop. This method is called *recursive feature elimination* and is available in `sklearn` through `RFE`.

Here we will use a `RandomForestClassifier` as the underlying model. As we saw in Section 12.3, random forests (RFs) operate by repeatedly working with random selections of the features. If a feature shows up in many of the component trees, we can use that as an indicator that a more frequently used feature has more importance than a less frequently used feature. This idea is formalized as the *feature importance*.

In [29]:

```
ftrsel = ftr_sel.RFE(ensemble.RandomForestClassifier(),
                     n_features_to_select=5)

res = ftrsel.fit_transform(wine_train, wine_train_tgt)
print(np.array(wine.feature_names)[ftrsel.get_support()])
```

```
['alcohol' 'flavanoids' 'color_intensity' 'od280/od315_of_diluted_wines'
 'proline']
```

We can also select features using a linear regression model. In the `sklearn` implementation, features are dropped based on the size of their regression coefficients. Statisticians should now read a warning in the End-of-Chapter Notes.

In [30]:

```
# statisticians be warned (see end-of-chapter notes)
# this picks based on feature weights (coefficients)
# not on significance of coeffs nor on r^2/anova/F of (whole) model
ftrsel = ftr_sel.RFE(linear_model.LinearRegression(),
                     n_features_to_select=5)
ftrsel.fit_transform(wine_train, wine_train_tgt)
print(np.array(wine.feature_names)[ftrsel.get_support()])
```

```
['alcohol' 'total_phenols' 'flavanoids' 'hue'
 'od280/od315_of_diluted_wines']
```

We can use `.ranking_` to order the dropped features—that is, where in the rounds of evaluation they were kept or dropped—without going back to the coefficients or importances of the models that were used along the way. If we want to order the remaining features—the keepers—we have to do some extra . work:

In [31]:

```
# all the 1s are selected; non-1s indicate when they were dropped
# go to the estimator and ask its coefficients
print(ftrsel.ranking_,
      ftrsel.estimator_.coef_, sep='\n')
```

```
[1 5 2 4 9 1 1 3 7 6 1 1 8]
[-0.2164  0.1281 -0.3936 -0.6394 -0.3572]
```

Here, the 1s in the ranking are selected: they are our keepers. The non-1s indicate when that feature was dropped. The five 1s can be ordered based on the the absolute value of the five estimator coefficients.

In [32]:

```
# the order for the five 1s
keepers_idx = np.argsort(np.abs(ftrsel.estimator_.coef_))
# find the indexes of the 1s and get their ordering
keepers_order_idx = np.where(ftrsel.ranking_ == 1)[0][keepers_idx]
print(np.array(wine.feature_names)[keepers_order_idx])
```

```
['total_phenols' 'alcohol' 'od280/od315_of_diluted_wines' 'flavanoids'
 'hue']
```

13.1.3 Integrating Feature Selection with a Learning Pipeline

Now that we have some feature selection tools to play with, we can put together feature selection and model building in a pipeline and see how various combinations do. Here's a quick baseline of regularized logistic regression on the *wine* data:

In [33]:

```
skms.cross_val_score(linear_model.LogisticRegression(),
                     wine.data, wine.target)
```

Out[33]:

```
array([0.8667, 0.95  , 1.    ])
```

You might wonder if selecting features based on that same classifier helps matters:

```
In [34]:
# do it
# theshold is "small" coeffs
lmlr = linear_model.LogisticRegression
ftrsel = ftr_sel.SelectFromModel(lmlr(penalty='l1'))

pipe = pipeline.make_pipeline(ftrsel, linear_model.LogisticRegression())
skms.cross_val_score(pipe, wine.data, wine.target)
```

```
Out[34]:
array([0.8667, 0.95  , 1.    ])
```

That's a definitive no. We'd have to dive into more details to see if keeping different numbers of features helped or not. We'll come back to that in a second. For now, we'll check if using a *different* learning model to pick features helps:

```
In [35]:
ftrsel = ftr_sel.RFE(ensemble.RandomForestClassifier(),
                     n_features_to_select=5)
pipe = pipeline.make_pipeline(ftrsel, linear_model.LogisticRegression())
skms.cross_val_score(pipe, wine.data, wine.target)
```

```
Out[35]:
array([0.8667, 0.9167, 0.9655])
```

Again, the answer is no. But it wasn't hard to do—and it *could* potentially help in other problems! Remember, it's easy to experiment with different learning pipelines. Let's switch to using an information-based feature evaluator:

```
In [36]:
ftrsel = ftr_sel.SelectPercentile(ftr_sel.mutual_info_classif,
                                  percentile=25)
pipe = pipeline.make_pipeline(ftrsel, linear_model.LogisticRegression())
skms.cross_val_score(pipe, wine.data, wine.target)
```

```
Out[36]:
array([0.9167, 0.9167, 1.    ])
```

It seems to help a bit, but I wouldn't read too much into it here. We'd need to do a bit more experimentation to be sold on making it part of our pipeline. Let's turn to fine-tuning the number of features we keep. We can do that with a `GridSearch` on the `Pipeline`.

In [37]:

```
ftrsel = ftr_sel.SelectPercentile(ftr_sel.mutual_info_classif, percentile=25)
pipe = pipeline.make_pipeline(ftrsel, linear_model.LogisticRegression())

param_grid = {'selectpercentile__percentile':[5,10,15,20,25]}
grid = skms.GridSearchCV(pipe, param_grid=param_grid, cv=3, iid=False)
grid.fit(wine.data, wine.target)

print(grid.best_params_)
print(grid.best_score_)
```

```
{'selectpercentile__percentile': 20}
0.9444444444444443
```

13.2   Feature Construction with Kernels

Now, we're going to look at some automatic methods for feature construction in the form of *kernels*. Kernels are a fairly abstract mathematical concept, so I'll take a few pages to describe the problem they solve and how they operate. We'll actually do a fair bit of motivation and background discussion before we get to see exactly what kernels *are*.

13.2.1   A Kernel Motivator

Let's start with a nonlinear problem that will give linear methods a headache. It's sort of like a Zen kōan. We'll make a simple classification problem that determines whether or not a point is inside or outside of a circle.

In [38]:

```
xs, ys = np.mgrid[-2:2:.2, -2:2:.2]
tgt = (xs**2 + ys**2 > 1).flatten()
data = np.c_[xs.flat, ys.flat]

fig, ax = plt.subplots(figsize=(4,3))

# draw the points
ax.scatter(xs, ys, c=np.where(tgt, 'r', 'b'), marker='.')
ax.set_aspect('equal');

# draw the circle boundary
circ = plt.Circle((0,0), 1, color='k', fill=False)
ax.add_patch(circ);
```

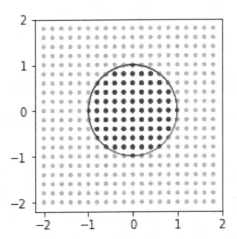

If we look at the performance of two linear methods, Support Vector Classifier (SVC) and logistic regression (LogReg), we'll see that they leave something to be desired.

In [39]:

```
shootout_linear = [svm.SVC(kernel='linear'),
                   linear_model.LogisticRegression()]

fig, axes = plt.subplots(1,2,figsize=(4,2), sharey=True)
for mod, ax in zip(shootout_linear, axes):
    plot_boundary(ax, data, tgt, mod, [0,1])
    ax.set_title(get_model_name(mod))
plt.tight_layout()
```

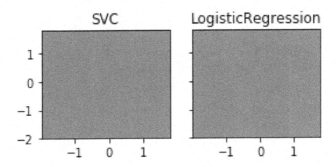

Both of them always predict *blue*—everything is labeled as being in the circle. Oops. Can we do better if we switch to nonlinear learning methods? Yes. We'll take a look at *k*-NN and decision trees.

In [40]:

```
# create some nonlinear learning models
knc_p, dtc_p = [1,20], [1,3,5,10]
KNC = neighbors.KNeighborsClassifier
DTC = tree.DecisionTreeClassifier
shootout_nonlin = ([(KNC(n_neighbors=p), p) for p in knc_p] +
                   [(DTC(max_depth=p), p)   for p in dtc_p ])

# plot 'em
fig, axes = plt.subplots(2,3,figsize=(9, 6),
                         sharex=True, sharey=True)
for (mod, param), ax in zip(shootout_nonlin, axes.flat):
    plot_boundary(ax, data, tgt, mod, [0,1])
    ax.set_title(get_model_name(mod) + "({})".format(param))
plt.tight_layout()
```

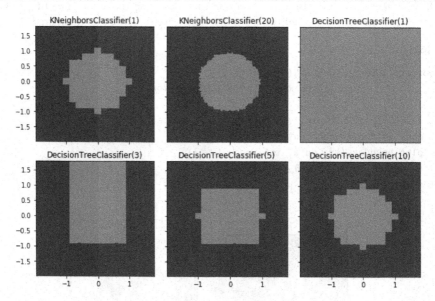

Our nonlinear classifiers do much better. When we give them some reasonable learning capacity, they form a reasonable approximation of the boundary between *red* (the outer area, except in the top-right figure) and *blue* (the inner area and all of the top-right figure). A DTC with one split—the top-right graphic—is really making a single-feature test like $x > .5$. That test represents a single line formed from a single node tree which is really just a linear classifier. We don't see it visually in this case, because under the hood the split point is actually $x < -1$ where everything is the same color (it's all blue here because of a default color choice). But, as we add depth to the tree, we segment off other parts of the data and work towards a more circular boundary. *k*-NN works quite well with either many (20) or few (1) neighbors. You might find the similarities between the classification boundaries `KNC(n_neigh=1)` and `DTC(max_depth=10)` interesting. I'll leave it to you to think about *why* they are so similar.

We could simply throw our linear methods under the bus and use nonlinear methods when the linear methods fail. However, we're good friends with linear methods and we wouldn't do that to a good friend. Instead, we'll figure out how to help our linear methods. One thing we can do is take some hints from Section 10.6.1 and manually add some features that might support a linear boundary. We'll simply add squares—x^2 and y^2—into the hopper and see how far we can get.

In [41]:

```
new_data = np.concatenate([data, data**2], axis=1)
print("augmented data shape:", new_data.shape)
print("first row:", new_data[0])

fig, axes = plt.subplots(1,2,figsize=(5,2.5))
for mod, ax in zip(shootout_linear, axes):
    # using the squares for prediction and graphing
    plot_boundary(ax, new_data, tgt, mod, [2,3])
    ax.set_title(get_model_name(mod))
plt.tight_layout()
```

```
augmented data shape: (400, 4)
first row: [-2. -2.  4.  4.]
```

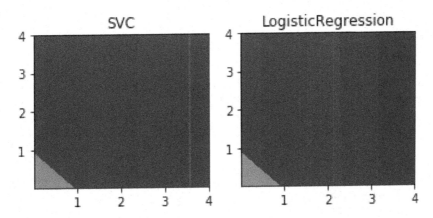

What just happened? We have reds and blues—that's a good thing. The blues are in the lower-left corner. But, where did the circle go? If you look very closely, you might also wonder: where did the *negative values* go? The answer is in the features we constructed. When we square values, negatives become positive—literally and figuratively. We've rewritten our problem from one of asking if $x^2_{\text{old}} + y^2_{\text{old}} < 1$ to asking if $x_{\text{new}} + y_{\text{new}} < 1$. That second question *is a linear question*. Let's investigate in more detail.

We're going to focus on two test points: one that starts inside the circle and one that starts outside the circle. Then, we'll see where they end up when we construct new features out of them.

In [42]:

```
# pick a few points to show off the before/after differences
test_points = np.array([[.5,.5],
                        [-1, -1.25]])

# wonderful trick from trig class:
# if we walk around circle (fractions of pi),
# sin/cos give x and y value from pi
circle_pts = np.linspace(0,2*np.pi,100)
circle_xs, circle_ys = np.sin(circle_pts), np.cos(circle_pts)
```

Basically, let's look at our data before and after squaring. We'll look at the overall space—all pairs—of x, y values and we'll look at a few specific points.

In [43]:

```
fig, axes = plt.subplots(1,2, figsize=(6,3))

labels = [('x',      'y',      'Original Space'),
          ('$x^2$', '$y^2$', 'Squares Space')]

funcs = [lambda x:x,     # for original ftrs
         lambda x:x**2]  # for squared ftrs

for ax, func, lbls in zip(axes, funcs, labels):
    ax.plot(func(circle_xs), func(circle_ys), 'k')
    ax.scatter(*func(data.T), c=np.where(tgt, 'r', 'b'), marker='.')
    ax.scatter(*func(test_points.T), c=['k', 'y'], s=100, marker='^')

    ax.axis('equal')
    ax.set_xlabel(lbls[0])
    ax.set_ylabel(lbls[1])
    ax.set_title(lbls[2])

axes[1].yaxis.tick_right()
axes[1].yaxis.set_label_position("right");
```

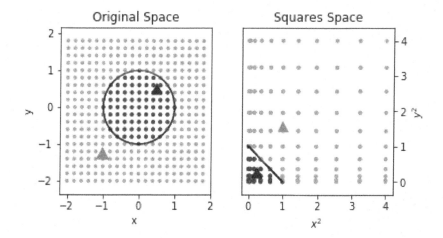

As we reframe the problem—using the same trick we pulled in Section 10.6.1 when we attacked the *xor* problem—we make it solvable by linear methods. Win. The dark triangle in the cirlce ends up inside the triangle at the lower-left corner of the *Squares Space* figure. Now, there are a few issues. What we did required manual intervention, and it was only easy because we knew that squaring was the right way to go. If you look at the original target `tgt = (xs**2 + ys**2 > 1).flatten()`, you'll see that squares figured prominently in it. If we had needed to divide—take a ratio—of features instead, squaring the values wouldn't have helped!

So, we want an *automated* way to approach these problems and we also want the automated method to try the constructed features for us. One of the most clever and versatile ways to automate the process is with *kernel methods*. Kernel methods can't do *everything* we could possibly do by hand, but they are more than sufficient in many scenarios. For our next step, we will use kernels in a somewhat clunky, *manual* fashion. But kernels can be used in much more powerful ways that don't require manual intervention. We are—slowly, or perhaps carefully—building our way up to an automated system for trying many possible constructed features and using the best ones.

13.2.2 Manual Kernel Methods

I haven't defined a kernel. I could, but it wouldn't mean anything to you—yet. Instead, I'm going to start by demonstrating what a kernel does and how it is related to our problem of constructing good features. We'll start by *manually* applying a kernel. (*Warning!* Normally we won't do this. I'm just giving you an idea of what is under the hood of kernel methods.) Instead of performing manual mathematics (x^2, y^2), we are going to go from our original data to a *kernel* of the data. In this case, it is a very specific kernel that captures the *same* idea of *squaring* the input features, which we just did by hand.

```
In [44]:
```

```
k_data = metrics.pairwise.polynomial_kernel(data, data,
                                            degree=2) # squares
print('first example: ', data[0])

print('# features in original form:', data[0].shape)
print('# features with kernel form:', k_data[0].shape)

print('# examples in both:', len(data), len(k_data))
```

```
first example:  [-2. -2.]
# features in original form: (2,)
# features with kernel form: (400,)
# examples in both: 400 400
```

That may have been slightly underwhelming and probably a bit confusing. When we applied the kernel to our 400 examples, we went from having 2 features to having 400 features. Why? Because kernels redescribe the data in terms of the relationship between an example and *every other example*. The 400 features for the first example are describing how the first example relates to every *other* example. That makes it a bit difficult to see what is going on. However, we can force the kernel features to talk. We'll do it by feeding the *kernelized data* to a prediction model and then graphing those predictions back over the *original data*. Basically, we are looking up information about someone by their formal name—Mark Fenner lives in Pennsylvania—and then associating the result with their nickname—Marco lives in Pennsylvania.

One other quick point: if you are reminded of covariances between pairs of features, you aren't too far off. However, kernels are about relationships between *examples*. Covariances are about relationships between *features*. One is between columns; the other is between rows.

```
In [45]:
```

```
fig, ax = plt.subplots(figsize=(4,3))

# learn from k_data instead of original data
preds  = (linear_model.LogisticRegression()
                      .fit(k_data, tgt)
                      .predict(k_data))

ax.scatter(xs, ys, c=np.where(preds, 'r', 'b'), marker='.')
ax.set_aspect('equal')
```

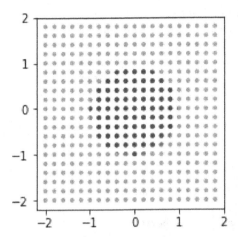

Something certainly happened here. Before, we couldn't successfully apply the LogReg model to the circle data: it resulted in flat blue predictions everywhere. Now, we seem to be getting perfect prediction. We'll take a closer look at *how* this happened in just a moment. But for now, let's deal with applying manual kernels a little more cleanly. Manually applying kernels is a bit clunky. We can make a `sklearn Transformer`—see Section 10.6.3 for our first look at them—to let us hook up manual kernels in a learning pipeline:

In [46]:

```
from sklearn.base import TransformerMixin

class PolyKernel(TransformerMixin):
    def __init__(self, degree):
        self.degree = degree

    def transform(self, ftrs):
        pk = metrics.pairwise.pairwise_kernels
        return pk(ftrs, self.ftrs, metric='poly', degree=self.degree)

    def fit(self, ftrs, tgt=None):
        self.ftrs = ftrs
        return self
```

Basically, we have a pipeline step that passes data through a kernel before sending it on to the next step. We can compare our manual degree-2 polynomial with a fancier cousin from the big city. I won't go into the details of the `Nystroem` kernel but I want you to know it's there for two reasons:

1. The Nystroem kernel—as implemented in `sklearn`—plays nicely with pipelines. We don't have to wrap it up in a `Transformer` ourselves. Basically, we can use it for programming convenience.
2. In reality, Nystroem kernels have a deeply important role beyond making our programming a bit easier. If we have a bigger problem with many examples, then constructing a *full kernel* comparing each example against each other may cause problems because of a very large memory footprint. Nystroem constructs an *approximate* kernel by reducing the number of examples it considers. Effectively, it only keeps the most important comparative examples.

In [47]:

```
from sklearn import kernel_approximation

kn = kernel_approximation.Nystroem(kernel='polynomial',
                                   degree=2, n_components=6)
LMLR = linear_model.LogisticRegression()
k_logreg1 = pipeline.make_pipeline(kn, LMLR)
k_logreg2 = pipeline.make_pipeline(PolyKernel(2), LMLR)

shootout_fancy = [(k_logreg1, 'Nystroem'),
                  (k_logreg2, 'PolyKernel')]

fig, axes = plt.subplots(1,2,figsize=(6,3), sharey=True)
for (mod, kernel_name), ax in zip(shootout_fancy, axes):
    plot_boundary(ax, data, tgt, mod, [0,1])
    ax.set_title(get_model_name(mod)+"({})".format(kernel_name))
    ax.set_aspect('equal')
plt.tight_layout()
```

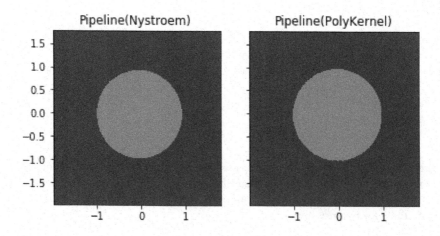

Here, we have performed a *mock up* of kernelized logistic regression. We've hacked together a kernel-method form of logistic regression. I apologize for relying on such rickety code for kernelized logistic regression, but I did it for two reasons. First, `sklearn` doesn't have a full kernelized logistic regression in its toolbox. Second, it gave me an opportunity to show how we can write `PlainVanillaLearningMethod(Data)` as `PlainVanillaLearner(KernelOf(Data))` and achieve something *like* a kernel method. In reality, we should be careful of calling such a mock-up a kernel method. It has several limitations that don't affect full kernel methods. We'll come back to those in a minute.

We've made some substantial progress over our original, all-blue logistic regression model. But we're are still doing a lot by hand. Let's take off the training wheels and fully automate the process.

13.2.2.1 From Manual to Automated Kernel Methods

Our first foray into a fully automated kernel method will be with a kernelized support vector classifier which is known as a support vector machine (SVM). We'll compare the SVM with the polynomial kernel we built by hand.

In [48]:

```
k_logreg = pipeline.make_pipeline(PolyKernel(2),
                                  linear_model.LogisticRegression())


shootout_fancy = [svm.SVC(kernel='poly', degree=2),
                  k_logreg]

fig, axes = plt.subplots(1,2,figsize=(6,3), sharey=True)
for mod, ax in zip(shootout_fancy, axes):
    plot_boundary(ax, data, tgt, mod, [0,1])
    ax.set_title(get_model_name(mod))
plt.tight_layout()
```

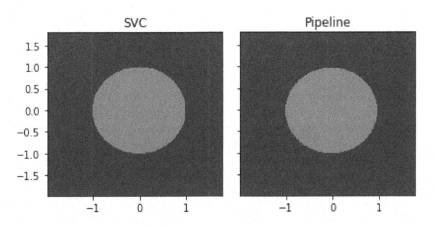

We've now performed a real-deal—no mock-up—kernel method. We computed a SVM with `SVC(kernel='poly')`. It has something pretty amazing going on under the hood. Somehow, we can tell `SVC` to use a kernel internally and then it takes the raw data and operates *as if* we are doing manual feature construction. Things get even better. We don't have to explicitly construct all the features. More specifically, we don't have to build the full set of all the features that a kernel implies building. We don't do it and `SVC` doesn't do it either. Through the *kernel trick*, we can replace (1) explicitly constructing features and comparing examples in the bigger feature space with (2) simply computing distances between objects using the kernel.

13.2.3 Kernel Methods and Kernel Options

Now, let's talk a bit about what kernels are and how they operate.

13.2.3.1 Overview of Kernels

Kernels may seem like a magic trick that can solve very serious problems. While they aren't really magic, they are really useful. Fundamentally, kernel methods involve two plug-and-play components: a kernel and a learning method. The kernel shows up in two forms: a kernel function and a kernel matrix. The function form may be a bit abstract, but a kernel matrix is simply a table of example similarities. If you give me two examples, I tell you how similar they are by looking up a value in the table. The learners used with kernel methods are often linear methods, but a notable exception is nearest neighbors. Whatever method is used, the learner is often described and implemented in a way that emphasizes relationships between *examples* instead of relationships between *features*. As we said before, covariance-based methods are all about feature-to-feature interactions. Kernel methods and the kernel matrices are about example-to-example interaction.

Up to now, we've been representing examples by a set of features—remember the ruler dude from Chapter 1?—*and then* compared examples based on the similarity or distance between those feature values. Kernels take a different view: they compare examples by directly measuring similarity between pairs of examples. The kernel view is more general: anything our traditional representation can do, kernels can do also. If we simply treat the examples as points in space and calculate the dot product between the examples— *presto!*—we have a simple kernel. In fact, this is what a *linear kernel* does. In the same way that *all*-Nearest Neighbors—that is, a nearest neighbors method which includes information from *everyone*—relies on the information from every example, kernel methods also rely on these pairwise connections. I'll make one last point to minimize confusion. Kernels measure similarity which *increases* as examples become more alike; distance measures distance-apart-ness which *decreases* as examples become more alike.

There's one last major win of the kernel approach. Since kernels rely on pairwise relationships between examples, *we don't have to have our initial data in a table of rows and columns to use a kernel*. All we need are two individuals that we can identify and *look up* in the kernel table. Imagine that we are comparing two strings—"the cat in the hat" and "the cow jumped over the moon". Our traditional learning setup would be to measure many features of those strings (the number of *a*s, the number of occurrences of the word *cow*, etc.), put those features in a data table, and then try to learn. With kernel methods, we can directly compute the similarity relationship between the strings and work with those similarity values. It may be significantly easier to define relationships—similarities— between examples than to turn examples into sets of features. In the case of text strings, the concept of *edit distance* fits the bill very nicely. In the case of biological strings—DNA letters like AGCCAT—there are distances that account for biological factoids like mutation rates.

Here's a quick example. I don't know how to graph words in space. It just doesn't make sense to me. But, if I have some words, I can give you an idea of how similar they are. If I start at 1.0 which means "completely the same" and work down towards zero, I might create the following table for word similarity:

	cat	hat	bar
cat	1	.5	.3
hat	.5	1	.3
bar	.3	.3	1

Now, I can say how similar I think any pair of example words are: *cat* versus *hat* gives .5 similarity.

What's the point? Essentially, we can directly apply preexisting background knowledge—also known as assumptions—about the similarities between the data examples. There may be several steps to get from simple statements about the real world to the numbers that show up in the kernel, but it can be done. Kernels can apply this knowledge to arbitrary objects—strings, trees, sets—not just examples in a table. Kernels can be applied to many learning methods: various forms of regression, nearest-neighbors, and principal components analysis (PCA). We haven't discussed PCA yet, but we will see it soon.

13.2.3.2 How Kernels Operate

With some general ideas about kernels, we can start looking at their mathematics a bit more closely. As with most mathematical topics in this book, all we need is the idea of dot product. Many learning algorithms can be *kernelized*. What do we mean by this? Consider a learning algorithm $\mathcal{L}$. Now, reexpress that algorithm in a different form: $\mathcal{L}_{dot}$, where the algorithm has the same input-output behavior—it computes the same predictions from a given training set—but it is written in terms of dot products between the examples: $dot(E, F)$. If we can do that, then we can take a second step and replace all occurrences of the $dot(E, F)$ with our kernel values between the examples $K(E, F)$. *Presto*—we have a kernelized version $\mathcal{L}_k$ of $\mathcal{L}$. We go from $\mathcal{L}$ to $\mathcal{L}_{dot}$ to $\mathcal{L}_k$.

When we use K instead of dot, we are mapping the Es into a different, usually higher-dimensional, space and asking about their similarity there. That mapping essentially adds more columns in our table or axes in our graph. We can use these to describe our data. We'll call the mapping from *here* to *there* a warp function—cue Piccard, "make it so"—$\varphi(E)$. φ is a Greek "phi", pronounced like "fi" in a giant's fee-fi-fo-fum. φ takes an example and moves it to a spot in a different space. This translation is *precisely* what we did by hand when we converted our circle problem into a line problem in Section 13.2.2.

In the circle-to-line scenario, our degree-2 polynomial kernel K_2 took two examples E and F and performed some mathematics on them: $K_2(E, F) = (\text{dot}(E, F))^2$. In Python, we'd write that as `np.dot(E,F)**2` or similar. I'm going to make a bold claim: there is a φ—a warp function—that makes the following equation work:

$$K_2(E, F) = \text{dot}\big(\varphi_2(E), \varphi_2(F)\big)$$

That is, we could *either* (1) compute the kernel function K_2 between the two examples *or* (2) map both examples into a different space with φ_2 and then take a standard dot product. We haven't specified φ_2, though. I'll tell you what it is and then show that the two methods work out equivalently. With two features (e_1, e_2) for E, φ_2 looks like

$$\varphi_2(E) = \varphi_2(e_1, e_2) \rightarrow (e_1 e_1, e_1 e_2, e_2 e_1, e_2 e_2)$$

Now, we need to show that we can expand—write out in a longer form—the left-hand side $K_2(E, F)$ and the right-hand side $\text{dot}(\varphi_2(E), \varphi_2(F))$ and get the same results. If so, we've shown the two things are equal.

Expanding K_2 means we want to expand $(\text{dot}(E, F))^2$. Here goes. With $E = (e_1, e_2)$ and $F = (f_1, f_2)$, we have $\text{dot}(E, F) = e_1 f_1 + e_2 f_2$. Squaring it isn't fun, but it is possible using the classic $(a + b)^2 = a^2 + 2ab + b^2$ formula:

$$\big(\text{dot}(E, F)\big)^2 = (e_1 f_1 + e_2 f_2)^2$$
$$= (e_1 f_1)^2 + 2(e_1 f_1 e_2 f_2) + (e_2 f_2)^2 \quad \star$$

Turning to the RHS, we need to expand $\text{dot}(\varphi_2(E), \varphi_2(F))$. We need the φ_2 pieces which we get by expanding out a bunch of interactions:

$$\varphi_2(E) = (e_1 e_1, e_1 e_2, e_2 e_1, e_2 e_2)$$
$$\varphi_2(F) = (f_1 f_1, f_1 f_2, f_2 f_1, f_2 f_2)$$

With those in place, we have

$$\text{dot}\big(\varphi_2(E), \varphi_2(F)\big) = e_1^2 f_1^2 + 2(e_1 f_1 e_2 f_2) + e_2^2 f_2^2$$
$$= (e_1 f_1)^2 + 2(e_1 f_1 e_2 f_2) + (e_2 f_2)^2 \quad \star\star$$

We can simply read off that $\star$ and $\star\star$ are the same thing. Thankfully, both expansions work out to the same answer. Following the second path required a bit more work because we had to explicitly expand the axes before going back and doing the dot product. Also, the dot product in the second path had more terms to deal with—four versus two. Keep that difference in mind.

13.2.3.3 Common Kernel Examples

Through a powerful mathematical theorem—Mercer's theorem, if you *must* have a name—we know that whenever we apply a valid kernel, there is an equivalent dot product being calculated in a different, probably more complicated, space of constructed features. That theorem was the basis of my bold claim above. As long as we can write a learning algorithm in terms of dot products *between examples*, we can replace those dot products with kernels, press go, and effectively perform learning in complicated spaces for relatively little computational cost. What kernels K are legal? Those that have a valid underlying φ. That doesn't really help though, does it? There is a mathematical condition that lets us specify the legal K. If K is *positive semi-definite* (PSD), then it is a legal kernel. Again, that doesn't seem too helpful. What the heck does it mean to be PSD? Well, formally, it means that for any z, $z^T K z \geq 0$. We seem to be going from bad to worse. It's almost enough to put your face in your hands.

Let's switch to building some intuition. PSD matrices rotate vectors—arrows drawn in our data space—making them point in a different direction. You might have rotated an arrow when you spun a spinner playing a game like Twister. Or, you might have seen an analog clock hand sweep from one direction to another. With PSD rotators, the important thing is that the *overall* direction is still mostly similar. PSD matrices only change the direction by at most 90 degrees. They never make a vector point closer to the direction opposite to the direction it started out. Here's one other way to think about it. That weird form, $z^T K z$, is really just a more general way of writing kz^2. If k is positive, that whole thing has to be positive since $z^2 > 0$. So, this whole idea of PSD is really a matrix equivalent of a positive number. Multiplying by a positive number doesn't change the sign—the direction—of another number.

There are many examples of kernels but we'll focus on two that work well for the data we've seen in this book: examples described by columns of features. We've already played around with degree-2 polynomial kernels in code and mathematics. There is a whole family of *polynomial kernels* $K(E, F) = (\mathrm{dot}(E, F))^p$ or $K(E, F) = (\mathrm{dot}(E, F) + 1)^p$. We won't stress much about the differences between those two variations. In the later case, the axes in the high-dimensional space are the terms from the p-th degree polynomial in the features with various factors on the terms. So, the axes look like e_1^2, $e_1 e_2$, e_2^2, etc. You might recall these as the *interaction* terms between features from Section 10.6.2.

A kernel that goes beyond the techniques we've used is the *Gaussian* or *Radial Basis Function* (RBF) kernel: $K(E, F) = \exp\left(\frac{\|E - F\|^2}{2\sigma^2}\right) = \exp\left(\frac{\mathrm{dot}(E - F, E - F)}{2\sigma^2}\right)$. Some more involved mathematics—Taylor expansion is the technique—shows that this is equivalent to projecting our examples into an infinite-dimensional space. That means there aren't simply 2, 3, 5, or 10 axes. For as many new columns as we could add to our data table, there's still more to be added. That's far out, man. The practical side of that mind-bender is that example similarity drops off very quickly as examples move away from each other. This behavior is equivalent to the way the normal distribution has relatively short tails—most of its mass is concentrated around its center. In fact, the mathematical form of the normal (Gaussian) distribution and the RBF (Gaussian) kernel is the same.

13.2.4   Kernelized SVCs: SVMs

In Section 8.3, we looked at examples of Support Vector Classifiers that were *linear*: they did not make use of a fancy kernel. Now that we know a bit about kernels, we can look at the nonlinear extensions (shiny upgrade time!) of SVCs to Support Vector Machines, or SVMs. Here are the calls to create SVMs for the kernels we just discussed:

- 2nd degree polynomial: `svm.SVC(kernel='poly', degree=2)`
- 3rd degree polynomial: `svm.SVC(kernel='poly', degree=3)`
- Gaussian (or RBF): `svm.SVC(kernel='rbf', gamma = value)`

The `gamma` parameter—in math, written as γ—controls how far the influence of examples travels. It is related to the inverse of the standard deviation (σ) and variance (σ^2): $\gamma = \frac{1}{2\sigma^2}$. A small γ means there's a big variance; in turn, a big variance means that things that are far apart can still be strongly related. So, a small `gamma` means that the influence of examples travels a long way to other examples. The default is `gamma=1/len(data)`. That means that with more examples, the default `gamma` goes down and influence travels further.

Once we've discussed kernels and we know how to implement various SVM options, let's look at how different kernels affect the classification boundary of the *iris* problem.

13.2.4.1   Visualizing SVM Kernel Differences

In [49]:

```
# first three are linear (but different)
sv_classifiers = {"LinearSVC"    : svm.LinearSVC(),
                  "SVC(linear)"  : svm.SVC(kernel='linear'),

                  "SVC(poly=1)"  : svm.SVC(kernel='poly', degree=1),
                  "SVC(poly=2)"  : svm.SVC(kernel='poly', degree=2),
                  "SVC(poly=3)"  : svm.SVC(kernel='poly', degree=3),

                  "SVC(rbf,.5)"  : svm.SVC(kernel='rbf', gamma=0.5),
                  "SVC(rbf,1.0)": svm.SVC(kernel='rbf', gamma=1.0),
                  "SVC(rbf,2.0)": svm.SVC(kernel='rbf', gamma=2.0)}

fig, axes = plt.subplots(4,2,figsize=(8,8),sharex=True, sharey=True)
for ax, (name, mod) in zip(axes.flat, sv_classifiers.items()):
    plot_boundary(ax, iris.data, iris.target, mod, [0,1])
    ax.set_title(name)
plt.tight_layout()
```

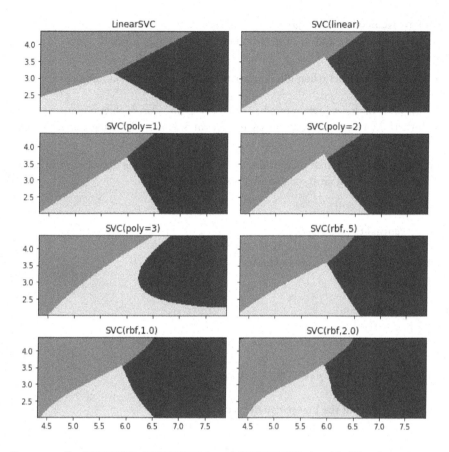

Conceptually, LinearSVC, SVC(linear), and SVC(poly=1) should all be the same; practically there are some mathematical and implementation differences between the three. LinearSVC uses a slightly different loss function and it treats its constant term—the plus-one trick—differently than SVC. Regardless, each of the linear options has boundaries defined by lines. There's no curve or bend to the borders. Notice that the SVC(poly=3) example has some deep curvature to its boundaries. The rbf examples have increasingly deep curves and a bit of waviness to their boundaries.

13.2.5 Take-Home Notes on SVM and an Example

Although this book is largely about explaining *concepts*, not giving *recipes*, people often need specific advice. SVMs have *lots* of options. What are you supposed to do when you want to use them? Fortunately, the authors of the most popular SVM implementation, libsvm (used under the hood by sklearn), have some simple advice:

- Scale the data.
- Use an rbf kernel.
- Pick kernel parameters using cross-validation.

For `rbf`, we need to select `gamma` and `C`. That will get you started. However, there are a few more issues. Again, a giant of the machine learning community, Andrew Ng, has some advice:

- Use a linear kernel when the number of features is larger than number of observations.
- Use an RBF kernel when number of observations is larger than number of features.
- If there are many observations, say more than 50k, consider using a linear kernel for speed.

Let's apply our newfound skills to the digits dataset. We'll take the advice and use an RBF kernel along with cross-validation to select a good `gamma`.

In [50]:

```
digits = datasets.load_digits()

param_grid = {"gamma" : np.logspace(-10, 1, 11, base=2),
              "C"     : [0.5, 1.0, 2.0]}

svc = svm.SVC(kernel='rbf')

grid_model = skms.GridSearchCV(svc, param_grid = param_grid,
                               cv=10, iid=False)
grid_model.fit(digits.data, digits.target);
```

We can extract out the best parameter set:

In [51]:

```
grid_model.best_params_
```

Out[51]:

```
{'C': 2.0, 'gamma': 0.0009765625}
```

We can see how those parameters translate into 10-fold CV performance:

In [52]:

```
my_gamma = grid_model.best_params_['gamma']
my_svc = svm.SVC(kernel='rbf', **grid_model.best_params_)
scores = skms.cross_val_score(my_svc,
                              digits.data, digits.target,
                              cv=10,
                              scoring='f1_macro')
print(scores)
print("{:5.3f}".format(scores.mean()))
```

```
[0.9672 1.     0.9493 0.9944 0.9829 0.9887 0.9944 0.9944 0.9766 0.9658]
0.981
```

Easy enough. These results compare favorably with the better methods from the Chapter 8 showdown on `digits` in Section 8.7. Note that there are several methods that achieve a high-90s `f1_macro` score. Choosing to use a kernel for its learning performance gains comes with resource demands. Balancing the two requires understanding the costs of mistakes and the available computing hardware.

13.3 Principal Components Analysis: An Unsupervised Technique

Unsupervised techniques find relationships and patterns in a dataset without appealing to a target feature. Instead, they apply some fixed standard and let the data express itself through that fixed lens. Examples of real-world unsupervised activities include sorting a list of names, dividing students by skill level for a ski lesson, and dividing a stack of dollar bills fairly. We relate components of the group to each other, apply some fixed rules, and press *go*. Even simple calculated statistics, such as the mean and variance, are unsupervised: they are calculated from the data with respect to a predefined standard that isn't related to an explicit target.

Here's an example that connects to our idea of learning examples as points in space. Imagine we have a scatter plot of points drawn on transparent paper. If we place the transparency on a table, we can turn it clockwise and counterclockwise. If we had a set of *xy* axes drawn underneath it on the table, we could align the data points with the axes in any way we desired. One way that might make sense is to align the horizontal axis with the biggest spread in the data. By doing that, we've let the data determine the *direction* of the axes. Picking one gets us the other one for free, since the axes are at right angles.

While we're at it, a second visual piece that often shows up on axes is tick marks. Tick marks tell us about the *scale* of the data and the graph. We could probably come up with several ways of determining scale, but one that we've already seen is the *variance* of the data in that direction. If we put ticks at one, two, and three standard deviations—that's the square root of the variance—in the directions of the axes, all of a sudden, we have axes, with tick marks, that were completely developed based on the data without appealing to any target feature. More specifically, the axes and ticks are based on the covariance and the variance of data. We'll see how in a few minutes. Principal components analysis gives us a principled way to determine these data-driven axes.

13.3.1 A Warm Up: Centering

PCA is a very powerful technique. Before we consider it, let's return to *centering* data which mirrors the process we'll use with PCA. Centering a dataset has two steps: calculate the mean of the data and then subtract that mean from each data point. In code, it looks like this:

In [53]:

```
data = np.array([[1, 2, 4, 5],
                 [2.5,.75,5.25,3.5]]).T
mean = data.mean(axis=0)
centered_data = data - mean
```

The reason we call this centering is because our points are now dispersed directly around the origin $(0, 0)$ and the origin is the center of the geometric world. We've moved from an arbitrary location to the center of the world. Visually, we have:

In [54]:

```
fig, ax = plt.subplots(figsize=(3,3))

# original data in red;
# mean is larger dot at (3,3)
ax.plot(*data.T, 'r.')
ax.plot(*mean, 'ro')

# centered data in blue, mean at (0,0)
ax.plot(*centered_data.T, 'b.')
ax.plot(*centered_data.mean(axis=0), 'bo')

#ax.set_aspect('equal');
high_school_style(ax)
```

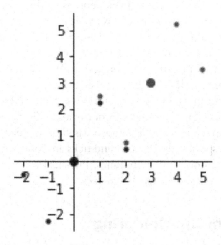

In Section 4.2.1, we discussed that the mean is our best guess if we want to minimize the distance from a point to each other value. It might not be the *most likely* point (that's actually called the *mode*) and it might not be the *middle-most* point (that's the median), but it is the *closest* point, on average, to all the other points. We'll talk about this concept more in relation to PCA in a moment. When we center data, we lose a bit of information. Unless we write down the value of the mean that we subtracted, we no longer know the *actual* center of the data. We still know how spread out the data is since shifting left or right, up or down does not change the variance of the data. The distances between any two points are the same before and after centering. But we no longer know whether the average length of our zucchini is six or eight inches. However, if we write down the mean, we can easily *undo* the centering and place the data points back in their original location.

In [55]:

```
# we can reproduce the original data
fig,ax = plt.subplots(figsize=(3,3))
orig_data = centered_data + mean
plt.plot(*orig_data.T, 'r.')
plt.plot(*orig_data.mean(axis=0), 'ro')

ax.set_xlim((0,6))
ax.set_ylim((0,6))
high_school_style(ax)
```

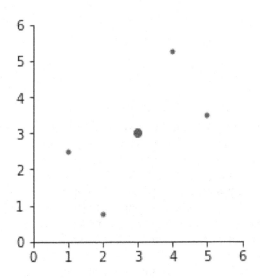

If we write this symbolically, we get something like: $D \xrightarrow{D-\mu} C_D \xrightarrow{C_D+\mu} D$. We move from the original data D to the centered data C_D by subtracting the mean μ from the original. We move from the centered data back to the original data by adding the mean to the centered data. Centering deals with shifting the data left-right and up-down. When we *standardized* data in Section 7.4, we both centered and *scaled* the data. When we perform principal components analysis, we are going to rotate, or spin, the data.

13.3.2 Finding a Different Best Line

It might seem obvious (or not!) but when we performed linear regression in Section 4.3, we dealt with differences between our line and the data in one direction: vertical. We *assumed* that all of the error was in our prediction of the *target* value. But what if there is error or randomness in the *inputs*? That means, instead of calculating our error up and down, we would need to account for both a vertical *and* a horizontal component in our distance from the best-fitting line. Let's take a look at some pictures.

In [56]:

```
fig, axes = plt.subplots(1,3,figsize=(9,3), sharex=True,sharey=True)
xs = np.linspace(0,6,30)
lines = [(1,0), (0,3), (-1,6)]
data = np.array([[1, 2, 4, 5],
                 [2.5,.75,5.25,3.5]]).T
plot_lines_and_projections(axes, lines, data, xs)
```

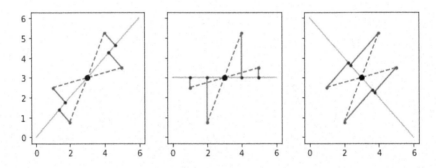

I've drawn three yellow lines (from left to right sloping up, horizontal, and down) and connected our small red data points to the yellow line. They connect with the yellow line at their respective blue dots. More technically, we say that we *project* the red dots to the blue dots. The solid blue lines represent the distances from a red dot to a blue dot. The dashed blue lines represent the distances from a red point to the mean, which is the larger black dot. The distance between a blue dot and the mean is a portion of the yellow line. Unless a red dot happens to fall directly on the yellow line, it will be closer to the mean when we project it onto its blue companion. Don't believe me? Look at it as a right triangle (using Y for yellow and B for blue): $Y^2 + B_{\text{solid}}^2 = B_{\text{dashed}}^2$. The yellow piece has to be smaller—unless red happens to be on the yellow line.

There are *lots* of yellow lines I could have drawn. To cut down on the possibilities, I drew them all through the mean. The yellow lines I've drawn show off a fundamental tradeoff of *any* yellow line we could draw. Consider two aspects of these graphs: (1) how spread-out are the blue dots on the yellow line and (2) what is the total distance of the red points from the yellow line. We won't prove it—we could, if we wanted—but the yellow line that has the *most spread-out blue dots* is also the one that has the *shortest total distance from the red points*. In more technical terms, we might say that the line that leads to the *maximum variance* in the blue points is also the line with the *lowest error* from the red points.

When we perform PCA, our first step is asking for this best line: which line has the *lowest error* and the *maximum variance*? We can continue the process and ask for the *next* best line that is perpendicular—at a right angle—to the first line. Putting these two lines together gives us a plane. We can keep going. We can add another direction for each feature we had in the original dataset. The *wine* dataset has 13 training features, so we could have as many as 13 directions. As it turns out, one use of PCA is to stop the process early so that we've (1) found some good directions and (2) reduced the total amount of information we keep around.

13.3.3 A First PCA

Having done all that work by hand—the details were hidden in `plot_lines_and_projections` which isn't too long but does rely on some linear algebra—I'll pull my normal trick and tell you that we *don't* have to do that by hand. There's an automated alternative in `sklearn`. Above, we tried several possible lines and saw that some were better than others. It would be ideal if there were some underlying mathematics that would tell us the best answer without trying different outcomes. It turns out there is just such a process. Principal components analysis (PCA) finds the best line under the minimum error and maximum variance constraints.

Imagine that we found a best line—the best single direction—for a multifeatured dataset. Now, we may want to find the *second*-best direction—a second direction with the most spread and the least error—with a slight constraint. We want this second direction to be perpendicular to the first direction. Since we're thinking about more than two features, there is more than one perpendicular possibility. Two directions pick out a plane. PCA selects directions that maximize variance, minimize error, and are perpendicular to the already selected directions. PCA can do this for all of the directions at once. Under ideal circumstances, we can find one new direction for each feature in the dataset, although we usually stop early because we use PCA to *reduce* our dataset by reducing the total number of features we send into a learning algorithm.

Let's create some data, use `sklearn`'s `PCA` transformer on the data, and extract some useful pieces from the result. I've translated two of the result components into things we want to draw: the principal directions of the data and the amount of variability in that direction. The directions tell us where the data-driven axes point. We'll see where the lengths of the arrows come from momentarily.

In [57]:

```
# draw data
ax = plt.gca()
ax.scatter(data[:,0], data[:,1], c='b', marker='.')

# draw mean
mean = np.mean(data, axis=0, keepdims=True)
centered_data = data - mean
ax.scatter(*mean.T, c='k')
```

```
# compute PCA
pca = decomposition.PCA()
P = pca.fit_transform(centered_data)

# extract useful bits for drawing
directions = pca.components_
lengths = pca.explained_variance_
print("Lengths:", lengths)
var_wgt_prindirs = -np.diag(lengths).dot(directions)
    # negate to point up/right

# draw principal axes
sane_quiver(var_wgt_prindirs, ax, origin=np.mean(data,axis=0), colors='r')
ax.set_xlim(0,10)
ax.set_ylim(0,10)
ax.set_aspect('equal')
```

```
Lengths: [5.6067 1.2683]
```

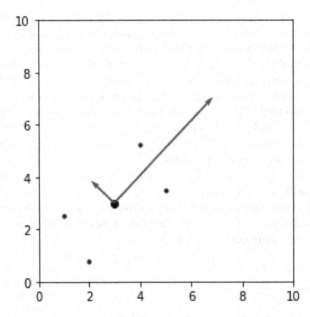

That wasn't too bad. If we tilt our heads—or our pages or screens—so that the axes are pointing left-right and up-down, all of a sudden, we've translated our data from an arbitrary orientation to a standard grid relative to the red arrows. We'll get to performing that last step—without tilting our heads—shortly. I'd like to take a moment and talk about the covariance of the results. In the process, I'll explain why I choose to draw the data axes with the lengths of `explained_variance`. As a warm-up, remember that the variance—and the covariance—is unaffected by shifting the data. Specifically, it isn't affected by centering the data.

In [58]:

```
print(np.allclose(np.cov(data, rowvar=False),
                  np.cov(centered_data, rowvar=False)))
```

True

Now, statisticians sometimes care about the total amount of variation in the data. It comes from the diagonal entries of the covariance matrix (see Section 8.5.1). Since `data` and `centered_data` have the same covariance, we can use either of them to calculate the covariance. Here's the covariance matrix and the sum of the diagonal from top-left to bottom-right:

In [59]:

```
orig_cov = np.cov(centered_data, rowvar=False)
print(orig_cov)
print(np.diag(orig_cov).sum())
```

```
[[3.3333 2.1667]
 [2.1667 3.5417]]
6.875
```

When we perform PCA, we get a new set of directions with the same total amount of variance. However, our directions will distribute the variance in different ways. In fact, we'll pile as much of the total variance onto the first direction as possible. That variance is completely related to the maximum variance/minimum error criteria we discussed earlier. In the next direction, we get as much of the left-over variation as possible, and so forth. If we add up all the variances of the new directions, we'll see that we get the same total.

In [60]:

```
EPS = 2.2e-16 # EPS (epsilon) is computer-sciency for "really small"
p_cov = np.cov(P, rowvar=False)
p_cov[p_cov<EPS] = 0.0  # throw out "really small" values
print(p_cov)
print(p_cov.sum())
```

```
[[5.6067 0.    ]
 [0.     1.2683]]
6.875000000000002
```

The diagonal values are the lengths that we used to draw the data axes. We also see that `cov(P)` has all zero entries off of the diagonal. We've eliminated the covariance between features. It is precisely because we chose directions via `PCA` that are not linearly related (they are at right angles) to each other. We've taken the liberty of replacing any suitably small values (less than `EPS`) with an exact `0.0`, primarily to deal with floating-point issues.

13.3.4 Under the Hood of PCA

We can take a quick look at what happens when `sklearn` calculates the PCA of a dataset.
The standard way to perform PCA relies on the singular value decomposition (SVD) of
matrices. I want to show off this process for three reasons: (1) the overall strategy and
algorithm is pretty straightforward, but it can be confusing to read about, (2) treating
tabular data as a matrix opens up a large window of opportunity to understand other
techniques, and (3) it is a great introduction to *why* you might ever want to study linear
algebra, even if what you really care about is *machine learning* and *data analysis*.

One of the major tools of linear algebra is *matrix decompositions* or *matrix
factorizations*—those are two names for the same sort of thing. When we decompose
something, we break it down into its component parts. When we factor an integer—a
whole number—we break it down into its component factors. $64 = 8 \cdot 8$ or $24 = 12 \cdot 2$
$= 3 \cdot 2 \cdot 2 \cdot 2 = 3 \cdot 2^3$. There are lots of ways to factor integers. We can seek pieces that
can't be broken down further: this is called a *prime factorization*. Or, we could simply ask for
any pair of two factors. Or, we could ask if the number can be factored into values that are
the same—is it a square, cube, etc.

Matrix decomposition or factorization is an equivalent process for matrices. We take a
known matrix and ask how we can break it down into more primitive, smaller, component
parts. What's interesting is that we can often talk about these parts in terms of how they
affect a scatter plot of a data matrix. For example, the SVD of a matrix essentially says that
any data matrix can be factored—broken down or separated—into three components: a
rotation or spinning, a stretching, and another rotation. Working backwards, if we start
with the most vanilla data we can imagine, and we rotate, stretch, and rotate again, we can
get any data matrix as a result. Another decomposition, the *eigendecomposition*, decomposes
a matrix into a rotation, a stretch, and then an *undo* of the first rotation. Let's examine
that here.

We'll need a quick helper that can rotate data points around the origin $(0, 0)$ by a given
angle:

In [61]:

```
def make_rotation(theta):
    ''' ccw rotation of theta when it post-multiplies
        a row vector (an example) '''
    return np.array([[np.cos(theta), -np.sin(theta)],
                     [np.sin(theta),  np.cos(theta)]]).T
```

With that, we can create some points that are equally spaced around a circle and set an
amount of rotation and scaling we want to perform:

In [62]:

```
spacing = np.linspace(0,2*np.pi,17)
points  = np.c_[np.sin(spacing), np.cos(spacing)]
    # sin/cos walk around circle
```

```
two_points = points[[0,3]]

rot = make_rotation(np.pi/8) # 1/16th turn degrees ccw
scale = np.diag([2,.5])
```

Then, we can put it all together to move from a vanilla circle to an interesting ellipse. Graphically, here's what it looks like:

In [63]:

```
fig, axes = plt.subplots(1,4,figsize=(8,2), sharey=True)

# original vanilla circle
axes[0].plot(*two_points.T, 'k^')
axes[0].plot(*points.T, 'b.')

# make a rotation
axes[1].plot(*np.dot(two_points, rot).T, 'k^')
axes[1].plot(*np.dot(points, rot).T, 'r.')

# stretch along x and y axes
axes[2].plot(*two_points.dot(rot).dot(scale).T, 'k^')
axes[2].plot(*points.dot(rot).dot(scale).T, 'r.')

# undo initial rotation
axes[3].plot(*two_points.dot(rot).dot(scale).dot(rot.T).T, 'k^')
axes[3].plot(*points.dot(rot).dot(scale).dot(rot.T).T, 'b.')

names = ['circle', 'rotate', 'scale', 'unrotate']
for ax,name in zip(axes,names):
    ax.set_aspect('equal')
    ax.set_title(name)
    ax.set_xlim(-2,2)
    ax.set_ylim(-2,2)
```

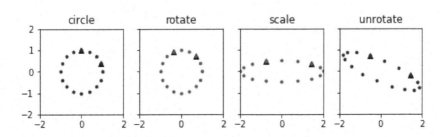

Now, what we did here is sort of the *opposite* of factoring a number: we multiplied things together, like going from 3 and 5 to 3 × 5 = 15. Normally, we're given interesting data that we can describe with the rightmost ellipse, and we want to work backwards to the uninteresting leftmost circle. If you wonder why we would go from something interesting to something uninteresting, it's because the things we learn along the way are the pieces that allow us to do the conversions from one graph to the next. These actions on the scatterplots are the *really* interesting bits. In fact, they are the bits we can use to compute a PCA.

To do that, I want to show that a few things are *the same*. However, when we talk about similarity, there are always constraints. When people say that I'm like my brother, they are typically talking about some specific characteristic like our humor or mannerisms. We actually look a bit different. So, really, when we say *the same*, we don't always mean *exactly the same*. Sometimes we mean *same up to some point or degree*.

Here's a mathematical example. Say you are 10 feet away from me. On a line, you could be in front of me, at me +10, or behind me, at me −10. So, you could be in two different spots, but it is correct to say that either is 10 feet away from me. *Ten feet away* determines where you are up to a plus or minus sign. If, instead, we were on a soccer field, you could be anywhere on a 10-foot circle around me. In that case, where you are is determined up to your angle-like position on a sundial or an analog clock face. Back to signs: you might remember that when you factored numbers in grade school, you did it with positive numbers: 15 = 5 × 3. In reality, you could also factor 15 as −5 × −3. Keeping the numbers positive meant you could give fewer, simpler answers because the legal space of answers was reduced.

Now, imagine we wanted to factor −15. We no longer have the luxury of staying positive. Our factoring has to include a negative value somewhere. As such, we could equally well use −5 × 3 or −3 × 5. We don't know where the −1 belongs. We face a similar issue when we compute the SVD. There are several places where signs can be flipped, and we get the same answer when we multiply things out, so either way is equally valid. The only problem is when two different methods try to do the SVD and pick different signs for the components. This difference means that when we say they give the *same* answer, we really mean that the answers are the *same up to some plus or minus signs*. To make up for that, we have the following helper routine that massages two different matrices into similar signs. It has a test on it that makes sure the matrices are numerically similar—have the same absolute values—before applying the sign fix.

In [64]:

```
def signs_like(A, B):
    ' produce new A,B with signs of A '
    assert np.allclose(np.abs(A), np.abs(B))
    signs = np.sign(A) * np.sign(B)
    return A, B * signs
signs_like([1,-1], [1,1])
```

Out[64]:

```
([1, -1], array([ 1, -1]))
```

So, let's compute the SVD of our centered data. Basically, instead of factoring a number $15 = 5 \times 3$ we are going to factor a matrix of our centered data: $D_C = USV^T$. We will compute the SVD and then show that we haven't lost anything. We can multiply together the components of the SVD—U, S, V^T—and we get back our centered data.

We do a few things in the code to simplify our lives. `full_matrices = False` and `S=np.diag(s)` makes the multiplication to reconstruct `centered_data` easier. We use `signs_like` to deal with the sign issue we discussed above. Lastly and confusingly, `np.linalg.svd` returns a flipped—actually *transposed*, with rows turned into columns and columns into rows—version of `V`. We indicate this by assigning that part to `Vt`, the `t` standing for *transposed*. To get `V` itself, we unflip it with `.T` by taking `Vt.T`. Flipping twice gets us back to the original. Sometimes double negatives are a good thing.

In [65]:

```
N = len(centered_data)

U, s, Vt = np.linalg.svd(centered_data, full_matrices=False)
S = np.diag(s)
print(np.allclose(centered_data, U.dot(S).dot(Vt)))
```

True

`svd` plus a bit of work gave us `U`, `S`, and `V`. These components can be almost directly compared with the results from PCA. Here we check the directions, the variances, and the adjusted data:

In [66]:

```
# align signs
# note: U.S.Vt won't give centered now because
# U, Vt work together and we monkeyed with Vt
_, Vt = signs_like(pca.components_, Vt)
V = Vt.T

# directions come from Vt;  amounts come from S
# divide by n-1 to get unbiased... see EOC
print(all((np.allclose(pca.components_,          Vt),
           np.allclose(pca.explained_variance_, s**2/(N-1)),
           np.allclose(P,                        centered_data.dot(V)))))
```

True

Now, recall that we can compute the covariance matrix from our centered data with a quick `dot`.

```
In [67]:
```

```
print('original covariance:\n', orig_cov)
print('centered covariance:\n',
      centered_data.T.dot(centered_data) / (N-1))
```

```
original covariance:
 [[3.3333 2.1667]
 [2.1667 3.5417]]
centered covariance:
 [[3.3333 2.1667]
 [2.1667 3.5417]]
```

So, we just computed the PCA of our data by computing the SVD of our data.

One other way to compute the PCA of our data is by computing the eigendecomposition (EIGD) of the *covariance matrix* of our data. There is a deep mathematical relationship and equivalence between SVD(data) and EIGD(cov(data)).

```
In [68]:
```

```
eigval, eigvec = np.linalg.eig(orig_cov)

# two differences:
# 1.  eigenvalues aren't ordered high to low (S from svd is ordered)
# 2.  final signs with SVD go through V *and* U, eigenvector is a bit
#     different
order = np.argsort(eigval)[::-1]
print(np.allclose(eigval[order], s**2/(N-1)))

_,ev = signs_like(Vt,eigvec[:,order])
print(np.allclose(ev, Vt))
```

```
True
True
```

When mathematicians talk about eigenvalues and eigenvectors, they immediately throw up the following equation: $Av = \lambda v$ where v and λ are respectively the eigenvectors and eigenvalues of A. Unfortuantely, they don't often talk about what it means. Here's a quick take:

1. Representing our data as a matrix organizes the data as a table *and* naturally places each example as a point in space.
2. The covariance matrix of our data tells us how we map—via multiplication—a set of plain vanilla points into the actual data we see. These plain vanilla points simply have a value of 1 for a single feature and zero elsewhere. As a matrix, it is called the identity matrix.

3. The eigenvalues and eigenvectors of the covariance matrix tell us what directions point the same way and how long they are, after being mapped by the covariance matrix. We can read $Cv = \lambda v$ as saying that multiplying by C is the same as multiplying by single value λ. This means that C stretches v the same as a *simple number* λ and doesn't point it in a different direction. Note, this only works for *some* v, not every possible v.

4. For our problem of finding the principal components—or the primary directions, if you will—we need exactly the directions that are not changed when mapped by the covariance matrix.

If this look at the mechanics of PCA has left your head spinning with singular eigens and vectored components and principal decompositions (none of which exist), keep these three things in mind.

1. Through linear algebra, we can talk about tables of data—matrices—the same way we talked about single numeric values in grade school.
2. Matrices can describe points in space and ways to manipulate those points.
3. We can break down complicated matrices into simpler matrices.
4. The simpler matrices are often related to problems we'd like to solve, such as finding best lines and directions.

These are the four reasons why you *might* want to dig into linear algebra at some point in your machine learning and data analysis studies.

13.3.5 A Finale: Comments on General PCA

We can now actually *talk* about what PCA does. Above, we talked about how centering and uncentering data can shift back and forth between data centered at 0 and data centered at its empirical—actually measured—mean. Then we dove into mapping data points to a line that minimizes the distances between the points and that line. That line is different from linear regression because linear regression minimizes the *vertical* distances between the points and the line, not the shortest-path distances to the line.

Now, what does PCA do? When we apply PCA to n features, and we take the first k principal components, we are generating a best—closest—k-dimensional object to the points that live in n-dimensional space. You might like to look at Figure 13.3 to reduce your confusion. Suppose we have 10 features and $k = 2$. Two dimensions give a plane, so when we perform PCA(k=2), we are finding the best plane (as in Figure 13.1) to represent the data that originally exists in 10 dimensions. If we take PCA(k=3), we are finding the best infinite solid (just like lines go on forever, imagine a 3D set of axes extending out forever) to map our points to. The concepts get pretty weird, but the take-home is that we *reduce* our data from 10-D to k-D *and* we try to keep as much information—specifically, as much of the total variance—in the data as possible. In the process, we keep our projected points as close to the originals as possible by minimizing the error (distance) between the originals and the projections.

One other way to view the PCA process is to consider it as one half of a cyclic process that takes us from (1) random white noise with *no* information in it to (2) interesting

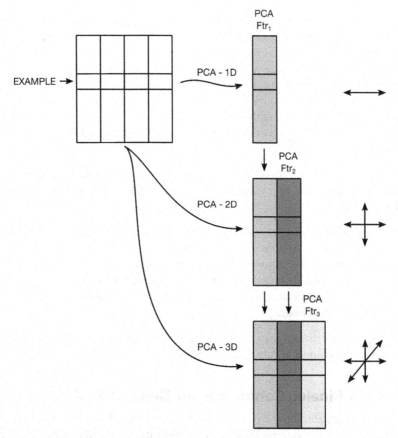

Figure 13.3   PCA reduces the dimensionality of our data, effectively reducing the number of conceptual columns describing each example.

empirical or generated data and (3) back to the white noise. $EIGD$ and SVD recover the stretching and rotating from that process.

13.3.6 Kernel PCA and Manifold Methods

Above, we discussed kernel methods and we said somewhat abstractly that as long as we can express a learning method as dot products between examples—not dot products between *features*, which is almost a covariance matrix—we can turn a vanilla method into a kernel method. It turns out that PCA is well poised to do that. Why?

Remember that taking the SVD(X) was like taking the $\mathrm{EIGD}(X^T X)$. Well, there's another relationship hidden in there. The calculations under the hood for SVD(X) (remember, we had a U and a V running around) *also* gives us $\mathrm{EIGD}(X X^T)$ which *precisely* describes a PCA version that operates between examples instead of between features. This same-but-different way of solving a problem—in some cases with more or less difference—is called *solving a dual problem* or simply *solving the dual* of an original problem. In mathematics, the term *dual* refers to an alternative but equivalent way of representing or solving a problem.

Standard principal components analysis finds good directions—data-defined axes—for the data by breaking down the covariance matrix. However, it does this by *implicitly* using the SVD of the data. We could consider that to be an unnecessary detail, but the covariance matrix is merely one way to capture the similarities in our data in a *feature-centric* fashion. As we discussed in Section 13.2.3.2, dot products and kernels give us another way to capture similarities—now in an *example-centric* fashion. The net result is that we can plug *kernels* instead of *covariances* into PCA and get out more exotic creatures that have an equally exotic name: *manifold methods*.

13.3.6.1 Manifolds

Don't be scared by the name *manifolds*: it is simply a fancy term for things that can clearly be *related to* points, lines, and planes but aren't exactly these things. For example (Figure 13.4), if I draw a circle and label it like a watch dial—I, II, III, etc.—and I am willing to break the circle at XII (noon), I can very easily connect spots on the circle to spots on a line. *The circle and the line share certain characteristics.* Namely, take the times near 3 o'clock. It's neighbors are at 2:59 and 3:01 (sorry, I can't write minutes as Roman numerals). Those neighbors are *the same* whether we draw the times as a circular watch-face or flatten them out as a timeline.

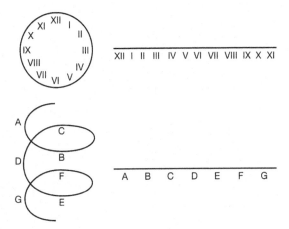

Figure 13.4   Viewing geometric objects as manifolds emphasizes the abstract similarity between different forms based on local neighbors. These neighbors remain unchanged by bending and looping.

Yes, you have a point: if we cut the watch face at the top, XII loses one side of its neighbors. Sacrifices must be made. As another example, if I unroll a lidless and bottomless aluminum can, I would have something looking like an aluminum cookie sheet—and again, away from the boundary where I cut the can, the local neighborhoods before and after the cut look very similar. In both cases, if I'm trying to deal with the mathematics that describe these things, I've reduced the complexity I have to deal with. I'm moving from curvy things to linear things. I'm afraid that I'm simplifying this pretty drastically—you can see the End-of-Chapter Notes for a technical caveat, if you care.

Here's a more complicated graphical example. `sklearn` can make a wonderfully complicated 3D dataset in the shape of an *S* that extends depthwise into a piece of paper it is written on. Here's what it looks like:

In [69]:

```
from mpl_toolkits.mplot3d import Axes3D
import sklearn.manifold as manifold
data_3d, color = datasets.samples_generator.make_s_curve(n_samples=750,
                                                          random_state=42)

cmap = plt.cm.Spectral
fig = plt.figure(figsize=(4,4))
ax = plt.gca(projection='3d')
ax.scatter(*data_3d.T, c=color, cmap=cmap)
ax.view_init(20, -50)
```

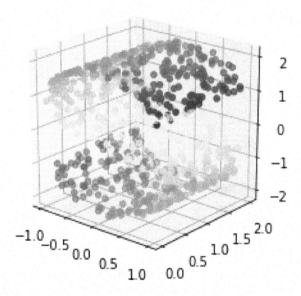

If it's a little hard to see, imagine someone took an *S* and smeared it depthwise from left to right. Now, take a moment and think about what that would look like if you flattened it out—perhaps by pulling at its ending edges like a string. Ideas? If you're stumped, we can let the computer do it for us.

```
In [70]:

fig, axes = plt.subplots(1,2,figsize=(8,4))
n_components = 2

# method 1:  map to 2D using isomap
isomap = manifold.Isomap(n_neighbors=10, n_components=n_components)
data_2d = isomap.fit_transform(data_3d)
axes[0].scatter(*data_2d.T, c=color, cmap=cmap)

# method 2:  map to 2D using TSNE
tsne = manifold.TSNE(n_components=n_components,
                     init='pca',
                     random_state=42)
data_2d = tsne.fit_transform(data_3d)
axes[1].scatter(*data_2d.T, c=color, cmap=cmap);
```

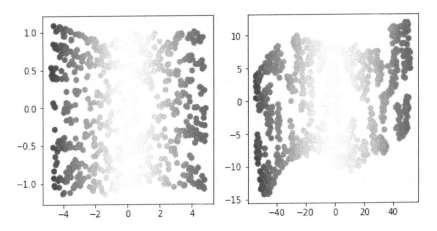

Surprisingly or not, we end up with a pair of *sort of* cookie sheets. It doesn't work out perfectly, but the algorithm is trying to reconstruct that flat cookie sheet from the complex bendy *S* in space. So, now, we have a very cool tool.

- PCA wants to find a best flat space—a line, plane, solid, etc.
- We can rewrite PCA to use dot products.
- We can replace dot products with kernels.
- Using kernels instead of dot products lets us effectively, and efficiently, work with nonlinear—curvy—objects.
- If we use the data-reducing capabilities of PCA with kernels, we can reduce our data from curvy manifolds to flat spaces.

There are several different *manifold methods* that aim at reducing arbitrary data down to some less complex space. Our example here used *TSNE* and *IsoMap*. Due to some clever mathematics, these methods can generally be described as PCA *plus* a kernel. That is, if we pick the right kernel and feed it to PCA, we get out the kernel method. Now, don't be misled. It may well be the case that it is preferable to use some custom code to implement a method. But it is equally important that to *understand* what these methods are doing and to compare them to similar techniques, we can show off the similarities by writing them all as variations on a theme—in this case, PCA plus different kernels. I won't go into the details of the kernels underneath these methods, but if you are curious, you can find the references in the End-of-Chapter Notes.

13.4　EOC

13.4.1　Summary

In this chapter, we've added some powerful—and in some cases, almost hypermodern—techniques to our toolbox. We have some ways of quantifying the contributions of features which we can use to select subsets of features that we hope are interesting and useful for learning. We can replace some of our manual feature construction steps with automatically applied kernel methods—whether the kernels are used with support vectors, principal components, or other learning models. We can also use SVMs and PCA as stand-alone tools to, respectively, classify examples and to redescribe our data explicitly for other processing steps.

13.4.2　Notes

Feature Evaluation Metrics　There are many feature evaluation metrics, but they are largely built from the same underlying toolbox of mathematical tools. If we expand out some of the components, we can start to see the mathematical similarities among these metrics. The dot product is a fundamental component: $\text{dot}(x, y) = \sum x_i y_i$, where x, y are features (columns).

- We didn't discuss the *cosine similarity*, but we'll see it in the next chapter. I'll start with it as a building block. Verbally, we can call the cosine-similarity a *(length-)normalized dot product*.

$$\cos(x, y) = \frac{\text{dot}(x, y)}{\text{len}(x)\text{len}(y)} = \frac{\text{dot}(x, y)}{\sqrt{\text{dot}(x, x)}\sqrt{\text{dot}(y, y)}} = \frac{\sum x_i y_i}{\sqrt{\sum x_i^2}\sqrt{\sum y_i^2}}$$

- We've seen the covariance before, but here's the formula in these terms. We'll use $\bar{x}$ to represent the mean of x. Verbally, we can call the covariance an *(average) centered dot product*. The average comes in when we divide by n.

$$\text{cov}(x, y) = \frac{\text{dot}(x - \bar{x}, y - \bar{y})}{n} = \frac{\sum (x_i - \bar{x})(y_i - \bar{y})}{n}$$

- The correlation combines these two ideas of centering and normalizing. Verbally, we can call the correlation a *centered cosine similarity*, a *(length-)normalized covariance*, or a *centered, (length-)normalized dot product*.

$$\text{cor}(x, y) = \frac{\text{dot}(x - \bar{x}, y - \bar{y})}{\text{len}(x - \bar{x})\text{len}(y - \bar{y})} = \frac{\sum(x - \bar{x})(y - \bar{y})}{\sqrt{\sum(x_i - \bar{x})^2}\sqrt{\sum(y_i - \bar{y})^2}}$$

- One last related measure is the linear regression coefficient we would get if we used x to predict y *without* an intercept (lrc_{wo}):

$$\text{lrc}_{\text{wo}}(x, y) = \frac{\text{dot}(x, y)}{\text{len}(x)} = \frac{\text{dot}(x, y)}{\sqrt{\text{dot}(x, x)}} = \frac{\sum x_i y_i}{\sqrt{\sum x_i^2}}$$

- When we have our usual linear regression coefficient estimated *with* an intercept term (lrc_{w}), we get several interesting relationships. I'll highlight two here: one that includes the correlation and one that shows this coefficient's relationship to a covariance that is normalized by the spread in x:

$$\text{lrc}_w = \text{cor}(x, y)\frac{\sqrt{\text{var}(x)}}{\sqrt{\text{var}(y)}} = \frac{\text{cov}(x, y)}{\text{var}(x)}$$

A wonderful, deep result in mathematics called the *Cauchy-Schwart inequality* tells us that $\sqrt{|\text{cov}(x, y)|} <= \text{var}(x)\text{var}(y)$.

In this book, I've completely avoided the issue of biased and unbiased estimates of standard deviation and variance. Basically, we have *always* divided by n in our variance calculations. For some purposes, we'd prefer to divide by $n - 1$ or even by other values. Dividing by $n - 1$ is called Bessel's correction. I'll leave it to you to find out more via Google or a statistically minded friend. However, I'll warn you that the calculation routines in `numpy` and friends can be inconsistent in their use of n versus $n - 1$. Read the documentation and default parameters very closely.

Formal Statistics for Feature Selection   Here are a few technical details about ordering features by r^2 for my statistical readers. The rank ordering of univariate F-statistics $F_i = \frac{\rho_i}{1 - \rho_i}(n - 2)$ is *the same* as the rank ordering of correlations $R_i^2 = \rho_i^2$. The algebra to show this is not hard. There are many relationships between formal statistical tests that can be made to determine the worth of features. The main tests are the t-test and ANOVAs. Some of the theory gets pretty deep, but you can get a quick overview by looking at Leemis and McQuestion's paper "Univariate Distributions Relationships" which has a wonderful graphic that is also available around the Web.

Our statistician friends should also be aware that in the statistical world an F-statistic is used in feature selection through a technique called *forward stepwise selection*. Forward stepwise selection is a *sequential* process which involves picking an initial feature f_1 and then *combining with* f_1 the feature which does best *in combination with* f_1 for learning. This is *not* what `sklearn` does. `sklearn` evaluates each feature individually, in isolation from all other features.

Metric Selection and Relationship to Tree-Splitting Criteria   One important special case of feature selection occurs when we select the features to divide our data in a decision tree. We tap-danced around this topic in Section 8.2. We can select features in several different ways. The major ones are the *Gini* and *entropy* measures based on the distributions of the target values. Briefly, for the probability of a class p_i, these look like Gini $= 1 - \sum p_i$ and entropy $= - \sum p_i \log(p_i)$. The entropy is used by comparing the entropy before the split with the weighted entropies after the split in a measure called the *information gain*.

Metric Selection Note: On Metrics and Models   While we separated our discussion of feature selection methods into those that used a model and those that didn't, the "modelless" methods are really using *some* model as their underlying intellectual foundation. For example, correlation is measuring how well a single-feature linear regression would do. Variance is measuring how well a single *value*—a mean—would do as a predictor. Mutual information measures are tied to the error rate of something called a *Bayes optimal classifier*; these are theoretical unicorns that are generally only constructable for toy problems—but they give us a formal notion of a "best" classifier. If you are a more advanced reader, you can find more details in a (heavy academic) paper "Feature Extraction by Non-Parametric Mutual Information Maximization" by Torkkola.

Kernel Notes   Why are 1-NN and a deep, high `max_depth` tree so similar for the circle problem? Both segment out many, many regions of space until there's only a small region to make a prediction for. 1-NN does this by asking for only a single close neighbor. The tree, ten nodes deep, does it by repeatedly cutting away more regions of space.

To give you an idea of what a kernel would look like on data that doesn't come prepackaged in a table, let's look at the *edit distance*, also called the Levenshtein distance. The edit distance between two strings is the number of insertions, deletions, and character substitutions needed to go from one string to another. For example, *cat* → *hat* requries one character substitution. *at* → *hat* requires one insertion of an *h* at the start. You can imagine that our phones' autocorrect feature is using something similar to fix our typos. This notion of distance can also be translated into a notion of similarity and used to define a kernel function between any two strings. Poof! We no longer need to explicitly turn the strings of text into features in a table.

Depending on your mathematical background, when you start seeing covariance matrices and kernels, you might start thinking about Gram matrices. And that can get *really* confusing because most writers define Gram matrices in terms of *column* vectors while we use rows as our examples. So, for our purposes, the usual Gram matrix can be used *directly* for kernels. However, if we want to talk about covariances, we have to take a transpose somewhere. With that in mind, Mercer's condition about the legality of kernels says: *the example-pairwise Gram matrix K must be symmetric positive-definite. A feature-pairwise Gram matrix* would be the covariance matrix.

SVM Notes   If you're going to use SVMs in general and `libsvm` in particular (even via `sklearn`), I'd recommend you read the `libsvm` user guide. It's not long. Here's the address: https://www.csie.ntu.edu.tw/~cjlin/papers/guide/guide.pdf.

In `sklearn`, `LinearSVC` uses squared hinge loss instead of the simple hinge. The change in loss, coupled with `LinearSVC`'s different treatment of the intercept term, really upsets some folks who are sticklers for the definition of what makes a support vector machine. I wouldn't stress about that, though those two facts will account for slight to significant differences between `LinearSVC` and `SVC(linear)`/`SVC(poly=1)`.

Technical Notes on PCA, SVD, and EIG   PCA on a dataset of n features can recover *up to* n directions. We'll get n directions if none of the input features are linear combinations of others.

The *best line* graphic was inspired by a great animation by user *amoeba* from a StackExchange discussion: https://stats.stackexchange.com/a/140579/1704.

Without getting into a whole lesson on linear algebra, we can give a quick overview of the mathematics that connect PCA, SVD, and EIGD. Again, this sort of answers the question, "Why would I ever want to study linear algebra?" Here goes.

We'll start with three quick facts:

- Some matrices are called *orthogonal* (yes, in the same sense of 90-degree angles). This means that their *transpose* acts like a numerical reciprocal $\frac{a}{a} = a^{-1}a = 1$. For an orthogonal matrix M_o, we have $M_o^T M_o = I$. I is the *identity* matrix. It is the matrix equivalent of the number one. Multiplying by I leaves the overall value unchanged.
- For all matrices, the transpose M^T trades rows for columns and columns for rows. With $M = \begin{bmatrix} 1 & 2 \\ 3 & 4 \end{bmatrix}$ we have $M^T = \begin{bmatrix} 1 & 3 \\ 2 & 4 \end{bmatrix}$.

- When we take the transpose of multiplied matrices—multiplication first, transpose second—we must swap the order of the inner matrices if we do the transpose first: $(M_1 M_2)^T = M_2^T M_1^T$.

That order-swapping shows up in several mathematical and computer-science operations. Here's a simple example with sorted lists and reversal. What happens if we reverse two sublists of an ordered list? Imagine we have $l_1 + l_2 = L$ and all three are in order (here, $+$ mean concatenation). If I reverse l_1 and l_2 separately and join them, $\text{rev}(l_1) + \text{rev}(l_2)$, I don't have a correctly reversed L. That is, $\text{rev}(l_1) + \text{rev}(l_2) \neq \text{rev}(L)$. Reversing is OK enough for l_1 and l_2 separately, but it falls apart when they are combined. To fix things up, I have to join together the reversed lists *in swapped order*: $\text{rev}(l_2) + \text{rev}(l_1) = \text{rev}(L)$. If you want to make that idea concrete, create two lists of names (Mike, Adam, Zoe; Bill, Paul, Kate) and go through the process yourself.

With those rules in mind:

- If we start with patternless data, W, our covariance matrix is $\Sigma_W = W^T W = I$.
- If we then stretch out the data with S, we get SW with covariance matrix $\Sigma_{SW} = (SW)^T SW = W^T S^T SW$.

- Then we can rotate it with an orthogonal R, giving RSW. Since R is orthogonal, $R^T R = I$. Its covariance matrix is $\Sigma_{RSW} = (RSW)^T RSW = W^T S^T R^T RSW = W^T S^2 W$.

Squaring a matrix is a bit complicated, but it turns out the S only has entries on its diagonal and squaring it means we just square the values on the diagonal. Crisis averted.

If we now work backwards, from the end data RSW and the end covariance matrix Σ_{RSW}, we have

- From EIGD on the covariance matrix: eig(Σ_{RSW}) gives $\Sigma_{RSW} V = VL$ or $\Sigma_{RSW} = VLV^T$.
- From SVD on the data matrix: svd(RSW) = $(UDV^T)^T UDV^T = VDU^T UDV^T = VD^2 V^T$.

Subject to a few caveats, we can identify RS—our stretching and rotating—with VL and VD^2. In the real world, we *start* with interesting data that comes to us in the form of RSW. We don't see the component pieces. Then we use SVD or EIG to *figure out* the RS that could conceptually get us from white-noise data to the data we observed.

PCA's Crew: PPCA, FA, and ICA   PCA can be related to several other techniques: *probabilistic PCA* (PPCA), *factor analysis* (FA), and *independent component analysis* (ICA). All of these techniques can be used in a fashion similar to PCA: create newly derived features and keep fewer of them than what we started with.

PCA is closely related to PPCA and FA. All of these techniques care about accounting for the *variance* in the data but they make different modeling assumptions about the nature of the covariance of the data being analyzed. PCA takes the covariance matrix as is. PPCA adds a shared random amount of variance to each feature. FA adds varying random amounts of variance to each feature.

ICA swaps out maximizing variance for maximizing *kurtosis*. There are other ways of describing and understanding ICA as well; ICA has an interpretation as minimizing mutual information. Kurtosis is a charteristic of distributions similar to the mean and variance. The mean is the center of the data and the variance is the spread of the data; kurtosis—loosely (there are several quibbles with most verbal descriptions)—describes how heavy the tails of the data are or how quickly the probability curve drops off to zero. Practically speaking, while PCA wants to find directions that account for variance and are orthogonal (uncorrelated) from one another, ICA wants to find directions that are maximally statistically independent from one another.

Manifolds   My discussion of manifolds blended the general idea of manifolds with the more specific idea of *differentiable* manifolds. Now you know why I didn't mention it in the main text. But the details are that manifolds have some nice equivalence with Euclidean space—our normal playground for graphing datasets and functions. Differentiable manifolds are a bit more strict: they have an equivalence with *linear* subsets of Euclidean space. If you recall your calculus, you took derivatives by approximating—with a line—the slope at very, very small intervals of a function. Differentiable manifolds extend that idea so we can perform calculus on weird mathematical objects—like models of black holes.

13.4.3 Exercises

1. We can use `GridSearch` to help us find good parameters for feature selection. Try using a grid search to find a good threshold for `VarianceThreshold`. Compare the result of learning with and without the removed features.
2. Look up the Anscombe datasets. Compare the variance, covariance, and correlation of the datasets. Consider yourself enlightened.
3. Take a second look at the two-feature mutual information example. What is the `mutual_info_classif` on `data**2`—that is, on the squares of the feature values? Why might we expect the information to be higher there? You might try on the regression problem also.
4. Constructing models to select features seems like a fairly heavyweight process. How do the execution times of some of the model-based feature selection techniques like `SelectFromModel` or `RFE` compare to simply running those models and calling it a day? Try learning on all of the features and compare it to a round of feature selection and then learning on just the selected features.
5. In the circle classification problem, the `depth=10` decision tree was not terribly circle-like. Does adding more data lead to a more circle-like boundary?
6. I claimed that the Nystroem kernel was useful to save resources. Demonstrate it. Compare the resource usage of full kernel and a Nystroem approximation.
7. Take some data—say a dozen rows from the *iris* dataset. Now, do a few things to it. Standarize the data and compute the covariance matrix of it; now compare with the correlation of the original. Compute the PCA on the standarized data and the PCA of the correlation matrix of the original.
8. `rbf` kernels are very powerful. Their main parameter is `gamma`. Evaluate the effect of changing `gamma` by looking at a complexity curve over different `gamma` values. Are bigger values of `gamma` more or less biased?

Feature Engineering for Domains: Domain-Specific Learning

```
# setup
from mlwpy import *
%matplotlib inline

import cv2
```

In a perfect world, our standard classification algorithms would be provided with data that is relevant, plentiful, tabular (formatted in a table), and naturally discriminitive when we look at it as points in space.

In reality, we may be stuck with data that is

1. Only an approximation of our target task
2. Limited in quantity or covers only some of many possibilities
3. Misaligned with the prediction method(s) we are trying to apply to it
4. Written as text or images which are decidedly *not* in an example-feature table

Issues 1 and 2 are specific to a learning problem you are focused on. We discussed issue 3 in Chapters 10 and 13; we can address it by manually or automatically engineering our feature space. Now, we'll approach issue 4: what happens when we have data that isn't in a nice tabular form? If you were following closely, we did talk about this a bit in the previous chapter. Through kernel methods, we can make *direct* use of objects as they are presented to us (perhaps as a string). However, we are then restricted to kernel-compatible learning methods and techniques; what's worse, kernels come with their own limitations and complexities.

So, how can we convert awkward data into data that plays nicely with good old-fashioned learning algorithms? Though the terms are somewhat hazy, I'll use the

phrase *feature extraction* to capture the idea of converting an arbitrary data source—
something like a book, a song, an image, or a movie—to tabular data we can use with the
non-kernelized learning methods we've seen in this book. In this chapter, we will deal
with two specific cases: text and images. Why? Because they are plentiful and have
well-developed methods of feature extraction. Some folks might mention that processing
them is also highly lucrative. But, we're above such concerns, right?

14.1 Working with Text

When we apply machine learning methods to text documents, we encounter some
interesting challenges. In contrast to a fixed set of measurements grouped in a table,
documents are (1) variable-length, (2) order-dependent, and (3) unaligned. Two different
documents can obviously differ in length. While learning algorithms don't care about the
ordering of features—as long as they are in the same order for each example—documents
most decidedly *do* care about order: "the cat in the hat" is very different from "the hat in
the cat" (ouch). Likewise, we expect the order of information for two examples to be
presented in the same way for each example: feature one, feature two, and feature three.
Two different sentences can communicate the same information in many different
arrangements of—possibly different—words: "Sue went to see Chris" and "Chris had a
visitor named Sue."

We might try the same thing with two very simple documents that serve as our
examples: "the cat in the hat" and "the quick brown fox jumps over the lazy dog". After
removing the super common, low-meaning *stop words*—like *the*—we end up with

	sentence
example 1	cat in hat
example 2	quick brown fox jumps over lazy dog

Or,

	word 1	word 2	word 3	word 4
example 1	cat	in	hat	*
example 2	quick	brown	fox	jumps

which we would have to extend out to the longest of all our examples. Neither of these
feels right. The first really makes *no* attempt to tease apart any relationships in the words.
The second option seems to go both too far and not far enough: everything is broken into
pieces, but word 1 in example 1 may have no relationship to word 1 in example 2.

There's a fundamental disconnect between representing examples as written text and
representing them as rows in a table. I see a hand raised in the classroom. "Yes, you in the
back?" "Well, how *can* we represent text in a table?" I'm glad you asked.

Here's one method:

1. Gather all of the words in all of the documents and make that list of words the *features* of interest.
2. For each document, create a row for the learning example. Row entries indicate if a word occurs in that example. Here, we use − to indicate *no* and to let the *yeses* stand out.

	in	over	quick	brown	lazy	cat	hat	fox	dog	jumps
example 1	yes	−	−	−	−	yes	yes	−	−	−
example 2	−	yes	yes	yes	yes	−	−	yes	yes	yes

This technique is called *bag of words*. To encode a document, we take all the words in it, write them down on slips of paper, and throw them in a bag. The benefit here is ease and quickness. The difficulty is that we *completely lose the sense of ordering!* For example, "Barb went to the store and Mark went to the garage" would be represented in the *exact same way* as "Mark went to the store and Barb went to the garage". With that caveat in mind, in life—and in machine learning—we often use simplified versions of complicated things either because (1) they serve as a starting point or (2) they turn out to work well enough. In this case, both are valid reasons why we often use bag-of-words representations for text learning.

We can extend this idea from working with single words—called *unigrams*—to pairs of adjacent words, called *bigrams*. Pairs of words give us a *bit* more context. In the Barb and Mark example, if we had *trigrams*—three-word phrases—we would capture the distinction of Mark-store and Barb-garage (after the stop words are removed). The same idea extends to *n*-grams. Of course, as you can imagine, adding longer and longer phrases takes more and more time and memory to process. We will stick with single-word unigrams for our examples here.

If we use a bag-of-words (BOW) representation, we have several different options for recording the presence of a word in a document. Above, we simply recorded *yes* values. We could have equivalently used zeros and ones or trues and falses. The large number of dashes points out an important practical issue. When we use BOW, the data become very *sparse*. Clever storage, behind the scenes, can compress that table by only recording the interesting entries and avoiding all of the blank *no* entries.

If we move beyond a simple yes/no recording scheme, our first idea might be to record *counts* of occurrences of the words. Beyond that, we might care about normalizing those counts based on some other factors. All of these are brilliant ideas and you are commended for thinking of them. Better yet, they are well known and implemented in `sklearn`, so let's make these ideas concrete.

14.1.1 Encoding Text

Here are a few sample documents that we can use to investigate different ways of encoding text:

In [2]:

```
docs = ["the cat in the hat",
        "the cow jumped over the moon",
        "the cat mooed and the cow meowed",
        "the cat said to the cow cow you are not a cat"]
```

To create our features of interest, we need to record all of the unique words that occur in the entire *corpus*. Corpus is a term for the entire group of documents we are considering.

In [3]:

```
vocabulary = set(" ".join(docs).split())
```

We can remove some words that are unlikely to help us. These throwaway words are called *stop words*. After we remove them, we are left with our vocabulary of words that show up in the corpus.

In [4]:

```
common_words = set(['a', 'to', 'the', 'in', 'and', 'are'])
vocabulary = vocabulary - common_words
print(textwrap.fill(str(vocabulary)))
```

```
{'cow', 'not', 'cat', 'moon', 'jumped', 'meowed', 'said', 'mooed',
'you', 'over', 'hat'}
```

14.1.1.1   Binary Bags of Words

With our vocabulary in place, some quick MacGyver-ing with Python gets us a simple yes/no table of words in documents. The key test is the `w in d` that asks if a word is in a document.

In [5]:

```
# {k:v for k in lst} creates a dictionary from keys:values
# it is called a "dictionary comprehension"
doc_contains = [{w:(w in d) for w in vocabulary} for d in docs]
display(pd.DataFrame(doc_contains))
```

	cat	cow	hat	jumped	meowed	mooed	moon	not	over	said	you
0	True	False	True	False	False	False	False	False	False	False	False
1	False	True	False	True	False	False	True	False	True	False	False
2	True	True	False	False	True	True	False	False	False	False	False
3	True	True	False	False	False	False	False	True	False	True	True

14.1.1.2 Bag-of-Word Counts

A tiny alteration to the first line of code gives us the *counts* of words in documents:

In [6]:

```
word_count = [{w:d.count(w) for w in vocabulary} for d in docs]
wcs = pd.DataFrame(word_count)
display(wcs)
```

	cat	cow	hat	jumped	meowed	mooed	moon	not	over	said	you
0	1	0	1	0	0	0	0	0	0	0	0
1	0	1	0	1	0	0	1	0	1	0	0
2	1	1	0	0	1	1	0	0	0	0	0
3	2	2	0	0	0	0	0	1	0	1	1

sklearn gives us this capability with CountVectorizer.

In [7]:

```
import sklearn.feature_extraction.text as sk_txt
sparse = sk_txt.CountVectorizer(stop_words='english').fit_transform(docs)
sparse
```

Out[7]:

```
<4x8 sparse matrix of type '<class 'numpy.int64'>'
 with 12 stored elements in Compressed Sparse Row format>
```

As I mentioned, since the data is sparse and sklearn is clever, the underlying machinery is saving us space. If you *really* want to see what's going on, turn a sparse form into a dense form with todense:

In [8]:

```
sparse.todense()
```

Out[8]:

```
matrix([[1, 0, 1, 0, 0, 0, 0, 0],
        [0, 1, 0, 1, 0, 0, 1, 0],
        [1, 1, 0, 0, 1, 1, 0, 0],
        [2, 2, 0, 0, 0, 0, 0, 1]], dtype=int64)
```

We see some slightly different results here because sklearn uses a few more stop words: *you*, *not*, and *over* are in the default English stop word list. Also, it's not obvious what the ordering of the words is in the sklearn output. But, it's all there.

14.1.1.3 Normalized Bag-of-Word Counts: TF-IDF

As we've seen in many cases—from means to covariances to error rates—we often *normalize* results so they are compared against some sort of baseline or other standard. In the case of word counts, there are two things we would like to balance:

1. We don't want longer documents to have stronger relationships with our target just because they have more words.
2. If words are frequent in *every* document, they no longer become a distinguishing factor. So, as frequency of a word increases across the corpus, we'd like the contribution of that word to drop.

Let's start by accounting for the frequency across all of the documents. We can compute that corpus-wide frequency by asking, "How many documents contain our word?" We can implement that as

In [9]:

```
# wcs.values.sum(axis=0, keepdims=True)
doc_freq = pd.DataFrame(wcs.astype(np.bool).sum(axis='rows')).T
display(doc_freq)
```

	cat	cow	hat	jumped	meowed	mooed	moon	not	over	said	you
0	3	3	1	1	1	1	1	1	1	1	1

Now, we're going to take a small leap and go from a corpus frequency to an *inverse* frequency. Normally, that means we would do something like $\frac{1}{\text{freq}}$. However, the usual way this is done in text learning is a bit more complicated: we account for the number of documents and we take the logarithm of the value. Our formula for inverse-document frequency will be $\text{IDF} = \log(\frac{\text{num docs}}{\text{freq}})$.

Why take the log? Logarithms have a magnifying and dilating effect. Basically, taking the log of values greater than one—such as a positive number of documents—*compresses* the difference between values, while taking the log of values between zero and one—such as one divided by a count—*expands* the spacing. So, the log here amplifies the effect of different counts and suppresses the value of more and more documents. The number of documents in the numerator serves as a baseline value from which we adjust down.

In [10]:

```
idf = np.log(len(docs) / doc_freq)
#  == np.log(len(docs)) - np.log(doc_freq)
display(idf)
```

	cat	cow	hat	jumped	meowed	mooed	moon	not	over	said	you
0	0.29	0.29	1.39	1.39	1.39	1.39	1.39	1.39	1.39	1.39	1.39

With this calculation, it's an easy step to create the *term frequency-inverse document frequency*, or TF-IDF. All we do is weight each word count by its respective IDF value. Done.

In [11]:

```
tf_idf = wcs * idf.iloc[0]   # aligns columns for multiplication
display(tf_idf)
```

	cat	cow	hat	jumped	meowed	mooed	moon	not	over	said	you
0	0.29	0.00	1.39	0.00	0.00	0.00	0.00	0.00	0.00	0.00	0.0000
1	0.00	0.29	0.00	1.39	0.00	0.00	1.39	0.00	1.39	0.00	0.0000
2	0.29	0.29	0.00	0.00	1.39	1.39	0.00	0.00	0.00	0.00	0.0000
3	0.58	0.58	0.00	0.00	0.00	0.00	0.00	1.39	0.00	1.39	1.39

Now, we haven't accounted for the unwanted benefits that longer documents might get. We can keep them under control by insisting that the total values across a document—when we add up all the weighted counts—be the same. This means documents are differentiated by the *proportion* of a fixed weight distributed over the word buckets, instead of the total amount across the buckets (which is now the same for everyone). We can do that with `Normalizer`.

In [12]:

```
skpre.Normalizer(norm='l1').fit_transform(wcs)
```

Out[12]:

```
array([[0.5   , 0.    , 0.5   , 0.    , 0.    , 0.    , 0.    , 0.    ,
        0.    , 0.    , 0.    ],
       [0.    , 0.25  , 0.    , 0.25  , 0.    , 0.    , 0.25  , 0.    ,
        0.25  , 0.    , 0.    ],
       [0.25  , 0.25  , 0.    , 0.    , 0.25  , 0.25  , 0.    , 0.    ,
        0.    , 0.    , 0.    ],
       [0.2857, 0.2857, 0.    , 0.    , 0.    , 0.    , 0.    , 0.1429,
        0.    , 0.1429, 0.1429]])
```

The sum across a row is now 1.0.

Our process mimics—inexactly—the same steps that `sklearn` performs with `TfidfVectorizer`. We won't try to reconcile our manual steps with the `sklearn` method; just remember that, at a minimum, we are using different stop words which affects the weightings used for the IDF weights.

```
In [13]:

sparse = (sk_txt.TfidfVectorizer(norm='l1', stop_words='english')
                 .fit_transform(docs))
sparse.todense()
```

```
Out[13]:

matrix([[0.3896, 0.    , 0.6104, 0.    , 0.    , 0.    , 0.    , 0.    ],
        [0.    , 0.2419, 0.    , 0.379 , 0.    , 0.    , 0.379 , 0.    ],
        [0.1948, 0.1948, 0.    , 0.    , 0.3052, 0.3052, 0.    , 0.    ],
        [0.3593, 0.3593, 0.    , 0.    , 0.    , 0.    , 0.    , 0.2814]])
```

14.1.2 Example of Text Learning

To put these ideas into practice, we need a legitimate body of preclassified documents. Fortunately, `sklearn` has tools to get it for us. The data is not installed with your `sklearn` distribution; instead, you need to `import` and call a utility that will download it. The following `import` will do the necessary steps.

```
In [14]:

from sklearn.datasets import fetch_20newsgroups
twenty_train = fetch_20newsgroups(subset='train')
```

The *Twenty Newsgroups* dataset consists of about 20,000 documents from 20 old–school Internet *newsgroups*. Newsgroups are a type of online forum that acts a bit like an email thread that multiple people can participate in at once. There are newsgroups for many different discussion topics: religion and politics are always particularly spicy, but there are groups for various sports, hobbies, and other interests. The classification problem is to take an arbitrary document and determine which discussion group it came from.

```
In [15]:

print("the groups:")
print(textwrap.fill(str(twenty_train.target_names)))
```

```
the groups:
['alt.atheism', 'comp.graphics', 'comp.os.ms-windows.misc',
 'comp.sys.ibm.pc.hardware', 'comp.sys.mac.hardware', 'comp.windows.x',
 'misc.forsale', 'rec.autos', 'rec.motorcycles', 'rec.sport.baseball',
 'rec.sport.hockey', 'sci.crypt', 'sci.electronics', 'sci.med',
 'sci.space', 'soc.religion.christian', 'talk.politics.guns',
 'talk.politics.mideast', 'talk.politics.misc', 'talk.religion.misc']
```

The actual contents of the examples are text emails including the header portion with a sender, receiver, and a subject. Here are the first ten lines of the first example:

In [16]:

```
print("\n".join(twenty_train.data[0].splitlines()[:10]))
```

```
From: lerxst@wam.umd.edu (where's my thing)
Subject: WHAT car is this!?
Nntp-Posting-Host: rac3.wam.umd.edu
Organization: University of Maryland, College Park
Lines: 15

 I was wondering if anyone out there could enlighten me on this car I saw
the other day. It was a 2-door sports car, looked to be from the late 60s/
early 70s. It was called a Bricklin. The doors were really small. In addition,
the front bumper was separate from the rest of the body. This is
```

Once we have the data available, we can almost instantly apply the TF-IDF transformer to get a useful representation of our documents.

In [17]:

```
ct_vect     = sk_txt.CountVectorizer()
tfidf_xform = sk_txt.TfidfTransformer()

docs_as_counts = ct_vect.fit_transform(twenty_train.data)
docs_as_tfidf  = tfidf_xform.fit_transform(docs_as_counts)
```

We can connect that data to any of our learning models. Here we use a variant of Naive Bayes:

In [18]:

```
model = naive_bayes.MultinomialNB().fit(docs_as_tfidf,
                                         twenty_train.target)
```

Now, you might ask if we can take all these steps and wrap them up in a pipeline. Of course we can!

In [19]:

```
doc_pipeline = pipeline.make_pipeline(sk_txt.CountVectorizer(),
                                      sk_txt.TfidfTransformer(),
                                      naive_bayes.MultinomialNB())
```

Before we ramp up for evaluation, let's reduce the number of categories we consider:

In [20]:

```
categories = ['misc.forsale',
              'comp.graphics',
              'sci.med',
              'sci.space']
```

We can even go one step better. `TfidfVectorizer` combines the two preprocessing, feature-extracting steps in one component. So, here is a super compact approach to this problem:

In [21]:

```
twenty_train = fetch_20newsgroups(subset='train',
                                  categories=categories,
                                  shuffle=True,
                                  random_state=42)

doc_pipeline = pipeline.make_pipeline(sk_txt.TfidfVectorizer(),
                                      naive_bayes.MultinomialNB())

model = doc_pipeline.fit(twenty_train.data, twenty_train.target)
```

And we can quickly evaluate the quality of our model:

In [22]:

```
twenty_test = fetch_20newsgroups(subset='test',
                                 categories=categories,
                                 shuffle=True,
                                 random_state=42)

doc_preds = model.predict(twenty_test.data)
cm = metrics.confusion_matrix(twenty_test.target, doc_preds)
ax = sns.heatmap(cm, annot=True,
                 xticklabels=twenty_test.target_names,
                 yticklabels=twenty_test.target_names,
                 fmt='3d') # cells are counts
ax.set_xlabel('Predicted')
ax.set_ylabel('Actual');
```

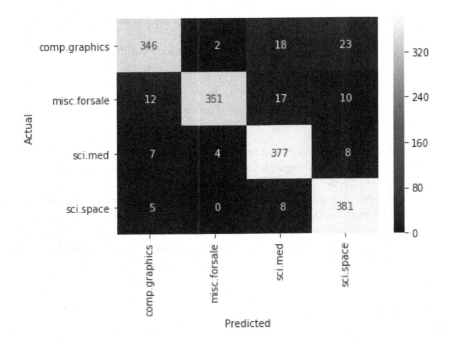

I hope that makes you smile. We've done *a lot* of work to get to this point. We are now putting together (1) feature engineering in the form of feature extraction from text documents to an example-feature table, (2) building a learning model from training data, and (3) looking at the evaluation of that model on separate testing data—all in about 25 lines of code over the last two code cells. Our results don't look too bad, either. Hopefully, you *understand* something about each of that steps we've just accomplished.

14.2 Clustering

Shortly, we are going to discuss some techniques to use for classifying *images*. One large component in that process is *clustering*. So, let's take a few minutes to describe clustering.

Clustering is a method of grouping similar examples together. When we cluster, we don't make an explicit appeal to some known target value. Instead, we have some preset standard that we use to decide what is the same and what is different in our examples. Just like PCA, clustering is an unsupervised learning technique (see Section 13.3). PCA maps examples to some linear thing (a point, line, or plane); clustering maps examples to *groups*.

14.2.1 *k*-Means Clustering

There are a number of ways to perform clustering. We will focus on one called *k-Means Clustering* (*k*-MC). The idea of *k*-Means Clustering is that we assume there are *k* groups each of which has a distinct center. We then try to partition the examples into those k groups.

It turns out that there is a pretty simple process to extract out the groups:

1. Randomly pick k centers.
2. Assign examples to groups based on the closest center.
3. Recompute the centers from the assigned groups.
4. Return to step 2.

Eventually, this process will result in only very small changes to the centers. At that point, we can say we have converged on a good answer. Those centers form the foundations of our groups.

While we *can* use clustering without a known target, if we happen to have one we can compare our clustered results with reality. Here's an example with the *iris* dataset. To make a convenient visualization, we're going to start by using PCA to reduce our data to two dimensions. Then, in those two dimensions, we can look at where the actual three varieties of iris fall. Finally, we can see the clusters that we get by using k-MC.

In [23]:

```
iris = datasets.load_iris()
twod_iris = (decomposition.PCA(n_components=2, whiten=True)
                          .fit_transform(iris.data))
clusters = cluster.KMeans(n_clusters=3).fit(twod_iris)

fig, axes = plt.subplots(1,2,figsize=(8,4))
axes[0].scatter(*twod_iris.T, c=iris.target)
axes[1].scatter(*twod_iris.T, c=clusters.labels_)

axes[0].set_title("Truth"), axes[1].set_title("Clustered");
```

You'll quickly notice that k-MC split the two mixed species the wrong way—in reality they were split more vertically, but k-MC split them horizontally. Without the target value—the actual species—to distinguish the two, the algorithm doesn't have any guidance about the *right* way to tell apart the intertwined species. More to the point, in clustering, there is no definition of *right*. The standard is simply defined by how the algorithm operates.

Although `sklearn` doesn't currently provide them as off-the-shelf techniques, k-MC and other clustering techniques can be kernelized in the same fashion as the methods we discussed in Section 13.2. In the next section, we are going to use clusters to find and define synonyms of *visual words* to build a global vocabulary across different local vocabularies. We will group together different local words that mean approximately the same thing into single, representative global words.

14.3 Working with Images

There are many, many ways to work with images that enable learners to classify them. We've talked about using kernels for nontabular data. Clever folks have created many ways to extract features from raw image pixels. More advanced learning techniques—like deep neural networks—can build very complicated, useful features from images. Whole books are available on these topics; we can't hope to cover all of that ground. Instead, we are going to focus on one technique that very nicely builds from the two prior topics in the chapter: bags of words and clustering. By using these two techniques in concert, we will be able to build a powerful feature extractor that will transform our images from a grid of pixels into a table of usable and useful learning features.

14.3.1 Bag of Visual Words

We have an overall strategy that we want to implement. We want to—somehow—mimic the bag-of-words approach that we used in text classification, but with images. Since we don't have literal words, we need to come up with some. Fortunately, there's a very elegant way to do that. I'll give you a storytime view of the process and then we'll dive into the details.

Imagine you are at a party. The party is hosted at an art museum, but it is attended by people from all walks of life and from all over the world. The art museum is very large: you have no hope of checking out every painting. But, you stroll around for a while and start developing some ideas about what you like and what you don't like. After a while, you get tired and head to the cafe for some refreshments. As you sip your refreshing beverage, you notice that there are other folks, also tired, sitting around you. You wonder if they might have some good recommendations as to what other paintings you should check out.

There are several levels of difficulty in getting recommendations. All of the attendees have their own likes and dislikes about art; there are many different, simple and sophisticated, ways of describing those preferences; and many of the attendees speak different languages. Now, you could mill around and get a few recommendations from those people who speak your language and seem to describe their preferences in a way that makes sense to you. But imagine all the other information you are missing out on! If there were a way we could translate all of these *individual vocabularies* into a *group vocabulary* that all the attendees could use to describe the paintings, then we could get everyone to see paintings that they might enjoy.

The way we will attack this problem is by combining all of the individual vocabularies and grouping them into *synonyms*. Then, every term that an individual would use to describe a painting can be translated into the global synonym. For example, all terms that are similar to *red*—scarlet, ruby, maroon—could be translated to the single term *red*. Once we do this, instead of having dozens of incompatible vocabularies, we have a single group vocabulary that can describe the paintings in common way. We will use this group vocabulary as the basis for our bag of words. Then, we can follow a process much like our text classification to build our learning model.

14.3.2 Our Image Data

We need some data to work with. We are going to make use of the *Caltech101* dataset. If you want to play along at home, download and uncompress the data from www.vision .caltech.edu/Image_Datasets/Caltech101/101_ObjectCategories.tar.gz.

There are 101 total categories in the dataset. The categories represent objects in the world, such as cats and airplanes. You'll see 102 categories below because there are two sets of faces, one hard and one easy.

In [24]:

```
# exploring the data
objcat_path = "./data/101_ObjectCategories"
cat_paths = glob.glob(osp.join(objcat_path, "*"))
all_categories = [d.split('/')[-1] for d in cat_paths]

print("number of categories:", len(all_categories))
print("first 10 categories:\n",
      textwrap.fill(str(all_categories[:10])))
```

```
number of categories: 102
first 10 categories:
 ['accordion', 'airplanes', 'anchor', 'ant', 'BACKGROUND_Google',
'barrel', 'bass', 'beaver', 'binocular', 'bonsai']
```

The data itself is literally graphics files. Here's an accordion:

```
In [25]:

from skimage.io import imread

test_path = osp.join(objcat_path, 'accordion', 'image_0001.jpg')
test_img = imread(test_path)

fig, ax = plt.subplots(1,1,figsize=(2,2))
ax.imshow(test_img)
ax.axis('off');
```

It's probably a reasonable guess that without some preprocessing—feature extraction—we have little hope of classifying these images correctly.

14.3.3 An End-to-End System

For our learning problem, we have a basket of images and a category they come from. Our strategy to make an end-to-end learning system is shown in Figures 14.1 and 14.2. Here are the major steps:

1. Describe each image in terms of its own, local visual words.
2. Group those local words into their respective synonyms. The synonyms will form our global visual vocabulary.
3. Translate each local visual word into a global visual word.
4. Replace the list of global visual words with the counts of the global words. This gives us a BoGVW—*bag of (global visual) words* (or simply BoVW, for *bag of visual words*).
5. Learn the relationship between the BoGVW and the target categories.

When we want to predict a new test image, we will:

1. Convert the test image to its own local words.
2. Translate the local words to global words.
3. Create the BoGVW for the test image.
4. Predict with the BoGVW.

The prediction process for a new test image relies on two components from the trained learning system: the translator we built in step 2 and the learning model we built in step 5.

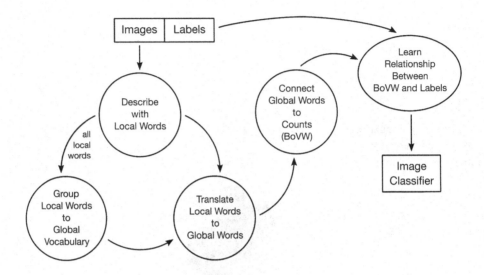

Figure 14.1   Outline of our image labeling system.

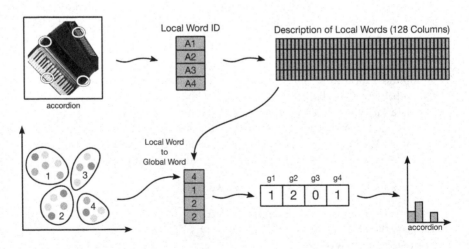

Figure 14.2   Graphical view of steps in of our image labeling system.

14.3.3.1 Extracting Local Visual Words

Converting an image into its local-word form is the one black box that we won't open. We will simply use a routine out of OpenCV, an image processing library, called `SIFT_create`, that can pull out interesting pieces of an image. Here, *interesting* refers to things like the orientations of edges and the corners of shapes in the image. Every image gets converted to a table of local words. Each image's table has the same number of columns but its own number of rows. Some images have more remarkable characteristics that need to be described using more rows. Graphically, this looks like Figure 14.3.

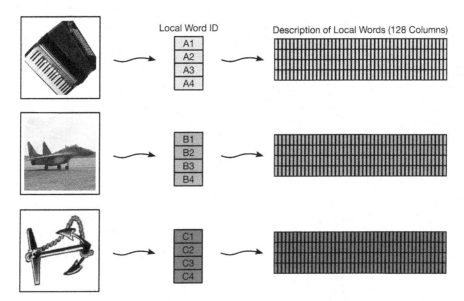

Figure 14.3   Extracting local visual words from the images.

We'll make use of a few helper functions to locate the image files on our hard drive and to extract the local words from each image.

In [26]:

```python
def img_to_local_words(img):
    ' heavy lifting of creating local visual words from image '
    sift = cv2.xfeatures2d.SIFT_create()
    key_points, descriptors = sift.detectAndCompute(img, None)
    return descriptors

def id_to_path(img_id):
    ' helper to get file location '
    cat, num = img_id
    return osp.join(objcat_path, cat, "image_{:04d}.jpg".format(num))
```

```
def add_local_words_for_img(local_ftrs, img_id):
    ' update local_ftrs inplace '
    cat, _ = img_id
    img_path = id_to_path(img_id)
    img = imread(img_path)
    local_ftrs.setdefault(cat, []).append(img_to_local_words(img))
```

Since processing images can take a lot of time, we'll restrict ourselves to just a few categories for our discussion. We'll also set a limit on the number of global vocabulary words we're willing to create.

In [27]:

```
# set up a few constants
use_cats = ['accordion', 'airplanes', 'anchor']
use_imgs = range(1,11)

img_ids  = list(it.product(use_cats, use_imgs))
num_imgs = len(img_ids)

global_vocab_size = 20
```

What do the local visual words look like? Since they are *visual* words and not *written* words, they aren't made up of letters. Instead, they are made up of numbers that summarize interesting regions of the image. Images with more interesting regions have more rows.

In [28]:

```
# turn each image into a table of local visual words
# (1 table per image, 1 word per row)
local_words = {}
for img_id in img_ids:
    add_local_words_for_img(local_words, img_id)
print(local_words.keys())
```

```
dict_keys(['accordion', 'airplanes', 'anchor'])
```

Over the three categories, we've processed the first 10 images (from the `use_imgs` variable), so we've processed 30 images. Here are the numbers of local words for each image:

In [29]:

```
# itcfi is basically a way to get each individual item from an
# iterator of items; it's a long name, so I abbreviate it
itcfi = it.chain.from_iterable
```

```
img_local_word_cts = [lf.shape[0] for lf in itcfi(local_words.values())]
print("num of local words for images:")
print(textwrap.fill(str(img_local_word_cts), width=50))
```

```
num of local words for images:
[804, 796, 968, 606, 575, 728, 881, 504, 915, 395,
350, 207, 466, 562, 617, 288, 348, 671, 328, 243,
102, 271, 580, 314, 48, 629, 417, 62, 249, 535]
```

Let's try to get a handle on how many local words there are in total.

In [30]:

```
# how wide are the local word tables
num_local_words = local_words[use_cats[0]][0].shape[1]

# how many local words are there in total?
all_local_words = list(itcfi(local_words.values()))
tot_num_local_words = sum(lw.shape[0] for lw in all_local_words)
print('total num local words:', tot_num_local_words)

# construct joined local tables to perform clustering
# np_array_fromiter is described at the end of the chapter
lwa_shape = (tot_num_local_words, num_local_words)
local_word_arr = np_array_fromiter(itcfi(all_local_words),
                                   lwa_shape)
print('local word tbl:', local_word_arr.shape)
```

```
total num local words: 14459
local word tbl: (14459, 128)
```

We've got about 15,000 local visual words. Each local word is made up of 128 numbers. You can think of this as 15,000 words that have 128 letters in each. Yes, it's weird that all the words have the same length . . . but that's a limit of our analogy. Life's hard sometimes.

14.3.3.2 Global Vocabulary and Translation

Now, we need to find out which local visual words are synonyms of each other. We do that by clustering the local visual words together to form the global visual word vocabulary, as in Figure 14.4. Our global vocabulary looks super simple: term 0, term 1, term 2. It's uninteresting for us—but we are finally down to common descriptions that we can use in our standard classifiers.

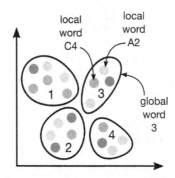

Figure 14.4 Creating the global vocabulary.

In [31]:

```
# cluster (and translate) the local words to global words
translator = cluster.KMeans(n_clusters=global_vocab_size)
global_words = translator.fit_predict(local_word_arr)
print('translated words shape:', global_words.shape)
```

```
translated words shape: (14459,)
```

14.3.3.3 Bags of Global Visual Words and Learning

Now that we have our global vocabulary, we can describe each image as a bag of global visual words, as in Figure 14.5. We just have to morph the global words table and image identifiers into a table of global word counts—effectively, each image is now a *single* histogram as in Figure 14.6—against the respective image category.

In [32]:

```
# which image do the local words belong to
# enumerate_outer is descibed at the end of the chapter
which_img = enumerate_outer(all_local_words)
print('which img len:', len(which_img))

# image by global words -> image by histogram
counts = co.Counter(zip(which_img, global_words))
imgs_as_bogvw = np.zeros((num_imgs, global_vocab_size))
for (img, global_word), count in counts.items():
    imgs_as_bogvw[img, global_word] = count
print('shape hist table:', imgs_as_bogvw.shape)
```

```
which img len: 14459
shape hist table: (30, 20)
```

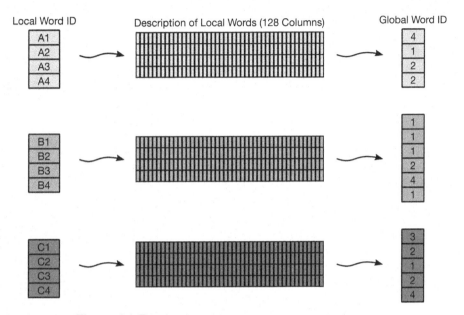

Figure 14.5   Translating local words to the global vocabulary.

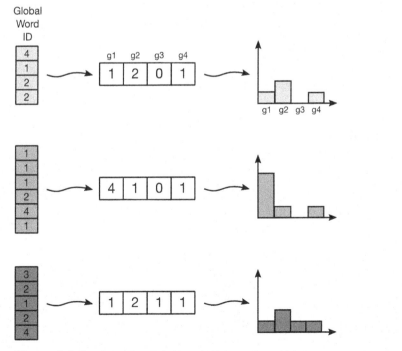

Figure 14.6   Collecting global vocabulary counts as histograms.

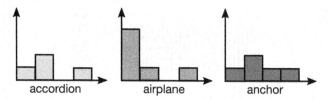

Figure 14.7   Associating the histograms with a category.

After all that work, we still need a target: the category that each image came from. Conceptually, this gives us each category of images as the target for a histogram-which-is-our-example (see Figure 14.7).

In [33]:

```
# a bit of a hack; local_ftrs.values() gives
# [[img1, img2], [img3, img4, img5], etc.]
# answers: what category am i from?
img_tgts = enumerate_outer(local_words.values())
print('img tgt values:', img_tgts[:10])
```

```
img tgt values: [0 0 0 0 0 0 0 0 0 0]
```

Finally, we can fit our learning model.

In [34]:

```
# build learning model
std_svc = pipeline.make_pipeline(skpre.StandardScaler(), svm.SVC())
svc = std_svc.fit(imgs_as_bogvw, img_tgts)
```

14.3.3.4 Prediction

Now we can recreate the prediction steps we talked about in the overview. We break the prediction steps into two subtasks:

1. Converting the image on disk into a row–like example in the BoGVW representation
2. Performing the actual **predict** call on that example

In [35]:

```
def image_to_example(img_id, translator):
    ' from an id, produce an example with global words '
    img_local  = img_to_local_words(imread(id_to_path(img_id)))
    img_global = translator.predict(img_local)
    img_bogvw  = np.bincount(img_global,
                             minlength=translator.n_clusters)
    return img_bogvw.reshape(1,-1).astype(np.float64)
```

We'll check out the predictions from image number 12—an image we didn't use for training—for each category.

In [36]:

```
for cat in use_cats:
    test = image_to_example((cat, 12), translator)
    print(svc.predict(test))
```

```
[0]
[1]
[2]
```

We'll take a closer look at our success rate in a moment.

14.3.4 Complete Code of BoVW Transformer

Now, you can be forgiven if you lost the track while we wandered through that dark forest. To recap, here is the same code but in a streamlined form. Thanks the helper functions—one of which (`add_local_words_for_img`) is domain-specific for images and others (`enumerate_outer` and `np_array_fromiter`) are generic solutions to Python/NumPy problems—it's just over thirty lines of code to build the learning model. We can wrap that code up in a transformer and put it to use in a pipeline:

In [37]:

```
class BoVW_XForm:
    def __init__(self):
        pass

    def _to_local_words(self, img_ids):
        # turn each image into table of local visual words (1 word per row)
        local_words = {}
        for img_id in img_ids:
            add_local_words_for_img(local_words, img_id)

        itcfi = it.chain.from_iterable
        all_local_words = list(itcfi(local_words.values()))
        return all_local_words

    def fit(self, img_ids, tgt=None):
        all_local_words = self._to_local_words(img_ids)
        tot_num_local_words = sum(lw.shape[0] for lw in all_local_words)
        local_word_arr = np_array_fromiter(itcfi(all_local_words),
                                           (tot_num_local_words,
                                            num_local_words))
```

```
        self.translator = cluster.KMeans(n_clusters=global_vocab_size)
        self.translator.fit(local_word_arr)
        return self

    def transform(self, img_ids, tgt=None):
        all_local_words = self._to_local_words(img_ids)
        tot_num_local_words = sum(lw.shape[0] for lw in all_local_words)
        local_word_arr = np_array_fromiter(itcfi(all_local_words),
                                           (tot_num_local_words,
                                            num_local_words))
        global_words = self.translator.predict(local_word_arr)

        # image by global words -> image by histogram
        which_img = enumerate_outer(all_local_words)
        counts = co.Counter(zip(which_img, global_words))
        imgs_as_bogvw = np.zeros((len(img_ids), global_vocab_size))
        for (img, global_word), count in counts.items():
            imgs_as_bogvw[img, global_word] = count
        return imgs_as_bogvw
```

Let's use some different categories with our transformer and up our amount of training data.

In [38]:

```
use_cats = ['watch', 'umbrella', 'sunflower', 'kangaroo']
use_imgs = range(1,40)

img_ids  = list(it.product(use_cats, use_imgs))
num_imgs = len(img_ids)

# hack
cat_id = {c:i for i,c in enumerate(use_cats)}
img_tgts = [cat_id[ii[0]] for ii in img_ids]
```

Now, we can build a model from training data.

In [39]:

```
(train_img, test_img,
 train_tgt, test_tgt) = skms.train_test_split(img_ids, img_tgts)
bovw_pipe = pipeline.make_pipeline(BoVW_XForm(),
                                   skpre.StandardScaler(),
                                   svm.SVC())
bovw_pipe.fit(train_img, train_tgt);
```

and we just about get the confusion matrix for free:

```
In [40]:

img_preds = bovw_pipe.predict(test_img)
cm = metrics.confusion_matrix(test_tgt, img_preds)
ax = sns.heatmap(cm, annot=True,
                 xticklabels=use_cats,
                 yticklabels=use_cats,
                 fmt='3d')
ax.set_xlabel('Predicted')
ax.set_ylabel('Actual');
```

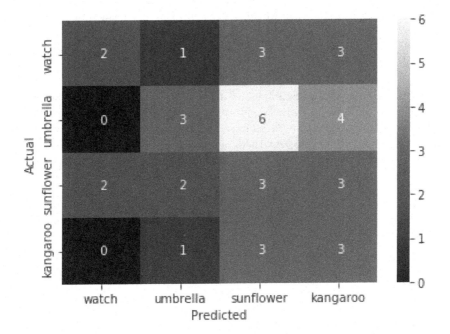

These results aren't stellar, but we also haven't tuned the system at all. You'll have a chance to do that in the exercises. The lesson here is that with a ~30-line transformer, we are well on our way to learning the categories of images.

14.4 EOC

14.4.1 Summary

We've taken an even-more-practical-than-usual turn: now we have some tools to work with text and graphics. Along the way, we explored some methods for turning text into learnable features. Then, we saw how to use characteristics of images—in analogy with words—to create learnable features from graphics. Coupled with a new technique called clustering, which we used to gather similar visual words together into a common visual vocabulary, we were able to classify images.

14.4.2   Notes

If you'd like to see the exact stop words used by `sklearn`, go to the `sklearn` source code (for example, on github) and find the following file: `sklearn/feature_extraction /stop_words.py`.

If we cluster over all of the features, we will get a single group (one cluster label) for each example—a single categorical value. You could consider performing clustering on different subsets of features. Then, we might get out *several* new quasi-columns containing our clusters with respect to the different subsets. Conceptually, using a few of these columns—several different views of data—might get us better predictive power in a learning problem.

Helpers   There are two quick utilities we made use of in our bag-of-visual-words system. The first is similar to Python's built-in `enumerate` which augments the elements of a Python iterable with their numeric indices. Our `enumerate_outer` takes an iterable of sequences—things with lengths—and adds numeric labels indicating the position in the outer sequence that the inner element came from. The second helper takes us from an iterable of example-like things with the same number of features to an `np.array` of those rows. `numpy` has a built-in `np.fromiter` but that only works when the output is a single conceptual column.

In [41]:

```
def enumerate_outer(outer_seq):
    '''repeat the outer idx based on len of inner'''
    return np.repeat(*zip(*enumerate(map(len, outer_seq))))

def np_array_fromiter(itr, shape, dtype=np.float64):
    ''' helper since np.fromiter only does 1D'''
    arr = np.empty(shape, dtype=dtype)
    for idx, itm in enumerate(itr):
        arr[idx] = itm
    return arr
```

Here are some quick examples of using these helpers:

In [42]:

```
enumerate_outer([[0, 1], [10, 20, 30], [100, 200]])
```

Out[42]:

```
array([0, 0, 1, 1, 1, 2, 2])
```

In [43]:

```
np_array_fromiter(enumerate(range(0,50,10)), (5,2))
```

Out[43]:

```
array([[ 0.,   0.],
       [ 1.,  10.],
       [ 2.,  20.],
       [ 3.,  30.],
       [ 4.,  40.]])
```

14.4.3 Exercises

1. Conceptually, we could normalize—with `skpre.Normalizer`—immediately once we have document word counts, *or* we could normalize after we compute the TF-IDF values. Do both make sense? Try both methods and look at the results. Do some research and figure out which method `TfidfVectorizer` uses. Hint: use the source, Luke.

2. In the newsgroups example, we used `TfidfVectorizer`. Behind the scenes, the vectorizer is quite clever: it uses a sparse format to save memory. Since we built a pipeline, the documents have to flow through the vectorizer every time we remodel. That seems very time-consuming. Compare the amount of time it takes to do 10-fold cross-validation with a pipeline that includes `TfidfVectorizer` versus performing a *single* `TfidfVectorizer` step with the input data and then performing 10-fold cross-validation on that transformed data. Are there any dangers in "factoring out" the `TfidfVectorizer` step?

3. Build models for all pairwise newsgroups classification problems. What two groups are the most difficult to tell apart? Phrased differently, what two groups have the lowest (worst) classification metrics when paired off one-versus-one?

4. We clustered the *iris* dataset by first preprocessing with PCA. It turns out that we can *also* preprocess it by using `discriminant_analysis.LinearDiscriminantAnalysis` (LDA) with a `n_components` parameter. From a certain perspective, this gives us a class-aware version of PCA: instead of minimizing the variance over the whole dataset, we minimize the variance between classes. Try it! Use `discriminant_analysis.LinearDiscriminantAnalysis` to create two good features for *iris* and then cluster the result. Compare with the PCA clusters.

5. We used a single, fixed global vocabulary size in our image classification system. What are the effects of different global vocabulary size on learning performance and on resource usage?

6. We evaluated our image classification system using a confusion matrix. Extend that evaluation to include an ROC curve and a PRC.

7. In the image system, does using more categories help with *overall* performance? What about performance on individual categories? For example, if we train with 10 or 20 categories, does our performance on kangaroos increase?

Connections, Extensions, and Further Directions

In [1]:

```
from mlwpy import *
```

15.1 Optimization

When we try to find a *best* line, curve, or tree to match our data—which is our main goal in training—we want to have an automated method do the work for us. We're not asking the hot dog vendor for a quick stock tip: we need an algorithm. One of the principal— principled—ways to do this is by assessing our cost and looking for ways to lower that cost. Remember, the cost is a combination of the loss—how well our model's predictions match the training data—and the complexity of the model. When we minimize cost, we try to achieve a small loss while keeping a low complexity. We can't always get to that ideal, but that's our goal.

When we train a learning model, one of the easiest parameters to think about is the weights—from linear or logistic regression—that we combine with the feature values to get our predictions. Since we get to adjust the weights, we can look at the effect of adjusting them and see what happens to the cost. If we have a definition of the cost—a cost *function*, perhaps drawn as a graph—we can turn the adjusting process into a question. From where we are—that is, from our current weights and the cost we get by using them—what small adjustments to the weights can we make? Is there a direction that we can go that will result in a *lower* cost? A way to think about this visually is to ask what direction is *downhill* on our cost function. Let's look at an example.

In [2]:

```
xs = np.linspace(-5,5)
ys = xs**2

fig, ax = plt.subplots(figsize=(4,3))
```

```
ax.plot(xs, ys)

# better Python:
# pt = co.namedtuple('Point', ['x', 'y'])(3,3**2)
pt_x, pt_y = 3, 3**2
ax.plot(pt_x, pt_y, 'ro')

line_xs = pt_x + np.array([-2, 2])
# line ys = mid_point + (x amount) * slope_of_line
# one step right gets one "slope of line" increase in that line's up
line_ys = 3**2 + (line_xs - pt_x) * (2 * pt_x)
ax.plot(line_xs, line_ys, 'r-')
ax.set_xlabel('weight')
ax.set_ylabel('cost');
```

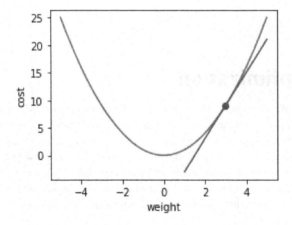

In this simple example, if we put an imaginary ball at the red dot, it would roll downward to the left. The red line represents the *slope*—how steep the blue graph is—at that point. You can imagine that if we are trying to find a low point, we want to follow the slope—with Jack and Jill down the proverbial hill. You might also find it reasonable to be *more confident* in our direction if the slope is steeper—that is, we can roll down the hill faster if there is a steeper slope. If we do that, here's one take on what can happen.

From the starting point of weight = 3 that we just saw, we can take a step down the hill by moving to the left. We'll take a step that is moderated by the slope at our current point. Then we'll repeat the process. We'll try this ten times and see what happens. Note that we could have picked the starting point randomly—we'd have to be pretty lucky for it to be the minimum.

In [3]:

```
weights = np.linspace(-5,5)
costs    = weights**2
```

```
fig, ax = plt.subplots(figsize=(4,3))
ax.plot(weights, costs, 'b')

# current best guess at the minimum
weight_min = 3

# we can follow the path downhill from our starting point
# and find out the weight value where our initial, blue graph is
# (approximately) the lowest
for i in range(10):
    # for a weight, we can figure out the cost
    cost_at_min = weight_min**2
    ax.plot(weight_min, cost_at_min, 'ro')

    # also, we can figure out the slope (steepness)
    # (via a magic incantation called a "derivative")
    slope_at_min = 2*weight_min

    # new best guess made by walking downhill
    step_size = .25
    weight_min = weight_min - step_size * slope_at_min

ax.set_xlabel('weight value')
ax.set_ylabel('cost')
print("Approximate location of blue graph minimum:", weight_min)
```

Approximate location of blue graph minimum: 0.0029296875

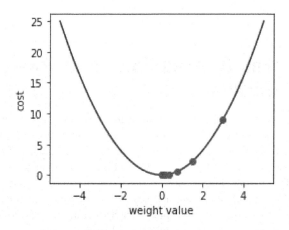

We gradually approach weight = 0 which is the actual minimum of the blue curve defined by weight^2. In this example, we never really went past the low point because we took relatively small steps (based on the `step_size = .25` in the `weight_min` assignment). You can imagine that if we took slightly bigger steps, we might shoot beyond the low point. That's OK. We would then recognize that the downhill direction is now *to the right* and we can follow that path down. There are many details I'm sweeping under the carpet—but we can eventually settle in on the low point. In reality, we might only get a value very close to zero—0.0000000001, perhaps—but that is probably good enough.

We can apply many different strategies to find the minimum. We don't have to do the downhill walking by hand—or even code it by hand. The general basket of techniques to do this is called *mathematical optimization*. We'll make use of one optimizer that is built into `scipy`, called `fmin`. Since that is a really boring name, we'll call it the `magical_minimum_finder`.

In [4]:

```
from scipy.optimize import fmin as magical_minimum_finder
def f(x):
    return x**2

magical_minimum_finder(f, [3], disp=False)
```

Out[4]:

```
array([-0.])
```

From a starting point of 3, `magical_minimum_finder` was able to locate the input value to `f` that resulted in the lowest output value. That result is analogous to what we want if we have weights as the inputs and a cost as the output. We now have one tool to use for finding minimum costs.

15.2 Linear Regression from Raw Materials

Now that we have a tool to minimize functions, can we *build a linear regression* system using that tool? Let's step back out to a 40,000-foot view of learning. When we try to *learn* something, we are trying to *fit* the *parameters* of a *model* to some *training data*. In linear regression, our parameters are weights (m, b or w_i) that we manipulate to make the *features* match the *target*. That's also a quick review of our most important vocabulary.

Let's get started by creating some simple synthetic data. To simplify a few things—and maybe complicate others—I'm going to pull a +1 trick. I'm going to do that by adding a column of ones to data as opposed to putting the +1 in the model.

In [5]:

```
linreg_ftrs_p1 = np.c_[np.arange(10), np.ones(10)] # +1 trick in data

true_wgts  = m,b = w_1, w_0 = 3,2
linreg_tgt = rdot(true_wgts, linreg_ftrs_p1)

linreg_table = pd.DataFrame(linreg_ftrs_p1,
                            columns=['ftr_1', 'ones'])
linreg_table['tgt'] = linreg_tgt
linreg_table[:3]
```

Out[5]:

	ftr_1	ones	tgt
0	0.0000	1.0000	2.0000
1	1.0000	1.0000	5.0000
2	2.0000	1.0000	8.0000

We've made a super simple dataset that only has one interesting feature. Still, it's complicated enough that we can't get the answer—the right weights for a fit model—for free. Well, we *could* by peeking at the code we used to create the data, but we won't do that. Instead, to find good weights, we'll pull out magical_minimum_finder to do the heavy lifting for us. To use magical_minimum_finder, we have to define the *loss* that we get from our *predictions* versus the real state of the world in the target. We'll do this in several steps. We have to explicitly define our learning model and the loss. We'll also define an ultra simple weight penalty—none, *no* penalty—so we can make a full-fledged cost.

In [6]:

```
def linreg_model(weights, ftrs):
    return rdot(weights, ftrs)

def linreg_loss(predicted, actual):
    errors = predicted - actual
    return np.dot(errors, errors) # sum-of-squares

def no_penalty(weights):
    return 0.0
```

Now, you may have noticed that when we used magical_minimum_finder, we had to pass a Python function that took one—and only one—argument and did all of its wonderful minimizing work. From that *single* argument, we have to somehow convince our function to make all the wonderful fit, loss, cost, weight, and train components of a learning method. That seems difficult. To make this happen, we'll use a Python trick: we will write one function that *produces another function* as its result. We did this in Section 11.2 when we created an adding function that added a specific value to an input value. Here, we'll use the same technique to wrap up the model, loss, penalty, and data components as a single function of the model parameters. Those parameters are the weights we want to find.

In [7]:

```
def make_cost(ftrs, tgt,
              model_func, loss_func,
              c_tradeoff, complexity_penalty):
    ' build an optimization problem from data, model, loss, penalty '
    def cost(weights):
        return (loss_func(model_func(weights, ftrs), tgt) +
                c_tradeoff * complexity_penalty(weights))
    return cost
```

I'll be honest. That's a bit tricky to interpret. You can either (1) trust me that `make_cost` plus some inputs will set up a linear regression problem on our synthetic data or (2) spend enough time reading it to convince yourself that I'm not misleading you. If you want the fast alternative, go for (1). If you want the rock star answer, go for (2). I suppose I should have mentioned alternative (3) where you would simply say, "I have no clue. Can you show me that it works?" Good call. Let's see what happens when we try to use `make_cost` to build our cost function and then minimize it with `magical_minimum_finder`.

In [8]:

```
# build linear regression optimization problem
linreg_cost = make_cost(linreg_ftrs_p1, linreg_tgt,
                        linreg_model, linreg_loss,
                        0.0, no_penalty)
learned_wgts = magical_minimum_finder(linreg_cost, [5,5], disp=False)

print("   true weights:", true_wgts)
print("learned weights:", learned_wgts)
```

```
    true weights: (3, 2)
learned weights: [3. 2.]
```

Well, that should be a load off of someone's shoulders. Building that cost and magically finding the least cost weights led to—wait for it—exactly the true weights that we started with. I hope you are suitably impressed. Now, we didn't make use of a penalty. If you recall from Chapter 9, we moved from a cost based on predicted targets to a loss based on those predictions plus a penalty for complex models. We did that to help prevent overfitting. We can add complexity penalties to our `make_cost` process by defining something more interesting than our `no_penalty`. The two main penalties we discussed in Section 9.1 were based on the absolute value and the squares of the weights. We called these L_1 and L_2 and we used them to make the lasso and ridge regression methods. We can build cost functions that effectively give us lasso and ridge regression. Here are the penalties we need:

In [9]:

```
def L1_penalty(weights):
    return np.abs(weights).sum()

def L2_penalty(weights):
    return np.dot(weights, weights)
```

And we can use those to make different cost functions:

In [10]:

```
# linear regression with L1 regularization (lasso regression)
linreg_L1_pen_cost = make_cost(linreg_ftrs_p1, linreg_tgt,
                               linreg_model, linreg_loss,
                               1.0, L1_penalty)
learned_wgts = magical_minimum_finder(linreg_L1_pen_cost, [5,5], disp=False)

print("   true weights:", true_wgts)
print("learned weights:", learned_wgts)
```

```
   true weights: (3, 2)
learned weights: [3.0212 1.8545]
```

You'll notice that we didn't get the exact correct weights this time. Deep breath—that's OK. Our training data had no noise in it. As a result, the penalties on the weights actually hurt us.

We can follow the same template to make ridge regression:

In [11]:

```
# linear regression with L2 regularization (ridge regression)
linreg_L2_pen_cost = make_cost(linreg_ftrs_p1, linreg_tgt,
                               linreg_model, linreg_loss,
                               1.0, L2_penalty)
learned_wgts = magical_minimum_finder(linreg_L2_pen_cost, [5,5], disp=False)

print("   true weights:", true_wgts)
print("learned weights:", learned_wgts)
```

```
   true weights: (3, 2)
learned weights: [3.0508 1.6102]
```

Again, we had perfect data so penalties don't do us any favors.

15.2.1   A Graphical View of Linear Regression

We can represent the computations we just performed as a flow of data through a graph. Figure 15.1 shows all the pieces in a visual form.

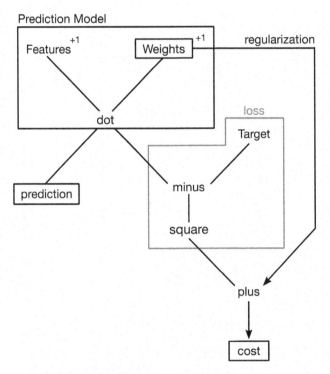

Figure 15.1   A graphical view of linear regression.

15.3   Building Logistic Regression from Raw Materials

So, we were able to build a simple linear regression model using some Python coding tricks and `magical_minimum_finder`. That's pretty cool. Let's make it awesome by showing how we can do classification—logistic regression—using the same steps: define a model and a cost. Then we minimize the cost. Done.

Again, we'll get started by generating some synthetic data. The generation process is a hint more complicated. You might remember that the linear regression part of logistic regression was producing the log-odds. To get to an actual class, we have to convert the log-odds into probabilities. If we're simply interested in the target classes, we can *use* those probabilities to pick classes. However, when we select a random value and compare it to a probability, we don't get a *guaranteed* result. We have a probability of a result. It's a random process that is inherently noisy. So, unlike the noiseless regression data we used above, we might see benefits from regularization.

In [12]:

```
logreg_ftr = np.random.uniform(5,15, size=(100,))

true_wgts  = m,b = -2, 20
line_of_logodds = m*logreg_ftr + b
prob_at_x = np.exp(line_of_logodds) / (1 + np.exp(line_of_logodds))

logreg_tgt = np.random.binomial(1, prob_at_x, len(logreg_ftr))

logreg_ftrs_p1 = np.c_[logreg_ftr,
                       np.ones_like(logreg_ftr)]

logreg_table = pd.DataFrame(logreg_ftrs_p1,
                       columns=['ftr_1','ones'])
logreg_table['tgt'] = logreg_tgt
display(logreg_table.head())
```

	ftr_1	ones	tgt
0	8.7454	1.0000	1
1	14.5071	1.0000	0
2	12.3199	1.0000	0
3	10.9866	1.0000	0
4	6.5602	1.0000	1

Graphically, the classes—and their probabilities—look like

In [13]:

```
fig, ax = plt.subplots(figsize=(6,4))
ax.plot(logreg_ftr, prob_at_x, 'r.')
ax.scatter(logreg_ftr, logreg_tgt, c=logreg_tgt);
```

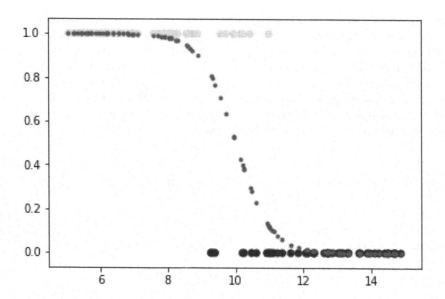

So, we have two classes here, 0 and 1, represented by the yellow and purple dots. The yellow dots fall on the horizontal line at $y = 1$ and the purple dots fall on the horizontal line at $y = 0$. We start off with pure 1s. As our input feature gets bigger, the likelihood of class 1 falls off. We start seeing a mix of 1 and 0. Eventually, we see only 0s. The mix of outcomes is controlled by the probabilities given by the red dots on the curving path that falls from one to zero. On the far left, we are flipping a coin that has an almost 100% chance of coming up 1, and you'll notice that we have lots of 1 outcomes. On the right-hand side, the red dots are all near zero—we have almost a zero percent chance of coming up with a 1. In the middle, we have moderate probabilities of coming up with ones and zeros. Between 9 and 11 we get some 1s and some 0s.

Creating synthetic data like this may give you a better idea of where and what the logistic regression log-odds, probabilities, and classes come from. More practically, this data is just hard enough to classify to make it interesting. Let's see how we can classify it with our `magical_minimum_finder`.

15.3.1   Logistic Regression with Zero-One Coding

We're not going to have much fuss creating our minimization problem. Our model—predicting the log-odds—is really *the same* as the linear regression model. The difference comes in how we assess our loss. The loss we'll use has many different names: logistic loss, log-loss, or cross-entropy loss. Suffice it to say that it measures the agreement between the probabilities we see in the training data and our predictions. Here's the loss for one prediction:

$$\text{log\_loss} = -p_{\text{actual}} \log(p_{\text{pred}}) - (1 - p_{\text{actual}}) \log(1 - p_{\text{pred}})$$

p_{actual} is known, since we know the target class. p_{pred} is unknown and can wave gradually from 0 to 1. If we put that loss together with target values of zero and one and shake it up with some algebra, we get another expression which I've translated into code `logreg_loss_01`.

In [14]:

```
# for logistic regression
def logreg_model(weights, ftrs):
    return rdot(weights, ftrs)


def logreg_loss_01(predicted, actual):
    # sum(-actual log(predicted) - (1-actual) log(1-predicted))
    # for 0/1 target works out to
    return np.sum(- predicted * actual + np.log(1+np.exp(predicted)))
```

So, we have our model and our loss. Does it work?

In [15]:

```
logreg_cost = make_cost(logreg_ftrs_p1, logreg_tgt,
                        logreg_model, logreg_loss_01,
                        0.0, no_penalty)
learned_wgts = magical_minimum_finder(logreg_cost, [5,5], disp=False)

print("   true weights:", true_wgts)
print("learned weights:", learned_wgts)
```

```
   true weights: (-2, 20)
learned weights: [-1.9774 19.8659]
```

Not too bad. Not as exact as we saw with good old-fashioned linear regression, but pretty close. Can you think of why? Here's a hint: did we have noise in our classification examples? Put differently, were there some input values that could have gone either way in terms of their output class? Second hint: think about the middle part of the sigmoid.

Now, let's see if regularization can help us:

In [16]:

```
# logistic regression with penalty
logreg_pen_cost = make_cost(logreg_ftrs_p1, logreg_tgt,
                            logreg_model, logreg_loss_01,
                            0.5, L1_penalty)
learned_wgts = magical_minimum_finder(logreg_pen_cost, [5,5], disp=False)
print("   true weights:", true_wgts)
print("learned weights:", learned_wgts)
```

```
true weights: (-2, 20)
learned weights: [-1.2809 12.7875]
```

The weights are different and have gone the *wrong* way. However, I simply picked our tradeoff between prediction accuracy and complexity `C` out of a hat. We shouldn't therefore read too much into this: it's a very simple dataset, there aren't too many data points, and we only tried one value of `C`. Can you find a better `C`?

15.3.2　Logistic Regression with Plus-One Minus-One Coding

Before we leave logistic regression, let's add one last twist. Conceptually, there shouldn't be any difference between having classes that are *cat* and *dog*, or *donkey* and *elephant*, or *zero* and *one*, or *+one* and *−one*. We just happened to use 0/1 above because it played well with the `binomial` data generator we used to flip coins. In reality, there are nice mathematical reasons behind that as well. We'll ignore those for now.

Since the mathematics for some other learning models can be more convenient using $-1/+1$, let's take a quick look at logistic regression with ± 1. The only difference is that we need a slightly different loss function. Before we get to that, however, let's make a helper to deal with converting 01 data to ± 1 data.

In [17]:

```
def binary_to_pm1(b):
    ' map {0,1} or {False,True} to {-1, +1} '
    return (b*2)-1
binary_to_pm1(0), binary_to_pm1(1)
```

Out[17]:

```
(-1, 1)
```

Here, we'll update the loss function to work with the ± 1 data. Mathematically, we start with the same log loss expression we had above, work through some slightly different algebra using the ± 1 values, and get the `logreg_loss_pm1`. The two `logreg_loss` functions are just slightly different code expressions of the same mathematical idea.

In [18]:

```
# for logistic regression
def logreg_model(weights, ftrs):
    return rdot(weights, ftrs)


def logreg_loss_pm1(predicted, actual):
    # -actual log(predicted) - (1-actual) log(1-predicted)
```

```
# for +1/-1 targets, works out to:
return np.sum(np.log(1+np.exp(-predicted*actual)))
```

With a model and a loss, we can perform our magical minimization to find good weights.

In [19]:

```
logreg_cost = make_cost(logreg_ftrs_p1, binary_to_pm1(logreg_tgt),
                        logreg_model, logreg_loss_pm1,
                        0.0, no_penalty)
learned_wgts = magical_minimum_finder(logreg_cost, [5,5], disp=False)

print("   true weights:", true_wgts)
print("learned weights:", learned_wgts)
```

```
   true weights: (-2, 20)
learned weights: [-1.9774 19.8659]
```

While the weights are nice, I'm curious about what sort of classification performance these weights give us. Let's take a quick look. We need to convert the weights into actual classes. We'll do that with another helper that knows how to convert weights into probabilities and then into classes.

In [20]:

```
def predict_with_logreg_weights_to_pm1(w_hat, x):
    prob = 1 / (1 + np.exp(rdot(w_hat, x)))
    thresh = prob < .5
    return binary_to_pm1(thresh)

preds = predict_with_logreg_weights_to_pm1(learned_wgts, logreg_ftrs_p1)
print(metrics.accuracy_score(preds, binary_to_pm1(logreg_tgt)))
```

```
0.93
```

Good enough. Even if the weights are not perfect, they might be useful for prediction.

15.3.3   A Graphical View of Logistic Regression

We can look at the logistic regression in the same graphical way we looked at the mathematics of the linear regression in Figure 15.1. The one piece that is a bit more complicated in the logistic regression is the $\frac{1}{1+e^{to}}$ form. You might remember that fraction as our logistic or sigmoid function. If we're content with using the name "logistic" to represent that function, we can draw the mathematical relationships as in Figure 15.2.

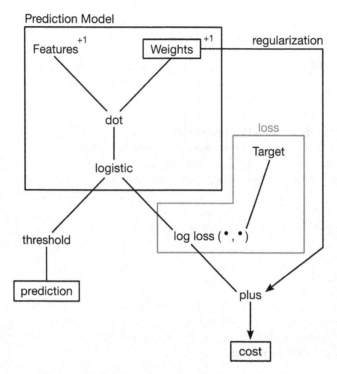

Figure 15.2   A graphical view of logistic regression.

15.4 SVM from Raw Materials

We've been on this journey for quite a long time now. I can't really pull any new tricks on you. You probably won't be too surprised if I tell you that we can do the *same* process with other learning models. In particular, let's see what SVM looks like when we build it from primitive components. Again, our only difference is that we'll have a slightly different loss function.

In [21]:

```
# for SVC
def hinge_loss(predicted, actual):
    hinge = np.maximum(1-predicted*actual, 0.0)
    return np.sum(hinge)

def predict_with_svm_weights(w_hat, x):
    return np.sign(rdot(w_hat,x)).astype(np.int)
```

SVM plays most nicely with ±1 data. We won't fight it. Since the SVM model is *just* the dot product, we won't even bother giving it a special name.

In [22]:

```
svm_ftrs = logreg_ftrs_p1
svm_tgt  = binary_to_pm1(logreg_tgt)   # svm "demands" +/- 1

# svm model is "just" rdot, so we don't define it separately now
svc_cost = make_cost(svm_ftrs, svm_tgt, rdot,
                        hinge_loss, 0.0, no_penalty)
learned_weights = magical_minimum_finder(svc_cost, [5,5], disp=False)

preds = predict_with_svm_weights(learned_weights, svm_ftrs)
print('no penalty accuracy:',
      metrics.accuracy_score(preds, svm_tgt))
```

```
no penalty accuracy: 0.91
```

As we did with linear and logistic regression, we can add a penalty term to control the weights.

In [23]:

```
# svc with penalty
svc_pen_cost = make_cost(svm_ftrs, svm_tgt, rdot,
                            hinge_loss, 1.0, L1_penalty)
learned_weights = magical_minimum_finder(svc_pen_cost, [5,5], disp=False)

preds = predict_with_svm_weights(learned_weights, svm_ftrs)
print('accuracy with penalty:',
      metrics.accuracy_score(preds, svm_tgt))
```

```
accuracy with penalty: 0.91
```

Now would be a great time to give you a warning. We are using trivial *true* relationships with tiny amounts of easy-to-separate data. You shouldn't expect to use `scipy.optimize.fmin` for *real-world* problems. With that warning set aside, here's a cool way to think about the optimization that *is* performed by the techniques you *would* use. From this perspective, when you use SVM, you are simply using a nice custom optimizer that works well for SVM problems. The same thing is true for linear and logistic regression: some ways of optimizing—finding the minimum cost parameters—work well for particular learning methods, so under the hood we *use that method*! In reality, customized techniques can solve specific optimization problems—such as those we need to solve when we fit a model—better than generic techniques like `fmin`. You usually don't have to worry about it until you start (1) using the absolute latest learning methods that are coming out of research journals or (2) implementing customized learning methods yourself.

One quick note. In reality, we didn't actually get to the kernelized version that takes us from SVCs to SVMs. Everything is basically the same, except we replace our dot products with kernels.

15.5   Neural Networks

One of the more conspicuous absences in our discussions of modeling and learning techniques is *neural networks*. Neural networks are responsible for some of the coolest advances in learning in the past decade, but they have been around for a long time. The first mathematical discussions of them started up in the 1940s. Moving toward the 1960s, neural networks started a pattern of boom-bust cycles. Neural networks are *amazing*, they can do *everything*! Then, a few years later, it becomes obvious that neural networks of some form can't do *something*, or can't do it *efficiently on current hardware*. They're awful, scrap them. A few years later: neural networks of a *different* form are *amazing*; look what we can do on brand-new hardware! You get the point. We're not going to dive deeply into the history that got us here, but I will now give you a concrete introduction to how neural networks relate to things you've already learned in this book.

First, we'll look at how a neural network specialist would view linear and logistic regression. Then, we'll take a quick look at a system that goes a good bit beyond these basics and moves towards some of the *deep* neural networks that are one of the causes of the current boom cycle in machine learning. A quick note: using neural networks for linear regression and logistic regression is sort of like using a Humvee to carry a 32-ounce water bottle. While you *can* do it, there are possibly easier ways to move the water.

With that introduction, what *are* neural networks? Earlier, we drew a diagram of the code forms of linear and logistic regression (Figures 15.1 and 15.2). Neural networks simply *start* with diagrams like those—connections between inputs, mathematical functions, and outputs—and then implement them in code. They do this in very generic ways, so we can build up other, more complicated patterns from the same sorts of components and connections.

15.5.1   A NN View of Linear Regression

We're going to start with linear regression as our prototype for developing a neural network. I'll redraw the earlier diagram (Figure 15.1) in a slightly different way (Figure 15.3).

To implement that diagram, we are going to use a Python package called `keras`. In turn, `keras` is going to drive a lower-level neural network package called TensorFlow. Used together, they massively simplify the process of turning diagrams of neural network components into executable programs.

In [24]:

```
import keras.layers as kl
import keras.models as km
import keras.optimizers as ko
```

Using TensorFlow backend.

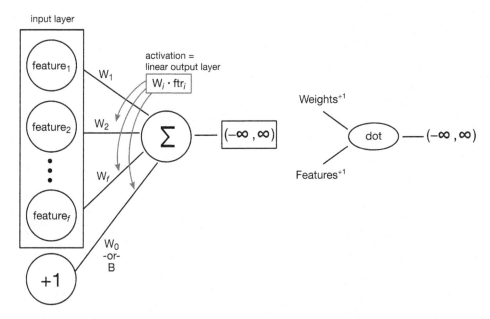

Figure 15.3   A neural network view of linear regression.

There are a number of ways to define and build a **keras** model. We'll use a simple one that allows us to **add** layers to a model as we work forward—from left to right or from input to output. This process is sequential, so we have to keep moving strictly forward. Now, it turns out that classic linear regression only requires one *work* layer. This work layer connects the inputs and the outputs (which are layers in their own right, but we're not concerned with them since they are fixed in place).

Back to the work layer: in Keras, we define it as a **Dense** layer. That means that we connect *all* of the incoming components together (densely). Further, we create it as a **Dense(1)** layer. That means that we connect all of the incoming components together into *one* node. The values funnel through that single node and form a dot product. That was specified when we said **activation='linear'**. If you're getting a distinct feeling of linear regression déjà vu, you're right. That's *exactly* what we get.

The last piece in our model builder is how we're going to optimize it. We have to define our cost/loss function and the technique we use to minimize it. We'll use a mean-squared-error loss (**loss='mse'**) and a rolling-downhill optimizer called *stochastic gradient descent* (**ko.SGD**). The *gradient descent* part is the downhill bit. The *stochastic* part means that we use only a part of our training data—instead of *all* of it—every time we try to figure out the downhill direction. That technique is very useful when we have a mammoth amount of training data. We use **lr** (learning rate) in the same way we used **step_size** in Section 15.1: once we know a direction, we need to know how far to move in that direction.

```
In [25]:
def Keras_LinearRegression(n_ftrs):
    model = km.Sequential()
    # Dense layer defaults include a "bias" (a +1 trick)
    model.add(kl.Dense(1,
                       activation='linear',
                       input_dim=n_ftrs))
    model.compile(optimizer=ko.SGD(lr=0.01), loss='mse')
    return model
```

The `keras` developers took pity on us and gave their models the same basic API as `sklearn`. So, a quick `fit` and `predict` will get us predictions. One slight difference is that `fit` returns a history of the fitting run.

```
In [26]:
# for various reasons, are going to let Keras do the +1 trick
# we will *not* send the `ones` feature
linreg_ftrs = linreg_ftrs_p1[:,0]

linreg_nn = Keras_LinearRegression(1)
history = linreg_nn.fit(linreg_ftrs, linreg_tgt, epochs=1000, verbose=0)
preds = linreg_nn.predict(linreg_ftrs)

mse = metrics.mean_squared_error(preds, linreg_tgt)

print("Training MSE: {:5.4f}".format(mse))
```

```
Training MSE: 0.0000
```

So, we took the training error down to very near zero. Be warned: that's a *training* evaluation, not a *testing* evaluation. We can dive into the fitting history to see how the proverbial ball rolled down the cost curve. We'll just look at the first five steps. When we specified `epochs=1000` we said that we were taking a thousand steps.

```
In [27]:
history.history['loss'][:5]
```

```
Out[27]:
[328.470703125,
 57.259727478027344,
 10.398818969726562,
 2.2973082065582275,
 0.8920286297798157]
```

Just a few steps made a massive amount of progress in driving down the loss.

15.5.2   A NN View of Logistic Regression

The neural network diagrams for linear regression (Figure 15.3) and logistic regression (Figure 15.4) are *very* similar. The only visible difference is the wavy sigmoid curve on the logistic regression side. The only difference when we go to implement logistic regression is the `activation` parameter. Above, for linear regression, we used a `linear` activation—which, as I told you, was just a dot product. For logistic regression, we'll use a `sigmoid` activation which basically pipes a dot product through a sigmoid curve. Once we put that together with a different loss function—we'll use the log loss (under the name `binary_crossentropy`)—we're *done*. In truth, we're only done because the output here is a probability. We have to convert that to a class by comparing with `.5`.

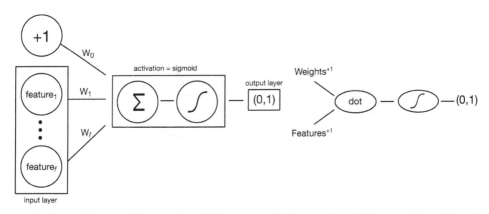

Figure 15.4   A neural network view of logistic regression.

```
In [28]:

def Keras_LogisticRegression(n_ftrs):
    model = km.Sequential()
    model.add(kl.Dense(1,
                       activation='sigmoid',
                       input_dim=n_ftrs))
    model.compile(optimizer=ko.SGD(), loss='binary_crossentropy')
    return model

logreg_nn = Keras_LogisticRegression(1)
history = logreg_nn.fit(logreg_ftr, logreg_tgt, epochs=1000, verbose=0)

# output is a probability
preds = logreg_nn.predict(logreg_ftr) > .5
print('accuracy:', metrics.accuracy_score(preds, logreg_tgt))


accuracy: 0.92
```

15.5.3 Beyond Basic Neural Networks

The single `Dense(1)` layer of NNs for linear and logistic regression is enough to get us started with basic—shallow—models. But the real power of NNs comes when we start having multiple nodes in a single layer (as in Figure 15.5) and when we start making *deeper* networks by adding layers.

`Dense(1, "linear")` can only perfectly represent linearly separable Boolean targets. `Dense(n)` can represent *any* Boolean function—but it might require a very large n. If we add layers, we can continue to represent any Boolean function, but we can—in some scenarios—do so with fewer and fewer total nodes. Fewer nodes means fewer weights or parameters that we have to adjust. We get simpler models, reduced overfitting, and more efficient training of our network.

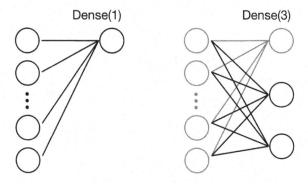

Figure 15.5   Dense layers.

As a quick example of where these ideas lead, the MNIST handwritten digit recognition dataset—similar to `sklearn`'s `digits`—can be attacked with a multiple working-layer neural network. If we string together two `Dense(512)` layers, we get a network with about 670,000 weights that must be found via optimization. We can do that and get about a 98% accuracy. The most straightforward way to do that ends up losing some of the "imageness" of the images: we lose track of which pixels are next to each other. That's a bit like losing word order in bag-of-words techniques. To address this, we can bring in another type of network connection—*convolution*—that keeps nearby pixels connected to each other. This cuts down on irrelevant connections. Our *convolutional neural network* has only 300,000 parameters, but it can still perform similarly. Win-win. You can imagine that we effectively set 370,000 parameters to zero and have far fewer knobs left to adjust.

15.6 Probabilistic Graphical Models

I introduced neural networks as a graphical model: something we could easily draw as connections between values and operations. One last major player in the modern learning toolbox is *probabilistic graphical models* (PGMs). They don't get quite the same press as neural networks—but rest assured, they are used to make important systems for image and speech processing and in medical diagnosis. I want to give you a quick flavor of what they are and what they get us over-and-above the models we've seen so far. As we did with neural networks, I'm going to show you what linear and logistic regression look like as PGMs.

Up to now, even with neural network, we considered some data—our input features and our targets—as a *given* and our parameters or weights as *adjustable*. In PGMs, we take a slightly different view: the weights of our models will *also* be given some best-guess form as an additional input. We'll give our model weights a range of possible values and different chances for those values popping out. Putting these ideas together means that we are giving our weights a probability distribution of their possible values. Then, using a processes called *sampling*, we can take the known, given data that we have, put it together with some guesses as to the weights, and see how likely it is that the pieces all work together.

When we draw a neural network, the nodes represent data and operations. The links represent the flow of information as operations are applied to their inputs. In PGMs, nodes represent features—input features and the target feature—as well as possible additional, intermediate features that aren't represented explicitly in our data. The intermediate nodes can be the results of mathematical operations, just like in neural networks.

There are some amazing things we can do with PGMs that we can't necessarily do with the models we've seen so far. Those models were easy to think of, conceptually, as sequences of operations on input data. We apply a sequence of mathematical steps to the inputs and, *presto*, we get outputs. Distributions over features are even more flexible. While we might *think* of some features as inputs and output, using distributions to tie features together means that we can send information from a feature to any other feature in that distribution. Practically speaking, we could (1) *know* some input values and ask what the *right* output values are, (2) *know* some *output* values and ask what the *right* input values are, or (3) *know* some combinations of inputs and outputs and ask what the *right* remaining input and output values are. Here, *right* means *most likely given everything else we know*. We are no longer on a one-way street from our input features going *to* our target outputs.

This extension takes us quite a ways past building a model to predict *a single* output from a group of inputs. There's another major difference. While I'm simplifying a bit, the methods we've discussed up until now make a *single, best-guess estimate* of an answer (though some also give a probability of a class). In fact, they do that in two ways. First, when we make a prediction, we predict one output value. Second, when we fit our model, we get one—and only one—best-guess estimate of the parameters of our model. We can fudge our way past some special cases of these limits, but our methods so far don't really allow for it.

PGMs let us see a range of possibilities in both our predictions and our fit models. From these, if we want, we can ask about the single most likely answer. However, acknowledging a range of possibilities often allows us to avoid being overconfident in a single answer that *might not be all that good* or *might be only marginally better than the alternatives*.

We'll see an example of these ideas in a minute, but here's something concrete to keep in mind. As we fit a PGM for linear regression, we can get a distribution over the weights and predicted values instead of just one fixed set of weights and values. For example, instead of the numbers $\{m = 3, b = 2\}$ we might get distributions $\{m = \text{Normal}(3, .5), b = \text{Normal}(2, .2)\}$.

15.6.1 Sampling

Before we get to a PGM for linear regression, let's take a small diversion to discuss how we'll learn from our PGMs. That means we need to talk about *sampling*.

Suppose we have an urn—there we go again with the urns—that we draw red and black balls from, placing each ball back into the urn after we recorded its color. So, we are sampling *with replacement*. Out of 100 tries, we drew 75 red balls and 25 black balls. We could now ask how likely is it that the urn had 1 red ball and 99 black balls: not very. We could also ask how likely is it that the urn had 99 red balls and 1 black ball: not very, but more likely than the prior scenario. And so on. Eventually we could ask how likely is that the urn had 50 red and 50 black balls. This scenario seems possible but not probable.

One way we could figure out all of these probabilities is by taking each possible starting urn—with different combinations of red and black balls—and performing many, many repeated draws of 100 balls from them. Then we could ask how many of those attempts led to a 75 red and 25 black result. For example, with an urn that contains 50 red and 50 black balls, we pull out 100 balls with replacement. We repeat that, say, a million times. Then we can *count* the number of times we achieved 75 red and 25 black. We do that *repeated sampling process* over all possible urn setups—99 red, 1 black; 98 red, 2 black; and so on all the way up to 1 red, 99 black—and tally up the results.

Such a systematic approach would take quite a while. Some of the possibilities, while strictly possible, might practically never occur. Imagine drawing (75 red, 25 black) from an urn with (1 red, 99 black). It might only happen once before the sun goes supernova. Nevertheless, we *could* do this overall process.

The technique of setting up all legal scenarios and seeing how many of the outcomes match our reality is called *sampling*. We typically don't enumerate—list out—*all* of the possible legal scenarios. Instead, we define how likely the different legal scenarios are and then flip a coin—or otherwise pick randomly—to generate them. We do this many times so that, eventually, we can work backwards to which of the legal scenarios are the *likely* ones. Scenarios that are *possible* but not *probable* might not show up. But that's OK: we're focusing our efforts precisely on the more likely outcomes in proportion to how often they occur.

Our urn example uses sampling to determine the percent of red—and hence also the black—balls in the urn. We do assume, of course, that someone hasn't added a *yellow* ball to the urn behind our backs. There's always a danger of an *unknown unknown*. In a similar way, sampling will allow us to estimate the weights in our linear and logistic models. In these cases, we see the input and output features and we ask how likely this, that, or another set of weights are. We can do that for many different possible sets of weights. If we do it in a clever way—there are many, many different ways of sampling—we can end up with both a good single estimate of the weights and *also* a distribution of the different possible weights that *might* have led to the data we see.

15.6.2 A PGM View of Linear Regression

Let's apply the idea of PGMs to linear regression.

15.6.2.1 The Long Way

Here's how this works for our good old–fashioned (GOF) linear regression. We start by drawing a model (Figure 15.6) of how the features and weights interact. This drawing looks an awful lot like the model we drew for the neural network form of linear regression, with the addition of placeholder distributions for the learned weights.

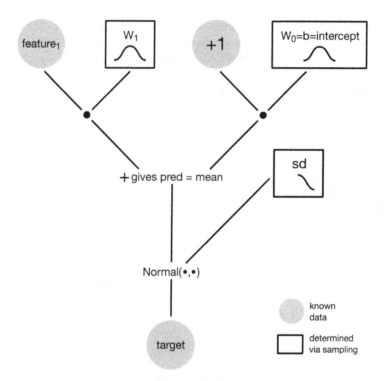

Figure 15.6 A probabilistic graphical model for linear regression.

Our major tool for exploring PGMs is going to be `pymc3`. The `mc` stands for Monte Carlo, a famous casino. When you see that name, you can simply mentally substitute *randomness*.

In [29]:

```
import pymc3 as pm

# getting really hard to convince toolkits to be less verbose
```

```
import logging
pymc3_log = logging.getLogger('pymc3')
pymc3_log.setLevel(2**20)
```

For most of the book, we've swept this detail under the carpet—but when we predict a value with a linear regression, we have really been predicting a *single* output target value that is a mean of the possible outcomes at that spot. In reality, if our data isn't perfect, we have some wiggle room above and below that value. This possible wiggle room—which GOF linear regression treats as the same for each prediction—is a normal distribution. Yes, it really does show up everywhere. This normal distribution is centered at the predicted value with a standard deviation around that center, so it shows up as a band above and below our linear regression line. Our predictions still fall *on* the linear regression line. The new component is simply something like a tolerance band around the line. When we look at linear regression as PGM, we make this hidden detail *explicit* by specifying a standard deviation.

Let's turn our diagram from Figure 15.6 into code:

In [30]:

```
with pm.Model() as model:
    # boilerplate-ish setup of the distributions of our
    # guesses for things we don't know
    sd        = pm.HalfNormal('sd', sd=1)
    intercept = pm.Normal('Intercept', 0, sd=20)
    ftr_1_wgt = pm.Normal('ftr_1_wgt', 0, sd=20)

    # outcomes made from initial guess and input data
    # this is y = m x + b in an alternate form
    preds = ftr_1_wgt * linreg_table['ftr_1'] + intercept

    # relationship between guesses, input data, and actual outputs
    # target = preds + noise(sd)   (noise == tolerance around the line)
    target = pm.Normal('tgt',
                        mu=preds, sd=sd,
                        observed=linreg_table['tgt'])

    linreg_trace = pm.sample(1000, verbose=-1, progressbar=False)
```

After all that, not seeing any output is a bit disappointing. Never fear.

In [31]:

```
pm.summary(linreg_trace)[['mean']]
```

Out[31]:

	mean
Intercept	2.0000
ftr_1_wgt	3.0000
sd	0.0000

Now *that* is comforting. While we took a quite different path to get here, we see that our weight estimates are 3 and 2—precisely the values we used to generate the data in `linreg_table`. It's also comforting that our estimate as to the noisiness of our data, **sd**, is zero. We generated the data in `linreg_table` without any noise. We are as perfect as we can be.

15.6.2.2 The Short Way

There are a lot of details laid out in that code example. Fortunately, we don't have to specify each of those details every time. Instead, we can write a simple formula that tells `pymc3` that the target depends on `ftr_1` and a constant for the +1 trick. Then, `pymc3` will do all the hard work of filling in the pieces we wrote out above. The `family=` argument serves the same role as our `target=` assignment did in our long-hand version. Both tell us that we are building a normal distribution centered around our predictions with some tolerance band.

In [32]:

```
with pm.Model() as model:
    pm.glm.GLM.from_formula('tgt ~ ftr_1', linreg_table,
                            family=pm.glm.families.Normal())
    linreg_trace = pm.sample(5000, verbose=-1, progressbar=False)
pm.summary(linreg_trace)[['mean']]
```

Out[32]:

	mean
Intercept	2.0000
ftr_1	3.0000
sd	0.0000

The names here are the names of the features. I'd be happier if it was clear that they are the values of the *weights* on those features. Still, consider my point made. It's reassuring that we get the same answers for the weights. Now, I brought up a benefit of PGMs: we can see a *range* of possible answers instead of just a single answer. What does that look like?

In [33]:

```
%%capture

# workaround for a problem: writing to a tmp file.
%matplotlib qt

fig, axes = plt.subplots(3,2,figsize=(12,6))
axes = pm.traceplot(linreg_trace, ax=axes)
for ax in axes[:,-1]:
    ax.set_visible(False)

plt.gcf().savefig('outputs/work-around.png')
```

In [34]:

```
Image('outputs/work-around.png', width=800, height=2400)
```

Out[34]:

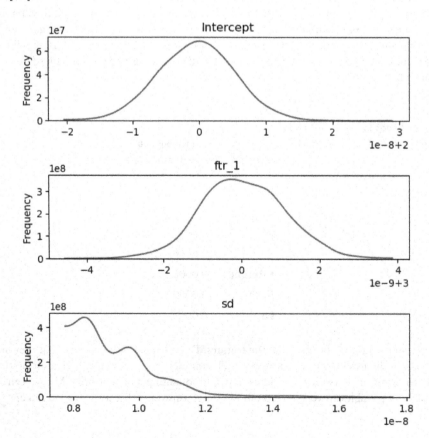

These graphs may be hard to read because the units are a bit wacky, but 1e-8 and 1e-9—one times ten to the minus eight and nine—are both approximately zero. So, those labels in the bottom right (the scale of the *x*-axis) are really funky ways of saying that the centers of the graphs are 2 and 3, exactly the values we saw in the previous table. The sd values are just little pieces sized like 1e-8—again, pretty close to zero. Good. What we see with the big bumps is that there is a highly concentrated area around the values from the table that are likely to have been the original weights.

15.6.3 A PGM View of Logistic Regression

Having seen the close relationships between linear and logistic regression, we can ask if there is a similarly close relationship between PGMs for the two. Unsurprisingly, the answer is yes. Again, we need only a tiny change to go from linear regression to logistic regression. We'll start by looking at a diagram for the PGM in Figure 15.7.

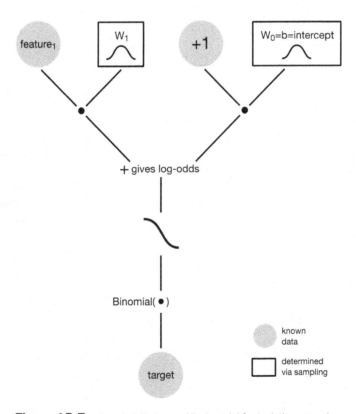

Figure 15.7 A probabilistic graphical model for logistic regression.

We can spin up almost the exact same model as linear regression except with a slightly different `family`: now we need to use `Binomial` as our target. Whenever you see binomial, you can immediately use a mental model of coin flipping. Since our logistic regression example has two classes, we can think of them as heads and tails. Then, we are simply trying to find the chances of flipping a head. Making that substitution—of the binomial distribution for the normal distribution—gives us the following code:

In [35]:

```
with pm.Model() as model:
    pm.glm.GLM.from_formula('tgt ~ ftr_1', logreg_table,
                            family=pm.glm.families.Binomial())
    logreg_trace = pm.sample(10000, verbose=-1, progressbar=False)
pm.summary(logreg_trace)[['mean']]
```

Out[35]:

	mean
Intercept	22.6166
ftr_1	-2.2497

Our results here are not *exact*: the true, original values were 20 and −2. But remember, our `logreg_table` was a bit more realistic than our linear regression data. It included noise in the middle where examples were not perfectly sorted into heads and tails—our original zeros and ones.

For linear regression, we looked at the univariate—stand-alone—distributions of the weights. We can also look at the bivariate—working together—distributions of the weights. For the logistic regression example, let's see where the most likely *pairs* of values are for the two weights.

In [36]:

```
%matplotlib inline

df_trace = pm.trace_to_dataframe(logreg_trace)
sns.jointplot('ftr_1', 'Intercept', data=df_trace,
              kind='kde', stat_func=None, height=4);
```

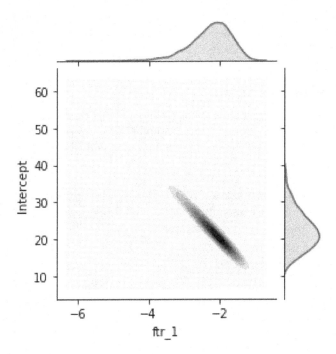

The darker area represents the most likely combinations of weights. We see that the two are not independent of each other. If the weight on `ftr_1` goes up a bit—that is, becomes a little less negative—the weight on the intercept has to go down a bit.

You can think of this like planning for a long drive. If you have a target arrival time, you can leave at a certain time and drive at a certain speed. If you leave earlier, you can afford to drive a bit more slowly. If you leave later—holiday craziness, I'm looking at you—you have to drive more quickly to arrive at the same time. For our logistic regression model, arriving at the same time—the dark parts of the graph—means that the data we see is likely to have come from some tradeoff between the start time and the driving speed.

15.7 EOC

15.7.1 Summary

We've covered three main topics here: (1) how several different learning algorithms can be solved using generic optimization, (2) how linear and logistic regression can be expressed using neural networks, and (3) how linear and logistic regression can be expressed using probabilistic graphical models. A key point is that these two models are very close cousins.

A second point is that *all* learning methods are fundamentally doing similar things. Here's one last point to consider: neural networks and PGMs can express very *complicated* models—but they are built from very *simple* components.

15.7.2   Notes

If you are interested in learning more about optimization, take a glance at zero-finding and derivatives in a calculus class or dig up some Youtube videos. You can get entire degrees in finding-the-best. There are people studying optimization in mathematics, business, and engineering programs.

Logistic Regression and Loss   With $z = \beta x$, probability in a logistic regression model is $p_{y=1} = \frac{1}{1+e^{-z}}$. That also gives us $p = \text{logistic}(z) = \text{logistic}(\beta x)$. Minimizing the cross-entropy loss gives us these expressions:

- For 0/1: $-yz + \log(1 + e^z)$
- For ± 1: $\log(1 + e^{-yz})$

When we go beyond a binary classification problem in NN, we use a one-hot encoding for the target and solve several single-class problems in parallel. Then, instead of using the logistic function, we use a function called *softmax*. Then, we take the class that results in the highest probability among the possible targets.

Neural Networks   It's really hard to summarize the history of neural networks in four sentences. It started in the mid-1940s and had a series of boom-bust cycles around 1960 and then in the 1980s. Between the mid-1990s and early 2010s, the main theoretical and practical hardware problems got workable solutions. For a *slightly* longer review, see "Learning Machine Learning" by Lewis and Denning in the December 2018 issue of the *Communications of the ACM*.

I mentioned briefly that we can extend neural networks to work with more than binary target classification problems. Here's a super quick example of those techniques applied to a binary problem. You can adjust the number of classes to work with larger problems simply by increasing `n_classes`.

```
In [37]:

from keras.utils import to_categorical as k_to_categorical
def Keras_MultiLogisticRegression(n_ftrs, n_classes):
    model = km.Sequential()
    model.add(kl.Dense(n_classes,
                       activation='softmax',
                       input_dim=n_ftrs))
    model.compile(optimizer=ko.SGD(), loss='categorical_crossentropy')
    return model


logreg_nn2 = Keras_MultiLogisticRegression(1, 2)
```

```
history = logreg_nn2.fit(logreg_ftr,
                         k_to_categorical(logreg_tgt),
                         epochs=1000, verbose=0)

# predict gives "probability table" by class
# we just need the bigger one
preds = logreg_nn2.predict(logreg_ftr).argmax(axis=1)
print(metrics.accuracy_score(logreg_tgt, preds))
```

```
0.92
```

15.7.3 Exercises

1. Can you do something like GridSearch—possibly with some clunky looping code—with our manual learning methods to find good values for our regularization control C?

2. We saw that using a penalty on the weights can actually hurt our weight estimates, if the data is very clean. Experiment with different amounts of noise. One possibility is bigger spreads in the standard deviation of regression data. Combine that with different amounts of regularization (the C value). How do our testing mean-squared errors change as the noise and regularization change?

3. Overfitting in neural networks is a bit of an odd puppy. With more complicated neural network architectures—which can represent varying degrees of *anything* we can throw at them—the issue becomes one of controlling the number of learning iterations (epochs) that we take. Keeping the number of epochs down means that we can only adjust the weights in the network so far. The result is a bit like regularization. As you just did with the noise/C tradeoff, try evaluating the tradeoff between noise and the number of epochs we use for training a neural network. Evaluate on a test set.

A

mlwpy.py Listing

```python
# common import abbreviations
import numpy as np
import matplotlib.pyplot as plt
import matplotlib as mpl
import seaborn as sns
import pandas as pd
import patsy

import itertools as it
import collections as co
import functools as ft
import os.path as osp

import glob
import textwrap

import warnings
warnings.filterwarnings("ignore")
# some warnings are stubborn in the extreme, we don't want
# them in the book
def warn(*args, **kwargs):  pass
warnings.warn = warn

# config related
np.set_printoptions(precision=4,
                    suppress=True)
pd.options.display.float_format = '{:20,.4f}'.format

# there are good reasons *NOT* to do this in any real production code
# for our purposes (writing a book with completely reproducible output)
# this *is* what we want
np.random.seed(42)
```

```python
# default is [6.4, 4.8]   (4:3)
mpl.rcParams['figure.figsize'] = [4.0, 3.0]

# turn on latex tables
pd.set_option('display.latex.repr', True)
# monkey-patch for centering Out[] DataFrames
def _repr_latex_(self):
    return "{\centering\n%s\n\medskip}" % self.to_latex()
pd.DataFrame._repr_latex_ = _repr_latex_

# only used once
markers = it.cycle(['+', '^', 'o', '_', '*', 'd', 'x', 's'])

# handy helper for displaying stuff
from IPython.display import Image

#
# sklearn's packaging is very java-esque.  :(
#
from sklearn import (cluster,
                     datasets,
                     decomposition,
                     discriminant_analysis,
                     dummy,
                     ensemble,
                     feature_selection as ftr_sel,
                     linear_model,
                     metrics,
                     model_selection as skms,
                     multiclass as skmulti,
                     naive_bayes,
                     neighbors,
                     pipeline,
                     preprocessing as skpre,
                     svm,
                     tree)

# the punch line is to predict for a large grid of data points
# http://scikit-learn.org/stable/auto_examples/neighbors
# /plot_classification.html
def plot_boundary(ax, data, tgt, model, dims, grid_step = .01):
    # grab a 2D view of the data and get limits
    twoD = data[:, list(dims)]
```

```
        min_x1, min_x2 = np.min(twoD, axis=0) + 2 * grid_step
        max_x1, max_x2 = np.max(twoD, axis=0) - grid_step

        # make a grid of points and predict at them
        xs, ys = np.mgrid[min_x1:max_x1:grid_step,
                          min_x2:max_x2:grid_step]
        grid_points = np.c_[xs.ravel(), ys.ravel()]
        # warning:  non-cv fit
        preds = model.fit(twoD, tgt).predict(grid_points).reshape(xs.shape)

        # plot the predictions at the grid points
        ax.pcolormesh(xs,ys,preds,cmap=plt.cm.coolwarm)
        ax.set_xlim(min_x1, max_x1)#-grid_step)
        ax.set_ylim(min_x2, max_x2)#-grid_step)

def plot_separator(model, xs, ys, label='', ax=None):
    ''' xs, ys are 1-D b/c contour and decision_function
        use incompatible packaging '''
    if ax is None:
        ax = plt.gca()

    xy = np_cartesian_product(xs, ys)
    z_shape = (xs.size, ys.size) # using .size since 1D
    zs = model.decision_function(xy).reshape(z_shape)

    contours = ax.contour(xs, ys, zs,
                          colors='k', levels=[0],
                          linestyles=['-'])
    fmt = {contours.levels[0] : label}
    labels = ax.clabel(contours, fmt=fmt, inline_spacing=10)
    [l.set_rotation(-90) for l in labels]

def high_school_style(ax):
    ' helper to define an axis to look like a typical school plot '
    ax.spines['left'].set_position(('data', 0.0))
    ax.spines['bottom'].set_position(('data', 0.0))
    ax.spines['right'].set_visible(False)
    ax.spines['top'].set_visible(False)

    def make_ticks(lims):
        lwr, upr = sorted(lims) #x/ylims can be inverted in mpl
        lwr = np.round(lwr).astype('int') # can return np objs
        upr = np.round(upr).astype('int')
```

```
        if lwr * upr < 0:
            return list(range(lwr, 0)) + list(range(1,upr+1))
        else:
            return list(range(lwr, upr+1))

    import matplotlib.ticker as ticker
    xticks = make_ticks(ax.get_xlim())
    yticks = make_ticks(ax.get_ylim())

    ax.xaxis.set_major_locator(ticker.FixedLocator(xticks))
    ax.yaxis.set_major_locator(ticker.FixedLocator(yticks))

    ax.set_aspect('equal')

def get_model_name(model):
    ' return name of model (class) as a string '
    return str(model.__class__).split('.')[-1][:-2]

def rdot(w,x):
    ' apply np.dot on swapped args '
    return np.dot(x,w)

from sklearn.base import BaseEstimator, ClassifierMixin
class DLDA(BaseEstimator, ClassifierMixin):
    def __init__(self):
        pass

    def fit(self, train_ftrs, train_tgts):
        self.uniq_tgts = np.unique(train_tgts)
        self.means, self.priors = {}, {}

        self.var  = train_ftrs.var(axis=0) # biased
        for tgt in self.uniq_tgts:
            cases = train_ftrs[train_tgts==tgt]
            self.means[tgt]  = cases.mean(axis=0)
            self.priors[tgt] = len(cases) / len(train_ftrs)
        return self

    def predict(self, test_ftrs):
        disc = np.empty((test_ftrs.shape[0],
                         self.uniq_tgts.shape[0]))
        for tgt in self.uniq_tgts:
            # technically, the maha_dist is sqrt() of this:
```

```
                    mahalanobis_dists = ((test_ftrs - self.means[tgt])**2 /
                                        self.var)
                    disc[:,tgt] = (-np.sum(mahalanobis_dists, axis=1) +
                                    2 * np.log(self.priors[tgt]))
                return np.argmax(disc,axis=1)

def plot_lines_and_projections(axes, lines, points, xs):
    data_xs, data_ys = points[:,0], points[:,1]
    mean = np.mean(points, axis=0, keepdims=True)
    centered_data = points - mean

    for (m,b), ax in zip(lines, axes):
        mb_line = m*xs + b
        v_line = np.array([[1, 1/m if m else 0]])

        ax.plot(data_xs, data_ys, 'r.') # uncentered
        ax.plot(xs, mb_line, 'y')       # uncentered
        ax.plot(*mean.T, 'ko')

        # centered data makes the math easier!
        # this is length on yellow line from red to blue
        # distance from mean to projected point
        y_lengths = centered_data.dot(v_line.T) / v_line.dot(v_line.T)
        projs = y_lengths.dot(v_line)

        # decenter (back to original coordinates)
        final = projs + mean
        ax.plot(*final.T, 'b.')

        # connect points to projections
        from matplotlib import collections as mc
        proj_lines = mc.LineCollection(zip(points,final))
        ax.add_collection(proj_lines)

        hypots = zip(points, np.broadcast_to(mean, points.shape))
        mean_lines = mc.LineCollection(hypots, linestyles='dashed')
        ax.add_collection(mean_lines)

# adding an orientation would be nice
def sane_quiver(vs, ax=None, colors=None, origin=(0,0)):
    '''plot row vectors from origin'''
    vs = np.asarray(vs)
    assert vs.ndim == 2 and vs.shape[1] == 2  # ensure column vectors
```

```python
    n = vs.shape[0]
    if not ax: ax = plt.gca()

    # zs = np.zeros(n)
    # zs = np.broadcast_to(origin, vs.shape)
    orig_x, orig_y = origin

    xs = vs.T[0]  # column to rows, row[0] is xs
    ys = vs.T[1]

    props = {"angles":'xy', 'scale':1, 'scale_units':'xy'}
    ax.quiver(orig_x, orig_y, xs, ys, color=colors, **props)

    ax.set_aspect('equal')
    # ax.set_axis_off()
    _min, _max = min(vs.min(), 0) -1, max(0, vs.max())+1
    ax.set_xlim(_min, _max)
    ax.set_ylim(_min, _max)

def reweight(examples, weights):
    ''' convert weights to counts of examples using approximately two
        significant digits of weights.

        there are probably a 100 reasons not to do this like this.
        top 2:
            1.  boosting may require more precise values (or using
                randomization) to keep things unbiased
            2.  this *really* expands the dataset to a significant degree
                (wastes resources)
    '''
    from math import gcd
    from functools import reduce

    # who needs repeated the least?
    min_wgt = min(weights)
    min_replicate = 1 / min_wgt # e.g., .25 -> 4

    # compute naive duplication to 2 decimal places
    counts = (min_replicate * weights * 100).astype(np.int64)

    # trim duplication if we can
    our_gcd = reduce(gcd, counts)
    counts = counts // our_gcd
```

```
    # repeat is picky about type
    return np.repeat(examples, counts, axis=0)

#examples = np.array([1, 10, 20])
#weights  = np.array([.25, .33, 1-(.25+.33)])
# print(pd.Series(reweight(examples, weights)))

def enumerate_outer(outer_seq):
    '''repeat the outer idx based on len of inner'''
    return np.repeat(*zip(*enumerate(map(len, outer_seq))))

def np_array_fromiter(itr, shape, dtype=np.float64):
    ''' helper since np.fromiter only does 1D'''
    arr = np.empty(shape, dtype=dtype)
    for idx, itm in enumerate(itr):
        arr[idx] = itm
    return arr

# how do you figure out arcane code?
# work inside out, small inputs, pay attention to datatypes.
# try outter and righter calls with simpler inputs
# read docs *in conjunction with* experiments
# [the docs rarely make sense - to me - in the abstract until I try
#  examples while reading them]

# the difference with a "raw" np.meshgrid call is we stack these up in
# two columns of results (i.e., we make a table out of the pair arrays)
def np_cartesian_product(*arrays):
    ''' some numpy kung-fu to produce all
        possible combinations of input arrays '''
    ndim = len(arrays)
    return np.stack(np.meshgrid(*arrays), axis=-1).reshape(-1, ndim)
```

Index

Q

VIDEO TRAINING FOR THE **IT PROFESSIONAL**

LEARN QUICKLY
Learn a new technology in just hours. Video training can teach more in less time, and material is generally easier to absorb and remember.

WATCH AND LEARN
Instructors demonstrate concepts so you see technology in action.

TEST YOURSELF
Our Complete Video Courses offer self-assessment quizzes throughout.

CONVENIENT
Most videos are streaming with an option to download lessons for offine viewing.

Learn more, browse our store, and watch free, sample lessons at
informit.com/video

Save 50%* off the list price of video courses with discount code **VIDBOB**